Education *for* Marriage

**SECOND
EDITION**

by

JAMES A. PETERSON

*Professor of Sociology
and Marriage Counselor
of the University
of Southern California*

Charles Scribner's Sons

NEW YORK

Printed in the United States of America
Library of Congress Catalog Card Number 63–10391

To My Family

AUDREY, JON, MARY, AND NANCY

for their many contributions to
the experience and insight
which have gone
into this book

FOREWORD

Henry J. Wegrocki, M.D.[*]

It is a paradox that, in an age when entry into even simple
occupations necessitates some training and preparation, the
initiation of the complex interrelationships which constitute marriage
is often accomplished blithely and without much real forethought. The
practicing psychiatrist, who sees a parade of pathetically incompatible
couples, too often realizes that he could have been helpful if he had
been consulted *before* marriage.

The prevention of potentially unsuccessful marital unions, and of the
misery they bring to all concerned, is one of the aims of Dr. Peterson's
Education for Marriage. The broad range of factors that make for
future compatibility, or incompatibility, is set forth comprehensively,
yet pithily. It is difficult for any author, unconsciously anchored, intellectually and emotionally, in the conceptual system of his particular
discipline or field of endeavor, to visualize marital problems except in
terms of his own familiar frame of reference. Dr. Peterson's background
in religion, psychological counseling, and sociology, as well as the
breadth of his own personal understanding, enable him to surmount this
tendency to unilateral emphasis. The comprehensiveness which results
is not, however, achieved at the cost of unity or organization, and the
book is unique, not only in its scope, but also in its organic wholeness
and its steady, and steadying, sense of direction.

Unique also, as a specific contribution, is the series of exercises in

[*] Associate Clinical Professor of Psychiatry, School of Medicine, University of Southern
California and Chief, Psychiatric Service, California Hospital, Los Angeles, California.

self-analysis appended to the various chapters. These are non-threatening in nature, but are provocative of further and deeper reflection on the issues of potential compatibility. If they only *raised* questions and doubts without pointing to a solution, they would still serve their purpose of increasing awareness of the various aspects of interpersonal adjustment that need to be evaluated before marriage is decided upon.

This preventive orientation is, however, secondary to a more basic, positive attitude toward the potentials of marriage. Dr. Peterson's effort represents a mental-hygiene approach in the fuller sense by its emphasis on the values and the development of cohesion in marriage. *Education for Marriage* succeeds excellently in prescribing the circumstances that make marital union an opportunity for a growing, greater, "other-centered" self-realization. Education, in any real sense, is a constantly evolving process. To deepen one's understanding is as important as to gain it. From this standpoint, this book has as much value for the already married as for the unmarried.

H. J. W.

PREFACE

To the Second Edition

THE SECOND edition of *Education for Marriage* has as a central
theme the rapid shifts in functions and roles in modern marriage. These transitions often result in conflict and tension between
husband and wife. Because the shifts have been so extensive and so
rapid, they have also contributed to the individual's anxiety about his
self-worth. This anxiety reinforces misunderstanding caused by role and
value differences. It is my conviction that preparation for marriage involves a profound and specific awareness as to what impact each of
these trends has made upon the individual. Without such awareness
the individual cannot clarify his own problems or understand another's.
Much of this book is focused on such sociological and psychological
awareness, which, if understood, might help the student gain that insight. But insight alone is barren unless it is accompanied by self-analysis
and conscious adaptation. In this sense the self-analysis schedules in
this book have more value than the research documentation that establishes the importance of each area of concern.

While much of both sociological and psychological research material
forms the foundation for this book, the particular way in which it is
used is the sole responsibility of the author. He is most grateful to
research specialists who have shared their studies with him and, through
him, with the students. Many students and their teachers responded to
a request for criticism of the first edition. The author appreciates their
help very gratefully.

JAMES A. PETERSON
1964

CONTENTS

CONTENTS

FIGURES

FIGURES

TABLES

TABLES

PART ONE

MARRIAGE IN TRANSITION

Introduction

NO INSTITUTION has changed as rapidly or as radically as has the American family since 1900. It has changed in structure and in function. Consequently, the roles of men and women in the family have been profoundly altered too. These shifts in family structure and function and the roles played by family participants are often the source of great difficulty in achieving family integration.

The first two chapters of this text have as their goal helping the student perceive clearly the nature of modern marriage so that he can consciously adjust to these changes and not be controlled by them. Considerable new research is introduced in these first chapters to illustrate the descriptions of these changes. Then the implications for family behavior involved in the shifts are studied. Chapter Three deals with the nature of affectional bonds between husband and wife. Some of the distortions and some of the more mature types of affection are analyzed to help the student develop an adequate expectation of what mature love may mean to him. This part, then, orients the student in comprehending modern family life and modern love.

3

CHAPTER 1

The Family in Transition

INTRODUCTION

THIS is a book about the only really important things in this world—human beings. Nothing on earth is as intricate or as sensitive as the human mind; nothing is as complex or as creative as personality. Man in his early years of childhood can incorporate the learning of past centuries into his life and yet anticipate the future in his values. In this sense he is bound by neither time nor space. Each generation adds new dimensions to man's understanding and new conquests of his environment. Today his creativity has resulted in such rapid changes in his environment that he is lagging in his social adjustment to those achievements. But students should realize that the scientific way of thinking that has altered the face of the earth has also developed more adequate ways for individuals to achieve inner security, intellectual growth and spiritual fulfillment. When the methods of science are applied to understanding human behavior and the way men and women interact in marriage, we have the means for greater personal development than ever before in history. The chapters of this book focus that understanding on growth sequences of life to help young men and women consciously build constructive futures, unfettered by fears and myths from their past; and to work to develop personalities so strong that they can add much to another in marriage and so mature that they can contribute to the growth of their children.

This is a book about the most important decision human beings ever make—the choice of a life partner. That single decision has many and

5

extended results. In choosing a mate one chooses at the same time the ancestors of his children and thus their potentials or their limitations; he chooses the mood and the atmosphere of his future home; the level of his future intellectual, aesthetic, and recreational life; his lifetime friends and a new family. In selecting his marital partner he is limiting or expanding his own possibilities for personality enrichment because one possible mate would stifle while another might inspire him. He will live the rest of his life in most intimate relation to the one who walks with him down the marriage aisle. Whether or not that choice is "for better or worse" depends on informed and mature attitudes.

This is a book about the way human beings can learn to adjust to the most important relationship in life—marriage. Society never automatically guarantees either success in marriage or parenthood simply because a couple get a marriage license. The high rate of divorce and separation attest to that. In a complex and changing social setting, marital success must be earned by thoughtful effort. To understand the conditions and attitudes which promote happiness in marriage is a prerequisite to good adjustment. The rewards for efforts at understanding are great because no other area of life is as crucial as marriage for the growth of individual self-esteem and lifetime satisfaction. No economic success, no material achievement, neither fame nor glory, can ever purchase love, trust, or tenderness. These come only as rewards for unselfish devotion. Without them life is cold and finally empty. A rewarding marriage can never result from an egocentric drive on the part of one partner for economic security; a successful marriage is rather a shared effort to win shared goals. Happiness in marriage cannot be achieved if one partner regards it as only a means for sexual convenience; it is realized only when the physical union expresses a tenderness that already exists. Mature marriage is the fulfillment of our deepest needs to be completely accepted as an intimate part of another's life, to be trusted by someone who knows us year after year; to be loved and to be cherished by someone who cares deeply and persistently—this is the meaning of the most satisfying kind of marriage.

In marriage the most epochal as well as the most elemental experiences of life challenge a man and a woman. The miracle of motherhood and fatherhood will be shared by most couples. Later will be added anxiety over illness or accidents to the children, concern for the development of their intellects and their characters, and eventually the poignant sense of loss when they must leave the home. Throughout life, husband and wife experience together success and sorrow, joy and disillusionment. More-

6

over, they will share themselves, spiritually, mentally, physically in a more complete way than with any other human being they will ever know. For monogamous marriage in one form or another seems to be the universal way in which our most basic affectional and social needs are met. So marriage is the most profoundly important venture of life. How adequately we are prepared for that venture will determine not only the success of our marriage, but also the quality of most of life's adult experiences.

The functions of marriage vary so much by cultures, that it is difficult to define marriage or the family in other than the simplest terms of association. For instance in the Fiji islands it was an affront to the islanders' sense of delicacy that a man ever remain under the same roof with his wife at night. He slept with other men at one of the public *bures* of his village. The Shastiki Indians of California had a town-lodge for women and another for men. A Zulu woman was not permitted to address her husband or even to speak of him to others by his name; to do so was punishable by death. In the Fijis brothers and sisters were not allowed to eat together, let alone talk to each other, so that family life in our sense did not exist. For this reason it is important to reduce definitions of marriage and the family to their most elemental meaning, and those of Burgess and Locke seem most appropriate. They define marriage as "the union, sanctioned by society, of men and women as husbands and wives."[1] The family is ". . . a group of persons, united by ties of marriage, blood or adoption, constituting a single household; interacting and communicating with each other in their respective social roles of husband and wife, mother and father, son and daughter, brother and sister; and creating and maintaining a common culture."[2]

THE FAMILY IN TRANSITION

No social institution has changed as radically as the American family in the last one hundred years. Whenever basic institutions are in process of change, individuals who are conditioned by and participate in those institutions change too. They develop different functions, new attitudes, changing roles and expectations of others. But college students who are aware that the marriages of their older brothers and sisters were the most

[1] Ernest W. Burgess, Harvey J. Locke, and Mary Margaret Thomes, *The Family, From Institution to Companionship*, 3rd ed. (New York: The American Book Company, 1963), p. 1. Reprinted by permission.
[2] Burgess, Locke and Thomes, pp. 1–2.

7

fragile in history need to know why this happened, why social change results in personal disorganization, and how they can avoid such catastrophic events in their own lives. In this material we will attempt to help the student identify the ways these basic changes influence him or her so that such awareness can prevent disaster. To understand those changes we have to look at the family as it changes over a period of time because the etiology of the family in transition is a process and a complex one.

SCIENTIFIC THINKING

Science has had a two-fold impact on the family. First, it has promoted the kind of systematic analysis of our material world that has resulted in inventions. Consider the way only one invention has altered the family. Baber describes the way electricity has revolutionized home tasks:

> Electric lights have removed at one stroke the labor in caring for kerosene lamps. Electric vacuum sweepers are making brooms obsolete. Electric toasters, grills, waffle irons, and percolators make it possible to prepare part of the meal while at table. Electric stoves need no wood box or coal scuttle to keep them going. Electric refrigerators reduce the work and disorder of the kitchen by their quiet efficiency. Electric washing machines and ringers remove most of the back break from "washday," and the electric iron lightens the next day's task. The electric sewing machine speeds the needlework, and the electric dishwasher gives relief from one of the most irksome of household tasks.[3]

The changes in life patterns resulting from this one invention are difficult to comprehend. Margaret Benz of New York University reports one study which shows that as late as 1940 preparation of food for a household took an average woman five and one half hours, but today the same task takes but one and one half hours.[4] Women consequently have been freed for more leisure time, for more education, and, as we shall see, for the acceptance of work outside the home. Boys and girls are released from "chores" so that on the one hand they too have more leisure time, but on the other

---

[3] Ray E. Baber, *Marriage and the Family*, 2nd ed. (New York: McGraw-Hill Book Company, Inc., 1953), p. 13. Copyright 1953, McGraw-Hill Book Company, Inc. Reprinted by permission of the publisher.

[4] Margaret G. Benz, "The Changing Role of Women in the Economic Life in the U.S.," Preparatory Paper for the National Methodist Industrial Relations Conference, Cincinnati, Ohio, October 30, 1958, p. 1.

a source of learning responsibility and working skills is lost to them. The automobile and the airplane have made us a mobile people, and this has helped to destroy the large, extended family of our grandparents. Contraception has resulted in a smaller family unit, which immediately changes parent-child relationships. Every invention is a challenge to the status quo of the family institution.

A second effect of the scientific way of life has been the growth of secularization, which means that institutions and values which previously were regarded with awe as inviolate are now thought of critically and skeptically. Science is not solely responsible for this process, but the inventions and discoveries it produces and the inquisitive nature of its inquiries both help to undermine and to question that which was unquestionable yesterday. So many of the standards of perfection, many of the mores, many of the values that were associated with yesterday's family are no longer held to be inviolate. Some part of the increment of premarital sexual relations, of adultery, and of divorce is related to secularization. Both the basic attitudes of science and the rapid growth of mechanization due to science has contributed to industrialization and urbanization.

INDUSTRIALIZATION AND URBANIZATION

When it became possible not only to invent new devices for meeting human needs, but to manufacture them in the mass in a large setting, industrialization led to urbanization. Only ninety years ago, in 1870, some 74.3 per cent of the people of the United States lived in communities of less than 2,500 persons, or on farms. The U.S. census showed that by 1950 some 63 per cent of the population were urban dwellers. With urbanization came compulsory education, which effectively changed the role of both men and women and their relationships. Furthermore nearly 30 per cent of the families in New York lived in apartments, multifamily dwellings which in terms of their cramped quarters and social isolation, resulted in new behavior patterns. Kingsley Davis points out that "urbanism forces individuals to cooperate with countless individuals who are not kinsmen . . . and in contrast to the conventional intimacy of the family creates rationalized, impersonal associations on the one hand and unconventional intimacies on the other." [5]

[5] Kingsley Davis, "Reproductive Institutions and the Pressure for Population," *The Sociological Review*, XXIX (1937), 295.

MOBILITY

Urbanization always involves mobility because workers have to move from the country to the industrial centers and from one place of work to another. We have become a nation on wheels. Not only do city dwellers change their place of residence once every three years, but the family car or other forms of transportation may carry us far from the home many times each year. The result for the family has been that the "family home" with all of its visible symbols of family continuity and solidarity has little meaning, that family members separate and search for stimulation and thrills individually and away from the family group, that the local community with its primary—or face to face—relations with members of the family has lost much of its power for social control, and that there has been an increasing opportunity for anonymity and participation in types of sexual and recreational behavior that would be condemned by the primary group. When a family moves its residence, its boys and girls have to give up their friends, churches, schools, neighbors, rooms and many other things. James S. Plant, a psychiatrist, noted that many of his patients came from mobile families, and concluded that "We have seen evidences in children that one such change in address involves inadequacy (or inferiority) very much more than insecurity, but that repeated situations of this sort very definitely begin to give the picture of insecurity in the child." [6]

To the extent that scientific thinking, industrialization, urbanization, secularization, and mobility have altered the family situation significantly, we would expect to find the structure, the processes and the values of family life radically changed. By family structure we mean the relatively permanent kind of relationships that exist between members. By processes we refer to the reciprocal interactions by which members of the family get their tasks accomplished and the way they are constantly influencing each other. By values we mean the norms, the purposes and goals that motivate and guide each person in the family. To understand the many ways in which the revolution in the American family will complicate our marriage, we must first see how our functions and roles have become confused to the extent that the structures of our relationships have shifted. To make these shifts obvious we will chart them graphically, then discuss

[6] James S. Plant, *Personality and the Cultural Pattern* (New York: The Commonwealth Fund, 1937), p. 107.

10

FIGURE 1. Transitions in Family Structure

THE FAMILY OF YESTERDAY

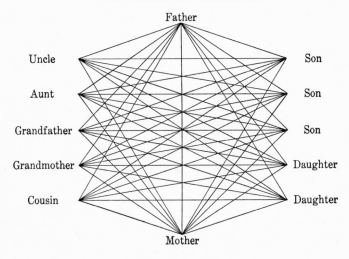

THE FAMILY OF TODAY

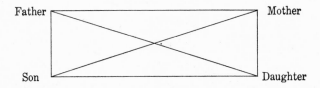

them, and try to make explicit the implications of the changes to each person living in the middle of the twentieth century.

SIZE

Young people entering marriage today expect on the average to be members of families that include only about half as many members as did those of their great grandparents. The average number of persons in the household in 1790 was 5.17, in 1850 it was 5.6, in 1900 it was 4.7, in 1950 it was 3.6, and in 1960 there were only 3.29 persons.[7] In the extended

[7] Figures for 1790 and 1850: Bureau of the Census, *A Century of Population Growth from the First Census to the Twelfth, 1790–1900*, 1909, p. 98; figure for 1950 from the Bureau of the Census, *Current Population Reports*, Series P-20, No. 38; figure for 1960 from *The Statistical Abstract of the United States* 1962 (eighty-third edition), No. 42, p. 44.

11

family, relationships were extensive and casual; today they are limited and intensive in the small nuclear family. The chart indicates complexity of interaction in a large family as contrasted to the paucity of contacts in today's family.

ORIENTATION

The results of this shift in size and closeness to other relatives is seen in the emotional life of the members of the family. Looking at the chart it is obvious, for example, that there will be more adult attention, many more adult demands and consequently more strain upon the children in the contemporary family structure.[8] In our grandparents' home there were so many males and females about that no one individual was pivotal for the personality development of the young. If father happened to be so hostile, or introverted, or preoccupied with outside interests that he could not be an identification figure for his son, there was always an uncle or a grandparent whose relationship with the boy would be intimate enough to furnish a masculine ideal. If mother was resentful or rejective of her daughters, an older sister, a grandmother, or an aunt would give the younger girls the emotional support they needed for effective maturation. Today the only male with whom most boys ever can identify is their father; and a mother is the only female most girls see consistently enough to basically influence them. So, if the father and mother are neurotic, or rejective, or their major orientation is outside the family circle, the children inevitably live a life barren of emotional warmth or possibilities for identification. This means that the small, nuclear family because of its structure involves really enormous demands upon its members for emotional responsiveness and exhibits an extraordinary sensitivity to failure on the part of the father or the mother in playing their modeling role effectively. The mechanics of sex identification and the development of character or conscience will be detailed in later chapters when the pivotal nature of the parental-child relationship will be emphasized. Here our pivotal point is that if the parents in the modern home do not fulfill a very much expanded role in interaction with their children, the result is disastrous because there simply is no one else in the life-space of the child

[8] James H. S. Bossard and Eleanor S. Boll, *The Sociology of Child Development* (New York: Harper and Brothers, 1959), pp. 53–56.

to make up for their deficiency. This is a major consequence of the size and the isolation of the modern family.

Partially because of the loss of the kinship and partially because of the isolation of urban living, a husband and a wife are also much more dependent on each other for the answer to emotional and social needs previously supplied by other adults. Much has been made of the fact that today women are often confused by the multiple roles they must play. They must be companions, partners, housekeepers, mistresses, mothers and wives. This is not really new because the wife of a farmer a hundred years ago was a partner in the farming enterprise, certainly a companion in some spheres of her husband's life, a mother, a mistress and a housekeeper. But what is unique is the degree to which she must fulfill all by herself these needs of her husband. His brother and his father and his close neighbors no longer furnish companionship. Previously the entire extended family formed a partnership in a husband's business; today he goes it alone, modified to the degree to which he can share with his wife. There were sons and daughters to help with the chores and the house. There were a great many more individuals about for the father as objects of both his negative and positive emotions. Today there is only the wife. Consequently the nuclear family must "turn in on itself" because there is no substitute. Unless the husband and wife share their problems, concerns, interests, frustrations and hopes, they will not be ventilated at all because one does not share these things with the casual acquaintance of the urban scene.

This then is what W. I. Thomas means when he says that the modern family is introverted. It has to turn in on itself to have its needs met, to demand greater participation in more areas by each member. Consequently to succeed, the modern family must depend upon individuals who have the mental and emotional breadth and maturity to meet these expanded expectations. And, as we shall presently see, these demands for broader and more mature parental and mate functions are imposed on men and women at a time when our culture perversely does not condition them to accept such challenges. Whatever else we say about the nuclear family in terms of its almost excessive demands on one man and one woman, we must also say that where they succeed in meeting the challenge, the rewards that come from a more profound interdependency are great indeed. But let us see what the social influences are that detract interest and concern from the family itself. We can understand this better when we visualize the many functional bonds that in the past knit the family together as a cohesive whole; today those or many of those functions are performed by out-groups, by societal organizations which not only do not contribute to family cohesion but in many ways compete with the family for the time, energy and loyalty of family members.

This chart illustrates the way in which basic functions that used to be a part of the cohesive, binding common life of the family now compete with the family or are relatively unimportant personal concerns. While protection of the family was a time-honored obligation in the past, the broken line indicates only a sporadic contact of the father with law enforcement agencies. The same is true of the shift in education. Until the opening of this century, mother and father had always been responsible for the education of their offspring. In the diagram on the left of Figure 2 below, education is shown as a part of the core of living experience of the

FIGURE 2. Shifts in Family Function

THE FAMILY AS THE PRIMARY
CORE OF LIVING EXPERIENCE

THE FAMILY AS A COMPETITIVE
INSTITUTION IN LIVING EXPERIENCES

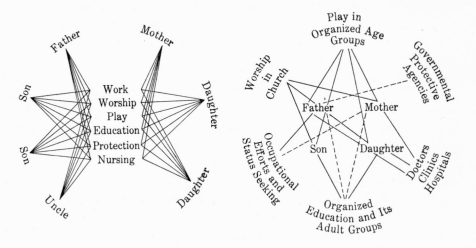

institutional family. This picture of family life is no longer accurate. As indicated in the diagram on the right of Figure 2 above, education is now peripheral to the family and each member of the family has an individual relation to this aspect of life experience. The broken line from parents to the educational institution is representative of the casual and intermittent contact of today's parent with those who educate his children. The contrast between these ways of living is also true of the way the modern family works, worships and plays. These were core functions of the family of yesterday; today they are allocated to community or governmental organizations. Thus participation in work, worship, learning or recreation no longer involves face-to-face family participation. When the family worked together on the farm or in a small store, they were bound together in great cohesion by a thousand daily worries, successes, or problems. Today father and sometimes mother may work at establishments twenty miles from home and even farther removed socially. Even if the members of the family have a healthy interest in the father's occupational task, there is generally no way in which they can share his work load. Their experiences are vicarious and peripheral.

The same analysis can be made of the way the shift from family worship and religious activities to the church has eliminated another bond of family interaction. The proponents of scientific religious education have imposed on church participation a rather rigid age classification, so that once the family has entered the front doors on Sunday morning, it disperses in all directions. In this sense the work of the church is actually divisive of family unity. The most comprehensive of all studies of the family and the church asked parents a question: "What kinds of things do you want your children to remember about your family when they grow up?" [9] They discovered that there was only a "small minority of parents (scarcely one in six) who wanted their children to remember most of all the Christian faith and the living of that faith . . ." [10] Furthermore, "relatively few parents (one in twenty) wanted their offspring primarily to remember the moral training of the family." This lack of desire does not mean that parents are not interested in their children's acquisition of the Christian faith or morality; it is rather evidence of the degree to which they have abdicated religion in the home. The same trend is reported by Catholic sociologists who report that

> . . . Catholic families have tended to entrust the entire formal religious training of their children to the [parochial] school. In a study of over 16,000 parochial school children entering first grade, we discovered that only a little over one-half knew how to make the Sign of the Cross, one-

[9] Roy W. Fairchild and John Charles Wynn, *Families in the Church: A Protestant Survey* (New York: Association Press, 1961), p. 136.
[10] Fairchild and Wynn, p. 138.

15

third could recite the "Hail Mary." . . . Knowledge of religious dogma is likewise deficient. . . . Specifically the failure of Catholic families to give their children adequate knowledge of family standards is reflected in the widespread demand for and introduction of marriage preparation courses in Catholic colleges and high schools.[11]

Furthermore, there is a significant difference in the quality of religious experience when it is practiced in the home by a family unit and when it is experienced in an institution outside the home. When religion was assiduously practiced in the home, the whole family as a unit shared in the experience; but in the church, worship, study and character education are fragmented experiences. While it is true that some of the major protestant denominations have recast their religious educational materials to stress home study and family interaction, this study is still infrequently practiced and does not yet involve the whole family. The church is a place where father goes to his men's club, mother for the women's fellowship, sister to youth meetings, brother as a member of the basketball team, and little Sue to Sunday School. And, if all the rest also go to Sunday School, they, too, go to separate rooms and study very diverse age-graded materials. Because of this fragmented experience, the church often takes single members of the family away at a time when the rest of the family is together. With all due regard to the contributions which religion makes to our general cultural life, it is important here to see that the church often conflicts with the family for the time and energy of members of the family.

Let us now turn to recreation and see whether or not we can document the same kind of shift from family-centered use of leisure time to activities outside the family. Almost all recreation of the family used to be home centered. This was partially because there was no commercial leisure-time industry, as at present with the movie theaters, bowling alleys, dance halls, cabarets, and golf courses to lure one away from the home. One of the other basic reasons was the lack of swift transportation which made even a short trip to town or city laborious and time consuming. Still another reason was the long work day, from sunup to sundown, which took so many of the twenty-four hours that there was neither time nor energy left for outside recreation. Neighborhood get-togethers included the whole family for quilting parties, barn raisings, square dances, or the festivities associated with weddings, funerals, or christenings. In the home itself playing instruments, singing, popping corn, cracking nuts,

[11] John L. Thomas, S.J., *The American Catholic Family* (Englewood, N.J.: Prentice-Hall, Inc., 1956), pp. 334–335. © 1956 by Prentice-Hall, Inc. Reprinted by permission.

making candy, playing such card games as "rook" occupied what few hours were left from a strenuous life.

All this has changed today. Entertainment has become one of the major industries of America. Instead of creating our own diversions, Americans hire someone else to plan them for us. Instead of joining in effective repartee we hire someone to say the whimsical or clever remark. Instead of exercising ourselves we sit in vast stadia and watch eleven members of a football team or nine members of a baseball team exert themselves, "pulling" for them in a purely vicarious manner. Inevitably commercial recreation made for individuation of interests, so that the family was divided in different interest groups away from home. There is some indication that we have reached the optimum in sex and age-stratified leisure-time pursuits and that such family interests as camping, backyard cooking, home projects, and travel may be easing the divisions caused by recreation in the last twenty-five years. But it is still true that the modern family is not united by consistent playing together. The family is still interested in recreation but in a very significantly different way. Instead of planning a game or activity that the entire family can enjoy, the emphasis is placed on enrolling Johnny in a Little League or Boy Scouts or Mary in tennis lessons or Girl Scouts. On the same day recently two different counseling clients said:

> "But I had a good life before I married, and I expected to continue my tennis, and boating with my friends. I thought my wife should accept that life."
> "Sure, she objects to my basketball playing three times a week and maybe I was a little dense to be gone so much doing it during the first months of my marriage but, hang it all, that's my life."

Insofar as playing together is a highly socializing form of family interaction, young people need to think about the importance of this loss to family growth in cohesion. More will be said about this subject in the chapter on children.

THE PERVASIVE INFLUENCE OF FUNCTIONAL CHANGES IN THE FAMILY

So far we have outlined by way of illustration some of the shifts in family function which have resulted from and then created the transition from the institutional to the companionship family. But every aspect of family life has been altered by this change. The relationship of parent to child has been subject to remarkable changes. The influence of the parent on marital choice has almost been reversed. Today few parents would have the temerity to select a mate for their boy or girl. The latter has almost unlimited freedom in making that choice. But to make that choice some new institutions had to be created, and since World War I dating and courtship activities have become a primary concern of almost all youth. These concerns have as their primary sociological function the sorting out and selection of appropriate mates.

When industrialization began to involve high mobility, the possibility of maintaining the extended family declined because ties and involvements with parents were sundered. Likewise, the very nature of housing in the urban scene made a two-family home almost impossible. With all these changes came a new feeling of the independence of the nuclear family, and, as a consequence, the emergence of interfamily hostilities with decidedly more poignancy. Mother-in-law may always have been a thorn in the side of a new bride, but the loss of primary relationships between future family relatives and the difficult tangential nature of interfamily contacts now give in-law interactions much potential for conflict.

CONCLUSION

If we are to live successfully in the twentieth-century family, it is necessary that we recognize how these functional changes have altered roles, values, and family patterns. In a sense the rest of this book details in depth the impact of family change on husbands and wives, children, and young adults. Although cultural discontinuities do not become obvious in a month or even in a year, you and I live in a time of dynamic change, of acceleration in mechanical and social inventions. We must understand the forms and the challenges of rapid social change if we are not to be the pawns of the disorganization that is always incident to it. We must remember that change is not nefarious in itself and that many of the shifts that do occur contain within themselves promise of healthier and fuller lives. To reap the benefits of these changes, young people must have a kind of poised creativity, sensitive to that which is novel, and they must be adept at making their lives congruous with the world in which they are destined to live.

READINGS

BOSSARD, JAMES H. S. and ELEANOR STOKER BOLL. *The Sociology of Child Development.* New York, Harper and Brothers, 1959, pp. 53–56. Copyright Harper and Row, Publishers.

BURGESS, ERNEST W., HARVEY J. LOCKE, and MARY MARGARET THOMES. *The Family, From Institution to Companionship,* 3rd ed. New York, The American Book Company, 1963, Chapter I.

KEPHART, WILLIAM M. *The Family, Society, and the Individual.* Boston, Houghton Mifflin Company, 1961, Chapter 8.

LOCKE, HARVEY J. *Predicting Adjustment in Marriage: A Comparison of a Divorced and a Happily Married Group.* New York, Henry Holt and Company, 1951, Chapters 1–3. Copyright 1951, Holt, Rinehart and Winston, Inc.

TRUXAL, ANDREW G. and FRANCIS E. MERRILL. *Marriage and the Family.* New York, Prentice-Hall, Inc., 1953, Chapter 16.

WINCH, ROBERT F. *The Modern Family.* New York, Henry Holt and Company, 1952, Chapter 14, Copyright 1952, Holt, Rinehart and Winston, Inc.

CHAPTER 2

The Changing Nature of Marital Roles

INTRODUCTION

IF the functions of any institution change significantly, it is inevitable that the part individuals play in that institution must also change in radical fashion. Furthermore, the importance of the family itself in the hierarchy of life-tasks may change in such a way as to make severe problems for the family itself. In this chapter we study the way in which a shift in function involves (a) conflict between commitment to the family and to other life-tasks, and (b) role conflicts within the family itself.

THE MEANING OF SOCIAL ROLE

When we speak of a social role, we are talking about the expectations that a social group turns towards an individual member of the group consequential to his particular place in the group. Newcomb defines this concept: "The ways of behaving which are expected of any individual who occupies a certain position constitute the 'role' (or, social role) associated with that position." [1] Role expectations represent the "ought to do" aspects of the role position, and role behavior is expressed by what the individual does in living up to those expectations.

---

[1] Theodore M. Newcomb, *Social Psychology* (New York: Dryden Press, 1950), p. 280. Copyright Holt, Rinehart and Winston, Inc.

CONFLICT BETWEEN FAMILY ROLES AND OTHER ROLES

Some reflection will make it clear that in the world of the institutional family of yesterday every social role, such as the part a man played in religion or in recreation, was still a family role. As these life functions were centered in the family, interaction centering about them involved all the members of the family and consequently enriched the total web of relationships. There could be almost no differentiation or fragmentation due to role-playing because the total family was involved. If a family was very religious or not religious, it was so as a unit. If a man had great ambition in his work, the entire family group became part of that effort. Furthermore, the various assigned or expected tasks of the family were so clearly understood and accepted by each member that conflict between them could scarcely arise. In addition, the cultural definition of roles was so specific that almost every individual's role expectations and behavior were congruent, and we may say there was a nice "fit" in social living.

Riesman's description of the power of the inner-directed norm is important because he has shown how the interiorized roles kept individuals hewing closely to a prescribed course throughout life. He uses the figure of an "internal gyroscope" which was powered by early training and governed by a profound sense of guilt to keep individuals geared to a pathway of industry, honesty and frugality.[2] Not only was a role well defined, but the individual suffered psychically if he did not live up to that role. It is significant that family stability and fidelity to family responsibilities were primary in the principles that spun the moral gyroscope of the inner-directed person. Even more significant is the concordance of principles in a homogeneous society where social controls reinforced the individual's conscience.

Today there is not only a confusion in society as to what principles are to be shared in the socialization process, but the goal of socialization itself has changed. Individuals are motivated not so much to "thine own self be true" but to be true to meeting the expectations of one's peers. The standards of self-esteem do not come from achieving notable conformance to inner ideals but rather to the approval of others. Thus, Riesman uses the term "other-directed" to designate a goal which is anchored in one's popularity or response from others.[3] Adjustment during child rearing, in

[2] David Riesman, Nathan Glazer, Reuel Denney, *The Lonely Crowd* (New York: Doubleday and Company, Inc., 1955), p. 41. Copyright Yale University Press.
[3] Riesman, Glazer, and Denney, p. 66.

21

the sense of getting along with others, becomes the concern of parents rather than the internalization of absolutes such as honesty, truth, and industry. The result is that contemporary man is not equipped by inner mechanisms (moral gyroscopes), but is rather possessed of "radar" which is sensitively tuned to the whims, wishes, and approval of others. The other-directed child has first to define what is good before he can work for it. His parents are of little help because of ambivalence grounded in "diffuse anxiety." So the modern child must find self-esteem outside himself, for there is nothing within that has ego significance.

Some important empirical proof of Riesman's position comes from recent studies of the values of college students. Jacob reports a study at a number of colleges that revealed that some 40 per cent or more of the students cheat. If given the task of proctoring an examination, 66 per cent of the students would not report an observed cheater if he were a personal friend, but 84 per cent would report the cheater if he were not a friend. However, if the proctoring student knew that his action in not reporting a friend would become known to the university, only 27 per cent said they would not report their friend. The conclusion of the study is that for college students self-interest comes first, then social acceptance, and finally moral principles.[4] The Cornell study confirms the conclusion that the students' ethical systems are undercut by other imperatives.[5] The point is further illustrated by Jacob's conclusions in terms of sexual and political values when he says:

> Permissiveness in regard to the conduct of others is as much a part of the American student's moral outlook as is the orthodoxy of his own code. Thus within the college, or rather the student community, no social sanctions attach to violations of the standards accepted by the majority. Freedom to deviate as an individual wishes is fully acknowledged.[6]

The wider implications of this type of characterless other-directedness of contemporary men and women will be considered later. Here, it is mentioned as it relates to the Riesman thesis of the vacuum of inner values. Instead, there is a kind of vacuum tube tuned to others to discover how the individual may please them. But the number and relationship of these

---

[4] Phillip E. Jacob, *Changing Values in College* (New York: Harper and Brothers, 1958), pp. 25–26. Copyright Harper and Row, Publishers.

[5] Rose K. Goldsen, *et al.*, *What College Students Think* (Princeton, N.J.: D. Van Nostrand Company, Inc., 1960), pp. 74–80. Copyright 1960, D. Van Nostrand Company, Inc. Reprinted by permission of the publisher.

[6] Jacob, p. 23. Reprinted by permission of Harper and Row, Publishers.

others have also changed. Because of the emphasis on social approval, children learn very early to seek self-esteem by playing roles which are responsive not to parents or parental ideals but to their peers outside the family circle.[7] So boys and girls are soon conditioned to find their worthfulness outside of the family setting.

If we relate this training for adjustment and source of ego-satisfaction outside the home setting to shifts in the function of the family, we can account partially for the "organization man" and the source of profound problems in the modern family. Let us consider only one aspect of role playing, that of the occupational role. To review . . . in the institutional family the occupational role was centered in the home and was really diffused to include a group instead of an individual. In the nuclear family the occupational role is played far from home and in a way that differentiates members of the family. Not only does the family not participate in a common economic enterprise, but it is also spatially and psychologically separated from it. But an even more significant aspect remains. If the individual is trained to find his self-esteem in areas away from the family, we must inquire into the relative emphasis which he can now place on his work role as contrasted with his family role. A case excerpt is instructive.

A young man of 30 appeared with his wife in the counselor's office for marriage counseling. The simple complaint of the wife was that soon after the marriage the husband had abandoned his courtship practices of affection and attention and was concentrating all of his efforts and energy on his job. In a sense she felt betrayed because his behavior before the marriage had been so dedicated that she at least felt there was no question of their companionship after marriage. The young man labeled his wife as a complainer, who "bitched" all the time so that she interfered with the peace of mind he needed to pursue his goals in life. After several interviews the young man remarked rather cynically that the counselor was not making much progress. The counselor freely admitted that this was so. The young man then said he had the formula for the success of the marriage. The counselor (refraining then from asking why he had not applied his formula and eliminated the necessity of visiting the counselor) was glad to listen to any solution. The young man said:

"I am already assistant secretary of my corporation. In seven or eight years one of the vice-presidents of the corporation will retire. I am going to have his job. I am going to have it if it means we can't have children, if I have to spend every evening and every week-end to get it. It is the only chance I'll ever have like this, and it is the only really important thing

[7] Riesman, Glazer, Denney, p. 74.

in my life. I won't have such an opportunity again, but I can always get another wife!" [8]

This was not the first time I had heard this statement or similar ones. Such statements mean for that young man that his occupational role takes precedence in weight over his role as a husband and potential father. If to our first chart we now add a section showing differences in family function, a comparison will reveal how the shift in role emphasis has influenced many families.

In the institutional family the entire family worked at the same project. On the farm the husband, the wife, and the children all had interrelated tasks which they could and did discuss. Today the father's work task is geographically and psychologically far removed from the family; his wife does her work apart from her husband; and the children rarely work at all. More important is the contention of many, and proved by case studies, that the weight of the work task in the man's hierarchy of values is far greater than the weight of his commitment to his family responsibilities. This is illustrated in the following diagram by the diameter of the arrows detailing a man's "connection" with each member of his family and his work.

FIGURE 3. Conflicts in Loyalties to Roles

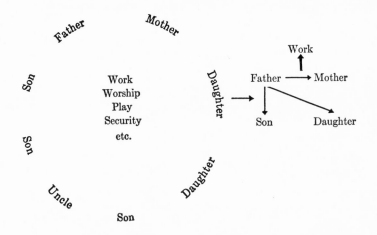

The significance of this shift of emphasis for the adjustment of modern men and women in marriage involves the following factors:

1. The occupational life today takes time away from the family. Not only does the husband (and sometimes the woman) work far away from home, but much of the man's nonworking hours are devoted to contacts or social activity revolving around his work goals.

2. Psychologically, the things to which modern men (and some modern women) attend are focused on work and not the home. Yesterday a young woman in my clinic vigorously condemned her husband because even when he was at home he could not think about or find interest in any phase of life except his work.

3. The immense drive needed to succeed plus the cost of anxiety attendant to the success-drive is such that many men complain of lack of energy to indulge in family activities.

4. As a man's primary motivation is related to other-than-family goals, his involvement and commitment to the family is diminished. Thus, a divorce or the psychic affairs at home are not viewed with the same degree of intensity they would have received fifty or a hundred years ago when the man was concentrating on achieving goals which were closely related to his status as a father and a husband.

THE CONFLICT OF ROLES CONTINGENT ON THE SHIFTING ROLE CONCEPTS OF MALE AND FEMALE

We have examined the effect on marriage of the decline in importance of family roles as contrasted with life roles. Perhaps more important has been the influence of role conflict between husband and wife on marital adjustment. Because of rapid changes in family structure and function, many men and women define the roles they expect to play in marriage very differently. If two individuals with great divergencies in their role expectations fall in love and marry, the result is inevitable role conflict. Insight into the reaction of a potential mate to the shifting functions of the male and female in marriage may assist one to act more successfully in making a wise marriage choice and in achieving greater marital stability. In this section of role analysis, we shall look at some of the troubles associated with differential role expectations.

Mangus has analyzed cases of marital difficulty in terms of the presence or lack of "harmony, consistency, and congruity among the role expectations of those participating in marriage." He explains his theory saying that:

> Marriage is viewed as a process of reciprocal role perceptions, understanding, and performance on the part of specific marital partners. The integrative or adaptive quality of the marriage is reflected in the degree to which relevant role expectations are shared between people in their lives. It is believed that the most pressing interpersonal problems in marriage arise out of the disparities among the role concepts and self-concepts that are pertinent to the marriage situation.[9]

The movement from the institutional form of the family toward the companionship or democratic form involved an extensive shift in the self-concept of women. The change in a woman's view of herself necessitated an adjustment on the part of men to that new role. That adjustment has been made in various ways: denial, ridicule, opposition, or acceptance. Some background is necessary for us to understand how profoundly the role of women has been altered in America in the last century.[10] In 1848 women came together at Seneca Falls to plan for a better day. The name given to their gathering, The Women's Rights Convention, is significant itself because the most significant report of that convention was on the absence of rights. Women then had a legal status not much different from the cattle they tended. Let us suppose that a woman inherited from her father 100,000 dollars. When she was married, the money immediately became the property of her husband to dissipate or utilize as he saw fit. Hawthorne's picture of *The Scarlet Letter* depicts the double standard of the day, for the very men who decreed that Hester should wear the letter "A" could commit the same act of adultery without condemnation. If a woman found some place to earn a little money, she could not legally sue for it because in the eyes of the law she was not a person. But her husband could go to court, collect the money, and keep it. She could not vote for a redress of her inferior position, nor could she raise her voice in any court in the land if her husband maltreated her children. The Bill of Rights rejected any claim she might have had. So did the Fifteenth Amendment in 1870. It was not until seventy years later that the Nineteenth Amendment gave women the rights of citizenship.

[9] A. R. Mangus, "Role Theory and Marriage Counseling," *Social Forces*, XXXV (1957), 200–209.

[10] Most of this material follows closely the role of women presented in Eleanor Metheny and James A. Peterson, *The Trouble With Women* (New York: Vantage Press, Inc., 1957), Chapter II. Reprinted by permission.

But even then women's rights were more theoretical than real. In 1920 a woman without training who had four or five children had few alternatives to staying with her husband, regardless of how sadistic or penurious he might be. However, with the development of universal education for women and their determination to break the locks which had confined them to their husband's homes, they ventured more and more into the business world.

> In the mechanized economy of the growing cities there were many jobs which required dexterity and intelligence rather than great physical strength. The rejected spinster who had formerly stitched out her despised life in the back bedroom of some male relative's home found new independence as the bravely pioneering "typewriter" in her stiffly starched waistshirt. The typist became the career girl. The career woman was soon joined by the employed wife, and then by mothers who returned to work after their children started for school.[11]

Now women had a new choice. It is probably responsible for a major part of the growing divorce rate. A woman who had previously worked and who found herself yoked to an irresponsible and petty man, now knew that she had a real alternative in leaving him and supporting herself and her children. The following case illustrates one such situation:

> Molly came to the counselor to discuss her future. She had recently filed for divorce and had no intention of returning to Jack, who had recently returned to her after three years in the army. The story she told related to conflict in role although it had many other aspects. Jack and Molly had never gotten along well during their eight years of marriage which preceded Jack's induction into the service. He was a swaggering lower-class individual with a high hostility quotient who expressed his irritation by acting it out. He would slap her or worse and then laugh when she cowered. But she soon had a family, and Jack kept her "barefoot and pregnant" so she was resigned to an unhappy life. She was especially fearful when Jack was drinking, and he drank every day.
>
> When Jack was called into the service, Molly had to find work, and she became quite an expert on the riveting machine. Her foreman gave her every encouragement to stay on after the war was over, but she did not know what to do. She soon made up her mind when Jack got home. He called her from his port of entry, asked her to quit her job that minute and come and get him. But he had been drinking, and Molly quite coldly told him to take the bus. She had to finish out her day. When she got home he

[11] Metheny and Peterson, p. 17. Reprinted by permission of the publisher.

was very nasty, demanded that she quit the next morning and said, "Things are going to get back to normal around here." When Molly saw the fear and revulsion in the eyes of her children, she went into the bedroom and packed her things. Then she moved, not into her mother's home, but closer to the aircraft factory.[12]

The last line is the significant one. Molly had a new alternative. She did not have to stay, nor did she have to move to her mother's home. She now could act as an independent person and, without fear, expect to make her own way. For the first time in history she could choose between staying in a bitter and destructive marriage or leaving, although this meant being away from her family while she was working. The developing economic status of women may be regarded as a lever for better marriages, or as an incentive to give up without trying to work out a difficult situation. But this new choice is one of the outcomes of woman's new role as a person in society, implemented by the opportunity for economic rewards outside the home.

After describing the promise of the new role for women, Metheny and Peterson conclude:

> In essence, then, the trouble with modern women is that neither the privileges nor the responsibilities of female human freedom have yet been clearly defined. Women have been promised the right to share equally with men in a democratic social order, but the meaning of that promise has not yet been fully interpreted. Full understanding of the interactions between equal but different female and male human beings has not yet been fully achieved. While new social and personal interpretations of equality are being established, women inevitably feel the pressure of many inconsistencies and contradictions in their modern lives.[13]

But if women feel contradictions, so do men. For dozens of centuries a sense of worthfulness came to a man who could take care of his wife and his children, all of whom were regarded by him as foolish and fragile. He was the intelligent one, the authoritative one, the strong one. The new role of women challenged all of these basic assumptions and brought to many men a profound anxiety about their masculinity. Then, in their need to defend their self-esteem, they became inordinately sensitive about the competition or contributions of women, and in many cases an intense role conflict ensued.

[12] From a case study in the author's files.
[13] Metheny and Peterson, p. 217. Reprinted by permission of the publishers.

This type of role conflict arises particularly in those cases where young men and young women have been raised in homes where the masculine and feminine norms were different. I will never forget the young man who came into my office shouting about his wife. I remember it very vividly because he pounded on the wall. The young man's agitation came because as he said:

> I just can't make any sense out of my wife. She wants to eat half the food, sleep in half the bed, use the car whenever she wants to. She talks about a partnership, but she refuses to go to work. What right does she have to half of my money if she doesn't earn part of it?

This young man had a mother who had always worked. And his sister, after she was married, had continued her job. All of his significant experiences with women were related to relatives who gladly and as a matter of course had worked for money. So he naturally felt that it was right for his wife to work. She, on the other hand, had never worked, her mother had always stayed home, and she had known very few women who regarded marriage as this kind of working partnership.

What empirical evidence is there that role conflict is related to marital adjustment? After all, these individual cases might be just that, individual and isolated and nonrepresentational. Several careful studies have been made which document the impact of agreement or lack of agreement in role behavior on marital adjustment.

THE KOTLAR STUDY [14]

The Kotlar study compared fifty adjusted couples as judged by the Wallace Adjustment test with fifty maladjusted couples secured from marriage counseling clinics. Both groups were middle class, Protestant, married about six years, with a somewhat higher educational and economic index than the average public. Kotlar used three instruments in her study, The Wallace Marital Adjustment Test, the Interpersonal Check List, and a Role Attitude Survey. The Wallace Marital Adjustment Test was used to validate the degree of difference in adjustment between the two groups. The ICL uses adjectives or short adjective phrases to permit the individual to translate his role perceptions and expectations into language

[14] Sally Kotlar, "Middle Class Roles . . . Ideal and Perceived in Relation to Adjustment in Marriage," 1961, unpublished doctoral dissertation, Libraries of the University of Southern California, Los Angeles, California.

and later to quantifiable material. The Role Attitude Survey further studies role differences between the two groups. Each husband and each wife checked items on the last two studies for both themselves and their mates. On the ICL they gave ratings for their perceived self, their ideal self, their perceived mate, and their ideal mate.

Kotlar was interested in testing Mangus' statement that the integrative quality of a marriage is reflected in the degree of congruence between the way a spouse sees himself as compared to the way he is seen by his partner. As Kotlar puts it:

> The hypothesis assumes that a low disparity between an individual's self-perception and his mate's perception of him was associated with good marital adjustment. The correlation between the couple's marital adjustment and discrepancy scores was found to be —30 and significant beyond the .01 level.* The hypothesis is accepted as valid according to the findings of this study. These findings concur with other research relating to this variable, and indicate a positive relationship between congruence of perception and good interpersonal relationships. The indications are that the adaptive quality of the marriage is reflected in the degree of similarity between the way each partner sees his own role and the way that role is perceived by his spouse.[15]

Kotlar also hypothesized that poor adjustment would result if a mate behaved in ways that violated the expectations of the mate. So the husband's role expectation for his wife was compared with the wife's actual role behavior. Her summary of her findings of this point are:

> The hypothesis had assumed that a low disparity between role expectation and role fulfillment was associated with good marital adjustment. This was accepted as the correlation between disparity scores and marital adjustment scores was found to be —.77. To the extent that we can generalize from the findings, we may say that if the individual perceives his mate as closely approximating his ideal for that marital role, this is significant for adaptive marital relations. However, where the disparity is great, the frustration of role expectations leads to disruptive interpersonal relations and makes for dissatisfaction with the marriage. This was supported by the Mangus study.[16]

The adjusted wives and husbands perceived their mates as approaching their expectations to a significantly higher degree than did the unadjusted

---

* Some of the statistical terms used in this book may be unfamiliar to the student. Their use is explained in Appendix II.

[15] Kotlar, p. 124. Reprinted by permission of Dr. Kotlar.

[16] Kotlar, pp. 139, 140.

spouses. This is simply to say that conflict in roles is related to lack of adjustment in marriage.

Kotlar's findings are similar to some of those of a Minnesota sample studied by an Iowa staff member who used the Wallace Adjustment Test and the Terman seven-point self-rating happiness scale. When 454 individuals who were former students at the University of Minnesota returned the adjustment test, they were divided into two groups, those who were "satisfactorily married" and "less satisfactorily married." [17] Then the ICL was sent to one of the spouses. When it was returned, another copy of the test was sent to the other. Men were thirty-one years old, women twenty-nine. Three-fourths were college graduates. Luckey's first hypothesis is almost identical to one of Kotlar's already considered:

> There is no difference in population means between two groups defined as satisfactorily and less satisfactorily married with regard to the degree of congruence between the concept each spouse holds of himself and the concept held by his marital partner.[17]

FIGURE 4. Perceived and Ideal Roles of an Adjusted Wife and Husband *

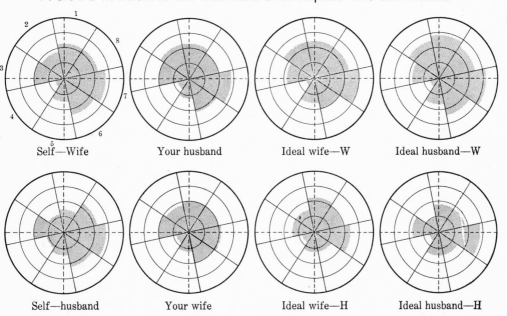

| Self—Wife | Your husband | Ideal wife—W | Ideal husband—W |

| Self—husband | Your wife | Ideal wife—H | Ideal husband—H |

* Figure is modified from Kotlar, Figure No. IV, p. 169.

[17] Eleanore Braun Luckey, "Marital Satisfaction and Its Association with Congruence of Perception," *Marriage and Family Living*, XXII, No. 1 (February, 1960), 49–54.

Luckey found in terms of testing this hypothesis that:

> In the group of married persons scoring highest on the marital satisfaction scale there was a significantly greater agreement of perception in regard to self by spouse.[18]

Both Kotlar and Luckey show that understanding the needs and expectations of the other leads to good adjustment.

Kotlar wished to help her readers understand graphically how differences in role as measured by the ICL could be portrayed; so she prepared on the ICL grid graphic representations of a happy and of an unhappy couple. Figure 4 represents a happy couple and Figure 5 an unhappy

FIGURE 5. Perceived and Ideal Roles of Unadjusted Wife and Husband *

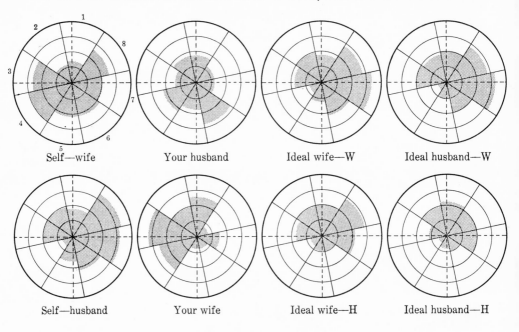

| Self—wife | Your husband | Ideal wife—W | Ideal husband—W |

| Self—husband | Your wife | Ideal wife—H | Ideal husband—H |

* Figure is modified from Kotlar, Figure No. IV, p. 170.

couple, i.e., one that was in therapy at a clinic or with a marriage counselor. To understand these charts more adequately, the meanings of the various segments are illustrated in Figure No. 6. The vertical axis is ordered along the domination-submission polarity with highest dominance

[18] Luckey, p. 54.

at the top. The horizontal axis is ordered along a love-hostility polarity with highest hostility and aggression to the extreme left, and high affiliative or love feelings on the extreme right.

F I G U R E 6. Personality Configuration from Interpersonal Check List *

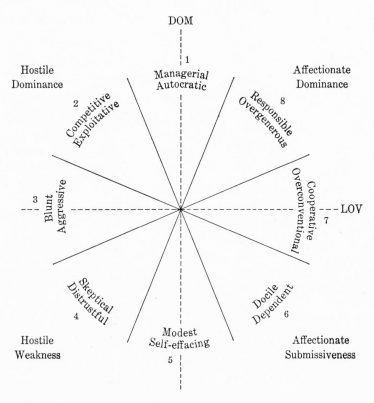

* Adapted from the Interpersonal Check List Illustrating the Classification of Interpersonal Behaviors into Sixteen Variable Categories, designed by members of the Kaiser Foundation psychology staff, appearing in Timothy Leary—*Interpersonal Diagnosis of Personality*— A Functional Theory and Methodology for Personality Evaluation. Copyright © 1957 The Ronald Press Company.

In analyzing Figure 4 which represents a happy relationship one notes:

1. The similarity of the role perceptions of the wife by herself and by her husband; there is no conflict in this relationship.
2. The similarity of the role perception of the husband by the wife and her ideal husband. He is generally a strong and affectionate man, and she wants him that way.

3. The similarity of the husband's perception of his wife as she is and the ideal he has for a wife. He would like her to be just a little less competitive and slightly more modest, but the differences are not marked.
4. Both husband and wife are fairly pleased with their own role performance. They do not feel that they have failed a great deal in matching performance with their own ideal. In general this husband and wife do not have, as far as role is concerned, much dissatisfaction with the self or the other.

By contrast Figure 5 which represents an unhappy couple presents many striking differences:

1. He sees himself as a very loving, tender person, but she sees him generally as a weak and docile individual. He gives himself great credit for strength, and she thinks he's dependent.
2. There is no similarity between the way the husband pictures his wife and the way he would like her to be ideally. He finds her hostile and distrustful, but he wishes she were loving and responsible.
3. There are also differences in the way she sees him and what she would like him to be as an ideal husband.
4. Neither one of them live up to their ideals for themselves, so that one can predict a certain amount of self-dissatisfaction which would indicate inner conflict. One positive note is the general congruity of their ideal patterns. If they could become what they would like to be, they would seemingly then please the other.

In summarizing this section of our study of modern role conflict, we may say that whenever there is wide diversity of definition of role expectation and consequently of role behavior, it can lead to difficulty in marriage. These recently developed studies of husband and wife roles have demonstrated that when there is wide diversity of role expectation as viewed by husband and wife, the result will be difficulty in marriage.

DEVIATIONS FROM CULTURAL ROLE DEFINITIONS AND MARITAL ADJUSTMENT

Is it possible in this shifting world of functions and roles to find any normative role definition on which any group of middle-class men and women would agree? Kotlar and others asked this question, and discovered that there not only was a new norm that is distinct from yesterday's ideal role expectation, but that deviations from the norm differentiated between the happy and the unhappy couple. Kotlar found that marital roles are defined more and more in terms of an equalitarian orientation in which extreme differences between the sexes in terms of function are being obliterated.[19] The ideals for both husband and wife were found in the affectionate-dominance quadrant which stresses strength and responsibility for both. The qualities subsumed here are: able to give orders, businesslike, can be frank and honest, can be strict if necessary, cooperative, eager to get along with others, is firm but just, is good leader, hardboiled when necessary, independent, likes responsibility, likes to compete with others, makes a good impression, is often admired and respected by others, is self-confident, self-reliant and assertive, stern but fair, sociable and neighborly, very respectful of authority, well thought of, and warm. On the other hand, a greater proportion of the unadjusted spouses saw themselves and/or their mates in the hostile-weak segment of the graph or in contradiction to the cultural norm. Therefore, in this study deviation from the norm was associated with poor adjustment.

Another study gives certain justification for holding this position. Yi-Chuang Lu reached similar conclusions in his investigation of the relationship of dominant-equalitarian-submissive behavior to marriage adjustment. He made an intensive study of some 603 husbands and wives selected from the Burgess-Wallin sample of 1,000 couples. As Burgess and Wallin had already studied the marital adjustment of these couples, it was only necessary for Lu to develop a scale by which to measure dominant-equalitarian-submissive roles and then to relate persons playing these roles to the adjustment scores. An index was developed consisting of sixteen items which had been selected out of fifty-two previously constructed questions.[20] After the dominant-equalitarian-submissive scores of these 603 couples were determined, they were then related to the marriage-adjustment scores by means of the two following tables, and were tested for statistical significance by means of the Critical Ratio formula (CR). A Critical Ratio of 2.0 was taken to mean that the statistic had a significance that could not be the result of chance. For both husbands and wives an equalitarian role was associated with the highest rating or adjustment.

[19] Kotlar, p. 155.
[20] Yi-Chuang Lu, "Marital Roles and Marriage Adjustment," *Sociology and Social Research*, XXXVI (July–August, 1952), 365.

T A B L E 1. Marital Roles and Husband's Marriage Adjustment *

Marriage Adjustment	Marital Role						Number of Cases
	Husband More Dominant		Equalitarian		Wife More Dominant		
	PER CENT	CR	PER CENT	CR	PER CENT	CR	
Poor	41.5	2.2	30.4	—	28.1	—	135
Fair	34.5	—	32.1	—	33.4	—	290
Good	29.8	—	39.9	1.8	30.3	—	178
TOTAL							603

* Yi-Chuang Lu, p. 365. Reprinted by permission.

In interpreting these data Lu says:

> An examination of Table 1 reveals that a negative relation exists between the husband's dominant role and his marriage adjustment. A larger proportion of those with "poor" adjustment fall in the "husband-more-dominant" group and a smaller proportion are found in the "equalitarian" and "wife-more-dominant" groups. In the husband-more-dominant group, only 29.8 per cent of husbands have made a good adjustment in marriage (CR 2.2) and 41.5 per cent a poor adjustment in marriage. The better the husband's adjustment with his wife, the higher the percentage of such cases falling into the "equalitarian" group. In the "equalitarian" group, 39.9 per cent of husbands make "good" adjustment with their wives, and only 30.4 per cent are poorly adjusted. The critical ratio of the difference between 39.9 and 30.4 is 1.8 which approaches significance. In the wife-more-dominant group, however, practically no difference is found in the husbands of the three degrees of marital adjustment.[21]

T A B L E 2. Marital Roles and Wife's Marriage Adjustment *

Marriage Adjustment	Marital Role						Number of Cases
	Husband More Dominant		Equalitarian		Wife More Dominant		
	PER CENT	CR	PER CENT	CR	PER CENT	CR	
Poor	43.0	—	22.2	—	34.8	2.2	135
Fair	31.0	−2.4	33.3	2.5	35.7	2.9	255
Good	33.8	−1.7	42.3	4.2	23.9	—	213
TOTAL							603

* Lu, p. 365. Reprinted by permission.
[21] Lu, p. 366. Reprinted by permission.

In interpreting these data Lu says:

> The figures in Table 2 indicate a definite relation between the husband's dominance in the marriage and the wife's poor marital adjustment. Of those wives who make "poor" adjustment in marriage, 43 per cent of their husbands are dominant. . . .
>
> In the "equalitarian" group there is an even more significant relation between the equalitarian role and the wife's good adjustment in marriage. Of those wives who make a "poor" adjustment in marriage, there are only 22.2 per cent playing equalitarian roles. . . . And of those wives who make good adjustment in marriage, an even higher proportion, 42.3 per cent, plays the "equalitarian" role. The critical ratio of the difference between 22.2 per cent and 42.3 per cent is 4.2.[22]

While these studies are suggestive, they should not be interpreted to mean that all dominant men and women will have problems in marriage. The relationships of dominant-compliant couples are analyzed in detail in Chapter Seven. These studies do call to our attention the need to be conscious of our role expectations in relationship to the intended mate. They show that role relationships are critical aspects of marriage, and need much premarital analysis. Still many individuals are happy even if they do not fit the central pattern. Kotlar summarizes her findings by saying:

> An indication of marital role norms is the similarity between adjusted and unadjusted spouses in the definition of ideal marital roles. Also the disparity between husbands and wives in terms of ideal role definitions did not differentiate between groups. That the cultural marital role has a more equalitarian orientation is revealed in the similarity of definition between the ideal husband and ideal wife role. Both marital roles are defined in terms of conventionality, self-confident independence, competent strength, and drive for status. . . . The significant relationship to marital adjustment was conformance with the cultural ideal of affectionate-dominance.[23]

COUNTER-ROLES IN MARRIAGE

Anselm Strauss has contributed a useful new concept in his notion of *counter-role*.[24] He defines counter-roles as all the sets of expectations in an

[22] Lu, pp. 367–368. Reprinted by permission.
[23] Kotlar, p. 201.
[24] Anselm Strauss, "The Development of Conceptions of Monetary Meanings in the Child," *American Sociological Review*, XVII (1952), 275 ff., and "The Learning of Roles and Concepts as Twin Processes," *Journal of Genetic Psychology*, LXXXVIII, No. 156 (1956) 211 ff.

interaction system other than those of the focal actor. Thus, in marriage the husband (if in interaction the focal actor) behaves in relation to his perception of the role response his wife will make to him. So husband and wife are "interlocked in more inclusive systems" than just their own individualistic patterns. They are tied together by the pattern of their reciprocal roles and counter-roles. The wife's counter-role behavior is complementary to the behavior of the husband and also contributory to it. He may "change his stance," or alter his behavior because of his sense of how his wife will react to his action.

The significance of Strauss' concept is that he sees the interaction of roles and counter-roles as a process moving toward greater cohesion, or if a mate is not sensitive in interpreting the probable response of the other, this insensitivity may interfere with the interaction. Strauss' emphasis is important because it introduces the *possibility of modification and adjustment* in role interaction. If the husband as focal actor changes his "lines" somewhat to make them more acceptable to his wife, and she then modifies her response, the result will be greater communication and congruent behavior. She will not be "misunderstood," and the possibility of joint action or consensus increases.

The significance of thinking of roles as adaptive and role enactment as a process is important. All of the research presented thus far makes it appear that a role is given and rigid, but Strauss sees roles as more fluid and changing. Indeed, his analysis makes it necessary for us to change our previous conclusion somewhat. It is now important for us to say that in many marriages it is probably not the role stance itself that is critical for good adjustment, but rather the ability of husband and wife to respond sensitively to the role of the other, and in so doing modify their own roles sufficiently to make compromise possible. So, if our general analysis of role interaction and role conflict has seemed rather bleak in promise, we conclude with this encouraging note: role interaction is a process. The process can be highly successful if we develop a sensitivity to the role or counter-role of the other. Individuals can do much themselves to learn how to be really attentive to the expectations of the other. One specific method for making progress here will be explained before the end of this chapter.

In this chapter we have tried to relate the shift in marital functions to changing role patterns. Can we relate this now to the task of young people as they prepare to make their choice, and then try to adjust in marriage?

PREMARITAL ROLE ANALYSIS

Our population is so heterogeneous that individuals who would be ranked at the opposite poles of the basic scales may be physically attracted and fall in love. The idealization which goes with romantic love tends to obscure the significance of basic differences until after marriage. The differences will then appear, in the early months of marriage or later, as very unwelcome surprises. It is one thing for a student to be convinced by theoretical studies or case analyses that discrepancies in role expectations can lead to serious marital conflicts and quite another to do anything in a meaningful way about this. The only solution to potential role conflict lies in long-term and comprehensive discussion of every area where such conflict might occur. Thus, a couple contemplating marriage may uncover differences in role definitions by talking about (1) the primary duty of the husband and wife, breadwinner, status-achiever, homemaker, sexual partner, business partner: (2) the extent to which the husband and wife are to participate in the work of the home, chores outside the house, chores inside the house such as dishes, cleaning and picking up: (3) financial duties, the extent to which the husband and wife participate in keeping financial accounts, paying bills, paying utilities, buying stocks etc.: (4) decision making, the extent to which the husband and wife agree on who is to have the final say and about what: (5) working with children, the degree to which the husband and wife are expected to discipline them, help them in such activities as Scouts, assist them in their studies, and play with them: (6) recreational plans, the degree to which the husband and wife expect to share with the other games, sports, the entertainment of friends, and of business companions. Any couple that earnestly explores what their expectations are regarding these areas with each other will soon discover any major value and role differences. These then can be probed and compromises attempted.

THE IMPACT OF ROLE CONFLICT ON MARRIAGE

If two individuals with rather divergent role expectations fall in love and marry, the result is poor adjustment. The shift presented in the charts may be regarded as polarities and may be arbitrarily scaled for the purpose of graphic presentation. We may represent the "institutional-companionship family transition" in the following way:

INSTITUTIONAL   COMPANIONSHIP

| 0 | 10 | 20 | 30 | 40 | 50 | 60 | 70 | 80 | 90 | 100 |

All of the other processes of transition may be similarly scaled. In analyzing a case study, it is possible to assign a hypothetical score of such scales to a man and a woman. Suppose that Mary Smith and Harry O'Brien, an engaged couple, be used as an illustration on the following scale.

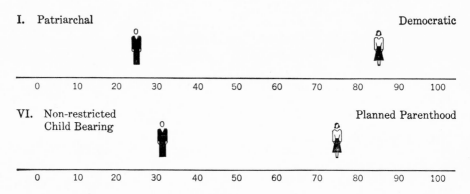

I. Patriarchal   Democratic

| 0 | 10 | 20 | 30 | 40 | 50 | 60 | 70 | 80 | 90 | 100 |

VI. Non-restricted   Planned Parenthood
     Child Bearing

| 0 | 10 | 20 | 30 | 40 | 50 | 60 | 70 | 80 | 90 | 100 |

It is obvious that these two individuals will have to face and resolve important differences before much cohesion is achieved in their marriage. Similar scales could be drawn from this case study to represent closeness or distance between the two principals in their role expectations and in their marriage philosophies, in their views of child guidance and discipline, in their social and religious attitudes, even in their ideas about recreation.

ROLE-CONFLICT AND CHILDREN

Suppose that Harry and Mary never come to understand the basic differences that separate them but, instead, drawn to each other by a "great love," get married. In due course, they have a child, Helen. Even before Helen is born, they have discovered that their thinking is very different on how decisions should be made, how children should be reared, what church they should attend, and so forth. While Helen is growing up, she finds no unified parental accord on her own behavior or on family matters. Her parents cannot even agree on how such accord should be reached because her father thinks that the man should be dominant and "lay down the law," while her mother thinks that the family should sit down together and discuss each problem as it arises, and that even the children should have some voice in the final decision. So Helen never learns what place either father or mother should have in the home. Beyond this, Helen goes to a school where there is little difference in the instruction given to boys and to girls. Some of the boys take homemaking, and some of the girls take shop. And when Helen visits the home of her friends, she finds the same kind of vagueness as to what men are expected to do and what women are expected to do. We may now indicate on the first scale what this conflict will mean to Helen.

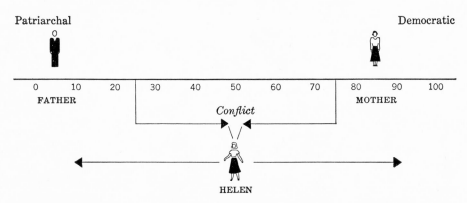

Helen is pulled in many directions. The ambivalence in her family becomes part of Helen. She may desire to play the right role, but she has no way of knowing what it is. When she begins to associate with males, she may not be sure how they should act. She knows how her father acted, and she knows that this resulted in conflict. She does not know how she should act. She knows what role her mother tried to play, and, consciously or unconsciously, she is apt to reject this role because it, too, led to conflict and unhappiness. Thus the original conflict of roles in her own family has weakened the presentation of family models for her guidance, and caused her to reject what she did see.

A great many young people today find themselves in Helen's predicament. Of course, other factors also play a part in this problem. Consider Helen's ability, or lack of it, to adjust sexually. She has been brought up in a society which has shrouded sex with the shadows of shame and silence. She knows little about it, and even what she knows may not be operative because of inhibitions derived from her parents and her peers. She is a victim of cultural lag. Society has set before her the goal of achieving more in her sex life than her mother or grandmother ever envisioned, but society has also presented her with attitudes which make it difficult for her to reach that goal. Likewise, in many other areas, conflicts between her parents and conflicting attitudes in society have now become conflicts within Helen herself. In some cases, these conflicts, in the family or in our culture, mean that no information is shared with young people. In this case, the need is to provide accurate and pertinent facts. This means that part of the purpose of education for marriage is to help young people orient themselves in a world of change. By being sharply aware of the ambivalences in their homes and in society, they are in a better position to deal intelligently with the problem of defining their own roles and values.

ANXIETY AND INSECURITY DUE TO CONFLICTING ROLES OF PARENTS

Suppose now that something different had happened in the social environment of Helen. Let us assume that the conflict in her home was so severe that her parents decided to separate. The environment during her first seven years was one of bitter quarreling, conflicts, and profound unhappiness. Then, at seven, she went through the trying experience, first, of the separation and, later, of the divorce of her parents. She had already, at seven years of age, become a fearful and anxious child because of these conflicts. Thereafter, she lived only with her mother who was bitter over the divorce, and who resented Helen. Helen knew neither the serenity nor the affectional responses which would have made it possible for her to develop a normal personality configuration. This chain of circumstances affected her in two ways. It gave her a morbid fear of marriage and a suspiciousness of men, instead of a happy image of what marriage might be. She developed a neurotic personality as a result of the stresses in her early life. In varying degrees, Helen's story parallels that of many young people who must themselves adjust in marriage. How valid this generalization is may be seen from the following chart which depicts the increase of divorce in the United States.

Of course, not all divorces are due to conflicts of role or to subsequent anxieties associated with the neurotic personality, but these are important among the factors associated with divorce. The same factors are also associated with many of those marriages which remain legally intact, but which have little cohesion and which offer little in the way of opportunities for the development of the personalities of parents and children. While the extent of emotional problems in contemporary society is difficult to measure, studies indicate that one family out of five will face an emotional problem of such severity that one of its members will have to be placed in an institution or require long psychiatric care. There is a direct relationship between immaturity in husband and wife and maladjustment in marriage. Some part of this maladjustment is due to role conflict between parents and within the individual.

FIGURE 7. Divorces in the United States per 1,000 marriages, 1885–1955 *

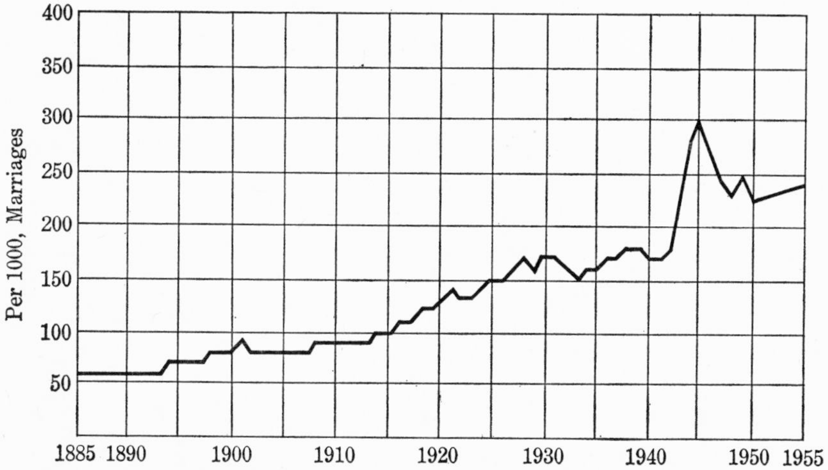

* Data from the *Statistical Abstract of the United States,* Bureau of the Census, Department of Commerce (1952), p. 59. The computation for 1955 is an extrapolation from numerical totals shown in NOVS *Special Reports,* XLVI, No. 12 (1957), 324–325.

CONCLUSION

This chapter has considered marital adjustment in relationship to: (1) the change in degree of loyalty to work roles as opposed to family roles, (2) the conflict that may result because of lack of congruence of role expectation and role behavior between husband and wife, (3) the effect of such role conflict on marital stability and on the marital expectations of children, and (4) ways of exploring role expectations before marriage to prevent role conflict. Insight about roles and skill in role adjustment is an important aspect of success in contemporary marriage.

READINGS

GOLDSEN, ROSE K., *et al.,* *What College Students Think.* Princeton: D. Van Nostrand Company, Inc., 1960.

JACOB, PHILLIP E. *Changing Values in College*. New York, Harper and Brothers, 1958.

KEPHART, WILLIAM M. *The Family, Society, and the Individual*. Boston: Houghton Mifflin Company, 1961, pp. 237–247.

MERRILL, FRANCIS E. *Courtship and Marriage*. New York: Henry Holt and Company, 1959, Chapters 12–20.

METHENY, ELEANOR and JAMES A. PETERSON. *The Trouble With Women*. New York: Vantage Press, 1957.

NATIONAL MANPOWER COUNCIL, *Womanpower*. New York: Columbia University Press, 1957.

PARSONS, TALCOTT and ROBERT F. BALES. *Family, Socialization and Interaction Process*. Glencoe, Illinois: The Free Press, 1955, Chapter 2.

RIESMAN, DAVID, NATHAN GLAZER, REUEL DENNEY. *The Lonely Crowd*. New York: Doubleday and Company, Inc., 1955.

CHAPTER 3

The Meaning
of Love

INTRODUCTION

In the last two chapters we have presented evidence of the radical transitions taking place in the functions and the roles of family members. We have noted some of the strains attending those changes, and their impact on marital adjustment. Certainly, one obvious implication of those facts is the need to have a sober and realistic philosophy of love which will assist and not inhibit a wise marriage choice and later adjustment. Marriage is changing. To adjust to it demands high common sense and insight. If this is true, we must now analyze the validity of the way young people think about love, or how they test the relationship between themselves in terms of its possible permanence.

Our society is a nation on the move in many ways. We are vigorously mobile, both horizontally and vertically. We mix every day with members of different races, religions, social classes. We dance at parties with potential mates who represent every region and every nationality. It is possible to be attracted to a great many of them, but it is probably not possible to be happily married to each one who is attractive. Consequently, the very heterogeneous nature of our social life makes it imperative that the philosophy by which we make our final choice illumine but not blind us. Young people thus need to understand "love." In this chapter we investigate the meaning of love and some of the distortions of love that destroy wise marriage choice and happiness in marriage.

A DEFINITION OF LOVE

There is no concept in the English language that is so difficult to define as "love." We may begin by saying that love is a term which describes the sentiments and strivings which bind together a man and a woman. Love is then a complex of feelings representing many aspects of male and female interaction. Waller and Hill have made an extensive study of what they call the *Components of Love,* and we will begin with their analysis. These authors include the following as essential elements of love:

(1) *A drive to repeat the family cycle;* one is motivated to repeat the pattern of childhood affection for the parent and to repeat the family experiences one had as a child.

(2) *Sheer sexuality;* part of the striving that is love roots in our hormonal systems. The reproductive drive is a very powerful one and accounts for much of the power love has to impel us.

(3) *Pride;* to marry and to reproduce brings us the approval of both parents and peers. Pride impels us not only to marry, but to marry "well."

(4) *Security in response relationships;* we find in marriage a consistent response and a permanence that allows us to trust the other and thus to entrust ourselves.

(5) *Economic striving;* to marry so that one is secure about the basic necessities of life not only for oneself but for one's children.[1]

Analysis of some of the research studies which will be cited later in this book results in the need to add the following elements to the above:

(6) *Emotional support;* every person needs comfort in distress, support in difficulty, understanding in trouble. He who meets these needs is very dear. Understanding involves concern for the mate's feelings, potential and individual growth.[2]

(7) *Appreciation;* this is the psychological product of companionship, it is the feeling about the history of shared experiences of excitement, joy and meaning. It is the pleasure in expectation of rewarding experiences to come.

[1] Willard Waller and Reuben Hill, *The Family: A Dynamic Interpretation,* rev. ed. (New York: Dryden Press, 1951) pp. 110–113. Copyright © 1951, Holt, Rinehart and Winston, Inc. Reprinted by permission of the publisher.

[2] *Emotional support* is not the same as *security.* By *security* we mean a consistent family structure on which we can depend; by *emotional support* we mean the qualitative aspect of emotional interdependence, the sensitivity to emotional need and the capacity to meet that need.

It is our contention that a love that can endure the vicissitudes of marriage must have all of these elements and that a relationship based on only one of them is very fragile. Thus, we discuss next the kind of attraction which is *only* sexual, or economic, or romantic as the kind of segmental striving towards another that often fails.

THE TENDER TRAP OF SEXUAL STRIVING

The first distortion of love to be considered is that of sexual attraction. Let us say quickly and emphatically that the erotic aspects of love are deeply rewarding and basic to any normal affectional relationship between a husband and a wife. We are referring here to love relationships based entirely, or nearly so, on physical attraction. Some young people today engage so completely in caressing and petting that the total goal of their relationship seems to be sexual stimulation. These persons are blinded by passion to the multiple factors involved in a love that will sustain a marriage. They seem only motivated by their hormones as though companionship, their economic future, and emotional contributions to each other mattered not at all. The enormous preoccupation of the American public with everything sexual makes it difficult for young people not to overvalue the physical part of love.

The distortion comes too because of the peculiar courtship customs of our society where mobility and anonymity and going steady seem to enhance the possibility of physical arousal whereas our value system denies such stimulations any release. This contradictory stimulation and repression serve perhaps to accentuate sexual strivings. It is instructive to note that early or teen-age marriage is related to going steady. These early marriages are very fragile. This may well illustrate our point that when one aspect of love becomes too dominant and the others are not developed or emphasized, love cannot endure. Marital love is poverty-stricken indeed if it is not based on strong physical desires, but it is equally poor if the only bond between husband and wife is physical.

THE DISTORTION OF LOVE FROM "OTHER-DIRECTEDNESS"

In our discussion of roles and role conflict we noted the pervasive nature of a social motivation to excel as defined as social or economic success. *Pride* in our achievement in the business or professional world and in our marriage is important to our self-esteem. But it may well be that this

47

motive has become for some too important, so that in critical ways it prevents us from achieving other aspects of love. Waller points out that pride really limits mate choice because we have to conform to peer and parental expectations, and this often leads to a marriage which precludes meeting our emotional needs. In this section we expand that thought to see how status-striving may truly inhibit a deeper and more responsive kind of relating.

Children and young people do not escape the contemporary ethos. They soon learn that they will be valued by their parents if they achieve a facsimile success predicated on the adult model. Young people must conform to their groups, live up to peer norms, and be accepted by their peers. But to be accepted means to be popular. As they move into junior high, being popular means being invited to parties, and very soon afterwards it means having dates, going steady, and then courtship. The most critical value in adolescence is to participate fully in what may be called the love games of the adolescent. Riesman summarizes his thinking about culture-transmission this way:

> Approval itself, irrespective of content, becomes almost the unequivocal good in this situation: one makes good when one is approved of. Thus all power, not merely some power, is in the hands of the actual or imaginary group, and the child learns from his parents' reactions to him that nothing in his character, no possession he owns, no inheritance of name or talent, no work he has done is valued for itself, but only for its effect on others. Making good becomes almost equivalent to making friends, or at any rate the right kind of friends. "To him that hath approval, shall be given more approval." [3]

In a sense, then, there is a subtle shift from the meaning of love relations as goals in themselves to a concept of them as games in which one achieves status for oneself. What often passes for love is not that at all, it is a play for prestige. We shall see when we analyze dating how insidious this kind of motivation is. The immense preoccupation with dating success, or the love game, is only another illustration of modern character knowing only how to exchange or to barter everything in life, material as well as spiritual. Young people "in love," then, are not really involved with each other; they are egocentrically conforming to group expectations. Fromm says:

[3] David Riesman, Nathan Glazer and Reuel Denney, *The Lonely Crowd* (New York: Doubleday and Company, Inc., 1955), p. 66. Reprinted by permission of Yale University Press.

Automatons cannot love . . . they can exchange their "personality pack-ages" and hope for a fair bargain.[4]

What we have suggested thus far is that the intensity of modern love may be understood partially by the need of young people to exhibit to others those ways of loving which are deemed superior by the group.

A phase of modern love is the distortion of the self which accompanies it, either in self-reference or in projection on the other person. An individual in love supposedly will repress negative aspects of his or her personality in order not to disturb the devotion of the other. This self-idealization is accompanied by a similar exaggeration of the other's good qualities and a minimization of the other's defects. From the point of view of the success motive, these forces can all be understood from the need to answer the cues of the other individual. Riesman mentions time and again the sophistication of young people in this game of adjusting to the suggestions of others. If success is threatened then by some behavior trait or some personality deviation, does it now follow that these young people have been trained in previous peer relationships to repress such behavior? What would be more logical? If one learns to be flexible in the "socio-metric peer" group, would it not extend to the "game" of love?

To whatever extent the basic affectional ventures of young people have been subverted towards egocentric success goals, competitiveness and distrust in male-female relationships must arise. In any case, the training young people have received in an "other-directed" society does not seem to equip them to furnish security or emotional support for others.

THE DISTORTION OF ROMANTIC IDEALIZATION

We have said that in terms of function the family is no longer the religious, social, recreational, and economic center it once was. Nor does it perform the educational, security or protective functions it once did. The two remaining functions, giving affection and sharing companionship, have become even more important today because of other trends in society. The industrialization of the Western world, the growth of urban centers of living, the emergence of scientific thinking, and the rise of secularization—all these have combined to produce other patterns of societal change. Modern urban man tends to be an isolated and lonely creature. Previously, men worked and worshipped, played and grieved, in a primary, or face-to-face, relationship with many individuals they knew

[4] Erich Fromm, *The Art of Loving* (New York: Harper and Brothers, 1956), p. 87.

and trusted well. These contacts provided support and close personal relationships which are not present in the great city or even the modern suburb. Burgess, Locke and Thomes summarize the importance of these core family functions as follows:

> "While various forces are decreasing the institutional significance of the family, it maintains its affectional and cultural activities. More and more the American family is becoming a union of husband and wife, parents and children, based on love, common interests, and companionship. Child development is affected by varied and important home activities. Perhaps the most significant are the attitudes, behavior, and relationships of the family which may be summed up in the phrase 'home atmosphere.' Family affection is, of course, the chief element here, but others of importance are family events and celebrations, family traditions and memories, and common interests and activities." [5]

It is precisely the pivotal importance of affection and companionship in happy marital adjustment that makes a pseudo-affectional philosophy so insidious a threat to wise marriage choice. We are referring to what is generally known as "romantic love." Romantic love is a form of camouflaged physical attraction which seems to preclude consideration of other more permanent phases of companionship and adjustment. The loneliness of city living accentuates the search for any type of response. Romantic love not only superficially meets this need, but adds the thrill of dreams besides. While romantic love seems to be related to the emerging function of the family as an affectional group, it actually distorts reality so much that a later and more permanent type of affection is difficult to achieve. Burgess and Locke summarize this problem as follows:

> Naturally, even where passion was deep and sincere, there was disillusionment when romantic impulses led to unions of persons of widely different temperaments, different cultural backgrounds, and different philosophies of life. It became evident that in many marriages, even if respect remained, romance had faded. The affinity theory was modified to demand either the continuance of romantic love in marriage or the dissolution of the marriage. . . . Increasingly in America and to some extent in other countries, the philosophy of romantic love is itself a major factor in the disillusion of one relationship and the consummation of a new union. [6]

---

[5] Ernest W. Burgess, Harvey J. Locke, and Mary Margaret Thomes, *The Family: From Institution to Companionship*, 3rd ed. (New York: American Book Company, 1963), p. 354. Reprinted by permission.

[6] Burgess and Locke, 1953 edition, pp. 321–328.

50

The first characteristic of romantic love is its emphasis upon the automatic nature of wise marriage choice as: "Love Is Just Around the Corner"; the "right one" exists and at the proper time will appear; "Some Day He'll Come Along"; he or she will appear, it might be added, under the most favorable romantic conditions; it will happen "Some Enchanted Evening" when "I'll Build a Stairway to Paradise." The second characteristic of such a love is that it is spontaneous. As soon as the two perfectly matched individuals come together, they know that they are destined for an exquisite and eternal love experience. "It Had to Be You." Thus, a mother told her doubting daughter that if the daughter had any reservations about her lover being the right one, then she would not marry him because one always knew, without question, when the right one appeared. A third aspect of this type of love involves a deep faith concerning the future. "I'll Always Be in Love with You." If one wishes for and then marries the predestined mate, one's marriage must inevitably be superbly successful. Many stereotypes are associated with romantic love. The man is always handsome, strong, and reliant; the girl—mysterious, alluring, and beautiful; the house—luxurious, chic, and commodious (a change from twenty-five years ago when the house was small and cosy, with porches and roses). No mundane problems of finance, illness, or conflict can ever upset this family unit, for somehow love immunizes the couple from all the negative aspects of common experience. It is obvious that this approach itself has become a factor in the deterioration of marriage, since it provides no rational, responsible view with which a couple may meet the impact of reality.

A couple recently counseled by the author illustrates this point. The girl had taken a premarital counseling class. She was a very good student, driven to study by the knowledge that her parents expected her to get straight A's. She spent too much time on her studies and too little in developing her social facility and acquiring her share of friends. Consequently, after graduation, when all of her classmates were getting married, she was without a fiancé. She had had two or three affairs; she had counseled about them, and in the calm atmosphere of the counseling office had soon found that she had exaggerated their significance. Then one day she came singing into the counselor's office. She had come, she said, not for counsel but to announce that she had found the one and only. She quickly recovered herself; she knew, she said, that ordinarily this meant that a couple was under the spell of the romantic notion of love and had temporarily lost any sense of perspective. But, she went on, their case was different. She had been standing on a pier when a small motor boat came rushing by. As it came close to her, it coughed and wallowed. The handsome youth standing in the boat looked up and caught her smiling at his dilemma. In that first glance, she said, there was so much mutual understanding that she knew they were destined for each other. Evidently he felt it, too, for he quickly leaped from the boat and stood beside her. This had been only ten days ago, and they were to be married in three weeks. She wanted to invite the counselor to the wedding because, she said, he had taught her so much about love and marriage. Growing more confidential, she asserted that this was truly the work of God who had revealed that she and her fiancé were meant for each other. They were duly married. Three weeks later they were in the counselor's office with serious problems.

This kind of love has been ironically labeled cardiac-respiratory love because it has certain physiological symptoms.[7] Young people who have "rounded their corner" and found their one and only have a breathlessness as though they had climbed to the highest peak in the Rockies. There is often palpitation and excitation which otherwise occur only when some great threat to existence is discovered. One is confounded by the brightness of the eye as though the person had a fever. Sometimes there are bursts of super-human energy and, at least verbally, those in love can conquer the world. There is ecstasy and euphoria to such an extent that the beloved seems to have transported one to a different world. There is also a certain schizophrenic reaction, a major loss of reality. Couples plan for a mansion full of children, but between them they couldn't buy a good meal. They eulogize the future, but pay no attention to major social, class, or religious differences between them. When leaving the other, the person in love remarks to himself what a remarkable transformation his beloved has wrought in himself. All of his neurotic tendencies are gone. All of his self-doubts are gone. He can move mountains. All of these psychic experiences make the moment supremely enjoyable.

OTHER EXPLANATIONS OF ROMANTIC IDEALIZATION

Many authors have attempted to account for the source of the power which is observed in the compulsiveness of those "in love." We have accounted for the loss of a sense of reality testing as a part and parcel of the

[7] This section follows a description of romantic love found in James A. Peterson, *Toward a Successful Marriage* (New York: Charles Scribner's Sons, 1960), pp. 35 ff.

extreme adaptability associated with searching for approval of others. But there are other and more searching explanations.

Waller has given the best description of the physiological factors,[8] and Burgess and Wallin describe the psychological aspects.[9] Physiologically, young people in our culture are ready for sexual experience long before they are socially ready to accept the responsibilities of marriage. They are sexually stimulated as they follow the patterns of modern dating which include necking and petting. The erotic urges are generally unfulfilled. The tension reduction that is essential if they are to live within tolerable tension limits is obtained by a psychic discharge in a displacement of libidinal energy into idealization of the mate and the relationship.[10]

Waller indicated the functional value of romantic idealization in our society as follows:

> One has to love in order to marry, but there are tendencies which oppose both love and marriage; one generates the commanding emotions of romantic love in order to overcome this opposition to a fundamental drive (i.e.) the sexual. Always there is a part of the man that loves, and another part that cries out against the slavery of love. The answer of the organism is to heighten the intensity of the emotion. When love choice was freed from the restrictions of the family and the tribe, the individual was set free in many others aspects as well. As individuation of life patterns increases, the person becomes increasingly unwilling to make the sacrifices involved in love and marriage and the upbringing of children. . . . A part of the individuated man struggles against paying the costs of love, bargains, exploits, and seeks its own interest. But the mating impulse is powerful, and, at least in persons who have been conditioned as we have, it is not satisfied by purely objective, touch and go, segmental relationships. Therefore the individual falls in love and disciplines his other behavior tendencies in the interest of the satisfaction of the one. The peculiar phenomenon known as falling in love is therefore a resultant of mental conflict; it emerges when sentiment-formation conquers the self-interest of the individual. . . . It (the euphoria of love) is the anesthetic which renders the amputation of our cherished habits painless.[11]

Bergler speaks of idealization as a form of derangement affecting both males and females, and as a psychoanalyst he sees the same kind of overvaluation of the loved one noted by the sociologists we have quoted:

[8] Waller and Hill, Chapter VII.

[9] Adapted from Burgess and Wallin, *Engagement and Marriage* (New York: J. B. Lippincott Company, 1953), Chapters III and IV. Reprinted by permission of the publishers.

[10] Waller and Hill, Chapter VII.

[11] Waller and Hill, p. 206. Reprinted by permission of Holt, Rinehart and Winston, Inc.

The man in love lives in an acute frenzy of love in a world of fantasy, in which the loved object of the moment seems to be the most beautiful, sublime, glorious in the world. If the rest of the world, which is not in love, tries to draw his attention to the defects and blemishes of the loved one, he denies them indignantly in a delusive rejection of reality. This world of fantasy is comprised of the lover's ideal and the feeling that the loved one is the material objectification of his ideal. The whole complex is likened to a psychosis, in so far as the lover denies reality. The lovers' protestation, "I shall always love you"—all this resembles more than anything else a psychotic state.[12]

Burgess and Wallin, sociologists, make two major comments regarding idealization. The first conclusion is that in our culture there are factors which lead to the depreciation of idealization so that "it is not the extreme in the majority of cases." These factors are: (1) the deductions from their theory of self-esteem; (2) the difference of idealization potential on the part of individuals; (3) the growth of standards of realism in our society and especially the application of such standards to affectional relationships; (4) the assumption that idealization only occurs when individuals are perfectionists; and, when they are not, idealization does not play a major role in the situation.[13]

The second conclusion of Burgess and Wallin is that idealization is the result of the continuous struggle for self-esteem. Following George Herbert Mead, they point out that the self normally included all the other selves with whom one is immediately identified. When we think highly of them, we are in reality thinking highly about our own self. Consequently, because of the motivation that comes from our need to bolster the self, we overvalue the personality and the achievements of the beloved. Our conception of what others think of him or her is also important, so that we would rationalize their failures or shortcomings to others. Thus, our tendency to identify becomes the explanation for our tendency to idealize.[14]

Robert Winch, a sociologist, treats romantic idealization as one facet of what he designates as the "romantic complex." He says: "In accordance with the 'love is blind' theme, a lover is able to see only the virtues of his love object, and indeed, he creates virtues invisible to the naked eye." [15]

[12] Edmund Bergler, *Unhappy Marriage and Divorce* (New York: International Universities Press, 1946). Reprinted by permission.
[13] Burgess and Wallin, pp. 222–223.   [14] Burgess and Wallin, pp. 220–221.
[15] Robert F. Winch, *The Modern Family* (New York: Henry Holt and Company, 1952), p. 363. Copyright © 1952 Holt, Rinehart and Winston, Inc. Reprinted by permission.

Having thus paid homage to the typical theme of romantic love, Winch goes on in a brilliant analysis to show the power of the mass media in our time in creating the attitudes and expectations of our young people. He thinks that culture has a large part in creating a myth of love.

There are also other psychological factors involved in the romantic entanglement. There is, for instance, the element of escape. Perhaps the most common escape would be from the uncertainty and confusion of dating competition. In our society the dating game is played with a good deal of anxiety. The anxiety is produced because worth or success is equated with many and valued dating contacts. The individual who dates the "wheel" or the "beauty" has higher status, but that very individual is always aware of the precarious nature of his ascendancy. For those who do not achieve the "inner circle," there is scheming and planning to gain the higher rungs of dating success. Many girls report that they are "tired" of the highly competitive and anxiety-producing strains of dating and would like to "settle down." To escape in such a way as to still achieve self-esteem is an important achievement. But the standards of dating are so high that to think well of one's final choice may of necessity include some idealization.

When Lillian entered the small, coeducational college which was not too far away from her home, she had expected that because of her family's social status she would quickly and easily be admitted into the inner circle of those who were considered to be the upper crust in the Freshman Class. Despite her relative attractiveness, however, she made no impression whatsoever and soon found herself drifting into something of an outsider group which considered itself patronizingly superior to the rest of the school. This included several boys and girls from the upper classes, and Lillian identified with them in her search for acceptance and approval. Living the so-called bohemian life affected by this group became her goal, and she considered her parents as very plebeian because of their objection to her spending the whole night playing records, reading and playacting. The parents would have probably been much more shocked if they had known that another aspect of her pattern of life included sexual relations with a boy who was the chief "wheel" of the group. There was much conflict with the family on the score of her mode of life and especially her passionate fixation on her boy friend, whom her parents regarded as simply an ill-bred individual. Her insistence that he was the acme of all that she admired intellectually and aesthetically brought panic to her parents. Fortunately, a summer position as a girls' camp counsellor put her in a different setting and with other opportunities for romantic involvements. As a result, Lillian was able to break the fixation which she had established, and as she herself expressed it, "I guess I was just having myself a fling." [16]

Lillian's idealization of the group into which she was accepted is an illustration of "other-directedness." There are other escapes. One may avoid all of the wear and tear of scholastic competitiveness if one makes a good marriage. Status attends both achievements. For not every young person enrolled in college or even high school has the intellectual requisites for successful academic pursuit. If their status in the eyes of their peers and parents depends on scholastic achievements, they may enthusiastically fall in love and idealize the love relationship, its importance, and the other person as a compensatory mechanism to justify failure in the scholastic area.

Consider again the various escapes from the home. If the home is a scene of marital conflict or child-parent conflict, it may be intolerable to live in such an atmosphere. A normal escape would be into a dreamworld. But if one can escape into a culturally acceptable dreamworld, this is doubly advantageous. Those who "fall in love" match the sordidness of their real emotional life with an imagined or projected loveliness of their marital future.

There is yet one aspect of idealization which has not been examined. Young people marry, according to Winch, because each fundamentally meets some of the needs of the other. In this total description of the facets of idealization, there ought to be some place for the very real satisfactions that come to individuals when they begin to interrelate with others on a very meaningful basis. When an individual finds profound satisfactions in the first efforts he makes in his chosen field, he can be observed singing songs or whistling or making pontifical statements regarding the usefulness of that profession. There is no doubt that the appreciation which attends any growth in positive relations is itself profoundly rewarding. When one has discovered a potential mate who helps one grow, it is not surprising that there should be a certain amount of euphoria attending both the discovery and the reinforcement of the judgment in experience. It is possible that for many couples this quieter type of emotional response is rightly interpreted as "being in love."

Although Burgess and Wallin [17] challenge the impact of romantic love on marital choice and, indeed, challenge the Waller thesis that idealization is significant in marital problems, another finding of their study is

---

[16] From a case study in the author's files.
[17] Burgess and Wallin, p. 394.

quite revealing. They asked young people if they should marry if they were not in love. Their findings follow:

TABLE 3. Percentages of 998 Engaged Persons Reporting Feelings About Whether They Should or Should Not Marry if Not in Love (by per cent)

	Men	Women
Yes	12.3	15.4
No	81.9	79.5
?	5.8	5.1

When we remember that many of these students were in graduate school and that this sample leans toward a highly educated and sophisticated group, such a large percentage confirms our hypothesis that romantic notions of love are important.

There is other objective evidence that we can assemble to attest to the validity of Waller's thesis.

THE KING STUDY [18]

One of the most penetrating studies of idealization as related to courtship has been made by Elsie King in her doctoral dissertation. King interviewed 215 couples who had just finished applying for their marriage licenses at the County Clerk's office in Los Angeles. They filled out a statistical information form and two copies of the Interpersonal Check List. This instrument has already been discussed in Chapter Two, but as King utilized other features of the checklist it is important to describe the test somewhat more fully.[19] The test not only measures individuals in terms of the two dimensions of dominance-submission and hostility-love, but it also determines the relative normality of individuals in terms of emotional stability. This factor of emotional stability is described by Leary in terms of adaptiveness or maladaptiveness. As norms for the middle-class population had already been established, King used these norms to measure the degree of lack of conformity to established patterns of the general populations of those in love. Intensity one items are checked

[18] Elsie King, "Personality Characteristics . . . Ideal and Perceived in Relation to Mate Selection," unpublished Ph.D. dissertation, Libraries of the University of Southern California, 1961.

[19] For a detailed history of the development of the ICL see Timothy Leary, *Interpersonal Diagnosis of Personality* (New York: The Ronald Press Co., 1957). Some material was presented in Chapter Two.

by 90 per cent of the population, intensity two items by 67 per cent of the population, intensity three items reflect very exaggerated or inappropriate degrees of the given relationship and are checked by 33 per cent of the population. Intensity four items, which reflect an extreme trait, are checked by 10 per cent of the population. In King's study, "realistic" attitudes are viewed as those that are adaptive; and "unrealistic" as those which are "maladaptive." These unrealistic attitudes are described as romantic idealization.

The results of the King study confirm the widespread presence of idealization. An average of 58 per cent of the sample perceive the mates in unrealistic terms, whereas 42 per cent see them in realistically oriented perceptions.[20] The following table indicates that females are more idealistic than males, but that both do distort.

TABLE 4. Sex Distribution of Perceptions of
Fiancé(e) by Per Cent *

GROUP	Realistic	Unrealistic
Males	.49	.51
Females	.34	.66
		$X^2 = 44.6$

* King, p. 100. Reprinted by permission of Dr. King.

Further analysis of the data revealed that while idealization is the characteristic of all social classes, it is more prevalent in the higher and lower occupational classes.[21] Winch and Peterson's theories that youth is more subject to unrealism are all rejected by the data.[22] King's study thus confirms the hypothesis that romantic idealization is a profound aspect of courtship in our society.

That idealization is not just the property of teen-agers can be found in the fact that older individuals, marrying for the first time, or previously divorced individuals both have special psychological needs which are met by idealization. Dr. King discovered that women are more prone to idealize than men in all social classes, races, educational levels, and religious groups. This study is the most careful analysis of idealization to date. There is some question as to whether the findings are biased by the proximity of the wedding date, but only another study can check this question.

[20] King, p. 129. [21] King, p. 131. [22] King, p. 131.

OTHER STUDIES OF IDEALIZATION

One of the explanations of romantic love is that it offers a neurotic escape from the pressures of competition in the status-dating game, from difficult environmental problems in school or work, or from a loveless home. Three studies have attempted to measure the degree of neurotic involvement of those who are intensely in love. Nimkoff and Wood [23] contrasted the personality scores of young people who were going steady at an early age, who had more "steadies" than the average, and who opposed their parents in their dating behavior. They found that these young people, indeed, were more emotionally maladjusted and socially "aggressive" than were others. In Kephart's study, which utilized the Bell Personality Inventory, similar conclusions are reached. Kephart found that

> . . . for both sexes, there was a negative correlation between number of times in love or infatuated and scores made on the Bell Personality Inventory; that is, those students who had a relatively large number of romantic experiences were those who made the poorest personality scores.[24]

On the other hand, negative evidence comes from Dean.[25] He found only the correlation between emotional adjustment and romanticism statistically significant. His study seemed to show that romanticism is more general among "lower-status" women, but other studies have not shown this to be the case. This study raises valuable questions regarding previous generalizations. There is one important difference in the design for this study and those of Nimkoff and Wood and the other one by Kephart. These two studies related emotional adjustment to past behavior, while the Dean study used an opinion type approach. It may be that future research will reconcile these studies. It is possible that checking a highly visible scale has difficulties which do not show up in reports of past behavior. While the Dean study cautions care in any final acceptance of the relationship of romanticism with emotional immaturity, the other studies point in the opposite direction.

It is possible now to generalize about the sentiment of love, in an effort to reconcile the various points of view that have been presented thus far in

[23] Meyer F. Nimkoff and Arthur L. Wood, "Courtship and Personality," *American Journal of Sociology*, January, 1948, p. 269.

[24] William M. Kephart, *The Family, Society, and the Individual* (Boston: Houghton Mifflin Company, 1961), p. 330.

[25] Dwight Dean, "Romanticism and Emotional Maturity. A Preliminary Study," *Marriage and Family Living*, Feb., 1961, pp. 44–45.

this chapter. In the first place, there is little doubt that Waller is right in stressing the sexual component in romantic love. The increasing freedom of young people in expressions of physical intimacy is well established. Nor can we question the power of the mass media in establishing patterns of interpretation of that sexual drive. Perhaps the degree of idealization is proportionate to the neurotic need for affection acceptance. In this case, the distortions are referrable to emotional imbalance. But an alternative explanation of equal value finds the motivation for "being in love" stemming from a need for peer acceptance. In this case, the distortions of idealizations are only illustrations of the way other-directed young people have learned to respond to the cues of others. The ease with which some young men can "pin a girl" or promise undying love as a preface for sexual exploitation would seem to illustrate this position.

We may interpret Burgess-Wallin's explanation of idealization as a method of finding self-esteem in terms of Riesman's thesis. Those who seek in love the enhancement of themselves are essentially egocentric individuals, and are fundamentally concerned with the view that others have of them. The mate in this case is an object to be chosen, manipulated or extolled in the interest of self. What are the results of romantic love, be it motivated (a) by frustration of sexual strivings, (b) by mechanisms designed to enhance self-esteem, (c) by attitudinal patterns learned from the culture through the mass media, (d) by the need for escape, (e) by response facilities already well learned in childhood to gain approval from their peer group and their beloved?

THE IMPACT OF ROMANTIC IDEALIZATION ON MARITAL ADJUSTMENT

The results can be generalized as follows: First, romantic idealization involves such distortions of personality that after marriage the two persons can never live up to the promise involved in those distortions. Second, romance is so myopic (blind) that such problems as temperamental or value differences, religious or cultural differences, financial, occupational or hereditary problems are rarely considered. If they are considered, they are glossed over. Third, romantic idealization gives such exaggerated expectations of sex and companionship in marriage that gross disillusionment may be inevitable. Fourth, romantic idealization often is an escape from negative or neurotic aspects of the personality which soon reappear after marriage with serious results. Fifth, romantic idealization sets a euphoric or erotic tone for a relationship which later proves a burden and a snare to good adjustment. Sixth, to the degree that romantic idealization represents the weather-vane type of other-directed adjustment in which love is a carefully played game, and self-interest is always paramount and determinative, a marriage which never does achieve deep involvement of one mate with another will result.

If anyone is tempted to interpret what has been said as a plea that young people should not enjoy love feelings or should try to decide on a marital partner by means of some algebraic formula, let us hasten to say that there is no such implication in this analysis of romantic idealization. Being in love is one of the great and ennobling experiences of the whole life cycle and because we deplore its excesses, we do not think it necessary to prohibit the entire experience. Let us consider two pilots who take their sail boats out on the rocky shore of the Pacific. One hoists full sail as soon as he acquires his boat and "beats up" the shore at full speed. Soon he has ripped his hull on a sunken reef or gashed a great hole because of an underwater collision with a jagged rock. He manages to struggle ashore with his boat destroyed and his feelings about sailing sadly mutilated. But another takes counsel before he goes out to sail. He buys a map of the region, locates the hazards and plots his course. Then he hoists only that sail which will enable him to control his boat, and he cruises carefully beside the reef and around the rock. In the end he enjoys the sail, he has a sense of having control of the expedition, and he comes back to harbor with positive feelings about the trip. But he does not give up sailing because there are hazards; he locates them and manages to avoid them. The course of true love, like sailing a rocky coast, never quite runs smoothly or straight. But still we sail, and we enjoy the wind in our faces and the journey. And still we love and enjoy the feelings of closeness and response which result. But because we are aware of the hazards, we go more slowly and we watch for the landmarks. We are aware of ourselves and aware of the meaning of our feelings. This awareness gives control over the situation, and we are not destroyed or wounded in our feelings because we are mature enough to ask questions occasionally and chart a course. To follow such a course is advisable in any human interaction; we should dare to venture, we should participate enthusiastically and with zest, but we should temper our feelings by answering questions raised by the head.

Nor should what we say be interpreted to mean that we should always move ahead with caution. There are altogether too many individuals in our society who have never learned to trust life or other individuals. They are cripples, persons who weigh every word they say, every choice they make, every chuckle that painfully escapes from their head. These are the men and women who have been so protected and cautioned all through their childhood that they have no spontaneity left. They cannot cry or hate or love. They are perfectionists who never permit anything challenging or impulsive to happen. Life to them is one long page of an accounting book. They sometimes get to the stage where love is a transaction: *I give you this and in return it is reasonable that you give me that;* but the glad, unreserved act of sharing is never theirs.

A MATURE LOVE

We began our analysis of love by analyzing the various elements that make up the full sentiment of love. Then we suggested that a relationship which was based on only one or several of these would not have enough meaning for a couple to survive. We discussed some of the distortions that develop when we stress only the sexual aspect, or social pride, or romantic, idealistic aspects of love. Considerable effort was made to bring research findings to bear on the importance of that conclusion, because we feel that the majority of early divorces could be avoided if they had been based on a more adequate love relationship. In the final section of this chapter we try, with the help of Fromm and Gibran, to describe in depth the meaning of mature love in marriage. We are relating these concepts of love to the problems of today.

Fromm has endeavored to state the dimensions of mature love. He defines it as:

> Love is union under the condition of preserving one's integrity, one's individuality. Love is an active power in man.[26]

This differentiates between "falling in" or "standing in." Love is giving. It is giving with no reference to an expectation of price, or reward. In the very act of giving I experience my strength, my wealth, my power.[27] Giving is growing, because in the act of giving I awaken potentials that had been dormant. One becomes more of a self through his sense of the needs of others and of one's capacity to meet those needs. Jesus told of the man who built barns to store his excess and when they were crammed full, he died. But he effectively died before that, because in his anxiety about adding to his wealth he lost the joy of sharing.

[26] Fromm, p. 20.   [27] Fromm, p. 23.

Love also involves "care, responsibility, respect and knowledge." Love is a deep and constant concern for those who care. There can be no scientific detachment in love, for it demands involvement to the degree that we work hard at love, and we work hard for those we love. As I have said in another place, the essence of responsibility is to be responsive, but to be able to be responsive is to attend to another, to care enough to listen with all our sense to his needs and wishes. This is to leave egocentricity behind and learn enough of the other to understand how their wishes make sense. In a sense, this is the understanding which comes to one who cares enough to really listen.

When one's wife greets him with listlessness and irritation, he needs to know her well enough to know that she is not really angry at him but that something has gone wrong during the day when he was not present. What she is really saying is that life has been rough and that she needs extra tenderness. But if one replies in kind and is only angry in turn, he has not understood. From this intimate kind of understanding comes deep respect. When we know an individual this well, we cannot but respect his achievements of spirit, regardless of the levels of his actions.

Fromm adds another thought. He feels that the Delphic oracle "Know thyself" is only half true. For we cannot know ourselves unless we love another, and out of that love comes a transcendental experience of knowing both another and ourselves. It seems essential to add to Fromm's analysis (and he certainly implies this) the importance of transcending petty, selfish, and anxious thoughts of self-reference before we can really love. Before we can "stand in" we have to be strong enough to make and sustain decisions. It requires a great soul to love in this sense. For we cannot lose ourselves in another or give ourselves without stint if every moment is devoted to shoring up the defenses of a weak ego. First we must be a self, we must be; then we have something to share.

The remainder of this book focuses upon the ways a couple may love. No marriage is adequate when both concentrate so completely upon individual interests that there is no common growth in sharing and companionship. Yet no marriage is adequate, either, when the basic personality potentialities of either partner are completely submerged in the demands of the family. Maximum life satisfaction, indeed maximum marriage success, comes when both partners develop optimum individual and group creativeness. Because this is a book concerned primarily with marriage and not with personality fulfillment, our main emphasis is upon growth in mutuality and cohesiveness. Yet a rewarding mutuality is predicated upon the degree to which the individuals involved have something to share.

That which does not exist cannot very well be shared. The counselor hears over and over again that marriage is boring, and family life is meaningless. But how it could be anything else, given the character structure of some of the individuals involved, is puzzling. A couple whose major aim in life is to find only new and more spectacular thrills may expect life sooner or later to fizzle out; a sparkler does not last forever. Young people preoccupied with the more superficial aspects of our culture, with its emphasis upon materialistic things and status, must one day discover, as Midas did, that such attitudes turn the rest of life into something hard and unlovely. Again those young people who approach love and marriage on the basis of romantic expectations cannot escape the day when they must summon the doctor for their mate or their baby; when their dreams of the little house are rudely shattered because of a down payment they cannot meet; or when divergent personality needs compel them to face fundamental conflicts. The abundant life does not come to those who have no abundance to share. One who does not really love himself cannot love others.

In this sense, all of human experience is a preparation for marriage. A class in education for family living may focus attention upon special areas such as economic or sexual adjustment, but it does little to alter the fundamental richness or poverty of the personalities involved. Hence, all college courses, including those in literature, art, music, recreation, anthropology, history, or science, etc., are preparatory to any interpersonal relationship because they add to character the dimension of depth. Likewise, all experiences which sensitize individuals to beauty or to fun, those which inculcate appreciations, or further intellectual interest are adding dimensions to the individual which later will add substance to his marriage. In this sense, no one can hope to teach another individual how to find success in marriage, for all of his past is involved.

The past continues to be important after marriage. "The oak tree and the cypress grow not in each other's shadow." One is reminded of the farmer who stood sorrowfully outside the state mental hospital shaking his head because he had just committed his wife. "How she could of caught this, I dunno. I kept her in the kitchen for forty years." Each individual must have freedom and time and opportunity to devote to his or her areas of creativity. There must be a respect for significant differences if the differences are to contribute to the enrichment of the union. If the wife loves the piano, she cannot indulge her joy in playing without an instrument or time to practice. If the husband realizes that music is an integral aspect of the personality of his wife, he will sacrifice so that she has an instrument and so that she has the time to play upon it. If he does this graciously and even enthusiastically, his wife's music will eventually add happy overtones to their relationship. She may paint, and in time the picture of their marriage will have deeper hues and better perspective. Individual achievement means individual contentedness which cannot but be reflected in a deeper unity. A union in which interests must be given up by one because of the demands of the other or of indulged children deprives the marriage of elements which can be ill neglected.

We are thus not discounting the basic need for each individual to drink from his own individual cup. This is necessary to avoid standardization and mediocrity. Procrustes saved money on beds, but his friends lost their lives when he made them fit his bed. Counselors have the task of helping individuals face their despair when they realize that their marriage partners seek to lop off attitudes, values, or interests which do not correspond to their own. This is not togetherness; this is surgery of a radical nature, and it strips the partner of individuality.

To achieve sympathetic understanding of one another, cooperation in planning, companionship in play and in sexual achievement, and love in family life is not easy in today's complex world. The radical differences in cultural backgrounds and consequently of expectations; the half-knowledge and hesitation in the realm of sex and reproduction; the impact of mass media with their insistent demands for conformity to hackneyed values and stereotypes; the constant threat of war and the surging rise of prices—all these combine to place the couple in a social environment of change and anxiety. To establish common interests and ways of solving problems is thus more difficult than it was a hundred years ago.

While modern marriage poses sharper problems, it also involves greater challenges to creativity. Young people today who achieve a happy marriage have attained something different in kind from marriages in the past because today neither economic necessity nor social control forces them to remain together when the gears do not mesh. Undoubtedly, this new freedom also results in more sensitive interrelationships in those marriages (and they are the vast majority) which succeed. Role and affectional problems then are serious challenges and opportunities which may result in greater progress.

At the same time, the confused state of values and social expectations in themselves render marriage somewhat more precarious than in past generations. Young people need to develop more mature personalities fitted for the acceptance of the responsibilities of marriage and parenthood, and they need to be more skillful in meeting particular problems of marital adjustment that will arise after the marriage service. Hence our concern with the development of those attitudes and increased knowledge of those facts which will be basic tools in giving love, once the marriage bonds have been established.

Marriage means interaction and communication and sharing. If these processes are at a maximum, a couple may be said to be truly married. But if they are at a minimum and both partners use the marriage relationship to satisfy only personal aims such as sexual fulfillment or economic support, there is little to keep the marriage together when adversity or conflict threaten it. Thus, a pivotal point in understanding success in marriage is to understand the means of achieving this kind of love in all aspects of the relationship.

> Then Almitra spoke again and said, And what of Marriage, master?
> And he answered saying:
> You were born together, and together you shall be forever.
> You shall be together when the white wings of death scatter your days.
> Aye, you shall be together even in the silent memory of God.
> But let there be spaces in your togetherness.
> And let the winds of the heavens dance between you.
> Love one another, but make not a bond of love:
> Let it rather be a moving sea between the shores of your souls.
> Fill each other's cup but drink not from one cup.
> Give one another of your bread but eat not from the same loaf.
> Sing and dance together and be joyous, but let each of you be alone.
> Even as the strings of a lute are alone though they quiver with the same music.
> Give your heart but not into each other's keeping.
> For only the hand of Life can contain your hearts.
> And stand together yet not too near together:
> For the pillars of the temple stand apart,
> And the oak tree and the cypress grow not in each other's shadow.[28]

[28] From Kahlil Gibran *The Prophet* (New York: Alfred A. Knopf, Inc., 1923). Copyright 1923 by Kahlil Gibran. Renewal copyright 1951 by Administrators C.T.A. of Kahlil Gibran Estate and Mary Gibran. Reprinted by permission of the publisher.

VISUAL AIDS

How Much Affection? Text-Film Department, McGraw-Hill Book Company, Inc., 330 West 42nd Street, New York 18, New York.

Is This Love? Text-Film Department, McGraw-Hill Book Company, Inc., 330 West 42nd Street, New York 18, New York.

READINGS

DWIGHT, DEAN. "Romanticism and Emotional Maturity: A Preliminary Study," *Marriage and Family Living*, Feb., 1961, pp. 44–45.

FROMM, ERICH. *The Art of Loving.* New York, Harper and Brothers, 1956.

KEPHART, WILLIAM. *The Family, Society, and the Individual.* Boston, Houghton Mifflin Company, 1961. Chapters 11–13.

KING, ELSIE. "Personality Characteristics . . . Ideal and Perceived in Relation to Mate Selection." Unpublished Ph.D. dissertation, Libraries of the University of Southern California, 1961.

ROCHE, PHILIP Q. *Man and Wife.* New York, W. W. Norton and Co., Inc., 1957, Chapter V.

WALLER, WILLARD and REUBEN HILL. *The Family: a Dynamic Interpretation.* Rev. ed. New York, Dryden Press, 1951, Part II. Copyright Holt, Rinehart and Winston, Inc.

WINCH, ROBERT F. *The Modern Family.* New York, Henry Holt and Company, 1952. Copyright Holt, Rinehart and Winston, Inc.

PART TWO

PREPARING

FOR MARRIAGE

Introduction

COLLEGE students in the sixth decade of the twentieth century are aware that the marriages of their older brothers and sisters are the most fragile in history. Those marriages are being broken at the rate of about one divorce for every four marriages. Statisticians indicate that the trend is toward more, and not less, frequent divorce. Yet, other factors—the trend toward equality and companionship in marriage, more adequate knowledge of reproduction and sexual adjustment, the decline in maternal and infant mortality, better management of sterility problems, the growing accumulation of insights into child psychology, consumer education, and other related phases of family life—promise for those who are adequately prepared a longer and more satisfying marital experience than that enjoyed by any past generation! It depends entirely upon the individual whether his marital venture will end in frustration or a vital and enduring relationship. This book was prepared to help students achieve the personal adjustment and the broad insight necessary for a permanent and happy marriage today.

Part II of this book is devoted primarily to an understanding of the way our

71

early experiences condition our expectations of the roles we are to play and our psychological readiness for marriage. This part of the book will have a double meaning for each student. It will help him to become a better parent when it is his turn to guide his children toward maturity. Also, by enabling him to analyze his own background, it may assist him to eliminate inhibitions, clarify his sense of his role, and grow in his ability to adjust to others, and to that extent help him to determine his own marital destiny rather than act the part of a puppet manipulated by strings attached to his past and to his culture. It is the goal of these chapters to enable young people to know themselves and their motivations so well that their ideas are not simply echoes of their peer group or their past, but creative efforts toward self-fulfillment.

The final value of this book does not lie in its ideas, its speculations, its statistics, or its quotations. It will mean much or little to the student in direct proportion to the extent that it stimulates him to become aware of his own needs and inhibitions, to clarify his expectations of role, to expand his capacity to relate to others, and to eliminate negative attitudes. If it is true that modern man is nervous and neurotic, anxious and fearful, it is also true that he is the most malleable creature on earth. He has the capacity to grow, to learn, and to adjust. This book proposes to help the student become the kind of person who can adjust well to marriage in an age when rapid social change puts a premium upon adaptability and creativity.

Each chapter in this section is followed by an exercise called "Self-Analysis." The purpose of this exercise is to enable the student to develop the ability to meet the demands of modern marriage that have been outlined in the chapter; to discover the degree to which he has acquired a mature definition of affection; to uncover his own expectations of role which may previously have been hidden and unexpressed; to overcome inhibitions due to ambivalences in his background at home and in society; to learn about modern family life so that he will adopt attitudes which will be productive of adjustment; and to analyze his own past in terms of becoming the kind of adaptable and creative person who can find success in the companionate and democratic family.

CHAPTER 4 | Factors in
Infancy

In an orderly development of our personalities, we prepare in a significant way for the next stage in our life. Each separate age has special challenges which enable us to expand our mastery of life and our relationship with others. Each presents special tasks for the family. A developmental task is defined as "a task which arises at or about a certain period in the life of an individual, successful achievement of which leads to his happiness and to success with later tasks, while failure leads to unhappiness in the individual, disapproval by society, and difficulty with later tasks." [1] The stages described by Duvall are:

Stage 1 Beginning Families (Married couple without children)
Stage 2 Childbearing Families (oldest child, birth to 30 months)
Stage 3 Families with Pre-School Children (oldest child 2½ to 6 years)
Stage 4 Families with School Children (oldest child 6½ to 13 years)
Stage 5 Families with Teenagers (oldest child 13 to 20 years)
Stage 6 Families as Launching Centers (first child gone to last child's leaving home)
Stage 7 Families in the Middle Years (empty nest to retirement)
Stage 8 Aging Families (retirement to death of one or both spouses) [2]

We begin our study of how you came to be the person you are with an analysis of the significant growth sequences of infancy, when the family was in the second stage.

[1] Robert G. Havighurst, *Human Development and Education* (New York: Longmans, Green and Co., 1953), p. 2.
[2] Evelyn Mills Duvall, *Family Development* (Philadelphia: J. B. Lippincott Company, 1957), p. 8. Reprinted by permission of the publisher.

INFANCY AS PREPARATION FOR MARRIAGE

Levy and Monroe say: "The child prepares for marriage during every moment of his waking hours, and perhaps also in his dreams." [3] How expectant parents feel about their coming child will determine how much love they will share with him. How much love they give the child is important in determining the child's growing capacity to show affection himself. The rejected child does not develop the response patterns that are essential for the intimate sharing of marriage. Initial child-training practices have an important bearing on later emotional development. In this chapter, important aspects of child rearing that have meaning for later adjustment are studied. The conclusions (reported about infancy) are widely held by psychologists who deal with the developmental problems of children; they are confirmed by the main body of experimental studies,[4] though further research is needed on each of the points to be considered.

A baby is a multiplicity of potentialities. The whole human past—centuries of constant growth of sensitivity and adaptation—is funneled to each infant. Twelve billion nervous cells have already "in utero" begun to develop patterns of responsiveness. The vast microscopic network of neurons provides both for automatic reaction and for poetic imagination. But a sterile or negative environment may blanket rather than fan the fires of creative growth.

PRENATAL INFLUENCES ON PERSONALITY

Recent studies have speculated about the influence of a mother's attitudes during pregnancy upon the child's personality. We are not thinking of the old wives' tale that the way a mother acts or thinks may mark the baby physically, but rather of scientific investigations of such factors as diet and emotional upset. Sontag studied prenatal influences from the standpoint of both nutrition and emotions, and concluded that there are ways in which the attitudes of the mother may make a permanent imprint

[3] John Levy and Ruth Monroe, *The Happy Family* (New York: Alfred A. Knopf, Inc., 1946), p. 18.
[4] An interesting critical review on the studies in this area has been made by Harold Orlansky in the *Psychological Bulletin*, No. 46 (1949) in which Orlansky concludes that experimental research contradicts the thesis that infant care is largely determinative of later personality, concluding that what happens during other periods is likewise important.

upon the psychic growth of the child. He also discusses the role of adequate nutrition in pregnancy and the relationship of this factor to ease of labor and the growth and health of the child.

> More recently investigators in Toronto compared the records of two different groups of infants. The mothers of both groups of infants lived during pregnancy on diets which were poor from the standpoint of vitamins, proteins, and minerals. One group of mothers, however, had their pregnancy diets supplemented by large amounts of vitamins. The infants of this group showed better growth during the first year of life and much less illness and in general were healthier children than those of the mothers whose diets had not been supplemented by vitamins. An additional fact of interest was that the labors of the mothers on the supplemented diets were *easier* and shorter than those of the women whose diets were non-supplemented.[5]

Modern nutritional science has enhanced the health of both the infant and the mother. It is no longer necessary for a mother to lose her vitality with each pregnancy. She is also healthier and happier because her obstetrician sees to it that she protects her own health as well as that of her child.

Sontag goes on in his article to consider what he terms "endogenous factors." He speculates about the possibility that the emotional reactions of the mother will produce physiological reactions which will in turn affect the fetus. Anxiety is not only a condition of the mind; it is also a state of the body. He thinks that he and his co-workers have discovered significant relationships between the body movements of the fetus and emotional stress in the mother:

> Another change which is apparent at birth in infants of mothers undergoing severe emotional stresses is in behavior, in total activity level. Such an infant is from the beginning a hyperactive, irritable, squirming, crying child who cries for his feeding every two or three hours instead of sleeping through his four-hour feeding. Because his irritability involves the control of his gastro-intestinal tract, he empties his bowels at unusually frequent intervals, spits up half of his feedings and generally makes a nuisance of himself. He is to all intents and purposes a neurotic infant when he is born . . . the result of an unsatisfactory fetal environment. In this instance, he has not had to wait until childhood for a bad home situation or other cause to make him neurotic. It has been done for him before he has ever seen the light of day.[6]

[5] Lester Sontag, "War and the Fetal-Maternal Relationship," *Marriage and Family Living,* VI (1944), 3. Reprinted by permission.
[6] Sontag, p. 4.

Mothers who resented their pregnancies and then felt guilty about that resentment would certainly be in such conflict that much anxiety might result. This anxiety in turn might affect the fetus as Sontag has indicated above. However, comparative studies need to be made in this area of prenatal influence before this conclusion can be recorded as truly scientific.

Almost all mothers are happy about their first pregnancy. Sears, Maccoby, and Levin studied 379 mothers by means of long, careful, intensive, tape-recorded interviews. They asked about their attitudes toward pregnancies. They found that 50 per cent were "delighted, very pleased; had been waiting and hoping for this"; 18 per cent were pleased but there was "no evidence of enthusiasm"; 15 per cent were pleased generally but had mixed feelings; 16 per cent were generally displeased or just displeased with no reservations, and the opinions of one per cent were not ascertained.[7] There was not so much happiness at the second pregnancy when only 34 per cent were "delighted" and some 34 per cent had mixed feelings or were displeased.[8] The degree of pleasure at the coming of a second child seemed to be a function of the length of interval between the coming of the first child and the beginning of the second pregnancy. Certainly having children is a primary goal of most women, however, and they were happy when they found they were to fulfill this expectation.

RELATION OF WORK TO CHILDBEARING

Sears was much aware of the possible conflict between a career and the motherhood role. He wondered if women who found satisfaction in a career would resent motherhood. His conclusions are that a woman's enjoyment of a job outside the home does not militate against her acceptance of motherhood. Only 6 per cent expressed any "real dissatisfaction" with the situation.[9] In fact, while only 29 per cent of the nonworking mothers were delighted with pregnancy some 48 per cent of those who had worked at some time were delighted.[10] In the next chapter we shall study the impact of working mothers on the psychological development of children. Here we have simply explored whether or not women become so involved with their work outside the home that they resent giving it up for a family. A large majority do not become so involved.

[7] Robert R. Sears, Eleanor E. Maccoby, Harry Levin, *et al.*, *Patterns of Child Rearing* (White Plains, New York: Row, Peterson and Company, 1957), p. 32. Reprinted by permission of Harper and Row, Publishers.

[8] Sears, Maccoby, Levin, p. 36.   [9] Sears, Maccoby, Levin, p. 47.

[10] Sears, Maccoby, Levin, p. 48.

THE BIRTH TRAUMA AND PERSONALITY DEVELOPMENT

At birth, one leaves the comfortable security of the uterus and is suddenly in a world where one must breathe and exert oneself to be nourished, where one experiences heat and cold, pain and discomfort. Birth is a formative crisis of life. The conditions which offset that shock are the warmth, the play, the tenderness, and the cuddling of the mother or substitute mother. Where those conditions are not present, the baby does poorly and, under severe circumstances, may die. At the turn of the century, a great many babies in the most privileged homes and in the best hospitals were dying in alarming numbers. No specific germ or genetic factor could be isolated to account for this mortality. The disease was known as marasmus, which is a term of Greek derivation meaning "wasting away." The only etiological factor that distinguished the care of these children from that of others was the fact that the carefully sterilized and scheduled babies were not rocked, cuddled, or loved. The disease came under control when a famous pediatrician wrote, so it is said, on the charts of such babies: "This baby is to be loved one hour a day."

Today this discovery has resulted in the well-known formula, TLC, or "Tender, Loving Care." Margaret Ribble is the most outspoken advocate of "mothering." In both an intensive study of 600 babies in New York and in a follow-up study in Berlin, Dr. Ribble found that babies who were not loved developed negativism in feeding habits and a depressive tone which she identified as infantile atrophy. Ribble's thesis has been widely accepted by child psychologists and pediatricians. The case study presented below illustrates her viewpoint:

> Little Bob was born in the maternity hospital where the writer was making studies of infants at the time. He was a full-term child and weighed six pounds three ounces at birth. During the two weeks' stay in the hospital the baby was breast fed and there was no apparent difficulty with his body functions . . . Both mother and child were thriving when they left the hospital.
>
> On returning home the mother found that her husband had suddenly deserted her—the climax of an unhappy and maladjusted marriage relationship. She discovered soon after that her milk did not agree with the baby. As is frequently the case, the deep emotional reaction had affected her milk secretion. The infant refused the breast and began to vomit. Later he was taken to the hospital and she wrote that she had been seriously ill and asked the hospital to keep the child until further notice.

In spite of careful medical attention and skillful feeding, this baby remained for two months at practically the same weight. He was in a crowded ward and received very little personal attention . . . The habit of finger sucking developed, and gradually the child became what is known as a ruminator, his food coming up and going down with equal ease. At the age of two months he weighed five pounds. The baby at this time was transferred to a small children's hospital, with the idea that this institution might be able to give him more individual care. It became apparent that the mother had abandoned the child altogether.

When seen by the writer, this baby actually looked like a seven months' foetus, yet he had also a strange appearance of oldness. His arms and legs were wrinkled and wasted, his head large in proportion to the rest of the body, his chest round and flaring widely at the base over an enormous liver. His breathing was shallow, he was generally inactive and his skin was cold and flabby. He took large quantities of milk but did not gain weight since most of it went through him with very little assimilation and with copious discharges of mucus from his intestines. The baby showed at this time the pallor which in our study we have found typical of infants who are not mothered, although careful examination of his blood did not indicate a serious degree of anemia. He was subject to severe sweating, particularly during sleep. A thorough study showed no indication of tuberculosis. The child's abdomen was large and protruding, but this proved to be due to lax intestinal muscles and consequent distention with gas and to a greatly enlarged and distended liver, which was actually in proportion to that of the foetus. There was no evidence of organic disease, but growth and development were definitely at a standstill, backward to lower and lower levels of body economy and function.

The routine treatment of this hospital for babies who are not gaining weight is to give them concentrated nursing care. They are held in the nurses' laps for feeding and allowed at least half an hour to take the bottle . . . This is the closest approach to mothering in a busy infants' ward. Medical treatment consists of frequent injections of salt solution under the skin to support the weakened circulation in the surface of the body.

With this treatment the child began to improve slowly. As his physical condition became better, it was possible for our research group to introduce the services of a volunteer "mother" who came to the hospital twice daily in order to give him some of the attention he so greatly needed. Her daily visits were gradually prolonged until she was spending an hour twice a day, giving the baby this artificial mothering. The result was good. The child remained in the hospital until he was five months of age, at which time he weighed nine pounds. All rumination and diarrhea had stopped, and he had become an alert baby with vigorous muscular activity. His motor coordinations were of course retarded. Although he held up his head well and looked about, focusing his eyes and smiling in response to his familiar nurses, he could not yet grasp his own bottle or turn himself over, as is customary at this age. The finger sucking continued, as is usually the case with babies who have suffered early privation.

In accordance with the new hospital procedure, as soon as the child's life was no longer in danger, he was transferred to a good, supervised foster home in order that he might have still more individual attention. Under this regime, his development proceeded well and gradually he mastered such functions as sitting, creeping and standing. His speech was slow in developing, however, and he did not walk until after the second year. The general health of this child is now excellent at the end of his third year; also his "I.Q." is high on standard tests, but his emotional life is deeply damaged. With any change in his routine or with prolonged absence of the foster mother, he goes into a state which is quite similar to a depression. He becomes inactive, eats very little, becomes constipated and extremely pale. When his foster mother goes away, he usually reacts with loss of body tone and alertness rather than with a definite protest. His emotional relationship to the foster mother is receptive, like that of a young infant, but he makes little response to her mothering activities except to function better when she is there. He has little capacity to express affection, displays no initiative in seeking it, yet fails to thrive without it . . .[11]

This case illustrates the emotional factors which Ribble feels influence all children in their physical and psychological health.

Rene Spitz reports a study which not only confirms Ribble's interpretation but gives statistical evidence about the physical results of mothering and the lack of it. She compared the rate of development and the mortality of babies in two institutions. The institutions were evenly matched so far as adequate nutrition, adequate medical care, hygiene and asepsis, and housing were concerned; but one kept the babies with their mothers and the other cared for them without the help of mothers. The mother-child relationship was then the independent variable. The children cared for with mothers were in an institution called "Nursery," those without mothers were in an institution called "Foundlinghome." At the end of the first year, the "developmental quotient" for "Nursery" children was about 98 and for the children in "Foundlinghome" about 70. But by the end of the second year, the quotient of the children in "Foundlinghome" had de-

[11] Margaret Ribble, *The Rights of Infants* (New York: Columbia University Press, 1943), pp. 4–7. Reprinted by permission of the publisher.

creased to 45; and the difference in mortality was so striking that we quote Spitz directly:

> The most impressive evidence probably is a comparison of the mortality rates of the two *institutions*. "Nursery" in this respect has an outstanding record, far better than the average of the country. In a five years' observation period during which we observed a total of 239 children, each for one year or more, "Nursery" did not lose a single child through death. In "Foundlinghome," on the other hand, 37 per cent of the children died during a two years' observation period.[12]

These studies indicate the importance of love at the beginning of life. There is reason to believe that love continues to be an essential, if not the most essential, ingredient in healthy living. The early relationship of a mother and child is of paramount importance in influencing the health and response patterns of her child. This relationship conditions the child's later ability to give and receive affection. We may agree with Orlansky that other periods of training are important for the adult personality, and still find with Ribble and Spitz that treatment in infancy is important. And for our purposes, in preparing our children for marriage or in reviewing our own backgrounds to determine our own preparation for marriage, it is not essential to say that one period or another is the most crucial.

CULTURAL DETERMINATION OF THE STYLE OF AFFECTIONAL RELATIONSHIPS

Maleness, femaleness, sex, and their interrelationship mean different things in different cultures. Our expectations in regard to specific patterns of sexuality depend in conspicuous degree upon the culture in which we live. Because cultures tend to bring their customs, their forms, and their expectations into alignment, we may find adult sexual roles symbolized and also created during infancy. We will now consider the specific way infant training conditions our style of affectional relationships as men and women. A given culture expects a particular type of affectional response and, so to speak, selects the type of training that will produce that response. Only in our century, when there is such confusion of expectations and when so much thought is given to childhood training, do we have an opportunity to influence consciously the way our children will regard sex.

[12] Rene A. Spitz, "The Role of Ecological Factors in Emotional Development in Infancy," *Child Development,* XX (1949), 149. Reprinted by permission of the Society for Research in Child Development, Inc.

By analyzing other cultures, Mead clarifies the way sexual responses are formed.[13] In developing her analysis of different types of sexual attitudes, Mead first studied infancy in the cultures of the South Seas.

The Arapesh carry their infants in soft net bags slung from their mothers' foreheads or on their fathers' shoulders. The baby to them is a fragile object. In the early months both mother and father concentrate on protecting and nourishing this vulnerable addition. The baby is fed at the breast often and tenderly, whether it demands food or not. Because it is satiated with food and because it is always tenderly carried, the focus of attention is upon its receptive mouth, a pattern which Margaret Mead thinks is easily transformed in the case of girls to sexual receptivity. On the other hand, Arapesh boys who have learned only to receive, never to grasp or demand, become frightened lovers, hunters, or entrepreneurs. The early training that so well conditions women for their role sexually and socially by stressing the complementary nature of human interaction prohibits men from those male forms of aggressiveness that in other cultures bring inventiveness and wealth.[14]

In contrast, the Iatmal baby is taught to demand. After the first weeks, it is placed some distance from the mother and must cry lustily to get any attention or food. Once it has attracted the mother's attention, it is fed with interest and adoration, but even though it is fed amply after its screeching insistence, its relationship with the breast is more energetic. Two other factors operate to make the mouth not only a receptive organ but also a demanding one. The infant is early given hard pieces of bird-meat, and later, cuts its teeth on shell ornaments. The child learns that anger and self-assertion are the attitudes that gain rewards. The child is regarded as an individual from birth. There is added to the receptive mood a demanding one, so that both the male and female learn to play more aggressive and positive social and sexual roles in life.[15]

Among the Mundugumor, women have a rejecting attitude toward both childbearing and nursing, and the way the child is handled depicts symbolically this rejection. The child is carried in a rough basket that is harsh to the skin, and nursing is brief and without tenderness. Out of this contest between mother and child come angry, conflict-minded adults, so that in later life "biting and scratching" are part of the foreplay of sexual activity. The acquisition of another wife by trading a daughter brings the father,

[13] Margaret Mead, *Male and Female* (New York: William Morrow and Company, Inc., 1949), pp. 64–70.
[14] Mead, pp. 65–67.   [15] Mead, pp. 68–69.

who wants a young mate, and the son into early enmity. The father, remembering his own bitter initiation into life, will treat his son harshly. The son, too, learns to be adequate in a desperate world where one may laugh while succeeding through conflict and anger.[16]

Thus every culture has a definite pattern of relationship between the sexes, and in every culture this pattern is both symbolized and perpetuated by the way babies are guided in their growth sequences. But what of our own culture—so much in flux? Does it exhibit a characteristic manner of molding response patterns?

In America, children are generally born to a mother who is either completely or partially under an anesthetic. She can consciously share very little of the birth experience. As soon as the baby is born, it is taken some distance from her and is placed in a nursery where it does not have that immediate closeness to its mother that Ribble has indicated is so important. Later this separation will be more obvious when the "mechanical perfection of a bottle" is substituted for the mother's body as the source of food and comfort.[17] Thus, instead of a complementary relationship between the mother's body and the child, there develops a dependence on an external device (the bottle) for meeting basic needs.[18] The baby early learns that mouths are not a way of "being with someone" but a way of existing in an impersonal environment.[19] So almost from birth the "deep structural difference between masculine and feminine roles is lost." [20]

These childhood conditioning experiences are only a small part of larger behavior patterns. Certainly, in America, we must take into account the Puritan heritage to explain the rejection of the body that is expressed by every attempt to substitute mechanical processes for bodily ones. What concerns us is the fact that in our culture the sense of maleness and femaleness is obscured in a general cultural emphasis on early denial of sexuality and sensuality. A student reported recently that, until she was sixteen, whenever her mother took her to visit a house where there was a baby, they quickly departed if the baby was having a bath or was nude. Happily, the modern trend is away from these traumatizing methods and toward closer physical and psychological relationships between parents and infant. Following the notable work of Grantley Read, many obstetricians are helping young mothers to face childbirth without fear. By becoming aware of the basic adequacy and preparation of their bodies for bearing children, these young women come to view childbirth as a natural,

[16] Mead, pp. 69–70.   [17] Mead, p. 260.   [18] Mead, p. 270.   [19] Mead, p. 272.
[20] Mead, p. 273.

healthy process and not as a threatening consequence of a long illness. Again, the institution of rooming-in procedures, by which the baby is placed in a crib beside the mother's bed shortly after birth and the nurse acts as teacher for both husband and wife, insures healthier emotional relationships. Again, the trend is away from mechanical methods of nourishing the child and is moving toward breast-feeding, for it has been found that breast-feeding not only immunizes the child against infant diseases but also against anxiety and fear.

SPECIFIC AREAS OF INFANT BEHAVIOR AND THEIR RELATIONSHIP TO LATER MARITAL ADJUSTMENT

The reader will remember that Margaret Mead felt the differences in satisfying the sucking need accounted for differences in later love relationships. Sucking seems to be a normal instinctive behavior pattern. It is the mechanism whereby the child receives nourishment. Since this is his primary concern in his first weeks, it is of primary importance from a nutritional point of view. Beyond this, sucking is also the first of the infantile bodily pleasures. Travis and Baruch say:

> Besides having his physical hunger satisfied, the baby also needs to suck for the pleasure of sucking. Sucking brings him closeness. It brings him comfort, it brings him his first sensory gratifications. Not only is sucking a means of livelihood, it is also a source of satisfaction in itself. He sucks not only to fill his stomach with food but also to fill his soul with peace.[21]

Ribble adds another thought about the emotional value of sucking:

> The mouth of the baby must have special consideration as an organ, the use and stimulation of which arouses the first sense of well-being and pleasure and definitely furthers mental development.[22]

Literally, the mouth furnishes the first "taste" of the outside world. Ribble concludes that the baby's initial security, or pleasure, satisfaction and success, is closely linked with his mouth activity.[23] Travis, Baruch and Ribble all are saying that sucking conditions the baby to regard the body as a source of pleasure and to accept life as good. It may thus have not only general but specific correlations with later acceptance of the mouth—as erotic zone of kissing—as pleasurable and good.

[21] Lee Travis and Dorothy Baruch, *Personal Problems of Everyday Life* (New York: Appleton-Century-Crofts, 1941), p. 46. Reprinted by permission of the publisher.
[22] Ribble, p. 32.   [23] Ribble, p. 23.

BREAST-FEEDING

If sucking is of vital importance in giving a child a sense of security and pleasure, it is reasonable to believe that this is related to the fact that such activity brings the child in reassuring and warm contact with the mother. This raises the question whether or not breast-feeding is superior to bottle-feeding. Ribble thinks that there is no room for doubt about this:

> Since sucking is a function which will soon be replaced, the best arrangement, where possible, is to follow Nature's clue. In normal breast feeding, which is without question the ideal form, at least until the teething period, the various instinctual hungers are self-regulated. The amount of flow of the mother's milk and the time and effort needed by the baby to extract it usually correspond nicely with his needs. The contact and fondling give the necessary passive stimulation. Artificial feeding immediately introduces the necessity for a careful regulation of sucking time coordinated with the flow of milk from the bottle. Holding, before and during the bottle feeding, is obviously necessary.[24]

Others are not quite so dogmatic about the importance of breast-feeding as compared to bottle-feeding when the bottle is held by the parent and the child is handled in a tender, loving way. Ross and Johnson summarize this point of view when they say:

> What happens to the infant in his first activity, eating, may lay down the basic pattern of behavior. When the child has a basic confidence in people, he no longer needs to waste his energy in trying people out, but can turn his interests to creative, productive pursuits. While breast feeding has advantages in that the mother has opportunity to be closer to the baby and thus to express her friendliness, bottle feeding can accomplish the same if the mother really loves her child and gives freely of her time and interest.[25]

Ross and Johnson might profitably have reviewed the differences in results of the varieties of breast-feeding in the tribes studied by Margaret Mead, for analysis of the experience of these tribes indicates that it is not breast-feeding itself but rather the attitude expressed by means of breast-feeding which determines the behavior patterns.

There is strong contrary evidence from the Sears study. They asked

[24] Travis and Baruch, p. 33. Reprinted by permission of the publisher.
[25] Helen Ross and Adelaide Johnson, "A Psychiatric Interpretation of the Growth Process in the Early Years," *Journal of Social Casework*, XXX (1949), 88. Reprinted by permission.

specifically about the effect of breast-feeding and the general conclusion of their study was that there is no *consistent* effect among all the children, although individual youngsters might have been affected. The following table illustrates differentials in behavior as related to children who were and who were not breast-fed.

TABLE 5. Relation of Breast-Feeding to Some Qualities of Child Behavior *

CHILDREN DISPLAY	Did Not Breast-Feed	Breast-Fed Less Than Three Months	Breast-Fed Three Months or More
"Some," "quite a bit," or "a great deal" of aggression at home	59%	58%	55%
"Considerable" or "high" conscience	24%	24%	27%
Moderate to severe feeding problems	40%	34%	41%
Bed-wetting at age five	22%	18%	14%
Strong emotional reaction to toilet training	11%	6%	16%
Number of cases	226	93	56

* Sears, Maccoby, Levin, p. 76.

There is no general effect as far as this sample is concerned. One other finding was that mothers who did not breast-feed had a significantly higher degree of discomfort about sex than those who did. This study throws considerable doubt upon Ribble's theories regarding the superiority of breast-feeding.

There are many unanswered questions about breast-feeding. We wonder if the modern emphasis does not make many women who cannot breast-feed their children feel guilty, though they should not, and actually mar their relationship to their children. We wonder what validity there is to the psychiatric interpretation of bottle-feeding—that it may represent, for women, a type of symbolic rejection of either their femaleness or of their children. We wonder what substance there is to claims that breast-fed children develop substantially fewer thumb-suckers than bottle-fed children. We wonder to what extent mothers' milk does immunize the baby to many diseases of childhood. The physiologists give some answers to this last question. Some of their research is indicated in the following quotation:

Human milk is specially adapted to the requirements of the human infant and so differs in some respects from that of all other animals. Cow's milk is most frequently substituted for human milk. The relative composition of the two can be seen in the following table.

TABLE 6. Composition of Human and Cow's Milk

	Human (Average) PER CENT	Cow's (Average) PER CENT
Water	88.4	87.1
Proteins	1.5	3.2
Fat	3.3	3.9
Lactose	6.5	4.9
Salts	0.3	0.9

In substituting cow's milk for human milk, the differences that must be taken into consideration are not only the different relative proportions but also the following: The difference in the proteins; the protein of human milk is one-third caseinogen and two-thirds lactalbumin, and that of cow's milk is five-sixths caseinogen and one-sixth lactalbumin. The difference is in the curds formed in the stomach; human milk curdles in small flocculi, and cow's milk curdles in large, heavy curds. The reaction of human milk is practically neutral, pH 7.0 to 7.2; cow's milk is slightly acid, pH 6.6 to 6.8 when first drawn, but the acidity increases on standing. Human milk is sterile, and cow's milk, due to the handling it undergoes, contains a large number of microorganisms. Pasteurization destroys the microorganisms usually found in milk, but unless it is done very carefully, it also destroys the vitamins. Human milk contains antitoxins and antibacterial substances that have been formed in the mother's blood; and as it is ingested directly from the breast, its germicidal power is at its height. Cow's milk may have germicidal value, but this soon deteriorates and usually is lost by the time it is given to the child.[26]

In the light of the Sears study we wonder what statistical proof there is for Ribble's assertion that breast-feeding is "the most important means of immunizing the baby against anxiety." [27] Since anxiety is the core problem of modern personality adjustment, such a sweeping statement is challenging, but no proof is offered to substantiate it. We wonder really

[26] Diana Clifford Kimber and Carolyn E. Gray, A.M., R.N., *Textbook of Anatomy and Psychology* (New York: The Macmillan Company, 1952), pp. 703, 704. Reprinted by permission.
[27] Ribble, p. 34.

how much validity there is to Mead's suggestion that "for the complementary relationship of the child at the breast is substituted a pattern that can easily be made an alternating one—'Give baby a cracker, baby give mother a cracker'—in which a satisfying object intervenes between the two, and deep structural differences between their masculine and feminine roles are lost." [28] There are a great many intriguing avenues for speculation in this area. Our conclusion is that in whatever way it may be performed—whether by fondling when feeding the baby from the bottle or by gentle handling when breast-feeding the baby, or by any of the subtle, unrecorded methods by which a mother influences her children—the ability to love must be developed.

THUMB-SUCKING

The only importance of thumb-sucking is the anxiety it produces in parents and the conflict that that anxiety creates between parent and child. Thumb-sucking may be thought of during its earlier manifestations as a natural response to the sucking need. Those who have sucked longer have had fewer behavior problems later. In early childhood, if thumb-sucking persists, it is generally a comfort-giving behavior pattern. Thumb-sucking worries many parents because they think it is unhygienic, unsightly, and productive of dental malocclusion. But dental damage rarely occurs when thumb-sucking is confined to the first two or three years before permanent teeth arrive. Furthermore, there is evidence to indicate that if the child is not thwarted in his early sucking needs, he will not thumb-suck later.

Primitive cultures recognized this need of sucking by furnishing the child with various types of pacifiers. Today the emphasis is generally to thwart any mouth activity—which is unfortunate in so far as it causes irritation to the child and a lack of oral satisfaction that may later interfere with normal affectional mouth activity.

THE IMPACT OF WEANING

Freud postulated that every person must enter and emerge from an oral phase in which the oral drive was recognized and satiated. If this satiation did not happen, the individual became orally fixated with dire consequences for the personality. Many researchers studied such aspects of oral

[28] Mead, pp. 272–273.

satisfaction as thumb-sucking and anxiety. They reinforced Freud's conclusions that unless the native oral drive was satisfied the child would find artificial substitutions. Sears wondered if perhaps the opposite might not be true. If one learns to get satisfaction from a repeated habit, might it not only be the learning due to habit which provided the trauma when the habit was interrupted? So in his various studies he tried to isolate the various factors involved in emotional upset at weaning. He found three: (1) the longer practice at sucking, (2) the more severe methods of forcing the transition, and (3) indecisiveness during the process, leading to confusion and frustration of the child.[29] In conclusion his study suggests that "the strength of the sucking habit, and the need to get food by sucking, are increased by more practice at sucking."[30] His statistics bear this out. This conclusion is important because in other areas of child development it is possible that habits or strong drives that have previously been accounted for as the result of inborn, almost instinctual needs actually are only the simple result of learning or habit formation. In this sense these conclusions on weaning are important because they introduce a new theory regarding child training.

TOILET TRAINING AND ATTITUDES TOWARD SEX

The psychoanalytical school of thought holds that another important aspect of infantile experience which is directly related to sexual attitudes in the mature person is that of bowel and bladder training. Two specific problems arise during toilet training. The first has to do with the attitudes of the parent toward the training, and the second has to do with the accommodation of the parent to the child's interest in his bodily processes. Educators have an important term to describe the situation in which there is a complex of factors in a learning situation. They say that "concomitant factors" are being learned. Bowel training involves other factors besides the control of the bowels in a manner approved by society. Because the evacuation organs are so closely associated with the genitals, any attitude associated with evacuation will tend to be transferred to sexual interests as a concomitant learning. Thus, when a mother teaches her child to conform in bowel training by shaming him for his mistakes or when she uses such terms as "nasty," "dirty," "bad" to describe her soiled child, she may unconsciously be teaching him attitudes toward sex in general.

[29] Sears, Maccoby, Levin, p. 92.   [30] Sears, Maccoby, Levin, p. 100.

If, because of social pressure, she feels compelled to establish training at an age when the musculature of the child is not ready for such effort, this experiment may result in permanent damage to the child's elimination apparatus. The watchwords for toilet training are casualness and patience, for toilet training that is premature or carried on with rigid and harsh attitudes may result in lifelong preoccupation with evacuation, compulsive ideas of cleanliness, stubbornness and stinginess, and hesitation in sexual acceptance.[31]

Let us test these theories by more empirical conclusions discovered again in Sears' study. He reports on the degree of emotional upset which accompanied toilet (bowel) training.

TABLE 7. Age at Beginning of Bowel Training: Relationship to Amount of Emotional Upset *

	AGE AT BEGINNING OF BOWEL TRAINING				
	Under 5 Months	5–9 Months	10–14 Months	15–19 Months	20 Months or More
Child showed emotional disturbance	35%	18%	29%	44%	19%
Number of cases	23	154	113	39	31
			$p = .05$ (F)		

* Sears, Maccoby, Levin, p. 113.

Age is not enough to account for differences in emotional upsets in training. Sears found that severity in training was an important factor, although mothers who put a good deal of pressure on their children did not achieve their goal any sooner, but they did arouse much more emotional upset. However, even this statement must be modified because even severe toilet training was traumatic only when the mother was *cold*. When she was warm and affectionate, the degree of severity did not result in emotional upset.[32] This is another insight into the importance of warmth in mother-child relations.

Closely related to the matter of toilet training is the handling of the child during that period when his attention is focused directly upon elimination as a pleasure. During this time he may dawdle over his performance and take pleasure in his productions. Sometimes he will smear, and at other times show attitudes towards his stools which are completely

[31] Travis and Baruch, p. 148.   [32] Sears, Maccoby, Levin, p. 125.

antithetical to the adult expectations of his mother or father. Again, if the pleasure associated with defecation is described as bad, the child may generalize that all pleasure is bad.[33] The wise parent is aware that the process of acculturation is a lifelong process and that attitudes of society will be accumulated later when the child is ready for social control. Such an attitude helps in maintaining the warmth which seems to inhibit trauma.

In their summary Sears, Maccoby and Levin characterize personality as a "cluster of potentialities for action." In our use of this material we are saying that there is developed in infancy a cluster of potentialities for effective interaction in marriage. When all of the significant qualities or factors in the parent-child relationship were considered, it was *the mother's warmth* or its opposite, *coldness,* that had the most influence in its effects on the child.[34]

Punishment is another important factor in child training and the conclusion regarding this is that it is "ineffectual over the long term as a technique for eliminating the kind of behavior toward which it is directed." [35] Important in describing the mother's personality qualities were her relationships with her husband and her judgment and acceptance of him.[36] It is impossible to isolate a mother from her own interaction with the total family. It is equally important to view a mother's warmth as something which includes the husband-wife warmth or coldness. So that, while mother's warmth may be most closely correlated with a child's future behavior, this factor is itself formed by and a parcel of the larger family qualities. In a sense, then, mother's warmth only mediates to the child the general warmth of life and love in the family itself. It is true that mother is the chief agent dealing with the child in his early months, but it is equally true that father, and father's acceptance of fatherhood and of a husband's role, does equally as much in determining mother's response to the child. It is not possible to think of mother and father or sib as distinguishable in their impact on the child. The child lives in a family. The family through individuals influences him or her.

The final analysis of a longitudinal study of five hundred delinquent boys by William McCord emphasizes these conclusions. In analyzing twenty years of accumulated material, these significant factors were found to account for the deviant behavior of these boys: (a) the mother's personality appeared to be most fundamental, (b) the father's personality

[33] Travis and Baruch, p. 150.   [34] Sears, Maccoby, Levin, p. 484.
[35] Sears, Maccoby, Levin, p. 484.   [36] Sears, Maccoby, Levin, p. 473.

had an important bearing, and (c) the child's home atmosphere "cannot be stressed too greatly." [37] These conclusions fit the general conditions found in the various studies reviewed in these pages.

The McCord study showed that mothers who were absent, passive, cruel, rejective, or neglectful produced criminal sons. It is certainly not proved that we can be completely sure of the implication from this study that such mothers are other-centered and get their satisfaction from other than home situations, but it adds weight to our analysis. These are the very attitudes we would expect if both father and mother are status seekers and alienated from home as a primary concern. And Sears' study certainly upholds our contention that to the degree mothers and fathers are not family-centered, great harm occurs.

CONCLUSION

American child care, in some of its phases, tends to use substitutes for the close body contact that Mead considers so essential to the development of our sexual selves. Insistence on cleanliness and bodily care has resulted in the daily bath, followed by an oil rub and the application of powder. During all this time, the baby is undergoing skin stimulation which is important to its circulation. Probably more important, however, is the sense of bodily well-being that results from this pleasant interlude with the mother. Ribble points out that thoroughbred kittens who are not licked by their mothers develop serious disorders or die, and that young anthropoid apes who are not groomed by their parents sometimes sicken and die. Most mothers talk to their babies when giving the bath or the oil massage, and this is a period of fellowship in which the baby acquires a sense of security and has a positive reaction to his new world.

None of these behavior sequences—nursing, toilet training, bathing or sucking—appears to be the single key to the development of emotional responsiveness. The mother who desires to nurse her baby but because of some illness is unable to do so need not think that her child will be only halfway emotionally developed. For a fundamental fact outweighs the importance of any one of these procedures: it is the loving and tender affection accompanying these activities that determines their value. Neither rocking nor breast-feeding assures the child of either emotional growth or physical health. It is the accepting and loving attitude which underlies these ministrations that gives them value. If this attitude is genuine, if the

[37] William McCord, *Origins of Crime* (New York: Columbia University Press, 1959).

mother has wanted and continues to want the child, if she accepts her own sexual role and is happy in it, we may be reasonably certain that the child will develop positive and constructive affectional attitudes. A mother may rock a baby and sing to it, but unless there is some rhythm in her life and a song in her heart, the experience will not be genuine. That is what Ribble means when she says:

> Obviously feeding, bathing, and all the details of physical care come in, but in addition to these duties which can easily become routine and perfunctory, we mean all the small evidences of tender feeling . . . fondling, caressing, rocking and singing or speaking to the baby. These activities have a deep significance.[38]

These early conditionings have determined in a major manner every adult's attitudes and expectations. The experiences of his own children in this period of infancy will, likewise, determine much of their adult life, including their basic emotional capacity, their verve for life, their sexual interest and fulfillment. Preparation for marriage begins at birth, and, today, we are beginning to know something of the crucial experiences which later will implement or inhibit emotional responsiveness and sociability.

SELF-ANALYSIS

The facts in this chapter will have little meaning for the reader unless they are specifically related to his own background, and little meaning for his children unless they are absorbed and become part of their attitudes.

By talking with older sibs, parents, uncles, or any other person who knew of our situation during infancy, we can gain some perspective regarding our earliest conditioning. The student may find that parents are eager to share their sense of joy about the early years. The following outline represents the first part of the self-analysis which will follow each chapter dealing with a person's developmental background.

OUTLINE OF SELF-ANALYSIS

I. EARLY FAMILY BACKGROUND . . . Mother and Father

A. Describe the courtship, engagement and early marital adjustment of your parents. What special problems did they have in their first year and years together? How were these problems resolved?

[38] Ribble, p. 9.

B. What seems to have been the personality characteristics of your mother during those years? Did she find the role of a wife and mother rewarding? Were there fears or traumas associated with motherhood? How would you characterize her in terms of (1) warmth, (2) permissiveness, (3) attitudes toward procreation and infant care?

C. Characterize the personality of your father during the first years of marriage. How did he adjust to the changes of marriage? Was he jealous of the children? Did he cooperate in their care?

II. EARLY MARITAL ADJUSTMENT

A. Can you describe the early ups-and-downs of your parents' marriage? Were there separations or quarrels? Were they "happy" or "strained" in relationships?

B. How did they solve the problem of dominance early in marriage? For instance, who *made* the decision regarding the number of children and when they should arrive?

C. In discussing the matter do you have a feeling that the children were an asset or a liability to the early union? Did the children interrupt plans and inhibit goals?

III. EARLY CHILDHOOD OR INFANCY TRAINING

A. How were you fed? Breast or bottle? Why? How long? Were you weaned at an early, middle or late stage? What special problems, if any, were there in the weaning process?

B. What kind of discipline was used very early in your life to get you to conform? Do you know what "psychology" your parents followed?

C. How were you trained in bowel and bladder control? When? Did you regress later? When? What special problems were there over these matters?

D. What illnesses did you have as a small child? Did they leave any residue of problems? How did your family handle these problems? Was there great anxiety about them?

E. How much "warmth" or "love" did you receive? From mother? From father? Do you think you were "spoiled"? Why?

IV. MEANING FOR YOUR PERSONALITY AND MARRIAGE

A. In what ways do you think the early family background of your mother or father influenced your progress toward the kind of maturity that means a good marriage?

B. In what sense do you think the "home atmosphere" influenced your feelings about your own worthiness as a person or about marriage?

C. How did the various methods used in child-training influence you as a person? As you look at the studies reviewed in this chapter, what are your ideas about the ways you now interact with others as related to infancy and early childhood?

VISUAL AIDS

Life with Baby, University of California Department of Visual Instruction, 405 Hilgard Avenue, Los Angeles 14, California.

Self Discovery In a Mirror, Encyclopaedia Britannica Films, 20 North Wacker Drive, Chicago 6, Illinois.

Baby's Day at Forty-eight Weeks, Encyclopaedia Britannica Films, 20 North Wacker Drive, Chicago 6, Illinois.

Preface to Life, Sundial Films, for National Institute of Mental Health, 341 East 43rd St., New York 17, N.Y.

READINGS

DUVALL, EVELYN MILLS. *Family Development*. Philadelphia, J. B. Lippincott Company, 1957, Chapter I.

MEAD, MARGARET. *Male and Female*. William Morrow and Company, 1949, Part II, Chapter III.

RIBBLE, MARGARET. *The Rights of Infants*. New York, Columbia University Press, 1943, Chapters II, III, and IV.

SEARS, ROBERT R., ELEANOR E. MACCOBY, HARRY LEVIN, *et al. Patterns of Child Rearing*. New York, Row, Peterson and Company, 1957, Chapters I, II, III, and IV. Copyright Harper and Row, Publishers.

SPOCK, BENJAMIN, M.D. *The Pocket Book of Baby and Child Care*. New York, Pocket Books, Inc., 1946.

TRAVIS, LEE and DOROTHY BARUCH. *Personal Problems of Everyday Life*. New York, Appleton-Century-Crofts, 1941, Chapters II and III.

WINCH, ROBERT F. *The Modern Family*. New York, Henry Holt and Company, 1952. Chapter VIII. Copyright Holt, Rinehart and Winston, Inc.

CHAPTER 5

Factors in
Childhood

INTRODUCTION

THERE is no major glandular or functional change that marks the transition from infancy into childhood. One week we are holding an infant, the next week a child is crawling by us. Childhood will be considered here as that developmental period from eighteen months to the beginning of puberty. Childhood is an important stage in the series of growth sequences that lead to later adjustment in marriage. Terman found happiness in childhood to be the most important of the background factors associated with marital adjustment.[1] Locke, too, discovered that a significantly larger percentage of those who were happily married than of those who were divorced, both men and women, reported their childhood as happy or very happy.[2] In this chapter we shall try to isolate some of the vital aspects of the years before adolescence that could explain more specifically those research findings.

It is not difficult to recall the deep emotions of childhood. Travis and Baruch describe childhood experience and its effect behavioristically:

> We have all lived through those long dark problems of childhood. Each and every one of us remembers at least in small proportion. We may say, "I was the world's worst." Or we may murmur, "I was really a good child; my problems were very mild." No matter which, we still remember. We remember, also, how we were handled when these problems were upon us.

[1] Lewis M. Terman, *Psychological Factors in Marital Happiness* (New York: McGraw-Hill Book Company, Inc., 1938), pp. 225–228.
[2] Harvey J. Locke, *Predicting Adjustment in Marriage: A Comparison of a Divorced and a Happily Married Group* (New York: Henry Holt and Company, 1951), pp. 107–108. Copyright © 1951, Holt, Rinehart and Winston, Inc.

We remember injustices. We remember righteous anger. We remember cajolings and less persuasive methods. We remember heads hung low, tears under hot lids, dry, set lips held from retort. We remember fury in return for fury. Penance, shame, regret. We remember what we did; what was done to us; what that did to us in turn—at least what it did to us at the moment. But almost never do we realize what it did to us for all time.[3]

"What it did to us for all time." That last arresting clause indicates that ten or twenty years after childhood we shall still be playing the roles we learned then and trying to work out in our marriages and in our relationship to our own children problems that came to us during these formative years. Life, to the child, may be a paradoxical experience. It is full of wonder and discovery; at the same time it is fraught with immense challenges, frequent misunderstandings, and painful adjustments. There is often the admixture of ringing laughter and bitter tears. As hour follows hour there is learning, learning by the tear ducts, the tensor muscles, the aesthetic sensitivities, the fingers, the tongue, and the heart. The mild-worded mother and the "manly, mean anger'd father," together with brothers, sisters, grandparents, uncles, aunts, and guests, are, during childhood, the dominant influences in molding personality.

But it need not be "for all time." For as we review the critical areas of our growth in our childhood we can see that some of the particular ways we were handled brought about particular results (we can see, too, how we may handle our own children differently and get different results). And, as we review these past hours of conditioning, the conditioning itself is modified. Travis and Baruch themselves suggest this possibility:

> And finally, we see that what has happened in the past needs to hurt us no longer. Reviewing the behavior problems of childhood is often akin to digesting food that has long lain heavily against one's diaphragm. We begin to see our own past behavior in a different perspective. We begin to see where present behavior has unsuspectedly been related to the past. We begin to see that how-we-are is related to how-we-were more than we guessed.[4]

THE PROCESS OF SOCIALIZATION

At eighteen months or thereabouts the infant begins to be mobile—begins to bump into chairs and into the world. His style of personality and

[3] Lee Travis and Dorothy Baruch, *Personal Problems of Everyday Life* (New York: Appleton-Century-Crofts, 1941), p. 129. Reprinted by permission of the publisher.
[4] Travis and Baruch, p. 130. Reprinted by permission of the publisher.

his bent of character are determined by the peculiar way in which he learns to adjust to others. This style and bent are determined partly by his "tempo," which is largely an inherited characteristic, but more importantly by the degree to which he is socialized. Winch defines the tasks presented to the growing child as these:

> (a) the incorporation into his behavior of a sufficient proportion of the parental discipline to enable the child to achieve a workable level of adjustment with his parents; (b) as a corollary of this, acceptance of the idea that a considerable number of "immediate" pleasures are to be foregone in the interest of some "future" gain; (c) the creation of the ego-ideal and the beginning of the struggle to realize it; and (d) integration into the appropriate age and sex groups.[5]

We should add to this list a fifth aspect of socialization, namely, the incorporation into his behavior patterns of an awareness of the generalized expectations of others sufficient to enable the child to communicate and to share.

The ability to play appropriate social roles is essential to normal adult life and certainly to marital life. Insofar as we must distinguish between appropriate *male* roles and appropriate *female* roles we add the need for sexual identification. Included in the adoption of appropriate social roles are the norms of society. We describe social norms as conscience when we are speaking of the way they are internalized within the individual. Much marital misery is associated with the union of individuals who do not possess consistent standards of behavior. Thus, what we shall discuss in this section is basic for marital adjustment. Therefore, in order to be good parents or to understand our own promise for marriage and parenthood, we need to look searchingly at the way we become human and humane.

The psychoanalysts long ago called this process *identification* and although our explanation is not exactly theirs, it is in debt enough to them to use the term. Our explanation is based generally on Mead, on Sears, and the neo-Freudians. We think that children have a need of perpetuating the pleasant and, for them, economical type of relationship they have in their earliest months with their mothers. Mother has met their every need and given them every kind of psychological comfort. Because the infant is helpless the mother must meet these obligations if the child is to survive. However, there are differences in attitudes of mothers and those who

[5] Robert F. Winch, *The Modern Family* (New York: Henry Holt and Company, 1952), p. 242. Coypright © 1952, Holt, Rinehart and Winston, Inc. Reprinted by permission of the publisher.

are cold and neglectful are not apt to establish the same kind of needs for the perpetuation of the relationship as are warm and kind mothers.

By the time the child becomes a toddler, his mother has spent a great deal of time with him. However, this situation changes if she begins to plan for another baby. But, whatever her condition, most mothers are happy to separate themselves to some extent from the baby who has literally consumed their time. So, quite naturally, they withdraw. But the child cannot accept the withdrawal. It means the loss of all past security, pleasure and ease. So the child, quite without rational syllogisms, casts about for means to re-establish that earlier state that was so comforting.

It soon becomes apparent to mothers that their children are developing *dependency* relationships and the mothers take this into account in either accepting it, rewarding it, or rejecting it.[6] If she rejects the child, he will increase his efforts at being close to her, i.e., being dependent. If she responds to his needs with affection, he will learn how to command affection from her and this will increase dependency.[7] However, if she vacillates, if he cannot be sure as to her response, he will become *anxious* and even more deeply dependent. If the child does not achieve enough response, he will now experiment with methods of winning again his mother's approval and closeness.

One of the ways he will do this is to try to be so much like his mother that she will approve of him and reward him with the closeness he covets. Thus, he tends to rehearse her behavior. He plays her role. He speaks to his peers using her language, her commands, her satisfactions. If he is playing with dolls he reproves and encourages as does his mother. He is internalizing her roles, her attitudes, her point of view. Thus he learns to be a civilized and conforming individual.

This process does well for a girl. She is admired and praised as she moves in her ways toward role playing as a woman. But, alas, when the little boy, expecting his due reward for mimicking mother, looks for approval, he is cut down with severe admonishment "not to act like a girl." This must puzzle him, particularly because he is becoming aware of the fact that there are others in his circle who seem to displace him in his mother's affection. There is a great, hulking figure of a male who comes in and out but who commands the kind of affection and service from his mother that he would like to have. The competitor for his affection is his father. At this

---

[6] Sears, Maccoby, Levin, p. 175.

[7] This section is a very much over-simplified summary of Sears' research. Students would do well to study his entire presentation of socialization and identification.

point the Freudians would introject the Oedipus complex with its emphasis upon sexual competition. It does not seem necessary to describe that theory here because what happens can be explained in interactional terms. It seems to us that the boy, upon seeing what kind of affection his father earns, would naturally try to behave in ways like his father so that he would be rewarded in the same way. So he becomes a little man. He cocks his hat like father, he sometimes embarrassingly swears like father, he growls like father, and he treats mother as father does. In other words, he identifies with his father. Then if his father is any kind of a man, he encourages the little fellow by sharing interest and fun with him. The boy discovers there are some things that men do that women do not, and not only enjoying these, but being praised for them, he is content to channel his development along male roles.[8]

THE GROWTH OF CONSCIENCE

If we can account for sex typing and male and female role playing as we have in the previous paragraphs, it will be apparent that the child will necessarily also internalize *norms* along with role attitudes and behavior patterns associated with those roles. The child learns to exercise control over the things his parents control. Sears adds a valuable insight at this point. He sees that the role practice to which we have referred may result in the "adoption of everything in the parents' behavior that the child perceives as appropriate to the parental role." [9] But, says Sears, children may have too much conscience, they may become *guilt-ridden* and rigid and inflexible. This attitude, in a highly mobile society with rapidly changing challenges and life patterns, is inhibiting. On the other hand, if the parents produce a child with a weak conscience he is controlled only by *expediency* and cannot be trusted.[10] We think there is a relationship here between McCord's findings of a profound relationship between a warm, loving mother and father and non-deviant behavior. For if parents are not those who inspire dependency, emulation, and identification, the child does not internalize values and may develop no conscience at all. Insofar as marriage involves a type of loving relationship that demands the highest type of trust and responsibility, it is immediately apparent what havoc follows marriage to an individual who has little or no conscience.

[8] The author is indebted to Dr. Simon Conrad, psychiatrist, and psychiatric consultant for the Peterson-Guedel Family Center, for explication of this point.
[9] Sears, Maccoby, Levin, pp. 390, 391.   [10] Sears, Maccoby, Levin, p. 391.

DEVELOPING A SENSE OF VALUES AND GOALS

Conscience of course involves the incorporation of a sense of right and wrong as related to specific behavioral situations. We shall speak more of this when we talk about the way character impinges on marital adjustment. Here we are concerned about the sharing by the parents of some values and goals by which the child *can judge future action*. We know we do not want our children to be delinquent, dependent, ineffective, shy or destructive, but what do we want? In another book I have suggested a positive way of looking at goals in child raising:

> Consider the following six objectives from the University of Chicago Parent Education Project:
>
> 1. Feelings of security and adequacy
> 2. Understanding of self and others
> 3. Democratic values and goals
> 4. Problem-solving attitudes and methods
> 5. Self-discipline, responsibility, and freedom
> 6. Constructive attitudes toward change
>
> Some parents may feel that this is not an adequate list of purposes for child-raising. Let us only say that it is a beginning and many parents would do well to use this list as a foundation for thinking through their own positive objectives so that they may finally come to work with their children *toward* something instead of always working *against* something that is vague and threatening but which they do not understand. One thing is certain. In a world where social change follows mechanical invention more and more rapidly, there is a *new need*. In those days if a boy was a carbon copy of his father he would succeed in life. But today our children live in a world in which *novelty* and *change* are the expected and a child trained only in his father's image is early made incompetent to live in his generation. It is a world in which the only appropriate mood is courage and adaptability. The wings of tomorrow will carry us to the uttermost reaches of space and probably disclose truth still undreamed of. No child anchored to the past by timidity or habit can enjoy this adventure into this unknown. The rather staid wording of the Parent Education Project really means that we lift our faces to the future with wonder, with zest and expectation, unafraid to brave the cosmic storms of space or the social revolutions that must inevitably accompany a brave new world. In such a society concern and concen-

tration upon minor habits is not nearly as important as the broader stimulation of the spirit to live—to live grandly, boldly, as though life were an adventure and not a trial. Children raised in such an atmosphere are not toppled by the winds of adversity nor do they cower before the unexpected.[11]

When we were discussing the meaning of love in Chapter Three we commented that in an other-directed society children are taught only one thing, to learn to respond to the cues of others, to conform for the sake of acceptance. But there is little substance to a weathervane. Whatever values parents have should be shared with children as sources of strength, and shared with the humility that will make it possible for the child to build on them in other directions without trauma.

DEVELOPING COMMUNICATION

The quantity and the quality of communication in the parental home and in the play group have a decisive influence later on, for social sharing is based on verbal and emotional communication. Communication means the sharing of symbols whose meaning is understood by those who participate. The meanings of symbols come to us as children when, through experience, we internalize what these symbols mean to others. Only when the symbol signifies to us an act yet to be completed does its meaning become clear. Until we learn that the muscle tension, the defiant pose, the tight lips, and the clenched fist mean that a blow is intended, we are not prepared to defend ourselves. In social communication our understanding of the meanings of gestures or word symbols enables us to imagine the response of others to our gestures or our words, and thus we anticipate the reaction of the other. This is the way we incorporate into ourselves the reactions of others. *Upon this fundamental process all interaction with others is based.*

It is obvious that the richer the variety of situations in which the child is placed the more adaptable will he be in marriage. The large family, variety of play and gang activities, freedom in emotional interaction—these are all critical factors in acquainting the child with the range of meanings associated with gestures and word symbols and enabling him, later on, to communicate effectively. The role we play at any given time is essentially the one which we imagine will bring us status among our

[11] James A. Peterson, *Toward A Successful Marriage* (New York: Charles Scribner's Sons, 1960), pp. 193–194. Reprinted by permission of the publisher.

fellows. Usually we discard a role which brings ridicule or disdain or increases the social distances between us and our playmates or our parents.

Adjustment in marriage depends on the degree to which the partners are "socialized." If they are to be emotionally responsive to one another, life must have taught them to laugh and to cry without fear, to love and to be tender without affectation or inhibition. If they are to understand the almost infinite moods, reactions, and needs of their mate, they must not have been isolated, in childhood and youth, from the floodtide of emotional experiences.

THE PLAY GROUP AND SOCIALIZATION

The group of children gathered under the tree discussing the problem of where to tie the swing is learning creative ways of group living—a learning that will play its part in group experience of marriage.

Socialization begins during those early months of transition from egocentric to group behavior. In this period the child discovers the importance of the demands of other individuals and learns that these others have rights and interests. If the social setting is a happy one, children learn that others also make contributions and that taking turns or sharing toys or cooperating in games increases their own satisfaction. The roles they choose to play are altered as some action on their part brings them either isolation or greater respect. Hence, one learns to limit one's demands, to consider the expectations of others, and finally to relate these to the interest of the group. Out of such experience comes social poise and adaptability. These characteristics cannot be taught—they are distilled from successful living and experience. Thus the play group and the family give the child practice in adjustment. He early learns to gauge his behavior by what that behavior elicits from others in the way of encouragement, reward, or punishment.

THE FAMILY AND SOCIALIZATION

The family is a school of living. Life in the family is without mask or "front." A child's brother may be quiet and respectful at school and a demon at home. His father may be a model of patience at the office but shout and swear while making repairs on the kitchen stove. His mother, when she is in society and with her friends, may carefully assume in her speech and tone of voice the exact attitudes her friends expect from a mother;

but at home, when the confusion and frustration are too great, she may abandon this role. Day by day, hour by hour, the child learns that life is a place of masks, poses, and roles, and he learns to adjust to this as reality. If, in later life, his own wife, now a mother, abandons the socially expected role of tenderness and patience and becomes upset and irritable, he will not be too shocked.

The experience of family life is deeply imbedded in the child's attitudes. If there is good humor and happy bantering, if the solemn moments of discipline are counter-balanced by the abandon of self-forgetting play, the child's expectation will be of a family life of fun and mirth intermingled only occasionally with shadows. For this child the family is fun. On occasion he will prefer the family circle to the gang; he will stop watching the TV screen to romp with Dad. On the other hand, if the family is dominated by conflict patterns, by repressed emotions or silent tensions, the child must inevitably internalize a less pleasant picture. Terman's study reinforces this point of view in his findings:

> The happiness of both spouses is positively correlated with attachments and also with lack of conflict. The correlations are highly reliable and are consistent in direction . . . The highest means (happiness scores) are for subjects reporting greatest attachment or least conflict, and they drop with considerable regularity as attachment decreases or conflict increases. The critical ratios of these differences run high. The data justify the assignment of fairly heavy weights in the happiness prediction scale.[12]

PARENTAL NEGLECT OR REJECTION

A boy was once referred to a counselor by a school because of his serious maladjustment. The boy had an acute shoulder tic; he could not communicate; he was listless and depressed. After a series of conferences in which his contribution was only a series of "uh huh's" and "huh uh's" he finally was induced to talk. After many weeks, he began to talk about recurrent dreams in which there appeared an enormous door which seemed very threatening to him. Persistent and patient examination revealed that there was indeed an important door in this boy's life. It proved to be the door to his father's study. When his father came home from his research laboratory, he would enter his study and shut the door. No one was permitted to enter or knock upon the door. Through the years the boy had come to hate that door and all that it symbolized in the way of affec-

[12] Terman, p. 215. Reprinted by permission of the publisher.

tional deprivation. Children hate doors, real or symbolic, that shut them out of the lives of their parents.

The mother who washes her children's clothes and cooks their meals, the father who provides for their present comfort and insures their future —such parents often think that they have thereby fulfilled their obligations; but they may have failed to give their children something even more important—time and attention. Without these, children grow up in emotional and spiritual isolation. We shall see later how urban life, with its media of mass communication and its commercial recreation, tends to accentuate this deprivation. Many modern parents do not give enough of themselves to enable even partial identification on the part of children. It is our belief, derived from careful analysis of case studies, that this can result in emotional impoverishment and insecurity.[13]

Other-directed parents, intent on "success" and "status" in work or community institutions other than the home, reject their children while rationalizing that they are earning the *things* the child needs. Studies of infancy cited in the last chapter indicate the possibility that rejection of children may result from their arriving when they are definitely not wanted. Plant stresses this point, putting it first among the four reasons he cites for the rejection of children. He thinks that if the first baby arrives before the parents are ready to give up their carefree childlessness, that baby is likely to be rejected.[14] Rejection may also occur if one parent is so preoccupied with the child that the other parent feels displaced and jealous. A third motivation for rejection is present if the child possesses some of the traits of one parent which are distasteful to the other. A further cause for rejection is the fact that pregnancy often focalizes a woman's lifelong resentment at being a woman.

DISCIPLINE AND THE PRODUCTION OF HOSTILITY

Winch has indicated that an internalization of discipline is the basis for adjustment between parent and child. The anxiety and basic hostility that threaten many marriages have their origin in the overall relations between parents and children. The growth of hostility patterns may conveniently be discussed as part of a consideration of discipline. Every parent has the obligation to help his child live comfortably with society's

[13] William Goldfarb, "Psychological Privation in Infancy and Subsequent Adjustment," *American Journal of Orthopsychiatry,* XV (1949), 247–255.

[14] James S. Plant, *Personality and the Cultural Pattern* (New York: The Commonwealth Fund, 1937), pp. 99–100.

rules. The parent who does not orient the child in terms of safety precautions, manners, laws, customs, and mores sends him into adult life without the moral and social equipment to adjust to the world. Yet no child automatically knows that such training is necessary for his future. He does not welcome the cultural straitjacket which is the price of admission to human society. He cannot naturally respond to all adult demands. Consequently, friction inevitably develops.

The way in which hostile and aggressive reactions of children to their parents' expectations are handled will affect their emotional security or adjustment. If the parents are understanding and permissive of the rebellion of an immature child and, as a result, consistently forgive the child's natural hostility, the child operates in a secure atmosphere in which he grows up with a minimum of neurotic results. But if parents are defensive and lack understanding, the child may be afraid to express his antagonistic and angry feelings and thus keep them to himself. He may fear that if he expresses these negative feelings he will be physically punished. He may fear that his parents will shame him for not having "proper respect," or that he might lose whatever affection his parents manage to give him. He may have tried to express his feelings and been made to feel "guilty," as if he were a bad person. Thus he stores up *repressed hostility*, a reservoir of hostility. It may never be expressed toward his parents; then it is very likely to be vented in later life on his business associates, his wife, and his own children. The mechanism here is laid bare in a case study in which the client said:

> The fact that my father gets so mad so easily and hollers has definitely created in me a feeling of inferiority, because in the past I've always been afraid of doing something which would make him bawl me out. Even though I no longer fear being bawled out, the attitude of being timid and the fear of making mistakes has clung to me to some extent. I'm too concerned with what people think of me and I'm usually worried about doing that which will please others and make others like me.[15]

This young man was afraid of his father. He could not talk back. Baruch reports a different type of father.

> As a final case in point, let's get back to our Heine who wouldn't eat and who had threatened to fling his food all around . . . Suppose now that Heine actually begins to throw his food around. This obviously won't do. It's destructive to the rug and furniture, and besides, a chicken bone might

[15] From a case study in the author's files.

land in father's eye. Heine's father is now on the spot; how can he continue to accept and mirror Heine's feelings and yet at the same time curb Heine's actions?

Here is father's opportunity to slip back into the good old ways of disciplining. He is, in fact, on the verge of this. He feels anger mounting inside him and he starts to think longingly of every threat in his vocabulary, from lambasting Heine to forbidding him ice-cream cones for a week. But he, too, remembers the new ways of discipline just in time:

> SEE how he feels.
> ACCEPT how he feels.
> REFLECT how he feels.
> Help him GET OUT THE POISON.
> If necessary, help him STEER his ACTIONS.

"Heine," Father says, his anger dwindling, "you're mad at me. It's not hard to see that. Why don't you tell me about it. You can say anything you feel like saying. It's okay to get out your anger in words. But I can't let you throw food around. Understand?"

Heine looks up challenging, "Suppose I do it anyway?" Heine's father notices quickly that there has already been a change in Heine. He is no longer concentrating on throwing the food. He is focusing on threatening his father. In other words, Heine is now using threats instead of food-flinging as a way of releasing his anger. This is the feeling that his father now mirrors.

"You want to threaten me, Heine?"

"I sure do. You're an old meanie. I'd like you to trip in the garden and get mud in your mouth. Old stinky mud. Old stinky—nice daddy!" And Heine bursts into a wide grin. "Come on, Dad, let's play kick-ball. I'll eat this here stuff up first real fast."

The crisis is past.

"But," you protest, "it doesn't work that way. If I'd forbidden him, my child would have gone right on throwing the food. I'd have had to resort to punishment, I know. The mere forbidding wouldn't have helped."

Heine's father had not, however, used mere forbidding. He had forbidden the action only. He had not forbidden the feeling. He had given Heine's feelings many chances to come out. The curtailment lay in the fact that they could not come out in this particular kind of action. If they had needed to come out further, they would have to be channeled into other kinds of action instead.[16]

---

[16] Dorothy Baruch, *New Ways in Discipline* (New York: McGraw-Hill Book Company, Inc., 1949), p. 97. Reprinted by permission of the publisher.

If the parent helps the child get the poison out day by day, it does not accumulate to complicate other adjustments. Furthermore, it does not accumulate to prevent normal affectional development. The child who can express open rebellion, anger, and resentment without fear of reprisal is also the child who will show a maximum of spontaneous love for his parents. Neurotic behavior often has its origin in the fact that many parents threaten their children in such a way that hostility and anxiety, and the consequent guilt feelings are never worked off. In a sense, every child must undergo constant frustration. As a result, he will be rather constantly hostile. These feelings must be allowed continuous expression.

Can we confirm these generalizations from our studies? There is some confirmation in the questions raised by Terman and Locke in regard to severe discipline. The relationship of a permissive home atmosphere to later marital adjustment is reported by these two investigators. Terman found that "firm but no harsh discipline" was the type associated with marital adjustment.[17] Locke concluded:

> A significantly larger per cent of both divorced men and women reported that they "never had own way" in their parental homes. "Usually had own way" was reported by a significantly larger per cent of both happily married men and women than by the divorced.[18]

Travis and Baruch report another study which bears directly on this point:

> A bit of interesting evidence comes from two hundred graduate students at Columbia University. Those students who, in their childhood, had been severely disciplined, managed to get over their "bad" behavior. But in the process they developed great animosity toward their parents. Quite naturally then, they also developed a tremendously large load of guilt feeling toward themselves. They owned up to having had strong desires to hurt, or even kill their parents. They wished their parents death through accident or disaster. They condemned themselves so mightily for such thoughts that they wished themselves dead. Many of them had seriously contemplated suicide. In contrast, where discipline had not been felt severe, the students were comparatively free from such feelings. Discipline which was resented had left its mark. It was succeeded by worse problems.[19]

It is probably accurate to say that Sears' findings present somewhat contradictory evidence for this point of view. He does not suggest com-

---

[17] Terman, pp. 228–236.
[18] Locke, p. 111. Reprinted by permission of the publisher.
[19] Travis and Baruch, pp. 285–286. Reprinted by permission of the publisher.

plete repression of hostility because "We are not suggesting that parents should band together in omnipotent suppression of every justifiable angry response the child makes. The right to be angry without fear or guilt is as inalienable as any other and more important than some." [20] But in concordance with his learning theory of motivation Sears shows that permissiveness toward aggression or anger simply encourages more aggression (toward parents). He found several factors that were statistically related to the growth of aggressive tendencies. He found them to be (1) permissiveness about aggression, (2) punishment for aggression, (3) physical punishment and (4) coldness on the part of parents. For both boys and girls the highest degree of aggressive behavior was associated with high permissiveness and high punishment.[21] This is obviously the most frustrating situation a child could face.

There is one criticism of Sears' research that may have a bearing at this point. His findings relate only to kindergarten children. We suspect that at least some of the children of his sample who seem now not to be aggressive have only learned to repress their hostility, and these feelings will impair interpersonal relations later in life. As his study was based on the reports of mothers when the child was five we could not expect the mothers to be aware of later problems. It is possible that some of the more aggressive children in his sample who ventilate their feelings while young may not need to be hostile later on in life. Yet Sears indicates that he is not saying all anger should be repressed and his final conclusion sounds much like that of Winch, who thinks that some of these matters are solved in terms of the economy of emotions which permit a family to live together on some basis of harmony.

Obviously hostility and its control are related to juvenile delinquency and we have further evidence from a follow-up of the Glueck study. This study scaled the most critical items of child-parent relationships as a predictive device to detect future delinquents. Again, the strictness of discipline and the use of harsh punishment was a factor. The predictive scales covered: (1) the degree of severity of punishment by the father, (2) the supervision by the mother, (3) father's affection, (4) mother's affection, and (5) the cohesiveness of the family. In 1958, a follow-up study on 1952 predictions made by the New York City Youth Board using these scales on a sample showed 93 per cent of the subjects reacting in conformity with early predictions! [22] While couched in different terms

[20] Sears, Maccoby, Levin, p. 269.   [21] Sears, Maccoby, Levin, p. 260.
[22] Maud M. Craig, "Six Years of a Validation Experiment on the Glueck Social Factors

this study conforms to the findings of the Travis-Baruch study. Harsh punishment is simply not an efficient way of achieving goals with children. Sears' summary comment is that "it is ineffectual over the long term as a technique for eliminating the kind of behavior toward which it is directed." [23] From all of our evidence it seems clear that there is agreement that non-punitive methods of getting compliance with parental standards is both more efficacious in getting results and without injurious side effects.

PARENTAL PROJECTIONS ON CHILDREN

Parents have special emotional needs which they often expect their children to meet for them. Exploited children are the boys and girls whose parents use them to make up for their own deficiencies, real or imagined. Such parents drive their children to embrace ambitions which they themselves could not realize. One of the most common illustrations of this tendency to relive one's life in that of one's child is to steer the child into the profession or occupation the parent desired but failed to enter; or parents may seek to improve their status in the accomplishments of their children. A student reports:

> When I was in the third grade I almost failed math—and this hurt my parents terribly. I had to struggle with math until I was a sophomore in college. I will always remember my parents' friends asking them if I was smart in this subject and they always had to apologize for me.

Another illustration is the mother whose undemonstrative husband had never given her an outlet for her affectional needs; thus she turned all of her love upon her little boy and made him dependent upon her. When the time came (around eight or nine) when he should have identified with his father, she blocked that transfer of affection. Later, when time for marriage approached, she found it impossible to surrender him to any other woman.

Unhappy mothers who have failed in several marriages sometimes want their children to reject marriage. When one of these children falls in love, the mother always finds something wrong with the intended mate. Or she may become ill so that her child will feel guilty if he leaves her.

Still another type of parent expiates a neurotic sense of guilt by bring-

Prediction Table of Juvenile Delinquency," speech delivered at American Association for Advancement of Science, Washington, Dec. 28, 1958. Mimeographed.

[23] Sears, Maccoby, Levin, p. 484.

ing up his children with extreme care lest they sin too. Children of such parents approach life with a perfectionism so rigid that they find marriage very trying. Others with a stronger ego develop patterns of distrust and deception toward their parents since they cannot live up to the high standards set for them.

Plant emphasizes the parents' need for projection when he says:

> There are few matters so common and impelling as the need that the individual has for mending the broken threads of his own life in the growing lives of those over whom he has a feeling of control. It is for this that the adult looks to family experience.[24]

SEXUAL DEVELOPMENT DURING CHILDHOOD

The general conditioning of the sensual self described in Chapter One becomes much more specific during childhood. The sexual interests of children seem to focus during the fifth, sixth, and seventh years upon their genitalia. After this comes the so-called "latency" period. The handling by parents of this interest in genitalia and sexual experimentation affects personality adjustment as well as sexual adjustment in marriage. Teachers of family-life courses in some high schools, in submitting curriculum materials, include such observations as these:

> Because of an unfortunate experience in another high school in our district, the word "sex" is not used in any of our schools, and consequently is omitted from this unit of study.

> As the school board has locked up any films on reproduction and has frowned on any instruction in the field of sex, we confine ourselves to the more sociological factors in marriage.

Students' reports indicate the same type of situation at home:

> I first learned of sex not from my parents but from a little French girl when I was in the fifth grade. What she told me shocked me terribly. I can remember telling her that "My parents never did that." Yet my parents never told me a thing about sex.

> The knowledge of sex that I acquired in the later years of grammar school and in the early years of high school was somewhat confusing. My parents, most especially my mother, suppressed sexual information or conversation.

> The information derived from classmates was not often of a wholesome nature but degraded sex considerably. Sexual information that I derived

[24] James S. Plant, "Mental Hygiene Aspects of the Family," *The Family*, April, 1932, pp. 39–45; May, 1932, pp. 90–99; June, 1932, pp. 118–126. Reprinted by permission.

from my parents was very inadequate; and that derived from my classmates was mostly inaccurate.

Inadequate and inaccurate! These are the words that most often occur
as young people describe their initiation into sexual knowledge. How important is this to marital adjustment?

It is important to keep the sexual factor in marriage in proper perspective. The statistical studies of Terman, Locke, and Burgess and Cottrell
are all in agreement that in marital adjustment the sex factor is secondary
to personality and interactional factors.[25] Nevertheless, as studies by
Davis, Schroeder, and Terman indicate, proper sexual education in childhood is significant in later marital adjustment. Bowman calls the attitude
of society toward sex "obscurantism," and points out that "marriage is the
only human endeavor in which ignorance is considered a virtue." [26]

There are many ways in which parents can contribute to the development of wholesome sexual attitudes on the part of their boys and girls.

1. They can try to talk freely with them at each stage of their development, answering their questions honestly but in keeping with the child's
comprehension.

2. Parents can supply the child with interesting books and pamphlets
written for various age groups. An example of such a book would be
Francis Bruce Strain's *Being Born*.

3. Parents can bring pets such as cats, hamsters, or rabbits into the
home and see to it that the children learn from the reproductive behavior
of these animals.

4. Parents can cultivate the confidence of their children so that when
the children hear obscene jokes or "gutter talk" the parents will have an
opportunity to correct misinformation and instill wholesome attitudes.

5. Parents who feel they are too inhibited themselves to discuss the
meaning of reproduction with their children can search out an understanding physician or psychologist who can talk with their children.

6. Parents can help mold public opinion so that schools and churches
will help boys and girls treat sexual topics as learning experiences in
realistic and meaningful ways.

One of the aspects of early sexual adjustment that must be discussed
is masturbation. Masturbation is universal but it is not an easy subject

[25] Ernest W. Burgess and Leonard Cottrell, *Predicting Success or Failure in Marriage*
(New York: Prentice-Hall, Inc., 1939), p. 347.
[26] Henry A. Bowman, *Marriage for Moderns* (New York: McGraw-Hill Book Company,
Inc., 1948), p. 311.

to talk about. Parents are sometimes upset at this practice and sometimes use harsh discipline to end it. The practice of masturbation itself has no harmful results unless it is practiced to great excess, but the sense of guilt associated with it may cause inhibitions in later life. If the child is made to feel that he is a criminal and a social outcast because of this experimentation, that feeling itself may impede his later effective sexual relations with his mate. A more important consideration for parents who find that their child masturbates is the question whether or not the practice is a retreat from life, a comfort-finding device used to compensate for life that has little joy and constant defeats. If masturbation is a compensatory outlet, the parent will do well to consider how the life of the family can be reconstructed so that the child no longer has a need for such physically soothing retreats.

The child sooner or later will hear from someone all of the myths concerning the damage done by masturbation. It is important for parents to reassure children about this point. If they cannot, the family doctor may well be asked to talk casually about it with the child.

PARENTS' SEXUAL ADJUSTMENT AND CHILDREN'S SEXUAL EXPECTATIONS

Specifically, too, the child has come to anticipate the meaning of marriage in the affectional relationships of mother and father. If they are cold and distant, if they rarely hug or kiss each other, if their marriage is polite, formal, and reserved, the meaning of this behavior is clear to the child. For although he may never hear them argue about their sexual life or other basic differences, he will be aware of the lack of tenderness and sense the barrenness of their marriage—and to some extent associate it with marriage in general. Marriage for him can hold no promise of deep and rewarding affectional patterns, for he has rarely felt the relationship to be one of tenderness. Some parents today are much concerned about being able to talk easily about sexual matters before their children. But this will never take the place of warm response patterns frequently exhibited. Travis and Baruch stress this factor:

> One thing we must take into consideration is that our children will not always hear nice things about sex. All the more must we counteract this. We must let them know that other people have varying ideas on this score, just as they have different ideas about sex—just as they have different ideas on countless other matters. Different religions, different prejudicial

slants, different opinions about politics, different ideas on sex—all these fit into the picture. Yet, even more important, we must give to our children a conviction that sex is essentially wholesome. This we will be able to do only as we work out our own conflicts about the part sex plays in our own lives. For proper sex education, then, the parent must see to his own sexual adjustment. After that, what he says, what he does, and how he feels will take care of themselves.[27]

EARLY HETEROSEXUAL EXPERIENCES

Heterosexual experiences come to children in the several guises in which they express their interest in learning more about the other sex and about sexual intercourse. The Ramsey study indicated that the early heterosexual activity of childhood involved most frequently manual exploration, direct observation of reproductive anatomy, exhibitionistic sex-play, attempts at intercourse, oral contacts, and other forms of experimentation. Table 8 taken from Ramsey's study indicates the number of boys involved and the percentage of these boys who had had some experience:

TABLE 8. Pre-Adolescent Heterosexual Play *

Age	Number of Boys Involved	Percentage with Some Experience	Increment at Each Age
5	286	2.4	2.4
6	286	16.8	14.4
7	286	24.8	8.0
8	286	34.8	10.0
9	286	41.2	6.4
10	286	46.9	5.7
11	280	52.5	5.6
12	235	58.3	5.8
13	122	66.1	7.8

* Glenn V. Ramsey, "The Sexual Development of Boys," *The American Journal of Psychology*, LVI, April, 1943, 226. Reprinted by permission.

By the age of 12, two-thirds of the boys had been involved in one form or another of sexual play with girls. One student reports this initiation into the "mysteries":

Sex as sex never actually entered my mind, but sort of accumulated. I never bothered to think about it. At one time (which I do not now re-

[27] Travis and Baruch, p. 302. Reprinted by permission of the publisher.

call) at the tender age of five or six my mother read a book especially prepared for children about the "birds and bees" which I forgot just as quickly. I specifically remember all the neighborhood boys and girls all assembled together and taking off their clothes. I was too young to know what it was all about although I felt it was "nasty" and it completely repulsed me; however, I never connected it with sex. At the age of ten my school teacher thought I needed to know so she explained everything to me with my full comprehension and I admit that the facts of life revolted me at first, but I do not feel this an unnatural reaction.

A counselor reports the following experience as fairly typical of the problems he must deal with in this field. A mother came to him because she had discovered her children in sexual play with two brothers from a nearby family. She reported what she had done. When she discovered the children, she sent the boys home, telephoned their mother, and took her own daughters into the house to talk with them. Her voice was full of tension and fear during this talk, which was for her, she said, the most important and the most difficult she had ever had. This troubled her. Because of her own upset emotions she found herself saying things she did not believe. She then forbade the girls ever to play with these boys again and kept her girls in the house for a week. The counselor knew that from this time on, unless the situation was corrected, those girls would never be able to confide in their mother regarding their sexual problems.

The boys had fared worse then the girls. Their father had given them a severe whipping and isolated them. Moreover, he felt so chagrined that he put his house up for sale and was planning to move out of the neighborhood. The counselor thought that unless these boys and girls received special help they would never completely overcome this traumatic introduction to their sexual selves. While no scarlet letter had been burned on their skins, an equal hurt had been inflicted on their psyches. Out of such experiences can come lasting repressions and inhibitions. Sex comes to be thought of as bad, sinful, something one does not discuss or think about.

Fortunate, indeed, is the child who grows up in the country. To him, sex is a natural and normal part of life. But for the urban dweller who never observes the processes of reproduction in nature and who is isolated from the births of his siblings, it may be difficult later to play an adequate role. This isolation makes it even more important for parents to instill an accepting attitude and wholesome knowledge of sex.

FAMILY RITUALS

As children grow older, certain ways of living and of responding in the family become rather permanently structured and take the form of what may be called rituals. Bossard and Boll have studied the integrative effects of the development of regular and expected modes of family life and have interpreted these in terms of preparation for marriage in *Ritual in Family Living*. Some of their conclusions are:

1. Many, perhaps most, family rituals develop with the coming of a child. Often they partake of the nature of a family drama, designed to impress the children. Many rituals center about the children; usually they participate in them.
2. Many family rituals cannot but make a vivid impression upon children. . . .
3. Many, if not all, of the family rituals recalled have pleasant associations. Often they center about holidays, birthdays, anniversaries, and other happy occasions. Because of the nature of family rituals—their recurrence, the sense of rightness which accompanies them, the pleasurable associations . . . they groove themselves deeply and pleasantly into the accumulating layers of the youthful mind, which constitutes the essence of the unconscious.
4. When the individual leaves home, a major part of the readjustment involves the change in ritualistic behavior. Marriage and the formation of a new family is such an occasion, obviously. Both mates bring with them to form the new family their respective experience. Similarity in such experience seems to be an important factor in making for marital success; lack of it appears to have the opposite effect.[28]

Rituals tend to promote family integration by producing "like-mindedness," by emphasizing "cooperation," by instilling a sense of "group participation," and by developing a sense of "rightness" that contributes to pride and interest in family life and achievement. For children ritual means an organization. Perhaps the most important of the rituals are those which center around the festival occasions of life—birthdays, vacations, and holidays. The tensions of ordinary living are relaxed as the family becomes a unified and organic group completely disposed toward making the occasion one of immense satisfaction. Much of life's meaning

[28] James H. S. Bossard and Eleanor S. Boll, *Ritual and Family Living* (Philadelphia: University of Pennsylvania Press, 1950), pp. 198–199. Reprinted by permission of the publisher.

comes out of these festival periods, and to secure the continuation of the meaningful experience is a strong motivation for marriage.

The interruption of family rituals by divorce has consequences for the child. Divorce results in the immediate cessation of many of the rituals —and of the structures of family living which have given security and meaning to the child's life. Of course, the problems associated with divorce go beyond this. The child may be attached to both parents: their separation throws him into conflict. In many cases there is a contest over the child's affection which makes him an unwilling pawn of adult bitterness. If the mother remarries, he may resent profoundly the coming of other children in a new marriage. He may feel that they "belong" more completely than he does. He will undoubtedly feel the differences between his status and that of children from unbroken homes. All of this may sometimes result in a tendency towards the rejection of marriage for himself, when—as a child—this is excessive, and sometimes in a general neurotic insecurity. Yet in some situations divorce is certainly preferable to keeping the child in a conflict situation all of his formative years.

Judson Landis' study of 295 university students, all children of divorced parents, indicates the degree of trauma associated with the breakup of their homes.[29]

He reports that there is a difference in reaction to divorce according to the degree of previous conflict in the home. If a child had considered his home a happy one, the emotional hurt was much greater than if he had regarded his home life as unhappy. Forty-four per cent of the students felt that they had been "used" by one or both parents. About a third of the students who had conceived their home life as happy were "astonished that parents were divorced," and 20 per cent "talked as though their parents were not divorced." Forty-five per cent of those who conceived of the home as having been happy reported no change in their feelings of security, but some 55 per cent reported that they were "less secure" or "much less secure." We know that in general these children from divorced parents are more divorce-prone than children from intact marriages. However, the greater awareness of the realistic problems of marriage may somewhat offset their insecurity. Landis found that 80 per cent felt the divorce had "made me more aware of the problems of marriage," and 75 per cent reported that "it has given me more determina-

[29] Judson Landis, "The Trauma of Children When Parents Divorce," *Marriage and Family Living,* XXII, No. 1 (February, 1960), 7–13. This is an excellent research report on many phases of post-divorce trauma.

tion to work at making a success of my marriage." Children from divorced homes do not need to repeat their parents' failures. But if such children are afraid of marriage or bitter about it, they sometimes need the help of a therapist to give them more realistic attitudes. We cannot change the past, but we can modify its power to continue to hurt us.

The difficulties entailed when the ritual in family living consists mostly of conflict are equally serious. Bossard thinks that "quarreling parents make quarreling children who grow up to be quarreling mates."[30] An excerpt from a case study indicates this:

> From early childhood I can remember the strained relation between my parents which frequently resulted in quarrels. When I heard my parents quarrel and almost come to blows I had a feeling that was close to terror —when I finished high school I was very insecure and had strong feelings of inferiority.[31]

Children from homes dominated by conflict sometimes are too eager for any kind of tenderness or too suspicious in dealing with others. Children from homes split by divorce or splintered by conflict may grow up as insecure persons and be timid in thinking about marriage. Others of different temperament master their feelings and indeed only achieve stronger motivations to build happier homes for themselves.

THE COMMUNITY AND ITS INFLUENCE ON THE CHILD

Today, influences outside the home likewise play a very important part in socializing the child and giving him attitudes which will be useful or demoralizing in a future marriage. As Waller points out:

> The role which the child plays within the family is not wholly a matter of family interaction. The entire family is involved in a number of processes of interaction in the community, in the social class, in the church, and in the economic system, and it is as true of the family as of any other group that its external relations determine its internal structure. The status which the child gains outside the family has its repercussions within it. The boy who distinguishes himself in athletics or in his studies is thought to reflect credit upon the entire family group, and his status in the family is correspondingly enhanced. The girl who disgraces the family may likewise find her family relations endangered. Similarly, the position of the family

[30] Bossard and Boll, pp. 254–255.
[31] Andrew G. Truxal and Francis E. Merrill, *Marriage and the Family* (New York: Prentice-Hall, Inc. 1953), p. 547. Reprinted by permission of the publisher.

117

in the community profoundly affects intrafamily relationships, and intra-family relationships affect the role of each member in the larger group.[32]

Today, the scout leader, the school teacher, the athletic director, the Sunday School teacher, and the probation worker exercise important influence on the child. As the family becomes more individualistic, the roles the child plays in groups outside the home become increasingly important in determining his attitudes. These again interact with his role as a child in the home.

Provided the child does not come from an emotionally impoverished home, all of these new experiences and roles add to his stability to adjust. The modern school with its "child-centered" approach, which aims to compensate for and ameliorate ego wounds suffered from the blows of early life, is important. The school's emphasis on communication and socialization contributes substantially to that type of maturity associated with wise marriage choice and optimum marriage adjustment.

CONCLUSION

The child assimilates, consciously or unconsciously, the attitudes, the values, and the roles of those about him—learning prejudices and stereo-types for or against affection and later marriage, maturing or growing fearful—all depending upon the stability and the values and the roles of the people who influence him most powerfully. Out of these many impacts grows a unique type of response, different from the response of anyone else in the world. This unique response pattern will also have its own special way of adjusting to situations, being confident or fearful, easy in interaction or inhibited in approaching interaction. He may accept sex as normal and wholesome or reject it as vulgar and indecent. But what-ever the experience gained through childhood, the individual has a his-tory by the time he comes to adolescence, a history that will affect this new and challenging period, and a history which will influence in every significant way his adjustment in marriage.

SELF-ANALYSIS: AUTOBIOGRAPHICAL STATEMENT

The analysis of the conditioning factors that operated during your childhood can be readily made by writing an autobiographical statement

---

[32] Willard Waller and Reuben Hill, *The Family: A Dynamic Interpretation*, rev. ed. (New York: Dryden Press, 1951), pp. 90–91. Copyright © 1951, Holt, Rinehart and Winston, Inc. Reprinted by permission of the publisher.

about your childhood experiences. Much of the material in this chapter will help the student recall significant areas of past experiences that were instrumental in forming current attitudes. As Travis suggested, once these are related to present behavior and present attitudes, they lose some of their power to control us. For convenience, the following outline is provided for self-analysis. This is a general outline, and each individual will think of additional important material.

In writing this statement, the student should remember that preciseness of phrase is not as important as freedom in the expression of feelings. If the student finds himself carried away by some memory, it is better to continue writing about this experience than to hold strictly to the outline.

   I. Family Background
- A. Describe your family configuration, your father, mother, or step-father or step-mother, your brothers and sisters, uncles, aunts, or grandparents who lived with you, and analyze their relationship to each other. Which siblings were older, which were younger than yourself? Give special attention to their emotional characteristics and attitudes, and to the "emotional climate" each created in the house.
- B. Indicate the relationship of each parent to each child, noting particularly any evidences of favoritism, hostility, dominance, rejection, and their effects. How warm were your parents?
- C. Analyze your relations with each of your parents during early and middle childhood, with your brothers and sisters; with uncles, aunts, grandparents, or others. If you were an only child or step-child, did deprivations result, and what close friendships or adjustments were made?
- D. What crisis did the family encounter during your early or middle childhood that influenced you? Give particular attention to deaths, divorces, economic failures, long illnesses, or separations.
- E. Analyze the degree of sociability that prevailed in your home with special reference to feelings of isolation or loneliness.
- F. What ritualistic behavior did your family have?
- G. How important were the festival occasions in your family?
- H. Analyze in what ways economic, social, or religious status influenced the behavior of the family.

   II. Developmental Aspects of Childhood
- A. How did your parents discipline you? Do you remember your reactions to that discipline? Were you more or less aggressive as a

result? Were you closer or farther from your parents as a result?

B. How dependent were you as a child? Was this an annoyance to your parents? How did they handle it?

C. Would you say that your parents were perfectionists in what they expected from you? What was the level of behavior and accomplishment that was expected? Were you often frustrated because you felt goals for you were too high?

D. What kind of a child were you temperamentally, emotionally, socially? Do you recall deep discouragement and/or real satisfaction during these years?

E. Did you have any specific problems such as enuresis, nightmares, fears during these years? Do they still bother you?

F. What are your happiest memories from childhood? Can you recall some of the periods of real elation and satisfaction?

G. Do you sense now that your parents and other contacts were giving you a strong and dependable sense of values during these childhood years? Did you develop a strong conscience?

H. How would you judge your strength as a person (your ego-strength) by mid-childhood? Did you begin adolescence with a fairly strong sense of security or not?

III. Social and Neighborhood Influences

A. How long did your family live in each house, each neighborhood, each city?

B. Did your parents own their home or rent?

C. Analyze the various neighborhoods in which you grew up, in terms of your relationship with other children and adults.

D. Which teachers, children, and activities exerted the greatest influence on your personality development and why? When?

E. Analyze your adjustment in the first six grades in school. Were you generally happy and secure while in school?

F. Describe the various play groups and gangs in which you participated as a child. What role did you play in them?

IV. Psychosexual Development

A. At what ages, on what occasions, and from what sources did you acquire information regarding sex during childhood?

B. How accurate was this information, and what was your reaction to it?

C. In what way did your relationship with your parents contribute to or retard wholesome development?

D. In what way did other children contribute to your sexual development or confuse you?

   E. What specific experiences did you have that gave you a sense of guilt, inhibition, or satisfaction with being a boy or a girl?
   F. In what way did your early religious education contribute to or detract from a wholesome development?
 V. Socio-Cultural Influences
   A. What clubs and groups did you belong to as a child? What positions of leadership did you hold in them? Were you happy in these groups?
   B. How many churches have you attended? What denominations? How often did you attend as a child? Were you happy in participating?
   C. What physical or social influences handicapped your early social adjustment?
   D. What social class did you belong to in the community?
VI. In what ways did these childhood experiences and contributing factors influence those attitudes that will be important in determining the degree of adjustment to your marriage?

AUTOBIOGRAPHICAL ANALYSIS

Once the autobiographical statement has been completed, it is important to analyze its meaning for marriage adjustment. Therefore, the last segment of the statement asks that this analysis be made. It is important in considering this to remember what sections of the statement were difficult, what areas of childhood memories were hard to recover or were recovered with some pain. For these are the areas in which we have had negative experiences and uncomfortable associations. If there are areas which we cannot remember at all, such a void may indicate either very traumatic experiences or no experience. In any case, we should give particular attention to such areas. The feelings that developed while writing this analysis are also important. There will be particular value in this effort if the material presented is talked over with the instructor of the course or a counselor, with particular emphasis upon those areas which produced marked emotional reactions. Once insight into present feelings and attitudes has been achieved, perhaps as the result of this study, a more mature attitude may result.

VISUAL AIDS

Films may be used to illustrate clearly some of the points raised in this chapter. The following films are suggested:

Feeling of Hostility, 1948, National Film Board of Canada, 1270 Avenue of the Americas, New York 20, New York.

Feeling of Rejection, 1948, National Film Board of Canada, 1270 Avenue of the Americas, New York 20, New York.

Overdependency, 1949, National Film Board of Canada, 1270 Avenue of the Americas, New York 20, New York.

The Family Next Door, Department of Administration and Leadership, National Council of Churches, 475 Riverside Drive, New York 27, New York.

READINGS

BOSSARD, JAMES H. S. *The Sociology of Child Development.* New York, Harper and Brothers, 1960, Parts I and II. Copyright Harper and Row, Publishers.

LOCKE, HARVEY J. *Predicting Adjustment in Marriage: A Comparison of a Divorced and a Happily Married Group.* New York, Henry Holt and Company, 1951, pp. 86–123. Copyright Holt, Rinehart and Winston, Inc.

PETERSON, JAMES A. *Toward a Successful Marriage.* New York, Charles Scribner's Sons, 1960, Chapters VIII and IX.

SEARS, ROBERT R., ELEANOR E. MACCOBY, HARRY LEVIN, *et al. Patterns of Child Rearing.* White Plains, New York, Row, Peterson and Company, 1957. Copyright Harper and Row, Publishers.

TRAVIS, LEE and DOROTHY BARUCH. *Personal Problems of Everyday Life.* New York, Appleton-Century-Crofts, 1941, Chapter VII.

WINCH, ROBERT F. *The Modern Family.* New York, Henry Holt and Company, 1952, Chapter IX. Copyright Holt, Rinehart and Winston, Inc.

CHAPTER 6

Factors in
Adolescence

INTRODUCTION

CHILDHOOD ends with the relatively tranquil years of eight through twelve. This last period of childhood is so harmonious that it is often described in literature as the golden period. It is a time of happy group activities in which earlier socialization problems have been largely solved, and the spurt of sexual interest manifested earlier has quieted and become latent. Parents find it difficult to give up the rich and rewarding fellowship of these years. But this period must end. Nature itself decrees it. The happy relationships of later childhood will disappear in the storm and stress of those turbulent experiences which mark the years from twelve to twenty.

In America, the adolescent lives in a tumultuous ambivalence. He feels new inner sexual tensions which discharge themselves in emotional outbursts or are dispelled through channels of high religious or moral idealism. The adolescent struggles with his new sensations from within even as he tries to adjust to new and vacillating expectations from without. For now he is expected to conform to adult behavior patterns for which he has no background of experience. While his biological development demands growing independence of action, he often encounters the resistance of his parents who resent his repudiation of the patterns of control which marked his childhood relations with them. The outcome of these years of struggle to achieve adulthood is decisive for marriage.

THE MEANING OF ADOLESCENCE

Adolescence is regarded chronologically as the years between twelve and twenty-one; physiologically as the time between the onset of puberty and the achievement of maximum physical growth; psychologically as the period of transition from childhood dependence to adult independence; socially as the period from the beginning of the loosening of home ties to the establishment of a new family unit.

The onset of puberty presupposes certain marked physiological developments which differentiate the adolescent from the child. Height increases most rapidly in boys from 12½ to 14½; in girls from 10½ to 14. Weight increases most rapidly in girls from 11½ to 14½ and in boys from 13 to 16. Furthermore, this weight is distributed on a changing bony structure. The boy's chest enlarges, his shoulders broaden; his hips become narrower, while his legs and arms grow longer and terminate in what seem to him, at the time, enormous hands and feet. The girl grows in a somewhat different way. Her hips become wider; and there is an increase in chest, shoulder, hand and foot size, but less marked than in the boy. Her weight is also distributed differently. The boy grows harder, more muscular, and straight, while the girl becomes soft and round in contour because of a layer of fat that is deposited under her skin. For this reason the boy comes to have a greater immediate strength while the girl develops greater reserves and has longer endurance.

The physical changes in both sexes are related to glandular developments. During childhood, the endocrine system, except for the thymus and pineal glands, is relatively inactive. Early in adolescence, the pituitary, thyroid, ovaries, testes, and suprarenals show a sharp upturn of activity. These glandular and physiological changes are related to sexual development. Boys and girls who develop faster in bone structure, height, weight, and endocrines also mature more quickly sexually. This onset of maturity is marked by menstruation for girls and sexual emissions for boys. Ramsey gives the indices of sexual growth by age groups: puberty and its physical changes appeared generally at ages 12, 13, and 14, but many boys did not mature sexually until age 15 and a few not until 16.[1]

In this study of 291 boys, Ramsey shows that the secondary physical changes such as voice-change and growth of pubic hair parallel the

[1] Glenn V. Ramsey, "The Sexual Development of Boys," *The American Journal of Psychology*, LVI (April, 1943), 217.

124

maturation of the sex glands. With sexual maturity inevitably come sexual sensations. To adjust to the inner promptings of these sexual pressures while at the same time adjusting to equally insistent social pressures, constitutes one of the main problems of adolescence.

DEVELOPMENTAL TASKS OF ADOLESCENCE

As the majority of individuals make their marital choices at the conclusion of adolescence, it is essential that those years see the development of personality competence. But what factors are the main components of competence? Foote and Cottrell think six factors account for success in interpersonal relationships: (1) health, (2) intelligence, (3) empathy, (4) autonomy, (5) judgment, and (6) creativity.[2] Duvall lists the following as essential achievements for teen-agers looking forward to adult life:

(1) Accepting one's changing body and learning to use it effectively.
(2) Achieving a satisfying and socially accepted masculine or feminine role.
(3) Finding oneself as a member of one's own generation in more mature relations with one's age mates.
(4) Achieving emotional independence of parents and other adults.
(5) Selecting and preparing for an occupation and economic independence.
(6) Preparing for marriage and family life.
(7) Developing intellectual skills and social sensitivities necessary for civic competence.
(8) Developing a workable philosophy of life that makes sense in today's world.[3]

Jersild devotes almost a third of his book on *The Psychology of Adolescence* to the analysis of problems involved in achieving emotional maturity during these years.[4] All of these factors are essential in the final preparation of any boy or girl for marriage, but some of them seem more critical than others. In this chapter we shall discuss the achievement of *independence, sexual identification, heterosexuality, emotional maturity, and a sys-*

[2] Nelson N. Foote and Leonard S. Cottrell, *Identity and Interpersonal Competence* (Chicago: The University of Chicago Press, 1955).
[3] Evelyn Duvall, *Family Development* (Philadelphia: J. B. Lippincott Company, 1957), pp. 294–297. Reprinted by permission of the publisher.
[4] Arthur Jersild, *The Psychology of Adolescence* (New York: The Macmillan Company, 1957), Chapters VII–X.

tem of values. These include all of Duvall's points except those relating to occupation and economic independence, and it is our contention that if an individual achieves independence and emotional maturity these will follow.

Foote and Cottrell use the word *autonomy* in a somewhat more inclusive sense than we are using the word independence, for they define that word as including a sense of self and a "stable set of internal standards." These are certainly important, but we choose to discuss them under a different heading because we feel that independence is a somewhat sharper psychological concept than "autonomy."

ACHIEVING INDEPENDENCE

Achieving independence would not be so difficult if all parents were sensitive to the developmental needs of their children.

Many parents, however, cannot and do not draw aside, happy that their child has grown beyond the need of their constant help. They have learned so well the role of being superior guides and have found such satisfaction in it that they continue to demand obedience all through adolescence; moreover, their own lives have been, up to this point, centered on their children, and allowing freedom to the children means to parents the loss of the most rewarding function they have ever had. Young people need to understand the emotional investment parents make in them; if they do, they will be more tolerant of what they sometimes regard as mere interference. Children, too, must remember that their parents grew up in a different cultural era; hence, their recollections of their own adolescence do not always give them an adequate base for understanding the new generation. Yet, studies indicate that many parents do well in trusting their young people. In a major study of 5,500 high school seniors in the state of Washington, Elias asked them to check each of nine areas of serious disagreement with parents. The percentages are surprisingly low—in only one area did more than 30 per cent disagree with their parents.

Elias also asked about the degree of respect which parents showed for their children's opinions and judgments, which is indirectly a measurement of recognition of the adolescent's need to gain independence. The high-school seniors answered this question as shown in Table 9 (p. 127).

These figures would indicate that many families are considerate of the opinions of young people. Still, for a sizable percentage of young people,

TABLE 9. Responses of 5,500 High-School Seniors Who Checked the Statement: "My parents respect my opinions and judgment." *

RESPONSE	Boys Per Cent	Girls Per Cent
All of the time	10.0	13.4
Most of the time	52.3	53.7
About half the time	27.5	23.8
Seldom respect their opinion	7.0	6.8
Never do	1.4	1.1

L. J. Elias, "High School Youth Look at Their Problems," State College of Washington, January, 1949.

there are problems involved in achieving independence. The following case study indicates some of the dynamics of this problem:

Mary is a girl of 21, a senior in college, of singular mental and artistic abilities. She can sing, dance, paint, play the piano, or write a script for a radio play. She has held many major positions on campus. Her classmates know her as one of the campus "wheels." What her classmates do not know is that this very chic girl does not select her style of hairdo, nor has she ever picked out a coat or a dress for herself. Her mother does this. When she makes major decisions regarding any organizational matters, it is only after a long distance telephone conversation with her mother. She has majored in telecommunications, but her mother made the choice because the mother owns a great deal of stock in a radio station in her city where she wants Mary to work.

Mary is often depressed. In such a mood she does not turn to her roommate or her house mother; she calls home and receives comfort. Mary's career, her looks, her religion, and her plans have all been determined by her mother.

Mary is engaged to a young man with a promising future. He has begun to resent Mary's dependency although he is not fully aware of the reasons for his increasing irritability. He does not know yet that Mary's mother has decreed that they must put off marriage until Mary has worked for two years after graduating. He does not know that when Mary objected to this, her mother immediately became ill and made Mary feel very guilty. He does not know that Mary was told over and over when she was a little girl that not to obey Mother, or to think ill of Mother was a very deep sin. He does not know that when Mary's mother decides they may marry she will also decide, as she has already intimated, that Mary and her husband must move to her community and live close to her.

127

Mary is becoming aware of what her mother is doing to her. While she feels guilty about it, she has begun to save part of her allowance and has purchased her first dress of her own choosing. And, although it depresses her to do so, she has been giving steady attention to the question whether it would be wise to live near home after marriage. Mary says, "I was always taught never to doubt Mother's wisdom. If I ever did when I was younger such a hurt and angry look came over Mother that I retreated, and I've retreated ever since."

Mary thinks she understands her fiancé's irritation. She says that when vacation comes she is going to fly home and talk to her mother about waiting two years to get married. She also says that this will be the hardest task she has ever undertaken and probably the most necessary. Mary has been trying to crowd five years of gradual growth towards independence into five months, and it has not been easy. Mary now understands the need to work through her emotional feelings whenever she must make a decision or oppose her mother. She still has the feelings, but she is on the road to being a person in her own right.[5]

Mary will become a person. She has had help. But there are a great many other adolescents who do not get help. To them, it seems right and proper to obey without question the dictates of their parents. These young people often lose opportunities for marriage because their prospective mates do not meet their parents' special expectations. These expectations often include a lifetime supervision of the married children and then of their grandchildren. One psychiatrist who specializes in marriage-counseling estimates that 75 per cent of his cases of marital maladjustments are the result of unbroken dependency patterns. While this psychiatrist's practice represents only a small segment of the population, it is probably true that many marital problems stem from such problems as Mary exhibits.

On the other hand, it is true that parents are often right about the lack of wisdom in their children's marriage plans. Young people are all too often so romantic that they fail to see obstacles to their future happiness. The parents who see these obstacles become alarmed, and often drive their sons and daughters further into mismatches by their criticism. These parents lost their opportunity years ago when they failed to shift gradually from dictators to advisors, from guides to companions. Now, when they attempt to give advice, the channel of communication is clogged with past bitterness and misunderstanding. Had the children been allowed

[5] From a case study in the author's files.

to make many minor decisions throughout childhood and early adolescence, they would have matured, and through learning from minor mistakes become prepared to make intelligent major decisions. Furthermore, the parents would have gained their children's confidence because they did not stifle them with anxious care. Young people who are allowed to grow and mature are really closer to their parents than those who are psychologically bound to them; those parents who cling too tightly to their children eventually destroy any possibility of love between them.[6]

Dependence operates in subtle ways. A young woman falls in love and tells her family that she wishes to announce her engagement. Immediately, the mother or father becomes agitated. Not wishing to face their need for the daughter's continued emotional servitude to them, the parent invents any number of rationalizations. "She must finish school." "She must work long enough to have some experience." "He is not frugal or saving, you will never have anything." "He is too frugal, you will never have any fun." "He is not intelligent enough." "His family background is poor." "His mother is a snob." "He may be called into service." All of these objections are repeated every day in one form or another. If reasoning does not work, emotional parents may feign illness or other special needs, thus inducing guilt feelings in young people. Translated into the truth, all of these phrases and actions say only one thing: "I can't bear to let you go."

Nor can we overlook the consequences of dependence in the marital relationship. The dependent adolescent is unconsciously looking for someone to lean on. He does not search for a companion, but for a foster mother. His life pattern is one in which a mother has always cared for him and made his decisions. He is not prepared to live in a companionship setting with vigorous give and take. He has nothing to give, and he has been protected from taking anything. For this reason, he needs and unconsciously searches for someone who will play the role of maternal protector all through life.

THE OVER-INDEPENDENT PROTEST

On the other hand there is a danger that a reaction to the struggle for independence will swing too far; Cole speaks of the problems of the type of individual who overcompensates because of parental dominance:

[6] Ernest R. Groves, *The Family and Its Social Functions* (Philadelphia: J. B. Lippincott Company, 1940), p. 429.

This type of unemancipated adolescent is seen in the boy who gets drunk, uses profanity, or has illicit sex relations as a means of demonstrating his independency to the world. When an over-attached adolescent sets out to break the bonds between himself or herself and the family by unwise and violent methods, it is generally because all ordinary methods have failed. A boy or girl rarely succeeds in growing up by such violent means; all he does is to build up a habit of childish resentment. The adolescent who is free to buy his own clothes (provided he keeps within his budget), free to bring anyone he will to his own house, free—within reasonable degrees of guidance—to choose his own work, and free to plan his own time, has adequate opportunity for self-assertion without going to such extremes. The boy who gets into serious difficulties in order to prove he is grown up is no more independent of his home than the boy who cannot make up his mind which book to read until he has asked his mother for her advice. One is positively conditioned, the other negatively; neither is mature and neither can regard his home objectively.[7]

Such a person generally makes a poor adjustment in marriage. In trying to get out of too tight a social contract at home, he has developed an attitude of contempt for all social obligations and responsibilities. Much of his behavior shows his lack of concern for the feelings or needs of others.

THE POSITIVE APPROACH TO PARENTS

In contrast to the over-dependent and the over-independent, there are the boys and girls who work with their parents well. The adolescent has the power to help create good relations. Where there is only a minor degree of dominance or conflict, he can often change the situation into a humorous one. Again, if the adolescent attempts to understand his parents' point of view, he can often by his own reasonableness effect a compromise and educate his parents to a better way. Adolescents should realize, too, that often verbal criticisms by their parents are only symbolic expressions of deep concern for their welfare. On many matters it is better for the boy or girl to accept advice graciously from his parents than to engage continuously in a bitter battle of wills. Finally, if efforts to work out the situation bring no results, the adolescent can suggest to his parent that the two of them talk with a counselor. Young people often take the

[7] Luella Cole, *Psychology of Adolescence*, 4th ed. (New York: Rinehart and Company, Inc., 1954), p. 340. 5th ed. © 1959, Holt, Rinehart and Winston, Inc. Reprinted by permission of the publisher.

initiative in improving family relations. They often forget that their child-hood assumption of the omnipotence of their parents is at least somewhat in error, and that some parents have profound problems of their own, some of them stemming back to the parents' own youth. Jersild points this out very sharply:

> Many of the adults who deal with adolescence are, to a degree, "adoles-cents" themselves. An adolescent's parents are themselves adolescent if they have conflicts and unresolved problems stemming back to their own adolescent years, such as problems pertaining to sex, work, responsibility for self and others, attitudes toward authority and the like. They are still struggling, in a sense, with their own adolescence if they are very depend-ent on the opinions of others, distrust their own judgment, feel a need to cling, like children, to others for support in what they think or decide to do. Such parents are likely to feel threatened when an adolescent brings up problems that are so much like their own.[8]

If young people take time to try a little to understand some of the prob-lems of their parents, they may find real reward for so doing.

ACHIEVING SEX IDENTIFICATION

It is imperative that during the period of physiological change into womanhood and manhood, corresponding changes in social roles take place. Menstruation indicates with finality that a girl is now a potential mother; an ejaculation indicates potential fatherhood for the boy. To achieve acceptance of our sexual selves is as important as gaining poise in our relations with the opposite sex. To some extent, these processes are interrelated, for those adolescents who are blocked socially in hetero-sexual development find it hard to accept their sexual capacities. Many case studies of adolescents with deviant sexual behavior indicate that when social adjustment with the opposite sex had not been achieved, such behavior was used as a substitute.

Menstruation. Menstruation often comes as a shock to those girls who have not had a normal expectation of puberty. The following case illus-trates something of the trauma introduced into a girl's life because her mother, her church, her school, and her community had failed to intro-duce her to facts she could not overlook or escape:

> Helen was the only daughter of Mrs. B. Mrs. B. had been divorced when
> Helen was 8 because of her own sexual inhibitions which had made her

[8] Jersild, pp. 259, 260. Reprinted by permission of the publisher.

marriage a period of physical frustration for her husband and a time of neurotic illness for herself. As a result she had been unable to share any kind of sexual information with her daughter. Due to a sense of failure, she embarked on a program of entrusting Helen to anyone else she could. Helen was kept in boarding schools during the school year and sent to a wealthy aunt's beach home during the summer. The summer when Helen was 12 she began to menstruate. She immediately thought she would die and confided in a girl friend who was slightly older. The girl friend told her about menstruation and took her to a drug store, but Helen was alarmed. She called her mother and asked her to come and get her. Mrs. B, not knowing the cause of her illness, immediately drove to the beach.

The aunt inquired of Mrs. B, after she had talked to Helen, what the trouble was. Mrs. B could not discuss it and assured the aunt that Helen had an intestinal upset and would be all right. The aunt, never hesitant to spend money if the cause was adequate, insisted on taking Helen to the doctor. Mrs. B was now put in a ridiculous situation but she eluded it by saying that perhaps Helen would be better off if she saw her own doctor who was familiar with her background. This peculiar conversation contrasted so sharply in Helen's mind with what her girl friend had told her that she now became even more anxious and was very happy about going home to see her physician.

But when they arrived home her mother showed no concern and told her that the trouble would be over shortly. It was, but both Mrs. B and the girl friend had forgotten to tell Helen that the trouble was to be a regular or an irregular regular one. So when Helen returned to the beach the same situation reoccurred with Helen now obsessed with fear concerning cancer. This time no reassurance would do, and a doctor had to be consulted. While this introduction to womanhood was only part of the conditioning process, it definitely contributed to a frigid sexual reaction on the part of Helen.[9]

Menstruation is a natural evidence of creativity. It is the process which monthly clears the uterus of stored material so that a fresh supply of food and nourishment may be gathered, in case a new life process is begun. As such, it is part of the cycle nature has developed in sharing with men and women the nurturing of another generation of human beings. It is true that in the past the days of the menstrual flow were regarded as "sick" days, but this is looked upon today as a psychosomatic reaction. Excessive pain or cramps are almost always due to attitudes and posture, not to any physiological condition. There is a special exercise called the "Billig

[9] From a case study in the author's files.

132

stretch," which can be described by any doctor, that has proved to be very helpful in relieving distress in this period. The modern girl has no need for either seclusion or special care during her menstrual period. She may swim, dance, and play, provided she does nothing to excess. Menstruation is a burden only if girls make it so. It should be regarded as an intrinsic part of the whole process of motherhood. Adolescents who have learned to regard it in this way rarely have any physical problems, or any psychological difficulties in accepting it.

Seminal Emissions. Seminal emissions are nature's way of relieving the excess of stored sperm. They may cause fear reactions on the part of maturing boys. While a few boys may regard nocturnal emissions as a welcome sign of maturity and future fatherhood, very often no thoughtful father or teacher helps them come to this conclusion. Instead, the natural questions motivated by "wet dreams" are answered by uninformed peers whose inadequate explanations may lead to guilt feeling or fear. Seminal emissions are as normal as menstruation and cause no physical damage.

Masturbation. As mentioned already in Chapter Five, most normal young people experiment with various sexual outlets before and during adolescence. The most common way of dealing with early sexual tension is through masturbation. Ramsey confirms the belief that masturbation among boys is practically universal. In the study mentioned previously he discovered both the onset and the incidence of masturbation. Over 98 per cent had masturbatory experience by the age of 15. All that was said in the last chapter about the harmlessness of this practice in childhood applies, too, during adolescence. However, masturbation comes to be more highly charged with emotion during these years because now both the girl and the boy are capable of an orgasm, which means for the boy an ejaculation and for the girl a series of pleasurable contractions of the muscles of the vagina. Ramsey makes the following significant comment after reviewing his material on masturbation:

> Before or soon after the onset of adolescence over 90 per cent of the boys reported masturbatory experience, which in the majority of cases ranged in frequency from one to four times a week. As socio-sexual forms of outlet were developed, the frequency of masturbation usually declined. Worry over alleged deleterious effects of masturbation was the most common sexual problem presented by these boys. The popular literature of sex-education and lecturers was primarily responsible for the widespread misinformation on this subject.[10]

[10] Ramsey, p. 232. Reprinted by permission.

TABLE 10. Source of Most Sex Information of 5,500
High-School Seniors *

SOURCE OF INFORMATION	Boys Per Cent	Girls Per Cent
Parents and adults at home	38.2	64.6
Church, Sunday school, minister	3.2	2.5
Older kids, magazines, movies	52.3	26.7
Class and supervised discussion	10.5	20.8
An adult counselor	8.7	6.4

* L. J. Elias. Reprinted by permission.

Erotic Feelings. Certain sensations, erotic in nature, bother the adolescent. The erection of the penis is often a source of shame to an adolescent boy as are feelings of erotic satisfaction that come from physical contact with a girl. Dancing sometimes proves a problem to very healthy young people who find themselves erotically stimulated by body contact. Yet these reactions are normal signs of developing womanhood and manhood. Common questions such as those that deal with menstruation, seminal emissions, masturbation, and sexual sensations might not cause anxiety if they were anticipated by parents or answered during early adolescence, but, unfortunately, these questions often are not answered. Elias found that for boys the source of information was most frequently their friends, but for girls the primary source was their parents.

Parents may try to discuss menstruation and reproduction, but Ramsey tells us that there are some things which seem tabu for discussion, such as masturbation, nocturnal emissions, contraception and prostitution.[11] Indeed, it is harder for young people to discuss masturbation than sexual intercourse. As Terman has indicated that frank and full discussion of sexual matters is correlated with good marital adjustment, this seems a serious problem. Ehrmann makes an important contribution in his study, showing that boys are more interested in specific and detailed information regarding female sexuality and sex techniques while girls focus their attention more generally on pregnancy.[12] Ehrmann indicates the importance of the parental contribution to sexual information when he points out that the males and females of his sample volunteered more comments about this background in their lives than about any other interest.[13] They

[11] Ramsey, p. 349.
[12] Winston Ehrmann, *Premarital Dating Behavior* (New York: Henry Holt and Company, 1959), p. 101. Copyright © 1959, Holt, Rinehart and Winston, Inc.
[13] Ehrmann, p. 102.

were particularly concerned about the attitudes of the parents, for they "did not seem to mind so much the omission of sex instruction, but they did seem to resent deeply the attempt by parents to depict sex as something horrible and sinful." [14] The meaning of Terman's and Ehrmann's findings is that students, during this first period of adulthood, must develop a normality to form a basis for good adjustment during adulthood.

ACHIEVING HETEROSEXUAL POISE DURING ADOLESCENCE

Independence and sexual adjustment have so far been discussed as important goals of adolescence. The third major area of growth for this age group that is specifically related to marriage is the achievement of poise and ease in associating with members of the other sex. During early childhood we fix our affectional patterns around our parents as love objects. In later childhood, we are members of a one-sex gang and we often focus our affectional life upon a "pal." Crushes and identifications with the same sex are normal in early adolescence or late childhood, but such fixations during later adolescence are very unhealthy. Individuals who fail in their attempts to relate to the other sex sometimes become homosexuals.

The period of middle and late adolescence is characterized by many affectional trials, by infatuations and quick love affairs. These are the trial runs of courtship. They serve a profound purpose in maturing our ability to get along with the other sex. And success in developing apt and secure relational abilities in this period has a strong bearing on success in marriage.[15]

How important it is to achieve poise and ease—and an ethical attitude in meeting and sharing with the other sex—is further indicated by the material in Table 11 which indicates the ranking of problems of 5,500 high school seniors (p. 136).

These seniors were very much concerned with the attributes of a good marriage as well as with their interaction with each other. The largest percentage of boys (13.9) and the largest percentage of girls (32.6) indicated that what constitutes a good marriage was their most important problem. "Going steady," "Can't date the right person," and "Not enough dates" ranked about even in importance for both. Roughly, 12 per cent of both the girls and the boys indicated that dating was a major concern.

[14] Ehrmann, pp. 102. 103.
[15] Robert O. Blood, Jr., *Anticipating Your Marriage* (New York: The Free Press of Glencoe, 1962), pp. 28–32. Copyright The Macmillan Company.

Ethical concerns such as "Proper sex relations," "Petting," "Right attitudes about sex" were not as important as problems but they did trouble many.

TABLE 11. Per Cent of 5,500 High-School Seniors Who Checked Certain Problems in Boy-Girl Relationships *

PROBLEM IN BOY-GIRL RELATIONSHIP	Boys	Girls
What makes a good marriage	13.9	32.6
Making a sucessful marriage	9.1	25.5
Going steady	12.9	13.3
Can't date the right person	12.7	12.5
Not enough dates	11.5	11.6
Break with girl, boy friend	9.0	13.4
How much intimacy to permit	6.9	14.7
Getting along with other sex	12.2	9.5
Not having (girl/boy) friend	9.0	8.4
Understanding about love	4.4	10.5
Should I get engaged	3.1	11.5
Not attractive to other sex	7.8	7.5
Right attitude about sex	7.9	7.3
Insufficient sex knowledge	7.6	6.9
"Going too far"	8.5	5.9
Sex problems	7.6	6.5
Uncomfortable with other sex	8.9	5.2
Wonder if anybody will want me	5.1	7.6
Learning about sex	6.4	6.4
(Girls/boys) on mind too much	7.5	5.2
Concerned about sex disease	6.4	4.1
"Necking, smooching"	4.8	5.4
Proper sex relations	5.5	4.3
"Petting"	3.5	3.9
Thinking too much about sex	5.9	1.6
Embarrassed about sex	2.8	3.6
(Boy/girl) friend stepping out	3.8	2.2
Too many dates	3.1	2.5
Self-abuse, masturbation	4.8	0.8
Not able to get married soon	3.3	1.2
Quitting school to get married	0.3	0.7

* L. J. Elias. Reprinted by permission.

While many of the topics in Table 11 receive specific consideration in the next chapter on dating, Elias' findings indicate how important many of these points of stress are to adolescents. It is interesting to compare this list of problems with those of the next age group, students in junior college. A list is prepared from a summary by junior-college teachers of Southern California, as shown in Table 12.

TABLE 12. Fifteen Dating Problems of Junior College Students of Southern California by Rank Order and by Per Cent for Men and for Women *

Rank Order	MEN'S PROBLEMS	Per Cent	WOMEN'S PROBLEMS	Per Cent
1.	Finances	34	Petting	36
2.	What to do (where to go)	29	What to do (where to go)	26
3.	Finding suitable girl	17	Conversation	12
4.	Conversation	15	Finances	12
5.	Petting	11	Getting the "wanted" man	8
6.	Asking for date (opportunity for)	10	Drinking	6
7.	Shyness	7	Time to come home	6
8.	Lack of time	6	Behavior—lack courtesy	6
9.	Getting too serious	6	Parent problems	5
10.	Transportation (distance too far; no car)	4	Getting too serious	5
11.	How late to stay	4	How to refuse or discourage	5
12.	Getting along with parent	4	Lack of opportunity	4
13.	Etiquette on date	3	No problems	4
14.	Girls spoiled (not punctual)	3	Shyness, or lack social skill	3
15.	Arguing, criticizing	2	Last minute dates	3

* Material arranged from data supplied by Junior College Teachers of Southern California. Material gathered in a joint research project in marriage-education classes.

It is obvious from this table that problems of conversation, of shyness, of what to do and where to go have not been finally settled even by late adolescence. The adolescent is concerned with these problems of developing into a person others will like. Consequently his speech, dress, manners, attitudes, and even morals are bent toward this goal. Some adolescents think that to be accepted is more important than to use good grammar, to wear clean clothes, or be dignified in bearing. These later will be the goal of young adulthood, but in the phase of seeking status they are sacrificed to the great god of conformity. Conformity means acceptance. Hence the precocious or withdrawn boy or girl who develops hobbies or pays too much attention to studies does so at the cost of ostracism. On the other hand, the most popular students are the friendly, enthusiastic, happy individuals who make others feel secure in their presence.

Whether these heterosexual contacts are initiated early or late, the ability to make them is crucial as training for marriage. To accept a member of the other sex as a stimulating companion, to be able to communicate without hesitation, to feel free and easy in his company are preliminary steps to the later achievement of the permanent companionship of marriage, of the ability to differ, to discuss, to plan, and to love without hesitations. Locke has studied the importance to marital adjustment of the solution to this problem of heterosexual poise. He measured the relationship of the number of friends before marriage to marital adjustment:

> A sociable woman, as measured by the number of both women and men friends, is a good marital risk. About 1 in 4 divorced women as compared to 1 in 7 married women reported "almost no" and "a few" women friends (per cents: 26.0 and 15.5, CR 2.1). This, of course, means that more happily married than divorced reported "several" and "many" women friends. Likewise "almost no" men friends were reported more frequently by divorced than by married women (per cents: 19.6 and 7.9, CR 2.8), with happily married more frequently reporting "several" men friends before marriage.[16]

Adolescents in an urban setting and, generally, members of small families find the development of sociability or heterosexual relations difficult. Nevertheless, to face the problem successfully is an important step toward later happy marriage.

ACHIEVING EMOTIONAL MATURITY

All of the studies of adolescence without exception indicate that one of the basic developmental tasks of this period is the achievement of a certain stability of the emotions. Jersild, who has studied this aspect of adolescence with perhaps more thoroughness than anyone else, speaks of the following areas of growth:

1. *The need to give and receive affection* . . . "No human being, during adolescence or later years, has so many resources within himself that he can live happily and healthily in emotional isolation from others." [17]
2. *Learning how to handle anger and hostility* . . . "The adolescent who is self-accepting is one who can face himself without guilt as a human being who becomes angry, who has a great capacity for anger, and who is likely to become angry in the future." [18]

[16] Harvey J. Locke, *Predicting Adjustment in Marriage: A Comparison of a Divorced and a Happily Married Group* (New York: Henry Holt and Company, 1951), p. 230. Copyright © 1951, Holt, Rinehart and Winston, Inc. Reprinted by permission of the publishers.
[17] Jersild, p. 141.　　[18] Jersild, p. 165.

3. *The ability to recognize and manage anxiety.*

Anxiety has been defined as "a kind of uneasines of mind or a kind of apprehension, irritability, foreboding, or distress arising out of disturbances within a person's inner life." [19] It is a distraught emotional condition arising when the "thoughts, feelings, and impulses that are out of harmony with what a person expects of himself are out of keeping with the kind of a person he would like to be in his own eyes or in the eyes of others." [20]

Anxiety has been called the hallmark of modern civilization. Anxiety is an emotional strait jacket that prevents expression of emotions, moving towards others, or creative mental life. It makes capable individuals fail and takes the zest out of whatever accomplishments are made despite the inner turmoil. It is painful for young people to be anxious, but it is sometimes more painful for them to look honestly at the reasons for their anxiety and so, instead of trying to face their inner conflicts or the demands of their environment honestly, they work out substitute ways of defending themselves against anxiety-producing situations. In the self-analysis provided in this book, we try to help students look courageously at those situations in the past and in the present which produce anxiety for them and make them ineffective. Jersild concludes that:

> In emphasizing the prevalence of anxiety in this way we are not simply trying to paint a gloomy picture of human existence. Actually, it is gloomier, if anxiety prevails, to deny or conceal it than to face it. It is much more hopeful and healthy to face the fact that many young people carry a burden of anxiety than to pretend that anxiety does not exist.[21]

In the next chapter on dating we shall see some of the elements of our courtship structure with its parental and peer insistence on "success" in dating as the *sine qua non* of adolescent prestige. This is an important factor in the growth of anxiety of both boys and girls in their interpersonal relationships. Another profound source of inner apprehension comes because of society's emphasis on the ultimate value of status as related to occupational achievement. This is a threat to many adolescents because they do not know that they can succeed when they enter the highly competitive world of work. Adolescents look to their parents to help them set realistic goals for the future. If the parents are anxious to push their youth into too early and too competitive dating situations, then the youth them-

---

[19] Jersild, p. 170.   [20] Jersild, p. 170.
[21] Jersild, p. 188. Reprinted by permission of the publisher.

selves must learn to control their anxieties or to seek help from others in this venture toward maturity.

The well-rounded person has developed enough ability so that he can: (1) Handle the problems that have come from the past and the ambiguities of the future with understanding and patience, (2) Accept responsibility and discharge it within boundaries set by the norms of society, (3) Enjoy an ever increasing scope of imaginative response to a disciplined curiosity, (4) Accept and enjoy growing sexuality, (5) Use and express feelings with the kind of freedom that involves responsible restraint, (6) Enjoy giving as well as receiving with growing sensitivity to the vital needs of others, and (7) Demonstrate the increased capacity for compassion, which is "a fellowship of feelings," which makes possible "the appreciation of the personal meaning and subjective reality of emotion—another's emotion. . . ." [22] Jersild regards compassion as the "ultimate and most meaningful expression of emotional maturity." [23] It is something like the response which the author has described as tenderness, the deepest and most satisfying warmth that can be expressed for and to another human being.

It is difficult for young people to be objective enough to understand how crucial personal growth is for every aspect of their lives. How mature we are in handling our emotions determines largely our poise in college, in an occupation, and surely in marriage. But emotional growth is not enough; beyond that a person's achievement depends on interpersonal competence, for we can be poised but ineffective. Nor is effectiveness by itself enough, for it may only mean that we can manipulate others. Compassion, when added to competence, means that our relationships will be lasting and good.

CONCLUSION

Adolescence is nearing its conclusion when a student enters college. How he has progressed in meeting the major developmental tasks in this stage of life will have much to do with his marriage success. He should have developed some competence in being (1) an independent and secure adult, (2) capable of accepting wholesome sexual roles, (3) secure in enjoying heterosexual sociability, and (4) far on the road towards emotional maturity. The purpose of the self-analysis schedule which follows

[22] Jersild, p. 201.   [23] Jersild, p. 203.

is to assess individual growth or retardation in meeting the developmental challenges outlined in this and earlier chapters.

SELF-ANALYSIS

The following outline, like the one at the end of the chapter on childhood, specifies important areas of growth that lead to marital adjustment. The student will want to add any experiences or facets of his life during adolescence which seem important to him but which are not in the outline.

I. Family Background
   A. Describe the following areas of interaction with your father during your adolescence:
      1. Use of car or home
      2. Choice of male or female friends
      3. Hours for study, hour to "get in "
      4. Clothes, make-up, habits, or mannerisms
      5. Recreational patterns
      6. Discipline
      7. Your developing independence
      8. Your father's help as a friend and counselor
   B. Describe the above areas of interaction with your mother.
   C. Describe any areas of conflict during this period with your brothers or sisters.
II. School and Neighborhood Influences
   A. Describe any problems in terms of adjustments in studying, use of time, relations with other students, reading or writing.
   B. Describe your relationships with your teachers during this period.
   C. Analyze your social adjustments during these years in terms of friendships and groups. Did you feel accepted or rejected?
   D. Were there any particular families or institutions in your neighborhood that influenced you?
III. Psychosexual Development
   A. Did you have a problem with inadequacy of sexual information during these years?
   B. What preparation had you had for these experiences? Did evidence of puberty (seminal emissions or menstruation) come as a shock or embarrassment to you?
   C. How did you handle your fears about masturbation?
   D. How troublesome to you were your first erotic feelings?

IV. Mood Reactions
   A. Did you tend to be cheerful, worried, fearful, depressive, optimistic?
   B. Were you burdened by feelings of insecurity, inferiority, self-doubt?
   C. Did you feel shy and self-conscious? How did you overcome these feelings?
   D. How great were your hostility feelings?
   E. Do you still feel guilty about the aggression you displayed during adolescence?
   F. Was it difficult to develop a sense of responsibility? Adequate use of time?
   G. Did you quarrel with any member of your family?
V. Social Values
   A. How did you decide your stand on sexual matters, smoking, drinking, gambling? Did problems arise?
   B. Did you struggle over religious ideas and ideals?
   C. Were you concerned about your choice of and future success in an occupation?
   D. Analyze any conflicts in values you had with your friends, your family, your school.
VI. Analyze the meaning of this developmental period in your life for marriage.

VISUAL AIDS

The Story of Menstruation, International Cellucotton Products Company, 919 N. Michigan Avenue, Chicago 11, Illinois.

You and Your Family, Association Films, Y.M.C.A. Motion Picture Bureau, 347 Madison Avenue, New York 17, New York.

Angry Boy, Mental Health Film Board, 164 East 38th Street, New York 16, New York.

Farewell to Childhood, International Film Bureau, Inc., 57 East Jackson Boulevard, Chicago 4, Illinois.

Children's Emotions, McGraw-Hill Book Company, Text Film Dept., 330 West 42nd Street, New York 18, New York.

READINGS

COLE, LUELLA. *Psychology of Adolescence*. 4th ed., New York, Rinehart and Company, Inc., 1954. Copyright Holt, Rinehart and Winston, Inc.

DUVALL, EVELYN. *Family Development*. Philadelphia, J. B. Lippincott Company, 1957, p. 8.

FOOTE, NELSON N. and LEONARD S. COTTRELL. *Identity and Interpersonal Competence*. Chicago, The University of Chicago Press, 1955.

JERSILD, ARTHUR. *The Psychology of Adolescence.* New York, The Macmillan Company, 1957, Chapters 7 through 10.

LANDIS, PAUL. *Adolescence and Youth.* New York, McGraw-Hill Book Company, Inc., 1952, Chapters 5 and 7.

WINCH, ROBERT F. *The Modern Family.* New York, Henry Holt and Company, 1952, Chapter 10. Copyright Holt, Rinehart and Winston, Inc.

CHAPTER 7 | Dating

INTRODUCTION

DATING provides the opportunity for the most important social relationship which a young person can have. Dating is important because of its contribution to socialization, to the maturing of personality, to the selection of a mate, and to subsequent marital adjustment. In this chapter, we study dating in terms of its function at different age levels and for different classes. We shall consider some of the problems associated with the present system of dating and some possible solutions to these problems. As Lowrie [1] has suggested, dating is a neglected field of study. There is little research material available on the subject. This chapter summarizes existing research and uses interviews and papers of young people as the basis for its generalizations.

THE BACKGROUND FOR DATING

Dating generally begins with puberty. But this statement neglects the important training that ordinarily precedes it. The last stage of childhood is marked by widespread participation in one-sex groups. In this pre-adolescent stage, the other sex is usually ignored. With the advent of puberty comes another type of gang in which boys and girls mix but do not pair off. Crist, in a study of 120 high-school students in the ninth through the twelfth grades of a university laboratory school,[2] concluded that successful early heterosexual social relationship was associated with

[1] Samuel H. Lowrie, "Dating, a Neglected Field of Study," *Marriage and Family Living*, X (1948), 90–91, 95.
[2] John R. Crist, "High School Dating as a Behavior System," *Marriage and Family Living*, XV (1953), 23–28.

enjoyment of the first dating experiences.[3] He also found that individuals who had not had previous conditioning in a mixed group were apt to be more anxious, fearful, and shy than those who had had frequent heterosexual contacts.[4] Hollingshead, in his study of many of the adolescents of Elmtown, found that early dating experience was characterized by overcautiousness in physical contact, shyness, difficulty in saying the right thing, and anxiety about proper behavior.[5] Duvall and Hill stress the fact that few schools or communities make adequate provisions for "this mingling of the sexes of different age groups, thus making dating more difficult." [6] Crist's study indicated the importance of the status achieved in other areas of interaction to the enjoyment on the first date.[7] There is agreement that successful heterosexual group activities are an important prelude to successful dating.

DATING IN JUNIOR HIGH SCHOOL

Duvall and Hill characterize dating in junior high as "fleeting affinities" and describe such dates as coke dates, being walked home from school, or other types of temporary try-outs of pairs.[8] The extent of dating in this age group varies with regional mores and with individual physical maturity. There is a difference of five years in the physical maturation of the sexes with girls maturing earlier on the average than boys. Hollingshead reported that by the time they enter high school, 43 per cent of the boys and 58 per cent of the girls have had at least one date. Crist found that dating in its earliest stages developed "primarily because the group expected it, not because of any particular interest in the girl or the boy in dating as such. . . ." [9] Mead thinks that this very early dating accentuates tensions and hostilities because boys, particularly, are not ready for such activity:

> During the very age when most of our comparative material suggests that boys are least ready to engage in sex activity in which they have to take the initiative, they are being drawn into a life that mimics the sex activities of late adolescence.[10]

[3] Crist, p. 25.   [4] Crist, p. 25.
[5] A. B. Hollingshead, *Elmtown's Youth: The Impact of Social Class on Adolescence* (New York: John Wiley and Sons, 1949), p. 224.
[6] Evelyn M. Duvall and Reuben Hill, *When You Marry*, rev. ed. (Boston: D. C. Heath and Company, 1953), p. 54.
[7] Crist, p. 24.   [8] Duvall and Hill, p. 55.   [9] Crist, p. 25.
[10] Margaret Mead, *Male and Female* (New York: William Morrow and Company, 1948), p. 280.

Despite the differential in physical and psychological maturity, Crist found that 87.9 per cent of this age group dated their classmates, while in high school only 54.7 per cent would select companions from their own grade.[11] These data indicate that much early dating is motivated by status considerations and may make for problems later by forcing individuals into situations for which they are not yet sufficiently mature. Early discouragement may be a factor in later withdrawal. McGuire reports an interview which illustrates the importance of a good beginning.

> Maybe I ought not to tell you—but, when I was a Freshman and a Sophomore [in high school], I didn't dress very nice or pay any attention to my figure. The kids didn't talk to me. I wasn't in any clique. Cliques are natural; you like some people better than others. So I turned to the skating rink. Because I didn't belong to any clique here at school I tried hard to make friends at the skating rink. Then I began to pay more attention to my clothes and my appearance. I worked into the crowd. Then—at school, when I looked better—the kids began to be more friendly to me. But you never really get in the top crowd if you don't start early.[12]

Status for dating may depend on an early acceptance by the "top crowd." It is not difficult to understand failures in development if considerations of social status force boys and girls to play roles for which they are not ready and for which they have had little preparation.

HIGH-SCHOOL DATING

The structure of dating in high school is very complex because it is related to clique formation, community class structure, and psychological maturity. Hollingshead identified 106 cliques in Elmtown, and concludes: "The adolescent clique and dating patterns are a reflection in large part of adult social structure." [13] McGuire emphasizes the following categories of cliques which seem to supersede community stratification:

> For convenience, the following terms are being used by research workers to designate the reference groups which mark the several categories of peer acceptance.
> 1. Wheels . . . "the active ones," "the top crowd."

[11] Crist, p. 25.
[12] Carson McGuire, "Family and Age-Mates in Personality Formation," *Marriage and Family Living*, XV (1953), 20. Reprinted by permission.
[13] Hollingshead, p. 242.

2. Brains . . . "Students," "good kids, but they don't know the score."
3. Outsiders . . . "skaters," "not in the crowd," but "they get around."
4. Mice . . . "quiet ones," "inoffensive," and "seldom heard."
5. Outcasts . . . "you don't want to be with them." [14]

There are a number of subdivisions of outcasts. McGuire describes these:

> Apparently, according to the interview data, there are at least two kinds of outcasts. A "drip" is a would-be wheel who "doesn't know how to run around." A "dope" is a would-be brain who arouses antagonism by parading his knowledge and by not knowing how to act appropriately when certain role behaviors are expected.[15]

The clue of "appropriate behavior" is important because it indicates that those who are psychologically inhibited or whose behavior patterns reflect class backgrounds that are out of harmony with the peer group cannot make the grade. Hollingshead confirms this in his study of cliques; for he found that the cliques in Elmtown reflected the social class structure.

We may now summarize the high-school dating structure. One is prepared or not for the dating experience, depending upon the opportunity to participate in heterosexual groups before dating. Dating takes place in cliques. Ability to participate in these cliques depends on psychological adjustment, upon membership in the social class structure, and upon the ability to fit into the peer pattern. Once a rating is established it is difficult but not impossible to move from one group to another. Our next task is to define dating in terms of patterns for different social classes.

HIGH-SCHOOL DATING AND SOCIAL CLASS

The life pattern of young people determines their dating behavior. The age at which they must accept adult status, find a job, and establish their own home has much to do with their dating attitudes. Hollingshead describes the lower-class youth of Elmtown as definitely looking forward to early marriage and early employment.[16] They leave school very early for casual employment in low-paid jobs. This fact is reflected in an emphasis on freedom of action and freedom from parental control at a much earlier age than for the middle- or upper-class levels.

Lower-Class Dating. This emphasis on freedom is reflected in the

---

[14] McGuire, p. 20.   [15] McGuire, p. 20.   [16] Hollingshead, p. 242.

ways of securing dates, dating behavior, and marital choice. Dates are "picked up" after cruising around in a car or visiting various ice-cream parlors or taverns which are known as centers for these youth. The boys may discuss the girls and make an agreement as to how they will pair off. The invitation is quite casual and may simply consist of a promise of a ride home or to a park. But implied in the ride home are many other things such as refreshments, necking, or sex activities.

Sexual activities among adolescents are more prevalent in the lower-class group than in any other. A Southern California teacher who daily counsels young people in this group explains something of their pattern and of the reasons for the pattern:

> The home is truly patriarchal in domination, especially those of the Slavs, Italians, Mexicans and Japanese. It is not uncommon for the girls to be forbidden to go on unescorted dates. If the girl wishes to see a boy, she must meet him at the dance, on the street corner, at a girl friend's house, or in a movie. Very few parents will allow their daughter to go on a date as we know it. A large number of girls and boys have intercourse before they reach high school or soon after reaching high school. These are some of the superficial reasons: the close living conditions of the lower economic classes, the low morals of their parents, the poor family life education in junior high school.[17]

It is apparent that the dating-sexual pattern of the lower class reflects the more casual sexual patterns of the parents. Going steady means engagement for these young people, and pregnancy is often the prelude to marriage.

Middle-Class Dating. Most of the literature on dating really deals with middle-class dating. Dating for this group can be divided into three stages: Cavan calls the first stage "the Ritual of Making a Date."[18] The boy must take the initiative although the girl has many opportunities of subtly indicating her interest in him. In contrast to the lower-class patterns, dates must be arranged somewhat formally to conform to middle-class standards. It is often easier for the insecure adolescent to "break the ice" and ask for a date on the telephone than in a face-to-face encounter, and consequently the telephone is a most important adjunct to dating. The telephone conversation is often prolonged and serves as a preliminary getting-acquainted

---

[17] From a case study in the author's files.

[18] Ruth Shonle Cavan, *The American Family,* 2nd ed. (New York: Thomas Y. Crowell Company, 1953), p. 309.

period. The telephone is also very useful in the development of the relationship, and for discussing the date afterward with various girl or boy friends. This often leads to friction with parents, who generally do not understand the function of the telephone in developing these relationships. Dates must be arranged some time in advance, for last-minute dates are regarded as fill-ins and are demoralizing to a girl's sense of prestige.

The second stage of the date is the sharing of some common activity such as a movie, a dance, a party, or a sports event. These events occur generally on Friday and Saturday nights and last considerably longer than week-day events. There seems to be an almost universal compromise between children and parents regarding hours. The hour to be home is one of the major points of conflict between adolescents and parents. Boys and girls feel that they will lose status if they cannot stay out as long as their peers do, and their parents feel that extremely late hours are injurious to the morals, education, and health of their growing sons and daughters. This often leads to quarreling, because two different sets of values are involved. The problem is most generally solved by a compromise—the young people agree to stay at home during school nights but are given considerable freedom on weekends when they do not have to get up early the next morning. Some communities try to establish norms.

The boys who excel in sports or dancing and display the height of sophistication and personality are the most popular, while girls with good clothes, a sparkling manner, and at least a minimum of prudery are the most popular with the other sex. During the social activity of the date, both boys and girls, if they are not going steady, will try to meet and favorably impress those who rank high on the prestige scale. This exploitation of the dating situation leads to such complaints as, for instance, that "the boy or the boys are fickle, they are always making a play for another girl or girls even when on a date with you." This competitive aspect of dating gives it an insecurity which is not always conducive to harmonious relationships.

In order to escape the competitive aspects of dating, many give up rather early in their dating career and escape by means of going steady. Cavan has summarized some of the mores which control going steady:

1. No boy other than the chosen one will ask the girl for a date; this rule is highly respected and rigidly followed. The girl, for her part, may not entice any other boy or show him favors.
2. The couple is always invited together to social functions; if one cannot attend, the other may not attend. They have become a social unit.

149

3. Symbols are exchanged, such as rings, class pins, club pins, bracelets with the owner's name inscribed, or sweaters. These symbols are not gifts; ownership remains with the original owner, the symbols are returned when the arrangement of going steady breaks up. In fact, the absence of the pin or ring signifies to the high school crowd that the two are no longer going steady.
4. Nonmaterial symbols are cultivated between the two. They may have a favorite song, a favorite seat in the motion-picture house, or a favorite place to park. They thrill to the sound of "our song" and resent innocent intrusion of another couple who happen to occupy the favorite seat or parking spot.
5. More intimacy is permissible and expected than on a casual date.[19]

Going steady is motivated by a sense of insecurity, by the prestige that comes to those who have a "steady," by new opportunities for parties, dinners, and other social events, and by its effect in enhancing the self-esteem of the individual involved.[20] But with these advantages come several disadvantages. Going steady involves tensions with parents who lament the limitations of experience inherent in going steady, a sexual tension because of the greater intimacy involved,[21] and a social tension as many of these young people soon tire of their companions and wish to dissolve the relationship.

Upper-Class Dating.　In the upper class, dating does not have the same motivation as in either of the classes already discussed. As prestige inheres in the social class itself, these young people are not ordinarily troubled about prestige or status. Furthermore, parental control operates in the selection of a mate, so that freedom of choice in dating and freedom of dating activity are much more circumscribed. Going steady is not part of the mores of this group. Many of the girls in this class attend girls' schools, and dating is restricted to highly controlled social occasions arranged by the school. Sexual experimentation is frowned upon because prestige is much associated with personal morality.

Much of the dating in this group is carried on at clubs and resorts where parents are present and a part of the social group.

Some upper-class young men have sexual liaisons with girls from the lower classes. They treat these girls with contempt but exploit them for sexual release. If the girls become pregnant, the parents of the boy arrange for an abortion or make a cash settlement with the girl. Marriage is never considered.

[19] Cavan, p. 314. Reprinted by permission of the publisher.
[20] Cavan, p. 315.　　[21] Cavan, p. 315.

COLLEGE DATING

Delora studied 120 college students to "ascertain the nature of ends, norms and status-role patterns of social systems of dating." The students in the sample were able to differentiate five types of dating which were definitive enough so that Delora could analyze the general expected patterns of behavior that clustered around each type. The students reported that, in general, these types were sequential but in some instances some stages were skipped. His findings are presented in the following table:

TABLE 13. Types of Dating Compared on Basis of Social Structure *

Type of Dating

Structural Element	Casual	Steadily	Going Steady	Engaged to Be Engaged	Engaged
End **	Getting acquainted	Entertainment Enjoyment	Companion-ship	Trial engagement	Getting ready for marriage
Norms	Impersonal Uninvolved Rational	Individualistic Free No commit-ment	Personalized Monogamous Intimate Emotional	Personalized Monogamous Intimate Emotional Oriented to future	Personalized Monogamous Intimate Emotional Oriented to future Rational plans
Status-Role	Initiation of action by male Dominance of male Authority	Initiation of action by male Dominance of male authority	Two way initiation of action Equal authority	Two way initiation of action Equal authority	Two way initiation of action Equal authority Male-female assumption of specific respon-sibilities

* Jack Delora, "Social Systems of Dating on a College Campus," *Marriage and Family Living*, XXV, No. I (February, 1963), 84. Reprinted by permission.
** The *Ends* of dating tended to be compounded as a couple moved from one type to the next.

Delora points out that each of these types has different types of goals, different norms, and that role function shifts with the degree of involvement and the goal of the interaction. He points out that failure to analyze dating in terms of a generalized function must "result in confusion." His finding that initiation of action shifts when couples go steady to *two way initiation of action* somewhat contradicts the theory that the individuals are by training either dominant or submissive. He indicates that the power role may vary depending on the degree of involvement. This is an important new finding and needs further research. If this statement is proved to be an accurate finding, much of our thinking regarding the role strain may be complicated by a further dimension: the expectation that as involvement increases the control role changes.

Delora found that *heavy petting* is associated with going steady and that intimacy increases after that as involvement increases. Insofar as female sexual expression is related to going steady, this factor involves the possibility already discussed in Chapter Three that the physical component of love is overstressed. It may become a means to sexual exploitation and later disillusionment, or it may be the distorted means to an unfortunate marital choice. Waller has pointed out the influence of one-sex groups in dating. If status and self-esteem are somewhat dependent on sexual exploitation, a college male may find it difficult to sort out his motives in his relationships with a girl. He may then go steady as the means to gratification or self-fulfillment with no regard for the personality outcomes of his partner. We will consider this problem again when we discuss the rating-dating complex.

Dating for college students involves a great many opportunities and some problems. It gives further opportunity for the growth of personality, for wider heterosexual contacts, for development of greater poise with the other sex, for greater discrimination in marriage choice, and for broad recreational experience. On the other hand, it produces insecurity for those who fail, it confronts almost every college student with sexual tensions, and it sometimes produces competitiveness between men and women.

THE DATING DILEMMA

Dating operates on an improvised basis with few mores thus far developed to regulate the behavior of young people. The result is that they must develop their own standards. They find themselves in the dilemma of being strongly stimulated sexually and yet expected to behave as though they were without sexual feelings. This dilemma means that they must exercise an unprecedented amount of self-control and make difficult personal decisions.

These decisions are not easily made today. We live in a social atmosphere heavily charged with sexual allusions and sexual stimuli. Lazarsfeld and Stanton conclude in their study of the lyrics of songs on the hit parade between January 1, 1941, and July 1, 1942, that of some ninety songs, eighty-three had lyrics with sex interest and only seven had no sex interest.[22] So the songs which young people sing, and which contribute to their expectations, directly or indirectly, motivate sexual activity. Movies stress the theme of sex. No advertiser is unaware of the advantage of an attractive pair of woman's legs in selling cars, refrigerators, or beer. Radio has its "lonely gal" with her insinuating, low, and husky voice, while the "Continental," who adjured his audience "not to be afraid because it's only a man's apartment," and then a little later whispers, "I ought not to do the things I do," was elevated to a national network on television.

The inference from these facts is that many consider sex to be the basic need and interest in life. Young people approaching later adolescence are bombarded with sexual allusions, suggestions, and stimuli. It is impossible for young couples today to escape making some decisions regarding sexual conduct.

These decisions are complicated by a number of factors. The first factor of importance is that for the first time in our society young people are relatively unchaperoned. They are permitted more freedom and are more mobile than at any time in history. A recent magazine article referred to the automobile as the "passion wagon." Young people may drive into the mountains, to the beach, to a resort, and may be completely alone for many hours without anyone noticing them, checking on them, or caring much about them. What happens in the car or in the mountains is not determined now by parents or by society but by the young people themselves. Hence, at the very time in their lives when young men are exceptionally virile and passionate, society has put them on their own.

If chaperonage is gone, so too are some of the other controls that formerly operated for restraint. Very few young people today are much concerned about venereal disease. The threat of these diseases, therefore, does not inhibit sexual behavior. Again, the fear of pregnancy is not as strong as it once was. Contraceptives have taken away some of the fear formerly associated with sexual intimacy. Social controls have also become less positive. Religion is not the force in inspiring prudent conduct that it was fifty or seventy-five years ago. Parents do not provide their

[22] P. F. Lazarsfeld and F. N. Stanton, *Radio Research, 1942, 1943* (New York: Duell, Sloan, and Pearce, Inc., 1944), p. 365.

children with either an understanding of their sexual feelings or a set of values to regulate those feelings.

A study in 1952 of the background of one thousand students of five college campuses of South Carolina indicated that only 385, or 38.5 per cent, of the students were given any sex education by their mothers and only 19.7 per cent by their fathers.[23] Thus, young people are open to stimulation and provided with opportunities for sexual experimentation; social controls that formerly guided them in this area are not supplied by either parents or society; and yet they are expected to conform to adult standards. This is the dilemma of dating.

In college, the dating dilemma is sharpened by still other factors. Sexual prowess or sexual experimentation seems to give status to individuals in groups such as fraternities or college cliques. A fraternity man, reporting on the impact of fraternity life on attitudes toward dating, says:

> Once the preliminaries are over and the fraternity man starts dating, he is likely to find that a flashy car and sporty clothes will increase his rating. However, this is greatly over-rated by critics of the system as well as by those members who are less fortunate. A degree of determination and some help from the brothers who have automobiles is all that is required to get over these obstacles. On the other hand, the new member will find that as time goes by, his standing among the brothers *within* his own fraternity will depend more and more on the frequency of his dates and the date-rating of the young women he does take out (that is to say, how attractive they are, and whether they belong to a big sorority). Furthermore, the number of sexual experiences he has had will definitely increase his standing. If there are no such experiences, as is the case in about two out of three college men [as shown in Table 14 (p. 155)], the tendency is for the individual to fabricate some or at least leave the implication that he "is the lover." [24]

Thus there is some tendency within groups to regard the sexually experienced as possessing some merit that the less sophisticated do not have. Consequently, there is some pressure to achieve status through actual sexual experimentation or fabricated reports of sexual activity.

How do college young people meet this situation? In the following table Landis and Landis compare two studies, one at Cornell and one at Michigan:

[23] R. Grann Lloyd, "Parent-Youth Conflicts of College Students," *Sociology and Social Research*, 36 (1952), 229.

[24] From a case study in the author's files.

TABLE 14. Per Cents of Students Checking Each of Four Statements Representing Attitudes on Premarital Sex Standards: 2000 Michian State College Students, 1947; 173 Cornell University Students, 1940–41 *

APPROVED STANDARDS	MEN		WOMEN		BOTH	
	M.S.C.	Cornell	M.S.C.	Cornell	M.S.C.	Cornell
	PER CENT	PER CENT	PER CENT	PER CENT	PER CENT	PER CENT
Sexual relations for both	16	15	2	6	12	9
None for either	59	49	76	76	63	65
For men only	10	23	15	11	12	16
Between engaged persons only	15	11	7	6	13	8

* Judson T. Landis and Mary Landis, *Building a Successful Marriage* (New York: Prentice-Hall, Inc., 1948), p. 121. Reprinted by permission.

In contrast to these figures are those of Kinsey. He reported that of his college interviewees some 44 per cent had had premarital intercourse by the age of twenty.[25] Burgess and Wallin's sample included only 22.4 men and 36.5 women who had a high-school education or less, so that their findings are generally comparable to those of Landis and Kinsey. The men in this sample were divided into 32.2 per cent who had not had premarital intercourse and 67.7 per cent who had; 53 per cent of the women had not had intercourse before marriage and 47 per cent had had such experiences.[26] Kinsey reported that about 83 per cent of men at the grade-school level and 75 per cent of men at the high-school level had had intercourse by the age of twenty.[27]

A summary of various studies follows:

Premarital Sexual Intercourse of College Students by Year of Study and Incidence

NAME	Date	Sample	Incidence (per cent)	
			MALE	FEMALE
Hamilton	1929	100	54	35
Terman	1938	760	61	37

[25] Alfred C. Kinsey, W. B. Pomeroy, and C. E. Martin, *Sexual Behavior in the Human Male* (Philadelphia: W. B. Saunders Company, 1948), p. 550.
[26] Ernest W. Burgess and Paul Wallin, *Engagement and Marriage* (Philadelphia: J. B. Lippincott Company, 1953), p. 28.
[27] Kinsey, *et al.*, p. 550.

Premarital Sexual Intercourse of College Students
by Year of Study and Incidence (continued)

NAME	Date	Sample	Incidence (per cent)	
			MALE	FEMALE
Kinsey (M)	1948	2308	44	( )
Kinsey (F)	1953	2070	( )	20
Burgess and Wallin	1953	580	68	47
Landis and Landis (M)	1953	600	41	( )
Landis and Landis (F)	1953	1000	( )	9
Ehrmann (Non-veterans)	1959	274	57	13

The differences in incidence can be partially explained by different average ages of the samples. Burgess and Wallin studied engaged couples and Terman's sample had a mean male age of twenty-eight and a mean female age of twenty-five. The vast majority of girls have intercourse only with their future marital partner so it is obvious that an engaged sample such as Burgess-Wallin's would show a higher incidence.

Conflict and confusion are inevitable when ethical decisions are demanded in an area of stress where a large group carries on an activity and a large group condemns that activity. Expectations necessarily vary, and individuals are at a loss regarding personal standards.

Dating and the Development of Ethical Standards. Seen in this broad perspective of changing and confused standards, dating becomes a process of establishing norms for lifelong ethical conduct. Young people must make up their minds about a wide variety of moral matters. The following excerpt from a girl's analysis of her own ethical growth indicates something of the scope of decisions facing contemporary youth:

When I first got to school I just took everything in my stride; nothing shocked me because I was expecting completely new experiences. I had been there ten days the first time someone offered me dope. Never in my life have I had the slightest inclination to try it, nor at that time I hadn't even any inclination to try liquor or cigarettes, but the casual way in which it and other things drifted through my environment left me with the feeling that though I certainly would not drop my standards, I was never shocked at anything anyone else did. For this reason my friends have always brought their troubles to me—at least half of my close friends had to get married.[28]

For that large part of the population which has had no instruction in sex either in the church, in the school, or in the home, dating becomes an experience of groping for permanent answers to the meaning of sex in life and its function in contributing to happy living. If one talks with young people on an intimate basis, he soon learns that this drive to establish standards is almost as great as the sexual drive itself. Leland E. Glover held interviews or received questionnaires from 1,289 college students who listed for him their chief problems. The result of this survey indicated that the largest number of students were concerned with values, ethics, and morals.[29] The sorority house discussion and the fraternity "bull session" have been much maligned for their preoccupation with sex. Those who listen to these discussions with an attentive ear are aware that the motivation for them falls under two headings: (1) the need for accurate information which the young people never had an opportunity to acquire, and (2) their eagerness for some norms for their own conduct. Society has freed the sexual impulse, but it has not given guidance which would assist young people in using their freedom with either accurate knowledge or well-defined values.

Insofar as the first expressions of sexual feelings or the first experiences of sexual contact are basic in establishing later attitudes toward the sexual phase of life, what happens during dating is of great significance for marital adjustment. These dating experiences may result in such disgust as to bring on frigidity or impotence, or they may result in standards adequate for later adjustment in marriage. Dating problems may make a person a physical wreck and burden him with doubts and guilt feelings. Most young people in college face weekly decisions as to how they will behave in the dating situation, and many of them have no background of parental guidance to help them. It is crucial, then, to recognize the importance of dating as preparation for marriage.

The Rating-Dating Complex. Dating inevitably reflects social goals. Some parents are more anxious that their girls and boys be popular than that they do well scholastically. This is the channel by which adult goals of prestige are transmitted to young people. So in a sense youth can be-

[28] From a case study in the author's files.
[29] Leland E. Glover, "The Teacher of Marriage and the Family as Counselor," unpublis' Ph.D. dissertation, the University of Southern California Library, 1950, p. 87.

come as "other-directed" as some adults. There is a great anxiety about being accepted, and to be accepted means to date. The degree *to* which a girl or boy is regarded as desirable as a dating companion is measured by a rating. When both parents and peers motivate a young person to measure their self-esteem by their acceptance in the dating field, it is not surprising that the rating-dating complex influences the development of sexual standards.

In observing groups of young people Waller noted that their dating conduct was often motivated by a desire to achieve high status on campus. The individual's desire to build up personal self-esteem through dating the most desirable persons is reinforced by the desire of his group to rate on campus. One student confirms this:

> This pressure is so great that when I entered a fraternity and was dating a girl from my high school who was not going to college it was suggested to me that I drop her and begin to date girls from _____ sorority. I liked the girl and wanted to go with her so I continued. But the pressure got so great from the fraternity that I finally had to give her up.[30]

This student thinks there is a discernible cycle in dating which starts out with a girl's being very popular, then descending in popularity, and finally, weary of the competition, wishing to find a more permanent status, focuses on marriage as a goal.

Dating, Rating, and Sexual Standards. Perhaps the struggle for prestige is so intense that many boys and girls are subtly aware that the entire dating relationship is exploitative in the sense that its ultimate purpose is not friendship or fun but achievement of status. How difficult it is to adjust to status demands is indicated in the following excerpt from a student's analysis of her reactions to the struggle for prestige:

> However, though I had made tremendous adjustments, I was not accepted by the rest of the school for being any different than I had been in the seventh grade. I made up my mind in high school it would be different, because new students would judge me on the present, not the past. By the second day of high school I had bids to five social clubs, and before the month was over I was going steady with one of the leading football players. I was no longer a nonentity. I joined two social clubs in the tenth grade and was in the height of my glory; but after six months I became very disgusted with the two-faced back stabbing that one had to engage

[30] Statement by a student in the author's files.

in to maintain prestige, and spent a couple of months being anti-social and not dating at all.[31]

Or, on a date, one is not motivated to contribute to the enjoyment of one's partner so much as to impress the other with a view to what each will say about the other later in the fraternity, sorority, or other group. Obviously those who lead the race for prestige are not under pressure to win favor by excessive petting or by permitting sexual intimacies. But those who do not measure up to the cited requirements for high rating and who feel desperate because of lack of status, or who are very insecure because of their inability to attract dates, may feel that dating is so important that they will use sexual means to attain a type of temporary popularity. Hence, the rating-dating complex has serious repercussions on those who are not so popular. This is particularly true of those individuals who have never had an adequate love response from parents. They may engage in sexual intimacies not only to gain status but also because it seems the only avenue open to the experience of kindness, closeness, and tenderness. The dangers of such conduct will be discussed later.

The Romantic Fallacy and Sexual Standards. It is possible, too, that the romantic nature of the dating ideals of today has much to do with accentuating the dilemma. Many young people find it difficult to escape romantic interpretations of affectional relationships. Consequently they expect that dating or heterosexual relationships will be based on romance. Sexual attraction is camouflaged under intense romantic feelings which many young people assume to be love. Hence, young people concentrate on a "line" or an "atmosphere" which does not stress happy recreation, stimulating conversation, or interpersonality exploration, but, instead, moods associated with moonlight and roses and thrills. They become more and more embroiled in relationships which have sexual connotations and involve sexual stimulation but which they think of in terms of romantic love. When their caresses and kisses reach the stage of producing compelling emotions they have no way to cope with them. Indeed, they often rationalize these unusual feelings as the normal flowering of a beautiful and supposedly lasting love. Some young people have indicated that while they consider promiscuous sexual relations completely immoral, they believe that when a couple are "deeply in love"

[31] Statement by a student in the author's files.

159

sex relations are natural and good. But what they are experiencing is not love involving the whole personality but an infatuation based only on sex attraction. Thus a lack of knowledge of the basic differences between love and infatuation often leads to overt acts that are not understood.

One antidote to domination by either the drive for status or the romantic fallacy is a private but frank appraisal of one's own values. If one chooses an occupation, one plots the necessary steps to achieve one's goal. Likewise, if one focuses his attention upon marriage he should be concerned with the steps necessary to achieve a happy union. When one has thought over his personal life very carefully and has arrived at a decision regarding his behavior in potentially dangerous areas, he is then prepared to handle with courage and imagination any situation which may arise. If he is confused about what he believes, he is very likely to be carried away by powerful emotions.

Physical Aspects of Dating. Because of what we have labeled the dating dilemma, it is well to consider the various solutions of the problem in terms of their later influence on marital adjustment. Dating behavior varies in intimacy from a verbal "good-night" to coitus. In between are the steps known as necking, petting, petting to climax. By necking is generally meant rather casual embraces and kissing. By petting is meant more passionate embraces, deep kissing (soul kissing), and caressing most of the body. By petting to climax is meant stimulation of the erotic zones of the body until orgasm occurs. Coitus is sexual intercourse. Various individuals set different limits for affectionate behavior. There is no sharp distinction between any of these stages, and all affectional responses lead to more passionate ones. Nature endowed us with a powerful drive to procreate and accomplishes this by making the effect of physical contact progressive and cumulative.

The demarcation between necking and petting is particularly hard to make, for couples going steady find it easy to pass from casual embraces and kissing to more passionate involvements. Petting is normally the foreplay before intercourse. In marriage, petting is essential to mutuality and is a part of the satisfaction of the normal sex act. But before marriage, when love play does not result in intercourse, petting represents an incomplete emotional adventure. Petting may be compared to the hypothetical experience of the couple who love good swing music and have purchased tickets to hear Duke Ellington give a concert. They look forward to the concert and build up their expectations. Excitement mounts as they enter the concert hall. They look at the program and see that some of their favorite numbers are to be played. The band walks in. There is a hushed silence and the great moment is at hand. Then an attendant comes on stage and announces that Duke Ellington has suddenly become ill and that the concert must be postponed. They go home frustrated and unhappy. But the next week comes the announcement that Duke Ellington is well again and tickets will be honored at this performance. Again they go to the concert with expectations even higher than on the first evening. They take their seats, the band marches in, there is silence as they await the appearance of the leader. Then the attendant comes on stage and announces that the orchestra leader has had an accident on the way to the theater and that there will be no concert. Again they go home, filled with chagrin and consternation. Suppose this happens a dozen times. The final conclusion of the couple is that the experience of going to hear Duke Ellington is a dismal one, that all they have got out of it is disappointment, and that they will have nothing to do with his concerts from now on.

Something similar but more devastating often happens when a couple pets continuously. Petting brings them to a high pitch of excitement in which every nerve cell is urging them to finish what they have begun. But they say "no." There is no normal outlet for their emotions, so they learn that sexual play of this kind is a frustrating and dismal experience. If petting continues throughout high school and throughout college, the whole condition response of the woman's body and to some extent of the man's, is to say "no" whenever strong sexual feelings or sensations arise. How is it possible, then, that they should on their wedding night be able to reverse this situation and say "yes"? The answer is that many cannot.[32] Under such conditions a certain degree of frigidity is unescapable, at least for some years.

Petting to Climax. If, however, the emotional pressure becomes too great and the couple determine that there must be some other answer they may pet to climax. Petting to climax may release dammed up emotional feelings but it may also cause numerous psychological problems. Recently, a girl who was about to cancel her "pinning" to a boy honestly faced this situation. She had a rigid set of morals which did not permit her to have coitus but under emotional pressure allowed her to pet to climax. During the next three months the couple practiced this intermit-

[32] Margaret Mead, *Male and Female* (New York: William Morrow and Company, 1949), pp. 294–295.

tently. In the meantime she began to raise a great many rather minor questions regarding her fiancé. She was not now altogether sure that he was careful enough about his dress. She was not sure that he could hold a steady job. She resented the fact that at home he paid too much attention to her folks and seemed to neglect her. At every conference with the counselor she brought up an increasing list of objections to marrying him. But all of these objections appeared to have originated at the time they had begun to pet to climax. Previously none of these faults had troubled her. The fact was that she felt intensely guilty and unhappy about this type of love play. She enjoyed petting physically but could not tolerate it ethically. Hence, she projected blame upon her boy friend but camouflaged the reason for it by stressing minor objections. She did not realize the degree to which her petting to climax was interfering with a growing love relationship.

A careful study of the degree to which college males and females engage in various types of lovemaking and the meaning to them of these activities has been made by Ehrmann.[33] He used two different schedules, Schedule A for the first 30 per cent of his sample and Schedule B for the remaining 70 per cent. The change was made because of pertinent suggestions of the interviewees themselves. Consequently his reports are divided into two groups but these groups supplied comparable data. Ehrmann is at first interested in the type of behavior that characterizes young people. Later we will note some of the conclusions reached on the basis of his facts. Several of his categories are contained in Table 15 and promote understanding of his data.

While some 65 per cent of the males had had sexual intercourse by the time of the study, only 13 per cent of the girls had engaged in that activity. Religious background made some difference, but the sample was largely Protestant; for males the percentages were Protestant 82, Roman Catholic 9, and Jewish 9; for females 78 per cent were Protestant, 7 per cent were Catholic and 15 per cent were Jewish. Bearing this in mind, the incidence of premarital intercourse for males associated with these three groups was 64, 61, and 88. The situation was somewhat reversed for females for the percentage of Protestant, Catholic and Jewish girls who had experienced coitus was 12, 21, and 11.[34] We shall comment later on Ehrmann's finding that the going-steady relation is the greatest determinant of female sexual activity but not for males.[35] On the other

---

[33] Winston Ehrmann, *Premarital Dating Behavior* (New York: Henry Holt and Company, 1959). Copyright Holt, Rinehart and Winston, Inc
[34] Ehrmann, pp. 88, 89.   [35] Ehrmann, p. 169.

TABLE 15. Stages of Premarital Sexual Behavior by Per Cent *

STAGES	Lifetime Behavior		Current Behavior	
	MALE	FEMALE	MALE	FEMALE
A. No dates within specified period				
Schedule AB	1	0	4	1
Schedule B	1	0	4	1
B. No physical contact or holding hands				
Schedule AB	2	2	5	4
Schedule B	2	1	4	3
C_1 Kissing and hugging				
Schedule AB	15	52	31	60
Schedule B	9	34	23	45
C_2 Boy fondling girl's breasts with his hands outside her clothes, as well as any activity in C_1				
Schedule AB	(Not included in Schedule AB)			
Schedule B	8	18	11	17
D. Boy fondling girl's naked breasts, as well as any activity in C_1 or C_2				
Schedule AB	4	8	5	8
Schedule B	4	5	5	5
E. Boy fondling girl's genitals or naked area around genitals, as well as any activity in C_1, C_2 or D				
Schedule AB	13	25	17	18
Schedule B	14	27	16	18
F. Sexual intercourse, as well as any activity in C_1, C_2, D or E				
Schedule AB	65	13	38	9
Schedule B	62	15	37	11

* Material adapted from Ehrmann, Tables 1.1, 2.2, and 2.3. For strict accuracy it should be noted that Stage C of Ehrmann's Schedule AB is the equivalent of Combined Stages C_1 and C_2 of Schedule B. There were 576 males and 265 females in the AB sample and 382 males and 200 females in the B sample. Reprinted by permission of Holt, Rinehart and Winston, Inc.

hand the "comparable social class of companion is more significantly related to the sexual activity" of males than females.[36]

One of Ehrmann's most significant conclusions has been his perception of significant differences in sexual codes. He finds that the "double

[36] Ehrmann, p. 169.

standard" which permits sexual activity only for the male is still held by 33 per cent of the males but by none of the females.[37] A conservative "single standard" that permits no sexual behavior to either boy or girl is held by 20 per cent of the males and 86 per cent of the females.[38] There is conversely a "liberal single standard" which permits both male and female to have premarital coitus. Forty-seven per cent of the males believe in this standard and 14 per cent of the females. However, there is a variation in the last standard, for 5 per cent of the men and all 7 per cent of the women permit sex only with lovers.[39] This classification is an important addition to our understanding of the mores of our generation. It indicates the demise of the old double standard and the emergence of new ethical points of view among young people in the direction of equality.

A further note from Ehrmann's conclusions may well serve to clarify the student's thinking and understanding of male and female differences. He finds that female sexual expression is "profoundly related to being in love and to going steady," but male sexuality is "more indirectly and less exclusively associated with romanticism and intimacy relationships." [40] And "the degree of physical intimacy actually experienced and considered permissible is among males *inversely* related and among females *directly* related to the intensity of familiarity and affection in the male-female relation." [41] This distinctly different value system may well account for the growth of guilt feelings encountered by Kirkendall as love relationships increase among those having premarital intercourse.[42] This finding enables us to understand some of the profound antagonism which develops between young men and young women in courtship. They have different value systems in regard to sex.

There is one final factor mentioned by another researcher of interest when discussing premarital sexual experimentation. This fact must certainly be considered in the thinking of young people in deciding upon their premarital standards. Kinsey and his associates found that women who had had premarital intercourse were about twice as likely to have extramarital affairs as were women who had not had premarital intercourse.[43]

[37] Ehrmann, pp. 187–189.   [38] Ehrmann, pp. 187–189.   [39] Ehrmann, pp. 187–189.
[40] Ehrmann, p. 269.   [41] Ehrmann, p. 269.
[42] Lester Kirkendall, *Premarital Intercourse and Interpersonal Relationships* (New York: The Julian Press, Inc., 1961). This is certainly an inadequate summary of an important research effort. The reader is urged to study the original statement by Kirkendall.
[43] Alfred C. Kinsey, Wardell B. Pomeroy, Clyde E. Martin and Paul H. Gebhard, *Sexual Behavior in the Human Female* (Philadelphia: W. B. Saunders Company, 1953), p. 427.

Premarital Coitus and Preparation for Marriage. Premarital coitus involves many difficulties. Coitus, to be successful, requires a sense of security in the future relationship of the personalities involved. Coitus involves some sensitive adjustments, and these can rarely be made before a couple lives together. Many who have undertaken a trial period of intercourse have been so unsuccessful that a relationship that had held great promise was never achieved.

Kirkendall in an interview study collected case histories of 668 premarital intercourse experiences as reported by 200 college level males. He attempted to discover the effects of premarital sexual intimacy upon the relationship in which it occurred. He studied the outcomes of six types of associations which involved contacts with (1) prostitutes, (2) pick-ups, (3) casual acquaintances, (4) dating partners for whom no affection was held, (5) dating partners for whom there was much affection, and (6) fiancées. He judged the effects of these associations in terms of the reaction of the young men to the experience and in some cases to the contribution of the sexual experience upon communication and other relationship factors. Table 16 (p. 166) summarized these findings.[44]

Some interesting findings seem to emerge from this study. (1) Where there is minimal emotional involvement, men are more likely to react with resentment and hostility toward sexual partners; but as they develop affection for the girl, negative feelings more often take the form of guilt. (2) As affection increases for the girl more concern is shown to protect her from pregnancy by her partner. (3) A very serious consideration in the total picture is the immaturity of the young people who were studied because (a) it is questionable if they can deal with the potential outcome of premarital sex and (b) they confuse passion with love.[45] (4) It is obvious from the statistics in Table 16 that most of the sexual experiences reported here did not contribute to a positive view of sex or to the growth of a relationship. Even for engaged couples premarital sex was satisfactory in less than half of the cases where some feeling was reported.

Kirkendall ends his study with some observations regarding the way we can use "our sexual endowments in the service of satisfying interpersonal relationships." He suggests:

1. Adherence to a value system which makes a concern for the improvement of interpersonal relations a paramount value.

[44] Kirkendall, Chapters I and II.   [45] Kirkendall, p. 159.

T A B L E 16. Impact of Premarital Sexual Experience on Two Hundred Young Men *

Female Partner (By Types)	Reaction of Males to the Experience (By Numbers)					Result in Terms of Communication
	Satis-factory	Mixed Feelings	Unsatis-factory	No Feelings	No Infor-mation	
Type I Prostitutes	6	9	19	2	2	No comment
Type II Pick-ups	8	9	22	15	6	Negative hostility at partner
Type III Casual Ac-quaintances	28	14	19	4	33	Negative hostility at Partner
Type IV Dating Partners (No affection)	No statistics—23 out of 87 subjects lost respect for partners					Some hostility but emphasis of subject's comments stresses total relationship more than previous types
Type V Dating Partners (Much affection)	Over one-half expressed some kind of negative personal feelings concerning effect of premarital intercourse					More mutuality than in previous types Some guilt reactions
Type VI Fiancées	10	6	3	4	5	Varying effects: Intercourse sometimes integrated into relationship; sometimes weakens it One-third expressed guilt

* This table is not found in Kirkendall's book but represents the author's effort at summarizing various aspects studied by Kirkendall.

166

2. Acceptance of the fact that the sexual impulse is essentially positive and life-giving in nature. Rather than fearing it, our task is learning how to direct and utilize it.

3. Much discussion and objective consideration of the nature of sex, and its place in relationships. These discussions need to cut across age and sex lines, and to be approached in the same manner as we approach discussions of other subjects.

4. Scrupulous care to avoid exploitive, self-centered use of sex.

5. Much attention to the ways in which satisfying and complementing sex roles can be developed.

6. The release of pressures and the elimination of commercial uses which attach extraneous values to sex.

7. A continuation of research which will increase insights into all aspects of human adjustment, including sex.[46]

Kirkendall's goals are the enhancement of integrity, self-respect and fulfillment of the individual person and a growth in closeness, trust and faith between persons.[47] As such his observations are directed toward a more responsible, less exploitative and more fulfilling use of sex both before and after marriage. Kirkendall's study emphasizes the fact that one significant factor involved in premarital sexual relations is the absence of many of the conditions which make of intercourse a binding experience of love. The couple rarely has a sense of privacy. They fear they may be discovered in one way or another. They seldom have enough time to become completely relaxed and to share enough things together to make intercourse a normal outcome of other experiences. Then, too, there is the fear of pregnancy. The only tested medical methods of birth-control—the diaphragm and contraceptive jelly—are not readily available to the unmarried. And in any case some danger of pregnancy always exists—a danger which produces both fear and resentment. Again, emancipated as educated young people sometimes are today, they still are the products of a culture which has put a taboo on premarital sexual relations. Thus they must carry on their sexual activities covertly and with much scheming. All of these factors go to create a situation which is so disturbing that coitus, instead of being a climax to love, becomes a difficult and disappointing experience. Because of these factors and because sexual relations are not automatically successful at first, even in the security of marriage, it is difficult to achieve desirable learning experiences from premarital coitus.

[46] Kirkendall, p. 252.   [47] Kirkendall, p. 7.

The aggressor in sex play may also be primarily concerned with his or her pleasure and not at all with the mutuality of the experience. Those who have been sexually exploited under the guise of love are likely to be very suspicious of the motives of other partners and somewhat insecure about their capacity to adjust sexually in marriage. They also may have doubts as to whether or not they should tell their future mates about such experiences and, if they do not, whether they will nevertheless be found out. For these reasons, premarital sexual experimentation is correlated with somewhat poorer adjustment in marriage. An analysis of other statistical studies of the impact of premarital sexual intercourse will be presented in the chapter on engagement, and so it is not included here.

Values in sex behavior differ for different classes and for different generations. Values are today much in flux. After a great many class discussions and individual consultations with students, the author has only admiration for the courage and insight with which most young people face the dating dilemma. Couples who feel confused or who feel that their dating experience is having some unfortunate results should talk with a counselor, so that their future relationship will not be endangered by guilt feelings or unconscious hostilities. Personalities are plastic, and difficulties that seem insurmountable may actually be overcome with the understanding help of a counselor.

Dating and Its Contribution to Wise Marriage Choice. Dating is an extremely useful experience if it used for the development of heterosexual poise and ease in communication. Those who concentrate entirely on necking and petting lose the chance of the personality development inherent in dating. For dating may be a school for marriage. During the dating period, young people may come to appreciate differences in masculine and feminine points of view. They may come to know as many different types of people as are represented in their college group. If they become acquainted with a diverse assortment of individuals, they will learn which types complement their own personalities. They will know with what type they feel most comfortable and which most stimulates growth. Conversely, those who concentrate on the physical relationship may be quite blind to the other areas of adjustment needed in a good marriage. The objective of dating, then, ought to be different from that of courtship wherein an individual is consciously trying to pick a marriage partner. Dating is most useful when it functions in maturing a person in the social aspects of his relationship to the opposite sex. If it is to do this, dating must result in several positive achievements: (1) the growth of ability to communicate, (2) the growth of new social and cultural interests, (3) the growth of personal attractiveness.

Dating and Communication. Through dating in high school and college young people should learn how to communicate with the other sex. Communication is a very basic process in marriage. Those who can make articulate their emotions, their tenderness, their enthusiasms, their ideals, their values, and their points of view are generally good marital risks because they have developed means of facing conflicts intelligently when they arise. Dating which is focused on companionship enables a couple to explore each other's points of view, to begin to appreciate the many differences of approach, and to learn to deal with differences constructively. In order to develop mutuality of thought and basic communication, it is best if both have an opportunity to express themselves regarding their intentions and feelings. Insofar as a couple frankly discusses the limits they will set in meeting the dating dilemma, they are developing the ability to be free in marriage when dealing with sexual problems. As was indicated at the beginning of the discussion of dating, shyness and awkwardness characterize first dating attempts. When the time for courtship arrives, ease and verve in communication should have superseded shyness.

Dating and the Growth of Interests. Dating ought to include activities that interest both parties and some things neither has explored before. Young people who have always listened to Beethoven's symphonies may also find modern music interesting. Those whose preparation for occupational life has been scientific do not detract from their lifetime goal if they develop an interest in one or more of the various art forms they may find at any good museum or art institute. Dancing the rhumba well does not preclude the possibility of enjoying some of the more intricate folk or square dances. The same thing is true of various sports. If a girl cannot play tennis, she may prove to be a very good competitor on the golf course or in the swimming pool. Imaginative dating may become an adventure. Many individuals tend to be inordinately provincial in their tastes in food—and in life. Likewise the fact that one has never engaged in folk dancing is no reason for not discovering whether or not it may add a new pleasure to life. Life may be a sweep of exciting experiences or it may be a routine of dull, repeated exercises.

Developing Dating Desirability. How do you rate as a date? Several studies have recorded those qualities which others desire in a date. Chris-

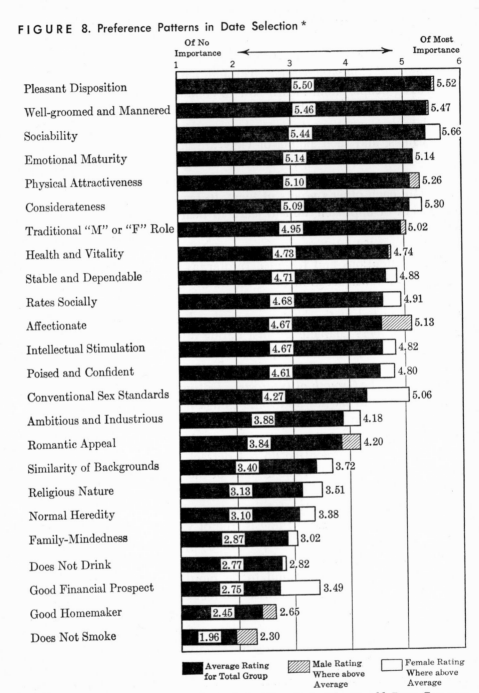

FIGURE 8. Preference Patterns in Date Selection *

Of No Importance ← → Of Most Importance

	Average	Full
Pleasant Disposition	5.50	5.52
Well-groomed and Mannered	5.46	5.47
Sociability	5.44	5.66
Emotional Maturity	5.14	5.14
Physical Attractiveness	5.10	5.26
Considerateness	5.09	5.30
Traditional "M" or "F" Role	4.95	5.02
Health and Vitality	4.73	4.74
Stable and Dependable	4.71	4.88
Rates Socially	4.68	4.91
Affectionate	4.67	5.13
Intellectual Stimulation	4.67	4.82
Poised and Confident	4.61	4.80
Conventional Sex Standards	4.27	5.06
Ambitious and Industrious	3.88	4.18
Romantic Appeal	3.84	4.20
Similarity of Backgrounds	3.40	3.72
Religious Nature	3.13	3.51
Normal Heredity	3.10	3.38
Family-Mindedness	2.87	3.02
Does Not Drink	2.77	2.82
Good Financial Prospect	2.75	3.49
Good Homemaker	2.45	2.65
Does Not Smoke	1.96	2.30

■ Average Rating for Total Group   ▨ Male Rating Where above Average   ☐ Female Rating Where above Average

* Harold T. Christensen, *Marriage Analysis* (New York: The Ronald Press Company, 1950), pp. 212, 213. Copyright 1950 The Ronald Press Company. Reproduced by permission of the publisher.

tensen made a study of 674 unmarried and unengaged university students who rated twenty-four items on a six-point scale according to what they considered most desirable qualities.

Figure 8 clearly indicates the premium put on companionship in dating. The 674 unmarried and unengaged Purdue University students, who rated these items on a six-point scale, stress those qualities which will make communication easy and stimulating. Some differences are interesting. Females obviously stress conventional sex standards, good financial prospects, ambition and industriousness, religious nature, considerateness and sociability, while the men stressed the affectionate and romantic aspects of a date, physical attractiveness, and "not smoking." However, in general, they agree. The student may well ask himself or herself the degree to which these qualities reflect his or her unconscious needs in a date.

One girl who sees the dating process with clarity and who very spontaneously and effectively outlines her own standards says:

> Most girls eighteen to twenty-one put a boy up to some kind of qualification standard they have developed through dating many boys. Even if the girl knows she isn't ready to think seriously because she wants to go three more years to college or wants a career, she is bound to set up standards. She spends many leisure hours in dreaming, formulating opinions on character, and comparing boys, so that the subject of dating is always in the back of her mind and affects many things she does.
>
> When a girl meets a boy, the first thing that is noticed is appearance. She likes someone who is neat, clean, and pleasant looking. The second thing would be friendliness, since by this quality we meet, talk, and arrange dates. When a girl is on the date, the first thing she notices is: "How does he treat me?" She knows whether or not he has her best interests at heart, whether he wants to please her, or whether he just wanted "a date" for some occasion. He should be considerate, kind, thoughtful, and respectful, and on this basis a true friendship could be started (providing the girl is the same way).
>
> In addition to the boy who has her best interests at heart and who is considerate, kind, thoughtful, and respectful, a girl likes a boy who is sweet and fundamentally gentle—a boy who is patient and understanding as well as helpful. Every girl likes someone who is sincere—whom she can believe, without getting too worried or jealous. Girls like a boy who is a true friend—one she can talk freely with, one she can share her thoughts with—one she can laugh or cry with, and one who is dependable and faithful, and the natural, wholesome and refreshing person, always rates high

because he acts natural. A girl can't help but go for a boy who visits and calls often, who is sentimental enough to show her he cares, who is capable of surprising her, and who shows he appreciates the "extra little things in life"—in other words, he puts the frosting on the otherwise plain cake. One of the most important, in fact very important, traits a girl should look for in a boy is his intelligence. A girl should be able to look up to a boy and he should be interesting and stimulating enough to grow with her as time goes by. Although it is good to have a boy whose temperament complements yours, it is not too good to have one whose views are radically different from yours. Having things in common contributes much towards the mutual fun and interest of two people, and is absolutely necessary.

Being able to get along in society is a very important trait. No relationship is good if it is selfish, and since no one can live without others, the aspect of association with others is extremely important. Girls like boys who can talk intelligently as well as be good listeners. However, a boy is not popular if he wants to be the big social ring leader and "run the show." A girl likes her date to have personality, wit, and humor and good manners, and she must feel proud to be with him. It is quite important that his personality and actions reflect his relationship with his girl; thus he makes her feel a sense of happiness—not jealousy or anxiety. No girl goes for a type of boy who is always trying to meet new date "material" and makes his intentions obvious. He should try to make a good impression on the friends of the girl as well as the girl herself by being attentive, thoughtful, and considerate. A good date has enough initiative, imagination, and sense of adventure to plan amusements with his friends. Actually, most girls agree that it is not where she goes but who she is with that counts, but she still likes to go places and see things as well as take time to enjoy her friendship by taking a walk or staying at home. No one likes to be taken for granted and no one likes to get into a rut or a hum-drum routine, and so that is why dates should be of *both* types. The amount of money spent is not the important thing. Girls naturally like the boys who have the same views on morals that they do and who are individual enough to do what is right instead of tagging along with the group.

To me the highest trait a boy can have is his realization of life on a spiritual basis. A girl respects a boy who has high ideals and the courage to live by his convictions and admit that sometimes he is wrong. A God-fearing boy knows how to be humble, forgiving, and kind to others, and he knows the value of faith and hope. His life reflects his beliefs and he has a much deeper relationship and bond to offer a girl—for his love is on the spiritual, not only the physical basis.

I realize that I have put up a pretty big order and I don't expect my best friends to be this perfect. But it does not hurt to know what is liked in a person. I don't feel that we always sit down and rate a boy, but we unconsciously love or "like" a person if he fits our major requirements without always realizing what happens.[48]

CONCLUSION

This chapter has presented the developmental nature of dating experiences, showing how dating behavior patterns are determined by peer and class groups. It has indicated something of the problems and opportunities in the dating system. The problems have to do with finding an answer to the sexual dilemma of dating and with the problem of status or rating in groups or cliques. Solutions to both of these problems involve the growth of communication and understanding between the sexes. Such achievements carry on into marriage to form a positive basis for good adjustment.[49] Failure in dating is likewise reflected in marriage, and is correlated with poor adjustment.

SELF-ANALYSIS

The following outline will help the student assess his own past for the way dating behavior has prepared him or her for a happy or an unhappy marriage. Those who discover areas in their past dating experience which seem to have set up inhibitions or left them without enthusiasm for married life will probably want to discuss this with the instructor or the marriage counselor. No past event necessarily predetermines failure in marriage, but certain events may make marriage adjustment difficult; the way may often be eased by frank discussion of the problem with an expert in the field.

  I. Dating Behavior
     A. High School Experiences
        1. Discuss your problems of dating while a freshman and sophomore in high school. Were you shy? Were you lacking in confidence? Were you insecure regarding dancing, talking, or other hetero-sexual activities?
        2. Discuss your problems of dating while a junior and senior in high school. Did you have enough dates? Had you at this time solved the problems mentioned above? Did you go steady?

[48] From a case study in the author's files.
[49] Robert F. Winch, *The Modern Family* (New York: Henry Holt and Company, 1952), p. 437. Copyright Holt, Rinehart and Winston, Inc.

Were you infatuated with one or more individuals? What did you learn in these experiences?

B. College Experiences
   1. Discuss your college experiences. In what ways do these experiences differ from those in high school?
   2. What pressures do you feel from your group, clique, or house in dating? What pressures are there to go steady? To be pinned? To be engaged?

C. Your Dating Problems
   1. Have you ever or have you often become so involved emotionally that sexual tension was a problem? What permanent results did your behavior leave with you that might influence your marriage?
   2. Do you feel that you have definite inhibitions or guilt feelings that were the result of that behavior? Have you discussed it with anyone?
   3. Do you feel that you have definite hostility feelings to the opposite sex which might have grown out of dating conflicts? How?

II. Values for Dating
   A. What values do you have with respect to:
      1. Necking
      2. Petting
      3. Petting to climax
      4. Premarital coitus
   B. Are you able to discuss these norms of conduct with another with whom you found a problem developing? Why? What resulted?

III. Goals for Dating
   A. What particular contribution do you expect from dating? Analyze yourself in terms of your ability to:
      1. Feel secure and confident when with a member of the opposite sex.
      2. Carry on an intelligent and animated conversation.
      3. Understand the other sex.
   B. Analyze the types of personality represented by those you have dated. Have you had contact with many different types? What type seems to be most stimulating to you? Do you need to date other types for further exploration?
   C. What is your pattern of dating? Do you always dance? Do you always go to a movie? Is dating contributing to your skills, culture and interests?

D. What are your norms? Do they satisfy your usual dating partner? What help do you need in sustaining your norms?

VISUAL AIDS

Wrong Way Out, Teaching Films Custodian, 25 West 43rd Street, New York 18, New York.

Youth in Crisis, Association Films, Y.M.C.A. Motion Picture Bureau, 347 Madison Avenue, New York 17, New York.

SPECIAL PROJECTS

1. Let every member of the class write a brief but complete summary of his or her standards for dating.
2. Appoint a committee to determine whether or not the "rating and dating complex" is a true picture of your campus. Who describes your campus norms most accurately, Blood or Waller?

READINGS

BURGESS, ERNEST W. and PAUL WALLIN. *Engagement and Marriage.* Philadelphia, J. B. Lippincott Company, 1953, Chapter 3.

CAVAN, RUTH SHONLE. *The American Family.* 2nd ed. New York, Thomas Y. Crowell Company, 1953, Chapter 12.

EHRMANN, WINSTON. *Premarital Dating Behavior.* New York, Henry Holt and Company, 1959. Copyright Holt, Rinehart and Winston, Inc.

KIRKENDALL, LESTER. *Premarital Intercourse and Interpersonal Relationships.* New York, The Julian Press, Inc., 1961.

LANDIS, JUDSON T. and MARY LANDIS. *Building a Successful Marriage.* New York, Prentice-Hall, Inc., 1948, Chapters 4 and 6.

TRUXAL, ANDREW G. and FRANCIS E. MERRILL. *Marriage and the Family in American Culture.* New York, Prentice-Hall, Inc., 1953, Chapter 8.

RECORDING

Sex Ethics and Behavior, Walter Stokes and David Mace, National Council on Family Relations, 1219 University Avenue, SE, Minneapolis, Minnesota.

PART THREE | FACTORS

IN MATE

SELECTION

Introduction

THERE is little to distinguish the courtship process from dating in our society. The majority of college women admit that for them college dating is courtship, if courtship be defined as activity directed toward the goal of marriage. It is true that there is a subtle difference between such purposive activity and dating with no other goal than that of having a good time. However, the dynamics of infatuation and sexual attraction are such that dating often turns out to be more goal-directed than is supposed, and couples who start off with a very casual relationship are surprised at the extent to which they rather soon find themselves emotionally interdependent. Likewise, the mores associated with going steady complicate the distinction between dating and courtship. Going steady, as we have seen, involves considerably more intimacy than casual dating. The goal of going steady might only have been adopted for the sake of convenience, but the emotional commitments associated with this relationship often lead to a courtship pattern. There is no way to mark decisively the step from dating to courtship, other than to say that courtship begins when one consciously begins to think of the partner as a possible life mate, and to order one's emotional relationships with this in mind. In Part III we study the decisive factors in a wise marriage choice.

CHAPTER 8

The Social Process of Mate Selection[*]

COURTSHIP is a process of interaction between a man and a woman. As the struggle for social status and personal prestige influences dating choice, it must inevitably also make an impact on mate choice. Both men and women in their early adult life are sensitive to the standards of approval of their classmates, their friends and their parents. They calculate not only their prestige at the moment but the likely status a possible mate may bring them after marriage. Thus, young women when asked about the qualifications for a mate inevitably list "ambition" as an indefinable attribute. But far more dynamic is the tenuous hold they feel they have on any one individual who has expressed a cautious interest in them.

Because their most basic feelings of self-esteem are involved in the judgment of others in relation to their mate choice and in relation to their ability to hold a lover, young people play a subtle ego-protecting game. Each of the partners endeavors to involve the other before giving an indication of his own interest. For if one should become more involved than the other, the other is in full command. So modern courtship involves masking true feelings and feints and ploys which keep young people defensive and insecure. If they are insecure because of these social and personal pressures, all of the other types of extraneous and

[*] This chapter was written with Henry J. Wegrocki, M.D., Ph.D., Associate Professor of Psychiatry, University of Southern California Medical School.

181

insidious forces that we have already described in discussing romantic idealization and the confusion of passion for love complicates the courtship process. Add to these difficulties the conflicting male and female standards of sexual permissiveness as well as different norms between those who believe in the double, the conservative single and the liberal single standard, and it is understandable that this courtship process is complex indeed. It is to their credit that so many young people have enough maturity to think clearly enough to make good choices.

MATURE MOTIVATION FOR MARRIAGE

In fact, where motivation for marriage and life is mature, none of these pressures is great enough to negate a basic evaluation of the goodness of another as a possible mate. For mature young people are not so insecure that they bow completely to the social pressures of others; nor do they need to escape in romantic idealization or succumb impulsively to physical or erotic drives. They learned long ago to postpone some satisfactions in order to earn greater rewards later. So they enjoy courtship, but they do not play games with the affections of others, nor do they panic at the thought of being single for another year. Secure in their own sense of worth, they can afford to wait for someone who has an equal degree of self-esteem. When they think they have found that person, they gladly share and give to him. In fact, such individuals think as frequently about their ability to meet the *needs of the other* as of their own desires. For they know that a half century of living with another person can be trying indeed if they do not feel profound satisfaction in making the other person happy.

In a sense then the great task of young people is to grow up so that they are stable enough to resist social, sexual, and romantic traps. It takes time to grow into that kind of maturity, so one safe caution is to avoid the more profound entanglements during teen years, when few individuals have achieved such emotional stature that they can keep perspective. It is helpful to zealously avoid the destructive games of courtship bargaining and exploitation, trusting that a worthy person will esteem honesty and sincerity in personal relationships. There is a great deal of trauma and resentment in modern courtship, and much of it comes from the artificial and insincere competition that characterizes present relationships. The mature individual can afford to be honest.

PSYCHOLOGICAL FACTORS IN WISE MARRIAGE CHOICE

Many individuals try to be honest, but their exaggerated emotional needs force them to act in ways that will guarantee an inadequate marital choice. Some motivations are neurotic, and we should be able to recognize these in ourselves or in others in order to avoid their consequences. If the choice of a partner is made on an unrealistic, accidental, or neurotic basis, marriage maladjustment is likely. Explorations of these areas must be made with a full realization that many roots of our personality patterns are buried in the unconscious, and some psychological digging is necessary to uncover all of a personality structure. Much that we offer by way of an explanation of our marriage choice is a rationalization simply because we do not know or we do not wish to look at our real motivation for marriage.

Thus a young woman who, from childhood on, had been dominated by a father who was a martinet, married a quiet and unassuming young man whose gentle nature was exactly the opposite of her surly father. But she was a submissive person herself because she had never been able to exhibit any initiative in her own home. She had only known a man who could and did handle all affairs at home and in the community. She soon found that while her new husband was kind, she could not respond to him emotionally or sexually. Her resentment of her father motivated her to marry his counter-image, but her past with her father made that man inadequate. But what did she say when she married this man? Did she recognize any of the above analysis? She did not. She said:

> Bill and I are almost perfectly mated. We've gone together for two years and never had an argument. The longer we know each other, the better we like each other. We have many common interests and as we have the same religion and education I don't think we could have found more ideal partners.

The young man, on the contrary, had had a weak man for a father and a mother who directed the life of the family. He resented his father for his weakness, but all his life he gave in to his mother. So he had to find a mate who was even weaker than he was. This he did, but when she constantly pleaded for help at home and with the children, he became uncomfortable because he had chosen a wife who needed more help than he could give. He did not recognize his true motivation any more adequately than did his wife. What these two did not realize was that they did not marry because of what the other mate promised them but rather to escape further humiliation from persons like their parents.

EGOCENTRIC MOTIVATION FOR MARRIAGE

Some individuals never grow up. They spend their lifetime as children thinking about and demanding things only for themselves. Because they may be well integrated around their own selfish goals, we do not call them neurotic; they can best be described as *egocentric* individuals.

It is surprising how an egocentric person can fool himself about the real meaning of his motivation. Years ago the wife of a busy political leader came for counseling. Her husband was literally never home, never with their children, and seldom with her. He was desperate for the status political success could bring to him, but he did not recognize this. Rather he spoke about his service to the people of his city, his many kind and helpful deeds for his constituents, his honesty and fairness as a public servant, and how much greater his contribution would be if he only earned more responsible positions. When he was asked about what "kind and helpful deeds" he had done for his children and wife, he dismissed this as unimportant. They should understand that he had to give all his life to others. For children needing a father figure and a wife needing at least some companionship, this rationalization was meaningless. It was difficult for this man—and it is difficult for each of us—to honestly face his own basic egocentricity. But when we do, we begin to be capable of real love and real growth.

MOTIVATION TO MARRY AS NEUROTIC ESCAPE

The neurotic factors which may color motivation for marriage may be anchored at varying depths of personality. Some of these factors have to do with the need for escape from unpleasant or domineering home situations.

A young, intelligent couple came to my office because of severe conflicts. They had torn the telephone from the wall, broken most of their dishes, and thrown large and small alarm clocks at each other. Investigation showed that they had married at seventeen and eighteen; had quickly borne three children and now at twenty-one and twenty-two were thoroughly dissatisfied with their children, their home, and each

184

other. Further probing revealed that they had married to escape intolerable home situations. The girl's parents were very religious. They felt modern dating was evil, lipstick was sinful, and the boy friend a personal emissary from Satan himself. The boy's parents took all the money he earned, denied him the use of the family car, and in general treated him as a ten-year-old. They had married to escape restrictions, but they found that marriage involves its own limitations, particularly where there are three small children. Each blamed the other very bitterly for their predicament. Actually the choice of a particular mate did not enter into the marital decision in any great degree. They both wanted to get away from home, and a marriage was one way to accomplish this goal. Other young people tire of academic or social competition and find marriage a socially acceptable escape. But marriage is never a haven or a refuge; for it has its own challenging tasks and responsibilities.

THE IDEAL IMAGE AND WISE MARRIAGE CHOICE

In the choice of a particular marriage partner, whatever neurotic tendencies an individual has are likely to express themselves. To a certain extent every individual carries within his mind an unconscious, or at least unverbalized, blueprint of the type of individual he would like to marry. This blueprint might have lines which are so deeply drawn in the unconscious that they are not modified by experience or time. On the other hand, the blueprint may vary with the time, circumstances, and stage of an individual's development. Thus a brilliant but insecure girl college student became depressed when her fiancé, a prominent athlete, broke his engagement with her to marry an outstanding girl on the campus. Her association with him had represented to her the achievement of a status that she did not feel within herself. A few years later, when her standard of values had changed, she made a satisfactory marriage with a man whom she had likewise known during her college days, but who had not appealed to her then because of his lack of status on the campus.

The broad range of cultural expectancies, such as age, race, religion, social level, physical appearance, size, and similar elements which also play a role in setting limits on the choice of a partner, will be considered in the next chapter. These elements, however, may be colored by neurotic factors. A New England spinster, for example, deprived herself of more than one opportunity for what might have been a satisfactory marriage, by reason of her particular social standards. These were emotionally exaggerated as a consequence of her deep sense of insecurity about her own personal value. Another lady from New England, on the other hand, made a point of marrying a man from a racial minority group, partly as an act of defiance against her very rigid, socially conscious parents, and partly because she felt identified with an individual who was discriminated against. She had been an only, but unwanted, child, and all her life had felt keenly a sense of parental rejection. Her marriage did not turn out satisfactorily because her husband had many neurotic tendencies and unconsciously resented the fact that she had married him out of sympathy. Paradoxically, his marriage to her, instead of increasing his own self-esteem, had merely lowered her status in his eyes. At the time of their marriage, the husband was a symbol of persecution and rejection to his wife—the unconscious image of her own inner rejected self.

This tendency to choose a partner who is, in a sense, a reflection of one's unconscious image of one's self is rather common. The ideal image in this case is the basic personality pattern of the self. In another instance, a brilliant but only moderately attractive young lady was married almost immediately after she was graduated from college to a man who was intellectually and socially her inferior. Obsessed with the idea that she was homely and undesirable so far as men were concerned, she became panicky at the idea of remaining unmarried. Because of her acute self-depreciation, she could not picture herself as being acceptable to anyone who was superior to her socially or intellectually. Shortly after her marriage, the gross disharmony between herself and her husband became apparent in a variety of difficulties. Such a case serves to illustrate the point made previously of the importance of establishing our sense of self-esteem before we venture into the marriage market.

THE PARENTAL IMAGE IN MARRIAGE CHOICE

The psychoanalysts have indicated that a mother or a father very frequently functions as the basic image for the blueprint of a future mate. Since parents play such an integral role in the personal development of an individual, it is not surprising that this should be so. An attractive, twenty-year-old mother was referred as a patient to a psychiatrist after the birth of her first baby because she developed a very severe depression with crying spells and a feeling of revulsion against her child. Psychiatric exploration revealed that she was an only child; she had been overprotected by her parents, and she had idolized her father. She had married, at eighteen, a man more than twenty years her senior and, like her father, a very successful business man. Until her pregnancy, the marriage was superficially successful, largely because her husband functioned so well as the friendly and considerate father-image. In her marriage she was thus still the little girl living with her father. This factor did not become apparent during her pregnancy, because the social circumstances of cultural expectancy contributed to give her a feeling that having a child was something particularly wonderful. She was much amazed at her emotional reaction at the birth of her son. A dream, which she had soon afterwards, illumined as well as anything could the basic anxiety factor involved in giving up the dependent little-girl role. She dreamed that she was holding her son in her arms and that suddenly he began to increase in size while she began to decrease in height. Within a few seconds her child was standing, holding *her* in *his* arms. This patient unconsciously wanted to continue to be the child, to prolong indefinitely the dependency relationship that she had with her father and the father-image.

In view of the extensive popular psychological literature about dependency, it might be well to point out that dependency is a normal need and that it is not, in itself, neurotic. Marriage provides an opportunity for an individual to satisfy legitimately his normal dependency needs. This issue was highlighted by the very intelligent mother of a young man who was having marital difficulties. John had always been very deeply attached to his mother and was very affectionate and demonstrative with her. The mother was a mature, well-balanced, extremely successful professional woman. She had been widowed early in life and for this reason had been driven all the closer to her son. Because of the son's attachment to his mother, he was called a "sissy" by his childhood friends. During adolescence, John attempted to compensate for his fear of femininity by particularly vigorous athletic activity. Throughout adolescence, however, his dependency upon his mother continued, although at a very subtle level. The son did not realize how very restrained he was in his emotional expression toward his wife because he had brought into marriage some of his earlier complexes about being considered masculine. With the intelligent help and cooperation of his mother, John was made aware of the factors responsible for his dependency upon her as well as with his inability to play a dependent role in relationship to his wife. There was a marked improvement in his marriage when he was able to allow his normal dependency needs to be satisfied by his wife rather than to interpret them as signs of a lack of masculinity on his part.

A *counter-image* can also exist. In such cases the individual looks precisely for the person who is entirely unlike the mother or the father. A young woman who believed herself to be rejected and unloved by her very rigid and puritanical minister-father married an emotionally expressive Latin—whose extreme possessiveness and jealousy became almost as intolerable as her father's unloving behavior.

THE MADONNA-PROSTITUTE PATTERN

The madonna-prostitute pattern is frequently seen in the blueprints of men. Women are frequently judged in terms of marriage material on the basis of their sexual accessibility. A middle-aged man fell deeply in love with a woman who refused his sexual advances despite the fact that she showed some response to his feeling for her. This refusal, along with her disapproval of his tendency to vulgarity and cursing, and her devotion to church and social work activities, corresponded with his picture of the ideal woman whom he had been seeking. They were married. Then, as so often happens in such cases, at the onset of sexual relations her image changed in his eyes because she reacted so intensely during sexual intercourse. Her reaction led him unconsciously to depreciate her, and he returned to his verbal habits of vulgarity and cursing which had been his lifelong pattern. This behavior produced so much stress and incompatibility that a separation resulted. A few months later, having realized how unreal his expectations had been, he wished to resume relations with his wife. She refused to return to him, whereupon he plunged into a depression and again over-idealized her.

The cases that have been presented show that the blueprint of a potential marriage partner, which an individual carries with him, includes many elements which are conscious and many which are unconscious. The unconscious elements, surprisingly enough, are often relatively obvious to the friends of the particular individual. The fact, for instance, that a girl has chosen to marry a father substitute is clear to her friends, yet quite unknown to her. In other instances a couple seems ideally matched, yet in the marital relationship unconscious factors emerge which indicate that the choice of a particular partner was neurotically determined. The question rises of what can be done to prevent a neurotic choice of a partner. There is no easy solution. Some of the unconscious elements

188

can be brought to light through interviews in premarital counseling. Hence, premarital counseling is extremely valuable. Specific ways of dealing with such problems in premarital counseling will be discussed later.

TEMPERAMENTAL FACTORS IN WISE MARRIAGE CHOICE

The factors responsible for an individual's motivation in getting married and for his choice of a particular partner are bound up with the total personality structure. We have indicated how two individuals entering into the continuous interpersonal relationship of marriage bring into it the psychological baggage of all their conscious and unconscious conditioning experiences since infancy. We must now discuss certain predominant temperamental inclinations and their meaning for wise marriage choice. These inclinations are often so interwoven into the fabric of an individual's personality that they cannot be readily separated. In some instances, however, temperamental factors play such an outstanding role that they may be considered in isolation for purposes of analysis.

INTROVERSION AND EXTROVERSION

Wide temperamental difference in introversion and extroversion, like all biologically derived personality differences, make for a very poor marital adjustment, unless they are compensated for by mutuality in many other areas. Minor differences, on the other hand, seem to act in a stimulating manner, such differences being complementary rather than conflictual. The introvert is pushed to play a role for which he is temperamentally unsuited and which causes him distress and a sense of tension, while the extrovert feels inhibited and chained in having to control his spontaneous, outgoing impulses. Thus, an introvert husband in his early thirties was able to have a happy marital life as long as he lived in close proximity to his parents and friends in whose company his wife could find a continuous satisfaction of her extrovert needs. When the husband's job required a transfer to California, and he was alone with his wife and child, many difficulties arose because the new pattern of life was not adequate for his wife. Her desire for external social life met with opposition on his part. The husband was angry at her disloyalty in preferring the company of others to his.

189

A middle-aged couple had made a relatively good adjustment while their two daughters were at home; later, when the daughters married and left town, the couple found themselves in conflict. Because of the husband's introvertive habits, the wife had actually lived through her daughters and found that adjusting to her husband's pattern was practically impossible because of her strong gregarious and social needs.

It is difficult to imagine how opposite are the attitudes of the extrovert and introvert. Waller discusses these differences in terms of fantasies:

> There are great differences in personalities in regard to types of fantasy and the importance of fantasy in the individual's life. In the so-called introverted personality, fantasy has great importance and is likely to be both clear-cut and unified. The extroverted person is likely to deny that he indulges in any fantasy at all, and certainly he sees little value in it. Boredom arises in the introvert from that which interrupts the flow of fantasy. The introvert is never bored when he is alone, but rather when the outer reality fractures the inner reality. The extrovert is bored and ill at ease when he has nothing outside himself to attend to.[1]

Temperamental difference presents a difficult problem for wise marriage choice. Some differences are stimulating and cohesive, but wide differences produce conflict. The problem is aggravated because during courtship basic temperamental moods are apt to be modified in the interest of pleasing the loved one. Romantic idealization often makes it difficult to sense these basic differences.

AGGRESSIVENESS AND PASSIVITY

Although they are associated with temperamental factors, the patterns of aggressiveness and passivity are far more colored by experiential elements. If aggressiveness is characteristic of the male partner, then the possibility of a good adjustment is present because of the cultural expectancy that the male will be the aggressive leader in the family. Modifications of this generalization will be considered in the next chapter. When the situation is reversed and the wife leads, there is much possibility for psychological mischief. For example, a young married couple in their twenties had a sizable problem. Despite having two children,

---

[1] Willard Waller and Reuben Hill, *The Family: A Dynamic Interpretation,* rev. ed. (New York: Dryden Press, 1951), pp. 63–64. Copyright © 1951, Holt, Rinehart and Winston, Inc. Reprinted by permission of the publisher.

the wife was extremely active in social and church work and was constantly serving as president or chairman of various organizations. This popularity provoked much joshing of the husband by his friends and was a source of constant marital disharmony since the wife's activity was interpreted by the husband as a reflection on his male leadership role.

DOMINANCE AND COMPLIANCE

In exploring particular personality backgrounds of aggressive and passive persons, one usually finds that the individual has played a consistently passive or aggressive role since infancy. Problems relevant to dominance and compliance, on the other hand, may be referred to experiential factors which provoke these specific kinds of integration. The cultural factor of expecting the male to play the dominant role complicates the dominance-compliance relationship. The brilliant woman, who is aware of her intellectual superiority over her husband in matters of judgment, will find herself in a difficult situation if she has to permit the husband to make important decisions. Many women believe it to be psychologically wise for a bright woman to "play down" her intelligence and to give her husband a feeling of superiority, but this sometimes is done at a great cost if there are no adequate compensations. In a truly harmonious marriage the problem of dominance and compliance is no problem because it is resolved by a mature distribution of responsibility, with each partner acceding to the other.

In some marriages the struggle for dominance finds resolution only in an armed truce. This type of neurotic competitiveness occurs more frequently in those instances in which the wife is incapable of playing any other than a dominant role. The popular or beautiful girl, for example, finds it difficult to adjust herself to a situation in which she is no longer receiving constant assurances of the really great value others put upon her. In one instance a very active and successful girl, a leader of the university campus, married an equally successful male leader and found it impossible to relinquish her dominant role. Unconsciously her revolt against what she conceived to be unwarranted male dominance reflected itself in sexual frigidity as a protest against her husband. This was extremely puzzling to her because of the fact that she had been able to achieve a high pitch of sexual excitement in situations associated with necking and petting. In exploring the background factors responsible for her marital maladjustment, it became obvious that her initial motiva-

191

tion for marriage was very egocentric and that she had chosen as a marriage partner a man who might be expected to enhance her personal prestige. When the wedding took place, it was considered an ideal marriage. Very soon after the honeymoon, her unconscious rivalry with males became overt—as a struggle with her husband over the question of dominance and compliance.

SADISM AND MASOCHISM

The pattern of dominance and compliance sometimes reaches profound neurotic depths when it expresses itself as sadism and masochism —as either a strong, inner, compulsive need to gain satisfaction by completely dominating and humiliating the other partner or, on the other hand, by inducing situations in which one will allow one's self to be dominated or humiliated. Psychological exploration often reveals that individuals with tales of prolonged suffering in a marital relationship have a subtle, unconscious, neurotic need for suffering.

DEPENDENCY AND INDEPENDENCE

The polarities of aggressiveness and passivity, dominance and compliance, are related to still another polarity, that of dependency and independence. Although the compliant individual is apt to be also a dependent one, this does not mean that the aggressive or dominant person is independent. Because dependency has been so much associated with neuroticism, there has been a tendency to regard its opposite, independence, as having the highest value. Actually, however, independence as well as dependency can reach neurotic proportions. The well-integrated, flexible individual is one who is capable of satisfying, in appropriate situations, his independence as well as his dependent needs. One thirty-year-old bachelor experienced severe anxiety-panic reactions in contemplating his engagement. The unconscious determinants of this anxiety during courtship had to do with his very strong dependency upon his parents and especially upon his mother. The assumption of a new role as a person upon whom someone else could lean was an unconscious threat to him involving the loss of a protective mother figure.

Another bachelor of similar age, although highly desirous of getting married, had a great deal of difficulty in achieving any close interpersonal relationship with women because he consistently played an "I don't care" role toward them, and, consequently, never gave them a chance to get close to him. In his particular case several experiences of rejection within his family and during adolescence had caused him to build a strong protective armor about himself. He protected his self-esteem by not allowing himself to become involved emotionally, despite the fact that deep within himself he felt the need for it. In courtship this type of person is often most attractive to the other sex because he seems to be hard to marry. Yet this aloofness is really an indication of a neurotic defense. No matter how attractive this type of personality configuration may appear to be, such an individual is a poor risk in marriage.

Of all the personality integrations which are productive of marital difficulty, dependency of a neurotic type is undoubtedly the most troublesome. Neurotic dependency patterns date back to early life and are associated with one of two extremes: the extreme of overprotection or the extreme of rejection. Overprotection is a subtle factor which may manifest itself as merely overconcern on the part of parents, especially the mother, creating an unhealthy atmosphere in which the individual unconsciously leans on the parents. Rejection, too, can occur in not too apparent ways. A mother in describing her daughter said, "We have given her everything all her life," without realizing that she had given the daughter no affectionate display or basic emotional acceptance. The daughter, a very attractive looking girl, unconsciously played the role of the striving "popular" girl during her adolescence and in her twenties in order to gain the approval of others and bind them to her. When she married at twenty-five, her pattern did not change, in fact it expanded. The husband, a very busy business man, was content to allow her to play this role since she was an excellent housekeeper and hostess. When she had reached her middle thirties, however, she began to experience a sense of emptiness in her pattern of living, realizing that her "social success" was rather hollow compensation for an inner feeling of sterility. Symptoms began to appear in the form of intense resentment toward her husband, as well as depressive episodes, which basically represented aggression turned toward herself. The case study revealed that her parents had never allowed her to develop any feeling of dependency upon them. She compensated by trying to bind others to her but found that they did not reciprocate when she wanted to lean on them. Some degree of symptomatic improvement was achieved when her husband began to play a more dominant role and allowed her to satisfy her dependency needs.

Farber has made a significant analysis of dependence by defining two modes of the dependency-independency relationship.[2] He identifies behavioral dependence as the material services which members of the family perform for one another: the wife as a homemaker and the husband as a provider. Emotional dependence involves the reliance upon the mate for much reassurance, approval, and security. Obviously, the outcome of marriage will differ for these differing types and degrees of dependency. Marriage at its best involves an interdependency in roles and in emotional response.

HOSTILITY AND WISE MARRIAGE CHOICE

In addition to prolonged or neurotic dependency, the emotionally immature individual may manifest immaturity in other ways which may be observed during courtship. The emotionally insecure individual who, consciously or unconsciously, depreciates himself is in a very vulnerable situation in a marital relationship because the intimacy of the relationship exposes his shaky security to threats. Under circumstances like this, such attitudes as suspiciousness, possessiveness, jealousy, and general defensiveness may develop. These are all reflections of the individual's own personal sense of inadequacy. A possessive, jealous, individual is practically saying to the world, "I think so little of myself that I resent it when, in any way, you show that you likewise think little of me." Some individuals who are flattered by the jealousy of their companions during courtship or engagement might better analyze the basic psychological determinants of this behavior. A young woman who gained the approval of numerous friends by extending herself showed how much she was motivated by a feeling of her own self-depreciation when, after marrying a very popular young man, she continued to flirt with other men. She was then trying to prove her attractiveness to herself. The same girl responded with jealousy and hysteria to any gestures of friendliness that her husband made toward other attractive women.

Such individuals are critical of everyone else, but anything remotely critical of their own behavior is regarded as extremely offensive. This type of reaction indicates the individual's neurotic need for reassurance and emotional security. Besides suspiciousness, jealousy, possessiveness, and defensiveness, hostility may also appear in other forms. One form of

[2] See the unpubl. dissertation (University of Chicago Libraries, 1949) by Bernard Farber, "A Study of Dependence and Decision-Making in Marriage."

hostility is that of nagging, or chronic irritability and dissatisfaction with the other partner. When this hostility, instead of being turned outward is for various reasons turned inward, it may take the form of moodiness and sulking. This type of hostility reaction can occur wherever frustration is involved; that is, in any situation where an individual is either prevented from satisfying a need or a drive or where he is forced to do something or behave in a way in which he has no spontaneous desire to do.

Marriage as a relation in which two people attempt to adjust to one another and to satisfy one another's needs is replete with situations involving potential frustrations. It is a mark of emotional maturity if the marital partners can tolerate and handle the frustrations they experience. In those instances in which the frustrated needs are neurotically colored, the possibility of having a frustrating situation is, of course, tremendously increased and the problem can rarely be resolved.

PERFECTIONISM AND WISE MARRIAGE CHOICE

An instance in point is the character integration known as perfectionism. A patient in her late twenties was referred by her lawyer for psychiatric examination because he believed that the marital problem between her and her husband was psychological and might be resolved. The husband in the case was a business man whose income had rather quickly changed from approximately $5,000 a year to around $75,000. His new status required him to entertain important clients. He did his entertaining for the most part in a hotel until he acquired a splendid new home. He then wanted his wife to entertain and be his hostess. Many dinner parties were planned, but practically all were cancelled because on the very last day the wife would insist that she simply couldn't get everything ready, that some small thing wasn't exactly perfect, that she couldn't quite decide what they should have, etc. Her behavior provoked intense resentment on the part of her husband and a great deal of alienation in their relationship. Finally he decided to consult a lawyer about a divorce. Inquiry into the wife's background revealed that, as a young girl, she had had a tendency to be quite fat. Because of her poor grooming she had been constantly called "sloppy Joe," and told that when she grew up no man could possibly be interested in her. When she reached adolescence, she overcompensated; she went on a rigid diet until she had slimmed down; she was extremely overcareful about herself in every

195

way and attempted so to dress and carry herself that no one would, in any sense, be justified in calling her "sloppy." With marriage and two children this pattern continued, but it caused no difficulty because no challenge was offered to her sense of security. When, however, her husband had provided the family with a large home and she was exposed to individuals toward whom she felt inadequate, her perfectionistic, neurotic trends came to the surface. Having gained an awareness of the roots of her perfectionistic orientation, she was able to modify it and to meet the social obligations of her husband's position.

This type of obsessive perfectionism is a mode of reaction to the inner anxiety associated with unconscious threats to the personality. Anxiety itself, in the emotionally immature individual, can assume the status of an obsessive, compulsive state. Hence, the "worry warts" who are nervously over-alerted as if every move and every day represented a possible threat to their security. One young wife suffered constant agonies because her husband, a real estate speculator, was so free about the manner in which he bought and sold property. For herself this freedom represented a chronic threat to security, and she thought that he did not love her because he refused to change his occupation. Equally immature, of course, can be the opposite of overanxiety, the characteristic of irresponsibility or at least the failure to assume responsibility implicit in the marital relationship. This difficulty sometimes takes place when both the husband and the wife work. The adjustment of one couple changed markedly soon after the wife became pregnant, since the husband then became the sole support of the family and resented the fact that now he had to assume responsibilities he found too burdensome.

The lack of a truly mature love relationship often underlies the emergence of the above symptoms of anxiety or perfectionism. The inability to forego selfishness and to achieve a truly mature love relationship, in which concern for and consideration of the other person are the important things, lies at the root of much marital disharmony. Many patients defend themselves stoutly against any implication that they aren't really showing much love for their partners. One such young man of twenty-four, whose wife was reacting nervously because he insisted on carrying on his bachelor mode of life with its freedom of movement and secretiveness, responded by saying, "Gosh, Doc, I don't see how you can say I don't love my wife. Why, when I was married just over a year ago, I couldn't sleep or eat well for two months before we were married. Naturally after a while we sort of got used to one another and I wanted to get together with my old gang again. I don't see why she should want to deprive me of my freedom entirely." The confusion of this young man is the confusion of the many who have married while in a disturbed emotional state. There is a distinct difference between the almost acute, obsessional anxiety which characterizes romantic love and the attitudes attendant upon a love which is directed primarily toward satisfying the needs and increasing the happiness of one's mate. When this primary orientation is not present, there is fertile soil for the development of multiple marital difficulties.

PSYCHOLOGICAL CHARACTERISTICS OF HAPPY AND UNHAPPY HUSBANDS AND WIVES

Many of the cases and much of the description relating to different temperamental and psychological postures in this chapter have inevitably been exaggerated as we have tried to describe them clearly. We do not want to give the impression that most young people exhibit these tendencies in the extreme. The normal college student exhibits some hostility, some perfectionism, some anxiety and some introversion or extroversion, but most do not possess these in the degree that would threaten a marriage. However, to be aware of personality tendencies permits more intelligent adaptation in any relationship. The goal of presenting this material is not to frighten the student, but help him be aware of the complexity of personality patterns. In this section of the chapter we present summaries of personality profiles that describe both normal and neurotic husbands and wives. Most students will find that they more or less are described by the characteristics of happy husbands and wives. If, however, they do find that they have some negative tendencies, then they should attend to the task of growing more mature.

Lewis M. Terman is noted for his study of psychological factors in marital adjustment. While these traits, to be described, existed in marriage (and were not observed before marriage), it is reasonable to assume that such deeply set behavior patterns as are indicated in his summary must have been present at the time of marriage. As we have pointed out, neurotic tendencies may be brought out or accentuated by marriage, but they are generally present by the time of courtship. Terman's summary of psychological factors in marriage may be used during courtship to insure wise marriage choice. Terman studied 792 couples. We present the material first for women and then for men.

Happily married women, as a group, are characterized by kindly attitudes toward others and by the expectations of kindly attitudes in return. They do not easily take offense and are not unduly concerned about the impressions they make upon others. They do not look upon social relationships as rivalry situations. They are cooperative, do not object to subordinate roles, and are not annoyed by advice from others. Missionary and ministering attitudes are frequently evidenced in their responses. They enjoy activities that bring educational or pleasurable opportunities to others and like to do things for the dependent and underprivileged. They are methodical and painstaking in their work, attentive to details, and careful in regard to money. In religion, morals, and politics they tend to be conservative and conventional. Their expressed attitudes imply a quiet self-assurance and a decidedly optimistic outlook on life.

Unhappily married women, on the other hand, are characterized by emotional tenseness and by ups and downs of moods. They give evidence of deep-seated inferiority feelings to which they react by aggressive attitudes rather than timidity. They are inclined to be irritable and dictatorial. Compensatory mechanisms resulting in restive striving are common. These are seen in the tendency of the unhappy wives to be active "joiners," aggressive in business, and overanxious in social life. They strive for wide circles of acquaintances but are more concerned with being important than with being liked. They are egocentric and little interested in benevolent or welfare activities, except in so far as these offer opportunities for personal recognition. They also like activities which are fraught with opportunities for romance. They are more inclined to be conciliatory in their attitudes toward men than toward women and show little of the sex antagonism that unhappily married men exhibit. They are impatient and fitful workers, dislike cautious or methodical and painstaking effort. In politics, religion, and social ethics they are more often radical than happily married women.[3]

The men, happy and unhappy, showed some of the same characteristics as the women, but there is sufficient difference to justify presenting Terman's findings.

Happily married men show evidence of an even and stable emotional tone. Their most characteristic reaction to others is that of cooperation. This is reflected in their attitudes toward business superiors, with whom they work well; in their attitude toward women, which reflects equalitarian ideals; and in their benevolent attitudes toward inferiors and underprivileged. In a gathering of people they tend to be unself-conscious and somewhat extroverted. As compared with unhappy husbands, they show supe-

[3] Lewis M. Terman, *Psychological Factors in Marital Happiness* (New York: McGraw-Hill Book Company, Inc., 1938), pp. 145–146. Reprinted by permission of the publisher.

rior initiative, a greater tendency to take responsibility, and greater willingness to give close attention to detail in their daily work. They like methodical procedures and methodical people. In money matters they are saving and cautious. Conservative attitudes are strongly characteristic of them. They usually have a favorable attitude toward religion and strongly uphold the sex mores and other social conventions.

Unhappy husbands, on the other hand, are inclined to be moody and somewhat neurotic. They are prone to feelings of social inferiority, dislike being conspicuous in public, and are highly reactive to social opinion. This sense of social insecurity is often compensated by domineering attitudes in relationships where they feel superior. They take pleasure in the commanding roles over business dependents and women, but they withdraw from a situation which would require them to play an inferior role or to compete with superiors. They often compensate this withdrawal by daydreams and power fantasies. More often than happy husbands, they are sporadic and irregular in their habits of work, dislike detail and the methodical attitude, dislike saving money, and like to wager. They more often express irreligious attitudes and are more inclined to radicalism in sex morals and politics.[4]

TABLE 17. Per Cents of Men and Women Indicating Various Needs They Wanted Satisfied in Marriage *

PERSONALITY NEED FOR SOMEONE TO:	Men	Women
Love me	36.4	53.5
Confide in	30.6	42.0
Show me affection	20.8	38.0
Respect my ideals	26.0	26.0
Appreciate my goals of achievement	28.3	24.0
Understand my moods	23.1	27.5
Help me make important decisions	15.0	32.5
Stimulate my ambition	26.6	21.0
Look up to	16.2	29.0
Give me self-confidence	19.6	24.0
Stand back of me in difficulty	16.2	25.5
Appreciate me just as I am	20.2	20.5
Admire my ability	18.5	19.5
Make me count for something	20.8	17.0
Relieve my loneliness	18.5	18.5

* Ernest W. Burgess, Harvey J. Locke, and Mary Margaret Thomes, *The Family, from Institution to Companionship,* 3rd ed. (New York: The American Book Company, 1963), p. 261. Reprinted by permission of the publisher.

[4] Terman, p. 155.

In addition to the basic polarities outlined above there are certain generalized health and psychological needs in life which must be considered in relationship to marriage. Most of these cluster around the wish for response and the wish for recognition. Marriage is important to personality fulfillment in so far as it enables each individual to complete himself through marriage. The particular way in which each individual feels such needs is unique *for himself, but he shares in the general group of wishes* which characterize almost every acculturated person. Straus in his doctoral dissertation, "A Study of Three Psychological Factors Affecting Choice of Mate," analyzes the Ideal Mate, the Parental Image, and Personality Needs. Burgess and Locke report an interesting response that Straus obtained when he asked engaged men and women to indicate various needs they felt marriage would satisfy. Analysis of the material in the preceding table indicates that for the individuals studied marriage meant basic personality fulfillment. Mate choice, then, partially involves satisfying by that choice individual personality needs.

PHYSIOLOGICAL FACTORS IN WISE MARRIAGE CHOICE

Problems in the physical aspects of wise marital choice occasionally arise as a predominant issue. These are referable to certain areas: 1, the general health of the potential partner; 2, the presence in the other person (or his/her blood relations) of disorders which might be regarded as hereditary; 3, doubts with reference to the dimensions of the sex organs.

A complete premarital physical examination and laboratory study would be a wise precaution to detect and control any disturbances in general health. A low thyroid condition or persistent anemia can be as provocative of marital maladjustment as over-protective in-laws. The number of mental, nervous, or physical disorders which are directly hereditary is extremely small. In a far greater percentage, the genetic factor operates as a *predisposition*. The relative chance of either a partner or a child inheriting the predisposition to a disorder depends on the genetic family history. Specific individual study of a person's family history is required. Recourse to competent psychologists, psychiatrists, or appropriate medical specialists would help resolve the issue. The problem of sex-organ dimensions, in their relation to a satisfactory sexual relationship or to childbirth, can most readily be handled by a gynecologist or a urologist. Sex-organ dimensions are very rarely a problem.

CONCLUSION

Wise marriage choice always involves the establishment of the emotional interdependence that results from mutuality in answering needs. Wise marriage choice therefore involves some awareness of one's own needs as well as of the needs of the beloved.

Courtship is marriage-goal-directed activity. The two basic factors involved in wise marriage choice during courtship are psychological and socio-cultural. This chapter has been concerned with a description of various types of personality configuration and needs which are the product of the psychogenic processes reviewed in the previous chapters and which determine the type of adjustment achieved in marriage. The fundamental needs of an individual, such as the need of being accepted, of feeling that one belongs, of experiencing and expressing affection in its various forms, of achieving approval and a sense of personal significance—all these are values to be incorporated into the goal of personal maturity and to be sought in a future mate. When the motivation for marriage and for courtship is egocentric or neurotic, when the choice of a partner is neurotically based, when an individual's personality integration is such that he is inhibited in achieving a true love relationship, then his or her prospects for a proper relationship diminish greatly. This chapter has attempted to mark out dynamic areas of personality functioning which are significant not only in marriage choice but in marriage itself. As such, it has meaning for personality growth of the self and the individual's awareness of the basic needs of his intended mate.

SELF-ANALYSIS

There are many inventories and projective tests to ascertain the degree of personality maturity an individual has attained.

The self-analysis proposed here is a subjective one and involves a careful judgment on the part of the student regarding the critical issues raised in the chapter. No great validity is claimed for this test. Its purpose is only to help the student become acquainted with his own needs and tendencies. You are asked to compare your own tendencies with those of an average person and then to make some interpretation regarding the meaning of those tendencies for marriage. On the following chart we assume the central point (0) is the point where most individuals fall. To the left are marks (—) which measure the degree to which you have one tendency and to the right are marks (+) which measure the degree to which you feel you have the opposite tendency in a greater degree than the average person. If necessary, refer to applicable material in other chapters in order to help you make your judgment.

Individuals can use this test to study their readiness for marriage and to reveal something of motivation for marriage choice.

I. EMOTIONAL MATURITY CHECK LIST

A. RELATIONSHIP TO FATHER

(−3)	(−2)	(−1)	0	+1	+2	+3
Great Distance	Very much Distance	Much Distance	Average Closeness	Much Closeness	Very much Closeness	Great Closeness

B. RELATIONSHIP TO MOTHER

(−3)	(−2)	(−1)	0	+1	+2	+3
Great Distance	Very much Distance	Much Distance	Average Closeness	Much Closeness	Very much Closeness	Great Closeness

C. EGOCENTRIC-OTHER-CENTERED

(−3)	(−2)	(−1)	0	+1	+2	+3
Great Concern for Others	Very much Concern for Others	Much Concern for Others	Average	Much Ego-centricity	Very much Ego-centricity	Great Ego-centricity

D. INTROVERSION-EXTROVERSION

(−3)	(−2)	(−1)	0	+1	+2	+3
Great Intro-version	Very much Intro-version	Much Intro-version	Average (Ambivert)	Much Extro-version	Very much Extro-version	Great Extro-version

E. AGGRESSIVENESS-PASSIVITY

(−3)	(−2)	(−1)	0	+1	+2	+3
Great Aggression	Very much Aggression	Much Aggression	Average	Much Passivity	Very much Passivity	Great Passivity

F. DOMINANCE-COMPLIANCE

(−3)	(−2)	(−1)	0	+1	+2	+3
Great Dominance	Very much Dominance	Much Dominance	Average	Much Compliance	Very much Compliance	Great Compliance

G. SADISM-MASOCHISM

(−3)	(−2)	(−1)	0	+1	+2	+3
Great Sadism	Very much Sadism	Much Sadism	Average	Much Masochism	Very much Masochism	Great Masochism

H. DEPENDENCY-INDEPENDENCE

(−3)	(−2)	(−1)	0	+1	+2	+3
Great Dependency	Very much Dependency	Much Dependency	Average	Much Independence	Very much Independence	Great Independence

I. HOSTILITY-FRIENDLINESS

(−3)	(−2)	(−1)	0	+1	+2	+3
Great Hostility	Very much Hostility	Much Hostility	Average	Much Friendliness	Very much Friendliness	Great Friendliness

J. GUILT-DEPRESSION

(−3)	(−2)	(−1)	0	+1	+2	+3
Great Guilt	Very much Guilt	Much Guilt	Average	Much Depressiveness	Very much Depressiveness	Great Depressiveness

K. PERFECTIONISTIC-IRRESPONSIBLE

(−3)	(−2)	(−1)	0	+1	+2	+3
Great Perfectionism	Very much Perfectionism	Much Perfectionism	Average	Much Irresponsibility	Very much Irresponsibility	Great Irresponsibility

L. TENSION-RELAXATION

(−3)	(−2)	(−1)	0	+1	+2	+3
Great Tension	Very much Tension	Much Tension	Average	Much Relaxation	Very much Relaxation	Great Relaxation

I. *EMOTIONAL MATURITY CHECK LIST* (*Continued*)

M. ANXIETY-CAREFREE

(−3)	(−2)	(−1)	0	+1	+2	+3
•	•	•	•	•	•	•
Great Anxiety	Very much Anxiety	Much Anxiety	Average	Much Carefree-ness	Very much Carefree-ness	Great Carefree-ness

N. FEARFUL-COURAGEOUS

(−3)	(−2)	(−1)	0	+1	+2	+3
•	•	•	•	•	•	•
Great Fearfulness	Very much Fearfulness	Much Fearfulness	Average	Much Coura-geousness	Very much Coura-geousness	Great Coura-geousness

O. REFLECTIVE-IMPULSIVE

(−3)	(−2)	(−1)	0	+1	+2	+3
•	•	•	•	•	•	•
Great Reflective-ness	Very much Reflective-ness	Much Reflective-ness	Average	Much Impulsivity	Very much Impulsivity	Great Impulsivity

II. Analysis
   A. To what degree do you think your closeness or lack of it to your father and mother will influence your marriage choice?
   B. What other elements go into your "blueprint" for a mate?
   C. How difficult was it to assess your egocentricity? Is this a problem?
   D. Does your degree of introversion-extroversion ever cause problems in relationships?
   E. Does your degree of aggressiveness-passivity involve relationship difficulties? How?
   F. Did you judge yourself to be a dominant or a compliant person? Why? What impact will this have on your marriage?
   G. Does your degree of sadistic-masochistic tendency ever cause problems in relationships? When?
   H. Why did you rate yourself as you did on the dependency-independence scale? What does this mean for marital choice? For marital adjustment?
   I. Give illustrations to justify your judgment about your relative hostility-friendliness rating. What basic meaning does this judgment have for your future?
   J. Did you find yourself generally a gay or a sober, depressed person? Do you feel you need to mature in this area?

K. Are you perfectionistic or irresponsible? What difficulties have this tendency caused you? Do you think your tendency here may cause difficulty in marriage?

L. Are you generally tense or relaxed? What situations cause tension? Why?

M. Where did you locate your degree of anxiety? How do you protect yourself against situations that cause anxiety? What escapes from anxiety do you have? Is this a problem?

N. Are you generally fearful or courageous? Has there been a marked change in this tendency in the last five years? Do you have specific fears about being adequate in courtship or marriage? If so, what are they?

O. Did you find that you were a reflective or an impulsive person? How well do you relate to the other type person?

P. What insight has this exercise given you for marital choice and marital adjustment?

Q. If you think you need advice, are you afraid to seek it? Why?

VISUAL AIDS

Are You Ready for Marriage?, Coronet Instructional Firms, Chicago, Illinois.

Choosing for Happiness (Bowman Series), McGraw-Hill Book Company, Inc., Text Film Dept., 330 West 42nd Street, New York 36, New York.

It Takes All Kinds (Bowman Series), McGraw-Hill Book Company, Inc., Text Film Dept., 330 West 42nd Street, New York 36, New York.

READINGS

BLOOD, ROBERT O., JR. *Anticipating Your Marriage.* New York, The Free Press of Glencoe, 1962, Chapters 1–5. Copyright The Macmillan Company.

BOWMAN, HENRY A. *Marriage for Moderns.* 4th ed., New York, McGraw-Hill Book Company, Inc., 1960, Chapter 5, "Dating and Engagement," pp. 125–149.

LANDIS, PAUL H. *Making the Most of Marriage.* New York, Appleton-Century-Crofts, 1960, Chapters 13–14.

LEMASTERS, E. E. *Modern Courtship and Marriage.* New York, The Macmillan Company, 1957, Chapters 4–8.

CHAPTER 9

Socio-Cultural Factors*

INTRODUCTION

HAPPINESS in marriage depends partly on the maturity of the individuals concerned and the way the configuration of personality of each partner meets the needs of the other in intimate communication. Adjustment in marriage also depends upon the way the attitudes, values, and roles of each match those of the mate. This chapter describes the areas of agreement which, research indicates, are related to happy adjustment as well as the areas of disagreement which are related to unhappiness. In Chapter One, some emphasis was put upon the transitional nature of contemporary family life. It was indicated there that two persons who expected different kinds of behavior from their mates would meet much conflict. Our society is very heterogeneous. Young people with dissimilar backgrounds and expectations are often in such close contact that they develop romantic attachments. The purpose of this chapter is to help young people orient themselves in terms of their sometimes unconscious role expectations and in terms of sociological insights which will enable them to choose a marriage partner wisely. It does not attempt to contribute to the adjustment of the problems indicated; that will be done in a later chapter. Here, consideration is given to patterns of

---

* This long analysis of choice of mate in these chapters may really be unnecessary! On May 9, 1962, *The New York Times* had an article entitled, "Color Test Found Clue to Marriage." The subheading read: "Psychiatrists See Pattern of Discord in How Couples Match Fabric Hues." The test involved asking each couple to agree on a match for a certain color swatch and studied their interactions in the process. So, if the test is perfected, perhaps we can simply choose mates by matching materials and switching swatches!

marital choice which would promote happiness or result in a failure to adjust.

The problem of the changing role of women as it relates to wise marital choice has several facets: the psychological tendencies of superiority, dominance, and competition discussed in the last chapter; the changing economic roles of women, which will be discussed in the next chapter; the way she and her husband define her place or her function in relation to her home, her community, and her children. This last role factor may be regarded as sociological and is considered in this chapter.

ROLE CONFLICT AND MARRIAGE CHOICE

Since the education of women in years past was so different from that of men, differences in role expectations were never a problem. (Men and women were expected to be dissimilar in educational background.) Today men and women receive essentially the same schooling from kindergarten through college, but the stereotypes which control the relationship of the sexes derive from the earlier period. Komarovsky says that, "Today the survival of some of these stereotypes is a psychological straitjacket for both sexes." [1] Two different studies show that 40 per cent of women and undergraduates are so aware of men's need to feel superior in ability that the women "play dumb" on dates, simulate ignorance about school subjects, and fail to win when they have the ability to win. [2]

The girls soon learn in the school of dating how to submerge any innate efficiency in sports or any native intellectual ability. Sixty-five per cent of the girls in one large Western school thought that to be outstanding in academic work diminished a girl's chances for dates. [3] To illustrate this problem, Komarovsky quotes a letter from a girl to her brother, the brother's answer, and the girl's reaction to his comment.

> What a wonderful evening at _____ fraternity house. You would be proud of me, Johnny! I won all the ping-pong games but one!
>
> "For heaven's sake," came the reply, "when will you grow up? Don't you know that a boy likes to think he is better than a girl? Give him a little

---

[1] Mirra Komarovsky, *Women in the Modern World* (Boston: Little, Brown and Company, 1953), p. 77. Copyright, 1953, by Mirra Heyman. This discussion closely follows Komarovsky's analysis of this problem.
[2] Mirra Komarovsky, "Cultural Contradictions and Sex Roles," *American Journal of Sociology* (November, 1946), p. 187.
[3] Komarovsky, *Women in the Modern World*, p. 82.

competition, sure, but miss a few serves in the end. Should you join the Debate Club? By all means, but don't practice too much on the boys."

The girl's reaction was as follows:

Believe me I was stunned by this letter, but then I saw that he was right. To be a success in the dorms one must date, to date one must not win too many ping-pong games. At first I resented this bitterly, but now I am more or less used to it and live in hope of one day meeting a man who is my superior so that I may be my natural self.[4]

In discussions in marriage classes, girls have reiterated this point of view over and over. They have also revealed the bitterness they feel about this contradiction. They are expected to develop skills and leadership ability, but when they succeed, as their parents and schools expect them to, their very success threatens their relationship with men. Komarovsky suggests one solution for this problem:

It may be conceded that in so far as the sexes are not protected from rivalry by the sharp demarcation in the ideals of feminine and masculine aptitudes, such rivalry may be on the increase. But the way to alleviate excessive competition is to attack its profound roots in the isolation, the insecurities, and the hostilities of men and women. Excessive competitiveness is also destructive between members of the same sex. Since it seems neither realistic nor idealistic to attempt to reverse the trends which have increased women's competence in traditionally "masculine" spheres, there remains only one thing to do: give the man fairer odds, by relieving him of the need to demonstrate superiority over women in intellectual aptitudes.[5]

The solution suggested by Komarovsky undoubtedly is for the long term, involving as it does a basic modification of the attitudes of both men and women. It has little relevance to the immediate problem of marriage choice. A more practical solution is suggested.

There is no more critical area of compatibility in marriage than that of role congruence. Consequently, it is essential in making a wise marriage choice to investigate the ways role expectations gear together or fail to mesh. In a sense the parts in life we wish to play make up our most important goals, and if we are teamed with another person whose goals contradict ours, conflict is inevitable. Some of the areas where role conflict

---

[4] Komarovsky, *Women in the Modern World*, pp. 81–82. Reprinted by permission of the publisher.
[5] Komarovsky, *Women in the Modern World*, pp. 86–87. Reprinted by permission of the publisher.

occurs are those of a woman's career, managing the family finances, disciplining and guiding the children, the initiation of affectional and sexual gestures, carrying on the chores of the home and community service, as well as problem solving and decision making. Many men like to believe that they want their wives to be their social and intellectual equals, but when it comes to "running things" they fall back on old role patterns. So conflict develops. But it would not develop if there had been long and careful discussion before the marriage as to superordination and family decision making.

Men and women, realizing they are living in a period of transition, will do well to explore in rather great detail their own and their partners' attitudes toward the woman's role. There is no pat solution to this problem, but a beginning can be made by bringing to the surface one's stereotypes and expectations about the role of the mate.

THE IMPORTANCE OF SOCIAL CLASS IN MAKING A WISE MARRIAGE CHOICE

The following case illustrates some of the problems involved in cross-class marriage:

> The problem which brought Henry and Marion into the counselor's office was a bitter conflict over the type of home to be purchased prior to their marriage. Marion was shocked because Henry did not know the period styles of architecture or furniture and hurt because he did not match her interest in these. Henry was shocked because of the importance Marion placed on such "unimportant details" and hurt because she was insisting upon teaching him all about architecture, furniture, decoration and other home concerns. Henry furthermore resented Marion's gentle admonitions regarding his manners and his vocabulary. Marion was troubled because of her parents' reaction to the way Henry always dressed. These two had been brought together because both were champion skiers and enjoyed this sport during every leisure hour they did not have to be in school. Their courtship had taken place in winter practically entirely on the ski lift, and their marriage had been arranged for spring. It was not until they began to make specific plans for their home life that important differences began to appear in almost every area of values. They belonged to widely different socio-cultural classes, and this difference accounted for Marion's lack of satisfaction with her fiancé's manners, speech, background, dress and interests. After exploring still other areas of values Henry and Marion

209

decided to break their engagement. Outside of skiing they literally did not speak the same language.[6]

Much of the literature about marriage choice deals with the controversy as to whether "like attracts like" (homogamy) or "opposites attract each other" (heterogamy). Hollingshead found that in 587 of 1,008 marriages, or 58.2 per cent, the partners came from the same class of residential area and presumably from the same social class. His study also indicates that when class lines were crossed, the man chose a woman from a lower class much more frequently than the reverse. Obviously, homogamy operated in about 60 per cent of the cases, heterogamy in about 40 per cent.

A comparable indication of the degree of cross-class marriage is found in the study by Centers who analyzed occupational levels and marital selection. The following table gives in percentages the mobility of various classes of men in terms of mate selection. The higher the occupational status of the husband, the more likely he is to chose a wife from a lower social class.

TABLE 18. Distribution of Marriages by Occupational Strata *

OCCUPATIONAL STRATA OF HUSBANDS	PERCENTAGE OF MEN WHO MARRIED WIVES		
	Above Own Level	At Own Level	Below Own Level
Business executives	0	15	85
Professional	7	25	68
Small business	11	40	49
White collar	37	23	40
Skilled manual	24	46	30
Semiskilled	49	41	10
Unskilled	60	40	0

* Richard Centers, "Marital Selection and Occupational Strata," *American Journal of Sociology*, 44 (1949), p. 533. Reprinted by permission.

The crucial question in these interclass marriages is the degree to which the incorporation in a marriage of different sets of values, attitudes, and expectations causes conflict and tension. Roth and Peck have analyzed the original schedules of the Burgess-Cottrell marriage-adjustment study and worked out the social-class placement from their data. Cavan has given graphic summary to their findings.

[6] From a case study in the author's files.

FIGURE 9. Marital Adjustment and Social Class *

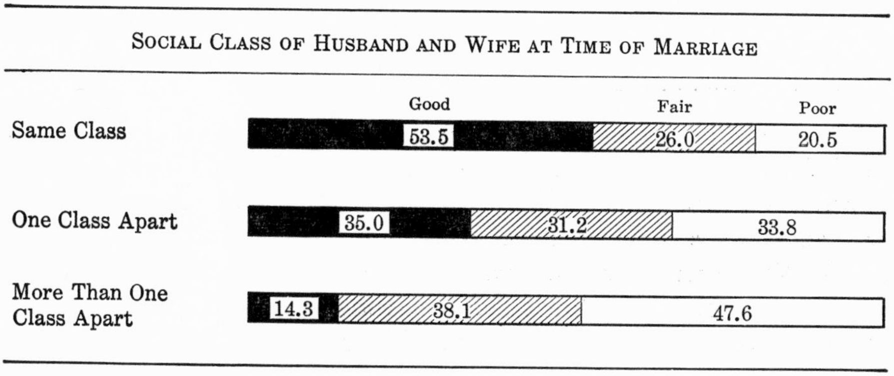

SOCIAL CLASS OF HUSBAND AND WIFE AT TIME OF MARRIAGE

	Good	Fair	Poor
Same Class	53.5	26.0	20.5
One Class Apart	35.0	31.2	33.8
More Than One Class Apart	14.3	38.1	47.6

* Ruth Shonle Cavan, *The American Family*, 2nd ed. (New York: Thomas Y. Crowell Company, 1953), p. 232. Reproduced by permission of the publisher.

Cavan follows the graph with this observation:

> This figure shows that intra-class marriages are preponderantly character-ized by fair or good adjustment; marriages with one class difference be-tween husband and wife are about equally divided between good, fair and poor adjustment; and marriages with husband and wife more widely sep-arated in social-class placement have almost half showing poor adjustment and a very low percentage with good adjustment.[7]

Burgess and Wallin's study indicated that cross-cultural differences are not only an important factor in broken engagements but that they in-evitably cause conflict in greater or lesser degree. While they think that some husbands and wives have the adjustive capacity to be tolerant of such difficulties, they also think that divergent cultures are apt to become minor or even major sources of irritation and resentment. They feel that such cultural differences as those in the areas of family background, reli-gion, nationality, education, and social class contribute to maladjust-ments.[8]

This discussion of social class and marriage choice indicates that a great many heterogamous marriages take place, but that they are often replete with irritation and conflict, and that in general the adjustment in such

[7] Ruth Shonle Cavan, *The American Family*, 2nd ed. (New York: Thomas Y. Crowell Company, 1953), p. 232. Reprinted by permission of the publisher.
[8] Ernest W. Burgess and Paul Wallin, *Engagement and Marriage* (Philadelphia: J. B. Lip-pincott Company, 1953), pp. 438–439.

211

marriages is not as satisfactory as in those in which class lines are not crossed.

TEEN-AGE MARRIAGE

The age of brides and grooms has been consistently dropping for the last half century. In 1890 the average age for men was 26.1 and for women it was 22.0 years. In 1960 the average age was 22.0 for men and 20.0 for women. More women were married at age 18 than in any other single year of life. We are concerned with what happens to these early marriages because they involve the future stability of the American home. We can cite the following research data about their likely outcome:

1. Burgess and Cottrell reported that wives under 16 and husbands under 22 tend toward poor adjustment and "in the great majority of cases there seems to be no doubt regarding the unfortunate effects of early marriage." [9]

2. Locke found that for those married only once, the differences between the mean age at marriage of married and divorced was very significant, 21.5 and 19.1 years.[10]

3. Glick summarized information gleaned from the national census material as showing that women who were still living with their first husbands in 1954 had married at an average age of 21.1 which was two years beyond the average age of women who had remarried. He also reported that the proportion of remarried women whose initial marriage had occurred when the woman was below age 18 was three times as high as for women whose first marital venture came between ages 22 and 24 years.[11]

4. Monahan studied all of the factors involved in all the marriages and divorces that took place in Iowa between 1945 and 1947. He found that when both the husband and the wife were 16 or younger at the time of marriage, the divorce ratio was 400 per cent higher than for marriages where husbands were from 20 to 26 years of age and wives from 22 to 24.[12]

[9] Ernest W. Burgess and Leonard S. Cottrell, *Predicting Success or Failure in Marriage* (New York: Prentice-Hall, Inc., 1939), p. 115.

[10] Harvey J. Locke, *Predicting Adjustment in Marriage, A Comparison of a Divorced and a Happily Married Group* (New York: Henry Holt and Company, 1951), p. 101. Copyright © 1951, Holt, Rinehart and Winston, Inc. Reprinted by permission of the publisher.

[11] Paul C. Glick, *American Families* (New York: John Wiley and Sons, Inc., 1957), pp. 56–58.

[12] Thomas P. Monahan, "Does Age of Marriage Matter in Divorce?", *Social Forces*, XXXII (October, 1953), 86.

5. In Landis' study of divorce rates of 3000 marriages of parents of college students the same trend appeared. When both parents were under 20 at the time of marriage 20 per cent were divorced but when they were from 20 to 25 at time of marriage only 10 per cent failed.[13]

6. Burchinal interviewed 60 girls who were married in high school. Some 55 of the 60 expressed regret that they had not completed high school before the wedding.[14]

If these early marriages are so hazardous why do they occur? There are many reasons and some of them have already been discussed. Certainly going steady at a young age brings with it an increasingly compelling involvement that motivates early marriage, nor should one forget the significance of greater sexual freedom and the some 200,000 illegitimate children born every year. Between one-third and one-half of all early teen-age marriages involve a premarital pregnancy. Of equal importance is the relative ease with which young men can find good jobs so that a period of saving is not regarded as essential before marriage as it was a hundred years ago. There is also the factor of anxiety and the need for the solace and warmth of a companion to buffer a changing and often ominous world. Many young people who marry when they are in their teens regard marriage as a haven to escape conflict, conflict with parents or with themselves. All of these factors are important although they may not all operate in a given case. But none of them can be said to reflect basically adequate motivation or the kind of marital choice based on mature considerations.

COLLEGE-AGE MARRIAGE

There is relatively little objective research material available regarding the fate of married college students. This is surprising because in 1957, 29 per cent of all male and 10 per cent of all female students were married and living with their spouses. The percentage is higher at some schools with large scale graduate programs. In 1960 some 35 per cent of all students at the University of Southern California were married, but the proportion was higher for graduate students and lower for underclassmen.

[13] Judson T. Landis and Mary C. Landis, *Building a Successful Marriage* (Englewood Cliffs, N.J.: Prentice-Hall, Inc, 1958), p. 156.

[14] Lee Burchinal, "Comparison of Factors Related to Adjustment in Pregnancy-Provoked and Non-Pregnancy-Provoked Youthful Marriages," *Midwest Sociologist*, XXI (July, 1956), 92–96.

Svend Rievier and Paul Trump, in early studies of the academic achievement of married veterans, showed that these students did a little better than their foot-loose contemporaries as far as grades were concerned. But veterans are a special class and we cannot generalize from their experience. Jensen and Clarke in a much more recent study (1958) found the opposite to be true, that unmarried males had better grades than their married fellow students. In their study they equated the two groups on ability.[15] Samenfink and Milliken undertook to clarify the contradictions between these reports. These two matched forty-one married male students, who had completed four years of academic work while married, with forty-one single men. The two groups were also matched in ability. The single students earned a cumulative grade point average of 2.46 in comparison to an average of 2.33 for the married men. This difference is not statistically significant but it does indicate at least some academic advantage for the single group. In a rather tongue-in-cheek conclusion the authors say,

> Therefore the marriage counselor, in response to the student who is concerned with the effect marriage will have upon his academic success, can hardly suggest that matrimony would be a panacea for grade improvement.[16]

Christensen and Philbrick were interested in general adjustment of student couples at Purdue University. Using a standard question from marital adjustment studies, they asked the married students whether, if they had it to do over, they would marry again while going to college. Three-fourths replied that they would, but 25 per cent felt the strain was too great and they would not.[17]

A great many married students have visited the office of the author during the last twelve years. Some of them wanted a divorce, and some of them wanted to improve their relationship. The highest incidence of problems of these students fell in the following categories.

1. *Role conflict.* Many of the men depended on the woman to earn the living and then felt very uncomfortable when she assumed the role of

---

[15] Vern H. Jensen and Monroe H. Clarke, "Married and Unmarried College Students: Achievement, Ability and Personality," *Personnel and Guidance Journal* (October, 1958), pp. 123–125.

[16] J. Anthony Samenfink and Robert L. Milliken, "Marital Status and Academic Success: A Reconsideration," *Marriage and Family Living,* XXIII (August, 1961), 226–227.

[17] Harold T. Christensen and Robert E. Philbrick, "Family Size as a Factor of Marital Adjustment of College Students," *American Sociological Review,* XVII (June, 1952), 306–312.

breadwinner. Some of them insisted on handling all of the money so as to maintain at least some symbol of masculine authority. They became very critical of the housekeeping efforts of the working wife. Some in their last year of professional training simply divorced their wives as a kind of gesture of denial of the wife's contribution. And almost all of these men resisted looking honestly at the motivation behind their irritation or hostility.

2. *Guilt reactions in regard to children.* A great many men reported negative reactions to the news that their wives were pregnant. They were afraid this would mean giving up their academic goals. Another group felt unhappy because the pressure of term papers and examinations prevented them from enjoying the companionship of their young sons and daughters. Many of them were annoyed (at the children and then at themselves) because their offspring interfered with careful financial plans, study hours, and recreational plans. If the wife had to work, they felt anxious and pressed because of the need to find competent baby sitters or nursery schools for quite young children. Christensen and Philbrick found comparable reactions in their study. Johannis, in his Oregon study of married students with children, found that two-thirds of these couples felt that children bring great stress.[18]

3. *Conflicts over leisure time.* This proves to be one of the vital conflict points of married students. A couple currently in therapy gave this initial picture to the counselor. The husband said:

"I want to tell you this is my only chance to be a professional man. I've got to study and study hard. All my wife wants to do is go to night clubs or play around. I can't do that and get my work done here. I'm desperate because she doesn't understand my values or my goals. When she gets on me for it I can't study. I just flunked an important test."

But the wife, who was working and paying their rent, food and tuition costs had a different story:

"I have never wanted just to party. I only ask that he show me some affection and some attention. If he would only look up from that _____ book when I get home from work or take fifteen minutes to take a walk with me at night. Before we were married, he had time to take me to dances and shows but now he doesn't even take time to look at me." Of course, many wives whose husbands *are not* in college say much the same thing but the problem is probably accentuated in the college setting. In a study to be found in a later chapter Gerson shows that the two-thirds of the married couples in college had less than 21 hours of leisure per week and a monthly budget allotment of $17.41, according to

[18] Theodore B. Johannis, "The Marital Adjustment of a Sample of Married College Students," *The Coordinator,* IV (June 4, 1956).

husbands, and $13.86 as reported by wives.[19] He concludes that it is not the amount of leisure time that is critical but rather attitudes toward it. I have found that even this is not so important as the general level of adjustment of the couple and the congruity of the two in terms of ultimate goals. But one common problem is the fact that the happy hours of dating often become tedious hours of concentration on work and study after marriage.

4. *Finances.* Many college marriages exist on the brink of financial chaos. This is not a disaster for those young people who are courageous and carefree, but for individuals who tend to be anxious this is a great millstone. They fear pregnancy so much that this fear interferes with a free and spontaneous sexual life. Financial worry leads to endless bickering over expenditures and turns love into conflict. There is no reason why parents should not go on making the same contributions they did before the marriage, but some feel that "now they are married the boy ought to support himself." Others will go on supporting the couple but insist on controlling their lives, and this is a high price to pay for economic assistance.

5. *Sexual adjustment.* In an unpublished study of one hundred married couples at the University of Southern California the writer was startled to see the numbers of couples who felt that studies and the college routine seriously interfered with their developing sexual life. Sometimes they mentioned the fact that the husband and wife lived different "shifts." While he studied at home, she worked, and when he was at school she rested. Others mentioned fear of pregnancy. Still others felt that fatigue associated with the girl's work or the man's studies interfered with full sexual expression. Some report that their lives are so full of nervous tension that they cannot relax. Whatever the cause, many of the couples reported that their sexual adjustment was far from adequate.

6. *Housing.* Campus marriages have come quickly to the attention of college administrators, and they have not been prepared either in accommodations or in attitude to deal with the problems of housing that confront college students. When we asked our one hundred couples what contribution the university could make to their comfort, a great many of them cited the need for low-cost campus housing facilities. Many of them are forced to live great distances from the campus. Others cannot find suitable housing at low cost. The housing secretaries do their best, but a university is not equipped to meet this new need. When we contemplate the increase of teen-age marriages and campus marriages, we are sure that colleges must revise many concepts of stu-

[19] Walter M. Gerson, "Leisure and Marital Satisfaction of College Married Couples," *Marriage and Family Living*, XXII (Nov. 1960), 360–361.

dent housing in order to provide comfortable and convenient apartments for the growing number of those who will go through college now as pairs and not as single students.

INTERRACIAL MARRIAGE AND MARRIAGE HAPPINESS

The problems associated with interracial marriage are social in nature. Biologists are in almost universal agreement that there is no genetic or organic problem associated with cross-racial marriages. However, in this country racial antagonisms and stereotypes infiltrate the cultural milieu so deeply that partners in an interracial marriage must face problems of segregation and great resentment. These prejudices may operate to strip the couple of membership in their own groups and to isolate their children. This causes difficulty in the adjustment of the partners to each other and to their groups.

Baber investigated interracial marriages over a period of several years. He studied forty-eight marriages and classified them according to sex and race.[20] He attempted to measure the happiness of this group of marriages by scaling it from 0 to 100—with 100 representing very happy; 75, moderately happy; 50, neutral; 25, very unhappy; and 0, very very unhappy—and arrived at the ratings for this group shown in Table 19. In general,

TABLE 19. Happiness Ratings of 48 Interracial Marriages *

	Number of Cases	TYPE OF MIXTURE MALE FEMALE	Happiness Rating
	18	Black X White	57
	7	White X Black	39
Both combinations	25	Black—White	52
	18	Yellow X White	67
	2	White X Yellow	100
Both combinations	20	Yellow—White	71
	3	Yellow X Black	75
All combinations	48	Black—White—Yellow	62

* Ray E. Baber, "A Study of 325 Mixed Marriages," *American Sociological Review*, II (October, 1937), 705–716. Reprinted by permission.

[20] Ray E. Baber, "A Study of 325 Mixed Marriages," pp. 705–716. Reprinted by permission.

217

he found that as dissimilarity in color and feature increased, the degree of marital adjustment or happiness decreased.

Baber compared this result with happiness ratings for intermarriages involving both nationality and religion and those involving only religion. The rating of interracial marriages is somewhat lower than that of nationality-religion cross marriages and lower yet than those involving religion only. For those involving religion only Baber found an overall happiness score of 73.[21]

Baber comments on the motivation for such marriages:

> In some cases, especially among college students, a mixed marriage springs partly from a protest against the prevailing pattern of race prejudice, the idealistic young people getting a certain satisfaction from defying public opinion. Or it may be a protest against the parental domination of a daughter who has been warned to have nothing to do with a cultured Oriental in whom she has become interested. Or again the unpopularity of a girl among her own kind may drive her to accept the attentions of attractive young men of another color. Certainly such a course is attention getting and is some compensation to the never-noticed person who thereby gains the spotlight. In cases where the "protest" motive is absent, the very fact that two persons of different race are willing to brave the unyielding opposition of all about them in order to wed may be evidence of an unusually strong personal attraction, and they may achieve happiness. Furthermore, such opposition makes them fully aware of the difficult adjustments ahead and may result in early and determined efforts to justify their decision. Such factors are favorable to adjustment, and occasionally they outweigh the heavy hand of prejudice.[22]

One of the factors frequently overlooked in thinking about inter-racial marriages is the reaction of parents and other relatives. Both often resent out-group marriages of any kind but most particularly interracial marriages which they may feel bring disgrace upon themselves. The following excerpt from a case study indicates something of this problem; the case involved a Negro girl and an Oriental boy:

> "I love Bob very much," the girl said, "but his mother has threatened to commit suicide if we get married. And I know of a similar case where a mother did just that. I don't want that on my conscience the rest of my life. Can't you see the mother and explain to her how much in love we are?" [23]

[21] Ray E. Baber, "A Study of 325 Mixed Marriages," pp. 705–716.
[22] Ray E. Baber, *Marriage and the Family*, 2nd ed. (New York: McGraw-Hill Book Company, Inc., 1953), p. 97. Reprinted by permission of the publisher.
[23] From a case study in the author's files.

Baber cites a case which indicates that the problem for the children of such a union is not only ostracism at school but sometimes trouble between the siblings themselves:

> In one case (W X B) the boy is white and his two sisters are dark. They quarrel a great deal, his most effective technique being to call them "nigger," which infuriates the girls and stirs up both the parents. In another (Y X W) the six-year-old daughter is called "chink" by her playmates at school. Her parents are ostracized by whites, and her Chinese father is "beaten up" periodically by her mother's brothers. The mother in another case (W X B) hates the daughter because she is light like her father yet will not let the girl marry a dark person. In one instance (Y X B) the wife had a daughter by her first marriage with a white man, and now in this second marriage the white daughter resents having a Chinese stepfather and half brother. Misery attends the mother in another union (B X W) because her little daughter hates her for being white and loves her father because he is black, as she is. Her little brother, however, loves his mother and hates his sister for hating and striking his mother. The mother "has no friends." Still another mother in a mixed marriage (W X B) is hurt because her daughters avoid introducing her to their friends but are eager to introduce their father and show him off.[24]

Interracial marriages cause difficulties in (1) alienating the parents, relatives, and past friends of the man and wife, (2) inviting the resentment and prejudice of communities and neighborhoods where racial caste systems are rigid, (3) causing the offspring of such unions extreme problems in adjusting to their peers and to their siblings. Baber rightly comments that such marriages are sometimes successful but that they are fraught with the problems outlined above in addition to normal problems of marital adjustment.

INTERFAITH MARRIAGES AND WISE MARRIAGE CHOICE

Interfaith marriages are marriages between any two people from such diverse religious backgrounds that their difference in religious values are possible causes of conflict. This may be a Catholic-Protestant, a Catholic-Jewish, a Liberal-Protestant–Fundamentalist-Protestant union, or the union of one who has a wide interest in religion and one who has none. There are a great many variations in loyalty to religious groups as well as in types of beliefs. Our analysis is confined to Catholic-Protestant inter-

[24] Baber, *Marriage and the Family*, pp. 95–96. Reprinted by permission of the publisher.

faith marriages (1) because they are the most numerous and (2) because more research has been done on this type. However, the type of approach used here applies to all forms of interfaith unions and may be applied by those couples who have questions regarding the outcome of their marriage.

What is the extent of such interfaith marriages? Clement S. Mihanovich, writing in a Catholic periodical in July, 1948, said: "Over 40 per cent of all Catholic marriages in 1946 were mixed marriages." [25] Paul Blanshard thinks that there are over 100,000 Catholic-Protestant marriages in the nation every year.

> There are more than 100,000 priestly mixed marriages a year in the United States and recently studies by priests show not only that such marriages are increasing rapidly in spite of ecclesiastical pressure, but also that a very large proportion of mixed families are lost permanently to the church.[26]

To the mixed marriages performed by priests must be added all those mixed marriages performed by Protestant ministers and justices of the peace. This would probably mean that 50 per cent of Catholic youth are marrying non-Catholic mates. Leiffer [27] made a special study of 6,236 families and found among them 743 families of divided religious loyalties at the time of marriage. Of these families some 444 were Protestant-Catholic unions.

Mihanovich, Schnepp, and Thomas have made a national study of the extent of mixed marriage. (See Table 20 from their study, p. 221.) Intensive studies of individual parishes seem to show that the mixed marriage rate may vary rather widely from one area to the next. Thus, in a study of a parish on the Atlantic seaboard, mixed marriages constituted about 50 per cent of all marriages; another parish, also in the East, gave a figure of 20 per cent. By diocese Thomas found rates ranging from 70 per cent to 10 per cent and noted a negative correlation between the proportion of Catholics in an area and the percentage of mixed marriages. Further, mixed marriage rates seem to be higher in the upper socio-economic classes and lower in areas occupied by cohesive ethnic groups. Thomas believes that the overall rate is increasing and offers five factors to support that position: (1) national groups are gradually fusing with the host

---

[25] Clement S. Mihanovich, *The American Ecclesiastical Review*, July, 1948.

[26] Paul Blanshard, *American Freedom and Catholic Power* (Boston: The Beacon Press, 1949), pp. 165–166.

[27] Murray H. Leiffer, "Mixed Marriages and Church Loyalties," *Christian Century* (January 19, 1949), pp. 87–90.

culture; (2) Catholic and non-Catholic interaction is increasing; (3) mixed marriages seem to have a cumulative effect; (4) there is increasing individualism in the selection of a marriage partner; and (5) the attitude of both Catholic and non-Catholic young people seems to be becoming more tolerant to mixed marriages.[28]

T A B L E 20. Mixed-Marriage Statistics for 7 Archdioceses and 43 Dioceses, 1934–1941 *

Year	TOTAL MARRIAGES	CATHOLIC MARRIAGES	MIXED MARRIAGES	
			Number	Per Cent
1932	59,329	42,196	17,133	28
1933	66,198	46,869	19,329	28
1934	91,179	67,844	23,825	25
1935	83,397	58,377	25,020	29
1936	90,712	63,651	27,061	29
1937	94,582	65,759	28,823	30
1938	92,198	64,044	28,154	30
1939	102,831	71,865	30,966	29
1940	114,985	79,153	35,832	30
1941	117,440	79,583	37,857	31

* From: Bishop's Committee on Mixed Marriages, "A Factual Study of Mixed Marriages" (Washington, D.C.: National Catholic Welfare Conference, 1943), p. 5. Reprinted by permission.

HAZARDS OF MIXED MARRIAGE

Some of the results of interfaith marriages are analyzed by these authors. They depend for their data on a study of a single parish made previously by one of them, Schnepp.[29] This study can be summarized by saying that while 6.1 per cent of Catholic marriages ended in divorce, some 12.5 per cent of mixed and 15.1 per cent of invalid marriages ended in divorce; from 30 to 40 per cent of non-Catholics were converted and from 20 to 30 per cent of the Catholics involved gave up their faith; only 51 per cent of the children of these mixed families attended Catholic schools. Even more important for future trends is the summary dealing with the marriages of children from mixed marriages:

[28] Mihanovich, Schnepp, and Thomas, *Marriage and the Family* (Milwaukee: The Bruce Publishing Company, 1942), pp. 202–203. Reprinted by permission.
[29] Gerald J. Schnepp, S.M., *Leakage from a Catholic Parish* (Washington, D.C.: The Catholic University of America Press, 1942).

221

Of 702 children whose parents were united in Catholic marriage, 425 or 60 per cent contracted a Catholic marriage; 206 or 31 per cent a mixed marriage, and 61 or 9 per cent an invalid marriage—of 200 children whose parents married mixed, 44 per cent contracted a Catholic marriage; 44.5 per cent contracted a mixed marriage and 11.5 per cent an invalid marriage—It seems fairly correct to say, then, that mixed marriages have bred mixed marriages in this parish. The proportion of Catholics to mixed marriages is approximately two to one when the parents' marriage was Catholic, and one to one when the parents' marriage was mixed.[30]

Three other studies which analyze the fate of these mixed marriages are summarized by Skidmore and Cannon, as shown in Table 21.

TABLE 21. Per Cent of Marriages of Mixed and Non-Mixed Religious Faiths Ending in Divorce or Separation in Given Studies *

RELIGIOUS CATEGORIES	LANDIS STUDY IN MICHIGAN		BELL STUDY IN MARYLAND	WEEKS STUDY IN WASHINGTON
	No.	Per Cent	Per Cent	Per Cent
Both Catholic	573	4.4	6.4	3.8
Both Jewish	96	5.2	4.6	
Both Protestant	2794	6.0	6.8	10.0
Mixed Catholic-Protestant	192	14.1	15.2	17.4
Both none	39	17.9	16.7	23.9
Protestant changed to Catholic	56	10.7		
Catholic changed to Protestant	57	10.6		
Protestant Father Catholic Mother	90	6.7		
Catholic Father Protestant Mother	102	20.6		
Father none Mother Catholic		9.8		
Father none Mother Protestant	84	19.0		

* Adapted from Rex Skidmore and Anthon S. Cannon, *Building Your Marriage* (New York: Harper and Brothers, 1951), p. 166. Reprinted by permission of Harper and Row, Publishers.

Peterson studied the impact of religion upon family adjustment of 440 persons selected on a cross-sectional basis from the County of Los Angeles. Religious histories were taken and the questions in the Burgess-Terman-Locke adjustment-scale were asked. From the answers to these questions basic adjustment scores were derived. When the individuals were grouped

[30] Schnepp, p. 209.

according to their religious backgrounds, mean adjustment scores were computed. It was evident from the study that religious groups differ significantly in the way couples belonging to those groups adjust in marriage. One finding was that interfaith couples have the lowest mean adjustment score of any group in the study. The following table indicates the mean Catholic-Protestant adjustment score as compared to the mean score of Catholics married to Catholics and Protestants married to Protestants.

TABLE 22. Interfaith Marriages Compared as to Adjustment Score with Catholic, Protestant, and Nonreligious Marriages *

ADJUSTMENT SCORE	CATHOLIC-PROTESTANT	CATHOLIC	PROTESTANT	NON-CHURCH
	Per cent	*Per cent*	*Per cent*	*Per cent*
Low adjustment	50	39	20	29
High adjustment	50	61	80	71

* James A. Peterson, "The Impact of Objective and Subjective Religious Factors on Adjustment in Marriage." Unpublished Ph.D. dissertation, University of Southern California Libraries, 1950, p. 196. Reprinted by permission.

There is only one state, Iowa, that asks about religious affiliation on its marriage and divorce forms. Chancellor and Monahan studied some 22,000 marriages and 5,000 divorces there.[31] They found that while only 27 per cent of the Catholics being married united with someone of another faith, some 55 per cent of the Catholics being divorced had intermarried. This study is more adequate methodologically than the others because this statistic includes all marriages, but the previous studies included only marriages with children. However, the end results are about the same, indicating that there are twice the number of divorces involving Catholics when they intermarry as compared to Catholics united with Catholics. There is still one other factor which must be mentioned. Catholics, because of their religious feelings about divorce, are underrepresented in divorce statistics and overrepresented in desertion. *The Annual Reports of Philadelphia Municipal Courts* indicate that in 1954 Catholics, who comprised 40 per cent of the population, contributed some 60 per

[31] Loren E. Chancellor and Thomas P. Monahan, "Religious Preference and Inter-Religious Mixtures in Marriage and Divorce in Iowa," *American Journal of Sociology* (November, 1955), p. 239.

cent of the desertion cases.[32] But we do not have a breakdown as to whether Catholic intermarriages were again overrepresented in those deserting. This is an important aspect of understanding the total outcome of interfaith marriage which needs exploration. Nevertheless, we can conclude that religiously mixed marriages are more likely to end in disaster than marriages of like faith. It is important to try to understand why this occurs.

These studies indicate that Catholic-Protestant marriages are very hazardous unions. For this reason most Protestant denominations and all Catholic groups strongly urge their members to marry within their own faith. Five general individual problems characterize this type of marriage:

1. *The Problem of Family Participation.* Where will the family of an interfaith marriage worship? This question was raised by Leiffer, who came to the conclusion that in general children go to the church of the mother, despite the fact that a couple married by a priest signs a pledge promising to bring up the children as Catholics. This may be one reason for the very high rate of divorce of Catholic men and Protestant women shown in the Landis study. In his study of 444 husbands in Catholic-Protestant marriages he found that 110 were no longer connected with their church and 124 had not attended in the previous year. Almost the same thing happened on a smaller scale with wives. Of 449 Catholic-Protestant wives, 60 had no denominational affiliation and 91 had not attended in the previous year. Three generalizations are possible: (1) a few individuals are converted to the spouse's faith, (2) many drop out of religious groups altogether, and (3) children tend to go with the mother to the church of her choice.

2. *The Problem of Family Planning.* Spacing children is an important concept which many Protestants accept but which Catholics, according to their church dogmas, may not. If a Catholic, under pressure from his or her Protestant mate, does accede to the use of mechanical or chemical methods of birth control, it is often with deep remorse and guilt.[33] To be married in the Catholic Church, a couple must solemnly promise not to use any *artificial form* of birth control. Artificial birth control is regarded as a serious sin in Catholic doctrine.

It is difficult for the average Protestant or Jewish young person to understand how strongly Catholics feel about birth control. To gain such

---

[32] *1957 Annual Report* (Philadelphia, Pa.: Philadelphia Municipal Court), p. 220.

[33] A copy of the agreement that must be signed by a Protestant when married to a Catholic in a Catholic church by a priest is included in Appendix I.

understanding they should read some of the official statements of the church or talk to priests about this matter. In an Encyclical letter Pope Pius XII described contraception as "intrinsically against nature," calling it "sinful" and "vicious," and concluding that it is a "grave sin." [34] One form of birth prevention is permitted by Catholic doctrine because it is regarded as a "natural" method. Catholics may use the "rhythm method" and avoid intercourse during that period when fertilization is most likely to occur providing that there are serious reasons for interfering with the possibility of conception. These are described by Pope Pius XII as (1) *Medical*, where childbearing may be dangerous to the health of the woman as in cases where she has heart disease, (2) *Eugenic*, where medical science indicates the child will inherit defects of a serious nature, (3) *Economic*, where there is grave financial difficulty and (4) *Social*, where, for example, there must be a long separation due to military or educational obligations. But because of the gravity of the decision to avoid children the matter should be talked over with a priest before this method is used.[35]

On the other hand the positive affirmation of Catholics is that their highest aim is the procreation of children, a privilege God shared with man, and this privilege may not be disregarded for the pleasure of individuals.

3. *The Problem of the Religious Pressures of In-Laws.* Some wives and husbands in interfaith marriages might adjust if left to themselves. In-laws have an interest in the life of their son or daughter and because their religious interests are so intense, they are often factors for disunity. A Catholic-Protestant couple contemplating marriage should assess what importance their parents' attitude will have in the religious lives of themselves and their children.

4. *Culture and Style of Life.* Religion is more than a special way of genuflecting or subscribing to creeds. It involves a whole cluster of attitudes and values. One church may use raffles to raise money and a church not far from it may preach against gambling. The Protestant church may have a large dinner serving turkey or a roast on Friday night, but the Catholic partner cannot attend that dinner. During Lent some Protestants deny themselves some luxury, while others do not. Almost all Catholics

[34] Encyclical Letter of Pope Pius XII on *Costi Connubi*, pamphlet (New York: Paulist Press, 1951), p. 17.

[35] Pope Pius XII, "Moral Questions Affecting Married Life—The Apostolate of the Midwife," a discourse given on Oct. 29, 1951, to delegates attending the Congress of the Italian Catholic Union of Midwives, pamphlet (New York: Paulist Press).

fast and make some personal sacrifice during the Lenten period. In these and hundreds of other ways religion is a strong cultural force in determining not only religious beliefs but specific family rituals and attitudes. Interfaith couples need to be aware of the many ways in which their religious background reflects a way of life.

5. *The Problem of the Wedding.* Most, but of course not all young people, like to be married in the church where they have spent their childhood and youth and to be married by their own minister. Protestant churches accept as binding and meaningful a wedding performed by a Catholic priest or a judge. Catholic churches regard weddings performed by Protestant ministers and judges as invalid and meaningless if one of those being married is a Catholic. The Catholic Church feels that to recognize such marriages as valid would be to indicate the religious validity of non-Catholics and this is contrary to Catholic doctrine that it is the one and the only true church. As a result, being married by a religious leader who belongs to any non-Catholic group is a gross sin and the person involved may be excommunicated on the grounds of apostasy. There is often disappointment and hurt for a couple who have difficulties over this rule of the church.

How can couples who feel that they are in love determine to what extent their religious differences will cause difficulties when they are married? These five areas of concern do not affect all individuals. For some with a Catholic or a Protestant background may have so little real interest in their religion that it will not affect their adjustment in marriage.

Not everyone who is a member of or who participates in a religious group does so with the same degree of zeal or intensity. A rough scale of this zeal follows:

Our Interest in Religion

Almost No Vital Interest	Some Interest	Much Interest	A Very Great Interest

Where one places oneself on this scale and where the intended mate is placed on the scale may suggest the degree to which the couple may be troubled about religious differences. If both fall at the end of the scale marked "Almost No Vital Interest," there would obviously be very little trouble no matter how great the differences between their alleged religions. On the other hand, if both had "A Very Great Interest" and then

226

differed significantly in their religious beliefs, the matter would call for greater exploration.

A second scale has to do with the degree of interest of the immediate relatives, for many parents will have a deep and constant concern for the welfare of their married children and for the religious education of their grandchildren. Therefore it is well to place the families on a similar scale:

Our Families' Interest in Religion

My Family	Almost No Vital Interest	Some Interest	Much Interest	A Very Great Interest
Intended Mate's Family				

By using these two scales and studying the type of their religious affiliation, young people can objectify the degree to which religion may be a problem in later adjustment, both for themselves and their families. A Catholic-Protestant couple contemplating marriage will do well to assess what importance their parents' attitude will have in their religious lives and those of their children.

The best safeguard against future difficulties is a full and frank discussion of religious beliefs and differences. Such a discussion will include the frank acknowledgement of any basic disagreements about the place where the marriage will take place, about birth control, the religious education of children, and the family's future religious life. The interest scales proposed above may help the couple determine to what extent differences will be major obstacles to their happiness. Insofar as possible they must think clearly about the future and project themselves into the role of parents and try to determine how they will feel then. There are many happy Catholic-Protestant couples who find that their fundamental beliefs are fairly similar and that their different religious traditions enrich rather than endanger their marital happiness.

RECREATION AND WISE MARRIAGE CHOICE

The use of leisure time is important in American life. Burgess and Wallin think that many of the conflicts about leisure-time pursuits reflect traditional sex differences in our culture as expressed in different degrees of interest and participation by men and women. Even during childhood the American boy is encouraged to participate in sports because to do so is a typically masculine pattern in this country, while the girl may be discouraged from such pursuits. Women supposedly like the gentler pursuits of the theater, or visiting friends, or dancing, while men are supposed to appreciate prize fights and baseball games.[36]

In marriage young people face the necessity of giving up some of their independent recreational behavior because, previous to marriage, recreation aside from dating is ordinarily a same-sex pursuit. Adjustment to a new type of leisure-time activity may be difficult. Two significant studies have attempted to analyze the result of difference in recreational habits on marriage adjustment. Locke in his study asked the following question:

> In leisure time both husband and wife prefer to be "on the go," both prefer to stay at home, one prefers to be "on the go," and the other to stay home?[37]

Another question in Locke's study dealt with agreement on recreation: the couple were asked to check on a six-point scale the degree to which they felt they agreed. Locke put the answers to all his adjustment questions in rank order of their importance in differentiating the happily married from the divorced. There were thirty-four items on this scale, and the question regarding leisure time quoted above rated in sixth place, while the agreement on recreation question rated in twenty-sixth place. It appears that differences in preferences in the use of leisure time are highly important in determining the adjustment of a man and wife.

It is obvious that stereotypes derived from past cultural traditions seriously hamper men and women in preparing for marital adjustment. In the face of such contradictions, young people need to assess very carefully their recreational backgrounds and activities to be sure of common interests after marriage.

MILITARY SERVICE AS A FACTOR IN WISE MARRIAGE CHOICE

Military service complicates both planning for marriage and adjusting to it. Perhaps the most serious complication is the impact military service has upon wise marriage choice.

[36] Burgess and Wallin, pp. 258–260.
[37] Locke, p. 374.

228

The feeling of desperation is one of the prime factors in the anxiety of college students as they contemplate the cold war and the relationship of a future marriage to military service. A new sense of time pervades society. The "now" is all important. As men continue to go into the service immediately upon graduation, the girls become more and more aware of the possibility of remaining unmarried and consequently take the initiative in speeding up courtship.[38] In college, as the junior and senior men face and discuss their future in the service, their girl friends may become very anxious about marriage. This anxiety is a major factor in promoting many marriages which would never have been contracted under peacetime conditions. One student summarized her feelings as follows:

> Though strictly speaking our time should not be called a time of war, still, it is an undeniable fact that since the beginning of World War II we have been in a continual state of emergency, which, if not actual war, at least produced the same effect. Certainly it can be said that for my generation the distinction is slight. It is true that some men are not called into service at all. It is true that some men serve their military duty stateside, never leave home and the girl they want to marry, and practice, while in the service, the profession of their choice. It is true that, for a fortunate few, military services offer the opportunity to receive free an education in just the technical skills needed to enable the young man to get ahead, and a salary while learning, but these are, I am afraid, in the minority. Men are still being conscripted into service; they still are sent suddenly overseas (even from the National Guard); they are still giving their lives on the battlefields; many of them are still going to come back and find adjustment difficult; careers are still being halted and opportunities hopelessly lost; girls are still having to adjust to no husband at all, a husband now and then, or a husband away. . . .
>
> Strangely enough, women are more fundamentally disturbed by war than men. Their loneliness, their sacrifice, and their fears may seem more obscure but they are very real to them. Women between 18 and 25 are hoping and dreaming of marriage opportunities. They know that chances dwindle after twenty-five. They realize that war diminishes man power and causes husband shortages. This causes a feeling of desperation. What to do? [39]

The following eight suggestions are in answer to that girl and to others who find themselves in similar situations. These suggestions are derived

---

[38] Evelyn M. Duvall and Reuben Hill, *When You Marry*, rev. ed. (Boston: D. C. Heath and Company, 1953).

[39] From a personal document written by a student in the author's files.

from experience in dealing with the problems of a great many young people who have had to make decisions about marrying when confronted with military service.

Beware of Extraneous Motivations. Because so many young men are being inducted into the various services, many girls and many young men feel panicky over their chances of marriage. One girl said recently:

> But I'm twenty-three. All the men my age are in or are going into the service. When they get out they will be interested in younger girls. If I am ever going to be married it is now or never.

This girl came for counsel because she was contemplating marrying a person about whom she had grave doubts. She may be married because of the pressure she feels simply to "get married now or never," but it will not be because she has built up a community of interest with the young man, or because she can confidently expect a long and happy future, but only because she feels desperate.

Insist Upon a Longer and Not a Shorter Courtship. The knowledge that so many hasty World War II marriages failed should be an object lesson. Because of the possibility that some inadequate motivations may be present in the developing love of a man and woman, they should test their affection over a longer period than might be necessary in a different situation. The selective service requirements are stable enough today so that most couples should be able to avoid hasty courtships and "quickie" marriages.

Be Realistic About the Problems Involved in Marriage Today. Couples who are to be married when the man is going into the service will further their adjustment immeasurably if they enter the situation realistically. There are many ways of insuring this adjustment. Young couples generally have friends who have been in the same predicament and have had to make similar decisions. A talk with such a couple should help them avoid unhappy "surprises" later on. Older couples who were in the same dilemma during World War II can also tell them, in realistic terms, of the difficulties that are likely to arise after marriage. Having learned what the problems are, the couple should have a thorough discussion of possible solutions—the problems include housing, the wife and work, the possibility of a child, and the readjustment after separation. If they meet these problems directly and courageously, they are not apt to suffer so much as those who never think about the negative aspects of the

230

days ahead. It should help later adjustment, too, if they will face honestly the problem of meeting their affectional needs while they are separated. Being separated is not an easy problem, but mutual agreement will help them face their days apart and help their readjustment when they are reunited.

Be Realistic About Yourself and Your Mate. Some persons are not capable of making the adjustment involved in a service marriage. No one can arbitrarily say that one person will or will not make a success of a trying situation. If a girl dislikes being uncomfortable, hates travel, is unwilling to uproot herself from her home community, objects to the unexpected, she needs to think twice about marrying a person who will be in the service for a number of years. On the other hand, the girl who is very adaptable, likes change, new experience and new surroundings, and finds joy in making new friends will probably not have too much trouble in adjusting to a marital situation that involves moving about. Comfort and order are very important to some people, but mean nothing to others. There are girls who look forward to "three years of gypsy life"—to the continual leaving and saying goodbye, the surprise visits, the unexpected leave—as a period in which "we shall achieve such security and oneness that it will see us through any adjustment problem that comes when we must settle down." Such girls have anticipated realistically the problems that are to come but welcome them as opportunities to test their mettle and to build a permanent structure of sharing. Anyone who has serious misgivings about his ability to live this way ought to face such misgivings honestly.

Build a Pair-Solidarity Before Marriage. There is no way of avoiding the problems that arise from living together. But problems can be anticipated and the unity of a couple strengthened before the wedding vows are spoken. If a couple can engage in different types of recreation before marriage, if they can spend much time discussing their future home and its requirements, if they can focus upon the problem of children and begin to plan the way in which they will guide those children, if they can search out the long-range values they will try to attain, if they can achieve a certain amount of adjustment of temperamental and personality differences, they will then have some background of unified interests and plans. There will then be some security and some stability in their marriage to hold them together when they are separated.

Use Available Premarital Counseling Facilities. Because of all the

231

complications which have been mentioned, it is essential for a couple to obtain as much premarital help as possible so that certain of the adjustments of marriage can be made with as much dispatch as possible. For example, it may be a cause of some anxiety to the wife to spend the months or years her mate is away wondering if they will ever achieve sexual compatibility. It is possible to make great strides if one works through such problems with a counselor. For example, if there is sexual inhibition as the result of earlier experience or home conditioning this inhibition may be modified before the ceremony ever takes place. The couple will better understand, too, that if certain adjustments are not made before they separate, this situation is normal and no cause for prolonged worry.

Choose with Care the Time for Marriage. The problem of adjusting to "boot camp" or to the early months in any of the services is difficult enough without the further problem of adjusting to a new marriage. Moreover, these first months of training are such that a couple can generally be together only a very small part of the time. It thus seems wise for the couple to marry either some months before or some months after induction. Even if they are in college and both are finishing their senior year, they might use the last semester or the last year for adjustment, and for building solidarity. If this arrangement is not feasible, it may be better to postpone marriage until after the period of basic training so that two adjustments do not come at once. Whether the wife should plan to work during the time immediately after marriage must be decided by the needs of the situation. Some branches and ranks of the service pay better than others. In all cases, the couple must abide by the regulations of the different services regarding marriage.

Consciously Emphasize Communication Even When Separated. If the man must go overseas or into some area where his wife may not follow him, they should work out ways of continuing their efforts to achieve unity. If the wife is working, she may save a little each week and put it aside as a sinking fund. The husband, too, may take pride in sending small sums to add to the fund. This growing nest egg may be earmarked for a home, or a start in business, or even a trip together. It does not matter much what the purpose of the fund is; the important thing is that it is an activity that both share during their separation. Again, they may read a number of books they have selected and write comments back and forth. They may decide that further enlightenment on marriage is in order and elect to read books about marriage. Their letters should be frequent and

232

filled with references to happy times in the past and the happy times they expect to have in the future.

The attitude each partner has toward the service itself is important. If they regard military service as an intolerable imposition by an arbitrary force, both will find the interval very difficult. On the other hand, if they believe that both of them are engaged in building a world in which their children can be free and family life can be more secure from the social and economic ravages of war, they will have common unity in a great cause. If the free forces prevail because of the dedication of young people, a new and richer world may emerge for all families of tomorrow.

Finally, it must be recognized that the present unsettled period may continue for some time. There is no use trying to escape the fact. Young people may be faced for years with the need to adjust to marriage while the man is in the service. The problems raised must be met courageously and creatively. There is no perfect solution. But if a couple determines to work out an answer in terms of their own personalities, using all of the resources offered by counseling facilities, a surprisingly well-adjusted marriage may result.

Every age has its traumatic experiences. The parents of this generation faced a great depression as well as two wars. Life must go on during disaster, depression, or war, and young people need not lament their lot. A period of difficulty may be a prelude to a period of profound happiness.

CONCLUSION

This chapter has presented material dealing with cultural definitions and expectations relating to the woman's role, interclass marriages, age difference in marriage, interracial marriages, interfaith marriages, service marriages, and recreation. Cultural stereotypes place burdens on marital adjustment. The roles prescribed by the stereotypes lag behind actual educational preparation for marriage, producing tension in marriage. On the other hand, in interracial and interfaith marriages cultural values and expectations are so diverse that adjustment is difficult. Young people need to orient themselves in view of their own cultural backgrounds so that they can predict what their reaction will be in relation to others of either similar or dissimilar backgrounds. Because of the heterogeneity of our culture a large segment of the population becomes involved in cross-class, or cross-religious unions. These place a special burden on the adjustment processes of marriage.

SELF-ANALYSIS

Obviously this analysis must be made not only for you but for your intended mate. The advantage of understanding your own value structure is that it enables you to compare it with that of the person with whom you must adjust in marriage. For those not contemplating marriage the self-analysis will help them realize more adequately their own expectations and goals. When woman's role is analyzed, by a man, he will think of his own attitudes toward woman's role, but the woman will try to make articulate her own concept of her own goals and wishes.

I. Woman's Role in Marriage:
   A. Should a woman assume an inferior role in
      1. Sports and recreational pursuits?
      2. Intellectual activities?
      3. Community leadership roles?
   B. In terms of decision-making should a woman have
      1. Equality with men?
      2. A subordinate role to men?

II. Social-Class Membership
   A. To what social class do you belong?
   B. What particular characteristics of your behavior pattern do you ascribe to membership in that social class?
   C. Do you aspire to move into another social class?
   D. What problems would moving into another social class bring to you?

III. Recreational Interests and Background
   A. During middle and later adolescence or young adulthood what specific skills and interests have you developed in the following areas of leisure-time activities:
      1. Sports?
      2. Intellectual pursuits?
      3. Aesthetic fields?
      4. Hobbies?
   B. During middle and later adolescence or young adulthood what specific skills and interests have you developed in these four areas that would appeal to a member of the opposite sex?
   C. During middle and later adolescence or young adulthood what

skills and interests have you developed in these four areas that would appeal not only to your mate but to children?

D. List the most rewarding activities you have shared in a mixed group during the last six months.

E. Remember, if you can, most of your dates for the past six months, and describe the types of activities they entailed. Are you satisfied with this report?

F. In general, are most of your leisure hours devoted to things you do yourself, or do you depend on the skill of others to amuse you?

G. Analyze your reactions when participating in a game.
   1. Are you primarily interested in winning or in sharing a good time?
   2. Are you a "good loser" or do you feel a little depressed at losing?
   3. Do you select activities to give you status or do you select them simply because they appeal to you?
   4. Can you spontaneously forget yourself in play? Or are you somewhat serious even in recreation?

H. Analyze your general reactions with a group
   1. Can you engage in happy "small talk"?
   2. Can you take a joke?
   3. Do you "banter" or "tease" in an easy way?
   4. Do you laugh easily, and often?

I. Analyze your present state of health in terms of your recreational life. Is your feeling one of physical buoyancy? Do you have energy and "bounce"? Are you keeping fit through sufficient exercise?

IV. Religious Participation and Interest.

A. On the scale provided on page 226 rate yourself on the intensity of your religious interests.

B. On the scale provided on page 227 rate your family on their religious interest.

C. Write out a simple statement outlining your expectations in marriage in terms of:
   1. The importance of worship, grace at meals, prayer for your incipient family.
   2. Your feeling regarding birth-control.
   3. Your feeling regarding the importance of religious education of your children; your desire as to the type of religious training they would receive.
   4. Your religious beliefs.

D. Write out briefly the ways in which the religious atmosphere of your childhood and youth makes important contributions to your cultural pattern of life.

VISUAL AIDS

One Marriage—Two Faiths, Methodist Publishing Company, Nashville, Tennessee

READINGS

BABER, RAY E. *Marriage and the Family.* 2nd ed. New York, McGraw-Hill Book Company, Inc., 1953, Chapter 4.

BOSSARD, JAMES H. S. and ELEANOR STOKER BOLL. *One Marriage, Two Faiths.* The Ronald Press, New York, 1957.

BURGESS, ERNEST W. and PAUL WALLIN. *Engagement and Marriage.* Philadelphia, J. B. Lippincott Company, 1953, Chapter 6.

KOMAROVSKY, MIRRA. *Women in the Modern World.* Boston, Little, Brown and Company, 1953, Chapter 3.

LOCKE, HARVEY J. *Predicting Adjustment in Marriage: A Comparison of a Divorced and a Happily Married Group.* New York, Henry Holt and Company, 1951, Chapter 5. Copyright Holt, Rinehart and Winston, Inc.

PETERSON, JAMES A. "The Impact of Objective and Subjective Religious Factors on Adjustment in Marriage." Unpublished Ph.D. thesis, University of Southern California Libraries, 1951.

SLOTKIN, J. S. "Adjustment in Jewish-Gentile Intermarriages." *Social Forces,* XXI (December, 1942), 226–230.

VINCENT, CLARK E. "Interfaith Marriages: Problem or Symptom." *Religion and the Face of America,* Jane C. Zahn, editor, Berkeley, University Extension, University of California, 1959, pp. 67–87.

CHAPTER 10

Economic
Factors

INTRODUCTION

WORK, money, economic roles and expectations, and occupational attitudes are important concerns for those who contemplate marriage. This chapter will deal with the problems involved in: (1) the way socio-economic factors are related to marital happiness; (2) the impact of occupational choice on marital adjustment; (3) the modern woman's role; (4) the impact of maternal employment on children and marital adjustment. These are all of critical importance because when one chooses a mate, he also chooses for life his security level and the specific pattern of life imposed by an occupation. Equally important for future marital adjustment is the attitude of husband and wife toward the wife's gainful employment and the impact this will make on child rearing.

ECONOMIC SECURITY AND MARITAL ADJUSTMENT

Economic factors have received much attention in marital studies. Terman studied 792 couples of early middle age from the upper-class.[1] He found that insufficient income was frequently mentioned as a negative factor in marriage. This factor was rated as one of the sources of trouble of 70.5 per cent of the husbands and 68.8 per cent of the wives. He found, however, that it was the way the income was handled rather than the actual amount that was important.

[1] Lewis M. Terman, *Psychological Factors in Marital Happiness* (New York: McGraw-Hill Book Company, Inc., 1938), pp. 167–171.

Burgess and Cottrell's study was of a middle-class sample of 526 couples who had been married five years or less when studied.[2] By using the statistical device of partial correlation, they were able to hold other major factors constant and so measure the importance of any one single item. When they followed this procedure for economic items, they found that the economic factor had little importance by itself but was a symbol of cultural and educational factors. Locke studied a fairly evenly divided sample of happily married and divorced families in Indiana.[3] His study represents the average population more adequately than any other major study. By asking the happily married group to name couples who were divorced, and then interviewing these, he obtained a matched sample. He asked these married and divorced families whether or not they believed their total income met their needs as families. He also asked them to judge the adequacy of income on the following scale: very adequate, adequate, inadequate, or very inadequate.

The happy group said, in general, that they considered their income adequate and the unhappy described their income as inadequate. Locke also found that certain indices of security—namely, possession of life insurance, savings at marriage, and accumulated savings at the time of the interview—were associated with good adjustment. He found, too, that those families that rated higher on rent, life insurance, utilities, and luxuries had better adjustment than those that rated lower on these items. Williamson's findings give moderate support to Locke's conclusion that security is associated with marital happiness.[4]

Three conclusions with reference to factors determining wise marriage choice emerge from these studies. The first is the very obvious conclusion that the security factor is important to the well-adjusted family. Steadiness of income is more important than size, but both Locke and Williamson indicate that adjustment is somewhat better as security increases. The second conclusion (from Terman) is the importance of management of income. Young people contemplating marriage need to know the skill with which the intended mate meets his or her obligations. It is important that at least one of the couple has some ability to manage well. The fol-

[2] Ernest W. Burgess and Leonard Cottrell, *Predicting Success or Failure in Marriage* (New York: Prentice-Hall, Inc., 1939), pp. 139–146.

[3] Harvey J. Locke, *Predicting Adjustment in Marriage: A Comparison of a Divorced and a Happily Married Group* (New York: Henry Holt and Company, 1951), pp. 268–297. Copyright © 1951 Holt, Rinehart and Winston, Inc.

[4] Robert Williamson, "Economic Factors in Marital Adjustment," unpublished doctoral dissertation, University of Southern California Libraries, June, 1951.

lowing excerpt from a premarital interview indicates an awareness of this factor:

> I suppose she wrote down on her form that I couldn't handle money. That's right. Money slips through my pockets like quicksilver through your fingers. I never have been able to save anything. I have a great time the first of the month and I starve the last week. That's one reason I'm marrying her. She will get my check and pay the bills.[5]

The third conclusion is that the economic backgrounds of the couple are more important than the actual security rating at marriage. Couples are apt to have problems if there are wide differences in their past economic experience because our expectations regarding the normality and use of comfort-providing items and luxury items are all contingent on family patterns. Baber comments on this problem:

> One common source of economic conflict is in the unequal economic status and habits of the husband and wife prior to marriage. When a young man with a small income marries a girl from a family of somewhat higher economic rank (not necessarily wealthy) who has been used to a higher standard of living than the young husband can afford, she is likely either to spend beyond his income or to become irked at the necessity of restraint. Before marriage, in the rosy haze of romance, it looks easy to economize, and she promises to be the most thrifty of wives. But habits of a lifetime are not easily changed, and what looked simple turns out to be a long, hard process of learning self-denial. It can be done, but the record of success is certainly below the one-hundred mark.[6]

Part of the conflict which Baber describes comes from the fact that different socio-economic class families use money, time, and things differently—so differently, in fact, that conflict is engendered when individuals who are used to different habits of spending, saving, and budgeting are included in the same family. This conflict has roots far beyond what Baber describes—the roots go into different living patterns and are sustained by different values. Olson has recently studied *patterns of responsibility distribution* in an urban setting due to the factor of socio-economic stratification.[7] He studied 391 specific families who represented

---

[5] From case study in the author's files.

[6] Ray E. Baber, *Marriage and the Family*, 2nd ed. (New York: McGraw-Hill Book Company, Inc., 1953), p. 229. Reprinted by permission of the publisher.

[7] Marvin E. Olson, "Distribution of Family Responsibilities and Social Stratification," *Marriage and Family Living*, XXII, No. 1 (February, 1960), 60–65.

different status levels. The study attempted to equate differences in the distribution of responsibility in the home for each class. The following table [8] summarizes the results:

TABLE 23. Mean Distribution of Responsibilities Within the Family by Status Levels

PERSON	STATUS LEVELS		
	High %	Middle %	Low %
Wife	50.7 **	58.5 *	61.0
Husband	32.3 **	36.7 **	31.9
Children	6.9 *	3.6 *	6.0
Outside	10.1 **	1.2	1.1

* P = .05.
** P = .01.

Reprinted with the permission of *Marriage and Family Living.*

Some conclusions are clear. There is an inverse relationship between status and responsibility for wives, but middle-class husbands take more responsibility at home than men from either high or low status levels. Thus, "it would appear that the companionship ideal of husband-wife sharing of home responsibilities has gained most acceptance in the middle class." [9] Conversely, a more traditional pattern of role-taking is present in the high and low status groups.

This study brought to mind a recent case of marriage counseling in which a middle-class couple were moving rather swiftly toward a higher status due to the nation's fixation on electronics. As this happened, the husband wanted to relegate all of the household tasks he had previously performed to servants or hired help. But his still middle-class wife pictured home as a place where a man exhibited interest by fixing things and sharing many tasks with her. She could not "eat the bread of idleness" and began to nag him about his lack of attention to his family. But he said he had such responsibilities now that he wanted to rest when he got home or search out some entertainment. The problem involved a shift of his concept of appropriate tasks for his role and how this conflicted with his wife's role expectations for him.

To the degree that this study accurately measures different norms of what is proper behavior and "work" for different socio-economic status groups, it shows how important not just the spending of money may be

[8] Olson, p. 63.   [9] Olson, p. 63.

but the whole concept of the use of energy as a potential area of discord for a man and woman coming from different classes.

OCCUPATIONAL LIFE AND WISE MARRIAGE CHOICE

Does it make any difference whether your husband-to-be is a plumber, a doctor, a school teacher, or a minister? Can the factors associated with his vocation seriously affect your life as his mate? These questions are frequently asked by young people when they become aware of the importance of occupational determinism in behavior patterns.

Three factors relating to occupational roles appear to be important to marital adjustment. One is the degree of stress associated with the vocation, since such stress may be reflected in tension in the home; the second is the requirement of the vocation in hours and mobility; the third is attitudes about life associated with specific occupations which may seriously affect marital adjustment. Adams reports on Lang's work that "in one study of more than 17,000 marriages, ratings on marital happiness were contrasted with fifty different occupations." The ten occupations [10] associated with the greatest happiness and those associated with the least happiness are given below:

Highest	Lowest
1. Chemical engineers	1. Gas station employees
2. Ministers	2. Truck drivers
3. College professors	3. Musicians
4. Teachers	4. Real estate salesmen
5. Engineers	5. Plumbers
6. Wholesale salesmen	6. Auto mechanics
7. Chemists	7. Carpenters
8. Accountants	8. General mechanics
9. Civil engineers	9. Traveling salesmen
10. Office workers	10. Laborers

Locke's study partially confirms this finding; he found that professional and semiprofessional vocations are associated with marital adjustment.[11] Weeks' study involved high-school students filling out questionnaires in Spokane, Washington. He related divorce to occupation as follows:

[10] Clifford Adams, *Preparing for Marriage* (New York: E. P. Dutton and Company, 1961), pp. 151–152. Reprinted by permission of the publisher.
[11] Locke, p. 271.

TABLE 24. Number of Divorces
per 100 Families,
by Occupation *

Professional	6.8
Proprietary	8.4
Clerical	10.4
Skilled	11.6
Semi-skilled	13.4
Unskilled	7.3

* H. Ashley Weeks, "Differential Divorce Rates by Occupations," *Social Forces*, 21 Oct., 1942, 332–337. Reprinted by permission.

Williamson's study is the most comprehensive attempt yet made to measure the economic and occupational factor in relation to marital adjustment. He studied a representative sample obtained on the basis of the Shevky-Williams analysis of the social areas of Los Angeles by securing a random sample within selected social areas. His sample consisted of about 140 wives and husbands from each of three areas. The Burgess-Terman-Locke adjustment scale was employed to obtain his judgment of the relative adjustment of the couples. This correlated occupational and income groups with adjustment scores.

Williamson found that belonging to the white collar, professional, and executive groups was significantly associated with marital happiness. He also found that occupations requiring more than 47 hours of work per week were associated with low adjustment scores. This probably means that too many hours away from home and great fatigue cause conflict.[12]

After reviewing all of his findings, Williamson states:

> From the findings it can be concluded that a positive relationship exists between marital happiness and occupational adjustment.[13]

May's summary of the experience of psychologists and counselors in dealing with marital maladjustment and vocation problems also indicates that frustration in one's occupation leads to some maladjustment at home.[14]

---

[12] Williamson, p. 159. [13] Williamson, p. 162.
[14] Mark A. May, *A Social Psychology of War and Peace* (New Haven: Yale University Press, 1943), p. 153.

THE STRESS-POTENTIAL OF OCCUPATIONS

The stress-potential denotes the degree of tension-producing strains in various occupations. The stress-potential of various occupations has never been accurately measured. Obviously, individual temperaments make such a measurement difficult. A phlegmatic person will not be as anxious in tension-producing situations as a more volatile one. It is certain that the man in a highly competitive business situation is confronted with a great many worries. This is true whether he is a small entrepreneur trying to make a small profit in a small store or an executive responsible to many stockholders for dividends. Many of these men think that their status depends entirely upon their economic success, and sometimes their wives are much concerned with "keeping up with the Joneses" in physical luxuries. Aristophanes once said that "Whirl is king," and he might have said it of our economic competition and its resultant personality tensions.

These tensions often bring conflict and quarrels into the home. It is not possible for a business man to express his frustrations or hostilities toward his business associates, customers, or employees. If he did he would lower the very status he is attempting to establish. He therefore tends to contain himself until he is in a more intimate situation where an explosion will not mar his opportunity for worldly success. As a result, his general hostility may be vented over small matters in the home and directed against the wife or the children. The marriage consultant often hears this phrase: "I cannot understand my husband, he is such a different person at work than he is at home." On the other hand, the wife may identify herself with her husband's economic problems so that his recital of difficulties falls on sympathetic ears, and they face the problems together.

The business man is not the only person in a tension-producing vocation. The doctor must share sorrow, shame, and despair with his patients and is faced with daily decisions which involve life or death. The minister shares a great many of the same anxieties with members of his congregation. Policemen have a vocation in which danger is a constant companion.

OCCUPATIONAL MOBILITY AND MARITAL ADJUSTMENT

The separation of the breadwinner from his wife and children may have a serious impact upon the family, as the following experience shows.

In the few situations where the man's work involved a good deal of traveling this became an additional hazard to the marriage in terms of aggravation of a problem already existing for other reasons. One young husband, for instance, complained bitterly that his wife was unwilling to leave her parents' home. He was a professional hockey player who had to travel considerably during the hockey season. Now it is certainly true that all wives whose husbands travel do not feel that they cannot establish a home of their own and must instead stay with their mothers; there must be some unusual parental ties involved when this occurs without other obvious reasons. But it also seems likely that this fact that the husband in this case was traveling a good deal of the time made it somewhat more difficult for the wife to break her tie with her parents' home and set up an independent establishment.[15]

In every economic group there seems to be a segment that is highly mobile; thus the tenant farmer moves on an average of once every three years, and many industrial workers must constantly shift to those areas where work is plentiful. Each move tends to have a disorganizing effect on the personality of individuals and on the family itself. For these reasons high job mobility may be said to be correlated with marital maladjustment.

On the other hand, Burgess and Locke contend that in certain circumstances mobility may be associated with an organizing and not a disorganizing effect on family relations.[16] They believe that travel such as honeymoons, vacations, or long trips may have a cohesive effect if the trip satisfies both partners. In the opinion of Burgess and Locke, temporary separations seem to have no disturbing effect on family relations and actually, in some cases, the return of the absent member enhances the pleasure of the association. Certain mobile families like gypsies and families in trailers seem to be highly organized. Finally, a family or members of a family which may have been highly disorganized in one locality, sometimes, in moving to a new location, find an opportunity for readjustment. Nevertheless, mobility is disorganizing, as Burgess and Locke point out:

> The chief disorganizing effect of mobility is that it individualizes the person by detaching him from his family and other personal associations.

[15] Florence Hollis, *Women in Marital Conflict* (New York: Family Service Association of America, 1948), p. 135. Reprinted by permission.

[16] Ernest W. Burgess, Harvey J. Locke, and Mary Margaret Thomes. *The Family, from Institution to Companionship*, 3rd ed. (New York: The American Book Company, 1963), p. 377.

This takes place (1) by the interruption of communication with family and friends, (2) by bringing the person into communication with those engaging in divergent practices, (3) by freeing him from primary social controls over his conduct, (4) by weakening personal attachments and loyalties to his family and friends, and (5) by increasing the opportunity of choice between various patterns of behavior.[17]

OCCUPATIONAL ATTITUDES AND MARITAL ADJUSTMENT

The third impact of an occupation upon marriage is that of attitude formation. Bogardus first called attention to the impact of occupations on attitudes and personality configurations. He found that the vocabulary, the frame of reference, the emphasis of thought are all greatly influenced by one's vocational group. One tends to have his social, his recreational, and his educational experiences within his own occupational group. Thus each vocational group develops its characteristic speech mannerisms, its own sources of authority, its own ethics, and its method of problem-solving. Unfortunately, we know almost nothing about the way occupational determinism affects marital adjustment. Some case studies have indicated that it plays a part in marital adjustment.[18] An engineer, in discussing the problem of his children, said:

> In engineering after we have studied the problem, we seek out the principle that is involved in the solution of that problem. When we have found the principle then we can easily deduce the solution. The same must be true about kids; there must be true principles. Once I have discovered them I think the rest will be easy.[19]

This engineer had had eminent success in hydraulics. His children, unfortunately, did not respond to the principles used in hydraulics, and his shifting search for the one scientific solution to their problems was rather hard on them.

Young men, in choosing their vocation, might well give some attention to the way various occupations will affect their family life. So, too, in selecting her marriage partner, a girl must realize that economic factors play a part in marital adjustment. The level of economic security implied in her fiancé's vocational choice and the occupational patterns peculiar

[17] Burgess, Locke and Thomes, p. 381. Reprinted by permission of the publisher.

[18] See particularly the notable series of marriage counseling cases presented by Dr. Maurice Karpf in *Marriage and Family Living*, XIV, No. 3 and No. 4, August and November, 1952, in which occupational attitudes are shown to be definitely involved in the conflicts presented.

[19] From a case study in the author's files.

to that choice should have some consideration. A minister's wife must be made of tough fibre, and her dedication to the church must be virtually as great as that of her husband if they are not to have serious difficulties in their marriage. The same is true of a doctor's wife. Perhaps the most important question to be asked is whether or not the occupation is stable, promising a fairly secure employment with consequent steadiness in income. When a man chooses a vocation he chooses a way of life. The wife, too, must of necessity elect his way of life when she chooses a given man.

THE CHANGING ECONOMIC ROLE OF WOMEN AND ITS MEANING FOR WISE MARRIAGE CHOICE

Hollis reports a case which displays some of the problems occasioned by women working or men's reaction to their working:

> This couple has been married for four years and there were two children— 3 and 2 years old. However, at the beginning of marriage Mr. F. was earning a small salary, and Mrs. F. had continued to work until the previous May, employing a housekeeper to care for the children and home. At that time Mr. F. had secured a better paying job, and the couple had agreed that it would be better for the children if Mrs. F. stayed at home. Now Mrs. F. complained that her husband was gambling and that they were much in debt and that there was constant quarreling; Mr. F. had threatened to leave. Mrs. F. was devoted to her husband, and greatly distressed at this possibility. As the caseworker listened to Mrs. F.'s spontaneous story, she noted that Mr. F. did not show any great change during the marriage. She noted, too, that Mrs. F. traced her anxiety about this back to the previous May. Mrs. F. did not make any connection between this and the fact that this was the very month she had stopped working. The case worker pointed out the coincidence and asked if Mrs. F. thought there might be a connection. It developed that Mrs. F. hated housework and that she had really been making something of a drudge of herself in an attempt to do a thoroughly good job even though she disliked it. It was also clear that this left her in a constant state of irritation and thus with less ability to tolerate her husband's carelessness about financial matters. Also, she seemed to miss the security of having some money she considered her own because she had earned it. Since Mr. F. had earlier no objection to Mrs. F. working, it seemed possible that the previous harmonious balance in the family might be restored if Mrs. F. returned to her former plan of employing a housekeeper and working outside the home itself.[20]

[20] Hollis, pp. 137–138.

FIGURE 10. Women in the Working Force, 1890, 1940, 1956 *

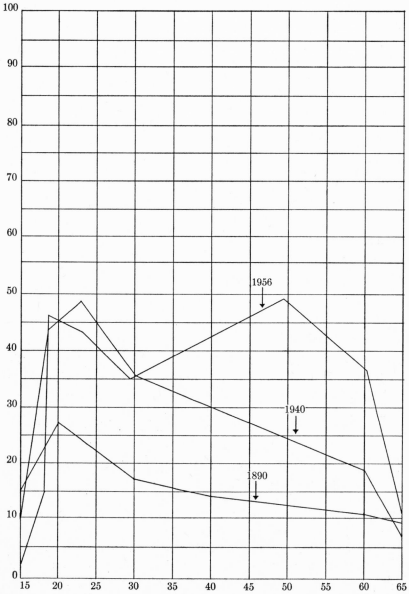

* Data from 1890 are from the 1890 Census Report and are for age groups 10–14, 15–24, 25–34, 35–44, 45–54, and 65 and over. Data for 1940 and 1956 are from the Census Current Population Reports and are for age groups 14–15, 16–17, 18–19, 20–24, 25–34, 35–44, 55–64, and 65 and over. *Womanpower*, National Manpower Council (New York: Columbia University Press, 1957), p. 126.

247

We have already indicated in Chapter Two that the shifting role of women from quiet, submissive persons toward assertive, self-confident individuals has changed the very nature of marital interaction. In this chapter we analyze the economic aspects of that role shift. Marital conflict over working or career wives is one of the basic incongruities of the contemporary family. Nowhere is the evidence of the shift in the economic role so dramatically shown as in the trends between the number of working women in 1890 and at the present time. The chart on page 247 graphically tells that story.

In 1890, 70 percent of all women workers were single because women stopped working when they married. But today over half of the working women are married, and more and more women never do leave the working forces. The figure shows that this is largely a phenomenon of the period during and following World War II. The authors provide this profile of the contemporary scene:

> An increasing number of girls go to work in their teens, with a temporary peak of nearly 50 percent participation in the labor force being reached at around 18 or 19. As they marry and begin to have children, more and more of them stop working. At the low point, around the age of 30 or slightly before, about one third of the women are in the labor force. After this point, more women return to work or go to work for the first time. The proportion in the labor force continues to rise to about age 60.[21]

What contributions do these women make to the national economy and to their individual families? Very few industries, schools, hospitals, or commercial enterprises could exist without them. Beyond this, "their substantial earnings have made it possible for millions of families to buy homes, automobiles, and household appliances, and to achieve higher standards of educational and health services. This higher level of consumer spending has helped to accelerate the expansion of the economy, which in turn has made a larger number of jobs available to women."[22] They earn about fifty billion dollars in wages each year.

Not all women work simply for economic rewards. A study of Cornell college women illuminates this point.

It is obvious that the mere earning of money plays a rather limited part in the total motivation for a woman's working. She wants to use her talents, develop her potential, help through her work, and serve people

[21] *Womanpower,* 129. Reprinted by permission of the publisher.
[22] *Womanpower,* p. 46.

much more than she desires rewards. Figures from our national economy reinforce this point.

When the family has no small children, the size of the husband's salary makes little difference on the incidence of the wife working. In those families in which the husband earns no more than $5,000, over half of the wives work.

TABLE 25. Importance of Various Occupational Requirements Among Women *
(Cornell Women, 1952: Total—420)

CONSIDER TO WHAT EXTENT A JOB OR CAREER WOULD HAVE TO SATISFY EACH OF THESE REQUIREMENTS	Percentage Ranking Each Goal As: HIGHLY IMPORTANT			
	First	Other High	Medium	Low
Goal Values				
Provide an opportunity to use my special abilities	29	56	15	1
Permit me to be creative and original	12	45	33	11
People-Centered Values				
Permit me to work with people rather than with things	24	40	22	15
Permit me to be helpful to others	11	44	36	10
Reward Values				
Stable, secure future	13	31	46	11
Chance to earn a good deal of money	3	20	56	22
Give me social status and prestige	1	16	55	28
Other Values				
Leave me free of supervision	2	31	54	12
Give me a chance to exercise leadership	–	27	54	18
Provide me with adventure	1	17	43	38

* Rose Goldsen, Morris Rosenberg, Robin M. Williams, and Edward Suchman, *What College Students Think* (Princeton, N.J.: D. Van Nostrand Co., Inc., 1960), p. 50. Copyright 1960. D. Van Nostrand Company, Inc. Reprinted by permission of the publisher.

About two-fifths of the urban families with total income between $4,000 and $7,500 would have had less total income than $4,000 if it were not for the earnings of other members of the family. In the group where the husband's income falls between $5,000 and $10,000, the number of wives that work decreases sharply, but where the husband earns over $10,000 the proportion of wives working was more than double the proportion of the husband who was in the $7,000 to $10,000 income range.[23]

These figures make no sense if we assume women want to work only because of economic motivations. This may be the strongest driving force for those wives whose husbands earn under $4,000 but certainly not for those whose husbands bring home over $10,000 a year.

What type of women are these men likely to marry? They probably want to marry educated and talented women. These women have invested sixteen or more years in acquiring skills and interests which cannot be expressed in the home, and it is true that women who work have had more schooling, on the average, than women who do not work.[24] Furthermore, they have their children later in marriage and in fewer numbers. A woman trained for technical work or intellectual contributions may feel that household chores fall short of using all of her potential. Again, the smaller apartments or homes of our urban world are so well equipped that a woman's work there is no longer from sun-up to sundown. Benz reports that a woman today needs to spend only an hour and a half in preparation for the meals of the day which in 1940 took five and a half hours.

It does seem paradoxical to train women to be competent public servants and, when they marry, ask them to give up these interests for tasks at home that are neither time-consuming nor very rewarding. There is vast role confusion about the future place of women in our culture.

But there does not seem to be much confusion in terms of trends of female employment. It is increasing far more rapidly than male employment. Between 1940 and 1950 the labor force increased by 8.6 million, but women contributed 55 per cent of the growth. Between 1950 and 1956 some 4.3 million individuals entered the labor force. Males made up only 1.2 million of that total, so the female labor force increased by 3.1 million. The best projections for the future indicate that 90 per cent, or nine out of every ten, of our school girls will work for remuneration some twenty years of their adult life.

The implications of these figures for marriage are obvious. If men hold role expectations for women that preclude their employment, and women are going to work, only conflict can result. On the other hand, if both

[23] Goldsen, Rosenberg, Williams, and Suchman, p. 72.
[24] Goldsen, Rosenberg, Williams, and Suchman, p. 80.

sexes can accept the pattern of life for a wife which gives her the most fulfilling experience, such a decision will contribute to richer marriages. It is important for wise marriage choice to have full and free discussion of career goals before marriage. The issue ought to be canvassed for role conflicts before marriage, and not after children are born. Benz feels that there are many positive benefits which come from this revolution in women's employment which can lead to a better life for both men and women. So much attention has been focused on negative aspects of maternal employment that the whole picture has not often been visualized. We shall paraphrase Benz's conclusion:

1. Labor-saving devices make the constructive use of leisure time a reality.
2. There is progress in viewing men and women's work as complementary, with less need for competition between the two sexes.
3. Wives working make it possible for men to achieve a higher education and more economic success later in life, and they have great satisfaction in doing this.
4. Men may live longer, have fewer pressure illnesses, not need to hold two jobs, because of the wife's help.
5. Marriage now can be a matter of choice and not so much a necessity for women.
6. With more real democracy in male and female relations, citizens will be better prepared to accept and carry the load of a democratic community.
7. With a high percentage of middle-aged women working there will be less domination by in-laws.
8. As women get out of the home, they can permit a father to have closer contact with his children, for they will not feel they are giving up their own limited prerogatives.
9. There will be less need and dependency during old age because both a man and wife will have contributed to social security.
10. Church and community activities will profit from participation by both men and women.[25]

With these positive insights, Benz can say finally that "as we look more closely at the changing role of women in the economic life in the U.S., it would seem that this dynamic, changing role represents the basis

[25] Margaret G. Benz, "The Changing Role of Women in Economic Life," paper read at the National Methodist Industrial Relations Conference, Cincinnati, Ohio, October 30, 1958, p. 5.

of a higher, more worthwhile and challenging standard of living for everyone." [26]

But what about the effect on children? We cannot conclude this discussion without surveying research about the impact of maternal employment on the next generation.

There is no more bitter indictment of modern women than the one which accuses them of shameful neglect of their children because they are so interested in money or a career that they spend their days working instead of staying home with their children. Some writers trace the rise in juvenile delinquency rates to the fact that many mothers are employed. As we have already indicated that more and more of our young women will be employed, it is necessary to make a careful analysis of the truth or irrelevance of these accusations. Often, stereotypes like the one ascribing social disaster as the inevitable result of maternal employment have little validity when scientifically studied. But if there is a connection between working mothers and juvenile delinquency, we should know this. What do we know about this controversial subject? Lois Meek Stolz of Stanford University has made a comprehensive review of the significant research findings regarding effects of maternal employment on children. [27]

Stolz reports on Nye's comprehensive study of factors related to working mothers. He sent questionnaires to over 2,000 mothers of children attending grades one to ten; some mothers were employed and some were unemployed. He found the working mothers had smaller families, more education and husbands who earned smaller salaries. The employed mothers visited less, telephoned fewer times, and spent less time playing cards, partying and watching television. A larger (but still small) percentage argued with their husbands, 14.9 per cent workers argued and 8.2 per cent non-workers argued. Again a larger per cent had considered divorce from their husbands (but again the differences are not great), 60.1 per cent and 46.6 per cent respectively. [28] The unemployed women desired more children, but more of them also stated that "children make me nervous." One direct conclusion is significant:

> A quasi-scale, composed of items from the favorable and unfavorable items, yielded no significant differences between the groups, but the

[26] Benz, p. 10.
[27] Lois Meek Stolz, "Effects of Maternal Employment on Children: Evidence from Research," *Child Development*, XXXI, No. 4 (December, 1960).
[28] Stolz, p. 753.

252

differences were in the direction of more favorable attitudes of employed mothers.[29]

Nye did some interesting sub-sampling. He discovered that "in small families, employed mothers are more likely to be well-adjusted to children than are nonemployed mothers, but the reverse is true in families with four or more children." [30] Nye himself concludes ". . . employment initially produces poorer adjustment to children, probably, related to role conflicts. As behavior becomes more congruent and as family expectations are modified, these conflicts are presumably decreased."

MATERNAL EMPLOYMENT AND JUVENILE DELINQUENCY

One of the most frequently repeated comments is that juvenile delinquency is caused by working mothers' neglect of their children. This is a serious charge, and it concerns a serious problem. The total rate of delinquency for the United States has doubled in one decade, from 1948 to 1958. In 1958, between 1,500,000 and 2,000,000 young people under the age of eighteen were involved with the police for misconduct. Over 600,000 of these appeared before the juvenile courts because of alleged delinquent behavior. At this rate, in the next decade, with no further increase in the basic rate, some 5,000,000 youths will be referred to the courts for delinquent acts.[31] Certainly it is important to assess the validity of the charge that maternal employment is a significant factor in the total etiology of delinquency. There have been several significant studies which have tried to test this relationship. They are condensed in the table on the following page which summarizes research on this issue.

It is clear that these findings are inconclusive and largely contradictory. After a close look at all such studies it seems fair to agree with Robison:

> It seems reasonable to conclude, on the basis of the evidence so far presented, that more definitive studies are needed before we can say *when* and *under what conditions*—the child's needs, the house setting, and the parent-child relationship—working mothers are a precipitating factor in either delinquent or disturbed behavior of a child.[32]

If there is no evidence for any relationship between maternal employment and juvenile delinquency, is there evidence that such activity re-

[29] Stolz, p. 753.   [30] Stolz, p. 754.

[31] "Report to Congress on Juvenile Delinquency," U.S. Department of Health, Education and Welfare, Children's Bureau, U.S. Govt. Printing Office 0-545966, 1960, p. 3.

[32] Sophia M. Robison, *Juvenile Delinquency, Its Nature and Control* (New York: Henry Holt and Company, 1960), p. 114. Copyright Holt, Rinehart and Winston, Inc.

253

TABLE 26. Maternal Employment and Delinquency by Per Cent

Name of Study	Number in Study	Employed Mothers	Nonemployed Mothers
Hodgkiss	362 Delinquent Girls	38	62
	362 Non-Delinquent Girls	29	71
Glueck *	500 Delinquent Boys	46.4	53
	500 Non-Delinquent Boys	46	54
Bandura and Walters	26 Delinquents	34	66
	26 Non-Delinquents	46	54

* The Gluecks found that a greater proportion of delinquents than non-delinquents had mothers who worked irregularly.

sults in psychological disturbances? Maccoby reviews the findings of studies relative to this question and concludes:

> Curiously enough the girls with working mothers seemed to have more disturbance in their relationship with their fathers than with their mothers. Possibly the mother's working in some way weakens the father's role in the family so that the daughter does not respect him as much as she might otherwise. An equally possible explanation, however, is that a number of mothers are working because their husbands are unstable, a quality which might produce negative feelings toward a man on the part of both wife and daughter. Until we can compare families which are initially similar in paternal stability and economic level, we will not know the effect of the mother's working *per se* on adolescent's adjustment.[33]

Rockman studied 400 serious cases of emotionally disturbed children who were under the supervision of the school's guidance staff. He studied four parental groups: (1) families in which mothers were full-time workers; (2) families in which the children were cared for by stepparents or guardians; (3) families in which there was no adult male; and (4) those families which were intact and the mother did not work. Some 288 of the disturbed children came from intact families and only seventy-two children had full-time employed mothers, so Rockman concludes:

> Apparently, there are many children whose mothers work, who do not present problems in school.[34]

[33] Eleanor Maccoby, "Children and Working Mothers," *Children*, V (1958), 84.
[34] Stolz, p. 759.

In a comparable study, Bandura studied thirty extremely aggressive and thirty extremely inhibited children. Only twenty-eight of these children had employed mothers and Stolz concludes that:

> Since the national average of working mothers of school children is about 40 per cent, we might assume conservatively that the working mothers in this community were not contributing more than their share of the extreme emotional problems of aggression and inhibition in children.[35]

If there is no substantial evidence regarding the harmful impact of maternal employment on adolescents or school children, we have yet to inquire about the influence that separation from the mother would have on quite small, preschool children. Siegel, Stolz, Hitchcock, and Adamson conducted such a study.[36]

They studied twenty-six matched pairs of five-year-olds in kindergarten. The children were carefully matched as to sex, age, occupation of father, number of siblings and ordinal position in the family. Data were obtained by means of recorded observations regarding behavior during four fifteen-minute periods of indoor activities. This study revealed *no differences* between the children of working and nonworking mothers for either boys or girls.

When we ask why there are not some differences between children of employed and nonemployed mothers, we find some answers in other research. Benz reports on an unpublished study by Langmuir at the Child Development Institute of Columbia.[37] In this study Langmuir found that employed mothers spend more hours per week with their children than do nonemployed mothers. One hundred mothers kept accurate time budgets. Half of them were employed and half were not. It was found that the employed mothers planned more carefully to be with their children and actually achieved more "withness" than the homemakers. It is noteworthy that the records show that to do this the working mothers gave up much social life. The study confirms the Gluecks' suspicion that we must determine the mothers' attitudes toward child raising if we are to make adequate comparisons. And we do well to remember Sears' emphasis on the critical importance of warmth in child rearing. If the dimension of warmth-coldness had been studied for both employed and nonem-

---

[35] Stolz, pp. 760–761.
[36] Alberta E. Siegel, Lois M. Stolz, E. Alice Hitchcock, and Jean M. Adamson, "Dependence and Independence in the Children of Working Mothers," *Child Development*, XXX (1959), 533–546.
[37] Benz, p. 7.

ployed mothers, we might find that it is not the *quantity of hours* spent in the same house but the quality of interaction that is the decisive factor.

We have one last question to ask. In a home where mother goes out to work, what impact does her working have on the role of expectations of boys and girls in the home? Hartley has done an exploratory study on children's role expectations in relation to maternal employment.[38] He found that "significantly more sons of working mothers than nonworking mothers assigned work roles to women," and significantly more daughters of nonworking mothers gave "housewife" their primary choice of what they wanted to do. Conversely, more daughters of working mothers said they thought they would continue to work after marriage. But Benz suggests that this may actually contribute to a successful transition in role definition rather than to role confusion:

> Probably one of the most frequent objections to the mother working outside the home is the confusion that it may cause in the minds of children as to the differentiation of the roles of men and women. . . . This is probably inevitable in periods of social change, such as that in which we are now living. A father today is not doing what his father did, and there is every reason to think that his son also will lead a very different work life. . . . There is every reason to believe that there will be less and less differentiation in the roles of men and women, as mechanization increases in the years ahead, but this does not need to make for insecurity and uncertainty.[39]

Although much research has been done in this field, it is obvious that not all of the factors that are important have been considered. Before any conclusion is attempted regarding the effects of maternal employment, we need studies in which the following factors are more definitively taken into account:

1. The degree of cohesion and warmth in the father-mother relationship.
2. The degree of congruence in work-role expectations of father and mother.
3. The effect of the warmth-coldness dimension on children of working and non-working mothers.
4. The emotional balance and the interest level of working and non-working mothers.

[38] Stolz, p. 778.   [39] Benz, pp. 7, 8.

Nevertheless, in summarizing the studies to date on different children of different ages, we must conclude with Stolz that:

> After reading these studies, it looks as if the fact of the mother being employed or staying at home is not such an important factor in determining the behavior of the child as we have been led to think. It might be more profitable to focus attention on the psychological conditions within the family, especially on the personal characteristics of the mother and the father and the kind of supervision and guidance which they provide, not only when the parents are at work but when they are at home as well.[40]

Still we do have some studies that specifically asked about the relationships of wives who work and marital adjustment and these need to be surveyed to complete our study.

THE MARITAL ADJUSTMENT OF WORKING WIVES

There is not much statistical information on the adjustment of working wives. Locke has collected data in two different studies, one in Indiana and a second (with Muriel Mackeprang) at the University of Southern California.[41] The second was devoted to measuring the adjustment of wives who worked and wives who did not. Both studies failed to show any statistically significant differences between the married women who worked and those who did not work. Locke is not convinced, however, that his findings reflect the true situation, for some persons when interviewed indicated that the wife's employment was a primary factor in the divorce:

> The first ten years of our marriage, my wife and me got along fine. I earned good money and managed it right. Then I lost my job and couldn't get another, and she got out and made money. She got independent. She wanted to run everything, and she was no manager at all. If she wanted anything, she would run up town and charge it.
>
> She would go to work and the kids would go to school, and I would be all alone. She wanted me to stay right at home, cook the meals, and do all the work. She would call up home to see if I was there. She wanted to boss everything.[42]

[40] Stolz, p. 779.

[41] Harvey J. Locke and Muriel Mackeprang, "Marital Adjustment and the Employed Wife," *American Journal of Sociology*, LIV (1949), 536–538.

[42] Locke and Mackeprang, p. 295. Reprinted by permission.

Locke found one interesting difference in opinion between the married and divorced samples in regard to the employment of women. In answer to the question directed to husbands, "If the wife worked during marriage, did the husband approve or disapprove?" a significantly larger percentage of divorced than of married men expressed disapproval. This introduces one of the basic components of the problem. In American culture it has been assumed that there is a wide difference in the economic roles of men and women, that it is the man's duty to provide well for his family and the woman's function to assume domestic duties. When these prototypes determine the attitudes of husbands or wives, a wife's working may be in conflict with the husband's expectations of what her role should be. If the man is somewhat sensitive about his own male role, this encroachment of the wife on a formerly masculine area may cause him to react violently. If she earns more than he earns, it may be especially traumatic for him. This point is illustrated by the following statement by Tead in a Washington address:

> It is of course trite and oversimplified to state the conflict as that between motherhood and a career. The dilemma is rather to be stated more profoundly as centering in decisions as to where, when, and how the drive to creativity, love, and self-growth is to express itself. In each individual case how are creative urges—psychological, intellectual, moral, and spiritual—*all* to get reasonably balanced and adequate expression? For many women in today's United States I venture that this dilemma is harder to resolve than for many men. One is prompted to say on their behalf as Antonio said of himself in *The Merchant of Venice:*
>
> > "And such a want-wit sadness makes of me
> > That I have much ado to know myself."
>
> I hasten to agree that the dilemma of this irrepressible conflict about the focus and flowering of creativity is not helped but hindered by the typical marital situation, if one can identify any situation as typical. I refer to the fact that men, broadly speaking, immersed in their own aggressive drives for creativity and for ego-maximizing in a competitive society, do not seem yet ready on as wide a scale as necessary to realize the deep roots of the woman's dilemma. Hence, they do not do what they might as husbands and as citizens to alleviate the contributing causes. There are still vast accumulations of male pride, possessiveness, false social standards, self-centeredness, and fearfulness of job competition, which aggravate the over-all social picture that women confront. These are a part of the social pattern she encounters. There is no solution, as affecting these negative

forces, which can come about without frank collaboration and a truer equal fellowship between the sexes both in the home and in the market place.[43]

On the other hand, if a woman is married to be "taken care of" and discovers that because of economic insecurity she must herself contribute to the support of the family, trouble may ensue. The important question is the attitudes the husband and wife have toward the proper role of married women in our society. Some agreement on this question ought to be reached before an engagement takes place.

This problem becomes even more acute for the woman who establishes herself in a career she enjoys and after some time gives it up for motherhood. She has had the satisfaction of accomplishment, the security of her own pay check, and the stimulation of those she worked with. All this she exchanges for the routine of keeping house and caring for children. This change involves readjustment of attitudes, reorganization of life patterns, loss of economic independence, disruption of daily patterns, loss of at least the intimacy of former friendships, and perhaps the development of a sense of injustice because being a woman means abandoning this rewarding and sometimes exhilarating work pattern. It is not that she does not appreciate homemaking. Her home may mean much to her. But having experienced the satisfaction of a man's world, it is most difficult to be wholly content with a homemaker's lot. This problem is growing more and more acute because an increasing number of college women are working after college and during the early years of marriage.

If the woman decides to combine motherhood and a career, she likewise faces much strain. Society still has a strong opinion about the right place for the wife and mother. Futhermore, society is very vocal about it, so that it is easy for all but the most calloused woman to have some guilt about the limitations work imposes on her care of her children. The problems associated with managing a successful home and being a mother while at the same time developing a career are many and complex, and there are no pat solutions for *them*. Girls of ability are inspired to look forward to performing a creative function, to achievement, to social status and responsibility, but the conditions they must meet in the responses of other persons and in situational stress often create a dilemma only the creative can solve. The tensions associated either with working for a time and then giving it up, or with trying to combine motherhood and a career need to be honestly and cogently discussed by future partners,

[43] Ordway Tead, *Social Patterns for Women: The Present and the Prospects.* Address, February 18, 1948, Washington, D.C. Mimeographed copy in the files of author.

so that dissension between the two will not add to the stresses already present in these situations. Modern young people will be concerned to protect the personality resources of the future wife as well as the needs of the future marriage.

Many of the complicated problems involved in the collision between the values of the woman who wants to work and the husband who thinks her place is in the home are illustrated in the following case adapted from Komarovsky:

> Mrs. Clark is a pretty and vivacious woman of twenty-nine, a mother of three children. She comes from a well-to-do Latin-American family. Her mother had two years of college and Mrs. Clark was sent to college in the United States. She married Mr. Clark, who still had four years of medical school ahead of him. Upon her graduation from college she went on to work for her M.A. and the young couple was supported by Mr. Clark's father.
>
> Serious sickness caused Mr. Clark to interrupt his studies for three years. In the meantime, their first child was born. When Mrs. Clark was offered a teaching job at a private school, Mr. Clark did not object to her accepting the offer, because he wished to lighten his father's financial burden. The practical problems were solved by the arrival of Mrs. Clark's mother, who, though residing elsewhere, arrived at the Clarks' apartment at 8:30 a.m. daily and stayed till 6:00, at which time both parents returned, one from the medical college and the other from her job. The birth of the second child did not change the arrangements. Mrs. Clark's mother gladly took over the additional duties, with the help of a maid.
>
> For Mrs. Clark her teaching job was not a regrettable necessity but the culmination of a lifelong ambition. As a child, her nickname was "the studious one" and the whole family was proud of her achievements in school. It was understood that she would go to college and she herself always planned to have a profession. Because she was quick and efficient she managed to be a good student and at the same time look and act like a "party girl" and have plenty of beaux. Even at present she gets a kick out of the amazed look on the faces of strangers when they learn that she is a mother of three children and a high-school teacher. She loves to teach and is working towards her Ph.D. in order to advance to college teaching.
>
> Mr. Clark, on the other hand, soon came to the conclusion that, even with the serious financial problems, he would rather go into debt than have his wife continue teaching. Mrs. Clark assured the interviewer that her husband suffered no practical inconvenience as a result of her working, neither did he have any worries about the children. He admired her mother and liked her way with the children. He returned to a clean house,

happy children, and a good meal. He himself had to work evenings and his wife's extracurricular duties on the job never interfered with his leisure. He needed her earnings and yet he wanted her to quit her job. It was "the principle of the thing."

"Why did you get married," he asked, "if you didn't expect to do your own housework and to take care of your children?" He is especially indignant on occasions when she returns too late to feed the children and put them to bed, even if she spent the morning with them, which her flexible hours allow on some days. "I can buy the help of a servant," she replies, "and do more interesting things. You should respect me all the more for it. As to putting the children to bed, how many of the women in your southern home town had 'mammies' who practically brought up their children? Why don't you accuse those mothers of shirking their duties?"

Mrs. Clark is bewildered by his attitude. Throughout her life, praise came to her through certain attainments, and now he "despises" what to her are her proudest accomplishments. "He never refers to my work as a profession, always as a job." When she jubilantly informed him of her promotion all he said was, "Now I suppose you will be even busier." His mother also looks at her as a "museum piece" or a "freak." Mrs. Clark always looked down upon women whose chatter was limited to a recipe for apple pie and gossip about maids. But her mother-in-law would drop a contemptuous remark about a "Ph.D. who doesn't know how to cook."

The marriage relationship of the Clarks is strained. Their conflicting values are doubly hard to reconcile because each has an emotional stake in his own version of marriage responsibilities.[44]

In a later chapter on marital adjustment some suggestions are made as to how men and women can solve some of the problems that accompany the employment of women.

CONCLUSION

In this chapter socio-economic factors of general importance for marriage, economic security, the style of life attendant upon participation in various occupations, the revolution in female work patterns and its meaning for marital choice, and the impact of these shifting roles for marital choice, child rearing and marital adjustment, have been studied. All of these need to be studied by young people in order to assess their future relationships wisely, and to become aware of the attitudes and needs of

[44] Mirra Komarovsky, *Women in the Modern World* (Boston: Little, Brown and Company, 1953), pp. 173–176. Copyright 1953, by Mirra Heyman. Reprinted by permission of the publisher.

potential mates and to be sure there will be mutuality of work-role expectations. The self-analysis schedule should help clarify our latent feeling about these important matters.

SELF-ANALYSIS

I. Our Socio-Economic Expectations
   A. Analyze your socio-economic expectations in life in terms of the ways of living that have characterized your background.
      1. In what socio-economic group were you raised? Have you always had access to all the luxuries you wanted?
      2. In what kind of house do you live? What kind of a car do you drive? How much spending money have you had for your own the last two years?
      3. How important do you feel these "things" have come to be for you? Do you feel you could live on a much lower scale for five years, for ten years, for life?
      4. What social-status values have come to you because of your socio-economic background? Is this important to you?
      5. If you are a girl, would you mind doing your own house cleaning, cooking, ironing, washing, if this is necessary? If a man, would you mind your wife doing this?
   B. Analyze the way you "dream" about your home, its furnishings, your own function in the home when you think about the future.

II. Your Occupational Expectations
   A. Analyze your thoughts about the general type of occupation you wish for yourself and your mate.
      1. What was your father's occupation?
      2. What values do you expect an occupation to provide?
      3. Do you have prejudices toward some types of occupation?
   B. If you are a male, note the contributions your chosen occupation will bring to your family in terms of
      1. Security
      2. Time schedule
      3. Stimulation of the job
   C. List the disadvantages your occupation will bring to your family in terms of
      1. Security
      2. Time schedule, trips, long hours, etc.
      3. Business pressure

III. The Changing Role of Women
  A. Analyze your reactions to the following possible roles of women:
     1. Those who make homemaking a career
     2. Those who work two or three years to get the family well started
     3. Those who work all the time except for certain months taken off for childbearing
     4. Those who are most interested in a career
  B. Do you believe that talented women should contribute those talents to society? Or do you think a woman's place is in the home?
  C. If a man, would you feel comfortable helping in the home if your wife worked? If a woman, would you feel comfortable if your husband did part of the housework if you contributed to the family income?

READINGS

HIMES, NORMAN and DONALD L. TAYLOR. *Your Marriage.* Rev. ed. New York, Holt, Rinehart and Winston, Inc., 1955, Chapter 14.

KOMAROVSKY, MIRRA. *Women in the Modern World.* Boston, Little, Brown and Company, 1953, Chapter 5.

LANDIS, JUDSON T. and MARY G. LANDIS. *Building a Successful Marriage.* 3rd ed. Englewood Cliffs, N.J., Prentice-Hall, Inc., 1958, Chapters 14, 15, 16.

LANDIS, PAUL H. *Making the Most of Marriage.* New York, Appleton-Century-Crofts, 1960, Chapter 26.

LEVY, JOHN and RUTH MONROE. *The Happy Family.* New York, Alfred A. Knopf, Inc., 1946, Chapter 6.

LOCKE, HARVEY J. *Predicting Adjustment in Marriage: A Comparison of a Divorced and a Happily Married Group.* New York, Henry Holt and Company, 1951, Chapter 13. Copyright Holt, Rinehart and Winston, Inc.

MAVITY, NANCY. "The Two Income Family." *Harper's Magazine,* December, 1951.

Womanpower. National Manpower Commission. Columbia University Press, New York, 1957.

CHAPTER 11

The Engagement Period

INTRODUCTION

BECAUSE of changes in mate-selection procedures, the engagement period in our society has become the last and major factor in wise marriage choice. In addition to being a testing period for the goodness of choice it serves as a planning period. This chapter analyzes the ways in which the engagement actually can be used for a fundamental evaluation of those basic interaction processes which contribute to good or poor adjustment in marriage and role playing. It goes on to discuss fundamental testing and planning procedures that help insure a successful transition into marriage. Waller stresses the usefulness of these months for the latter goal when he says that engagement serves "the need of cushioning the sharp transition from youth to adulthood, from the stage of single irresponsibility to that of married responsibility and the need for group sanctions to justify the shifts in activity and changes in role which accompany the assumption of mature adult responsibilities." [1]

Hart speaks of the testing function of engagement saying that "The engagement might well be characterized, then, as the period during which the idea of marriage with this particular mate is being explored as

---

[1] Willard Waller and Reuben Hill, *The Family: A Dynamic Interpretation*, rev. ed. (New York: Dryden Press, 1951), p. 220. Copyright © 1951, Holt, Rinehart and Winston, Inc. Reprinted by permission of the publisher.

a working hypothesis."[2] Waller also mentions this testing aspect of modern engagements:

> It is quite apparent from the foregoing functional analysis that the engagement activities which would serve the social structure best in our society are poorly communicated in the "promise to marry and engaged to be married" ideas. The mergent idea of engagement is of an arrangement that is constantly being re-evaluated with the possibility of being broken. It is a tentative agreement to marry if in the experiences of play acting permaritally the permissible marital roles prove promising for future relations.[3]

The accuracy of this analysis has been substantiated by the Burgess-Wallin study of engagement. This study followed 1,000 couples through engagement and the first five years of marriage. Of the sample only 22.4 per cent of the men and 36.5 per cent of the women had a high-school education or less.[4] Consequently it represents a highly educated college group. Protestants predominated with 42.5 per cent of the men and 57.5 per cent of the women coming from that group; 14.9 per cent of the men and 13.9 per cent of the women were Catholic; 18.8 per cent of the men and 19.7 per cent of the women were Jewish; the remainder stated that they had no religious affiliations.[5] The 666 couples who eventually married and were included in the follow-up study of their early marital adjustment had known each other, on the average, for 45.0 months, had been keeping company 31.5 months, and had been engaged 13.2 months.[6] Their unions had not been "runaway, overnight" affairs. In summarizing their findings regarding the function of the engagement period, Burgess and Wallin prove their contention by citing engagement fatalities; 24 per cent of the men and 36 of the women reported prior broken engagements. In addition, 15 per cent of the couples broke their engagements while the study was going on.[7] The engagement period thus may be regarded as the final factor in wise marriage choice.

LENGTH OF ENGAGEMENT

If the engagement period is regarded as the final testing period for marriage, it should be long enough for this process to take place. Further-

[2] Hornell Hart and Ella Hart, *Personality and the Family* (Boston: D. C. Heath and Company, 1935), p. 142.
[3] Waller and Hill, pp. 226–227. Reprinted by permission of the publisher.
[4] Ernest W. Burgess and Paul Wallin, *Engagement and Marriage* (Philadelphia: J. P. Lippincott Company, 1953), p. 54.
[5] Burgess and Wallin, p. 55.   [6] Burgess and Wallin, p. 56.
[7] Burgess and Wallin, pp. 272–273.

more, if the thesis that engagement is a "working hypothesis" is correct, it will follow that long engagements are correlated with later marital success. Burgess and Cottrell found that as the length of the engagement increased the average adjustment score was higher.[8] Terman's study likewise showed that very short engagements were unfavorable and long engagements favorable to marital adjustments.[9]

Bowman objects, however, to a too dogmatic conclusion regarding long engagements:

> We may, however, set up some very rough criteria and say that an engagement is too long if there is an excessive amount of nervous tension generated; if the couple experience a sense of frustration; if they become more than usually tired of waiting; if they grow discouraged; if they become indifferent to one another; if they begin to accept the status quo as a substitute for marriage and lose interest in the latter; if the engagement constitutes more than a relatively small fraction of the total period from meeting to wedding. This is a dogmatic statement and we have no substantial evidence on which to justify it. We wish to counteract the opinion so commonly expressed among students to the effect that on the basis of a few months' courtship a couple may without risk enter upon an engagement of several years' duration.[10]

It must always be remembered that the conclusions of research studies are based on averages. It is certainly possible that a young couple who are more apt than others at communication and more relaxed in sharing affectional relationships may accomplish this "dress rehearsal" for marriage in a shorter time. There is a rhythm in growth of cohesion for couples and this rhythm may vary from couple to couple. There is no need to assume that what is essential for one or for most relationships is necessarily best for all. Duvall and Hill give some functional criteria which may be helpful to young people thinking about the duration of their engagement:

> Engagements need to be long enough to act as a screening device to alienate and separate incompatible couples who would otherwise marry, only to separate more painfully after some years of marriage. The answer to the question of length of engagement is given best, not as a number of

[8] Ernest W. Burgess and Leonard S. Cottrell, *Predicting Success or Failure in Marriage* (New York: Prentice-Hall, Inc., 1939), pp. 167–168.

[9] Lewis M. Terman, *Psychological Factors in Marital Happiness* (New York: McGraw-Hill Book Company, Inc., 1938), pp. 198–199.

[10] Henry A. Bowman, *Marriage for Moderns* (New York: McGraw-Hill Book Company, Inc., 1948), p. 249. Reprinted by permission of the publisher.

months or years, but in terms of the indefinite "long enough." The engagement, then, should be long enough to perform the many functions of testing, discussing, learning, fighting, and loving which underlie successful marriage.[11]

GOALS FOR THE ENGAGEMENT PERIOD

The assumption underlying the approach to engagement as a working hypothesis of marriage is that the intimacy and new status accorded a couple during engagement enable them to test their relationship in ways that were not possible previously. There are other essential factors which are tested in an engagement and which do not play such a part in early courtship. The clue to the nature of these factors appears in Waller's term, premarital play-acting. This play-acting has to do with the actual planning for and solving of situations which will be faced in matrimony. Previously, during courtship, the attention of a couple has been centered upon the personality and background factors which operate to draw them together in a developing love situation. But during engagement, the focus is upon whether or not that love relationship has the resources and the strength to weather the problems of marriage. In this respect new elements related to the future become more important. The new elements that are specially tested during engagement are the adaptability of the individuals, their facility in communication, their adjustment to reality, and their ability to solve problems.

ADAPTABILITY

The transitional nature of contemporary family life plus the heterogeneous nature of a social group often brings together individuals with diverse religious, cultural, social, and economic backgrounds. Individuals in love often bring to their engagement conflicting expectations of the roles they will play as husband and wife, as parents, and as members of the larger community. When such a couple are engaged and face the reality of their coming marriage, they tend to focus their attention on the way they will act after marriage. The extent to which they can adjust to differences will determine the success of their engagement and is a measure of later marriage success. The extent to which they can adjust is largely a function of their flexibility or adaptability. This quality is not

[11] Evelyn M. Duvall and Reuben Hill, *When You Marry*, rev. ed. (Boston: D. C. Heath and Company, 1953), p. 89. Reprinted by permission of the publisher.

267

much tested when they are making love or seeking to impress each other. But when they face actual planning for the future, their adaptability comes to the fore.

Burgess and Wallin analyzed the way engaged couples face disagreement and stress. They measured the extent of agreement and disagreement on such questions as dates with one another, demonstration of affection, arrangements for marriage, religious matters, table manners, attitudes toward conventionality, recreation, philosophy of life, money, ways of dealing with in-laws and friends.[12]

Some 1.7 per cent reported that they "always agreed" on all items, 18.5 per cent reported that one "always agreed" and the other "almost always agreed," but nearly four-fifths of the couples stated that they disagreed on one or more items and one half reported disagreements in one to four areas of their relationships. This means that adjustment between these partners must involve the modification of individual expectations and adaptation to the other's role.[13]

Important differences in attitudes and values face the majority of engaged couples in our day. If these differences cannot be solved or resolved the relationship will not endure. On the other hand, couples with seemingly great divergencies of background and interests may be successful if they are highly adaptable. Burgess and Wallin account for the successful adjustment in marriage of some couples who rated low on their engagement-adjustment scores by suggesting that one or both members may have had a general personality pattern of adaptability.[14]

Locke found, too, that adaptability was associated with marital adjustment.[15] He measured adaptability by the capacity for "giving in" in arguments, not being dominating, slowness in getting angry, and quickness in getting over anger.

Burgess and Wallin list the conditions of adaptability as empathy, flexibility, command of appropriate attitudes and roles, and the motivation to adjust. They define empathy as "the ability to recognize and appreciate the motivation of the actions of others."[16] Flexibility is the capacity to vary one's responses in interpersonal relations, a capacity which is partly psychogenic.[17] Motivation to adapt means the drive that

---

[12] Burgess and Wallin, p. 246.   [13] Burgess and Wallin, p. 247.

[14] Burgess and Wallin, p. 520.

[15] Harvey J. Locke, *Predicting Adjustment in Marriage: A Comparison of a Divorced and a Happily Married Group* (New York: Henry Holt and Company, 1951), p. 205. Copyright © 1951, Holt, Rinehart and Winston, Inc.

[16] Burgess and Wallin, p. 624.   [17] Burgess and Wallin, p. 626.

impels the marriage partners to work at adapting their behavior to that of the other person. By command of appropriate responses is meant the possession of responses which can be integrated with the understanding of the behavior of the mate. Adaptability can be increased most by improving awareness of appropriate responses.[18] This can be accomplished in marriage by learning by experience the roles, attitudes, and responses appropriate to the spouse's behavior, and it can be enhanced in marriage classes by stressing the significance of adaptability in situations which can be productive of future misunderstanding and conflict. Engagement is important not only in testing but also in developing adaptability.

COMMUNICATION

Being able to adapt to another person depends largely on understanding that person's needs and expectations. Unless role expectations are communicated in engagement neither person will learn how the other needs to adjust.[19] The basic need for affection in marriage will not be met unless the marriage partners are able to communicate their sentiments of devotion and tenderness. Karlsson thinks that communication is basic to marital adjustment. He says: "In order to perform the marital operation efficiently it is necessary for the spouses to be able to predict what the other one will do next. Such prediction requires communication of intentions." [20]

Before engagement, communication regarding role expectations is generally not adequate. Often it is not satisfactory during the engagement period either. During this period, if it is to be a testing period, a couple must discuss all of the important areas of married life. The following excerpt from a case study indicates the importance of communication in engagement adjustment:

> *Girl:* I listed, in the things I wanted changed, a more masculine support from Herb. We are going to be married in a month and we haven't yet found a place to live. Last Saturday I had to get a paper, I had to find the ads for apartments to rent, and I had to suggest we go looking. He is supposed to take the lead in those things and I resent having to do it.

[18] Burgess and Wallin, pp. 639–640.
[19] George Karlsson, *Adaptability and Communication in Marriage* (Upsala: Almquist and Wiksells, 1951), p. 33.
[20] Karlsson, p. 33.

Man: I thought about looking for an apartment but I didn't know what she wanted me to do about it. I resented her hauling out the paper and suggesting that we had better find an apartment. There are a lot of things I'd like to do but I don't know what to expect from her. I did suggest some things about the wedding and she seemed to resent that.[21]

In this case the role expectations were quite similar but a lack of communication caused friction and resentment. Often the counselor functions in such a case to clear the channel so ideas flow more freely between the partners.

Karlsson developed an index to measure the degree of communication. He brought together a number of items such as talking about children, work or finances, appreciating the work of the mate, criticizing the mate, praising the mate, or playing with children. He then asked whether a change in the behavior of each mate was wished for by the other. He measured the amount of communication in the marriage by comparing the answers of the husband and wife and noting the degree to which each understood the wishes of the other.[22] The communication index thus constructed showed a high correlation with marital adjustment. Karlsson believes that this indicates an association between communication and marital satisfaction, and that the communication index can be used in predicting marital adjustment.

Locke also measured the relationship of intimacy of communication to marital adjustment. He investigated items dealing with face-to-face communication, loss of unity through decline of communication, sympathetic understanding, frequency of kissing, talking things over together and engaging in outside interests together. His index of items includes that of affectional communication as well as verbal. His conclusion supports that of Karlsson.

> Intimate, friendly, and prolonged communication between a husband and a wife tends to weld them together, whereas a decided decline in this type of communication tends to break up existing attachments. This conclusion was supported, in part, by items in the questionnaire, but was supported to a much greater extent by the case materials secured in the interviews.[23]

Waller thinks that communication is a stabilizer of interaction for the engaged pair:

[21] From a case study in the author's files.   [22] Karlsson, pp. 132–133.
[23] Locke, p. 246. Reprinted by permission of the publisher.

Since there is so much to learn, so many differences of background to be accepted, understood, and accommodated, and since pluralistic ignorance (the uncertainty of each concerning the real attitudes of the other) has so completely characterized dating and courtship relations, communication becomes a major process of stabilization in engagement.[24]

Couples that develop ease of communication in engagement are beginning the adjustment process which will be important in their later marriage.

ADJUSTMENT TO REALITY

Courtship is apt to be a time of over-idealization. It is important during the engagement period that a realistic appraisal of the future mate take place so that there will be few "surprises" when marriage actually begins. During courtship, idealization, whether due to the frustration of sexual drives as suggested by Waller or the need for self-esteem as suggested by Burgess and Wallin, has tended to distort and obscure the real self of the future mate. Furthermore, each party in courtship tends to obscure his or her negative qualities in order not to threaten the developing affectional relationship. The love relationship thus tends to develop between two masked individuals. Each person actually wears a double mask, one self-imposed and the other created by the lover. It is obvious that, if marriage choice is to be adequate, it must involve stripping away these masks.

This adjustment to reality takes place in many situations. During courtship both partners present themselves with as much glamour and appeal as possible. Life cannot be lived on this plane. During engagement, society sanctions more intimate contacts so that each may see the other, as Waller says, "without makeup." During courtship such matters as religious differences are largely ignored but in the engagement period some settlement must be made regarding the use of birth-control, the religious education of children, religious rituals in the home, and philosophies of life.

To adjust to reality involves conscious planning on the social, economic, religious, ethical, and recreational planes. The decisions that are reached need not be final. But in discussing such problems, the masks come off, communication begins on a level of reality, and practice in adapting takes place.

[24] Waller and Hill, pp. 236–237.

PROBLEM-SOLVING

In companionship marriage, the way a couple goes about problem-solving often determines the success or failure of the marital union. As society today does not furnish cultural answers to problems, most young couples must improvise their own solution. Communication is essential, so is adaptability, and facing reality helps the couple make wise decisions. The manner in which a young man and woman face problems involves establishing an approach, a way of meeting difficulties. The pattern worked out during engagement is most likely to be the pattern to be followed during marriage.

There are many alternative methods of decision-making. None of them is superior to the other. This is because of the difference in background expectations of individuals. A girl coming from a first-generation German home in which the family stability patterns involved the dominance of the father is not prepared to enter a democratic structure. She has had a happy home experience in which the father was the master. In her own home she will expect the husband to take the lead. In some cases the boy who has been brought up by a mother with a very strong personality will be more comfortable in a home in which his wife takes the lead. In general, however, the well-adjusted American family follows democratic procedures and shares decision-making, depending on consensus rather than on autocratic rule. This generalization is supported by the following data from Locke: Some 62.3 per cent of the married men and 66.9 per cent of the married women, but only 35.9 per cent of the divorced men and 36.3 per cent of the divorced women, reported democratic methods of making decisions. Equally significant differences between the married and divorced samples were found in the areas of disciplining children, affectional behavior, religious behavior, and recreation for both men and women. Thus democratic relationships are clearly associated with success in contemporary family life.

Locke concludes that: "democratic relationships, as measured by reported equality in taking the lead, were decidedly more prevalent among happily married than divorced couples." [25], *

While the method of making family decisions may vary from family

[25] Locke, p. 262.

* The relationship of democracy to successful marital adjustment is described more fully in Chapter Twenty.

272

to family, the most important consideration is that decisions be made. If matters that cause disagreement are shunted out of consciousness because they threaten the affectional relationships, the relationship itself is weak. If partners become angry whenever a problem arises, they will have little or no basis for wise decision-making during their marital experience. It is imperative that in facing reality during the engagement period, the man and woman explore their problem-solving abilities and seek to establish the type of approach to decision-making which corresponds to their role expectations and in which both feel comfortable.

TABLE 27. Per Cent of Happily Married and Divorced Reporting Democratic Relationships in Given Situations, with Critical Ratios of the Difference of Per Cents *

SITUATIONS	MEN			WOMEN		
	Married	*Divorced*	*CR*	*Married*	*Divorced*	*CR*
1. Making family decisions	62.3	35.9	3.2	66.9	36.3	4.7
2. Disciplining the children	55.2	40.5	1.9	58.3	22.0	4.8
3. Handling money	50.9	38.1	—	58.1	34.8	3.7
4. Affectionate behavior	59.9	41.0	2.5	59.0	33.3	3.7
5. Religious behavior	52.9	38.9	—	59.7	25.0	5.0
6. Recreation	57.6	42.6	2.0	54.2	36.4	2.7
7. Meeting people	40.4	32.3	—	42.6	33.7	—

* Adapted from Harvey J. Locke, *Predicting Adjustment in Marriage*, New York, Henry Holt and Company, 1951, p. 263. Copyright © 1951, Holt, Rinehart and Winston, Inc. Reprinted by permission of the publisher.

The couple that builds problem-solving patterns efficiently during the engagement period is laying a firm foundation for the growth of cohesion during marriage. Honest facing of differences involves compromises, but the compromises result in cohesion. In most cases the achievement of the democratic approach during engagement will insure good marital adjustment. At the end of this chapter there is a simple inventory which may help couples to determine the degree of their communication, their relationship to real problems, and their problem-solving techniques. It may be useful to some couples to test the quality of their engagement behavior as preparation for marriage.

BROKEN ENGAGEMENTS

According to Burgess and Wallin, about one-third of the young men and one-half of the young women in their sample had had one or more broken engagements. More and more young people are willing to break an engagement rather than face a broken marriage later in life. Sometimes it is difficult for a girl who has made a formal announcement of her intention to wed, who has been feted by her friends, and who has organized her future plans around a particular man, to break off relations with him. But if she finds that they cannot adapt to each other, that communication is difficult, that role expectations are very diverse, and that their problem-solving techniques do not work, it is better to suffer the trauma of sending back engagement presents than to pack them away after a divorce.

Burgess and Wallin found that broken engagements were due to the following disruptive factors: (1) slight emotional attachment, (2) separation, (3) parental opposition, (4) cultural divergencies, and (5) personality problems.[26] In the first case the strength of and the degree of communication of affection is related to engagement success. The importance of face-to-face communication (as Locke indicates) is vital to the development of engagement success. Burgess and Wallin's evidence both from interviews and from statistical analyses indicates that parental opposition is an important factor in engagements that fail. Locke's data confirm the importance of this factor. He found that parental approval or disapproval of the prospective mate differs considerably between the married and the divorced persons in his Indiana study.[27] The following table compares the Burgess-Cottrell study with Locke's Indiana and Swedish studies in regard to parental approval of the future mate.

Adjusted men and women in all three studies reported significantly greater parental approval of mates than did the unadjusted men and women.

FACTORS IN ENGAGEMENT FAILURE

Burgess and Wallin measured cultural divergencies by studying differences in religion and differences in leisure-time interests. They found that couples with the same religious affiliations showed fewer unbroken

[26] Burgess and Wallin, p. 273.   [27] Locke, p. 119.

274

engagements (73.1 per cent) than those of mixed faith (58.8 per cent).[28] Similarly, couples with differences in leisure-time interests, indicating different cultural backgrounds, show the same kind of percentages of disrupted engagements.

TABLE 28. Per Cent of Adjusted and Unadjusted Reporting Parental Approval of Mate before Marriage: Three Studies *

STUDY	MEN			WOMEN		
	Adjusted	Unadjusted	CR	Adjusted	Unadjusted	CR
Chicago study (Burgess-Cottrell)	87.3	68.2	4.3	80.8	62.2	3.8
Indiana study (Locke)	76.8	51.9	4.6	82.3	45.6	7.1
Swedish study (Locke)	85.8	60.0	4.0	90.5	66.1	4.4

* This table was prepared by Harvey J. Locke for the annual Research Lecture at the University of Southern California, May, 1953.

Burgess and Wallin conclude that people with important personality problems tend to break engagements: men who are dependent, promiscuous, insecure, or contented with the less-demanding bachelor state; young women who have over-idealized or have been over-attached to their fathers, who are afraid of sex or childbirth, and who have such high standards for a mate that their fiancés cannot meet them.[29]

Other personality problems that make for engagement failure listed by Burgess and Wallin are incompatibility of temperament, unsatisfied personality need, and the career interest of either man or girl. As these have been discussed in the chapters on psychological and economic factors in wise mate choice, they will not be described further here.

When it appears that prolongation of the engagement is not wise because the couple cannot adjust well to each other the engagement must be broken. This may be done by one or the other or by mutual consent. It may be done by breaking completely and at once or by "tapering off" the relationship. There is much diversity of opinion on this point. Bowman feels that it is better to break sharply and be free of a burdensome situation. Burgess and Wallin give the values of both procedures but stress the diminution of emotional turmoil for the rejected person when

[28] Burgess and Wallin, p. 289. [29] Burgess and Wallin, pp. 278–279.

the slower procedure is followed. Every situation should be viewed as creatively as possible by the individuals involved and the method chosen which will be least painful. Young people need to anticipate the feelings of remorse and chagrin that follow a broken engagement. However, if the act of breaking an engagement can be regarded as a learning process, as a step in wise marital choice, it may serve to promote more discriminating choices in the future. Burgess and Wallin suggest that an increase in the rate of broken engagements may well result in a decrease later in the divorce rate.

ADJUSTING TO A BROKEN ENGAGEMENT

The most extensive study conducted regarding the trauma of broken love relationships is that of Kirkpatrick and Caplow at the University of Minnesota.[30] They did not limit their study to engaged couples but to couples who were certainly so serious that their findings have meaning here. Their study showed that about half of the students had no permanent emotional hurt but that it took the rest from several weeks to a year to heal the wound. Judson Landis in another study of 1,095 students found that two-thirds of the students were over the emotional impact of the breakup in less than six months but that it took longer for the others.[31] In fact 12 per cent indicated that they still had the aftereffects two years later. Kirkpatrick and Caplow studied adaptive measures designed to enable adjustment to the loss. They discovered the following mechanisms of adjustment listed by order of importance:

1. Remembering only pleasant things.
2. Dreaming about partner.
3. Daydreaming.
4. Frequenting places with common associations.
5. Preserving keepsakes.
6. Reading over old letters.

Landis adds that about two-thirds begin dating others to help forget the lover. Half of his subjects tried to avoid meeting the lover, but the other half of his sample schemed to do so.

Burgess and Wallin analyzed the process by which an engagement

[30] Clifford Kirkpatrick and Theodore Caplow, "Courtship in a Group of Minnesota Students," *American Journal of Sociology*, LI, 114–115.

[31] Judson Landis and Mary Landis, *Building a Successful Marriage* 3rd ed. (Englewood Cliffs, N.J.: Prentice Hall, 1958), p. 148.

is broken as (1) Growing difficulties developing into misunderstandings and quarrels, (2) the verbal breaking of the engagement, either abruptly or over a period of time, (3) the emotional crisis, the duration and seriousness of which is due to many things including the awareness of the partner that the break-up was imminent, (4) the rebound experience, escape into a new love affair and (5) the evaluation of the engagement experience in terms of the future.[32] This study reveals that some students become more cautious but others become cynical. One such student stormed into my office just after his girl had told him she loved another and was breaking their engagement. He said:

> What makes women behave this way? I never looked at another girl after we were engaged but evidently she just used me to meet others. It's a whole year out of my life but that doesn't mean anything to her. I won't get caught by another woman this way. From now on I'll do the ditching and in the meantime I'm going to get everything I can out of women.

A perplexing problem is how to reveal to the other that ardor has cooled and what seemed to be a wise choice no longer seems advantageous. Some students say that it is best to be very honest about it and chop it off immediately so that they do not have to play games trying to express affection they do not feel and make plans they know they will never see fulfilled. But other students caution that a sudden break is too drastic and hurtful and that sometimes what seems like an impossible obstacle in a relationship can be corrected, and a couple should not break up at their first impulse in that direction. There are good reasons for doing it either way. Perhaps the soundest advice is to combine honesty with a true regard for the other person and end the relationship in a way that seems least likely to cause deep wounds.

IMPORTANT CONSIDERATIONS FOR ENGAGEMENT BEHAVIOR

There are a number of other areas of behavior and planning which are important for a couple to consider. The first of these is sexual behavior during engagement.

Sexual behavior during courtship has already been considered so that this discussion is limited to the effect of sexual activity on engagement success and on later marital success. Burgess and Wallin found that those who did not have intercourse with future mates tend to have the highest

[32] Burgess and Wallin, pp. 297–301.

engagement-success scores. Men who had never had premarital inter-course had a mean engagement-success score of 155.5 as compared to a mean score of 145.5 for those who often participated in premarital coitus. For women the scores were: never, 154.3 and often, 147.4. Never having premarital intercourse is associated with engagement success.[33]

The next question deals with the relation of premarital sexual inter-course to marriage adjustment. Burgess and Wallin related sex histories to four criteria of success in marriage: (1) marital happiness, (2) general marital satisfaction, (3) love, and (4) marriage-permanence scores. De-tailed statistics are given only in regard to the relation of love scores in marriage to premarital intercourse. The love score was scaled as 0 to 13. Under 9 was considered a low score and from 12 to 13 was regarded as a high score. Forty-nine per cent of the husbands who had never had pre-marital intercourse with their mates fell into the high category of love scores as compared with 25.8 per cent of those who had.[34] The statistics indicate that those men who had had intercourse seemed more likely to fall into the low love-score class and much less likely to be included in the high-score group. The same characteristic pattern is revealed in the case of women. Sixty-two per cent of the women who had never had premari-tal coitus fell into the high category of love scores as compared with 49 per cent of those who had frequently had premarital intercourse.[35]

Burgess and Wallin summarize premarital relationships between spouses and the other adjustment indices as follows: "In general the other meas-ures of marital success have the same relation as the love scores to fre-quency of premarital intercourse with spouse . . ."[36]

Burgess and Wallin conclude from these data that: "Summarizing roughly, the result of different studies, although not decisive, supports the conclusion that husbands and wives with no experience of premarital intercourse have the higher probability of marital success. . . ."[37]

Kinsey also analyzed the premarital experience of 5,774 females in re-lationship to marriage. His findings are the most detailed to date, but they are limited by the nature of his sample for (a) his subjects are all volunteers, (b) 3,138 are below the age of twenty-five, and 1,927 are be-low the age of twenty, (c) 3,313 or 58.2 per cent are not or never have been married, (d) only 445 of the 4,922 have ever been divorced, sepa-rated, or widowed, (e) 75 per cent have some college or post-graduate

---

[33] Burgess and Wallin, pp. 297–301. [34] Burgess and Wallin, pp. 368–369.
[35] Burgess and Wallin, p. 369. [36] Burgess and Wallin, p. 369.
[37] Burgess and Wallin, p. 370.

study and only 17 per cent are limited in education to high school. This means that Kinsey's conclusions regarding the effect of premarital sexual intercourse on marriage are based on about 40 per cent of his volunteer sample, or those married.

Kinsey found that nearly 50 per cent of the females in his married group had coitus before they were married.[38] Of these, 46 per cent had coitus only with their future husbands, 13 per cent had it only with other males, and 41 per cent had coitus with both fiancé and other males.[39] Only 30 per cent of the grade-school group had had premarital coitus as compared to 47 per cent of the high-school and 60 per cent of the college group.[40]

On analyzing Kinsey's figures we find that 468 did not have orgasm in premarital intercourse, and 614 did have orgasm from one to twenty-five-plus times in premarital intercourse. The lowest rate of orgasm in marriage is not for those who never had premarital intercourse but for those who had coitus which did not result in orgasm. The physiological or psychological factors involved in the reactions of these women were not analyzed.

A considerable number of premarital sexual experiences results in pregnancy. Kinsey's sample included 2,094 single, white females who had had coitus and for whom he had data on pregnancy. The number of pregnancies was 476, or 18 per cent.

It is important to point out here that these findings are all averages. Some couples who had had very frequent sexual relations were included in the most successful engagement and marriage groups; some couples who were continent fell into the lowest engagement and marriage-adjustment groups. Each couple has different cultural and ethical backgrounds.

There are two other considerations which young couples must bear in mind as they are trying to decide whether to have sexual intercourse during the engagement period. We have just been pointing out the large percentage of engagements that fail and are broken. No one has done a study yet to determine if engagements in which there was coitus leave a heritage of greater disillusionment than those where the couple did not become that intimate. But many individuals in counseling sessions following the breakup of an engagement have accused the other of only getting engaged for the purpose of exploiting the other. Now this may be an un-

[38] Alfred C. Kinsey, W. B. Pomeroy, C. E. Martin and P. H. Gebhard, *Sexual Behavior in the Human Female* (Philadelphia: W. B. Saunders Co., 1953), p. 286.
[39] Kinsey, Pomeroy, Martin and P. H. Gebhard, p. 336.
[40] Kinsey, Pomeroy, Martin and P. H. Gebhard, p. 293.

fair evaluation, but it does indicate the degree of bitterness that may be present when a girl gives herself to a man with the understanding that they are going to be married, only to find later that he has chosen another. At least it is wise for couples to admit the possibility that their engagement may fail and to ask themselves if they wish to consummate their sexual lives with this possibility in mind. Some counselors feel that the sexual strain of modern engagements is so great that, unless there is sexual relief, quarreling may lead to a breakup of the engagement. On the other hand, it is also necessary to record the fact that for some individuals guilt over sexual experimentation and doubt over compatibility may also lead to the same result.

The second consideration has to do with the possibility of pregnancy before the marriage. Here a couple should ask themselves if a premarital pregnancy will cast any shadow upon their wedding and, more importantly, destroy any of their early plans. Most couples try not to have a baby the first year because of the difficulty of early adjustments. That this factor has some importance is seen in Christensen and Meissner's study which showed that the divorce rate was more than twice as high for those marriages where the conception happened before the wedding than it was for marriages in which the girl became pregnant some time after the wedding date. The respective percentages were 18.54 and 8.95.[41] We assume that some of these marriages were "forced marriages" and would not have occurred if it had not been for the pregnancy, but it is also possible that some of these failures represent the inability to adjust to marriage when the girl has the additional burden of becoming a mother. Perhaps the safest rule to follow here is to suggest frequent and honest communication about the problem, to try to find the appropriate response to assure the longtime happiness of the engagement partner, and to adapt to the needs of the other. On the other hand, it is well to remember that for the average person intercourse in engagement is not correlated with engagement success or marital success.

PREPARING FOR MARRIAGE DURING THE ENGAGEMENT PERIOD

In moving from "irresponsibility to that of married responsibility" a young couple must undertake a variety of tasks which they have never

[41] Harold T. Christensen and Hanna H. Meissner, "Studies in Child Spacing: III—Premarital Pregnancy as a Factor in Divorce," *American Sociological Review*, XIX, No. 6 (December, 1953), 641–644.

faced before. Of course the major one has to do with the way in which each cherishes and enhances the personality of his mate. But other responsibilities must be faced to make the other person secure and comfortable. The couple must locate a house or an apartment. They must determine to some degree how they will manage their finances and their time. They have to decide when they wish to begin a family. Today most couples discuss the question of the young wife working and how long she will continue to work. Most couples talk long and earnestly about the perpetuation of premarital patterns of interpersonal relationships, such as the advisability of keeping their old friends, whether they should have a "night out," and what they will do about keeping the respective in-laws happy. There are legal chores which help to indicate their seriousness in working toward a marriage: they must plan to change or write a will, change over their insurance, open joint bank accounts, transfer their investments or savings, etc. And it is in discussing these practical matters that a couple may gain in their ability to communicate, to solve problems, and to make mutual decisions. They also test their ability to disagree, to compromise, and to learn to think as a pair. In working out adequate plans for the future, many couples have found that premarital counseling is an invaluable help.

PREMARITAL COUNSELING

Premarital counseling is a relatively new step in preparing for marriage. The Roman Catholic Church has instituted a Pre-Cana conference during which those who are soon to be married receive specific instruction regarding marital adjustment. Many Protestant ministers have been trained in clinical psychology and in the sociology of the family, and are prepared to assess carefully any problem areas the couple recognize in their relationship. Many colleges have instituted courses in marriage. The instructors of these courses serve formally or informally as marriage counselors on their respective campuses. Some private agencies have developed premarital counseling programs. One of the oldest of these is the American Institute of Family Relations in Los Angeles. The Marriage Council of Philadelphia has developed a notable program of premarital counseling under the direction of Emily Mudd.

The work of Burgess and Wallin already cited proved that it is possible to predict the probability of happiness in marriage from a marriage-prediction schedule consisting of five parts: background factors, personality traits, engagement relations, engagement adjustment, and anticipated contingency factors. This text is being widely used to help locate areas in which growth is essential before marriage takes place. A couple should seek counsel with their minister or priest, a marriage counselor, and a gynecologist. The contributions of the three will now be discussed. It is not assumed that the average couple has great problems that will burden their marriage if they do not seek help. It is assumed that premarital counseling can help every couple to clarify their conceptions of what to expect in marriage and improve their adjustment.

THE MARRIAGE COUNSELOR

The marriage counselor may use a group of tests, such as the Burgess-Wallin predictive test mentioned above, to determine degrees of compatibility and readiness for marriage. Certainly he will consider background factors, psychological and cultural factors, the problem-solving patterns of the partners, as well as any specific difficulties they themselves bring to him. In addition he may explore with the couple attitudes which lead to cohesion in marriage and, on the other hand, situations which are commonly disruptive unless they are met with intelligence and understanding. The engagement-adjustment test used by the author in premarital counseling is appended to this chapter. It measures communication, agreement on role, values, and decision-making.

PREMARITAL TESTS

Two temperament tests widely used by marriage counselors are the Johnson Temperament test and the Guilford-Zimmerman Temperament Survey. Both reveal basic temperament trends of which it is important to be aware before marriage. The tests are given to the two partners and the profiles are then superimposed one upon the other. The results reveal areas of divergence, and degrees of divergency, that might be troublesome in marriage if not anticipated and dealt with. The Guilford-Zimmerman test reveals personality patterns in terms of polarities—activity-inactivity, restraint-impulsiveness, ascendancy-submissiveness, sociability-shyness, emotional stability-emotional instability, objectivity-subjectivity, friendliness-hostility, thoughtfulness-thoughtlessness, cooperativeness-criticalness, and masculinity-femininity. If the difference is not too great the counselor will interpret it as complementary. Such a difference will add to the interest and strength of the marriage. If the difference is very great, however, possible friction is indicated, and the couple will want to develop ways of dealing with it. The use of the temperament survey often helps couples to face problems which previously they had felt emotionally but were unable to define intellectually. This is particularly true of the masculinity-femininity index. Society is passing through a period of changing roles, of confused meanings of dominance, submission or equality, of inferiority and superiority. Consequently such a survey often serves to bring latent problems into the open. To take such a test and talk through the meaning of any problems revealed by the test often quiets doubts and helps the couple achieve new patterns of understanding.

The profile chart (Fig. 11) is an actual picture of the way in which one couple relates temperamentally. The prognosis for that marriage is in general very good. The differences in traits are not marked but neither are the similarities so great as to indicate that the partners will be bored with each other. Both are emotionally stable, sociable, friendly, and thoughtful. They are cooperative, and have enough energy to match one another rather well. However, the chart indicates—in the last column— that the woman rated very high on masculinity, the man correspondingly low. Exploration of this contrast indicated a latent but potential conflict. The girl had been a leader in high school, in college, and in groups, and she was used to taking the lead. The man, while moderately successful in his undertakings, had not developed into a leader. He had often resented her taking the lead but had refrained from discussing it for fear of marring their otherwise admirable relationship. When the survey brought the issue to the surface, the man poured out his feelings. His resentment was quite apparent. Surprisingly, she, too, had been secretly troubled by what she thought was his lack of purpose. Having spent several hours discussing the problem with the counselor, they made a specific plan for a more democratic approach to difficulties, and the danger of what might, in marriage, have developed into a major conflict in role-playing was ameliorated by communication before the wedding. Sometimes, the temperament survey will reveal profound submissiveness, emotional instability, or much hostility and intolerance. In such cases it is well for the individuals involved to discuss their future with a person capable of helping them develop more adequate personality resources for marriage. They will probably be referred, for more comprehensive counseling, to a psychiatrist or a clinical psychologist.

Sexual factors in premarital counseling. The marriage counselor will want to discuss quite specifically with the couple the adequacy of their

FIGURE 11. Profile Chart for the Guilford-Zimmerman Temperament Survey Showing Differences in Temperament between a Man and a Woman *

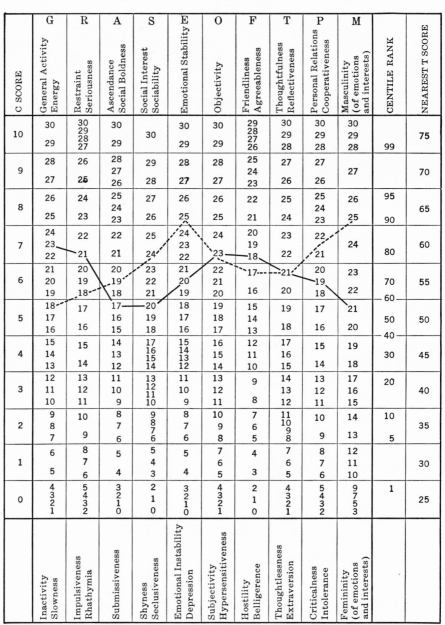

* Beverly Hills, California: Sheridan Supply Company, 1949. Reprinted by permission.

284

knowledge about sexual intercourse and reproduction. Although sexual matters are discussed rather freely in a few academic circles, we cannot assume that the average young person has escaped traumatic experience or that he is well-informed. The chapter on adolescence indicates that this fact has been demonstrated by a number of studies. Therefore, previous to marriage, the couple will need to discuss with a counselor many of the more intimate details of sexual relations which have not been covered in family conferences (if any) and in peer "bull sessions." The counselor may share with the couple a number of books which deal adequately with the subject as well as outlining for them the major prerequisites of sexual enjoyment. These points are fully discussed in a subsequent chapter on sexual adjustment in marriage.

Some aids have been produced which help young people evaluate their information and their attitudes about sex. The Sex Inventory X and Y prepared by the Marriage and Family Council of Durham, North Carolina, has been put to use by a great many ministers, doctors, and marriage counselors. Form Y of this test is a four-page booklet with vocabulary tests and an ingenious device for determining whether or not the testee understands what happens in intercourse and in childbirth. Form X is longer and more comprehensive.

Form X consists of eighty multiple-choice questions which are designed not only to show the couple's familiarity with sexual terms but to enable them to grow toward a fuller understanding. Two questions picked at random indicate the quality of the sexual inventory and its usefulness in assisting a couple to measure the degree of their knowledge and to become even more familiar with important facts.

24. Of the following, which is most closely related to a happy sexual adjustment in marriage?

A. The amount of sex relations wanted by both husband and wife.
B. The intensity and the length of the sexual climax.
C. The wish to be together after sex needs are satisfied.
D. The length of time spent in sex relations and the amount of sleep afterward.

60. How does being unresponsive

A. Makes pregnancy impossible.

in sex relations affect a woman's
ability to become pregnant?

B. Greatly reduces ability.
C. Has no effect on ability.
D. Makes pregnancy more likely.
E. The effect depends on the kind of man she marries.

The counselee is asked not only to pick out the right answer to the question submitted but to circle questions which puzzle him or her. Many counselors give this test to all couples who come for pre-marital consultation and then use it as the basis for discussion of any areas in which doubts or questions exist. While this test is very useful, it does not take the place of the study of basic physiological material or of consultation with someone skilled in sexual counseling.

While the counselor will pay attention to the degree to which the couple understands sexual facts, he will be more concerned with the overtones of the conversation. He will listen for indications of inhibition or fear. If he finds such indications, he will then structure his relationship with the couple to help them overcome such obstacles to happy marriage.

The marriage counselor will also inquire about the practical side of the coming marriage—financial plans, housing plans, budgets, time budgets, and other forms of planning that make adjustment more fruitful and reduce anxiety. Finally, he will ask the couple to return after they have been married for a few months to discuss any obstacles to happiness which may have arisen during the early adjustment period.

All marriage counselors recommend that every couple have a thorough physical examination and have several sessions with a gynecologist prior to their marriage. In some cases the couple may raise questions regarding their capacity to bear healthy children which can only be answered by a doctor skilled in genetics. In all cases the couple will wish to discover any abnormalities which might temporarily interfere with the consummation of their marriage, as well as those which would endanger their chances of having children or be obstacles to full sexual togetherness. Both the man and the wife will wish to enter marriage in optimum health, and such an examination will assure them that they have no physical condition which needs correction. Included in the examination will be the routine blood test which is almost universally required by law today. This test checks for venereal diseases, but young couples may request that it be extended so as to isolate any special problems such as the RH factor.

Duvall and Hill have listed desirable steps to be included in a premarital physical examination of the future husband and wife:

Premarital Physical Examination

1. Medical history including the previous sex history of both the man and the woman, possible hereditary problems in either line, and the menstrual history of the woman.
2. Clarification of any item or questions one or both members of the couple bring in, along with any that arise during the consultation. Selected books may be recommended as helpful.
3. Brief review of the anatomy and physiology of both male and female genital systems in the human (with charts or films if desired).
4. General physical examination, including blood and urine studies, heart, lung, and pelvic conditions, and search for any possible pathologies in both the man and the woman.
5. Pelvic examination of the woman with special attention to the condition of the vaginal orifice and the adequacy of the vagina for sexual intercourse.
6. Possible instruction in hymen dilation, where indicated and compatible with the attitudes of the couple.
7. Examination of the clitoris, and plan for freeing the clitoris as indicated.
8. Laboratory study of cultures from vagina and cervix with especial concern for the presence of gonorrheal infection, with immediate program of treatment if tests are positive.
9. Examination of the male genitalia with laboratory tests and a program of treatment for possible infection. (Sperm count and motility may be included if desired.)
10. Blood tests for the detection of syphilis in both individuals. Positive findings are followed at once by adequate treatment. No evidence of the disease is the clean bill of health required in most states before the license is issued.
11. Discussion of plans for contraception, as requested, with particular reference to the initial period of the marriage and the religious factors that may be pertinent: (a) plan for plotting the "safe period" if rhythm method is to be used, or (b) fitting a diaphram if religious and personal factors allow it.
12. Specific advice on vagina lubricants and coital procedures as requested and indicated.[42]

Such a thorough examination takes care of all physical factors as well as helping the couple deal with doubts which may have been troubling them.

The Minister, Priest, or Rabbi. It is thoughtful to consult the minister, priest, or rabbi some time previous to the actual date of the wedding.

[42] Duvall and Hill, p. 123. Reprinted by permission of the publisher.

Religious leaders are busy people, and they need to know the dates of wedding rehearsals and ceremonies in sufficient time to fit them into their schedules. The minister, priest, or rabbi will arrange for one or more consultations with the couple previous to the rehearsal.

During these consultations the clergyman will talk with the couple about their preparation for marriage, their religious problems or outlook, and the meaning of the ceremony itself. If the minister functions as a marriage counselor he may give the couple some of the tests that have been reviewed earlier in this chapter. He will also help the couple review arrangements for the wedding and the honeymoon.

GROUP PREMARITAL COUNSELING

One of the promising movements to aid young people to prepare more adequately for marriage is premarital group counseling. The author has conducted five such groups in which the stress was put on sharing needed information and on discussing problems which were distressing the group. Levine and Brodsky have recently evaluated their experience of conducting eight such groups.[43] They ranged in size from two to six couples, but the therapists found that the optimum number for good results is four couples. They held a series of three sessions and dealt with love, sex, and parenthood. At the beginning of each session a brief presentation was made. This was followed by discussion. The author conducted his groups in similar fashion but devoted more time to the presentation of pertinent information and had ten sessions with each group. Levine and Brodsky, as well as the author, discovered that there is a very grave lack of factual information among engaged couples, and that often their information is distorted. This leads to anxiety since the couple looks forward to marriage as an unknown and sometimes threatening situation. In group therapy, individuals can voice their fears and ask questions about things they do not understand. The value of the group seems to be that to some extent it reduces fear, guilt, and conflict as well as helping individuals to set somewhat more adequate goals for marriage.

CONCLUSION

The most useful function of the engagement period is the final and essential test it permits of the relationship of the future husband and wife.

[43] Lena Levine and Jeanne Brodsky, "Group Premarital Counseling," *Mental Hygiene*, XXXII (April, 1953), published by Planned Parenthood Federation of America.

During the engagement period, the euphoric nature of the love relationship can be set aside, and the partners can explore and measure their capacity for communication, adaptability, and problem-solving. If a couple finds that the divergences are too great, it is well to break the engagement—in the most constructive way possible. On the other hand, achievements in communication, accommodation, adaptation, and problem-solving during engagement create a solid foundation for the initiation of married life. The general engagement inventory that follows is designed to help a couple test their development in cohesion and problem-solving as well as their agreement on values and attitudes. It summarizes points considered so far as essential to courtship, wise marriage choice, and engagement adjustment.

Analysis of Your Interaction with Future Mate

I. Agreement on economic matters with future mate.
   A. Approximately how many times have you discussed your future financial plans and problems?———
   B. What has been the result of these discussions: (1)———new insights for both; (2)———happy agreement; (3)———temporary disagreement; (4)———bitter disagreement.
   C. Have you discussed   Have you reached agreement on
      1. A budget   Yes———No———   Yes———No———
      2. Savings   Yes———No———   Yes———No———
      3. Wife's working   Yes———No———   Yes———No———
      4. Buying a home   Yes———No———   Yes———No———
      5. Who will manage
         the money   Yes———No———   Yes———No———
      6. Your occupational
         plans.   Yes———No———   Yes———No———
      Which of these caused conflict? ————————————
      Which of these would you like to discuss? ——————

II. Agreement on matters of recreation with future mate.
   A. Approximately how many times have you discussed your future recreational plans and problems?———————
   B. What has been the result of these discussions: (1)———new insights for both; (2)———happy agreement; (3)———temporary disagreement; (4)———bitter disagreement.

289

C. List the recreational activities of your future mate that you do not participate in:

3. _____

1. _____ 4. _____

2. _____ 5. _____

D. List the recreational activities that are important to you that your future mate does not participate in:

1. _____ 3. _____

2. _____ 4. _____

E. List the different recreational activities in which you and your intended mate have participated as a couple more than once in the last six months:

4. _____

1. _____ 5. _____

2. _____ 6. _____

3. _____ 7. _____

What conflicts do you have over recreation? _____

Which of these would you like to discuss? _____

III. Agreement on religious matters.

A. In what church did you receive your childhood religious training?_____. How intensive was it?_____.

B. At present to which religious group do you belong?_____.

C. Approximately how many times have you discussed your future religious plans?_____.

D. What has been the result of these discussions? (1)____new insights for both; (2)____happy agreement; (3)____temporary disagreement; (4)____bitter disagreement.

E. Have you discussed   Have you reached agreement on

1. Religious education of children	Yes____No____		Yes____No____	
2. Grace at meals	Yes____No____		Yes____No____	
3. Attendance at church	Yes____No____		Yes____No____	
4. Birth control	Yes____No____		Yes____No____	
5. Who will marry you	Yes____No____		Yes____No____	
6. Your basic religious ideas	Yes____No____		Yes____No____	

Which of these caused conflict? _____

Which of these do you wish to discuss? _____

How often have you worshiped together in the last six months?__

F. Rate on the scale below your religious interest:

Intense interest   Average interest   Little interest

_____

G. Rate your future mate's interest on the scale above.

IV. Agreement on children.
   A. Approximately how many times have you discussed children and how they will be raised?_____.
   B. What has been the result of those discussions: (1)____new insights for both; (2)____happy agreement; (3)____temporary disagreement; (4)____bitter disagreement.
   C. Have you discussed   Have you reached agreement on
      1. Methods of
         discipline   Yes____No____   Yes____No____
      2. Number of
         children   Yes____No____   Yes____No____
      3. Sex education   Yes____No____   Yes____No____
      4. Allowances   Yes____No____   Yes____No____
      Which of the above caused conflict? _____
      Which would you like to discuss? _____

V. Agreement on demonstrations of affection.
   A. Approximately how many times have you seriously discussed the degree of sexual intimacy you should permit while going steady, being pinned, or being engaged:_____.
   B. What has been the result of these discussions: (1)____new insights for both; (2)____happy agreement; (3)____temporary disagreement; (4)____bitter disagreement.
   C. Have you discussed   Have you reached agreement on
      1. Petting   Yes____No____   Yes____No____
      2. Petting to climax Yes____No____   Yes____No____
      3. Premarital inter-
         course   Yes____No____   Yes____No____
      4. Birth control   Yes____No____   Yes____No____
      5. Achieving good

sex relations
in marriage   Yes——No——   Yes——No——
6. Demonstrations of
affection   Yes——No——   Yes——No——

D. How free have you been as a couple in demonstrating affection: (1)——very inhibited; (2)——somewhat inhibited; (3)——quite free; (4)——very free.

E. How free have you been as individuals in demonstrating affection by your verbalizations of love: (1)——very inhibited; (2)——somewhat inhibited; (3)——quite free; (4)——very free.

Which of these caused conflict? ————————————

Which of these would you like to discuss? ————————

VI. Agreement on matters relating to in-laws.

A. Approximately how many times have you seriously discussed your relations, now and in the future, with your in-laws: ——.

B. What has been the result of those discussions: (1)——new insights for both; (2)——happy agreement; (3)——temporary disagreement; (4)——bitter disagreement.

C. Have you discussed   Have you reached agreement on
1. Proximity of your
home to in-laws   Yes——No——   Yes——No——
2. Your dependence
on parents   Yes——No——   Yes——No——
3. Degree in-laws
may interfere in
marriage   Yes——No——   Yes——No——
4. How to achieve
happy relations
with in-laws   Yes——No——   Yes——No——

Which of these caused conflict?————————————

Which of these would you like to discuss?————————

VII. Agreement on matters relating to emotional understanding.

A. Approximately how many times have you discussed the degree to which you understand each other's emotional needs and meet them? ————————————————————————

B. What has been the result of these discussions: New insights for

292

both——, happy agreement——, temporary disagreement ——, bitter disagreement——.

C. Have you felt:

1. Any need to be better understood   Yes—— No——
2. Any need for more warmth and closeness   Yes—— No——
3. Any need for more tenderness   Yes—— No——
4. Any blocks in expressing your own feelings   Yes—— No——
5. Any hostility over courtship conflicts   Yes—— No——

Which of these caused conflict or withdrawal ——————

Which of these would you like to discuss ——————

VIII. When you discuss a problem can you talk: (1)——very easily; (2)——easily; (3)——with some difficulty; (4)——with great difficulty.

IX. As you think about the conflict noted previously, how would you characterize your method of settling disputes: (1)——future wife gives in; (2)——future husband gives in; (3)——matter is never settled; (4)——matter is settled by give and take; (5) ——some matters are avoided which tend to cause unhappiness. In these disputes what is the result: (1)——quick forgiveness; (2)——period of feeling estranged; (3)——an agreement to forget the matter; (4)——an attempt later to solve the problem. In these disputes can you: (1)——easily express resentment; (2)——sometimes express resentment; (3)——rarely express resentment.

X. Indicate your degree of agreement on the following items:

	Always agree	Almost always agree	Occasionally disagree	Almost always disagree	Always disagree
1. Drinking					
2. Petting					
3. Gambling					
4. Smoking					
5. Friends					

6. Politics

7. Money

8. Amount of time
spent together

XI. Please list the things which have troubled you regarding your coming marriage:

Please list the irritations or annoyances which occur when you and your intended mate are together:

XII. If you could make your mate "to order" what things would you change about him or her:

If you could relive your courtship with your intended mate, what things would you not do or do differently from what actually occurred:

XIII. Please rate yourself and your future mate in terms of the following items. Make a "Y" for yourself and an "M" for future mate in the column which most nearly indicates the degree to which you and your mate possess each trait:

Items	Very much so	Con- siderably	Somewhat	Not at all
1. Dominating				
2. Submissive				
3. Anxious				
4. Irritable at times				
5. Moody				
6. Depressed at times				

7. Angers quickly

8. Nervous

9. Jealous

10. Conventional

11. Dependent

12. Hostile

13. Ambitious

14. Sympathetic

15. Forgiving

16. Affectionate

17. Tender

18. Considerate

19. Companionable

20. Flexible

21. Takes responsibility readily

22. Creative

23. Domestic

24. Adaptable

PROJECTS

1. Interview your married friends and bring back a report to the class regarding wise steps to be taken during the engagement period.
2. If you are engaged, ask your instructor to give you the Burgess-Wallin Premarital Prediction schedule or the Preston Premarital Counseling schedule and discuss with him areas of improvement.
3. Let the class take the Sex Inventory and discuss any questions that result from taking the test.
4. Ask a gynecologist to come and speak to the class on the values of a premarital examination.

VISUAL AIDS

Are You Ready for Marriage?, Coronet Instructional Films, Chicago.

READINGS

BOWMAN, HENRY A. *Marriage for Moderns.* 4th ed. New York, McGraw-Hill Book Company, Inc., 1960, Chapters 8 and 9.

BURGESS, ERNEST W. and PAUL WALLIN. *Engagement and Marriage.* Philadelphia, J. B. Lippincott Company, 1953, Chapters 5, 8, and 12.

CHRISTENSEN, HAROLD T. *Marriage Analysis.* New York, The Ronald Press Company, 1950, Chapter 9.

JOHANNIS, THEODORE B., JR. and KARAN MANEY. "Financing Student Weddings," *Journal of Home Economics,* LI, May, 1959, 362–364.

LOCKE, HARVEY J. *Predicting Adjustment in Marriage: A Comparison of a Divorced and a Happily Married Group.* New York, Henry Holt and Company, 1951, Chapter 12. Copyright Holt, Rinehart and Winston, Inc.

MACE, DAVID R. *Marriage.* New York, Doubleday and Company, Inc., 1952, Chapter 7.

SKIDMORE, REX and ANTON CANNON. *Building Your Marriage.* New York, Harper and Brothers, 1951, Chapters 11 and 13. Copyright Harper and Row, Publishers.

WALLER, WILLARD and REUBEN HILL. *The Family: A Dynamic Interpretation.* Rev. ed. New York, Dryden Press, 1951, Chapters 12 and 13. Copyright Holt, Rinehart and Winston, Inc.

PART FOUR

THE

ACHIEVEMENT

OF MARITAL

COMPATIBILITY

Introduction

THE REMAINDER of this book focuses upon the ways a couple may achieve marital compatibility. No marriage is adequate when both concentrate so completely upon individual interests that there is no common growth in sharing and companionship. Yet, no marriage is adequate, either, when the basic personality potentialities of either partner are completely submerged in the demands of the family. Maximum life satisfaction, indeed maximum marriage success, comes when both partners develop optimum individual and group creativeness. Because this is a book concerned primarily with marriage and not with personality fulfillment, our main emphasis is upon growth in mutuality and cohesiveness. Yet rewarding mutuality is predicated upon the degree to which the individuals involved have something to share.

To achieve sympathetic understanding of one another, cooperation in planning, companionship in play and in sexual achievement, cohesion in family life is not easy in today's complex, urban world. The radical differences in cultural backgrounds and consequently of expectations; the half-knowledge and hesitations in the realm of sex and reproduction; the impact of mass media with their insistent demands for conformity to hackneyed values and stereotypes; the constant threat of war and the surging rise of prices—all these combine to place the couple in a social environment of change and anxiety. To establish common interests and ways of solving problems is thus more difficult than it was a hundred years ago.

While modern marriage poses sharper problems, it also involves greater challenges to creativity. Young people today who achieve a happy marriage have attained something different in kind from marriages in the past. Neither economic necessity nor social control forces them to remain together when the gears do not mesh. Undoubtedly this new freedom results in more divorces but such freedom also results in more sensitive interrelationships in those marriages (and they are the vast majority) which succeed. These problems then are challenges and opportunities which may result in greater progress.

At the same time the confused state of values and social expectations in themselves render marriage somewhat more precarious than in past generations. Young people need to develop more mature personalities fitted for the acceptance of the responsibilities of marriage and parenthood, and they need to be more skillful in meeting particular problems of marital adjustment that will arise after the marriage service. Hence, our concern with the development of those attitudes and increased knowledge of those facts which will be basic tools in achieving cohesion once the marriage bonds have been established.

CHAPTER 12

The Wedding
and the
Honeymoon

INTRODUCTION

IT is generally felt, at least by women, that the wedding and honeymoon experiences are the most momentous and meaningful of any in life. We propose to look at these events in this chapter in such a way that each couple can find meaning in them. Not every couple recalls with relish the frantic pace before the wedding or the early adjustment days with ecstasy. This is perhaps due to lack of wise preparation and to unrealistic expectations. Perhaps through discussion we can not only help make these days memorable but add some significance to them.

GETTING THE LICENSE

It is a good thing that most couples plan to get their license some time before the ceremony because they have time to forget that aspect of getting married. The majority of couples who have mentioned obtaining a license have been a little troubled at the memory. They go hand in hand to take the first step toward culminating a lifetime of dreams and they end up generally in a shabby, smoke-filled office where granting a license is just another business transaction. If we were to make a list of the insensibilities of government agencies, the provisions for granting marriage licenses would be high on the list. Some couples are just startled at the contrast between their mood and that of this office; others feel letdown and disappointed.

Some are even more disappointed because they neglect to check into the laws that govern the granting of permission to marry. Modern marriage law is a product of early Teutonic, Roman and Hebraic customs which have been modified by the impact of Christianity and more recently by the shifting roles of women and children. A summary of current marriage law follows, but every couple should make inquiry regarding these statutes in their own states.

AGE LIMITS FOR MARRIAGE

In America, the marriage statutes have generally raised the age limit of fourteen for boys and twelve for girls which characterized both Roman law and the English common law. Usually the law sets the minimum age of marriage without consent of parents at eighteen for girls and twenty-one for boys. Some states require both the girl and boy to be twenty-one. Even if parents consent, many states do not permit boys below eighteen or girls below sixteen to marry.

PROHIBITIONS ON MARRIAGE

Consanguineous marriages (or marriages of blood relatives) have been prohibited since ancient times due to the chance that relatives carry similar hereditary traits in their germ plasm. All states prohibit the marriage of close blood relations, including marriage between brothers and sisters, mothers and sons, fathers and daughters, aunts and nephews, uncles and nieces, grandmothers and grandsons, grandfathers and grand-daughters—with the exception of Rhode Island which permits the marriage of Jewish uncles and nieces. Twenty-nine states prohibit the marriage of cousins or of brothers and sisters of half-blood.

In the past two decades many health regulations have been introduced into marriage requirements. Seven states prohibit the marriage of those with transmittible disease in the infectious stage. Five states require examinations for venereal diseases, twenty-nine states specify such an examination for syphilis, and other states have similar laws although eight states still do not prohibit the marriage of those who have not presented evidence of being free from venereal diseases. All states regulate the marriage of the mentally ill, seventeen will not issue licenses to epileptics, and three prohibit the marriage of the feeble-minded unless they have been sterilized.

The third area of prohibitions has to do with racial regulations. Thirty states prohibit interracial marriages. The southern states have been most concerned to prohibit the marriages of Caucasians and Negroes while the western states have statutes prohibiting the union of Orientals and Caucasians. The recent Supreme Court decision in California which declared such laws unconstitutional may affect the constitutionality of all other laws which prohibit interracial marriages.

COMMON-LAW MARRIAGES

Common-law marriages are recognized in twenty-one states. A common-law marriage is one in which any agreement to marry is followed by cohabitation as man and wife. Three requirements must be met: (1) no existing impediments (under legal age, no existing marriage, no feeble-mindedness or other specified prohibitions); (2) agreement in the present tense (a promise to marry at some future date is insufficient); (3) holding forth as man and wife, that is, signing a hotel register, establishing credit at a grocery or department store, renting a house, etc. It is important for college youth to recognize these measures by which they can unwittingly be faced with the accomplished fact of common-law marriage. In such marriages no license or ceremony is required. Arizona, Illinois, Missouri, and New York have now declared such marriages "null and void" and it is likely that other states will follow suit because the state can have little or no control over such unions.

ELOPEMENTS

Some couples for various reasons do not want a public wedding in their own community. They may feel that the cost in time and money is exorbitant. They may be trying to overcome opposition of parents or their group. Sometimes they are so anxious to be married that the legal requirements in their own state seem too frustrating. They do not want to wait. Other couples are impulsive, and some want to keep their marriages secret for employment, educational, or other reasons. The best study of elopements was done by Popenoe who found that the motivations for 738 of these marriages were: [1]

[1] Paul Popenoe, "A Study of 738 Elopements," *American Sociological Review*, III (Feb., 1938), 48.

1. Parental objections   46 per cent
2. Avoidance of publicity   20 per cent
3. Economy   12 per cent
4. Pregnancy   8 per cent
5. Others   14 per cent

In studying the results of these elopements in terms of later marital adjustment, he judged that 46 per cent were happy, 9 per cent were doubtful, and 43 per cent were unhappy. He concludes that a preplanned and formal wedding is more conducive to later happiness.

THE MEANING OF THE WEDDING

A wedding is a very complex social function. It involves a great many people who care deeply about the participants. Therefore, there is a good chance for conflict about wedding plans and for sensitive reactions on the part of those who may feel slighted. Some parents use the event as part of their maneuvering for social prestige, and so they are very concerned about the most trivial details of etiquette. Sometimes it seems that the selection and supervision of the photographer is more important than the basic commitment the young people are making. If the parents are "organization" men and women, the young couple will hear much about the invitation list and its value.

A wedding is, however, not primarily a social event; it is an hour when two people vow that regardless of the vicissitudes of life they will be loyal to each other. It is the hour of climax to months and months of growing towards each other in trust and confidence. Of course, it should be well ordered, but if the preparations are so tense that the couple worries all through the service, something meaningful is lost. In planning for the wedding, primary focus should always be on its significance rather than on its showiness, on the meaning more than on its munificence!

The wedding has several purposes. One is to comply with society's regulation that a couple legitimatize their marriage. Another is to secure the blessing of friends and church upon what is regarded as a supremely important event. Still another is to undergird the importance of marriage with symbolic and meaningful ritual. The wedding ceremonializes the final step from singleness to married living. Religiously, the wedding brings the blessings of God through the church to the couple. It is generally recognized that weddings performed in the home or in the church have an aesthetic quality which is missing when a couple elopes or is married by a justice of the peace.

WEDDING FINANCES

Weddings at home with simple flower settings cost about one tenth the cost of elaborate church affairs. In New Haven, Hollingshead found the median cost of weddings was $775. In that city 46 per cent of the weddings were financed by the bride's parents. This is the traditional expectation. They pay for the wedding and the groom pays for the honeymoon. The actual size of the wedding may reasonably be determined by the wishes of the couple and by their economic circumstances. Some couples have reported that they were so lavish in their wedding and honeymoon plans that they existed in rather dire poverty for the next six months! They also said that their parents and others had protested, but that "no one could tell us anything then, and now we wish we had listened." Because the wedding is the joining together of a young man and woman, they ought always to have the final word about arrangements.

THE DATE OF THE WEDDING

Ordinarily the date of the wedding is determined by the menstrual cycle of the bride, and the date is set so that it will not coincide with her menstrual period. Sometimes, however, other considerations are important, such as the attendance of family and friends, or the work schedule of the groom. Then, too, there is the question of the honeymoon. In our society it is customary for the groom and bride to go away for a period of early adjustment. If the man is working, the wedding must take place at a time when it is feasible for him to be absent from his job.

The date ought to be determined far enough in advance so that all arrangements can be made easily and without undue haste, so that all participants can plan their attendance, and so that invitations can be sent out in time.

THE PLACE OF THE WEDDING

The place of the wedding has been given considerable attention in studies of marital adjustment. Locke's study is summarized in the following table:

TABLE 29. Per Cent of Happily Married and Divorced Married
in a Given Place or by a Given Person *

PERSON OR PLACE	MEN		WOMEN	
	Married N 173	Divorced N 161	Married N 171	Divorced N 183
At home	27.7	15.5	29.2	14.8
At church	12.7	9.3	11.1	8.2
By judge	1.2	2.6	1.2	0.5
At minister's home	38.7	39.1	40.4	46.5
By justice of peace	13.3	29.2	11.7	27.3
Elsewhere	6.4	4.3	6.4	2.7
	100.0	100.0	100.0	100.0

* Harvey J. Locke, *Predicting Adjustment in Marriage: A Comparison
of a Divorced and a Happily Married Group* (New York: Henry Holt
and Company, 1951), p. 238. Copyright © 1951, Holt, Rinehart and
Winston, Inc. Reprinted by permission of the publisher.

Being married by a justice of the peace is unquestionably associated
with maladjustment. Marriage at home, in a church, or at the minister's
home is associated with marital adjustment. The high incidence of marriages performed in the minister's home in Locke's table is probably referable to the region in which his study was made and would not apply in
many localities.

THE WEDDING SERVICE

Churches have different types of wedding ceremonies. While the Nup-
tial Mass of the Roman Catholic Church is markedly different from the
silent, or nearly silent, marriage of Quakers, both have some symbolism
in common. In an effort to interpret some of the symbolisms, a Protestant
wedding service is reproduced below with interpolations explaining the
background of some of its parts.

At the time appointed for the marriage ceremony (*the time appointed
means following the seating of the bride's mother, the singing of one or
two special songs such as "Oh, Promise Me," and the wedding procession
which consists first of the minister and the men of the bridal party and
then of the women of the bridal party*) the persons united shall stand,
the man on the right, and the woman on the left, and the minister shall
say:

Dearly Beloved: We are gathered in the sight of God and in the face of this company to join together this man and this woman in holy matrimony which is ordained of God and is to be honored by all men. Therefore it is not by any to be entered into unadvisedly, or lightly, but reverently, discreetly and in the fear of God. Into this holy estate _____ and _____ come now to be joined.

Then the minister shall say to the man:

Will you take this woman to be your wedded wife, to live together in the holy estate of matrimony? Will you love her, comfort her, honor and keep her, and forsaking all others, keep you only unto her so long as ye both shall live?

The man shall answer: I will.

Then the minister shall say to the woman:

Will you take this man to be your wedded husband, to live together in the holy estate of matrimony? Will you love him, comfort him, honor and keep him, and forsaking all others, keep you only unto him so long as ye both shall live?

The woman shall answer: I will.

Then the minister shall say: Who giveth this woman to be married to this man?

Then the father (*or uncle, brother, or friend*) shall say: I do; or by a sign, or by putting the hand of the bride into that of the groom shall give her away. (*In ancient times this was the whole of the marriage service. The father placed their hands together reverently and they were married. This symbolizes the surrender of authority from one family to another. It means that the father now commits the happiness of his child whom he has reared from infancy into the keeping of another. In recent years the words used have been changed, so that in some services the father says: "Her mother and I," thus recognizing the part the mother has played in the daughter's development.*)

Then the minister shall require the couple to repeat the vows as follows:

I, _____, take thee, _____, to be my wedded wife, to have and to hold, from this time forward, for better or for worse, for richer or poorer, in sickness and in health, to love and to cherish till death do us part, and thereto I plight thee my troth. (*Some couples prefer the word "faith" here.*)

I, _____, take thee, _____, to be my wedded husband, to have and to hold, from this time forward, for better or for worse, for richer

307

or poorer, in sickness and in health, to love and to cherish till death do us part, and thereto I plight my troth. (*Or "faith."*)

At this time the best man shall give the groom the ring, the groom shall give it to the minister, the minister shall give it to the bride and the bride shall return it to the groom who then places it on the finger of the bride. (*This symbolic ring service unites friends, God, family, and the couple in a circle of blessing and of love. The ring which is itself a circle makes a wider circle joining all of these in the new configuration of the new family. This most beautiful symbolism is often not known by those who participate in the service.*)

The man shall say as he holds the hand upon which he has placed the ring:

> With this ring I thee wed, and to thee I will be true, in name of the Father, and of the Son, and of the Holy Spirit. Amen.

If there is a second ring in a double-ring service, the same service is repeated. (*A variation consists of the minister taking the ring to the altar and blessing it before he gives it back to the man to put on the finger of the girl; or in a double-ring service, before it is given back to the girl to put on the finger of the man.*)

After this the minister shall say: Let us pray. (*In the unified type of service the bride and groom remain before the minister and simply bow their heads, but in the divided service they go to the kneeling bench provided for this purpose and kneel in front of the minister. In recent years many couples have asked that the "Lord's Prayer" by Malotte be sung before the wedding prayer is said by the minister.*)

Following the prayer the minister shall say:

> For inasmuch as _____ and _____ have consented together in the holy wedlock, and have witnessed the same before God and this company, and have pledged their faith each to the other, by the authority committed unto me, I pronounce that they are man and wife. Whom God hath joined together, let no man put asunder.

After this the minister shall say the closing benediction and the couple close the ceremony with a kiss which is followed by the recessional in which the bride and groom go down the aisle together followed by the entire wedding party.

There are many other details involved in planning a wedding, and these should be thought of merely as details. The important part of the marriage is the dedication of one individual to another in a reverent and beautiful way. But when the romantic dreams of the "march in the gown" or the social prestige factors involved in the "great ceremony" occupy the attention, a wedding loses much of its special value to the couple.

The details of wedding courtesy such as the giving of gifts, the arrangement of the reception line, etc. need give us little concern here. The minister who performs the ceremony is well equipped to guide a couple when necessary. Many large department stores now maintain special wedding counselors who can advise skillfully concerning what is regarded as proper at a wedding. Yet one fact needs to be mentioned. The bride is right no matter what she desires. If she wants to rewrite the marriage service or dispense with the reception, that is her prerogative. The reactions of her friends may not be positive, but if she wishes to add to the meaning of the occasion in any way, she may rightfully do this. The guiding principle is that the wedding should be as meaningful as possible.

THE RECEPTION

Most couples plan to have a reception following the wedding service where they can informally greet their guests and receive congratulations. In some cases the reception goes so long and is so pretentious that the couple is completely exhausted, and the honeymoon becomes a convalescence instead of a happy beginning of married life. In fact one marriage counselor quite seriously lists *Recuperation* as the primary function of the modern honeymoon. Says he:

> The first service of the honeymoon is to provide a chance to rest after the strenuous activities of the previous days and weeks. No matter how simple or well-planned the wedding, it is inevitably fatiguing . . . when the guests have gone, the feeling of exhaustion sweeps in. The honeymoon bed then looks inviting not alone for sexual intimacy but for just plain sleep.[2]

This fatigue may be inevitable, but a longer period of planning and some limitation to the reception activities might make the honeymoon more than a rest period.

THE HONEYMOON

How indispensable is a honeymoon? Most young people think it so because at least 80 per cent go on one. Bron has studied reactions to

[2] Robert Blood, *Anticipating Your Marriage* (New York: The Free Press of Glencoe, 1962), p. 95. Copyright The Macmillan Company.

honeymoons more thoroughly than anyone else.[3] He reports that 74 per cent described their honeymoon as a complete success. On the other hand, some 68 per cent felt that a honeymoon is not "indispensable" to a happy marriage. When the couples of his sample reflected on it, some 80 per cent thought it false that "there is no more ideal happiness in all married life than during a honeymoon." [4] But despite the fact that about half of Bron's women reported that they did not achieve complete sexual satisfaction on the honeymoon, it was still a time of joy and delight. The honeymoon is a time of privacy when *adjustments only begin.* If this is the expectation, happiness will follow.

The purpose of the honeymoon is to facilitate the transition from individual patterns of behavior to group behavior. It is a special period in which in privacy and isolation the couple take the first steps in adjustment to shared living, not only sexually, but in every other way. For this reason a honeymoon should be planned to produce a maximum of growth toward solidarity. It is a period of major importance in every couple's life for it represents the culmination of years of expectations and hopes. What are the conditions which will facilitate these adjustments?

If the honeymoon is meaningful, it is a period in which each of the partners concentrates upon the other; thus mutuality in marriage gets an early emphasis. Hence, honeymoons planned in conjunction with long business trips or research projects fail in purpose because they divide the attention of one or both partners. Honeymoons involving extensive travel or busy schedules likewise do not give the partners sufficient opportunity for quiet explorations of each other's personality. This is one period in life which should be completely free of every obligation. The couple should focus on sharing sexually, and on companionship socially. It is a time when nothing else matters.

This early adjustment involves the location of the honeymoon. Obviously it should be a place that both enjoy. Students seem always to disagree regarding the selection of the honeymoon spot. About a fourth of the girls want to be completely surprised and know nothing about the place the man has selected. Another fourth want to know in general whether it is at the beach, in the city, or in the mountains so that they can bring appropriate clothes. The other half would like to have a voice in planning where to go. Whatever the wishes of the girl, she should be

---

[3] Stanley R. Bron, "Note on Honeymoons," *Marriage and Family Living* (Summer, 1947), p. 60.
[4] Bron, p. 60.

consulted as to her preferences regarding the share she wants to play in selecting the place. If the man selects the place, it should be with a full realization of the general attitudes of his bride. And wherever the couple go, they should leave word with some trusted relative or friend so that in case of emergency they may be quickly reached.

In planning for the honeymoon, the place chosen should be commensurate with the couple's resources. Some couples splurge to the extent that they are impoverished for the next six months and have no money for continued fun after the honeymoon. One of the early accomplishments in the wise use of resources may be the agreement that is reached about an appropriate place for the honeymoon and its length. There is no "good" rule for these matters because they will vary in terms of a couple's background and resources.

It is better for a honeymoon to start immediately after the wedding. Honeymoons which are postponed for a month or six months do not perform the same function as those which enable the couple to begin marriage alone. If a man's work interferes with the possibility of an immediate honeymoon, it is better to shift the date of the wedding so that it corresponds with his vacation.

More important than the details of time and place are the attitudes with which a couple begin married life. Even though they have been most thorough in preparing for marriage, there is apt to be some anxiety about the initial steps in achieving sexual happiness. If, however, they have fully discussed this, and if they have prepared themselves with as much knowledge as possible, they need not be too concerned. Many couples are happy on their honeymoons even if they do not find complete sexual success at first. The attitude of mutuality, the attitude of tenderness, the attitude of patience—these are as reassuring as actual sexual attainment. Any type of adjustment as complex as sexual compatibility may take time. Patience will enable the couple to take any problems in their stride with confidence that they will be worked out later.

Furthermore, a considerate and extensive effort on the part of each of the partners to bring pleasure to the other in all phases of the honeymoon will make their sexual experiments meaningful even though not as completely satisfying as they will be a year later. The excitement of the wedding and the reception sometimes brings on the menstrual cycle two weeks early, and this, of course, interferes with the initiation of sexual contact. But if the couple have a sense of humor and if their love is firmly rooted, this will not mar their honeymoon.

CONCLUSION

The initiation of compatibility during the engagement period, during the planning for the wedding, during the epochal moments of the wedding itself, and during the honeymoon is an important step toward further enlarging the degree to which the couple share each other. There will be problems in each of these periods, but if the problems are faced frankly and openly their discussion and solution will be steps to unity.

The wedding and honeymoon can promote growth in the relationship of the couple providing that they use good judgment in planning and financing these events. If they are realistic in considering that these weeks are only the first in half a century of living together, they will not be impatient if all is not achieved before they must leave their hideaway for home. Because beginning life in a new home as a married couple has its own significant satisfactions, we turn to these in the next chapter.

READINGS

BOWMAN, HENRY A. *Marriage for Moderns.* 4th ed. New York, McGraw-Hill Book Company, Inc., 1960, Chapter 9.

DUVALL, EVELYN and REUBEN HILL. *When You Marry.* Rev. ed. Boston, D. C. Heath and Company, 1943, Chapters 9 and 10.

LANDIS, JUDSON T. and MARY G. LANDIS. *Readings in Marriage and the Family.* New York, Prentice-Hall, Inc., 1942, Chapter 6.

LANTZ, HERMAN R. and ELOISE C. SNYDER. *Marriage.* New York, John Wiley & Sons, Inc., 1962, Chapter II.

LOCKE, HARVEY J. *Predicting Adjustment in Marriage: A Comparison of a Divorced and a Happily Married Group.* New York, Henry Holt and Company, 1951, Chapter 11. Copyright Holt, Rinehart and Winston, Inc.

CHAPTER 13

The Early
Adjustments
of Marriage

INTRODUCTION

FOR many couples the early months of marriage are just as meaningful and euphoric as the days of the honeymoon. Many couples report that they were so eager to get into their first house or apartment that they came home a little early from the honeymoon. In truth, it is really these early months in their own home that are the culmination of much of the earlier fantasy and anticipation of both the man and the woman. Because they have thought much about the way they would function in the roles of husband and wife, they are delighted to begin to play out those projections. So, in a sense, this is the real beginning of their marriage, for now they entertain their friends, decorate their house, and begin in earnest the business of adult living. Most couples look back upon these first months when they are beginning their life together as among the happiest of their marriage. They associate their effort with the happiest memories of their own former homes.

This period of time is also of critical importance because the *patterns of living together set during these early months are those that are likely to endure for the whole of marriage.* That this period is difficult for some couples can be seen in the analysis of the number of divorces that occur during the first two years. We shall presently discuss this fact. Because of the importance of this period in establishing the dimensions of the relationship and because so many marriages fail in these first months, this chapter is devoted to analyzing the response patterns and to providing solutions to many problems. It is hoped that this discussion will help the young people to solve their problems positively and together in their struggle for security.

THE VALUE OF MARITAL EXPECTATIONS

Baber deplores the one-sided emphasis upon the problems of adjustment at the beginning of marriage. He stresses the prophylactic power of the expectation of success.[1] For a long time the bride and groom have been looking forward to their marriage, to living in a home of their own, to their happiness together. There is a rush of enthusiasm which is strong enough to carry a couple through the accommodation process of early marriage. There will be disagreements, but their joy in their new status is a power for the maintenance of early marital stability.

While such an estimate of the euphoria of marriage as a positive force may be correct, it cannot obscure the fact that many couples do fail to make the early adjustments of marriage. The following table indicates the divorce rate by years of marriage:

TABLE 30. Per Cent of Divorce by Duration of Marriage *

Years Married	Per Cent of Total Divorces	Cumulative
1 or Less	16.0	16.0
2 or Less	10.0	26.0
3 or Less	8.5	34.5
4 or Less	7.4	41.9
5 or Less	6.2	48.1
6 or Less	5.4	53.5
7 or Less	5.3	58.8
8 or Less	5.3	64.1
9 or Less	4.7	68.8
10 or Less	3.2	72.0
11 or Less	2.5	74.5
12 or Less	2.5	77.0
13 or Less	2.4	79.4
14 or Less	2.2	81.6
15 to 19	7.8	89.4
20 to 24	4.7	94.1
25 to 34	4.6	98.7
35 and Over	1.3	100.0

* Novs, *Special Reports*, XLVI, No. 4, 1957. Table computed from Table 5, 102–103.

[1] Ray E. Baber, *Marriage and the Family*, 2nd ed. (New York: McGraw-Hill Book Company, Inc., 1953), p. 173.

Landis studied 409 couples to discover the length of time it took these couples to work out various adjustments in marriage. Husbands and wives responded individually so that a check could be made upon their answers. The remarkable aspect of Figure 12 is the high percentage of couples

FIGURE 12. Length of Time Required for Adjustment in Six Areas of Marriage *

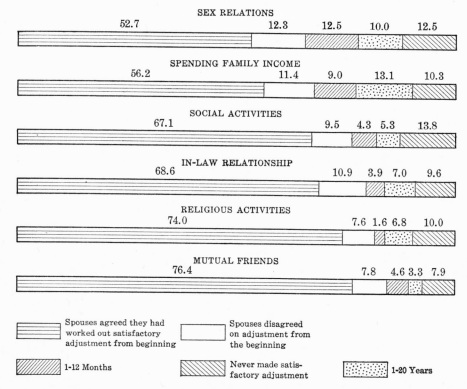

* Adapted from Judson T. Landis' study, "Length of Time Required to Achieve Adjustment in Marriage," *American Sociological Review*, XI, 666–77 (December, 1946). Reprinted by permission.

who reported agreement from the start. Agreement on mutual friends was the least troublesome item, and sexual adjustment was achieved last.[2]

Baber believes that the difficulties of early adjustments in marriage are partially due to the way each partner has oversold himself in an effort to impress the other during courtship.[3] Waller and Hill hold that the

[2] Judson T. Landis and Mary Landis, *Building a Successful Marriage* (New York: Prentice-Hall, Inc., 1948), p. 243.
[3] Baber, p. 172.

315

type of solidarity peculiar to the honeymoon and early months of marriage must break down because no one can continue to live at such a high emotional pitch. When this happens, conflict appears.[4] No matter how successful the engagement process of exploring the reality of the other person, marriage is an undefined situation and each person has a new status which involves playing a new role.[5] Even if each person knew the other well before marriage, each was still a single individual. In marriage each is forced to adjust to a person he could not know completely before the wedding and adjust to that person in a new situation. For the marriage partner is also trying to discover the limits and the most satisfactory directions of role playing in this new way of life. If this redefining of the situation and the role of the self in relation to the emergent role of the mate is not worked out during the first months of marriage, it may never be worked out.

The Landis study indicates that couples who had not worked out adjustment in the early part of marriage had a lower adjustment score than those who had. The following table indicates the relation between the length of time needed to make adjustments in six areas of marriage and marital happiness:

TABLE 31. Self-Rated Happiness of 409 Couples Reporting Various Lengths of Time Required to Make Adjustments in Six Areas *

LENGTH OF TIME REQUIRED	Very Happy	Happy	Average
Satisfactory from beginning	53	35	12
1–12 months	50	34	16
1–20 years	35	44	21
Never	19	35	46

* Judson T. Landis and Mary Landis, *Building a Successful Marriage*, 3rd ed. (Englewood Cliffs, N.J.: Prentice-Hall, Inc., 1958), p. 408. © 1958 by Prentice-Hall, Inc. Reprinted by permission of the publisher.

Landis reports the same correlation in terms of sexual adjustment. Those whose sexual adjustment was satisfactory from the beginning rated themselves 53.3 very happy, 35.3 happy, and 11.4 average in happiness. On the other hand those who rated their sexual adjustment as never satisfactory indicated their marriage as 11 very happy, 36 happy, and

[4] Willard Waller and Reuben Hill, *The Family: A Dynamic Interpretation*, rev. ed. (New York: Dryden Press, 1951), p. 253. Copyright © 1951, Holt, Rinehart and Winston, Inc.

[5] Waller and Hill, p. 254.

53 average in happiness. Happiness in marriage is related to solving adjustment problems during the settling down period of marriage. If adjustment problems persist, there is a tendency for those marriages never to be happy.

PERSONALITY CHANGES AFTER MARRIAGE

In the transitional period following marriage many aspects of an individual's personality change in response to the new role required by marriage. Waller emphasizes both the reappearance of old patterns and the emergence of new behavior responses.[6] As one settles down to marriage the tenderness and ecstasy of voice and manner give way to more casual approaches. Likewise, if one has been egocentric, or dependent, or introvertive, these tendencies, suppressed during courtship, reappear. The husband and wife tend to approximate in their new relationship the roles they learned in their childhood from interaction with their parents. Their parents are the only models they have ever known.

In assuming the role of husband and wife, each partner also takes on new tasks, or a constellation of new tasks. These demand a different type of attention and attitude than did the ways of behaving before the wedding. Waller mentions the wife who becomes concerned over the material things in the household and who is upset by the first scratches on her furniture.[7] If she concentrates very much upon her role as a housewife she will inadvertently lose some of the charm that she had for her husband when she played more consistently the role of a companion.

Values change after marriage. One of the surprises after marriage is the constant awareness that now neither person can plan his recreation, his diet, his religious life, his hourly routine, or anything else as he once did. The other person must always be considered. Waller illustrates the shift in values by analyzing changes in leisure-time activities of bachelors and married men.[8] Bachelors may pursue thrills, drink, and stay out late. The married man works in his garden, washes his car, and tends to his economic commitments. The married man finds new interests and new satisfactions. Some of these satisfactions come from curbing the egocentric self-indulgences which characterize single life. Day after day he gives up interests, time, money, pleasures, for the sake of the whole family.

[6] Waller and Hill, p. 261.   [7] Waller and Hill, pp. 262–263.
[8] Waller and Hill, p. 262.

The immediate rewards of this self-denial are not great.[9] Yet out of such sacrifices family unity is born.

There is a change in the newly married's interest in other people. If the married man no longer needs the thrill-seeking of his bachelor days, he will not have as much in common with his bachelor friends. Anyway, having a wife precludes his taking much part in bachelor activities. Or in bachelor talk, particularly the carefree talk about erotic experiences that single men indulge in, for after marriage there is a rather sudden shift toward regarding as privileged material the same type of experiences at home. Again, he considers his status, and individuals faced with the early adjustments of marriage are not apt to talk very freely about their difficulties to people outside the intimate family circle. This comes about, too, because when one is married one has a stake in the preservation of the moral order. The young married adult who has paid little heed to conventional standards of sexual conduct before marriage begins to have more concern for these standards.[10]

There is also a shift from a picture of the self as a glamorous, exciting lover to that of a husband who must earn a living and face a lifetime of unromantic episodes. This is part of the disillusionment of early marriage. This disillusionment evolves, however, not only from the more realistic picture that one has of his lifetime partner but also from a clearer view of the self. For the same self that existed before it was idealized by the devotion of the other in courtship is recognized again.[11] Psychiatrists find that the motivation for those who cannot accept the ordinary pace of marriage, and who must suffer a perpetual sense of frustration in their marriage or compensate for it by a series of extramarital affairs, comes largely from a sense of inferiority or dissatisfaction with the self.[12] Divorce rarely helps this type of person.

THE DYNAMICS OF EARLY MARRIAGE [13]

We here summarize the conclusions reached by Burgess and Wallin in their study of dynamics of early interaction. Previous to this study, no

[9] Waller and Hill, p. 264. [10] Waller and Hill, p. 267.

[11] John Levy and Ruth Munroe, *The Happy Family* (New York: Alfred A. Knopf, Inc., 1946), p. 67.

[12] Levy and Munroe, pp. 67–68.

[13] This heading is a modification of the chapter heading entitled "The Dynamics of Marriage" from Ernest W. Burgess and Paul Wallin, *Engagement and Marriage* (Philadelphia: J. B. Lippincott Company, 1953). The nature of the sample raises some questions about the accuracy of generalizing upon their findings in terms of marriage as a whole. They are cer-

research material was available that dealt in detail with the interaction during the early years of matrimony. Burgess and Wallin limited their study of marriage to 666 couples who had been married from three to five years. This material is exceptionally valuable, for Burgess and Wallin have outlined, on the basis of statistical analysis and interview material, those factors they believe to be most important in determining early adjustment in marriage. They summarize their findings as follows:

Those factors which are essential to happiness in the initial years of marriage were found to be: (1) love and affection, (2) satisfactory sexual relations, (3) emotional interdependence, and (4) temperamental interaction. When there was mutual love and affection the marriage was integrated and developed, but when there was indifference or hostility the conjugal relation was frustrated and disrupted. When sexual relations were enjoyable the result was integration, but when there was sexual dissatisfaction the partnership was disrupted. Mutual dependence was developmental, emotional independence was disruptive. Compatibility of temperamental interaction was an integrative factor while temperamental incompatibility was frustrating to the couple.[14]

THE ESSENTIAL FACTORS IN MARITAL ADJUSTMENT

Material already presented from Karlsson and Locke has pointed up the importance of communication of ideas and affection in marriage. This is another way of saying that companionship (in America, at least) is the most essential requisite for happy marriage. Burgess and Wallin propose the theory that "love, mutual enjoyment of sexual relations and emotional interdependence are typically the strongest social-psychological factors holding the married couple together and making for happiness and satisfaction in that relation." [15]

Love. Love is defined by Burgess and Wallin as "the inner feeling of affection, rapport, and attachment." [16] They hold that the type of love which makes for mutual success in middle-class America is not romantic infatuation but rather "friendship deepening into love." This has its origin in the companionship of courtship and engagement, and deepens during the early years of marriage. The following quotations from interviews

tainly applicable to a study of early marriage interaction. Quotations from this book are reprinted by permission of the publisher, J. B. Lippincott Company.
[14] Burgess and Wallin, p. 418.　[15] Burgess and Wallin, p. 419.
[16] Burgess and Wallin, p. 419.

indicate something of the change that comes into the love relationship during the early years of marriage:

> *Husband:* I am more in love now. At that time it was a romantic love. Now it is something deeper. It is a mutual understanding of each other; a faith in each other; a companionship. When we are apart we yearn to be together. She has said she is more in love now than ever.

> *Wife:* I think my love has grown stronger. I think it is a different kind. In the first place, I think it is a much more sensible kind. I think it is truer and more understanding.[17]

These interviews and others which Burgess and Wallin record seem to indicate that as romantic love diminishes, companionship and affectional love increase. These authors measured on a scale the degree of companionship in marriage and thus determined a companionship score for each couple. They then correlated this companionship score with the couple's love score. In this way they attempted to discover any association between the growth of love after marriage and the degree of companionship which existed. They found the correlation between the companionship score and love to be +.39 for husbands and +.40 for wives.[18] Statistically, this indicates that there is an association between these two factors which cannot be accounted for by chance. In our society, according to this study, satisfactory love relationships are related to the development of companionship. Newly married couples concerned about a solid beginning will certainly strive for growing companionship.

Sex Relations. It is the thesis of Burgess and Wallin that sexual adjustment is a function of growing adjustment and relatedness in other aspects of marriage. They also believe that satisfying sexual relations "markedly reinforce" love. The following interviews indicate that passion may draw a couple together but becomes less important after marriage; then the sexual relation is a way of expressing affectional feelings. The following excerpts from interviews express this well:

> *Wife:* My idea of love goes much deeper than even companionship and understanding. I have found love to be not merely an attraction, but something live and growing that makes you forget yourself in an effort to bring complete happiness to your husband—to do things with him and for him that will make his whole being glow with the warmth of satisfaction. We have so many times said to each other that the love we had when we were first married seems so small compared to the love we have come to know now. Sex life is not merely the physical satisfaction that

[17] Burgess and Wallin, p. 420.   [18] Burgess and Wallin, p. 421.

I thought it was going to be, but is an expression of love—a much needed outlet for deep-rooted emotion.

Wife: Sexual intercourse is the only complete way of demonstrating your affection for a person. I would feel pretty deprived if I could not express my affection for my husband in that way, because I would feel that any other expression would be inadequate.

Husband: My love for my wife has changed from the physical attraction to an increase in appreciation for her personality as a whole.[19]

Burgess and Wallin remark that for "practically all couples" sex is secondary to companionship and other aspects of marriage. The following brings out this fact even more strongly. It compares the association of love and of sexual adjustment to happiness scores in the marriage.

Love is associated with happiness in marriage for men by the Pearsonian Correlation figure of .65 and for women by the figure of .63. Sexual adjustment is correlated with happiness for husbands by a score of .45 and for wives by a score of .29. The nearer the Pearsonian Correlation approaches 1.0 the greater is the association of the factors under investigation.[20] Burgess and Wallin state that these are statistically significant differences which tend to support the theory that companionship love is more important than sex for marital adjustment.

In the early years of marriage, passion and physical satisfaction recede into the background, and sex as an expression of developing companionship takes its place. This conclusion is justified by the many cases in which sexual adjustment is indifferent or inadequate but in which other binding factors make the love relationship a strong one. Whether or not sexual deprivation would alter marital adjustment over a longer period of years is not known and could not be known from this study. But companionship love is evidently a more dynamic factor than sex in the early interaction of married couples. Nevertheless, young couples need to utilize every resource to develop a mutually satisfying sexual relationship.

Two aspects of the demonstration of affection illustrated by the interview material given by Burgess and Wallin are interesting because they seem to underline material presented previously in this chapter. The first has to do with carrying out in marriage roles played in the parental family. It was suggested by Waller that there is a strong tendency to approximate these roles because they are the only models that the young

[19] Burgess and Wallin, pp. 421–422.   [20] Burgess and Wallin, p. 423.

husband or the wife know. The following interviews seem to confirm this explanation of some behavior in marriage:

> *Woman:* Our families are not particularly demonstrative. If anything, the opposite. Neither of us has gone for anything like demonstration of affection.

> *Woman:* I am inclined to be indifferent about demonstrations of affection. This seems to run in our family; we never were. He is demonstrative. I like it, but I don't give it. He likes to get it very much.[21]

The second important insight gained about demonstration of affection is that it changes significantly after the honeymoon or early months of marriage. This is part of the settling-down process. However, if this tendency goes too far, and the relationship becomes too casual the partners, and particularly the wife, may come to resent the lack of demonstration of affection:

> For the first one or two years after our marriage we used to go out the twentieth of every month, our wedding anniversary. One month we both forgot, but it made no difference. We now usually congratulate each other and sometimes do, and sometimes don't, make an occasion of it—I bake a cake or we have wine with our dinner.

> *Woman:* Demonstration of affection is not nearly as important as it was when we were first married. It is natural for us to show affection. If he leaves for a few hours and he does not kiss me, I don't notice that.[22]

Burgess and Wallin conclude that "a display of love does not in itself insure the growth of a warm feeling between husband and wife." [23] They also think that demonstration of affection is "integrative but not dynamic." This is evidently an impressionistic conclusion because they present no statistical evidence comparing the importance of demonstrations of affection with that of love or sexual adjustment. Their case-study material indicates that demonstrations of affection are much prized in early marriage—particularly by the wife. The development of a pattern of emotional response should be a goal of early adjustment.

Emotional Interdependence. Emotional interdependence is defined as the expectation and reception of sympathetic understanding, encouragement, and expressions of appreciation.[24] Three patterns are possible. (1) both emotionally dependent upon each other, (2) one

---

[21] Burgess and Wallin, p. 424.   [22] Burgess and Wallin, p. 424.
[23] Burgess and Wallin, p. 425.   [24] Burgess and Wallin, p. 425.

emotionally dependent, and (3) both more or less emotionally independent. Of these three patterns the first is the most integrative as far as marriage is concerned. This conclusion is based on impressions as no statistical measure of the three patterns of interdependence is offered.[25] An excerpt from an interview indicates how in early marriage the partners come to meet each other's needs.

> *Wife:* I need sympathy and encouragement. I think he gives it very well. Better now than when we were first married because we understand each other better. That goes for him too. He needs encouragement. When we were first married I didn't realize I should encourage him about little things such as writing a paper or speaking in public. . . .[26]

In this case the development of appropriate response patterns to fit the need of the partner occurred when mutual understanding increased. This somewhat modifies the theory of disillusionment, for in many cases it is only after the removal of masks that partners come to understand the real needs of each other and to react constructively to them. In other cases the husband and the wife may wish for sympathy or encouragement and not receive it because the other mate cannot temperamentally or emotionally meet the need. Again, an emotionally dependent spouse may be married to one who is entirely self-sufficient. Another situation occurs when both members of the union are self-sufficient. Burgess and Wallin conclude that when this is so, one condition for integrating the marriage is lacking because the unification which comes from mutual encouragement and the sharing of sympathetic understanding is absent.[27] Certainly all that has been said in the chapter on "The Social Process of Mate Selection" would apply here. A great deal more specific attention needs to be given to the ways in which individuals with different personality configurations adjust in early marriage. Burgess and Wallin's study concludes that failure to obtain emotional support in marriage is frustrating.[28] Specific concentration on discovering the deepest needs of the mate in the early months of marriage will be correspondingly rewarding.

Temperamental Interaction. The term "temperamental interaction" is not defined by the writers but is said to be employed in the broad sense of "popular usage." The descriptions subsumed under this title are really temperamental and emotional interactions for they deal not only with

---

[25] Burgess and Wallin, p. 425. [26] Burgess and Wallin, p. 426.
[27] Burgess and Wallin, p. 429. [28] Burgess and Wallin, p. 429,

such items as introversion and moods but also with hostility, anger, resentments, and other emotional responses. An analysis of a case with adaptations made by interviewees in adjusting to temperamental or emotional disharmonies in engagement and early marriage was presented in Chapter Eleven.[29]

In some cases temperamental differences prove to be integrating because they are complementary. Burgess and Wallin conclude that marital clashes should be appraised in terms of their long-run effect.[30] So appraised, they indicate that many husbands and wives wish to solve marital clashes for "they realize that they are subject to control." These interviews serve to underline what has been said earlier in the chapter about the new problems of personality and interpersonal relations that appear after marriage. Here the will to understand and adjust appears important to early marital adjustment.

OTHER FACTORS IN ADJUSTMENT

The four factors already considered are regarded by Burgess and Wallin as being *essential* and *indispensable* for marital adjustment.[31] The factors to be considered next, cultural interaction, stimulation of interests, domesticity, and expectation of the continuity of the union, must also be present to assure marital unity. They are not, however, of such great consequence as the four items already considered and will not therefore receive as much attention.

Cultural Interaction. Husband and wife must adjust differences in culture during their early marital life. After marriage the process of conflict, accommodation, and assimilation develop as an effort to adjust to differences in cultural backgrounds. In accommodation the husband or the wife agrees to tolerate differences. In assimilation one member of the couple becomes converted to the attitudes and habits of the other. A third possible solution is for the couple to discover a new pattern which is more imaginative and satisfying than either of the old ones. In conclusion Burgess and Wallin say that the best test for measuring the cultural interaction of husband and wife is to discover whether their interests and values are mutually stimulating and promote their individual personality development.[32]

Stimulating Interests. Burgess and Wallin found that common in-

---

[29] See Chapters Eight and Eleven for analyses of temperamental interaction.
[30] Burgess and Wallin, p. 436.   [31] Burgess and Wallin, p. 437.
[32] Burgess and Wallin, p. 467.

terests may be classified in terms of the degree to which they bind couples together. They suggest the following classification:

(1) Little or no binding effect: sports and games
(2) Some binding effect: friends, reading and dancing
(3) Considerable binding effect: music, theater, church
(4) Great binding effect: same or similar professional interests, active community service, devotion to a common cause.[33]

It is interesting to raise the point as to whether a sample containing individuals who had been married twenty or more years would not result in the transposition of some of these ratings. However, during early marriage it appears that music, the theater, religion, similar professional interests, active community service, and devotion to a common cause are the more dynamic types of common interest. Burgess and Wallin stress the point that in some cases any common interest such as bridge or golf may be as integrating as those mentioned. It is probable that this rating of the binding effect of common interests reflects the high educational status of the Burgess-Wallin interviews. In marriage the development of a group of common interests to expand the areas in which the couple is interdependent is important. The newly married couple need to make explorations during their early adjustment in order to locate a maximum number of jointly enjoyed pursuits.

Domesticity. In discussing domesticity Burgess and Wallin state that while a chief factor in the success of marriage is the extent to which domesticity reinforces the other factors which are components of companionship, nevertheless, home-centered activities should not be carried to the point where they would mean the complete exclusion of interests outside the home.[34] Thus the ideal situation for the development of the marriage is one in which the vital domestic interests are primary but in which there is time and energy left for participation in one or more educational or cultural activities significant for the personality development of husband and wife.[35]

Burgess and Wallin found that domesticity could be described in six pattern types. These six patterns may be put on a continuum from the most to the least preoccupation with family services.[36] In analyzing the relationship of these six patterns to marital success, they conclude that "the extremes of domesticity and nondomesticity may be inimical to

[33] Burgess and Wallin, p. 462. [34] Burgess and Wallin, p. 445.
[35] Burgess and Wallin, pp. 445–446. [36] Burgess and Wallin, p. 446.

success in marriage, and the golden mean which integrated domestic and vital outside interests appears most favorable to marital adjustment. . . ." [37]

It is not easy for a young couple to emerge from a period of almost complete concentration upon courtship and create a new domestic life. In so doing they must balance domesticity with social life, recreational life, aesthetic life, and many other forms of stimulating activity. Burgess and Wallin's emphasis on the "golden mean" stresses the importance of both personality fulfillment and family cohesion.

Expectation of Continuity. The factor of expectation of continuity is related to Baber's emphasis upon the expectation of success in marriage. However, Burgess and Wallin relate their expectation to conventionality and identification while Baber refers to the emotional thrust of premarital hopes. Conventionality refers to the degree to which a person identifies his values with the standards and values of society. The religious factor is an important aspect of conventionality for the couple who happen to belong to the Roman Catholic, Episcopal, or any other church group that puts powerful sanctions on couples for the continuity of marriage. But if too great emphasis is put on living up to conventional standards, companionship goals may suffer.[38] Conventionality is certainly not the potent force it was in past generations in holding an incompatible couple together. At best, expectation of continuity is a static and stabilizing factor when it is based on the degree of conventionality of the couple, their sensitivity to what people say, or their conformity to ideals of duty learned in the parental home or other character-building institutions.[39] On the other hand, in marriages that grow in cohesion, each comes to identify his interests, his goals, his future with his mate. In the Burgess-Wallin interview material this identification finds expression in the married partners' consciousness of the merging of personalities, reaffirmation of love, and in planning for the future.[40] If the expectation of continuity is based on shared experience, on the identification of the husband with the wife, then it is not a static but a dynamic factor in integration.

INTRUSIVE FACTORS

If you have thought about the factors that we have been considering so far, you might think that the social situation of the couple or their re-

---

[37] Burgess and Wallin, pp. 450–467.   [38] Burgess and Wallin, p. 451.
[39] Burgess and Wallin, p. 467.   [40] Burgess and Wallin, p. 454.

lationship to others than the mate had no relevance to their early adjustment. However, young couples do not live in isolation and their intimate adjustments which we have considered are related to such things as their role adjustments, in-law relationships, and other social factors. So, to complete the picture, this part of our analysis is devoted to the way these matters play an important part in early adjustment. We shall study first the impact of role expectations.

Early Role Conflicts. We have already analyzed in Chapter Two the way in which the shifting roles of men and women affect their marriages. Here we focus on some of the specific problems that attend early adjustment. A short case is instructive in helping us understand the dynamics of such conflict.

Bill and Mary had come to the counselor for premarital counseling. They were as mature as any young couple the counselor had seen. They were eager for any kind of information or testing that would enhance their marital adjustment. When they finished their counseling, the counselor would have predicted an excellent relationship for them. But in six months they were back in the office, disillusioned and dismayed.

Mary explained that she was working and, consequently, there were things at home that sometimes did not get done. She had to use frozen meals, and the dusting was put off. Her husband did not help her but he was very critical of all she did at home. If she wanted to do housework on weekends, he resisted it because he always wanted to go to the beach or visit relatives or go to an athletic event. But when he got home at night he would wet his finger and go around the house hunting for dirt or dust and observing anything that was not picked up. This became a regular routine for him and he would be very unhappy if everything was not immaculate. She said he had a better eye for dirt than her mother and "that was something."

Bill put all the blame on Mary. He said he had emphasized before marriage how much he cherished a clean house. He recited the virtues of his mother. But when the counselor mildly asked him why, when his wife was supporting the family, he did not help with the housework he bristled with annoyance. This was not his role, and he had a great deal of graduate study. His profound emotional reaction to this gave the counselor the clue, and in a series of meetings the young man was much surprised to discover his real feelings. Mary and Bill had agreed that she would work and he would study, but he did not realize how much her pay check hurt him. When he realized that his negative reactions really stemmed from his insecurity about his masculinity, he apologized to Mary and they both felt

327

better about it. In working with Mary, ways were explored to help Bill feel that he was still the "head of the house" and a worthy person despite the fact that a woman was supporting him.[41]

We must never forget that both the husband and the wife adjust not only to each other but to their own expectations in marriage. During the early months there is a degree of sensitivity about adequately playing these roles that often causes trouble. It is this sensitivity that gives poignancy to any work demands that seem to deny either of the partners the time they feel that is rightfully theirs. I have in mind a second couple. The need of the young man to think of himself as a successful businessman nearly destroyed the marriage. The girl reported their situation this way:

> As soon as we got back from the week of honeymoon I just didn't see Bob. He is affectionate enough when he gets home late at night, but he's a different man from the one I knew when we were going together. Now he's serious and so worried about his business. When I try to talk to him, he resents my interrupting his thought. He's always got papers or something from the office. If someone calls, he's eager to go and talk with them. It's just as though I were a piece of furniture now. But when I complain he says he's doing all this for us. But there isn't any "us" as far as I'm concerned. I got married for some companionship, and I'm not going to put up with this.[42]

On more mature reflection, she decided to put up with it until we could work it out with Bob. It took some time, but he finally was able to see that the patterns of life he was establishing really did not involve much of marriage. It is in this way that "organization men" sometimes lose a marriage partner or reduce their marriages to meaningless limits of interaction. One young couple recently decided that the girl must give up a well paying job and stay home because her work took her away from the house during the only hours when her husband could be there. They decided to try to live on his part-time earnings rather than risk the happiness of the early years of a marriage in which they only said "hello" to each other at breakfast.

There is another area of role functions where some disagreement often occurs. This has to do with household tasks, and who does them. Living in a house demands hundreds of common chores. Some of them have been done traditionally by the husband and some by the wife. Recently a young wife described her predicament to me this way:

[41] From a case study in the author's files.   [42] From a case study in the author's files.

I hoped John would be a different sort around the house than Dad. You know Dad would never lift one finger to do anything. He said his function was to earn the money, and he was not going to be bothered taking out the garbage, mowing the lawn, or anything like that. And you know, John is just like that! I'm tired of living in apartments. I lived four years in one while in school, and now I want a home, but John says positively we will not move into a home until he can hire someone to cut and water the lawn, paint the fences and keep things up. I've always dreamed about having a home, and this is real hard for me. I guess, though, it's lucky I had the father I did because I can at least understand how a man can feel this way.[43]

This young man absolutely refused to lift a hand at home. In another case a girl resented her husband's neglect very, very much because her father had delighted in working around the house, and her picture of home life included the expectation that the husband would do all these things. It is important in working out the economy of the household that both the wishes of the wife and the husband be considered.

Of course, in terms of basic role conflict the conviction on the part of the male that his desire is the only important one may be the really dynamic aspect of any situation. If he feels that to be comfortable, he must exercise a patriarchal type of role, but his wife wants him to exemplify what we have called companionship roles, there is sure to be trouble. Jacobsen found in his study of one hundred married and one hundred divorced individuals in Ohio that the divorced people characteristically had combined men with patriarchal role expectations and the women with democratic ideals.[44] Burgess and Wallin have not commented on this aspect of marital difficulty, but they have stressed the importance of interdependence in marriage. This kind of role conflict brings trouble in problem solving and in decision making. Furthermore, many young couples are unconsciously fearful that marriage will submerge their individuality, and so they deliberately strive to play such determined roles that this will not happen. This need to be independent may make them behave in autocratic and unreasonable ways and make of the early months of marriage a battleground. In all of these aspects of role playing, a kind of tentativeness and a responsiveness to the expectations of the other will help overcome conflicts.

In-Law Difficulties. In-laws can be fun and they can be difficult. In

[43] From a case in the author's files.
[44] Paul H. Jacobsen, "Differentials in Divorce by Duration of Marriage and Size of Family," *American Sociological Review*, XV (1950), 150.

Duvall's study based on reports from 1,337 subjects, there were 345 who had no problems at all to report, but the rest listed problems of varying degrees of difficulty.[45] This means that 992 had problems. Mother-in-law was named by 491, or 36.8 per cent of the total group, as the most difficult person with whom to deal. Sister-in-law accounted for 20.3 per cent of the citations, brother-in-law a mere 5.4 per cent, and father-in-law only 5.0 per cent. It can readily be seen that for some reason the female side of the family causes most of the problems, at least on the surface where they can be detected readily. But how important are these conflicts to marital adjustment generally?

Landis and Landis asked couples who had been married for an average of twenty years to list their most serious problems in achieving happiness; the women mentioned in-law relationships second and the men listed them third.[46] In a follow-up study, 544 couples who were in the early years of marriage were asked the same question. These couples gave the in-law problem first place in their list of difficult situations. The following figures give specific statistical details of these 554 marriages.[47] When the

FIGURE 13. Happiness and In-Law Relationships *

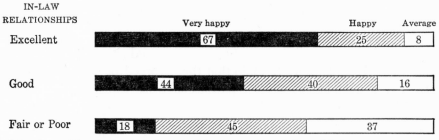

* Landis and Landis, p. 407. Reprinted by permission of the publisher.

in-law relationships were excellent, 67 per cent of the marriages were very happy, but when the in-law relationships were poor only 18 per cent of the couples were very happy.

It is essential in interpreting these percentages to recall the point made in Chapter Eight regarding the problems associated with dependencies in marriage. Part of the in-law adjustment problem is a reflection of that basic psychological difficulty. Another part of the problem of the in-law

[45] Evelyn Millis Duvall, *In-Laws: Pro and Con* (New York: The Association Press, 1954), pp. 187–188.
[46] Landis and Landis, *Building a Successful Marriage*, p. 407.
[47] Landis and Landis, p. 407.

is derived from the differences in family customs, rituals, and values which separate the parent-in-law and the child-in-law.

One of the tasks of the early years of marriage is the establishment of a deep emotional relationship between the partners, and it is easy for either party to resent any obvious display of deep attachment for outsiders. If dependency by a partner does exist, it may prove exasperating to the other mate, particularly if the young people live with or near the parents on whom one is dependent.

Finally, one should bear in mind that the stereotype of in-law relationships is one of the most powerful of our day and that, consequently, even when there would otherwise be no great problem, fears and uncertainties based on that cultural stereotype may actually produce difficulties.

Conflicts About Friendships with the Opposite Sex. Still another type of domestic difficulty involves interest or communication with "the other woman" or the "other man." We are not referring here to affairs, for we shall consider that subject when we come to sexual adjustment. We are interested just in relationships that a man has with an old girl friend, or his secretary, or even with one of his wife's friends, for this is often the cause of great tension, particularly early in marriage when the partner is still unsure. Levy and Munroe discuss this problem as follows:

> There is also the question of glamour outside of marriage. An old song runs:
>
>> If in your heart one corner lies
>> That has no room for me
>> You do not love me as I deem
>> True love should ever be . . .
>> You do not love me, no!
>> Bid me goodbye and go.
>
> To this exacting young lady I reply: "Bushwah." No man is so deeply in love with his wife that he loses his eye for a pretty pair of legs wherever he finds them—unless he's the sort of man who never notices his wife's legs either. A lady with a worried air said to me: "Whenever I'm feeling particularly keen about my husband, I start behaving like a school girl with other men, kissing in the moonlight and that sort of nonsense. I fall for sweet nothings like a ton of bricks. Does that mean I don't love my husband?" Not at all. Happily married people are by no means impervious to the romantic attractions of outsiders. Indeed, I sometimes think that the woman who has developed strong sex feelings in the arms of her husband is somewhat more susceptible to other men than the woman to whom sex has proved a disappointment. Moreover, however attractive a husband

may be, he is, ipso facto, not a new story, and we have already described the contribution sheer novelty makes to the love relationship. If we were picking reading matter for a winter in Little America, we would take with us the Bible and Shakespeare and the *Iliad*. We recognize and enjoy their permanent value. Here at home the most highbrow literati are not above chuckling over an ephemeral paragraph in the *New Yorker*. Flirtations are ephemeral, but many married folk find them amusing and seem to be none the worse for them.

When the marriage is really stable, however, these extra-marital adventures are not compulsive. We can take them or leave them with small disappointment. We can be pleasantly thrilled about the other woman without for a moment considering throwing over our marriage for her or even changing our affection for our wife . . .[48]

But if one partner is the least bit insecure or jealous, such adventuring causes rifts that are hard to heal. Many marriages apparently are not "really stable" and consequently are damaged by flirtations or even a passing interest in other individuals. A man, and to a certain extent a woman, who has just been married has been used to the ways of courtship and it takes a while before the old habits of pursuit disappear (or are repressed). But a young husband and wife would do well to discuss very precisely early in marriage what they expect of each other in this regard. Once having made an explicit agreement, they will have a standard by which to judge their own and their mate's conduct, and what could be a cause for friction will disappear.

CONCLUSION

Early marital adjustment is a time of great joy. It is also a period of learning and experimenting with adjustment processes. The results tend to persist throughout marriage. Such adjustments are inevitable, and they involve modifications of personality values and role expectations. The important areas where a couple should strive for maximum growth have been outlined. Attention has been given to intrusive factors and persons that may cause friction unless intelligently handled. When some patterns of interaction like these have been established, and the couple begin to feel some real degree of security with each other, they are ready to begin the next stage of family development. They then think about enlarging the circle of their love and their family in terms of having a child. The considerations that have to do with that decision are the subject matter of

[48] Levy and Munroe, pp. 78–80. Reprinted with the permission of the publisher.

the next chapter. It is a period of life that has as much adventure, satisfaction, and reward as any that comes before or after.

VISUAL AIDS

Who's Right? McGraw-Hill Marriage Series, McGraw-Hill Book Company, 330 West 42nd Street, New York 36, New York.

READINGS

Baber, Ray E. *Marriage and the Family.* 2nd ed. New York, McGraw-Hill Book Company, Inc., 1953, Chapter VI.

Blood, Robert O. Jr. *Marriage.* New York, The Free Press of Glencoe, 1962, Chapter 10. Copyright The Macmillan Company.

Burgess, Ernest W. and Paul Wallin. *Engagement and Marriage.* Philadelphia, J. B. Lippincott Company, 1953, Chapter XIV.

Landis, Judson T. and Mary G. Landis. *Readings in Marriage and the Family.* New York, Prentice-Hall, Inc., 1952, Chapter VII.

Waller, Willard and Reuben Hill. *The Family: A Dynamic Interpretation.* Rev. ed. New York, Dryden Press, 1951, Chapter XIII. Copyright Holt, Rinehart and Winston, Inc.

CHAPTER 14

Planning for
Children in
the Home

INTRODUCTION

THERE is no creativity in life that is comparable to that of giving life to another human being. If couples exult in their first months of establishing a home, the time comes when they look forward with equal joy to adding to the members of the group who live there. Members of every segment of society believe that children fulfill the final meaning of marriage. Yet, as we shall see, there are differences in the degree of satisfaction children bring. This chapter presents ways by which we can make the experience of parenthood more rewarding.

MARITAL ADJUSTMENT AND THE DESIRE FOR CHILDREN

What is the relation of marital adjustment to the desire for (and the having of) children? Burgess and Cottrell discovered a high correlation between happiness ratings and the desire for (and having) children. The following figure shows that for some men and women desire for children is a factor associated with marital adjustment or maladjustment. This figure shows that where the marital adjustment is poor no children are desired, and when children are present they contribute to greater dissatisfaction.

334

On the basis of a very careful statistical study called the Indianapolis Fertility Study, Robert B. Reed found an increase in marital adjustment with increasing success in controlling fertility according to the desires of the couple.[1]

FIGURE 14. Desire for Children and Marital Adjustment *

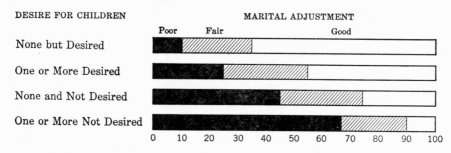

* Ernest W. Burgess and Leonard Cottrell, *Predicting Success or Failure in Marriage* (New York: Prentice-Hall, Inc., 1939), p. 260. Reprinted by permission.

We may conclude then that those couples who have not achieved good adjustment and who do not feel capable of assuming the responsibility of child rearing find in children an additional source of anxiety and conflict, while those who want children may expect that a child will add to their total adjustment. Furthermore, even for those families that want children, there is a vast difference in the degree of satisfaction they bring, which is directly related to their ability to space the births.

If, then, the contribution of children to marital adjustment depends upon success in controlling fertility, we must explore the possibilities of that control. It is seen from both the Reed and the Burgess-Cottrell studies that children who are not wanted not only contribute to family disorganization but, even more important, the children may receive poor psychological conditioning because of their rejection and because they are reared in an unhappy family. For couples who are in conflict or for some other reasons are not ready to have offspring, to insist that they do so will further impair the marriage. Sentimental persons who wish to foist parenthood on reluctant individuals may accomplish the very opposite of their ultimate goals. A short excerpt from a case history of a troubled marriage illustrates this point.

[1] Robert B. Reed, "The Interrelationship of Marital Adjustment, Fertility Control, and Size of Family," *Social and Psychological Factors Affecting Fertility*, VIII (New York: Milbank Memorial Fund, 1948), 423.

I suppose that although our problem seems to be a sexual one, it has some roots far back in our marriage. Part of the trouble I lay at the door of a doctor who gave me some mighty bad birth control advice when we were about to be married. The result was that I got pregnant on my honeymoon, and I have always resented that doctor and that pregnancy, and I suppose I have rejected the child, too.[2]

Our emphasis then must be upon the education of the generation that must bear the responsibility of procreation so that they will be both mature enough to want to undertake the responsibility of rearing children and intelligent enough to welcome these children into a well-adjusted home. We must, in the light of these findings, enable young people to plan child spacing so that the children will be desired and not rejected. If, however, the situation between the husband and wife has already deteriorated, children cannot mend the marriage. Sears discovered too that if there is already a "good deal of tension" between the husband and the wife, the wife rejects the idea of having a child or more children because more children tie "her more strongly to a marriage which she has begun to feel is a poor one." [3] But if the bond is close between them, she *may* want children who *may* resemble him or who will complete their family circle.

ORDINAL POSITION, CHILD SPACING AND MARITAL SATISFACTION

In the study of child-rearing patterns which we have already described in Chapter Four, Sears found that most couples were extraordinarily delighted with the discovery that they were going to have their first child. Eighty-one per cent were either generally pleased or completely delighted to know that the wife was pregnant.[4] Only 18 per cent were either displeased or registered mixed feelings. But the situation was different for succeeding children. In general, only 32 per cent were delighted to know that a second child was coming. Why the difference? We get a clue from the following table which indicates that it is a matter of timing.

[2] From a case study in the author's files.
[3] Sears, Maccoby, and Levin, *Patterns of Child Rearing* (New York: Row, Peterson and Company, 1957), p. 42. Copyright Harper and Row, Publishers.
[4] Sears, Maccoby, and Levin, p. 36.

T A B L E 32. Mother's Attitude Toward Pregnancy in Relation to the Age of the Next Older Child by Per Cents *

MOTHER'S ATTITUDE TOWARD PREGNANCY	AGE OF NEXT OLDER CHILD WHEN THIS CHILD WAS BORN			
	21 Months Or Less	22–31 Months	32–55 Months	55 Months Or More
Delighted	9	28	42	52
Generally Pleased	23	39	35	16
Mixed Feelings or Displeased	68	31	23	32
Not Ascertained	—	2	—	—
Total	100	100	100	100
Number of Cases	34	54	92	31

$$p < .01$$

* Sears, Maccoby and Levin, p. 40. Reprinted by permission of the publisher.

This chart shows that the degree of pleasure at having second or later children is related to "ordinal position" and the length of time between the arrival of the children. One has only to look at the fact that when there were only 21 months between the birth of the two children there was a large proportion of the mothers (68 per cent) who were either displeased or who had mixed feelings, in contrast to the few (23 per cent) who had similar feelings when the births were spaced from 32 to 55 months apart, to recognize how important child spacing may be. The greater the distance between children the greater the number of mothers who are delighted with another pregnancy.

CONTRIBUTIONS OF CHILDREN TO PARENTS

What specific contributions do children make to the well-integrated family? Bossard tells us more than anyone else what profound increments come to the family with the birth of children. We all have certain vague notions of the "joys of parenthood," but few of us have tried to define sharply what those joys are. Bossard does just this. He begins his analysis by stating what he calls the Law of Interaction.[5] The law is stated thus:

[5] James H. S. Bossard and Eleanor Stoker Boll, *The Sociology of Child Development*, 3rd ed. (New York: Harper and Brothers, 1960), pp. 134–138. Copyright Harper and Row, Publishers.

With the addition of each person to a family or primary group, the number of persons increases in the simplest arithmetical progression in whole numbers, and the number of personal interrelationships within the group increases in the order of triangular numbers. So:

Number of persons 2, 3, 4, 5, 6, 7, 8
Number of personal relationships .... 1, 3, 6, 10, 15, 21, 28.

The relationships between a husband, wife, and one child are diagrammed this way:

But if two more children are added to the diagram expression, the dynamic interaction of these five looks like this:

    The result of this multiplication of interactions may be considered in terms of our earlier discussion of the socialization of children. Obviously, from the standpoint of the child, the growing number of contacts with diverse individuals gives the child a growing fund of experience with others on which to base later social responses. It may likewise broaden the perspective and total emotional capacity and life of the parent.[6]

    A second aspect of growth in family life is the "Expansion of Family Interests." Bossard lists many of the new elements that become important upon the birth of a child such as finance, insurance, home ownership, assessment of the community, religious education. Even more important is the new stake the parent has in the "shape of things to come" because the world of which he is a participating citizen will be the environment of his child. Interests such as peace or public health which before had been given nominal attention take on deeper significance. We may conclude that the addition of children means the growth of a more profound general philosophy of life.

    [6] Bossard and Boll, p. 139.

The third point is that of the lasting emotional satisfactions derived from parenthood. Here we quote Bossard directly:

> The child not only broadens the interests of parents in the community and social matters of all kinds, but gives to most parents emotionally satisfying interests of long duration. Nothing is perhaps more essential to a happy life than such interests. . . . Emotional exploitation of children is news; behind the news are innumerable parents who find in their interest in children deep and abiding satisfactions without exacting any crippling bondage. This is the essence of normal and happy parenthood.[7]

There are many women who, during their childbearing years, are so content with their own personal achievements that any vision of their future needs is obscured. When they become older and lonely they may wish they had not concentrated so completely upon personal goals and had included children in their total life pattern.

A fourth concomitant of the rearing of children is the persistent stimulus to a more mature spiritual and intellectual life. Not only do children ask innumerable questions of philosophic or religious profundity, but they pose questions of value in terms of guidance situations. What shall I tell my daughter about drinking at sorority parties? What kind of training will best enable her to fit into our materialistic culture in terms of money stewardship? No parent may escape the consequences of the answers to both questions. They will be indelibly reflected in later life decisions of the child. Consequently the parent must grow even though he is reluctant to face ethical or spiritual questions dormant since his own childhood.

Bossard stresses two other important contributions of children to parental growth; one is the growing insight into life's processes, and a second is an insight into the meaning of life itself. There is a final point which is implied but not directly stated by Bossard. This is the contribution of parenthood to the cohesion of husband and wife, irrespective of what the children directly contribute to the parents. With the introduction of children into the family the focus of attention shifts partially from an emphasis upon the pleasures or the needs of husband and wife to the needs of the child. This shift of emphasis may of course introduce new aspects of conflict if there is jealousy toward the child, or if the parents' philosophies of child rearing are very widely different. But in most cases both parents begin to plan for the child and the future. Furthermore, even if

---

[7] Bossard and Boll, pp. 139–140. Reprinted by permission of the publisher.

their own interests are rather widely dissimilar in other areas they plan for the child together, enjoy him together, and, if he is ill, worry together. The depth of their identification with the child gives this unity a special meaning. Thus, children may contribute much to the elimination of conflict by sublimating minor personal considerations to the larger concern with the child. Bossard concludes:

> This, then, is the real end of life, that we receive, as it were, the torch from one generation, to carry it over to the next generation. This is what the child brings, in some varying form of expression, to each parent who has the capacity to perceive it.[8]

In establishing a frame of reference for the family, the conclusion is reached that children add many dimensions of value to the home and to the personalities of parents, contribute to the cohesion of the parents, and add to the general investment of citizens in their communities. This means that family planning is based on the realities of personality interaction. With this background of appreciation of the contributions of children the problem of their spacing can now be discussed.

SPECIFIC CONSIDERATIONS IN PLANNING FOR CHILDREN

Early Marital Adjustments and the First Child. There are many considerations which need emphasis in discussing family planning. The first important factor in the spacing of the family is that of timing the arrival of the first child to give it maximum psychological security. This is not always easy because no matter when the first child comes, there is a certain quotient of inexperience which can be overcome only by trial and error. Nevertheless, the arrival of the first child should be postponed until the emotional nest is ready for him. It is unfortunate if the first child arrives so soon that he is a victim of the normal conflicts incident to early adjustment in marriage. Individuals with well-defined values will have conflicts because the man and the woman rarely have had identical backgrounds. If they quarrel in the course of compromising these differences, they are not abnormal. But it is unfortunate if these conflicts affect the emotional security of their first child. It is therefore wise to postpone the coming of the first child until the first general adjustments of marriage have been completed.

Finances and the First Birth. A second consideration involves fi-

[8] Bossard and Boll, p. 144. Reprinted by permission of the publisher.

nances. Very few young couples begin marriage with sufficient savings to be able to underwrite children immediately. If a couple have a child in the first nine or ten months of marriage, this upsets their plans to lay aside sufficient funds to meet new expenses of marriage and, specifically, the expenses of a child. Today many new wives expect to work so that they may have the money to make a down payment on a house or a car, or to have a baby. If these plans are interrupted by a child, the parents will generally not welcome him as wholeheartedly as they would if his coming had been more in keeping with their schedule.

Sexual Adjustment and First Births. A third consideration involves sexual adjustment. The advent of pregnancy may mar the growth toward sexual adjustment. A client said recently:

> We really have never had time to get adjusted. My three pregnancies came so close together that, since the beginning of our marriage, I have been pregnant most of the time. I think that is one reason why we are so badly adjusted. The first pregnancy came before we had adjusted sexually and when I became pregnant we didn't make much progress.

The most extensive study of the interval between marriage and first birth has been made by Christensen in a study based on a sample of 1,670 marriages. This 1939 study involved Mormon individuals who lay great stress on early and large families. Christensen concluded:

(1) The modal interval between the marriage of parents and the birth of their first child was about ten or eleven calendar months.
(2) The trend from 1905 to 1935 was toward a lengthening of this interval.
(3) Heterogeneity between husband and wife, as to both age and pre-marital residence, was associated with the long time-intervals.
(4) In general, the older the couple at marriage the longer was the interval between that marriage and the birth of a first child.
(5) The occupations of farming and unskilled labor were associated with short intervals and the skilled and professional occupations with long intervals.
(6) Relief work was associated with disproportionately short time-intervals.
(7) Urban dwellers showed longer intervals than did the residents of rural communities.[9]

[9] Harold T. Christensen, *Marriage Analysis* (New York: The Ronald Press Company, 1950), p. 363. Copyright 1950 The Ronald Press Company. Reprinted by permission of the publisher.

A couple who have saved enough so that financial strain does not undermine the joy of having a child, and who have adjusted psychologically and sexually so that the child does not threaten future growth in adjustment are ready for parenthood. On the other hand, would-be parents should not wait too long. Their pattern of living should not become so fixed that it is difficult for them to adjust to an infant.

Time-Interval Between Children. A fourth consideration is the time-interval between children. There should be enough time so that the couple is ready financially for the second child. The first child should be old enough when the second pregnancy starts so that the mother does not have to lift and carry him everywhere. Again some time should elapse to allow the mother to regain her health. Obstetricians in general think that at least two years should elapse between births. Infant death rates are definitely higher when children are more closely spaced, probably because the mother has not fully recovered her strength. Another factor has to do with the relationship between the children. Children who are too far apart definitely do not have common interests or the degree of companionship which characterizes siblings born closer together.

Total Size of Family. The fifth consideration has to do with the total number of children desired by a family. The following table shows the size of the family from 1790 through 1960. Family size decreased from 4.1 persons in 1930 to 3.38 persons in 1960.

There is no question that all intelligent individuals must now give at-

TABLE 33. Average Number of Persons per Family Household in the United States, 1790–1960 *

Year	Persons per Family	Year	Persons per Family	Year	Persons per Family
1790	5.7	1880	5.0	1920	4.3
1850	5.6	1890	4.9	1930	4.1
1860	5.3	1900	4.7	1940	3.8
1870	5.1	1910	4.5	1950	3.6
				1960	3.38

* Figure for 1790–1900 from U.S. Bureau of Census, *A Century of Population Growth from the First Census of the United States to the Twelfth, 1790–1900,* 1909, p. 96; 1900–1920 from the *Fourteenth Census of the United States, 1920, Population, General Report and Analytical Tables,* 2, p. 1266; 1930 and 1940 from the *Sixteenth Census of the United States, 1940, Population, Families, Size of Families and Age of Head,* p. 4; 1950, *Bureau of the Census, Current Population Report,* Series, p. 20, No. 38; 1960 from *1961 Statistical Abstract.*

tention to the burgeoning birth rate and its meaning for economic prosperity and world peace. At the present rate of growth there will be over six billion people on this planet by the year 2000, and 13 billion by the year 2050. If we take our own ratio of births to deaths from 1953 to 1956 and project that rate of increase to 2050 we will have one billion persons in the United States. The population of the world is expanding so rapidly that the gross national product per individual goes down. At it goes down, desperation increases. The great explosion many persons fear is not that of the atomic bomb but the increase in homeless and underfed men and women who in their misery will challenge the stability of civilization all around the globe. While different individuals will make different kinds of suggestions regarding solutions to this problem, no moral man can any longer evade trying to find solutions to the dilemma. It is true that the United States is the most fortunate of all nations economically, but it may not be true that we will continue to be so if no attention is paid to this problem. In the meantime, increasing numbers of people is one of the most pressing problems the world generally faces.

DIFFERENTIALS IN THE BIRTH RATE

There are wide differences in the fertility rates of contrasting groups in the United States, but these differences are not as great as they used to be. In 1953 the crude birth rate for the nation was 25.0. Kirk reports, on the basis of a careful inference from tabulations given in the *Official Catholic Directory*, that the crude birth rate for Catholics for 1953 was 35.0 per 1,000.[10] He estimates that while Catholics made up 19.5 per cent of the total population, Catholics contributed 27.3 of the births.

The birth rate varies also in terms of educational levels, but this difference has been narrowing. Grabill, Kiser and Whelpton report that:

> Thus, the 1940–50 per cent increases in cumulative fertility rates tended to be largest among women who finished college and the smallest among those of "none or elementary" status. As a result there has been a substantial narrowing of the fertility differentials by education since 1940.[11]

Between 1935 and 1940 the net replacement rate was 48 per cent below a replacement figure but from 1945 to 1950 college graduates were re-

[10] Dudley Kirk, "Recent Trends of Catholic Fertility in the United States," *Current Research in Human Fertility* (New York: The Milbank Memorial Fund, 1955), p. 101.
[11] Wilson H. Grabill, Clyde V. Kiser and Pascal K. Whelpton, *The Fertility of American Women* (New York: John Wiley and Sons, 1958), p. 386.

producing at a rate 9 per cent above the number needed for replacement of the population through births.[12] Childbearing is definitely more popular with college graduates than it has been for many decades.

The birth rate also varies according to ethnic group, occupation of husband, participation in the working force, rural or urban residence and other factors. In speaking of more general considerations Grabill, Kiser and Whelpton conclude:

> The Bureau of Census estimates that the population may contain from 207 to 228 million persons in 1975; according to Whelpton's projections these figures are reasonable but so are estimates as high as 243 million and as small as 193 million. Business conditions, the international situation and attitudes toward family size will no doubt have much influence on fertility and population growth.[13]

It is not possible to be more precise but at the moment larger families are now more common than twenty years ago. In speaking of this factor Christensen says:

> It is conceivable, however, that a reversal in some of the fertility differentials would be of benefit to society. From the standpoint of economic welfare it would be better if those who could most afford it would have more children, and those who could least afford it, fewer children. From the standpoint of cultural opportunity it would be better if the well educated would play a larger role in reproduction, and the uneducated a smaller role. Since economic success and higher education are at least partially selective, it follows that a reversal of present birth rate differentials in these areas would be eugenically beneficial. There is need for some kind of public policy and educational program directed toward these ends.[14]

FAMILY PLANNING AND CONTRACEPTION

If it is wise to postpone the advent of the first child and to protect the health of the mother between births, it is important to know how this may be done. There are various methods of contraception or birth control. The history of birth control is as old as marriage itself but only today has science provided adequate methods. In discussing the various methods of birth control we shall relate them to religious groups. These groups have varying attitudes toward contraception.

[12] Grabill, Kiser and Whelpton, p. 388.
[13] Grabill, Kiser and Whelpton, p. 302. Reprinted by permission of the publisher.
[14] Christensen, pp. 358–359.

Birth control is still a controversial subject. Recently the Roman Catholic Church reaffirmed its historic position, with certain clarifications. It declared that the only methods of contraception permitted were the rhythm and the temperature methods, both of which require the exercise of self-control; and that even these methods were not to be used indiscriminately but only for a "grave" reason such as serious economic stress or a condition of health which made childbearing dangerous. No mechanical or chemical methods may be used, only the spiritual method of self-denial.[15]

The Temperature Method. The temperature method of birth control is based upon continence during the period immediately before and after ovulation. If one asks how one is to know whether or not ovulation has taken place, the answer is that a new method of using temperature charts assures this knowledge. We now know that temperature varies rather precisely with changes in the menstrual cycle as indicated in the following diagram.

FIGURE 15. Temperature and the Menstrual Cycle

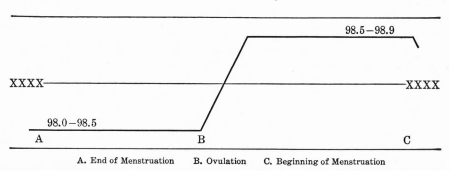

A. End of Menstruation   B. Ovulation   C. Beginning of Menstruation

At the conclusion of each menstrual cycle the temperature falls to some point below normal (Point "C"). At ovulation it begins to rise and remains steady until the next menstrual period when it drops again. If a woman keeps a careful record of her temperature for several months she will be able to tell precisely the day when ovulation occurs, at Point "B." She is fertile after ovulation.

This method has helped those couples who were having difficulty achieving pregnancy so to time their coitus that they would have a maximum chance of insuring pregnancy. Furthermore it is a very inexpensive

[15] *The Tidings* (Catholic publication of the Los Angeles Diocese of Catholic Churches), November 14, 1951.

test of pregnancy, for every woman who keeps such a chart knows that if her temperature stays up for several weeks she is probably pregnant, unless some factor such as a cold or other infectious condition influences her condition.

The Rhythm Method. The second method which is approved by Catholics is the rhythm method, so called because of the regularity of the menstrual cycle. This is the method which Pope Pius XI approved in his encyclical on marriage of December 31, 1930, when he stated:

> Nor are those considered as acting against nature who in their married life use their right in proper manner, although on account of natural reasons of time and of certain defects, new life cannot be brought forth.[16]

This method depends again on exact knowledge of the menstrual cycle. This information may be obtained by keeping a careful record of the cycle for some months previous to marriage. When this is done the period when fertilization may take place can be predicted.

The ovulation period for a woman with a normal menstrual cycle of 28 days is from 12 to 16 days prior to the first day of menstruation. However, since the spermatozoa sometimes live for three days, three additional days must be added to the 16-day period, making it 19 days. In calculating the period of possible impregnation one counts back from the next expected period. Thus the time-interval when pregnancy would be possible is from 12 to 19 days before the first day of the next expected menstruation. Thus a woman who is on a regular 28-day cycle and expects to to menstruate on November 28 can determine her fertile period by counting back 19 days (or to November 9). Fertilization presumably is possible during this period. It is represented on a calendar in Figure 16 (p. 347).

The immediate objection to this plan is that it does not take account of irregularities in the monthly cycle. Specialists in the rhythm method however have worked out a way of meeting this problem—by keeping track of the degree of irregularity and compensating for it in the schedule. Thus, assuming that a woman with a 28-day cycle actually varies now and then by five days, the variation is taken care of by adding 5 days to the 7 which are ordinarily considered fertile or unsafe. That is, the unsafe period is 12 days in length and will end on November 22. One may thus adjust to any irregularity by incorporating into the schedule the maximum number of days of variation.

[16] T. S. Welton, *The Modern Method of Birth Control* (New York: Grosset and Dunlap, 1943), p. 148.

FIGURE 16. Fertility and the Menstrual Cycle

NOVEMBER						
SUN.	MON.	TUES.	WED.	THURS.	FRI.	SAT.
		1	2	3	4	5
6	7	8	*First day of Fertility* 9	10	11	12
13	*14*	*15*	*Last day of Fertility* 16	17	18	19
20	21	22	23	24	25	26
27	*Expected Menstrua- tion* 28	29	30			

Couples must not expect too much certainty from the rhythm method. Anyone who practices it should seek the help of a competent physician in charting the calendar plan. Dickinson and Wood, after a lifetime of study, conclude that:

> Those who have been taught that no method but observance of the safe period, the sterile period, is right, may give a year's study to a calendar marked with the date of each period, and then take advice as to whether the wife's regularity is such as to warrant a test of this method. It has not lived up to claims, as there are enough women who do not produce the egg on the usual calendar date near the mid-month (and with no way of telling who is uncertain) for the risk is still considerable.[17]

[17] Leland Foster Wood and Robert L. Dickinson, *Harmony in Marriage* (New York: The Round Table Press, 1948), p. 86. Reprinted by permission.

It is also true that ovulation may be stimulated or retarded by sudden surges of emotion and perhaps by intercourse itself. Again, the appearance of fraternal twins indicates that often two eggs are released in the same month and at different times. This may account for the number of children conceived during the so-called safe periods. Significant research is going on, and the rhythm method, when it is perfected, may offer a very adequate method of birth control.

There are some disadvantages to all types of birth control and there are some serious drawbacks to the use of the rhythm method.[18] (1) The necessary abstinence for a minimum of eight days each month and for a long post partum period is difficult for many men and women and (2) the method is relatively inefficient and can be used successfully only by women with quite regular cycles. (3) It has a high failure rate; in one study it was found to be fourteen per 100 years of coital exposure.[19] This rate of failure is twice as high as that of other types of birth control.

General Acceptance of Mechanical or Chemical Methods of Birth Control. Only a generation ago Margaret Sanger was sent to prison for the "crime" of sending out birth control information. Since then all but two states have legalized such information. The extent of approval of birth control by the general public is indicated by Table 34 (page 349) which summarizes findings of polls regarding various aspects of contraception. This table shows that as early as 1943 some 85 per cent of all women, and 69 per cent of all Catholic women, believed that birth control information should be made available to married women. In 1947, 64 per cent of all women, and 57 per cent of Catholic women, stated that they would approve having government health clinics furnish birth control information to married people who want it.

The meaning of this table is that the great majority of American women approve of birth control, although only yesterday the mores condemned it. An even more persuasive proof of the acceptance of birth control is the fact that women of all positions and educational attainment are controlling the size of their families.

General Knowledge of Birth Control. How accurate is the birth control information of the average American family? Dr. Earl Koos studied a typical small industrial community in the northeastern part of the United States to get an answer to that question. He discovered that one

---

[18] Alan F. Guttmacher, "The Control of Fertility," *Sterility*, ed. by Edward T. Tyler (New York: McGraw-Hill Book Company, Inc., 1961), p. 364.
[19] Guttmacher, p. 364.

out of three couples either have no knowledge of modern birth control methods or use methods regarded as inadequate by scientists. When those individuals, such as Catholics, who have religious objections to birth con-

T A B L E 34. Findings of Polls of Public Opinion on Birth Control, 1936, 1943, and 1947, for Given Groups *

QUESTION AND RESPONSE	PER CENT OF GIVEN GROUPS				
	All	College	High School	Grades Only	Catholic
1936. Do you believe in the teaching and practice of birth control? (General population sample)					
Yes	63	—	—	—	—
No	23	—	—	—	—
Don't know	14	—	—	—	—
1943. Do you believe that knowledge about birth control should or should not be made available to all married women? (Women, age 20–35, general population)					
Should be available	85	93	—	70	69
Should not	10	5	—	18	24
Don't know	5	2	—	12	7
1943. (If "should" above) Do you believe that knowledge about birth control should or should not be kept away from unmarried women? (Women, age 20–35, general population)					
Should not be withheld	70	—	—	55	59
Should be	23	—	—	34	34
Don't know	7	—	—	11	7
1947. Would you approve or disapprove of having government health clinics furnish birth control information to married people who want it in this country? (General population)					
Approve	64	76	70	—	57
Disapprove	23	18	19	—	26
No opinion	13	6	11	—	17

* From Ernest W. Burgess and Harvey J. Locke, *The Family* (New York: The American Book Company, 1953), p. 454. Reprinted by permission. Table does not appear in 1963 edition.

trol are eliminated from the sample, two out of five couples who would accept and use contraceptive methods do not have the necessary information. Of the sample of 514 families, one-fifth (71 Catholic and 33 Fundamentalists) rejected birth control on religious grounds. Of the remaining 410 families, who had no objection, 96 reported no direct information about contraceptive methods, 76 reported using methods of "limited or no value" and in some cases "potentially injurious." Thus, some 175 families did not know about birth control or 33 per cent of the families involved in the whole study and 42 per cent of the 410 families who had no religious objection to the practice of contraception.[20]

Mechanical and Chemical Methods of Birth Control. The only safe procedure for any woman to follow is to visit an *informed* physician (not all of them are well trained in the use of contraceptives) and allow the the doctor to prescribe the method best suited for her physical structure. In Yarros' study of 12,500 cases, not a single woman was injured in any way by the use of contraceptive devices recommended by competent physicians.[21] There are some birth control methods that are dangerous and some totally ineffective. Only a physician should make a specific recommendation to an individual who may have unique problems. Having said this, we will review types of contraceptives and present some of their advantages and disadvantages.

THE DIAPHRAGM

The diaphragm occludes the cervix from the vaginal canal and thus prevents semen from entering the mouth of the cervix. It is used with a spermacidal cream or jelly that is placed on the lip of the diaphragm and some in the center of the dome so that there is always double protection. It has several distinct advantages:

1. It is probably the most effective type of contraceptive now generally in use. (The pill may be more effective. At present studies indicate that this may be so but they are not yet conclusive.) It has a failure rate of 6 per 100 years of coital exposure among well-motivated, intelligent persons. The failure rate is higher among "poorly motivated, underprivileged" persons.
2. There is no dulling of sexual sensation caused for either partner by its use.
3. It may be inserted regularly on retiring so there is no need for irritating delays due to last minute preparations.[22]

---

[20] *Planned Parenthood News*, VII (Spring, 1954), 5.
[21] Rachelle Yarros, *Modern Women and Sex* (New York: The Vanguard Press, Inc., 1953), p. 147.
[22] Guttmacher, p. 357.

The main disadvantages are that it must necessarily be fitted by a doctor and used consistently. Some women may not like the task of inserting the diaphragm and some do not have the intelligence or motivation to use it well.

THE JELLIES AND CREAMS

Some doctors have found the use of the spermatoxic jellies and creams so effective that they are now recommending the use of certain of these without the diaphragm. The studies are inconsistent, but "it seems likely that among highly motivated, intelligent couples the standard creams and jellies are slightly less effective than either the condom or the diaphragm but give superior protection when compared to the more complicated methods in poorly motivated, unintelligent patients."[23] Some women and men object to excessive lubrication, and others to the fact that it must be used much closer to the time of sexual relations.

THE CONDOM

The condom is by far the most popular of the more effective methods of birth control. It is made of latex or rubber or animal membrane.[24] It must, however, be used according to specific directions by a physician to prevent failure. It has some disadvantages:

1. It often dulls sensation so that in some men an erection cannot be maintained.
2. It may diminish sexual satisfaction in the female enough to prevent orgasm.
3. It prevents couples from remaining together after intercourse because it then may slip off.

The condom, when used according to a physician's precautionary rules, probably has a pregnancy rate of six or below per one hundred years of coital exposure.[25] But in "unsophisticated groups" the rate is twice as high.

The Oral Steroids (The Pill). The U.S. Food and Drug Administration approved for sale in 1960 a contraceptive pill. Two types of oral steroids, norethynodrel and norethindrone, have been tested thoroughly. Both function by inhibiting the gonadotropic cells of the anterior pituitary, thus eliminating the production or maturation of ova.[26] The reports

[23] Guttmacher, p. 362. [24] Guttmacher, p. 359. [25] Guttmacher, p. 360.
[26] Guttmacher, p. 367.

about the effectiveness of the pill are in disagreement. Pincus summarized four studies on 635 women in Puerto Rico and Haiti and found that the pregnancy rate was only 2.7 per one hundred years of coital exposure.[27] Tyler and Olson, experimenting with five different compounds, reported a rate of 8.6, but pointed out that of the five, norethindrone and norethyno-drel were "more effective in inhibiting ovulation than the others."[28] So if we had the separate rates for those two they might compare with Pincus' reports. Tyler and Olson also reported fewer side effects of spotting, irregular menses, nausea, headache and some dizziness with these two drugs. Pincus found some of the patients in the four studies he surveyed dropped out because of those side effects, but he reported no significant change in the well-being or libido of his patients except for some tendency to gain weight.[29] Many women have reported improved sexual life because they felt the pill assured them of no pregnancy until they were ready for it.

While the oral method is new and requires much investigation before we will know enough about it to describe adequately its long-term effects, it is the most promising step in contraception for many years. One preliminary study already has reported that over 1,000 women using this method showed less cervical or uterine cancer than a comparable age group not using it. Of course such a study must be replicated before we know whether this result came as the concomitant of sample selection or if there is some dynamic factor inhibiting carcinogenic growth.[30]

Inferior or Disapproved Methods

THE DOUCHE

In one study the pregnancy rate of women using the douche for contraceptive purposes was thirty-six which is extremely high.[31] It has disadvantages in timing and in the method itself that renders it inadvisable.

COITUS INTERRUPTUS

This simply means withdrawal of the penis just before ejaculation. Two studies rank its pregnancy rate at seventeen and thirty-eight, which means that it is extraordinarily inefficient.[32] Furthermore, it destroys much of the joy in intercourse for both the man and the woman.

---

[27] Guttmacher, p. 367   [28] Guttmacher, p. 368.   [29] Guttmacher, p. 369.
[30] Reported personally to the author by Henry Olson, M.D.
[31] Guttmacher, p. 363.   [32] Guttmacher, p. 365.

INTRAUTERINE STEMS AND RINGS

These have physiologic consequences such as endocervicitis, irregular bleeding, erosion of the tissue or general irritation. They seem not to be effective.

General Standards for Contraception. Whatever birth control method is chosen, it should measure up to certain standards which have been rather carefully stated by Bowman:

1. It should be relatively effective, that is, as effective as modern medical science can make it. No method is entirely fool-proof. The methods most commonly recommended by informed physicians and reliable clinics, when used with intelligence and care, are nearly enough 100 per cent reliable to make possible the removal of all fear of unwanted pregnancy.
2. It should be relatively easy to use, simple and readily understood.
3. It should be readily available and relatively inexpensive.
4. It should be aesthetically acceptable to both parties and repugnant to neither.
5. It should permit normal, satisfactory, successful sexual adjustment.
6. It should have no harmful results. The contraceptive should contain and entail no chemical or mechanical irritant that may give rise to infection or poisoning.
7. It should be temporary, in the sense that its use may be terminated at will. Permanent sterilization, though it is a means of preventing conceptions, is not considered contraception.[33]

The temperature method, or the rhythm method, or chemical or mechanical contraceptive devices may all be regarded as means of promoting family adjustment and stability. Birth control provides that sense of security in which a husband and wife may achieve maximum sexual joy without inhibiting fear of unwanted and unwise pregnancies. On the other hand, research is daily contributing to the fulfillment of the longing of husband and wife for children. In many cases careful study based on birth control research has resulted in a baby when hope for one was almost gone. Everything possible should be done to determine whether or not sterility can be overcome. It has already been suggested that the use of the temperature method was helping some previously infertile couples to have babies. Since 1949 the number of infertility clinics in the

[33] Henry A. Bowman, *Marriage for Moderns,* 4th ed. (New York: McGraw-Hill Book Company, Inc., 1960), p. 457. Reprinted by permission of the publisher.

United States increased from 67 to 151 in 1954. In a nationwide survey Dr. Mary Steichen Calderone discovered that among 13,051 patients some 3,026 pregnancies, or one out of four, resulted. Dr. Calderone believes that if the results of only the last five years had been reported the ratio would be higher because of improved methods and greater knowledge. Thus, many couples who have been disappointed at not achieving parenthood may with help become parents.

STERILITY AND ADOPTION

No matter how competent the medical advice followed, there will still be a number of families who will remain sterile. Fortunately, however, a sterile family need not always remain childless. There are many parentless children who need to be adopted and given a normal chance for healthy character development. In a sense the purpose of adoption is to bring together under the most promising circumstances the homeless child and the childless adult. The mid-century White House Conference on Children and Youth came to the conclusion that about 38,000 children are adopted each year.

HESITATIONS ABOUT ADOPTING A CHILD

Because barren couples may long for a child, many of them welcome an adopted baby into their home. One of the questions which is often important to would-be adoptive parents is whether they have the capacity to accept fully and love as their own a child not related to them by birth or marriage. Many adoptive parents who later had children of their own have been asked whether or not there was any difference in the degree of love which they felt for their adopted and their natural children. In every single case these parents replied that they felt no such difference. When pressed as to what they would do if they had to make a choice, almost all of them replied that they would probably keep the adopted child. The question was an invidious one but they went on, in their answers, to say that the reason they felt this way was that the adopted child had come to them at the time of their greatest need and loneliness.

Bearing a child or adopting a child does not necessarily make the child one's own except in a legal sense. The child becomes a part of the parent only when the parent has given to the child tender care, deep affection, and much time. Neither the personality of the child nor the nature of

354

his adult values is determined at birth. Both are the products of interaction with others and in particular of interaction with parents. A child's bringing up is far more crucial to his personal happiness and to his worth as a member of society than his biological parentage. In every real sense the adoptive child is truly the child of the parents who share with him their lives, their ideals, and their values. Those childless couples who hesitate to adopt a child because they are afraid that they may never feel that such a child is really theirs do not fully understand the dynamics of personality growth.

Laws protect adoptive parents so that the natural parents cannot demand custody of their child. Adoptive parents need to investigate the specific laws of their state on this point but generally, if the seal of law is placed upon the new relationship between the child and the adoptive parents, legal responsibility is permanently established. Through the adoption process the child's natural parents generally waive all rights to the child, and the adoptive parents assume all the rights and obligations of parenthood. However, parents should consult with a lawyer or social agency to clarify their rights when adopting a child. The child after adoption bears the name of his new family. This family has sole right to the custody of the child and to his services or earnings as a minor. Finally, the adopted child shares in the rights of inheritance.

RECOMMENDED ADOPTIVE PROCEDURES

As the result of careful study of problems that have risen in the past, the United States Children's Bureau has set up certain standards which should guide adoptive procedures.

1. The termination of parental rights is as important as the establishment of new parental ties by adoption and should be safely guarded.
2. Placement for adoption should be made only by an agency authorized to make such placements by the state department of public welfare.
3. Adoption proceedings should be in a court of record having jurisdiction over children's cases, in the home state of the petitioners for adoption and preferably in the local community in which they live and are known and where the child is properly before the court.
4. In every proposed adoption of a child the court should have the benefit of a social study and a recommendation made by the state department of public welfare, or by a local department of public welfare designated by the state welfare department.

5. Consent to adoption should be obtained from the natural parents, or if their parental rights have been legally relinquished or terminated, from a person or agency having legal responsibility for the child and the right to consent to adoption.
6. Court hearings should be closed to the public, and the records, because of their confidential nature, should be protected.
7. A period of residence in the adoptive home, preferably for one year, should be required before the hearing on the petition, so that the suitability of the proposed adoption may be determined.
8. In the event a final decree is not entered, provision should be made for the removal of a child from a home found to be unsuitable and for his care and guardianship after his removal.
9. Safeguards should be provided in related laws, such as those affecting relinquishment of parental rights, regulations of child-placing services and determination of guardianship and custody of all children, to assure the welfare of the child in all such matters as well as in the adoption proceedings, and to define the rights and the obligations of the parents.[34]

Given these principles, we can study the exact procedure of an adoption and discover whether or not the interests of the child and of the new parents are safeguarded. After a couple has decided to adopt a child, certain alternatives are presented. The prospective foster parents may visit a friend who is a doctor and ask him to use his good services in finding them a baby. They make it known in the community that any unmarried pregnant girl can expect them to take good care of her in return for her baby. These are called independent adoptions. For reasons that will be discussed later these methods are not recommended.

The best method of adoption is through a recognized social agency. The couple calls and makes an appointment for an interview with one of the workers of the agency. During this first meeting they give their reasons for wanting a child and something of their background. In the course of this preliminary interview they fill in a first form which gives essential information regarding their place and type of residence, their citizenship status, their financial resources, their medical history, and physical descriptions of themselves and of any other persons living in the family. The worker describes the way the agency operates and discusses the remaining steps necessary before an application for a child may be entered.

After the initial interview and the completion of the first form a social worker is sent out from the agency to visit the home. She is interested

[34] *Essentials of Adoption Law and Procedure* (Washington: United States Children's Bureau, Publication No. 331, 1949), pp. 2–4.

in both the physical and the psychological attributes of the home. While some couples seem apprehensive about this visit, they should remember that the social worker is trained in making the parents feel at ease and never expects the extraordinary either in home facilities or in personality maturity. After this first visit to the home the agency studies the material it now has on the family and decides whether or not the couple seem to be good parental prospects. If the decision is a positive one, the couple is now sent an "Application for Child."

Following the receipt of the application the worker visits the home a second time and discusses any problems that may seem important to the couple or to the agency. A statement is then obtained from the couple's doctor explaining reasons for the inability of the couple to have a a child of their own. This statement is put in the agency's files.

Some question whether such an exhaustive study is really necessary, but all of this information is important in matching the child and the parents in appearance, intelligence, religion, temperament, and personality. Every possible avenue is explored which may lead to a successful and happy relationship between the child and his adoptive parents.

Even more careful scrutiny is given the children who have been placed in the care of a placing institution. As soon as children enter the institution they have a very careful physical examination. This is soon followed by an equally careful psychological study. The children are also observed by several pediatricians and social workers. No child is ever placed until those who have supervised him are convinced that he has a reasonable expectation of success in the new home situation.

Introduction to the baby that the agency has selected for them, needless to say, is one of the very high points in the life of a childless couple. A special room is generally provided for this purpose. After the social worker "introduces" the baby to its possible parents, the couple and baby are left alone to get acquainted. The parents need not take the baby recommended to them, but they generally do. However, if they take the child home, they are only prospective parents for the next year. Technically they are on probation. If, during that year, the couple decide that they cannot manage this particular child or do not feel close to him for some other reason they do not have to keep him. During this year the couple is visited four times or so by a worker from the agency who observes the progress in the growing relatedness of child and foster parents. If this worker discovers that the parents and child are basically incompatible or for some other reason that it is not in the interest of the couple or the

357

child to continue the relationship, the child may be removed from the home. It is, perhaps, unnecessary to add that this seldom happens because of the care with which the child has been placed.

At the end of the year the agency restudies the total situation and makes a recommendation for the guidance of the court which must approve the adoption.

When this final study has been completed the parents petition the court of jurisdiction for the adoption. The court considers the petition in a private hearing. The judge has a history of the child and his development, a copy of the home study and a recommendation of the state department of social welfare as well as the formal petition for adoption. If the judge, upon considering all of the evidence, favors the petition, he issues a court order granting the adoption. The adoption is now legally consummated, and the child belongs completely to the adoptive parents.

Independent Adoptions. An independent adoption is defined as an adoption which is negotiated directly between the natural parent or parents or their representatives and the adoptive parents. In many states independent adoptions are not permitted. In some states the law requires that the transaction take place within the legal framework provided by the state department of public welfare so that the one year waiting period and visits to the home are still required. What is not required is the very careful study of both foster parents and the child to be sure that they are matched to the degree that a happy relationship will result. As a result, the risk in independent adoptions is great, as indicated in the conclusions reached by the Citizens Committee on Adoption of Children in California which studied independent adoptions over a two-year period. The conclusions, statistical and qualitative, were as follows:

> Statistical information was furnished by the Department (California State Department of Public Welfare) on 13,802 California Independent Adoption Cases Terminated in 1948. From these data it was learned that 44 per cent of the parents placed their babies in the year, but that intermediaries placed 56 per cent of them. A total of 60 per cent of all the mothers were 24 years of age and under. Unmarried mothers equalled 39 per cent. At the time of investigation by the State Department 45 per cent of the mothers were not acquainted with the couple who had petitioned to adopt their children.
>
> These four statements alone raised questions about the urgency of the need of these young, unmarried mothers for good services in making the decision to give away a child forever, and the necessity for knowing these

children and the family adopting them. Of these 3,802 babies placed in independent adoption, 42 per cent were placed by married couples. This also raised questions about the reasons why families give up their children, the necessity for knowing these families and helping them to determine if this is the best plan for their family life.

The fact that, following investigation, the State Department of Public Welfare recommended denial or dismissal for 23 per cent of the independent adoption petitions means that in one year 872 children were in adoptive homes which were not suitable for them, or their parents changed their minds about adoption, or they were not legally free for adoption, or their adoptive parents decided they did not wish to proceed with adoption. The result—uprooting of family ties, new adjustment, sorrow and heartache for 872 children, their natural parents, and adoptive parents. Who knows if these changes in decision were right for the natural parents, the child, or adoptive parents, and if the services of a case work agency might not have helped before the second break in family ties was made? Who knows how many of these parents and children could have been helped by preventive services but who, for lack of such help, may later come as deeply disturbed people to social agencies.[35]

The advantages of agency placements as compared with independent adoption procedures (as shown by this study) are amply clear. Young couples eager for a baby should not be so eager as to neglect the warnings of this study. Carelessness in placing or receiving children in adoptive homes may mean much heartache and personality disruption later.

It is now rather universally recognized that an adopted child should be told that he is adopted and told very early in his relationship with his parents. One adoption agency releases the child to the parents with the understanding that the parents will tell the child he is adopted before he is three years of age. There are many positive ways in which this can be accomplished. Some mothers stress the fact that while other children just come, an adopted child is special because he has been "chosen." But the way the adoption is explained does not seem to be the important issue. The important fact for the emotional security of the child is that he shall be dearly loved; that every day of his life the tenderness and closeness of his relationship with his parents will assure him that he truly belongs. No word or phrase or illustration can ever substitute for emotional security based on feelings of closeness and love.

[35] Mary Stanton, *Gleanings From Twenty-Two Months of Activity* (The Citizens' Adoption Committee of Los Angeles, June, 1952), pp. 11–12.

CONCLUSION

Both children and the desire for children contribute to family happiness. Careful spacing of children appears to be essential to the health and happiness of both siblings and parents. Hence the need for employing methods of birth control—according to the dictates of conscience or religion. Because some married individuals will be permanently sterile, it is important to study adoption procedures.

PROJECTS

1. Take a census of the class to discover how many are only children, or first- or last-born in a larger family. Discuss the special problems in maturing that come to a child because of his ordinal rank in the family.
2. Ask a member of the sociology department to come to class for a discussion of population problems. Ask him about the contention of some eugenicists that the "best strains" are breeding themselves out of existence.
3. Ask a gynecologist to come to the class to discuss reasons for sterility, and to indicate the usefulness of the temperature and rhythm methods in assisting such couples in achieving a pregnancy.
4. If a discussion of religious approaches to birth control develops, list the many positive points on which all religions agree.
5. Plan a field trip and visit several adoption agencies. Be sure that the visits are arranged so that individuals will be there who can explain thoroughly the work of the agency.
6. Ask a representative of the Public Welfare Committee of your state or of your county to come and discuss the problems of adoption with the class.
7. Discuss the question of what actually makes a child a real son or daughter of its parents.

READINGS

Bowman, Henry A. *Marriage for Moderns.* 4th ed. New York, McGraw-Hill Book Company, Inc., 1960, Chapter 13.

Brooks, Lee M. and Evelyn C. Brooks. *Adventuring in Adoption.* Chapel Hill, University of North Carolina Press, 1939.

Cady, Ernest and Frances Cady. *How to Adopt a Child.* New York, William Morrow & Co., 1956.

Guttmacher, Alan F. "The Control of Fertility." *Sterility,* ed. Edward T. Tyler. New York, McGraw-Hill Book Company, Inc., 1961.

LANDIS, JUDSON T. and MARY G. LANDIS. *Building a Successful Marriage.* 3rd ed. Englewood Cliffs, N.J., Prentice-Hall, Inc., 1958.

LOCKBRIDGE, FRANCIS. *Adopting a Child.* New York, Greenberg Publishers, 1947.

STONE, HANNAH and ABRAHAM STONE. *The Marriage Manual.* New York, Simon and Schuster, Inc., 1953, Chapter 5.

PAMPHLETS

Essentials of Adoption Law and Procedure, U.S. Children's Bureau, No. 331, 1949.

The ABC of Foster Family Care for Children, U.S. Department of Labor, U.S. Government Printing Office, 1936.

CHAPTER 15

The Process
of
Reproduction*

INTRODUCTION

REPRODUCTION is a completely natural process and the most essential one in the whole life cycle. The infinitely complex system of human reproduction incorporates the creative adaptations of hundreds of years of change. The intricate interplay of psychological, glandular, nutritional, and muscular factors involved in the conception, nourishment, and birth of a child is a masterful achievement. To be familiar with the properties of the reproductive cells, the ovarian cycle, the process of fertilization, the growth of the fetus, and the birth process not only adds to our sense of wonder but increases our trust as well.

Some young people, either ignorant or negatively conditioned, lack this basic trust that makes their approach comfortable and exciting. These remarkable processes are studied in this chapter so that students can (1) build greater confidence and eliminate unnecessary worry about reproduction and (2) develop the kind of informed background which will enable them to be more intelligent and to behave more wisely when their turn comes to be parents than past generations.

THE REPRODUCTIVE CELLS

The changing physiological relationships of so many different organs in the reproductive process are indeed involved. It is something of a

* In the first edition, this Chapter was written with Dr. Nadina Kavinoky, M.D.

miracle that a child is ever conceived! At the onset of the process the cyclical functioning of the anterior pituitary gland must stimulate the ovary to produce an egg, and it then turns to the task of influencing the uterus to be ready to receive the egg once it has been fertilized. The egg itself must undergo radical transformations as it changes and matures, and it must move to a singular site in the Fallopian tube at the precise time healthy sperm in sufficient numbers are present for impregnation to occur. Then the zygote (as the fertilized egg is called) must move down an unobstructed Fallopian tube to the uterus, where conditions must be right so that it may attach itself and begin the long process of interaction with the mother's body. It must be nourished and carefully protected for the nine months of its growth period. Finally, at term, there must be a safe delivery. We shall consider each one of these sequences of development. First, let us try to understand the way the egg and the sperm develop in response to the stimulation of the gonadotropic secretions of the anterior pituitary gland.

The cells which become ova or sperm are called germ cells. In human beings they develop directly from the tissues of the developing ovary or testis.[1] During the development of the egg and sperm cells there is a reduction in the number of chromosomes. In human beings the normal somatic cell contains forty-eight chromosomes but the reproductive cell (gamete) has but twenty-four. When the male and female cells join, the zygote that is formed has forty-eight chromosomes. The egg develops within a follicle in the ovary called the Graafian Follicle as illustrated in Figure 17. This follicle grows in size as the egg matures. As the egg is maturing, pituitary hormones become more concentrated and eventually liberate the egg by breaking down the follicle wall. The space previously occupied by the egg is now filled by a special kind of cell (the Luteum cells) and the follicle is now called the Corpus Luteum. If fertilization occurs, the Corpus Luteum becomes active and remains active throughout pregnancy, but if the egg dies the Corpus Luteum degenerates. Figure 17 from Barth illustrates the ovarian cycle in mammals.

The growth of the Graafian Follicle is stimulated by a hormone secreted by the pituitary FSH or Follicle Stimulating Hormone. The growth of the Corpus Luteum is stimulated by a second hormone from the pituitary designated LSH or Luteum Stimulating Hormone. The relationship of these hormones to the ovarian cycle is indicated in Figure 18 from Barth.

[1] Barth, p. 14. (See footnote for Figure 17, page 364.)

FIGURE 17. The Ovarian Cycle in Mammals *

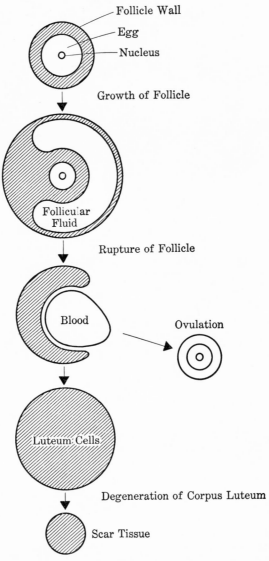

* Source: Lester George Barth, *Embryology* (New York: Henry Holt and Company, 1949), p. 21. Copyright 1949, revised and enlarged, 1953, Holt, Rinehart and Winston, Inc. Reprinted by permission of the publisher.

Male Reproductive Cells. The male reproductive cells are called sperm. They are produced in the male gonads called testes. They form in very small tubes within the testicles. These tubes are coiled and are very long. The sperm pass from these tubes into the epididymis, and then into the vas deferens, while still immature. When orgasm occurs the sperm are mixed with the secretions of the seminal vesicles and prostate gland. These secretions are a whitish, thick fluid called semen.

FIGURE 18. The Pituitary and the Ovarian Cycle *

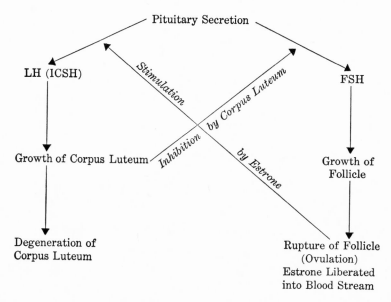

* Barth, p. 23. Reprinted by permission of the publisher.

The sperm is a tadpole-like cell microscopic in size, being about 1/500 inch long. It has some power of locomotion because of a long tail that lashes about, driving the sperm forward. Mammalian sperms contain a hormone-like substance called hyaluronidase which plays a part in fertilization. This is an enzyme which may facilitate fertilization by breaking down jellies about the egg. Thus in experiments in the artificial insemination of rabbits, if a seminal fluid containing low concentration of sperm is used the results are negative; but if a sperm extract containing hyaluronidase is added to the sperm, fertilization takes place.

INSEMINATION

In sexual intercourse the sperm are deposited in the vaginal canal. Each ejaculation contains about three hundred million sperm, and if the concentration of sperm is less than forty million per milliliter sterility is indicated.[2] The ascent of the sperm through the uterus to the Fallopian tubes is very rapid.[3] This rapidity of ascent is thought to be due to the action of the sperm's flagellum, to uterine and tubular contractions, and to celiacy movements of the oviduct-epithelium.[4] How much time is required for the sperm to travel to the tube is not exactly known, but Selye reports that mobile sperm were found in the tube in a dog and a guinea pig twenty minutes after copulation.[5]

THE PROCESS OF FERTILIZATION

Many sperm, it is thought, reach the surface of the egg at about the same time. However, when one sperm begins to penetrate the cellular wall of the ovum a "wave of negativity" develops throughout the ovum which excludes all other sperm.[6] The egg reacts to the sperm by forming a fertilization cone which engulfs it.[7] The tail of the sperm drops off, and the nuclei of the egg and sperm move together and fuse. The chromosomes pair off so that the forty-eight chromosomes contained in the separate sperm and egg now become twenty-four pairs in the zygote (the fertilized egg). The first cell division then takes place, and some remarkable changes occur. There is a great increase in the rate of oxygen consumption by the fertilized egg, probably 500 per cent.[8] There is a measurable increase in heat production. The cell membrane of the zygote becomes more permeable to allow for a freer exchange of substances through the membrane. The viscosity of the protoplasm of the cell increases—which perhaps is essential for cell division. The joining with the sperm vitalizes the egg, and sets in motion new and dynamic processes.

SEX DETERMINATION

Male students who are wondering if the changes in the role of females are going so far as to obliterate most of the differences between male

2 Barth, p. 45.　　3 Barth, p. 52.
4 Hans Selye, *Endocrinology*, Aeta Endocrinologica, Université de Montreal, Montreal, Canada, 1947, p. 816.
5 Selye, p. 816.　　6 Barth, p. 46.　　7 Barth, p. 46.　　8 Barth, p. 47.

and female function are assured that one function in life will always be theirs! They will always determine the sex of their children. All ova are similar in that they carry only one type of sex-determining chromosome, type X. Sperm, on the other hand, bear one of two types, either an X or a Y chromosome. When the ova and sperm both bear the X chromosome, the result of the combination XX is always a female. When the ova and sperm bear different chromosomes, the XY combination always results in a male.

However, if the male becomes too proud over the fact that he is the sole source of the sex of his children, he should remember that the Y chromosome, to which he owes his gender, is considerably smaller than the X chromosome and does not carry as many genes. Consequently, some of his son's characteristics will be determined solely by his wife's genes, but his daughter will always be a product of the interaction of both parents in all respects! This has genetic meaning because some characteristics that come from hereditary sources are sex-typed, and thus must occur more frequently in the male than in the female.

PREGNANCY

When the egg is fertilized in the oviduct it must move to the uterus if a normal pregnancy is to occur. If for some reason the egg is implanted in the wall of the Fallopian tube, this condition is called an ectopic or tubular pregnancy and requires surgery as the body cannot maintain a growing fetus in this location. In human beings implantation in the uterus usually occurs between the sixth and ninth day after mating.[9] The implantation consists of the zygote burying itself in the uterine wall and is called nidation. The fertilized egg secretes a gonotropic hormone which stimulates the Corpus Luteum to increase in size and to persist throughout pregnancy.[10] The Corpus Luteum then supplies the progesterone and estrone essential for the maintenance of the uterine wall. It also prevents further ovulation and inhibits contractions of the uterus.[11] During the latter half of pregnancy the placenta itself produces both progesterone and estrogen and takes over the function of the ovaries, the Corpus Luteum, and the pituitary. In human beings the glandular extracts produced by the placenta must be supplemented by a vitamin K which is essential to early embryonic development in mammals.[12]

[9] Selye, p. 818.   [10] Barth, p. 260.   [11] Barth, p. 262.   [12] Barth, p. 264.

Presumptive and Positive Signs of Pregnancy. What bodily changes indicate that a woman is pregnant? There are certain signs which are presumptive and others that are positive. The presumptive signs are morning sickness, cessation of menstruation, increased frequency of urination, increased size of the nipple, the breasts, the vaginal lining, and the abdomen, increased vaginal secretion, and higher temperature. One or the other or several may be present in other bodily states, but when they occur all together they are highly indicative of pregnancy.

Signs which are almost indisputable are the heartbeat of the baby, the discernible shape of the fetus, fetal movements, and the appearance of the fetus in an X-ray.

This information is important for young couples newly married or soon to be married. The excitement of the wedding and the beginning of sexual life may temporarily upset the menstrual cycle, or result in other changes which are often misconstrued as meaning a pregnancy. Then the anxiety occasioned by fear of pregnancy may further delay menstruation, so many weeks of needless worry are encountered. As a result, many unnecessary abortions have been performed on single and newly married women. If there is any question of pregnancy it ought always to be confirmed by a pregnancy test. There are many adequate and simple pregnancy tests.

Tests for Pregnancy. There are three old and two relatively new tests for pregnancy. Ascheim and Zondek demonstrated a test in 1928 which is 99 per cent accurate. Five mice are injected with the woman's urine six times in forty-eight hours. A sixth mouse is not injected, for comparison as a control. If the five mice develop indications of ovulation, it means that a pregnancy hormone is present in the injected urine. The Friedman test is similar but varies in that only one injection of urine is necessary, and a rabbit is used instead of mice. This test is almost 100 per cent accurate. When a third animal, the South African clawed frog is used, pregnancy is established if the frog expels eggs in large number.

The first of the new tests is the temperature test which has already been described. A continued high temperature in the absence of a cold or infection after the normal time for menstruation has passed indicates pregnancy. This is often called the "poor man's Friedman test." A second test now used involves the presence of estrones in the saliva. The level of estrone is apparently increased during pregnancy so that a chemical analysis which precipitates out the estrones in the saliva has proved to be a very effective method of determining pregnancy. Some work is also being done on ascertaining the sex of the child by a subtle means of staining the precipitate. Experiments indicate, however, that this test is not effective until after the sixth month.

MEDICAL PROGRESS AND PREGNANCY

One of the reassuring factors in considering reproduction today is the significant progress of medical science in the last century. In 1882 a book called *The Physical Life of Woman* by George Napheys, a doctor, went into its third edition; 150,000 copies had already been sold. The publisher of the book declared that it "may justly claim to count among the classics of American literature." The volume was constructive in temper, and it probably contributed a great deal to women seventy-five years ago. We quote it now only to show the progress medical science has made. In speaking of the influence of habitual mental conditions of the mother on the child Dr. Napheys gives several interesting illustrations:

> Dr. Demangeon of Paris quotes, in his work on the Imagination, the *Journal de Verdun,* as mentioning the case of a child, born at Blois, in the eyes of which the face of a watch was distinctly seen. The image was situated around the pupil, and the figures representing the hours were plainly perceived. The mother had experienced a strong desire to see a watch while she was pregnant with this child.[13]
>
> Professor Dalton of New York states that the wife of the janitor of the College of Physicians and Surgeons of that city, during her pregnancy dreamed that she saw a man who had lost part of the ear. The dream made a great impression upon her mind, and she mentioned it to her husband. When her child was born, a portion of one ear was deficient, and the organ was exactly like the defective ear she had seen in her dream.[14]

The learned doctor had a solution for these problems.

> Unfortunately all parents are not beautiful. Yet all desire beautiful offspring. The body of the child can be influenced by the mind of the parent, particularly of the mother. . . . A Roman magistrate, little, ugly, and hunchbacked, had by his wife a child exactly resembling the statue of Aesop. Frightened at the sight of this little monster and fearful of becoming the father of a posterity so deformed he went to consult Galen, the most distinguished physician of his time, who counselled him to place three statues of love around the conjugal bed, one at the foot, the others

[13] George H. Napheys, *The Physical Life of Woman* (Philadelphia: H. C. Watts Company, 1882), p. 187.
[14] Napheys, p. 183.

one on each side, in order that the eyes of his young spouse might be constantly feasted on these charming figures. The magistrate followed strictly the advice of the physician, and it is recorded that his wife bore him a child surpassing in beauty all his hopes.[15]

Napheys felt it was important to have beauty about not only at the time of insemination but also during pregnancy.

> During pregnancy the mother should often have some painting or engraving representing cheerful and beautiful figures before her eyes, or often contemplate some graceful statue. She should avoid looking at, or thinking of ugly people, or those marked with disfiguring diseases. . . . She should avoid ungraceful positions and awkward attitudes as by some mysterious sympathy these are impressed on the child she carries.[16]

Such were the myths that governed the men who cared for our grandparents. Today such myths have been discarded. Beyond that, painstaking research has found the cause of many pregnancy disorders, and these have been eliminated. Hospital facilities and their use have both increased. Consequently the infant death rate has declined from around 100 per 1,000 live births in 1915 to under 23 per 1,000 in 1960. The maternal death rate has declined from about 60 per 10,000 live births to 6.1 in 1950. Week in and week out, our medical scientists are studying ways of making childbirth safer. They have accomplished a great deal already.

DEVELOPMENT OF THE HUMAN EMBRYO

The human embryo develops in relationship to the placenta. (The early cell implants itself and forms roots in the uterine wall. These roots eventually become the placenta.) The placenta is a disc-shaped organ about nine inches in diameter and an inch thick. It is an extension of the umbilical cord. Where the placenta comes in contact with the uterine wall it has a great many root-like projections which spread out in all directions. These projections have thin membranes which lie in the lacunae (or lakes of blood) supplied by the mother for the nourishment and for the elimination processes of the embryo. Until the third week the embryo receives no food from the placenta but feeds on "debris" that results when certain cells break down at nidation and also on a diffusion of products from the

---

[15] Napheys, p. 127.   [16] Napheys, p. 141.

uterus.[17] After the third week the embryo receives food from the placenta.

The Placental Function. The placenta carries many substances necessary to the fetus and some that are harmful. Ordinarily only small molecules can penetrate the placental screen of three layers of cells which is placed between the maternal and fetal blood streams.[18] Carbon dioxide and oxygen have no difficulty in crossing the placenta. Ammonia, urea, and uric acid pass through easily. Glucose, amino acids, and a few red blood cells pass. Sometimes larger molecular substances such as the anti-RH factor and the German measles germ penetrate and cause difficulty. The placenta thus not only is the channel for food but functions to defend the fetus from destructive influences.

The Growth of the Embryo. In the five or six days in which this new cell is carried along the tube on its way to the uterus, the cell begins to divide into two, four, and more cells. By the time it arrives at the uterus it looks like a raspberry—although much smaller.

Due to the effect of hormones, another miraculous process is going on in the uterus itself. The lining cells begin to enlarge and fill with glycogen, a form of sugar, which nourishes the new life. More mucus is secreted, the blood vessels increase, and more blood is brought to the lining of the uterus. All this in preparation to receive, nurture, and permit the fertilized ovum to imbed and grow.

At this stage, if we could look inside the nest called the uterus, the embryo would look like a pearl on a maroon velvet background.

The mass of cells comprising the embryo at nidation is divided into three sections. One has a yoke-like substance to feed the embryo until enough capillaries and vessels surround it and form a pool through which oxygen, iron, and other food may be obtained. Another section starts the development of the placenta, the organ which in a few months will filter the food from the mother's blood and carry it through the fetal blood vessels in the umbilical cord to the fetus. In a few weeks this will be a pale pink fluffy sac filled with fluid, all prepared to protect and nourish the embryo. The third part contains the cells which will develop into the fetus. These will divide into three major divisions, thus, beginning the grouping of the cells to form skin, bone, muscles, brain, and other nerve tissue which will form the various organ systems of the body. Each of these systems has cells with highly specialized functions.

The male and female sex organs originate from the same group of cells.

[17] Barth, p. 276.   [18] Barth, p. 276.

The shape and organization of the reproductive organs, whether male or female, will depend on the sex-determining chromosome derived from the father's spermatozoa. All other physical and mental characteristics are derived from the chromosomes of both mother and father.

The growth and development of the different organs goes on for about 267 days from ovulation or 280 days from the beginning of the last menstrual period if it was in a twenty-eight-day cycle. During all this time the mother's body is not only giving nourishment to her child, but her hormones are continuing to help it grow. By the third month, many rudimentary organs are developed. They continue to grow and by birth the digestive system of the baby can digest milk and distribute calcium to the bones and nerves.

While the baby has been cuddled up inside of the sac filled with fluid, it has been protected by the fluid and by the muscles of the uterus and abdomen. These formed an original shock absorber. The muscle wall has developed and increased many times in size and power. This is necessary to achieve the birth process itself. In the vaginal canal, the tissues have become softer, more elastic, and lubricated. All of these many processes go on quite automatically and efficiently until the infant is ready to be born. What signal is given or what organ gives it is not known, but a signal is automatically given when it is time for birth. Mechanisms are set in motion, and the birth process begins: Figure 19 shows the position of the baby prior to birth. About two weeks before labor the baby has settled and its position is lower in the pelvis. The process of lowering is called lightening.

THE BIRTH PROCESS AND LABOR PAIN

In late pregnancy small pains and pressure signify that the opening in the cervix is beginning to thin out, stretch, and open. The mother may be conscious of scarcely anything more than a backache. When the opening has increased from ⅓ cm. to about 5 to 6 cm., or from ⅛ of an inch to about 3 inches, the rhythmic contractions of the uterus increase in frequency, strength, and discomfort. The manner in which the cervix dilates and prepares for the passage of the baby is indicated in Figure 20. The contractions last a minute or two, and the woman relaxes several minutes between contractions. The contractions become more frequent until the fetus is delivered.

THREE FIGURES
EXPLAINING THE BIRTH PROCESS

Reprinted from the *Birth Atlas*
with the permission of the
Maternity Center Association, New York City

FIGURE 19. Fetus at Term before Beginning of Labor

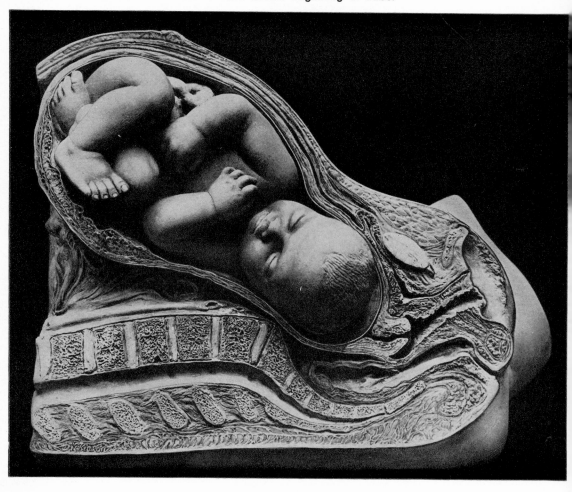

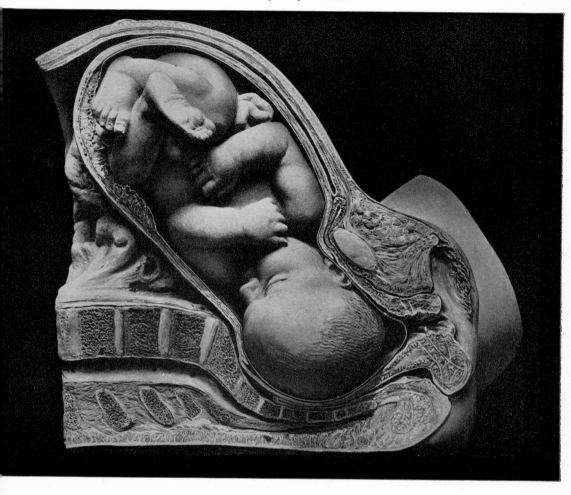

FIGURE 20. Labor: Cervix Completely Dilated

FIGURE 21. Labor: Birth of Shoulders

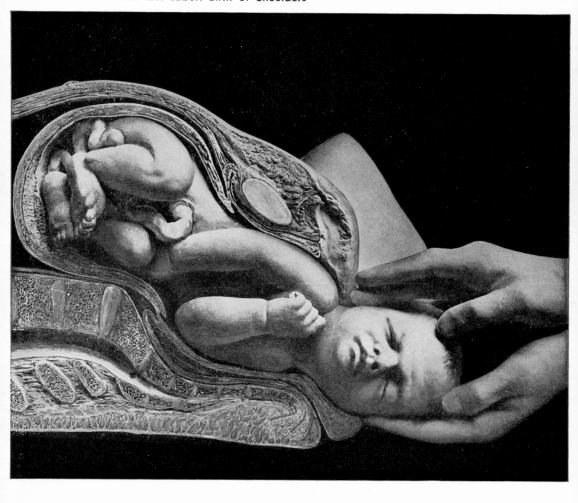

The actual pain or discomfort which accompanies the birth process varies. Some women have accustomed themselves to falls and bruises and have developed the ability to grit their teeth. Others have not outgrown crying even at the anticipation of pain. Some weep and worry, and dread the birth process because of the descriptions given them by their mothers or friends. One such woman did not recognize her actual labor pains. Her idea of the torture she was expecting, the "terrible time" she had heard about, was so much more agonizing than the pains she was having that she failed to recognize that she was in labor.

There is no question that fear, apprehension, and tension increase the sensation of pain, and that the anxiety so often associated with labor prevents relaxation and rest between contractions.

The initial phase of labor involves a twofold muscular reaction of the uterus. The muscles at the lower end of the uterus develop during pregnancy to hold the heavy baby. These muscles keep the baby from descending for nine months. During the birth process they must relax and allow the cervix to expand so that the baby may pass through. Thus, these muscles give way while the muscles that run longitudinally are contracting and forcing the fetus downward. If the mother is a victim of fear, the lateral or horizontal muscles cannot relax and the other muscles must struggle against them. Fear thus not only causes pain but prolongs labor.

When the cervix is completely dilated the baby's head passes through the cervix and into the vaginal canal. As the head presents the largest diameter at birth, once the head is born the body follows easily. Figure 21 shows the doctor assisting during the final stage of the baby's birth. A few minutes after the baby is born, the placenta is delivered. This is generally called the afterbirth.

Besides her emotional attitudes, a woman's nervous threshold also influences her ability to adjust to labor pains. The lack of Vitamin B and calcium often results in hypersensitive nerves. Inflammation of the reproductive organs increases the pain. Disproportion between the fetal head and the mother's pelvis may prolong the labor. The only general statement we can make about labor pains is that they apparently differ with each individual case. Nevertheless, a good attitude and knowledge of what is going on seem to lessen the discomfort.

Years ago, most women suffered during labor. Neither doctor, midwife, nor helping neighbor gave any sedative. Now a new era has arrived. Hospitals have trained anesthetists, and doctors and nurses understand the psychological need for reducing unnecessary tension. The mechanism in the reproductive system works so efficiently that 85 per cent of pregnant women give birth normally, 10 or 11 per cent have slight complications and 4 or 5 per cent have serious complications.

Complications that do occur in childbirth are often due to disease in other organs, such as anemia (which is a lack of hemoglobin or iron in the blood), RH difficulties, or toxins which result from chronic disease in the head, lung, or diabetes. That is why the obstetrician checks the blood and examines the urine every few weeks. Most of the complications can be prevented and steps can be taken to relieve any abnormal situation so long as it is revealed by a thorough medical examination *before* pregnancy.

"CHILDBIRTH WITHOUT FEAR"

In this country and in England the theory of natural childbirth has become accepted largely through the efforts of Dr. Grantly Dick Read. This process is much misunderstood. It really means putting the patient at ease throughout the pregnancy so that she will not waste energy through fear. She learns to relax her muscles as well as her mind. However, Dr. Read gives anesthetics or sedatives to many of his patients.

There is no doubt that it is best for the mother to be relaxed throughout the birth process. If a patient's doctor thinks the mother should have a mild sedative or anesthetic, his advice should be followed—especially if stitches are necessary to help the pelvic organs return to normal size after delivery. Because there are many factors which must be considered at the time of birth, it is not wise to be too rigid about sedatives. If the expectant mother chooses a well-trained doctor, she should give him her full confidence and intelligent cooperation.

Labor pains are due to hard contractions of the muscles of the uterus. There is no sensation of pain with the early contractions. Just before birth, the pains may last thirty to forty seconds and come every minute or two. Thirty to forty per cent of women can deliver their children without an anesthetic. Mothers seem to receive much satisfaction in consciously participating in the birth process. Joy and pride in the new baby appear on the mother's face almost before the last pain disappears. But whether a sedative is used or not, Dr. Read contributes much when he suggests that understanding the birth process and learning how to relax before birth takes place will contribute to ease of childbirth.

374

ROOMING-IN

Rooming-in is another new practice (or the revival of a very old one) which helps the father and mother learn how to care for their baby. After the birth of the child the infant is placed in a crib next to the mother's bed in the hospital. Diapers and other necessary items are within her reach. She can easily swing over her bed the plastic box containing the baby. Under the guidance of a trained nurse, the new mother learns to feed, change, bathe and cuddle her baby. The father, when he comes in, also takes part in caring for the baby. Thus he gets to know his child from the start, and at the same time learns how to prepare its formula and change its diapers. All of this is possible because the nurses become teachers. More and more hospitals are using the rooming-in procedure.

Conditions today are quite different from those our parents knew. Courses in home economics, even the diets printed in our magazines and newspapers, have contributed to more intelligent nutrition. A higher standard of living has made nutritious food available. Home-nursing courses as well as courses in child care and development have helped mothers to become skilled and relaxed. Red Cross courses for prospective fathers have helped them understand the process of pregnancy, labor, and infant care. Learning these skills together has not only prevented problems between mother and father, it has created more fun all around. It is easier to learn the intelligent way than through trial and error.

NURSING

After a few hours of rest, many mothers are ready to nurse their babies. Many of them during pregnancy have gently massaged and exercised their nipples so that the infant can grasp them easily.

There is emotional satisfaction in being able to nurse the new baby— pride in watching a baby thrive on the mother's milk, and the added satisfaction of holding the baby closely and cuddling it. This can and should also be part of bottle-feeding if the mother cannot nurse. However, the sucking satisfaction seems to be greater in nursing. Moreover, nursing and the pelvic exercises are factors in helping the uterus absorb and discard the extra cells and shrink back to normal.

During the nursing period, the progesterone hormone is at a high level of efficiency. That is why many women do not menstruate for several months after giving birth. However, nursing mothers do sometimes menstruate, and no one can depend upon nursing as an effective means of birth control.

POSTNATAL CARE

The reproductive organs return to normal in a matter of weeks. The stitches are usually healed in less than a week. But in the first few months after the birth of a baby, the menstrual periods may be very irregular. Some women start to menstruate at six weeks, others a month after they stop nursing. Here again, each individual case is different. The irregularity itself occurs because of the variation in the time necessary for the mother to re-establish a normal functioning of her endocrine glands.

During pregnancy and nursing, the progesterone hormone is more active. Slowly the estrogen phase comes back, and menstruation then becomes normal, followed by a greater desire for intercourse. Some women develop a greater capacity to respond sexually about a year after pregnancy than they had before they conceived. There is a maturing benefit from the increased hormone activity during pregnancy. Fertility generally also increases as a result of this great endocrine activity.

After the arrival of a baby, the contraceptive diaphragm, if it is used, should be refitted, since pregnancy may cause some change in the size and arrangement of the pelvic organs.

STERILITY

Sterility is of two kinds, voluntary and involuntary. This section is concerned only with couples who want a child and are disappointed that conception has not occurred. How serious a problem this is can be inferred from the fact that two hundred couples apply for every child available for adoption. While it has been estimated by some that involuntary infertility characterizes at least seventeen per cent of the child bearing population, a more conservative figure of twelve per cent is probably more accurate today. Adequate medical intervention can help almost half of these achieve their goals of parenthood.

Infertility is not a female problem alone. Indeed, some organic failure on the part of the male may be considered the primary cause of sterility in at least forty per cent of the cases and as a "contributory causative factor" in sixty per cent of infertile matings.[19]

[19] Edward T. Tyler, ed., *Sterility* (New York: McGraw-Hill Book Company, Inc., 1961), p. 1.

In a study of a series of 687 couples at the Tyler Clinic it was found that where the sperm count remained below twenty million per milliliter, there was considerably less chance for conception.[20] Thus, in a sample of 103 patients where the sperm count ranged between one and twenty million per milliliter, only 11 per cent of the patients concerned became parents, but in a sample of 232 patients where the sperm count was above one hundred million per milliliter, some 38 per cent achieved pregnancy.[21] In addition to the number of sperm, attention must be given to the total volume of the ejaculate, to the mobility, vitality, and morphology of the sperm.

Ordinarily, an evaluation is made first of the husband because if he has no sperm at all or is very, very low this condition must be studied and remedied before any success can be expected.

Furthermore, this examination is relatively simple, in contrast to many of the more complicated procedures used in the evaluation of female aspects of infertility. Men sometimes resent any examination, feeling that a low sperm count would cast some reflection on their level of masculinity. But masculine characteristics are referable to the interstitial cells in the testes, and there is no correlation between fertility and physiological features of masculinity.

For the female, studies are conducted to determine if the following requisites are present:

1. Normally functioning ovaries, in which every month the Graafian Follicle is followed by subsequent Corpus Luteum development.
2. A normal uterus.
3. A clear pathway from the vagina to the upper end of the Fallopian tube for the sperm, and for the zygote when the egg has been fertilized.
4. A "receptive genital tract" with a chemical constitution which permits the sperm to live.
5. Adequate protection and nourishment of the embryo and fetus, by means of the amniotic sac and the placenta.
6. A safe delivery.[22]

Careful and appropriate tests have been developed to check each factor mentioned above. For instance, in studying tubal potency there are two tests: the Rubins test in which the measure of pressure of gas introduced into the genital track records inadequate or obstructed passageways, and hysterosalpinography where the tubes and uterus are x-rayed to locate

[20] Tyler, p. 2.   [21] Tyler, pp. 14, 15.
[22] Tyler, p. 3. Reprinted by permission of the publisher.

any closures. Chemical analysis determines the relative hostility of the vaginal environment for the sperm. Each of the factors are studied, appropriate remedial steps are taken, and the removable difficulties eliminated.

Do marital adjustment and emotional factors play any part in infertility? Several studies indicate that these are basic, causative factors in infertility because emotion can influence the hyperthalamus which in turn influences the anterior lobe of the pituitary which controls the ovarian functions. Thus, severe marital conflict and/or severe intrapsychic stress can result in (1) inadequate performance of the endocrine system which in turn inhibits good ovarian function, (2) tubal closure or spasticity preventing the egg and sperm from meeting, or (3) the inhibition of the kind of sexual adjustment essential for conception. Some physicians now include a study of marital and personality integration as an integral part of any infertility examination.

One simple fact may be useful for those about to be married or just married. One of the real variables of fertility is age. If pregnancy is postponed too long, it may be difficult to attain. Couples who put off having children until they have a big car, some stock and a home sometimes never do have children to enjoy that home. But how long this matter can be postponed depends on many variables such as health, sexual maturity, and the reproductive organs of the female.

ABORTION

There is much confusion and lack of knowledge about many matters of sex, particularly about birth control and abortion. Birth control, or contraception, is the prevention by mechanical or chemical means of the meeting of the sperm and the ovum. Abortion is the destruction of the fetus by surgery—in other words, the prevention of birth *after* fertilization has taken place.

There are several types of abortions, and these should be clearly defined and understood. 1. Criminal abortion is an operation that is illegally performed to stop a pregnancy. Thousands of women annually die of hemorrhage or infection after a visit to an abortionist—a racketeer who performs an operation to terminate an unwanted pregnancy. Many women survive but suffer such damage to their reproductive organs that they are subject to inflammation, poor ovarian function, complicated labor in later pregnancies, or even sterility. Abortions may also give rise to guilt feeling, frustration, painful intercourse, and frigidity.

2. Spontaneous abortion occurs of its own accord. The causes are not always known. It usually takes place in the early months of pregnancy and is not considered dangerous if medical care is sought immediately.

3. Therapeutic abortion is surgical abortion performed in a hospital with the consent of a consulting committee of the staff to terminate a pregnancy which would endanger the patient's life. Such abortions are often recommended for women with tuberculosis or certain types of heart disease.

There are many factors to be considered before an abortion is performed (even a therapeutic abortion). A woman should realize that unless the operation is absolutely necessary and recommended by competent physicians, her health, her sexual relationships, her fertility, and even her life may be endangered.

CONCLUSION

Every advance in scientific knowledge gives us new awareness of the way nature has equipped men and women so that life may go on. In this chapter some of the aspects of reproduction such as fertilization and the birth process have been described. Today young people, since they are informed about reproduction, can prepare realistically for parenthood.

PROJECTS

1. Visit the local health department and ask for statistics on mother and infant mortality. Chart the decline in deaths of both mothers and babies.
2. Ask an obstetrician to visit the class to discuss modern views of childbirth and to describe advances in modern obstetrics.
3. Ask some new mother who previously had the course in marriage to discuss the manner in which she prepared for childbirth.
4. Visit a modern hospital and observe how this hospital provides for its mothers and babies.

VISUAL AIDS

Labor and Childbirth, Medical Films, Inc., San Francisco.

READINGS

BARTH, LESTER GEORGE. *Embryology.* New York, Henry Holt and Company, 1949. Copyright 1949, revised and enlarged, 1953, Holt, Rinehart and Winston, Inc.

BOWMAN, HENRY A. *Marriage for Moderns.* 4th ed. New York, McGraw-Hill Book Company, Inc., 1960, Chapter 15.

READ, GRANTLY DICK, M.D. *Childbirth Without Fear.* London, William Heinemann, Ltd., 1947.

SELYE, HANS. *Endocrinology.* Aeta Endocrinologica, Université de Montreal, Montreal, Canada, 1947.

TYLER, EDWARD, editor. *Sterility.* New York, McGraw-Hill Book Company, Inc., 1961.

CHAPTER 16

Achieving Sexual Maturity in Marriage

INTRODUCTION

THE attainment of sexual compatibility is an important factor in achieving cohesiveness in marriage. It is the climax in the development of the relationship of sharing and trusting. It is the most intimate form of tender and loving communication. Optimum sexual satisfaction comes only to those couples who have found optimum happiness in all other areas of their lives. The mood and the extent of all other adjustment determines the fullness of sexual expression. For this reason sexual success is almost always a function of adjustment in other areas of living. That sexual satisfaction is something more than a phase of the reproductive function may be concluded because men and women desire to be together physically without reference to the possibility of impregnation and regardless of pregnancy. Sexual love both perpetuates the family through reproduction and solidifies the marriage bonds.

PHYSICAL ASPECTS OF COITUS

There are many facts about the sexual capacity of human beings which, if understood, would help young people in approaching the physical side of marriage. The first is that through millions of years nature has been perfecting the sexual organs of man and woman so that they have become both more sensitive for pleasure and better adapted for complete union.

The penis becomes enlarged for coitus and extends forward at an angle which rather exactly matches the structure of the vagina of the wife. The glans, the end of the penis, is full of nerve endings and is one of the centers of sexual pleasure for the male. The two testicles, which hang in the sac or scrotum back of the penis, produce two things: the spermatozoa which fertilize the egg and the male sex hormones which circulate in the male's bloodstream and impel him toward sexual activity. Thus, male sex organs are not only structured for sexual intercourse, but manufacture materials which stimulate sensitivity and vigor.

The female sex organs are no less developed. The vagina consists of the vulva, or the outer lips, and the inner lips. At the upper junction of the inner lips is a small but important organ called the clitoris, which resembles a very small penis and in which there is also a concentration of nerve endings. The function of the clitoris is to promote enjoyment and orgasm. The clitoris is the most sensitive of all the female sexual organs and seems to have no other function than to provide sexual pleasure. The interior of the vagina is lined with a group of muscles which are perfectly structured for both childbirth and intercourse. These muscles have rugae or muscular folds which may expand to accommodate a large penis or contract to enfold a smaller one. They adjust to the male organ. Thus fear about difference in size is generally needless, for nature provides for this contingency. This means that not only are the male and female organs slanted to mate most closely, but their structure is adaptable so that the closest sort of physical union has been provided for.

It might seem that the closeness of the organs would cause friction in the back-and-forth motion of intercourse. But nature has provided for this contingency. The inner vulva contains glands which, during sexual stimulation, provide a lubricating fluid that not only enables the husband to make an easy entrance but facilitates a close but pleasurable union between the penis and the walls of the vagina. It is important that sufficient love play should precede the entrance so that there is a state of readiness on the part of the female structure to welcome the male organ.

DIFFERENTIALS IN MALE AND FEMALE SEXUAL-RESPONSE PATTERNS

A second characteristic of the male and female sexual systems is the differential in response patterns. This may be represented by the following figure.

FIGURE 22. Intensity of Male and Female Sexual Desire

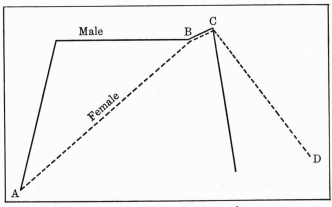

Length of Time for Arousal

A. Beginning of love play   C. Orgasm
B. Intromission   D. Detumescence

The male is very easily stimulated to sexual activity. This may be accomplished by a kiss, by some expression of tenderness, or even by the thought of his wife. He is then almost instantaneously ready for intercourse, but his wife does not respond so quickly to the same type of stimulus.

The female must be gradually roused by gentle caresses, many kisses, and fond words until she is ready for coitus. If we assume that the period from the first erotic impulse at "A" in Figure 22 to the time when the wife is sufficiently aroused for intercourse at "B," it might seem that this difference indicates a difficult problem. But closer study of the facts indicates that this period of caressing, kissing, fondling, spoken appreciations and endearments is one of the most important in marriage. Such love play contributes to the general intensity of the couple's feelings and makes coitus a time of meaningful joy. Far from being a mistake, this difference introduces into marriage a period of profound value.

We may assume that the same may be said of the period from "C" to "D." A man's feeling subsides very quickly after orgasm, but a woman's feelings may not. This means that there is not only a need but an opportunity for further expression of love during this period of after-play.

Kinsey has charted differences in erotic response between men and women. He used a threefold table to illustrate each of these differences —rated as definite and/or frequent, some response, and never. In the following adaptation of his findings we have combined the first two ratings and eliminated the "never" as this would obviously be the sum of the other two subtracted from 100 per cent.

These fourteen items indicate the degree of difference which Kinsey illustrates in some thirty-three individual sets of data. In response to only three of these items (moving pictures, reading romantic literature, and being bitten) were as many females affected as males. Women then are not as prone to be sexually stimulated by psychological factors as are men. Women are aroused chiefly by tactile stimulation of erotic zones. Men may be aroused by both tactile and psychological factors.

T A B L E 35. Summary of Differences in Psychologic Factors in Sex Response for Men and for Women, by Per Cent *

| EROTIC STIMULUS | Percentage responding to stimulus | |
	Females-%	Males-%
1. Observing the opposite sex (clothed or nude)	58	72
2. Observing own sex	12	16
3. Observing portrayals of nude figures	12	54
4. Observing genitalia of opposite sex	48	Many
5. Observing own genitalia	9	56
6. Observing commercial moving pictures	48	36
7. Observing burlesque and floor shows	14	62
8. Observing portrayals of sexual action	32	77
9. Observing animals in coitus	16	32
10. Fantasies concerning other sex	69	84
11. Reading literary materials	60	59
12. Stimulation by erotic stories	14	47
13. Arousal from sadomasochistic stories	12	22
14. Responses to being bitten	55	50

* Adapted from Alfred C. Kinsey, et al., Sexual Behavior in the Human Female (Philadelphia: W. B. Saunders Company, 1953), Chapter 16. Reprinted by permission.

SEXUAL ADJUSTMENT AND GENERAL MARITAL ADJUSTMENT

A third factor involved in achieving good coital adjustment relates to the totality of other adjustments. Man is the only animal in which psychological moods affect sexual functioning. In a man or a woman, thought or memory may influence glandular and emotional reactions. Consequently, conflicts over money or religion, neglect or discourtesies, quarrels and hurts will in time have an adverse effect on sexual harmony. While sexual difficulty is often caused by a lack of sufficient knowledge and a lack of acceptance of sex, it is also often caused by a failure in the general relationship of marriage. One reason why it appears that sexual adjustment is difficult to achieve is that failure in any one, or several, of the other major areas of adjustment is reflected in physical relationships. Generally a couple which has achieved a satisfactory cooperative framework in which to face all their other problems will find a minimum of difficulty in coming together sexually.

Some confirmation of this point of view is found in the research of Burgess and Wallin. They asked whether or not the sexual adjustment of a couple could be predicted from a knowledge of their general marital success. That sexual love is only a part of the total affectional pattern is indicated by the relationship they found between happiness scores and sexual-adjustment scores. Men with low happiness scores also had low sexual-adjustment scores. Wives with high happiness scores also had high sexual scores, and the women who had high happiness scores seldom fell into the low bracket of sexual scores (11.2 per cent).[1] This seems to indicate that good sexual relationships are barometers of the degree to which companionship and trust have been established.

This means that mutuality must pervade all the relationships in marriage if it is to be achieved physically. Marriages in which the principals are egocentric or neurotic, or use marriage either to satisfy personal needs or to satisfy dependency cravings, will miss the essential element of sharing. This lack will almost always be reflected sexually, for individuals without the experience of sharing other things will not share in sex either. A disturbance of relationship in social, economic, religious, or recreational areas will be a block as far as sexual compatibility is concerned. While there are couples who manage to find some sexual joy even though other aspects of their marriage are unhappy, we may still say that the third general prerequisite to sexual harmony is a growing harmony in all the other phases of living together. On the other hand, sex harmony also releases strains in other relationships so that there is a reciprocal action.

[1] Ernest W. Burgess and Paul Wallin, *Engagement and Marriage* (Philadelphia: J. B. Lippincott Company, 1953), p. 692.

GLANDULAR FACTORS IN SEXUAL RESPONSE

The fourth factor involved in achieving sexual satisfaction is knowledge and acceptance of certain physiological factors. A couple need always to keep in mind that the man and the woman respond to a different type of stimulus. The woman responds to gentle stimulation of lips, the neck, the ear lobes, and the breasts. The nipples, the lips of the vagina, and the clitoris are all especially sensitive. Nearly every part of the body is active during sexual play: the glandular system, the nervous system, and the muscular apparatus. The entire bodily mechanism comes to be more and more involved as passion increases. A male's excitable areas are generally localized, but the woman's erogenous zones are extensive and diffused. This makes for a different rhythm in the development of full sexual response, but as we have already pointed out, the male also has the capacity to sustain his passion over a long period of time and thus can enable his mate to reach the stage at which the sexual act will be satisfying to both.

But there is also a difference in terms of the degree to which the male and female are capable of responding at any given time. A male's sexual interest is subject to variation. His general state of health, his immediate energy or lack of it, the length of time since the last experience of coitus— all these have their effect. Such conditions also affect a woman, but because of the normal monthly cycle associated with preparation for pregnancy, her sexual desire sweeps in and out like the tides. She is also more sensitive to conflict and friction. But even more important is the relation of sexual desire to the menstrual cycle. Figure 23 shows the relationship of hormones to the menstrual cycle of a woman.

This figure indicates that during all of the period between the menses, the little gland called the Graafian Follicle and Corpus Luteum, which encases the developing egg, secretes estrogen. Estrogen is a stimulant and so works upon the whole glandular system that during this period the female is predisposed to more sexual excitement. It is as though nature had provided not only that the egg should be produced during this period, but that the same organ which develops the egg should so influence the feelings of the female that she is eager and ready for impregnation. So, during the period after menstruation and before ovulation, the secretion of the estrogen hormone into the bloodstream makes the female more responsive to love overtures. It is during this period that most women experience orgasms of considerable intensity.

386

At ovulation the production of estrogen decreases, and the Graafian Follicle changes its form and function and becomes the Corpus Luteum. This small gland produces progesterone, a drug with a sedative influence, which by inhibiting too great excitement and diminishing in some degree the sexual response, promotes the motherhood function of the uterus and the body. The production of progesterone continues until the egg is either fertilized or dies. If the egg dies, the Corpus Luteum ceases to manufacture progesterone, and this brings on the menstrual flow. During the period when the hormone progesterone is active the emotional response of the female is that of a mother. During this period she may not have an orgasm or the orgasm may be of considerably less intensity.

FIGURE 23. Hormonal Curves of the Normal Menstrual Cycle *

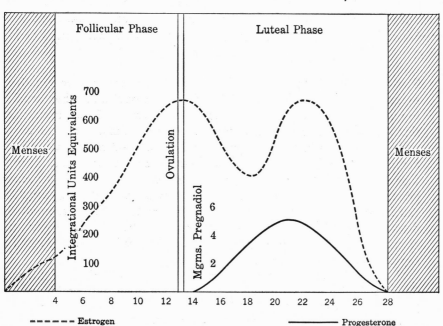

* Adapted from August A. Werner, M.D., *Endocrinology, Clinical Application and Treatment* (Philadelphia: Lea and Febiger, 1942), p. 305. Reprinted by permission of the publisher.

Thus after ovulation a woman's sexual response is modified by the hormone content of her system in such a way that her response is not as passionate as it is during the first period of her monthly cycle. Yet sexual relations during this period may be rewarding and meaningful even if the response is not so vigorous.

This means that a couple should not "worship" the orgasm. It is clear that from the standpoint of the endocrine system it may even be unwise to expect it. Furthermore, if too much stress is put upon achieving an orgasm, a couple's love-making may become so artificial and so strained that the natural spontaneity of the act will be destroyed. Love-making and coitus ought to allow the emotions to be fully expressed, and too much concern that the act end in an orgasm or that the orgasms be simultaneous may inhibit a couple from a full and free sexual expression. Sometimes the reward of intercourse will only be the tender closeness and the satisfaction of having given joy to the mate.

Hannah and Abraham Stone have discussed this question thoroughly in their excellent book, *The Marriage Manual*. This book is written in the form of a conversation in which the patient asks questions and the doctor answers. The discussion of the effects of orgasm incapacity runs as follows:

> First of all, I should like to stress the fact that if a woman responds actively to the sexual embrace and takes pleasure in the sexual union, her inability to reach an orgasm may not be of any serious import. Please understand that even if a woman does not attain an intense culmination, it does not mean that she does not derive a great deal of gratification from the sex act. Some women, indeed, are not at all aware of any orgasm problem until they learn about it from a conversation or book, and then they become greatly worried because they believe that they are not obtaining complete satisfaction from their sex experiences. As a matter of fact, some of the descriptions in the literature about the manifestations of the orgasm are often more poetic than real, and they sometimes lead men and women to expect sensations which are but rarely experienced.
>
> If an actual orgasm deficiency exists, however, the effect of this condition upon the woman would depend largely upon the intensity of her sexual desires and the degree of her excitation at the time of the relation. If her sexual impulse is weak, or if she has been aroused but little, the absence of the orgasm will hardly have any harmful effects. On the other hand, if she has been very much stimulated, the failure to reach a climax may leave her in a state of frustration which may prove physiologically and emotionally disturbing. During erotic excitation there is a marked local congestion of the sexual organs as well as a general physical and emotional tension. With the completion of the act, if an acme is reached, there is a gradual release of detumescence, and this is followed by a sense of fulfill-

ment and relaxation. In the absence of an orgasm, however, the relief is not complete, and the woman may remain for some time in an unsatisfied and restless condition. Repeated experiences of this kind may eventually lead to various nervous or sexual disturbances.[2]

Orgasms and Sexual Happiness. What is the relation of orgasms to marital success? What percentage of times of intercourse must result in orgasm for the woman if the marriage is to succeed? There is some factual material on this point. From a study of one hundred husbands and one hundred wives, G. V. Hamilton concluded tentatively that at least 20 per cent of the copulations must end in orgasms for the female if the marriage is to be successful.[3] In a study of 792 couples Terman found that 8.3 per cent never achieved orgasm, 25.1 per cent sometimes did, 44.5 per cent usually did, and 22.1 always did.[4] Orgasm apparently is one of the two sexual factors most importantly related to marital adjustment. Both of these studies indicate that it is perhaps unreasonable to expect that most women will achieve orgasm in every copulation. Orgasm capacity in women increases with age and marital experience. It is important that young people recognize this fact, lest they expect too much and regard as disappointing experience which is wholly normal.

LOVE PLAY AND SEXUAL ADJUSTMENT

The fifth factor in achieving sexual harmony is the development of love-play techniques which will bring an ultimate amount of pleasure to both the husband and the wife. Twenty-five years ago most of the books dealing with marital adjustment gave detailed instructions regarding various aspects of sexual play. This type of instruction often leads to strained procedures which are destructive both to sexual spontaneity and to personal fulfillment.

All delicate human achievements require experimentation and artistic improvisation. When Leonardo da Vinci painted a picture, he experimented with various colors, hues, and brush techniques until he achieved a masterpiece. His paintings are different from any others because they

[2] Hannah and Abraham Stone, *The Marriage Manual* (New York: Simon and Schuster, Inc., 1952), pp. 265–267. Copyright 1935, 1937, 1952, 1953 by Simon and Schuster, Inc. Reprinted by permission of the publisher.
[3] G. V. Hamilton, *A Research in Marriage* (New York: Albert and Charles Boni, 1929), Chapter 22.
[4] Lewis M. Terman, *Psychological Factors in Marital Happiness* (New York: McGraw-Hill Book Company, Inc., 1938), pp. 373–377.

are unique combinations of line, color, and composition. Love-making is just such a delicate art. To achieve maximum creativity every couple must work out their own patterns of approach and response. To the extent that these patterns are standardized and do not express the couple's sincere and natural feelings, they are awkward and inhibiting.

Nevertheless, there are some general points which every couple should know, not as rules of procedure but as background information. The first of these is the assurance to the woman that any erotic gesture on her part is not only permissible but will increase both her husband's and her own pleasure during pre-play and during actual intercourse. Nothing that is right for the man to do is wrong for the woman. During the early part of the love relationship she may be somewhat timid about expressing her love, but after greater intimacy is achieved, she may take an active part. At times, in fact, her initiation of love play will bring profound psychological pleasure to the male, in letting him know that he is wanted. Furthermore, the wife will wish to indicate to the husband those gestures of endearment which are most stimulating to her. The husband likewise will indicate to the wife which acts on her part are most pleasing to him. Strangely enough, such an important aspect of marital life as making love often receives the silent treatment even though both partners are relatively passionate and relatively emancipated from fear or repression. Nothing indicates so fully the degree of our cultural repression of sex as the stumbling way couples experiment sexually when frank discussion would solve any difficulties and add new understanding. It is a sign of the changing role of women in our society that they may look forward to being sexually active and share as creative partners.

What is right for the husband in terms of love play must also be permissible and desirable for the wife. But what is right? Young people entering married life are often troubled by fear of perversions or manipulations which are not generally discussed in adolescent conversation. In general nothing is wrong in sexual play which is not painful, which is aesthetically appreciated, and which does not substitute a type of foreplay for coitus itself. Furthermore, what is considered right during one period of the developing love relationship may not seem right at another. A couple will normally utilize a more varied repertoire of stimulating acts after they have been married ten years than earlier. The main criterion for love play is that it express the mutual desire of the couple and that it be spontaneous, creative, and tender.

If love play is varied, so is the time required for full tumescence of the male and female. Love play will vary according to variations in general sexual intimacy, in experience, in fatigue, and in frequency of intercourse. The ideal to be reached is the profound understanding of one another's reaction so that each responds to the other's need without hesitation.

A further point of information often sought by young people in pre-marital conferences is whether or not it is possible to determine at what period of love play coitus should begin. Men who are considerate of their mates are very often troubled by this point because they wish to begin intercourse only when their mates are ready. If a couple is able to communicate at all, there will be many ways in which the wife can indicate readiness, and her cooperation at this point often relieves the mate of considerable anxiety. Psychologically a state of deep excitation indicates such readiness. Physically the secretion of a mucoid from the glands of Bartholin makes the opening to the vagina moist and facilitates the penetration of the penis. The alert male will soon become aware of these signs and learn to time the consummation of the sex act without difficulty. The male may also want to know when an orgasm has taken place in the female. Ordinarily a strong orgasm can be felt by the penis because it consists of muscular vaginal contractions. At other times, when the orgasm is less marked, the male will know that it has occurred by a general relaxation of the whole body of his mate. In the male an orgasm is the ejaculation of the seminal fluid in a series of spasmodic contractions of the penis. A male's sexual excitement lessens very rapidly after his orgasm, and his general relaxation is unmistakable to his mate.

SEXUAL INHIBITIONS AND SEXUAL RESPONSE

The sixth general factor in achieving full sexual expression is that of overcoming sexual inhibitions. These are of different degrees and have their roots in different experiences for almost every person. Our society has shrouded sexual activity in secrecy. Children learn early that sex is some special type of experience which, even if it is discussed at home with Father and Mother, is not to be discussed with other children. When other children discuss it, they do so *sub rosa* and with a peculiar tone in their voice. This is the generalized experience of almost all children in our country. This heritage of Puritanism has caused a general repression of sexual expression. In addition, almost all young people have a history of personal incidents which have produced an accumulation of fear and wonder with regard to sexual intercourse.

Early experiences of masturbation or of heterosexual love play may have also contributed a sense of guilt and shame. Severe punishment for quite natural sexual investigation leads to sexual fears for some. In many churches sex is linked to sin. In some cases long continued petting experiences have so conditioned an adolescent to saying "no" to his intense sexual drives that he cannot let go once marriage has taken place. More profound causes of sexual repression lie in deeply etched memories of an unhappy home which was sexually starved or identifications with a mother or father who had been hurt by the other sex. There are innumerable specific psychological conditioning factors which may reduce the ability of individuals to respond satisfactorily.

In general, where a lack of sexual response exists, it is wise to consult two different types of specialists. In the first place, a gynecologist should be consulted to determine whether or not any physical factor might account for the lack of response. If the gynecologist's examination proves negative, and he finds no physical reason for a lack of response, he may refer his patient to a marriage counselor. The counselor and the patient will explore then all of the processes of marriage reaction to determine whether or not the lack of response is due to other maladjustments in the marriage. The counselor will also determine whether or not the couple understand the physiological facts of intercourse and love-making. He may then explore the background of the patient to discover any traumatic experiences which might account for the lack of sexual feeling. If he discovers that the root of the difficulty is some repressed psychological pattern, he will probably refer the individuals to a psychiatrist for deeper therapy. Almost all couples have the potential for a gratifying sexual experience, but they may need the help of one or more of these specialists in order to overcome background impediments to sexual compatibility. They should not feel embarrassed by this but seek such help as they need.

FEAR OF PREGNANCY AND SEXUAL RESPONSE

The seventh factor which frequently comes to the marriage counselor's attention is a lack of response due to fear of pregnancy. Nothing is so constrictive of sexual freedom as the continual fear on the part of a woman that she may become pregnant when she does not feel ready for pregnancy. Locke found this a significant factor in his study. He quotes one divorced woman as saying, "I was scared all the time I'd get pregnant. I didn't like to have intercourse because I was scared. I had a child every year." [5] Here again a different approach is needed for different groups. For young people who are Catholics or who belong to other religious groups which do not approve of the use of birth-control measures to delay the beginning of a family or to space or limit the family, the solution is to be found in a full understanding and appreciation of the philosophy of their church. The Catholic who does not feel ready to have children or mature enough to give them a good start in life should not marry until ready to accept the responsibilities of a Catholic marriage. Married Catholics who find themselves rebelling against the possibility of a large family must talk with their priests until they come to accept fully the philosophy by which they live. This in turn will eliminate fear of child-bearing and consequently give full freedom to sexual togetherness.

For Protestants and others who have no ethical feelings against birth control, the selection of a reputable gynecologist and the willingness to follow his instructions implicitly, as well as the understanding of the method of birth control he prescribes, will serve to eliminate fears of pregnancy. Sometimes coitus interruptus is practiced—the withdrawal of the penis just before ejaculation. Such a practice is universally unsatisfactory to both the female and the male and may lead to profound sexual dissatisfaction if not to neurotic reactions. If such a fear of pregnancy exists, it is well to face it very frankly and to deal with it honestly within the frame of ethical reference of the couple.

FATIGUE AND SEXUAL ADJUSTMENT

An eighth factor in achieving sexual completeness is that of conserving enough psychic and physical energy so that there is a reserve for expenditure in coitus. One of the great modern enemies of good marital relations is fatigue. The investment by both male and female of most of their resources in the great struggle for power, prestige, and wealth leaves very few resources for any other development. Here, however, we are concerned only with the general depletion of the libido which comes from much anxiety over status or economic position.

Some gynecologists are very much concerned today over this problem as it relates to women in the working force of America. They have no prejudice against women working, but they report more and more cases of sexual incompatibility which seem to be caused by no more complex a

[5] Harvey J. Locke, *Predicting Adjustment in Marriage: A Comparison of a Divorced and a Happily Married Group* (New York: Henry Holt and Company, 1951), p. 144. Copyright 1951, Holt, Rinehart and Winston, Inc.

factor than the serious depletion of strength caused by the stresses and strains of labor. They feel that women who sacrifice their sexual vitality by working are paying a very large price for added income because of innumerable tensions which must result. The same problem likewise occurs with men who suffer from a lack of potency because they are excessively involved either in work or in extra-curricular activity. Wilhelm Stekel introduces his two-volume work on *Impotence in the Male* with these words:

> In men love-inadequacy is increasing to an alarming degree, and impotence has come to be a disorder associated with modern civilization. Every impotent man forms the nucleus of a love tragedy. For impotence makes marriage impossible, or may be the cause of an ill-fated one; it also undermines the health of the woman and has an equally pernicious effect upon the mental life of husband and wife. The percentage of relatively impotent men cannot be placed too high. In my experience, hardly half of all civilized men enjoy normal potency. . . . The hypertrophic cultivation of the "will to power" has brought in its wake a situation wherein the majority of civilized men have neither time nor energy left for love.[6]

The problem here is so to budget energy and time that enough is left for marital relations and that this important phase of life is not a mere afterthought.

THE ENVIRONMENT AND SEXUAL RESPONSE

Ninth and related to this factor of energy is the pleasantness of surroundings. Cleanliness of both body and environment is an essential factor in the total list of factors necessary for sexual gratification. A messy bedroom added to a home in disarray is not conducive to the relaxation that ought to surround the sexual act. Strong body odors are not conducive to thoughts of endearment. Privacy is essential to complete abandon. A recent case illustrates the importance of this factor. A young couple came to the counselor because of a pronounced case of frigidity on the part of the wife. It was not too difficult to discover that the frigidity was rooted in her fear that her two sons who were old enough "to notice things" might wake up while the parents were having intercourse. They slept in the same bedroom. In another case, the wife's temporary frigidity was traced to the fear that her mother, sexually frigid herself, would walk

[6] Wilhelm Stekel, *Impotence in the Male* (New York: Liveright Publishing Corporation, 1939), I, 1–5. Reprinted by permission.

into their home without knocking, and discover her and her husband making love.

FREQUENCY OF SEXUAL INTERCOURSE

Young people often ask about the relationship between frequency of intercourse and adjustment in marriage. Frequency of coital experiences varies a great deal with individual couples and for the same couple. While the typical couple has sexual relations two or three times each week, each individual couple report changes in their own experiences. Blood thinks that:

> Happiness depends less on the absolute frequency of intercourse than on the relationship between actual and preferred frequencies.[7]

Even the difference between actual and preferred frequency may be due to other factors than amount of innate sexual desire. Even if a husband or a wife are not especially in the mood for intercourse, and they love each other enough to want to contribute to the other's happiness, they will not reject the overtures of the other. Conversely, if a man or woman is sensitive to the needs of the beloved, the one in need will not insist on coitus when the other is completely fatigued or unhappy. We would add a further qualification to what Blood says by adding that happiness depends on the consideration and kindness by which differences in preferred frequencies are handled. If husband and wife are relating to each other well in most of their marital experiences, they generally do not find that any difference in libido destroys their marriage.

PSYCHOLOGICAL SECURITY AND SEXUAL RESPONSE

The need for psychological security is of extraordinary importance to a woman. If she cannot feel that her husband truly loves her and would stand by her under any circumstances, she finds it difficult to give herself sexually to him. Quite frequently failure in sexual response is caused by a conflict in values, due to an assumed responsibility for the other's habits, morals and social views.

A daughter of a professional family of urbane ways was married to a farm reared high school teacher of much professional promise. She felt

[7] Robert O. Blood, Jr., *Anticipating Your Marriage* (New York: The Free Press of Glencoe, 1962), p. 368. Copyright The Macmillan Company.

responsible for his further growth in the social graces. He used his knife for purposes she knew could be better served by the fork. They, together with their minister, had acquired an insight into the ideal literature and spiritual point of view in sexual growth in marriage. This young wife brought her problem of unfulfilled sexual expectations to the marriage counselor.

Knowing the theory of value conflicts, the counselor soon helped the young wife to express her anxieties for her husband's professional growth, so dependent in her own way of feeling, upon his need for understanding concerning table manners. Once she saw the futility of taking responsibility for "changing him" she started to relax. She soon saw that if she wanted to continue as his teacher, she would find a conflict in giving herself completely in marriage. Within three weeks she had worked through her conflict and reported a satisfactory sexual response.

Many students learn to face the possibility of conflict over habits and attitudes before marriage. They learn to recognize the conflict in roles, conflict in duties, conflict in values for what they are, and then resolve them before marriage.

LIFE PATTERNS OF SEXUAL RESPONSE

In discussing the developing love play of a couple, we have referred to the growing intimacy and the more complete surrender that comes after a period of sexual experimentation. We say "a period" advisedly because this period varies from months to many years. Many women report that "it took a few months for me to awaken sexually." Others report that their ability to respond developed gradually. One gynecologist reports that society has been so repressive of the female's sexuality that her development is in general about ten years behind that of her husband. Kinsey comments on this fact as follows:

> One of the tragedies which appears in a number of the marriages originates in the fact that the male may be most desirous of sexual contact in his early years, while the responses of the female are still undeveloped and while she is still struggling to free herself from the acquired inhibitions which prevent her from participating freely in the marital activity. But over the years most females become less inhibited and develop an interest in sexual relations which they may then maintain until they are in their fifties or even sixties. But by then the responses of the average male may have

396

dropped so considerably that his interest in coitus and especially with a wife who has previously objected to the frequencies of his requests, may have sharply declined. . . .[8]

While tragedy seems a strong word for this lack of harmony, Kinsey reinforces our point of the discrepancy between men and women in the rate of sexual interest at different age levels. The problem is to minimize the inhibitions and to develop such sexual acceptance that the wife will have early emancipation from inhibition, and the husband, consequently, will not be thwarted in his sexual attentions to his wife.

It would seem that Kinsey's estimate was somewhat pessimistic; certainly it would be pessimistic for an alert young couple who focused on developing their love to its maximum extent. The present generation of young people have available to them many new books, many new courses in marriage, better counseling by doctors and ministers, so that the period of latency may be considerably reduced. It is also well to recognize the differential between a man's acceptance and readiness for full sexual participation and that of his wife. Understanding his wife's natural lag in sexual awakening would tend to relieve the husband of much anxiety about his love-making ability and his wife of self-doubt. The differential in the male's and the female's achievement of full sexual response may be indicated as follows:

FIGURE 24. Male and Female Patterns of Sexual Response *

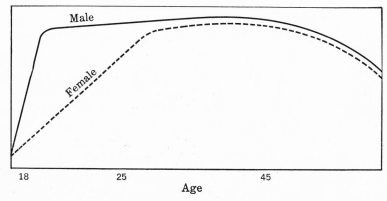

Male

Female

| 18 | 25 | 45 |

Age

* Prepared by the author on the basis of interviews with gynecologists, case studies, and Kinsey's conclusions.

[8] Alfred C. Kinsey, W. B. Pomeroy, C. E. Martin and P. H. Gebhard, *Sexual Behavior in the Human Female* (Philadelphia: W. B. Saunders Company, 1953), p. 353.

In interpreting this figure, we are assuming that if marriage occurs at eighteen, the man will in a few months develop completely his sexual powers. It is true that during the years new values will accrue to coitus, and the act will become more meaningful because of added compatibility in other areas of life. But as far as depth of passion is concerned, a man reaches the acme of his sexual prowess very early. The woman, on the other hand, may not develop her full sexual capacity until she is twenty-five. The apt lover will recognize the differential and not inhibit her further by his misunderstanding of this basic fact.

A second observation on this life cycle of sexual response is directed toward the gradual decline that occurs after the age of forty. Potency does not suddenly diminish during either the male or female climacteric. The change of life known in the female as the menopause occurs in most women between the ages of forty-five and fifty; a similar but less well defined change takes place in males at a slightly older age. In both instances the reaction is due to a combination of atrophy of the reproductive organs plus a psychological awareness of decreasing life function. In the woman, breasts gradually shrink, weight is gained in the abdomen, the voice may deepen, and hair may appear on the chin and neck. These changes may bring about a general nervousness and irritability. Generally most women go through this transition without medical treatment, although in cases of extreme tension both endocrine and psychological therapy prove helpful. In the male there may be a temporary loss of virility and fertility with prostate gland complications. Those men who have been most potent sexually may feel the most severe disturbances during this period, and some may resort to extra-marital affairs in an effort to compensate for their threatened loss of manhood.

Sexual activity should not be discontinued during these periods of natural change. Orgasms achieved during these months do much both to restore confidence and to relax tension. Knowledge of the fact that sexual desire and sexual satisfaction continue on about the same level after the climacteric may in itself be reassuring to both a man and a woman. The menopause is by no means the end of the love relationship, despite popular stereotype notions to that effect. Furthermore, the man and woman who have achieved a full and satisfying sexual union may look forward to a far milder period of stress during the transition period. It is as though nature rewarded those who developed their physical possibilities.

While these various factors will tend to enhance the sexual adjustment of a man and wife by releasing their full sexual potential, it is important

398

to stress the fact that after all of these factors are taken into consideration there will still be in some marriages some basic differences in intensity of sexual interest. Locke reports that while happily married men and women indicated "about the same" sex interest to a much greater extent than did divorced men and women, there were happily married couples who registered differences. In commenting on this Locke says:

> The informal material secured in the interviews reveals that husbands of the happily married occasionally had a stronger desire for intercourse than that of their wives. Other things in the marriage seemed to compensate for the relatively low sex interest of the wife.[9]

This seems to mean that, even though there is a difference in sexual desire, accommodation can be made, providing other basic adjustments have been made in the marriage.

FACTORS INVOLVED IN AFFAIRS

An affair is defined by Cumming as a relationship having durability, emotional involvement, some stability, but it does not necessarily involve sexual intercourse.[10] He found the majority of cases involved sexual intercourse, but a minority did not, as the following table indicates.

T A B L E 36. Degree of Sexual Contact Involved in Affairs *

DEGREE	MALE		FEMALE		TOTAL
	No. Cases	% Cases	No. Cases	% Cases	% Cases
Intercourse	34	73.7	32	59.1	66.0
Sex play only	2	4.3	6	11.1	8.0
No sex	4	8.6	12	22.2	16.0
No indication	6	13.0	4	7.4	10.0

* Cumming, p. 9.

When one inquires why individuals turn from their mates to others for sexual or emotional satisfactions, one sees that this is not generally due to poor sexual relations in marriage. Only one-third of the men and sixteen per cent of the women would in these affairs give poor marital sex

[9] Locke, pp. 141–142.
[10] Gordon Cumming, "A Study of Marital Conflicts Involving an Affair by One of the Partners," unpublished masters thesis, University of Southern California Libraries, Los Angeles, California, 1960.

adjustment as the basic reason for their involvement. The following table gives reasons for affairs as reported by the participants.

Cumming was interested in determining whether men and women involved in affairs were emotionally unstable. To answer this question, he studied clients at the American Institute of Family Relations who had affairs in relation to their scores on the Johnson Temperament Analysis Test and on the Minnesota Multiphasic Personality Inventory. He compared

TABLE 37. Reasons Given by Marital Partners Involved in Affairs for Beginning the Affair *

REASON	HUSBAND		WIFE		TOTAL
	No. Cases	% Cases	No. Cases	% Cases	% Cases
Poor marital sex	15	32.6	9	16.6	24.0
OM/OW a challenge	3	6.5	0	0.0	3.0
In "love"	8	17.3	12	22.2	20.0
Mate not affectionate	6	13.0	6	11.1	12.0
Marriage never good	3	6.5	12	22.2	15.0
Enjoy OM/OW company	2	4.3	7	12.9	9.0
Sympathy for OM/OW	2	4.3	1	1.8	3.0
Revenge	0	0.0	2	3.7	2.0
No specific reason	7	15.2	5	9.2	12.0

* Cumming, p. 11. OM = Other Man. OW = Other Woman.

these subjects with two different norms established in independent studies. He found that the MMPI comparisons showed that:

> In light of the results presented in this chapter concerning the scores of the subjects they definitely display personality deficiencies as measured by this personality inventory. Since the sample is relatively small, it would not be valid to draw hard and fast conclusions regarding the personalities of marital partners involved in affairs. It does seem valid, however, to point out some of the findings with relation to the MMPI scores.
>
> 1. On all scales except the masculinity-femininity interest, more than 18 per cent of the subjects scored above 70.[11]
> 2. Four scales displayed special significance—depression, paranoia, schizophrenia, and especially psychopathic deviate. The last scale may well be worthy of further study as a diagnostic measure for the affair-prone-personality.

[11] Given certain qualifications, normal subjects would be expected to score below 70 on all of the scales.

400

3. The total profile of the subjects' scores was indicative of an abnormal personality.
4. The MMPI profiles of 40.7 per cent of the subjects were rated as abnormal when judged by the formula derived by Meehl.
5. The marital partners involved in affairs received almost three times as many MMPI scores above 70 as a group of Northwestern students.
6. On the MMPI the mean scores on all but two of the clinical scales (Hs; Mf) were more than one standard deviation above the mean.
7. The MMPI scores of the subjects showed significant variance from the norms established by two independent studies on all but two of the clinical scales (Hs; Mf).[12]

The same pattern was characteristic of the Johnson Temperament Analysis when "more than 40 per cent of the subjects received scores above 80 on four of the nine scales—Active, Cordial, Sympathetic, and Aggressive."[13] As this is certainly a preliminary study, one may not generalize that those who carry on affairs are all psychologically maladjusted, but the evidence from this pioneering study seems to indicate that these persons do not need a new partner as much as they need therapy. One psychiatrist who has studied divorce persistently upholds this view of affairs.

> The most eloquent and convincing testimony to the fact that infidelity rests on an unconscious structure is supplied by the arguments of comparatively young men caught in a conflict. . . . The fact that a neurosis is involved here is quite obvious, though not to the victim. Unconsciously, the man still adheres to the infantile fantasy of sex—the forbidden. The girl friend is neither more charming nor more exciting than the legitimate wife. She has only one asset: she fits into the fantasy of the forbidden.[14]

SOME PSYCHOSEXUAL PROBLEMS

There are a number of sexual difficulties encountered by young couples that have been labeled as impotency, frigidity, and premature ejaculation. Some awareness of the dimensions of such difficulties can help young people face them and go to the proper source for help. Most of these difficulties can be resolved without long psychotherapy, but some may represent such a profound history that long-term psychiatric intervention is indicated. In the following discussion both types are described.

Impotency. Problems of potency in the male are generally indicated

[12] Cumming, p. 61.   [13] Cumming, p. 98.
[14] Edmund Bergler, M.D., *The Revolt of the Middle Aged Man* (New York: Hill and Wang, 1957), pp. 195–197.

when there is a total or partial inability to produce or sustain an erection.

Situational or Transitional Impotency. Impotency may be relatively situational and may be easily handled when it is due to extreme fatigue, to a particular individual stress in the current situation, or to some glandular deficiency which is capable of medical therapy. This type of impotency is encountered frequently during the honeymoon when very sensitive men who have had great determination not to displease their mate or who feel that they may fail to be the "man" are not potent. Many times individuals who have a strong superego have, during adolescence, not been able to follow through in a sexual situation, and this has produced a kind of circular anxiety pattern which has predisposed failure in other situations. Such anxiety is mobilized by the prospect of marriage. Sometimes the answer is as simple as the fatigue and anxiety associated with a great wedding where there is much tension and a great deal of alcohol. Such impotency is frequently associated with the Prostitute-Madonna image.

> Jack's presenting problem when he visited the counselor premaritally was an almost compulsive fear of impotency during marriage. His history revealed a very religious background in which virginity had been vigorously recommended both in church groups and in the home. He had been repeatedly told that only "bad" girls permitted sexual intimacies. Consequently, he invented an elaborate system of differentiation between the types of womanhood based on their sexual availability. But when he tried to have intercourse with one of those whom he "literally despised," he failed in the effort. This failure motivated him to try again with a different person. But this time the anxiety about his performance on the first occasion prevented his completing the act, and he became depressed. This circular reinforcement of failure went on and he never did achieve an erection with a girl before marriage. However, he had many erections and masturbated with pleasure. The later facts were used for support while the dynamics of his feelings about women in general were explored. He had no trouble during his honeymoon, and he has since produced two fine children.

Impotency That Is Associated with Profound Neurotic Trends. Impotency can also represent the failure of the individual to move through various phases of his psychosexual development. Here, an investigation of the resolution of the Oedipus situation is paramount, because the girl friend or future wife is unconsciously equated with a sister or a mother, so that the incest tabu prevents a libidinous gesture. In other cases, where the mother has been particularly hostile or rejective, the fiancée may become the object of the hostility, residual from infancy and childhood, toward the mother. In this case, the man may "punish" his wife by becoming impotent and denying her the satisfactions of sexual expression or the tenderness associated with sex.

Premature Ejaculation

SITUATIONAL OR TRANSITIONAL-PREMATURE EJACULATION

While premature ejaculation is generally viewed as a neurotic manifestation, there are occasions when this is not true. In those instances of premature ejaculation associated with premarital sexual experiences or with the first weeks of marriage, such lack of control may be due simply to situational anxiety or again to lack of experience. Most men fail to "last" very long at the beginning of their sexual life. They have been waiting a long time for the fulfillment of their male potential, and they are not sophisticated regarding methods of prolonging intercourse. During the period of the first months of marriage, this problem may be met by the use of an anesthetic preparation for the penis, by wearing one or two condoms, or by more frequent attempts at intercourse. Frequently, all that needs to be done is to have intercourse twice in each evening when it is desired. A case follows:

> Bill requested a private conference during one of his joint interviews with his girl friend. He was ill at ease during the interview and talked about many routine matters until finally, before the close of the hour, he confided that he had a great anxiety about being able to satisfy his wife in the coming marriage because he felt he was "triggered" sexually. During petting sessions he would "come" very fast and he thought this would cause difficulty. He was advised to pet or have intercourse early in the evening and then again later at leisure. In his follow up interview three months later, he indicated that this procedure had helped and they were not now having any difficulty.[15]

PREMATURE EJACULATION THAT IS ASSOCIATED WITH NEUROTIC TRENDS

Very often, premature ejaculation is a way of injuring the wife or of symbolically giving vent to profound guilt over sex. Such an individual is saying to himself, "I will do it . . . I must do it, but I will get it over with

---

[15] From a case in the author's files.

as soon as possible." Or this problem may be related to castration worries, or it may reflect extreme self-condemnatory attitudes associated with previous toilet training so that the sexual act is emotionally associated with soiling or with something that has been fixated in his mind as "dirty."

Frigidity

Frigidity means the inability of a wife to respond to sexual stimulus. Psychiatrically, it is interpreted more strictly as meaning the inability to have orgasm, but here we shall treat it in the more general sense. It has again either a superficial or a profound history.

FRIGIDITY THAT IS DUE TO CULTURAL OR SITUATIONAL STRESSES

A great many women, and probably the majority, are frigid at the inception of their sexual attempts. There are many possible reasons for this early lack of response, particularly:

(a) ignorance of what is "expected" of them
(b) a long history of repressing sexual feeling during courtship
(c) the whole religious or cultural emphasis of their past upon virginity and the "evil" of sex
(d) fear of immediate pregnancy
(e) the general difference between men and women in terms of developing sexual responsiveness as to age levels

With gentle, tender care in his approaches, a man may overcome this kind of frigidity in marriage without psychotherapy. However, during the period before marriage both individuals need to be made aware of differentials in response so that their growth together, while slow, may be accepted and not cause difficulties. The author counsels a great many couples where the man is impatient with his wife and decides that she is frigid, so he abandons his efforts to woo her. She in turn begins to question herself and her capacities. Intercourse becomes less frequent, there is less loving and both resign themselves to an inadequate sexual experience when this is totally unnecessary.

If men and women are aware of the normalcy of a time interval between the inception of sexual activity and the achievement of full responsiveness, anxiety will not complicate the problem.

Although the term "frigidity" usually has reference to the fact that there is a lack of erotic response, it is almost always assumed that this lack of response by the woman is a defect or at least is something which is missing. This is not necessarily true. If one has the opportunity to question a large number of individuals in the gynecological clinics of general hospitals, one very frequently will be confronted with only a blank stare at any implication that the wife is supposed to experience pleasure out of a sexual relationship.

Mary was a person in this category. She came from the Middle West to California when she already was a married woman with several children. In the community where she was raised, sex was very definitely a taboo subject and not only was it something not to be discussed, but on the occasions when any reference was made to it, it was taken for granted that sexual reaction in intercourse was something which was shameful to even contemplate and that the "good" woman was one who basically "gave in" to her husband to satisfy his "animal needs." Mary was a very surprised person to discover, in the community setting into which she came in California, that sex was not a taboo subject and that women not only had sexual responses, but were supposed to enjoy them. This environment was sufficiently disinhibiting to her that she discussed it with her husband. John had never heard of a woman having any kind of sexual response and he was much amazed, on inquiring of his own co-workers, that women experience an orgasm. In trying to develop some technique for helping his wife achieve this new kind of experience, he was able to get her somewhat aroused sexually, but was not able to induce an orgasm. As a result of this, with repetition of sexual acts, she began to develop nervous tension, insomnia, and irritability. Because of this, she was referred for psychotherapy. No profound psychological exploration was necessary in her case since the inhibitions to her sexual expression were basically cultural ones, rather than any profound problems anchored in subconscious neurotic factors. With the cultivation of a somewhat different philosophy of life and the opportunity under very special circumstances to attempt a sexual and second honeymoon, she was able with the cooperation of her husband to start achieving orgasms regularly and thus to overcome the frigidity which at the beginning she did not even know she possessed.[16]

FRIGIDITY THAT IS ASSOCIATED WITH PHYSIOLOGICAL DIFFICULTIES

We do not need here to enter the controversy regarding the value of a *clitoridean* climax as contrasted to a vaginal orgasm. But there are two aspects of the problem which need to be emphasized. In a few cases, the clitoris is "hooded" and a slight operation or "circumcision" promoted

[16] Case contributed by Henry J. Wegrocki, Ph.D., M.D.

more response on the part of the woman. Ordinarily, the physician would care for such a situation in his part of the premarital preparation. A second type of failure to respond may be referrable to the failure of the muscles of the vagina to be well-toned or developed. Dr. Arnold Kegal has done much in this field. He feels that if the pubococcygeous muscle is thin, weak or atrophied, the woman is not apt to have any vaginal sensations during intercourse. Dr. Kegal discovered, in dealing with incontinence, that when he strengthened this muscle to promote better control of the urinary function, the women he worked with simultaneously reported greater vaginal responses. Dr. Paul Popenoe believes that young people should be apprised of the need for the woman to develop this muscle and that if the man is tender and kind, ideal conditions are established for its development. The author feels that much more material needs to be surveyed before this becomes a standard part of premarital instructions.

FRIGIDITY THAT IS ASSOCIATED WITH NEUROTIC PERSONALITY CONSTELLATIONS

The more serious type of psychosexual frigidity has deeper intrapsychic roots. It often inheres in the too close identification by the wife with her father, so that all of the defenses organized in childhood against infantile sexual aims involving the father operate now in reference to the husband. Again, a profound hostility toward the father can be represented in the marital union as a revenge through the means of frigidity. There are many deep etiological aspects of frigidity which can only be uncovered by very lengthy psychotherapy or analysis.

CONCLUSION

Nature has endowed men and women with very adequate sexual organs, but culture has not always given them wholesome attitudes. Still, if men and women realize the differences in their sexual rhythms and arousal patterns, if they are happy in other marital relationships, if they have some creativity in their love-making, if they overcome fears of pregnancy and insecurities, if they are healthy and not perpetually fatigued, if their home is orderly and their privacy assured, they may look forward to a lifetime of happy sexual interaction.

In all love-making that is on a high level of adjustment, there is much complementary interaction. The husband and wife receive the utmost pleasure from this interaction when they are assured of the complete fulfillment of their partner. In the mature sexual relation this effort to please the other brings profound psychological closeness between the two. The sexual act is thus both an expression and an undergirding of companionship love. Such mutuality is one of the most rewarding gifts of life.

PROJECTS

1. Take an anonymous ballot of the class to determine the degree of sexual instruction each has received from home, church, and school. Report on and discuss the results.
2. Discuss ways of sharing sexual information with children and discussing problems with adolescents so that sexual inhibitions may be ameliorated.
3. Pass a question box around the class and ask each student to drop in one or two questions regarding coitus which may have been troubling him.
4. Discuss the place of "bull sessions" in fraternities or sororities in terms of the adequacy of information shared in such groups.
5. Discuss the difference between a series of dating "affairs" in college and those described by Cumming for mates.
6. Using the graph in Figure 22 as a factual summary, how far should women go in attempting to harmonize their patterns with men? Does this relate to the double standard?

READINGS

BOVET, THEODOR. *A Handbook for Marriage*. New York, Doubleday and Company, Inc. (A Doubleday Dolphin Book, C23), originally published as *Love, Skill and Mystery*, New York, Longmans, Green and Company, Ltd., 1958.

ELLIS, HAVELOCK, M.D. *The Psychology of Sex*. New York, Emerson Books, Inc., 1938.

EXNER, M. J., M.D. *The Sexual Side of Marriage*. New York, W. W. Norton and Company, Inc., 1932.

KINSEY, ALFRED C., W. B. POMEROY, C. E. MARTIN, and R. H. GEBHARD. *Sexual Behavior in the Human Female*. Philadelphia, W. B. Saunders Company, 1953.

LOCKE, HARVEY J. *Predicting Adjustment in Marriage: A Comparison of a Divorced and a Happily Married Group*. New York, Henry Holt and Company, 1951. Copyright Holt, Rinehart and Winston, Inc.

STONE, HANNAH and ABRAHAM STONE. *The Marriage Manual*. New York, Simon and Schuster, Inc., 1953.

CHAPTER 17

Economic
Contributions
to Family
Cohesion

INTRODUCTION

THE American people are the most fortunate economic group in
the world. On the whole, the average American has a higher living standard than any person has ever had in history. Indeed, the average middle-
class family today has a better diet, better health care, more adequate
housing, wider communication, and more diversified recreational opportunities than the kings and nobles of several hundred years ago. Yet, as
we get more and more, we seem to want more and more; and money and
its management are constant sources of unhappiness in a large number of
American families. On the other hand, economic insight, cooperative
planning, and management skill reinforce the bonds of love and affection
that hold families together.

CONFLICT OVER MONEY IN MARRIAGE

Innumerable surveys indicate the importance of money as a factor in
marital maladjustment. Wilson, in her study of college women, found
money and its management to be among the most frequent sources of
futility—with some thirty-eight out of fifty women mentioning money

as a problem. Only parental relationships and sexual adjustment ranked higher—these two being stressed by forty out of the fifty women.[1]

TABLE 38. Major Areas of Disagreement in Urban Families *

AREA OF DISAGREEMENT	PROPORTION OF WIVES MENTIONING	
	First	At All
Money	24%	42%
Recreation, companionship	16	30
Children	16	29
Personality characteristics	14	28
In-laws	6	10
Roles	4	7
Miscellaneous (religion, politics, sex)	3	5
None, not ascertained	17	17

* Robert O. Blood, Jr., *Anticipating Your Marriage* (New York: The Free Press of Glencoe, 1962), p. 292. Copyright The Macmillan Company.

This study shows how wives rank the areas of disagreement with their husbands. Money is by far the most significant item, being mentioned as the greatest area of disagreement almost twice as frequently as any other single item. Locke found that a significantly higher percentage (80.6) of married than divorced men (35.1) rated their wives "very satisfactory" in managing the affairs of the home.[2] In Pace's study of 951 former University of Minnesota students, management of money ranked as the number one cause of marital conflict.[3] There is no doubt that skillful home management and financial planning contribute to marital adjustment; poor management and no planning to poor adjustment.

ECONOMIC SECURITY AND MARITAL ADJUSTMENT: THE "CLASSICAL" STUDIES

In demonstrating the specific ways in which socio-economic factors are associated with marital adjustment, those studies generally regarded as "classic" in the field of family adjustment will be considered. Terman

[1] Pauline Park Wilson, "College Women Who Express Futility," *Contributions to Education*, No. 956 (New York: Bureau of Publications, Teachers College, Columbia University, 1950), p. 54.

[2] Harvey J. Locke, *Predicting Adjustment in Marriage: A Comparison of a Divorced and a Happily Married Group* (New York: Henry Holt and Company, 1951), p. 282. Copyright Holt, Rinehart and Winston, Inc.

[3] Robert Pace, *They Went to College* (Minneapolis: University of Minnesota Press, 1941), p. 82.

studied 792 couples of early middle age from the upper-class or upper-middle class.[4] Since more than 80 per cent were white-collar workers, generalizations based on his findings do not apply to the general population. Terman found that insufficiency of income was frequently mentioned as a negative factor in marriage. Some 70.5 per cent of the husbands and 68.8 per cent of the wives checked this item. Inadequate income very definitely differentiated the high from the low happiness groups. Terman stated that it was the way in which income was handled rather than the absolute size of the income that was important in relation to marital happiness.

Burgess and Cottrell's study included a sample of 526 middle-class couples who had been married six years or less.[5] These couples were studied by means of questionnaires. By use of the statistical device of partial correlation, other major factors of adjustment were held constant. Burgess and Cottrell found that the economic factor was of almost no importance. Locke, studying two groups, one happily married and the other divorced, in Indiana, asked his interviewees to indicate whether their income was very adequate, adequate, inadequate, or very inadequate.[6] The happy group considered their income adequate; the divorced described theirs as inadequate. Locke also found that certain indices of security, namely possession of life insurance, possession of savings at marriage, and accumulated savings at the time of interviewing were all associated with good adjustment. Furthermore, he found that the families on a higher level in terms of rent, life insurance, utilities, and luxuries were happier than those on a lower level.

WILLIAMSON'S STUDY

The most comprehensive study of the economic factors in marriage has been made by Williamson.[7] He studied three diverse social areas of Los Angeles. His sample included 420 persons, and each of them was individually interviewed. His study was, therefore, not subject to the criticism leveled at other major studies—that the sampling was too limited.

[4] Lewis M. Terman, *Psychological Factors in Marital Happiness* (New York: McGraw-Hill Book Company, 1938).

[5] Ernest W. Burgess and Leonard Cottrell, *Predicting Success or Failure in Marriage* (New York: Prentice-Hall, Inc., 1939).

[6] Locke, p. 297.

[7] Robert Williamson, "Economic Factors Associated with Marital Adjustment." Unpublished doctoral dissertation, University of Southern California, June, 1951.

Williamson likewise used more careful differentiations of economic factors than did previous investigators. For this reason his study, while not conclusive, is highly valuable. Concerning the amount of income he concludes:

> This factor was found to be associated with marital success, although the results were not conclusive. Incomes of less than $463 (per month) prevailed among the unhappy individuals. Conversely there was a larger percentage of happy husbands and wives in the income bracket of $463 and above. Although the differences did not reach a high level of significance, they were impressive compared to other studies, in which almost no relationship was found between income and marital happiness.[8]

His specific findings in terms of individual economic items are clearly set forth in Table 39. This table shows that an average income of over

TABLE 39. Percentages of Happy and Unhappy Husbands and Wives Regarding Given Economic Items with Critical Ratios *

ITEM	HUSBANDS' RESPONSES			WIVES' RESPONSES		
	Happy	Unhappy	CR	Happy	Unhappy	CR
Amount of average monthly income ($445 or less)	57.3	70.8	−1.7	61.2	75.4	−1.7
Renting (as against owning one's home)	27.9	50.0	−2.8	27.7	45.9	−2.3
Mobility (moving two or more times during the last 3 years)	34.0	52.4	−2.2	27.9	43.9	−1.5
Amount of savings ($600 or more)	72.4	49.8	2.0	75.0	51.3	2.2
Amount of indebtedness (less than $300.00)	81.6	57.8	3.3	79.2	54.7	3.4
Amount of insurance (over $5000.00)	63.9	55.2	1.0	72.6	53.1	−3.9

* Data adapted from Williamson, p. 152.

$445 a month, home-ownership, small indebtedness and insurance over $5,000 are associated with happiness in marriage. Williamson developed what he termed a "security rating" of high, medium, and low derived from a composite of economic items. Williamson concludes:

> There was the highest proportion of happy husbands and a still higher proportion of happy wives among the highest security ratings. (Percent-

[8] Williamson, p. 143.

ages for the husbands: 31.8 and 19.1, CR 1.7; for the wives: 36.5 and 16.1, CR 2.7.) Medium security was also associated with significantly happy marriages. (Percentages for husbands: 47.1 and 30.9, CR 2.1; wives: 47.1 and 25.5, CR 1.2.) Most critical, about twice as many of the unhappy marriages were found among the individuals with low security ratings. (Percentages for husbands: 21.2 and 50.0, CR —3.8; for the wives: 16.5 and 48.4, CR —4.2.) [9]

Williamson's findings seem to give moderate support to Locke's findings that security or a higher economic level is associated with marital happiness.

However, it is not only the question of what the mate is able to provide that is important. More important is the question of what his own background, his youthful training, and his family experiences have led him to expect as normal in the way of provision. Certainly those marriages are difficult in which a young woman from a wealthy background marries the son of a plumber. For our idea of what is normal in the way of comfort-providing items, luxury items, food, and housing is contingent upon our family and social background.

PSYCHOLOGICAL ASPECTS OF FINANCIAL PROBLEMS

There is no question that many of the studies of marriage have missed the most basic aspect of the relationship of money to marital adjustment. The difficulties in marriage over money are not generally due to lack of techniques; they are due to the more basic psychological patterns of individuals which motivate destructive monetary policies. A few vignettes from current counseling cases will clarify the meaning of this hypothesis.

Mary and Bill have been married for eight years. They have a five-year-old boy. Mary has worked all of the eight years with the exception of six months when William, Jr. was born. She worked to give her husband a professional degree in law. During the last year of their marriage, conflict was so rampant Mary asked Bill to leave. Bill had become very critical and sullen. During the separation, Bill gave Mary no money and made no effort to heal the rift between them. Mary visited a marriage counselor, but Bill would not keep his appointments. When it seemed inevitable that only a divorce might resolve the conflict, the couple tried to discuss a settlement. Bill kept saying over and over, "I don't owe you a cent, not a cent." When it appeared that the court would impose regular payments, he declared he would leave the state.

[9] Williamson, p. 154.

Bill's problem was not money. He was a very insecure man, and the knowledge that he owed all of his training to his wife troubled his feelings of self-esteem. While he often accused his wife of monetary irresponsibility, these charges were pure projections of his own shame at not being able to control his own impulsive spending. When he said that he did not owe his wife a cent, he was really saying that he knew he owed her a great deal, but this was so painful he had to deny it. While one might feel his refusal to pay child-support was sadistic punishment because the good work of his wife made him feel so obligated, this refusal probably represented rather his terror of all responsibility. He could not tolerate the thought of a regular payment to his child or anyone else. He had married a strong, competent wife because he was weak. In time her competence so highlighted his incompetence that he came to hate her. He could not admit his weakness to a counselor or to himself, so he had to rationalize his bad behavior by blaming someone else. This extreme resistance eliminated all hope for reconciliation. But the friends of this couple were convinced the trouble was money!

Another case illustrates the same labeling of psychological difficulties by affixing the dollar sign in front of them.

John and Helen had another problem. John was an executive of a large Chicago corporation and drew a salary of over twenty-five thousand dollars a year. They came for help because of a myriad of problems including concern over a sixteen-year-old daughter who had negative reactions to a painful abortion. But most of the first and second hours were given to recriminations about money. Inspection of the financial program of the family revealed grave problems. They were spending twice as much as they should on transportation. The husband felt that he had to drive a Cadillac, and his wife wanted and got a luxurious station wagon. Both the husband and the wife entertained lavishly. They always paid the check at business or social luncheons. Their personal allowance items were astronomical. The family was so unhappy that the children were insecure and anxious. They sometimes could not study, and sometimes they refused to study as punishment of their parents. So the parents hired tutors for them. Some of the children, like the sixteen-year-old girl, had to have intermittent psychotherapy, and this was expensive. John said he was an executive and consequently he was entitled to live like one. If his wife brought a casserole dish or any "second-rate" type of meat, he angrily pushed back his chair and left for a restaurant where he could get a steak. So the food budget was too high. Each member of the family blamed the other.

413

It does not take long years of psychiatric training to realize that these monetary problems represent various aspects of individual and family disorganization. The use of expensive cars, the spending of money on food to insure respect points to a vast need for reassurance. The cost of tutors and psychologists, in this case, is a direct result of the damage a hostile family brings to children. Much of the impulsive spending of the husband and wife came in efforts to compensate by gifts for hostile thrusts against the mate or children. When a child broke or lost something, the parents were so severe that this promoted lying on the part of the child. The father had such an obsession about "taking care of things" that every other member of the family hated all his gifts and their sumptuous home. In working with this problem, the counselor had to deal with very profound intrapsychic problems of inadequate self-images and conflicting role expectations. This family, too, stated during their first hour that one of their main problems was money. These cases tell us one important thing about finances. The significant aspect about finances is not how much money we have but, rather, what kind of motives direct the *use* of what we earn. Where those motives are neurotic like those of John or Bill, there will always be trouble in using the resources of the family. Yet money management is complicated, and even for families with more normal motives some training is essential.

ECONOMIC MANAGEMENT AND MARITAL ADJUSTMENT

It is important to investigate the use—or misuse—of money and its relation to marital adjustment. Money may be said to have been "earned" if by wise management the total overhead of a home is substantially reduced. If a wife, by studying weekly sales and watching price differences in various stores, spends 30 per cent less on food than she might have spent, she has "earned" that much. If she cleans her own dresses and shines her own shoes, the saving is likewise money "earned." Hence, wise management must be considered "earning." A family which had an unexpected and costly illness adjusted quite satisfactorily by several measures; combining trips and saving gasoline, using two rooms instead of seven for study and recreation in the evening, doing a good many tasks that had been done by others previously, and by making shopping an exercise in financial wizardry. The most important change to be observed in the family was not a lowering of its standard of living but an improvement in family unity.

414

PLANNING THE FAMILY ECONOMY

The term budgeting has had a very narrow connotation in the minds of the general public. Because of the concern for the "almighty dollar," budgeting has been thought of exclusively as a way of using that dollar more intelligently.

Each of us has six sorts of things in life which he may spend:

Time: days, weeks, months, years; vacation, minutes while waiting, and so on.

Energy: as expressed in interests whether these are physical, intellectual, social, spiritual, or other.

Abilities: talents, aptitudes, skills, poise, and so on.

Space: such as is within his control, walls and floor space in his own room and office, desk, drawers, shelves, closets, owned ground, seats at performances; there are many examples.

Property: tools, clothing, house, whatever one legally owns or controls.

Money: negotiable papers, cash, excess materials which can be sold or traded, and so on.

This sixth resource is different from all the others. It is worthless in itself. It can be so spent as to increase the others. With it we can often buy materials, inventions, or services which make our own time, energy, abilities, space, or property go much further. Or it can be spent so as to decrease our resources considerably without rendering equivalent value. Examples are buying a house too large for our needs, sustaining a meaningless membership in an expensive club, subscribing to a fat magazine with indifferent contents, and maintaining a hobby dealing with trivial things.[10]

Families sometimes sacrifice happiness and security because of environmental pressures for status. So many families "keep up with the Joneses" either consciously or unconsciously that the force of social competition is very marked. Advertising men are aware of this fact and use it to make sales. When television first became popular, one firm's advertisements proclaimed that children who did not have a set were underprivileged. In our materialistic culture we often buy for purposes of ostentation rather than for pleasure or usefulness. Money and things

[10] Regina Wescott Wieman, *The Family Lives Its Religion* (New York: Harper and Brothers, 1941), p. 116. Copyright Harper and Row, Publishers. Reprinted by permission of the publisher. See also pp. 176, 177.

have become synonymous with success. Some wives who do not have the latest refrigerator, washing machine, dryer, garbage-disposal unit, deep freeze, television, radio, car, mangle, etc. may feel inferior to those who have these things. Today such women do not depend upon their education, or charm, or kindliness to win position. They buy it. Some husbands, too, find that the size of the car they drive makes a greater impression than their character, or the wholesome growth of their children. In such a social-economic environment one values in a mate initiative and the desire to get ahead—and accumulates things as if they were a substitute for personal growth or family happiness.

The way income is managed has some bearing on marital adjustment. The family that is always overburdened with debt, never able to meet an economic crisis, anxious and strained at the thought of taxes or Christmas is not likely to be too well adjusted. A good credit rating is commendable and is very useful. But the family that is making so many installment payments that it cannot afford enough milk or a trip to the beach has mortgaged itself too deeply. To carry on family life without any financial plan may be as unwise as allowing the financial outlay to be dictated by competition for status. On the other hand, to follow a budget too rigidly may also bring maladjustment.

The virtue of a budget is that it necessitates the thinking through of family values—it also reflects that thinking. The family which sets its sights early upon long-range goals—a home, foreign travel, retirement income—is likely to achieve them. The children's education and the family security should be provided for in an adequate savings or insurance program. Where no long-term values are projected, no outstanding achievement of family goals or security can result. Likewise, decisions about the amount of income to be devoted to individual family pleasure and the amount to be allotted to the community chest, the Red Cross, the church, savings bonds, etc. are important, for they reflect the attitudes we have toward money and income. In the home that is sensitized to human need beyond its walls there is a continuous feeling of stewardship. The family council that decided to cut down on the allowances of each individual for recreation for a month in order to help tubercular Italian children, or an orphanage, is teaching spiritual values in a dynamic way. Budget sessions in a family may serve as schools in decision making, and at the same time create ties which bind the family more closely together.

Thus, a budget involves far more than just planned spending. Equally important are the factors of planned saving, of long-time goals, of indi-

416

vidual needs and family unity. A budget of a family with outdoor recreational interests will be much different from the budget of a family that is interested in art, music, and literature. One interest is not better than another, merely different. Some wives, perhaps most wives, will get their greatest pleasure from time-saving equipment and from clothes; for others a new assortment of oil paints, and money to be used to participate in art groups and to make trips, will take precedence.

It is generally recommended that a budget be based on past expenditures. In plotting these expenditures there must be an earnest endeavor by the family group to meet the dynamic interests of each of its members. Budgeting may then contribute to family unity and to personality growth.

THE FLEXIBLE BUDGET

No look at family finance has a reality basis unless it is related to the family cycle and its shifting demands. The family develops and grows, and each period requires new developmental tools involving a new expenditure of time and money. As we have said previously, Duvall divides the family cycle into eight periods.[11] (See page 73.)

She studies the financial needs which attend each of these stages. In talking about the family with teenagers she describes the financial stresses as follows:

> The teenage family feels pressures for physical expansion and renewal of its facilities. Junior campaigns for a new car. Sally needs a party dress. The refrigerator is no longer large enough to meet the demand for snacks and meals of the many appetites represented in the family. It would be nice to have another bathroom, or a second TV set, or a deep freeze, or a rumpus room, or a den where mother and father could find some place to call their own when the teenagers are entertaining, or some new furnishings to replace "this old stuff" that is suddenly so hideous in adolescent eyes. All the while, father sees costs of college, social life, and weddings ballooning up ahead of him.[12]

Each period has its own demands so that good economic planning not only is flexible enough to adjust to changing needs but to anticipate large future expenditures such as college tuition and retirement income. Harmony in spending patterns also depends fundamentally on agreement on

[11] Evelyn Miller Duvall, *Family Development* (Philadelphia: J. B. Lippincott Company, 1957), p. 8.
[12] Duvall, pp. 310–311. Reprinted by permission of the publisher.

long-term purposes and goals for the family group. When these are well defined their achievement rests upon careful planning, not rigid rules. Consider for instance the fact of differential expenses for different months. During some months costs are low, during others they are exorbitant. The following figure gives a somewhat oversimplified picture of this fact.

FIGURE 25. Peaks in Yearly Spending *

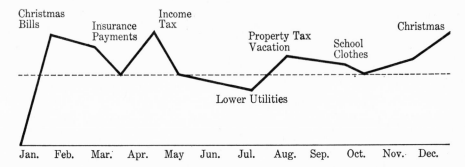

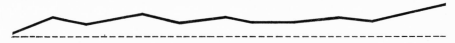

* From James A. Peterson, *Toward a Successful Marriage* (New York: Charles Scribner's Sons, 1960), p. 116. Reprinted by permission of the publisher.

Couples who have their finances under control can save during the low cost months for the higher expenditures during others. Thus instead of squeezing or borrowing three hundred dollars for Christmas or income taxes, twenty-five dollars are set aside each month; so when December comes the money is available. If such savings are planned, the figure representing the leveled off monthly costs looks like this: *

FIGURE 26. Peaks When Spending Is Leveled Off *

* Peterson, p. 116. Reprinted by permission of the publisher.

If we put together the desire to meet both life goals and yearly costs on an intelligent and sinking fund principle, we may now illustrate the monthly allocation of funds as follows:

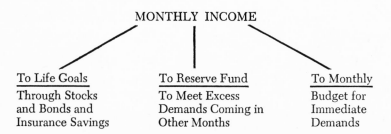

MONTHLY INCOME

To Life Goals	To Reserve Fund	To Monthly
Through Stocks and Bonds and Insurance Savings	To Meet Excess Demands Coming in Other Months	Budget for Immediate Demands

Such a plan eliminates unnecessary money costs involved in excessive borrowing to meet each high leap in costs. It also contributes to peace of mind regarding future demands.

We have not yet spoken about the constant monthly costs such as food, housing and transportation because such a discussion needs to be related to an understanding of the family cycle, the life goals, and the need to even out the annual expenditures. Nevertheless it is true that the rent or house payment comes with regularity every thirty days so it is essential to understand the wide variety of expenditures involved in living together. These items are generally listed as follows:

1. Utilities, rent or house payments
2. Taxes: federal, state, automobile, real estate, special
3. Transportation
4. Food, including dairy products and eating out
5. Medical, dental, and drug expenses
6. Household expenditures: brooms, paint, light bulbs, etc.
7. Furniture: new or replacement or repair including drapes, etc.
8. Personal allowances for each member of the family
9. Benevolence or gifts to the community chest, church, etc.
10. Advancement: education, magazines, books, lectures, etc.
11. Recreation, including hobbies, trips, some dinner parties
12. Clothing, including dry cleaning, pressing, etc.
13. RESERVE to equalize monthly costs of the family. This is the item which provides for high costs in subsequent months.
14. RESERVE for life goals. This obviously includes long-term savings and life insurance.

419

420

T A B L E 40. Budget for Family of Three at Five Income Levels *

Expenditures, monthly	In Dollars					By %				
Weekly income	$ 49.15	69.23	92.31	115.38	138.48					
Monthly income	200.00	300.00	400.00	500.00	600.00	200	300	400	500	600
Annual income	2400.00	3600.00	4800.00	6000.00	7200.00	2400	3600	4800	6000	7200
Taxes: fed. & state income, soc. sec.	12.17	32.92	52.43	71.00	91.13	.06	.11	.13	.14	.15
Housing, utilities, household operation	45.15	56.50	68.00	79.35	89.95	.23	.19	.17	.16	.15
Food (including meals away from home)	64.30	81.75	98.35	112.85	124.20	.32	.27	.25	.23	.21
Clothing	15.80	26.15	36.05	45.75	56.75	.07	.09	.09	.09	.10
House furnishings and equipment	9.15	13.25	17.80	22.65	27.65	.05	.04	.04	.05	.05
Car and transportation	15.45	27.60	40.60	53.90	65.30	.08	.09	.10	.11	.11
Personal care	3.95	5.75	7.30	8.75	10.10	.02	.02	.02	.02	.02
Medical and dental care	9.45	12.05	14.30	16.75	19.05	.05	.04	.04	.03	.03
Advancement, recreation	8.75	14.65	19.40	24.30	29.55	.04	.05	.05	.05	.05
Gifts and contributions	4.10	6.70	9.70	13.15	17.10	.02	.02	.02	.03	.02
Savings and life insurance	9.95	20.05	32.55	47.05	63.40	.05	.07	.08	.09	.10
Miscellaneous	1.78	2.63	3.52	4.50	5.82	.01	.01	.01	.01	.01
Totals	200.00	300.00	400.00	500.00	600.00	100	100	100	100	100

* This budget is computed from a 1956 statement by the Security–First National Bank of Los Angeles Research Staff, using the modified form of the Heller Committee Study for San Francisco. From Peterson, p. 119.

15. Contingency fund [13]

Is there such a thing as a standard budget? There is not because every budget must represent an answer to the needs of all individuals in the family, and needs differ. As the author has said elsewhere:

> Every budget must represent the vital interests of the individual for whom it is prepared. There are some families who abhor keeping up a home. They want to be free from all the details, expenses, and time involved in caring for a house of their own. They keep housing costs at a minimum and allocate such funds to travel or other expenditures which mean more to them. There are some families who do not like active recreation, who find their maximum pleasure in reading, in a library, and in music. Much of their recreation budget is then diverted to what we have called the advancement fund. To other families clothes are more important than music or dancing lessons. There is no uniformity about human needs or satisfactions, and an adequately prepared budget is one which guarantees to each member of the family the maximum opportunity to develop his or her interests and fulfill his or her needs. One, therefore, hesitates to recommend any standard type of budget to any individual family. The expenditure of funds ought to represent the determination of the values and interests of the group of people by long discussion and planning.[14]

But having given this word of caution, it seems desirable to present a model budget simply for comparative purposes and with the understanding that it is not recommended for one single person. It is, moreover, a composite budget, having been determined by studying the average expenditures of a great many people in recent years. No final figures can be given for yearly reserves or life-time reserves because these will vary a great deal from family to family, and not all the families in the past have refined their economic thinking to this point.[15]

INSURANCE

The young man who has been married for five years and has two children is aware that his family's lifetime goals could not be met if something happened to him. Life insurance helps him plan for such a contingency. The general principle behind any insurance policy is that many individuals contribute on a sharing basis to modify the risk to any one person. Cohen clarifies the functions of insurance as protection and savings and outlines the types of insurance:

[13] Peterson, pp. 117–118.   [14] Peterson, pp. 118–119.   [15] Peterson, p. 120.

There are only three basic types of policies: (a) term, which is temporary protection, (b) straight life, which is lifetime protection with savings values, (c) endowment, which is mostly savings with protection until the endowment matures. Every other type of policy is a variation or combination of the three basic types. Bear in mind that for your insurance premium dollar, the policy that provides the most protection provides little or no savings, while policies that maximize savings give you relatively less insurance protection for your money. As you progress through life your initial need for maximum protection will change until savings receive more emphasis than protection.[16]

Cohen has prepared a chart of costs.

TABLE 41. What Various Policies Cost *

(Approximate Annual Premiums for $1,000 of Insurance)

TYPE OF POLICY	AGE AT WHICH POLICY IS ISSUED					
	20	21	22	23	24	25
Five year term .... (Renewable and convertible)	$ 5.65	$ 5.70	$ 5.80	$ 5.90	$ 6.00	$ 6.10
Ten year term .... (Renewable and convertible)	6.80	6.90	7.00	7.10	7.20	7.30
Straight life	14.15	14.50	14.85	15.25	15.65	16.10
Life-paid-up-at-65	16.20	16.60	17.10	17.60	18.15	18.70
20 payment life	25.85	26.30	26.75	27.25	27.75	28.30
Retirement income at 65 (Male)	25.50	26.30	27.15	28.05	29.05	30.15
20 year endowment	46.95	47.00	47.05	47.10	47.15	47.20

* Rates shown are approximate premium rates for life insurance protection. Rates of "participating" policies would be slightly higher but the cost would be lowered by annual dividends. "Non-participating" policy premium rates would be somewhat lower than those shown and no dividends would be paid. Cohen, p. 17.

The costs, however, are relevant to the amount of savings involved in each policy. The following table and interpretation helps visualize these differences in return.

This table shows what $100 a year will buy in various types of insurance, enables you to compare and contrast the different types of policies according to (a) amount of protection provided, (b) savings feature, and (c) ability to provide a monthly income at retirement. In your twenties, probably policies which maximize protection will interest you most in view of new and growing responsibilities. From 35 to 50 the savings element is

[16] Jerome B. Cohen, *Decade of Decision* (New York: Institute of Life Insurance, 1958), pp. 16–17. Reprinted by permission of the publisher.

TABLE 42. What $100 a Year Will Buy *

(Starting at Age 22)

	Annual Rate per $1,000 of Insurance	Amount of Ins. $100 a Year Will Buy †	Cash Value at Age 65 per $100 Annual Premium	Monthly Life Income at Age 65, Men (10 Years Certain)
1. Term (5 year renewable & convertible)	$ 5.80	$17,241	—	—
2. Term (10 year renewable & convertible)	7.00	14,286	—	—
3. Modified 5 (minimum policy $2,000)	11.88 1			
	17.24 2	5,800	$3,567	$22.47
4. Straight life	14.85	6,734	4,141	26.09
5. Straight life (with 20 year family income rider)	18.30	5,464	3,360	21.17
6. Straight life (with 20 year family maintenance rider) . .	20.00	5,000	3,075	19.37
7. Life-paid-up-at-65	17.10	5,848	4,298	27.08
8. 20-payment life	26.75	3,738	2,747	17.31
9. Endowment at 65	19.60	5,102	5,102	32.14
10. 20-year endowment	47.05	2,125	—	—
11. Retirement income at 65 (male)	27.15	3,683	6,095	38.40
12. Retirement income at 65 (female)	29.85	3,350	6,265	39.47

* Cohen, p. 26. Reprinted by permission of the publisher.
† Most policies are issued in $1,000 units or in multiples of $500.
1 1st year.   2 Thereafter.

likely to assume more importance and significance. From 45 or 50 on, retirement income will become a major concern. In no one period will only one of these three basic elements be the sole concern; all need to be considered together in developing any insurance program, but as you walk through life this emphasis will change. The early concern with protection, which is the preoccupation of your decade of decision, will never give way completely, but it will yield its number one role in emphasis first to savings, and then later to retirement income.[17]

Families differ from one another in their values and in their needs. They also differ in their ability to visualize the whole life cycle and plan intelligently for each stage. Modern insurance underwriting has become increasingly complex as it seeks to differentiate special needs of families.

[17] Cohen, pp. 25–26. Reprinted by permission of the publisher.

For this reason it is possible for husbands and wives to find help for their particular problems by enlisting the expert advice of an insurance agent or a financial counselor.

HEALTH INSURANCE

The increased cost of medical care in the last ten years has been greater than the increase of any other kind of expense. Using 1947–49 as a base, medical care costs rose 51 per cent by January 1, 1960. The total amount spent on medical expenses in 1959 was $18.3 billion or about 6 per cent of the total personal budget of the American public. In 1957 one out of every eight Americans was hospitalized. Some 500,000 families had medical costs equaling or exceeding 100 per cent of their incomes.[18] In order to equalize these risks, by 1959 nearly 128 million Americans were enrolled in some voluntary health insurance group. How popular health insurance has become can be seen from the following figure:

FIGURE 27

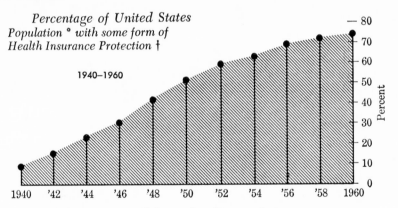

Percentage of United States Population * with some form of Health Insurance Protection †

1940–1960

* Population consists of the total civilian population.
Source: Health Insurance Council and U.S. Department of Commerce, Bureau of the Census.
† Graph from *Source Book of Health Insurance Data* (New York: Health Insurance Institute, 1960), p. 9.

Cohen describes the types of medical insurance as follows:

There are five basic types of voluntary health insurance. *First,* and oldest is *loss-of-income* insurance, also known as disability insurance. This pays

[18] Cohen, p. 27.

benefits when you are unable to work because of sickness or accident. Developed more than 60 years ago, this type of insurance and similar salary continuation plans now protect some 40 million employed persons. In the days when the costs of medical care were much lower than they are now, the problem which loomed largest in illness or accident was the loss of wages or salary during the period necessary to regain one's health. Policies of this type provide as much as 75 per cent of a wage earner's normal earnings for a specified period of disability.

The *second* kind of health insurance is *hospital expense insurance*. This pays the cost of room and board in the hospital. Depending on the policy, it may cover all or part of the total hospital expense. Under insurance company plans, you are allowed so much per day for your hospital room and board up to a maximum number of days, usually ninety or one hundred and twenty. In addition there is usually a lump sum payment to cover certain hospital facilities such as use of the operating room, anesthesia, x-rays, drugs, etc. Hospital expense insurance is the most widely held of all types of health insurance. Blue Cross is the organization that pioneered in the development of hospital expense insurance although a majority of insurance companies now sell it and it has become part of the total health insurance package.

The *third* type of health insurance is *surgical expense insurance*. This pays all or part of a surgeon's fee for an operation. Almost all policies, whether those of insurance companies or of Blue Shield, contain a schedule which lists the usual kinds of operations and the amount which the insurer will pay for each type.

The *fourth* type of health insurance is *general medical expense insurance*. This pays for visits to a doctor's office or for his visits to you at your home or in a hospital. Either the company that issues the policy or the Blue Shield organization will usually pay from $3 to $5 per visit. The maximum number of calls for each sickness or injury is specified in the policy, so the patient won't be tempted to pay an undue number of visits to the doctor. One policy declares: "Allowances for both office and house visits provide for one visit a day up to a maximum of 30 visits in each contract year for each member."

The *fifth* type of health insurance is *major medical expense insurance*, sometimes known as catastrophe insurance. None of the policies described earlier are designed to meet the needs of those who are hospitalized for long periods, and whose surgical bills exceed the amounts provided in the schedule of surgical insurance policies. Nor were these policies designed to meet the expenses of those who require extensive treatment by medical

425

specialists. To meet this need a different type of policy, known as major medical expense or health catastrophe insurance, has been developed over the past decade. Today it is very popular. Over 15,000,000 people already have this insurance.[19]

It may be difficult for young people who are normally very healthy to visualize medical costs. Since in most cases their parents have provided all dental and medical care, the young man or woman has not had to confront medical costs. The following table may help them to realize the importance of careful planning:

TABLE 43. Personal Consumption Expenditures by Types of Product *

Type of Product	Personal Consumption Expenditures (Billions of Dollars)	Percent of Total
Food	70.2	21.3%
Household Operation	45.9	14.0
Transportation	40.7	12.4
Housing	42.2	12.8
Clothing, Accessories, and Jewelry	33.9	10.3
Recreation	19.4	5.9
Personal Business	20.6	6.3
Medical Care †	19.6	5.9
Alcoholic Beverages	9.9	3.0
Tobacco	7.5	2.3
Personal Care	5.2	1.6
Religious and Welfare Activities	4.7	1.4
Private Education and Research	4.5	1.4
Foreign Travel and Remittances—Net	3.0	.9
Death Expenses	1.6	.5
Total	328.9	100.0%

Source: United States Department of Commerce.
* Table from *Source Book of Health Insurance Data* (New York Health Insurance Institute, 1961), p. 50.
† Includes expenses for health insurance.

A great many industrial and commercial firms are now including some form of medical insurance as part of the remuneration for a job. However, the coverage of these plans varies greatly, and individuals would do well to review their health insurance programs with some qualified expert, so that they have an insurance plan congruent with their needs.

[19] Cohen, pp. 28–32. Reprinted by permission of the publisher.

HOUSING

The problem of housing is always a critical one for newly married couples. They usually live on a small salary so that they cannot afford to rent or buy a house during the first years of marriage. Because there is some financial strain in these early years, to live with their parents may seem a logical choice. But in many cases the problems created overshadow the financial gain. A better solution is to find a small apartment within their means. This may seem a great sacrifice, but the gain in privacy and self-respect makes it worthwhile.

After several years of saving, it is possible for most couples to accumulate enough money to make a down payment on a house. At this point it is important for the couple to include in their financial plans all of the extra costs that ownership of a home entails. They must plan carefully to meet the costs of insurance on the house, taxes, utilities, maintenance, and interest. It is not satisfactory for a couple to compare the cost of the rent of an apartment to payments on the mortgage on a house. Ownership of a home involves additional expense which may make such a purchase a much larger total expenditure. Couples should study, too, the cost of borrowing the money. There is a large difference in total cost depending on whether one can obtain an FHA loan or whether one has to pay very high interest rates. What they can spend for a home depends entirely on their other financial obligations. Nevertheless, the accepted rule of thumb is that one can buy a home costing twice as much as he receives as annual income. So if a young couple earn five thousand dollars, they would be safe in purchasing a ten thousand dollar house.

INSTALLMENT BUYING

While it is important to consider the total cost of a house, or an automobile or a TV set, it is just as important to consider the use of credit in a wise financial plan.

Although a budget offers a skeleton framework upon which to build a sound financial life, it is not enough in itself to guarantee efficient money management. Some large items such as cars or homes cannot be paid for directly or immediately, and for these a good credit rating is important. The whole credit structure allows us to have more and to have it sooner.

On the other hand, credit ratings allow us to purchase large items over many future months, and charge accounts make it easy to pick up a load of drugs, household accessories, or groceries without paying too much attention to the total costs. Consequently, a great many individuals keep accumulating charge accounts and installment payments until there is nothing left of their paychecks. It is not uncommon for the counselor to encounter families whose total amount of payments for the month is more than the monthly salary. The author has even seen several families whose total monthly payments were far more than the combined income of both the husband and wife. Certainly, the problems of those who have over-extended their buying make it imperative to think seriously about the wise use of credit.

CREDIT

It is not difficult to borrow money. There are a great many different sources which should be investigated before one borrows. For example, a friend recently purchased a home. He found alternative ways of securing the money. An FHA loan together with the insurance for repayment would cost him 5¾ per cent interest. To get the loan, however, he had to do about five hundred dollars' worth of preventative termite work on the property. This did not seem to be a happy solution to his problem, so he investigated other sources of loans.

He found he could secure a bank loan for 6.6 per cent interest and he could get this loan without doing the five hundred dollar pest control work. It would seem obvious that he should take the second loan and not add the five hundred dollars to his initial cost of the home. He decided, however, to work out the difference in total payments between the 5¾ and 6.6 interest rates and found that even after he paid the five hundred dollars for termite prevention, he would still, over the years, save over eleven hundred dollars in interest if he took the FHA loan. He did.

Not every person can qualify for an FHA loan, however, and these loans are not available for other kinds of purchases. Some sources of credit (such as credit unions) are available only to specific individuals who happen to belong to a particular organization. Banks (as well as the FHA) very frequently loan only when adequate collateral is at hand. Young couples frequently do not have such collateral and cannot qualify. If they can qualify for credit service on bank loans, they may find these less expensive than other types of credit.

Small Loan Companies. To meet the needs of such individuals, many

428

small loan companies have developed in the nation. Because the risk is considerably higher in these loans and because it costs more to service many small loans, a higher rate of interest must usually be charged.

Loans through some sources carry a loan charge which is not included in the interest rate at all. The author recently negotiated for a loan at a very attractive interest rate, but his enthusiasm was dulled by a rather high charge made by the lending institution for arranging the loan. For these reasons it is always wise for a borrower to investigate very carefully the total transaction.

A small loan company offers a second advantage in terms of service. Sometimes couples need money quickly to meet an emergency. While negotiations at a bank or similar institution might require considerable investigation, the small loan companies offer much faster response. This advantage is often worth a good deal to people under stress or even looking at an opportunity for advancement.

Many young couples who are very inexperienced in financial transactions might do well to take advantage of companies that have counselors who will integrate the immediate loan into the total budget of the couple. Such counselors thus not only help a couple with an immediate problem but contribute to their long-range security as well. This is to the advantage of the company because it also often facilitates prompt payment as well as engendering goodwill. Most banks also have financial counselors who will help couples choose a wise financial plan.

There is no question that a good credit rating helps the young couple establish themselves in a well equipped home. On the other hand, if they overextend themselves they may lose their earlier investments and their credit rating. To resist the temptation to start out with everything they want where that would mean financial crisis is the mark of maturity.

SAVINGS

To save a certain amount of money each month is to attain some future goal for the family. There are a great many goals that require such a large expenditure that they can be obtained only after a systematic savings program. Most students list the following as lifetime goals: (1) a comfortable home, (2) a certain number of children, (3) adequate dental and medical care for the family, (4) travel in this country and abroad, (5) a college education for *their* children, and (6) sufficient retirement income for old age. Each person adds to this list his own individual goals which may range from a library of books to an annual hunting trip in Canada. But such goals are not reached automatically. They are accomplished by systematic saving.

There are many ways to save. In a sense, the monthly payment on a house is saving because usually the value of the house goes up as the mortgage goes down. Investment in real estate seems to be one way to offset inflation. As the value of dollars goes down, the value of real estate increases. This is also true to some extent of well-selected stocks and bonds if they are held long enough. Money deposited in savings accounts gains interest, but a great many persons who saved dollars toward their old age in the thirties and forties have less in the way of real value in those dollars than they had twenty or thirty years ago. This is also true of endowments and other forms of insurance which are primarily investments for the future.

Young parents who are anxious to start saving for their children's education must be aware of rising educational costs. They may find that the money they have set aside for their children's college education has decreased in value while the costs of a college education have increased. Only wise investment can offset these trends. College students who are majoring in business education or law may have enough insight to handle savings in an adequate way, but many students would do well to take courses in consumer problems and personal finance. There are investment counselors who are skilled in meeting the special problems of inflation. A few dollars spent in saving wisely safeguards the future.

CASH RESERVES

In addition to planning for lifetime security it is wise to be prepared for minor emergencies which occur in all families. An adequate budget will spread out over the entire year such major expenditures as insurance, taxes, Christmas spending, vacation costs, medical and dental expenses. But there are other emergencies such as unexpected trips when a member of the husband's or wife's family becomes suddenly ill or dies, costs involved in moving because of promotion to a new and perhaps better job, and many other expensive items which cannot be budgeted or anticipated. For this reason most financial advisors recommend a savings fund immediately available or a maintained surplus in the checking account equal to two months' salary. This sum is generally adequate to meet most emergencies not covered by health, accident, or unemployment insurance.

A further benefit of such a margin is the sense of security it gives the family.

THE ROLE OF THE EMPLOYED WIFE

The wife who works outside the home has special problems. One of these is to adjust to the attitudes of her husband. Unless he understands her double responsibilities and is cooperative in meeting the pressures of running the home on a reduced schedule, the working wife may quickly become frustrated. If the husband's concept of the role of woman is such that he cannot tolerate the thought of a wife earning money, that idea will undoubtedly lead to friction. Again, if he is insecure, he may regard the success of his wife's occupational venture as a threat to his own ego. On the other hand, if he regards her contribution to the family income as a constructive help and reciprocates by lending a willing hand about the house, no problem is likely to occur. While the question of a man's attitude toward his wife's working is of great importance, there are other factors of equal weight. One of the taunts thrown at women who work is the assertion that they cannot be good mothers. This depends upon the woman. If a woman likes her work, she may be able to give her children more affection than if she were tied down at home. One does not have to spend hours and hours with children in order to assure them of security. The essential need is to share a great number of happy experiences and to have a secure relationship with them. On the other hand, if the mother comes home fatigued and irritable, her exhaustion offsets any economic assistance her employment may yield for the family. Thus, no generalization as to the desirability of women's working is possible. Much depends upon the temperament, the vitality, and the capacity of the individual woman. Her employment may add value to affectional relationships at home or detract from them. It is unfortunate, of course, if the mother's perspective is so shallow that she works only in order to supply her children with things that she herself never had. Neither maturity nor affection can be purchased, and this bitter lesson is sometimes learned too late. On the other hand, as Mavity points out, many women today have no alternative to working; this is the price they pay for having children since the family income will not support them otherwise. Komarovsky shows that the outstanding statistical fact about working wives is the low earnings of the husbands.[20]

[20] Mirra Komarovsky, *Women in the Modern World* (Boston: Little, Brown and Company, 1953), p. 107. Copyright 1953, by Mirra Heyman.

The question is more acute when a woman wants to invest her life in a career rather than in a family. There may be some basic insecurity in her attitude toward rearing children, or she may simply have such an interest in some vocational field that she does not want to be burdened at all by children. Then, too, not every woman can be an adequate mother. But such women are few. Marriage normally implies having children. Most husbands marry with this expectation, and even the husband who does not have a great interest in children at the beginning of marriage often develops it later. If a career woman marries with the intention of remaining childless, this fact should be made clear before marriage. On the other hand, there is no good reason why a woman cannot combine a career with motherhood provided she has the strength and the emotional equipment for both. It is something of an anomaly that many girls who are highly trained in college, and make brilliant starts in their chosen profession are expected to give up their work when they marry. Many women have much to contribute to science, to art, to literature. It is difficult to believe that marriage, *ipso facto,* must eliminate the possibility of making such contributions.

If, on the other hand, a couple organize their marriage on the basis of the wife's working, certain alterations in family habit patterns must be made. The selection of reliable domestic help is of first magnitude. The willingness of the husband to participate in family chores must be assumed and realized. Mavity comments on this point:

> The postwar husband feels no ignominy in running the washing machine or taking clothes to the Laundromat, starting dinner, or pushing the vacuum cleaner. Executive efficiency in the household is not a sex attribute, and many men who take the common-sense view that they should share in the housework if their wives share in the production of income, have demonstrated that freedom from hidebound traditional procedures can be turned to good account. They see the problems of household management with fresh eyes. They discover shortcuts, tighten schedules, and invent improved procedures. "Woman's work was never done," perhaps because she followed deep-rutted grooves and did not try to invent new methods of getting the work done more quickly.[21]

The family time-budget must be planned with as much care as the financial budget (if not more) so that a maximum number of hours may be spent in family activities. In fact when the wife works and a time

---

[21] Nancy Mavity, "The Two Income Family," *Harper's Magazine* (December, 1951), p. 60. Reprinted by permission of the publisher.

budget is used, the total time invested in family activities is often greater than when the wife does not work and, therefore, uses her husband's free hours to get away by herself or with him.

The general acceptance of women in the working force may be regarded as a force for better adjustment in marriages. When a woman had no alternative to marriage, there was little she could do if there was great unhappiness in the home. Today the situation is changed. The result of women's work is that a man can no longer run roughshod over his wife's feelings or needs. She is in a bargaining position which means that he must expend greater effort to make the marriage last. In the long perspective this fact should make for the permanence of marriage, even though conflict over wives working may be a factor in the current unprecedented divorce rate.

The basic point of this discussion is that there is no such thing as a "woman's place." Men and women are involved in a spectacular social change by which the status of women is undergoing more radical transformation than it has in the last five thousand years. The woman who leads this procession may marry a man who is threatened and bewildered by her new role; and often she does not have any firm convictions herself about the meaning of her action. We are moving from a very, very old concept of woman's rights and place to a very modern one. This generation is still involved in experimentation. Young people should realize that what is basically important is not the criticism of what they do but their adjustment to each other. If this adjustment is good, they need not be concerned with the value judgments of others. They should also realize that there are few available patterns to guide them. This is a period of change, but that change also has much promise of happiness and marital success.

CONCLUSION

Family financial planning ought to result in two achievements, (a) adequate provision for the individual needs of the members of the family and (b) adequate provision for the basic needs of the family as a whole. Such plans should help each person develop his potentialities and his feeling of independence and security. When a family budget does not provide allowances for every member, it is too tight and may become a source of friction instead of a means to greater cohesiveness. Likewise, the budget is not adequate unless it provides well for the general needs such as food, housing, and transportation of the whole family. This dual goal helps the family keep in mind two purposes; the goal of individual personality fulfillment and the goal of family cohesion.

The way money and security are handled may weaken or strengthen individual growth and family unity. A budget should be a medium whereby the family plans together for the achievement of individual and family goals. The budget will not in itself solve every problem of finance for the family. Wise buying practices as well as wise planning for the future require careful practice and study. Study must be given also to ways of adjusting to the problems that arise when a wife works. Society is in a period of transition. The shifting roles and values do not make for automatic adjustment. The couple who can intelligently plan their time and the use of their money will discover that the effort used to do so will be a positive factor in their growing happiness.

PROJECTS

1. Plan a budget based on the average salary of last year's seniors.
2. Find booklets in your bank on savings and investment. What investments protect against inflation? Have half of the class budget one month and keep detailed records of expenses. The other half of the class use check book only. Compare results.
3. Collect monthly family budgets from married college students. Compare these with Table 40. Then study the budgets of young growing families reported in *Changing Times*, July, 1959, pages 15–17. Can you readily discern which families have a psychological problem rather than a purely money problem?

READINGS

COHEN, JEROME B. *Decade of Decision*. New York, Institute of Life Insurance, 1958, pp. 16–17.

COHEN, JEROME B. and ARTHUR W. HANSON. *Personal Finance—Principles and Case Problems*. Rev. ed., Homewood, Illinois, Richard D. Irwin, Inc., 1958.

LOCKE, HARVEY J. *Predicting Adjustment in Marriage: A Comparison of a Divorced and a Happily Married Group*. New York, Henry Holt and Company, 1951, Chapter 13. Copyright Holt, Rinehart and Winston, Inc.

TROELSTRUP, ARCH W. *Consumer Problems and Personal Finance*. New York, McGraw-Hill Book Company, Inc., 1957, Chapters I, II, III, and IV.

WILSON, PAULINE PARK. "College Women Who Express Futility." *Contributions to Education*, No. 956. New York, Bureau of Publications, Teachers College, Columbia University, 1950, Chapter V.

CHAPTER 18

Religion and the Family

INTRODUCTION

WHILE companionship and the transmission of culture are the two central functions which characterize the contemporary family, analysis of case-study material reveals that there are other binding forces which can contribute to the solidity of marriage. In this chapter the religious aspects of marriage will be studied to discover how they may affect stability in the marital union.

More than ninety million persons in the United States belong to religious organizations. An additional large group of individuals do not hold church membership but participate to some degree in religious activities. A third group of adults no longer participate, but as children were associated with a church and received some degree of religious education. Beyond this, all of us live in a democratic society whose laws, spirit, and mores are largely an outgrowth of the close relationship of religion to life during the most formative decades of the nation's history. The influence of the Hebraic-Christian tradition is so pervasive in our national laws, ideals, and customs that even the agnostic is largely the product of a religious background.

It is reasonable to think that an institution with such a wide and historic function in all human culture and in our own civilization has many influences upon the family.

THE RELIGIOUS CONTRIBUTION TO MORAL VALUES

Religion is a way of bringing some organization and meaning to the infinite number of experiences which happen to us in life. Religious values absorbed in the home give the individual a philosophy or a system of values which enables him to look at life with serenity and confidence. The White House Conference on Children in a Democracy stresses the contribution of the home by saying: "Here the foundations are laid for the moral standards that are to guide his conduct through life." [1] Later the Midcentury White House Conference added that parents who have achieved personality integration on the basis of ethical or religious convictions are able to share these with their children.[2]

RELIGION AND HAPPINESS IN THE HOME

Stone studied the relationship between church participation and social adjustment of high-school and college youth in Washington. This study disclosed that two-thirds of the boys who said that they were active in religious activities also indicated that their home life had been very

FIGURE 28. Percentage of Washington State College Students, Classified by Participation in Religious Activities, Giving Specified Answers to the Question, "Generally, how happy has your home life been?" *

Participation in Religious Activities	Number of Cases	"Very happy"	"Fairly happy"	"Fairly or very unhappy"
BOYS				
Very Much	88	66	28	6
Somewhat	219	58	37	5
Very Little	241	54	40	6
Not at All	158	48	40	12
GIRLS				
Very Much	128	73	21	6
Somewhat	325	74	22	4
Very Little	196	65	27	8
Not at All	50	58	30	12

* Carol Larson Stone, *Church Participation and Social Adjustment of High School and College Youth* (Washington Agricultural Experiment Stations, Institute of Agricultural Sciences, State College of Washington, Rural Sociology Series on Youth, No. 12, Bulletin 550, May, 1954), p. 15. Reprinted by permission.

[1] "White House Conference on Children in a Democracy," (Washington: United States Children's Bureau Publication No. 272, 1942), pp. 185–186.

[2] *A Healthy Personality for Every Child, Fact Finding Report, A Digest,* Midcentury White House Conference on Children and Youth (Raleigh, N.C.: Health Publications Institute, Inc., 1951), pp. 53 ff.

happy. On the contrary, Figure 28 indicates that about half of those who participated little in church activities considered their homes to be very happy. The figure indicates that the same conclusions were reached for girls.

Stone also found that those high-school and college students who took part in church activities tended to come from homes which were better adjusted than the homes of those who did not participate in religious activities, took part more frequently in school activities, and had a larger circle of friends; and that high-school seniors who shared in church activities had a more wholesome attitude toward "helping their fellowman" and were worried less about problems than those who were not so active. On the basis of her study Stone concluded that young people who participate regularly in church activities will have fewer problems of adjustment in their homes, in their relationships with their peers (their own age group), and in school situations than do those who take little or no part in church activities.[3]

CHURCH MEMBERSHIP, RELIGIOUS ACTIVITY, AND MARITAL ADJUSTMENT

Locke's study indicates that religion is correlated with marital adjustment. He presents two tables which show the relationship between church attendance and marital adjustment. Table 44 (page 438) for the last half of marriage shows that a much larger percentage of the divorced men and women attended church once a month or less while a much larger percentage of the married men and women attended church four or more times a month. This means that fairly steady church attendance is associated with happy marriage.

An analysis of Locke's figures also indicates that when both marriage partners belong to the same church they tend to be happily married while if they belong to different churches or if they do not belong to any church they tend to be in the divorced group. This is shown in Table 45 (page 438) for men and women which compares those who were married and divorced, according to church affiliation.

When both were members of the same church 96 men and 95 women were happily married and only 45 men and 55 women were divorced. But when neither was a member of any church the proportion was re-

[3] Stone, p. 28.

TABLE 44. Regularity of Church Attendance of the Happily Married and Divorced during Last Half of Marriage, by Per Cent, with Critical Ratios of the Difference of Per Cents *

ATTENDANCE MONTHLY	MEN			WOMEN		
	Married N 163	Divorced N 160	CR	Married N 166	Divorced N 182	CR
None	18.4	46.9	5.5	12.7	37.9	5.4
Once or less	28.2	28.1		29.5	27.4	
2 or 3 times	19.6	14.3		16.2	15.5	
4 or more times	33.8	10.7	5.0	41.6	19.2	4.6

* Harvey J. Locke, *Predicting Adjustment in Marriage* (New York: Henry Holt and Company, 1951), p. 241. Copyright © 1951, Holt, Rinehart and Winston, Inc. Reprinted by permission of the publisher.

versed with only 19 men and 20 women in the happily married group as compared to 41 men and 42 women in the divorced group.

These statistics are corroborated by a recent report on a marriage-

TABLE 45. Comparison of Married and Divorced Men and Women in Relation to Types of Church Affiliation *

CHURCH AFFILIATION		Married N = 278	Divorced N = 268	Critical Ratio
One a member	Men	22	37	2.3
Other not a member	Women	26	48	2.37
Both members of same church	Men	96	45	5.4
	Women	95	55	5.21
Neither one members of any church	Men	19	41	3.3
	Women	20	42	2.66

* Harvey J. Locke. Adapted from data used in the study, *Predicting Adjustment in Marriage*, but not reported in that study.

counseling experiment conducted by the Oklahoma City Family Clinic. This clinic, utilizing lawyers, ministers, teachers, business men, and doctors tries to effect reconciliations of couples having marital difficulties who are referred to it by judges and school teachers. The clinic had dealt with 250 couples at the time of the report. Forty per cent were separated, 11 per cent were divorced, 23 per cent had divorces pending. The Clinic was able to save 225 of these marriages or nine out of ten.[4]

[4] DeWitt Reddick, "They Give Marriage a Second Chance," *Child Family Digest*, X, No. 2 (February, 1954).

Only three of these families were attending church when they came to the clinic; the experience of the counselors was that participation in church activities was conducive to reconciliation. Reddick says:

> The Family Council has found that reconciliation becomes almost a certainty if they (the clinic) can persuade the couple to become active in church.[5]

One of the most comprehensive studies in marital adjustment is that of Chesser, who reported in 1957 on data secured from 6,000 marriages.[6] He reports that the highest percentage of happy marriages is found among Protestants (known in England as Non-Conformists), a smaller percentage in the Church of England, and the smallest degree of happiness was discovered in the group that had no religion at all.

In Weeks' analysis of the divorce rate of parents of 6,500 school children in Spokane, Washington, he showed that 24 per cent of marriages of parents without religion ended in divorce in contrast to a failure rate of 17.4 per cent for interfaith marriages. But when both husband and wife were Catholic only 3.8 per cent failed, and when husband and wife were both Protestant some 10.0 per cent failed.[7] These facts indicate that religious participation may be an important factor in marital adjustment, and we need to analyze to what degree this is true.

SPECIFIC RELIGIOUS GROUPS AND MARITAL ADJUSTMENT

As society becomes increasingly diversified in its degrees of education, urbanization, and sophistication, it is impossible for one single type of institution to meet all the needs of all the people. For some individuals liberal religion speaks with a foreign accent and for others an orthodox or conservative approach has lost all value. Consequently religious needs today can only be met by many different types of religious institutions. If it is true that we have many sects and many denominations, it is also true sociologically that these arose to meet different demands from different elements in society. All of them, however, cherish the home and all of them contribute in some ways to the preservation of a sense of sacredness of the home and to the cherishing of the marriage vows. Dr. Samuel Kincheloe has summarized the contribution of churches in general:

---

[5] Reddick, p. 43.

[6] Eustace Chesser, et al., The Sexual, Marital and Family Relationship of English Women (New York: Roy Publishers, 1957).

[7] H. Ashley Weeks, "Differential Divorce Rates by Occupation," Social Forces, XXI (March, 1943), 336 ff.

However pessimistic anyone may be regarding the influence of churches in our society he must recognize that they are dealing with the formation of attitudes, opinions and, eventually, personalities, and doing so with impressive procedures. . . . Churches in our urban society have specialized in the transfer of a great tradition, a "gospel," and according to H. Paul Douglass, a veteran student of church life in America, have done so on a "very profound level." [8]

While the influence of the church is on a profound level, it must necessarily be different to meet different needs. Whether the church is a small rural one-room type or a great city Cathedral, if people come consistently one may be sure both of them are serving basic human needs, and one of these needs is conservation of family life. The following material on churches deals with both their positive and their negative contributions to the family. However, as will be seen when the chapter is finished, the positive contributions are deep and significant.

The findings of Reddick, Locke, and Stone are valuable because they indicate statistically the importance of religion in family life. However, religious groups vary in their beliefs and attitudes, and consequently in their impact on family cohesion. It is important for the student to understand the different orientations of religious groups, and their contributions. In the following pages the association between specific religious approaches and marital adjustment will be presented in terms of case studies and statistical analysis.

The religious groups referred to in this study are not discrete denominational groups. The author is unwilling to name any particular denominations that "fit" the types described here. There is wide diversity even within denominations. Southern churches vary greatly from Northern churches of the same denomination. Many denominations in the East and and Middle West are so different from sister churches on the West Coast that members who transfer from one section to another are not at home. Each individual church has its own history of conservatism or liberalism which sets it off as distinctive from other churches in the denomination. Hence it is more helpful to describe types of churches than to speak of Congregationalists, Methodists, Catholics, etc. The categories proposed here have been utilized in a study of religion and the family and have proved to be of some utility. Individuals who come from different religious groups may relate their own experience to the category into which

[8] Samuel C. Kincheloe, *The American City and Its Church* (New York: Friendship Press, 1938), p. 152. Reprinted by permission.

it fits. The religious groups are placed on a scale; the categories are the sect, the orthodox-conservative, the authoritarian-institutional, the liberal, the Jewish, and the agnostic or non-church groups.

DESCRIPTIONS OF TYPES OF CHURCHES

The Sect Group.   Sect churches are those which are characterized by emotional participation, emphasis on the supernatural, a withdrawal from life, and an otherworldly motivation. These groups tend to secure their members by a cataclysmic emotional experience of conversion. Their definition of happiness always has reference to a code of conduct which will earn eternal life by avoiding sin and by definite acceptance of a "truth" as revealed to that group alone. They interpret the Bible literally and only according to their own "revelation" of what the Bible means. Their hymns dwell on the sinful nature of man, the great moment of being "saved," high hopes of future "glory," and the evil of "worldly" pleasures. The church is the focus of family life and of life in general. Sects are as a rule extremely puritanical and tend to destroy any recreational life for the family. Members of sects may sacrifice family interests to church interests.

Sexual adjustment for young people reared in sect groups is likely to be very difficult. A report of the adolescent history of a girl reared in this type of church illustrates this impact:

> When M. . . . was fourteen years of age she was called upon to speak in Sunday School regarding the evils of dancing. M. . . . had no hesitancy in doing so. She was well informed. She knew all about the lascivious nature of natural man and natural woman and she knew what happened when those "natural" impulses were stimulated. She knew that dancing was a form of petting that stimulated sexual desire in both boys and girls. Dancing meant such close physical contact that it could be regarded in almost the same category as promiscuity. Without doubt it was one of the special tools of the devil to entice youth to sin. Therefore no good Christian boy or girl would ever give way to the temptation to join in Satan's dance. M. . . . gave this address with conviction and with sureness. It was received by the congregation as a sure testimony that "grace" had come to M. . . . What it meant in terms of M. . . .'s later marriage adjustment never occurred to that congregation. M. . . . was speaking "truth." [9]

The Conservative-Orthodox Group.   The conservative-orthodox group has the same type of authority for its religious beliefs as the sect group.

[9] From a case study in the author's files.

Members believe the Bible to be inspired and hold closely to a literal interpretation, although allowance may be made for some deviation in interpretation. In general, the denominations that tend to be subsumed under this heading are the older, more historic groups which still cling to an "orthodox" position but have mellowed to the point of associating with other groups, although they still insist on the uniqueness of their "truth." These groups tend to be legalistic and to have a forbidding ethic, with much reliance for its enforcement on fear of future punishment. They also have a very imposing structure of "should nots" and regard happiness as the result of a rather rigid adherence to institutional codes. This group, however, tends to emphasize thoughtfulness in creed, and does not stress the highly emotional kind of conversion. Their members come as the result of a "letter" or by education in the creed.

This group tends to make much of doctrinal points of view and such outward forms of piety as prayer and church attendance. Sex is often linked with sin in the preaching and the educational work of these churches, which makes adjustment in marriage difficult. The following excerpt from a completed counseling record illustrates such a case:

> This case was referred by a lawyer in Chicago, who called to ask if the counselor would see a girl who had called on him to ask about preventing a divorce. The family consists of Marjorie, the wife; Henry, the husband; and two children, one four and the other twenty months. She had had Junior College training, but the husband had only had four years of high school education. They lived in a duplex owned by her parents, who lived in the other half. The two sides were connected by a door which was never locked.
>
> The focal problem of this case was twofold: in-law trouble and sexual maladjustment. Ever since Marjorie and her husband had moved into the duplex the in-laws had taken over financially for them. They had provided financial help all through the marriage. Although this was done in a kindly way, it still proved to be a club. Marjorie and Henry had no sexual life whatsoever. They had had no sexual contact for over three months; they had had it seldom before that and it was so upsetting to Marjorie that she developed a migraine headache whenever her husband kissed or caressed her.
>
> Marjorie's early life had been very restrictive. She had a set hour to get into the house. She was not allowed to go to movies or to dance. So she lied about it and then lied again to get out of the lie. Her mother thought dancing very immoral and irreligious. Marjorie thought her mother went

"hog wild" over religion. So Marjorie always had to go to her mother's church, which was of the conservative-orthodox type we have described, with great emphasis on the sin of dancing, card playing, movies, sex, and drinking. Furthermore, her mother insisted that this church only had the answer to the need for salvation and everyone outside it was condemned to hell.

Marjorie was an only child, but she felt she had never been loved; in fact, she remembered wondering if she really would ever know what the meaning of love was. Her mother would never allow her to kiss her or anyone else, on the theory that there were "bugs" which one would get. As a small child she remembered that she had not been allowed to see a boy baby until he was diapered. She never had seen a naked boy and felt very guilty because she often wondered what her father really looked like. In high school, when she discovered some things about sex she became very frightened. She was frightened not by the facts themselves but because her mother might find out that she knew these facts. Even though she was married and the mother of two children, she felt that her mother would be very much happier if she could feel that Marjorie knew nothing about sex. She knew that when she kissed her husband she made it as brief as possible lest her mother or father come in, which they did without knocking. All in all, her rigid religious and home background combined to inhibit her almost completely in the area of sexual acceptance and somewhat in the area of social adjustment.[10]

There were many important factors in this case; chief among them was an extreme dependence upon the parents which involved an acceptance of the general puritanism of the parents' religious group. This puritanism includes not only renunciation of sex but disapproval of activities such as card-playing, dancing, and going to the movies, which in our society are means of developing sociability, making friends and finding a mate. Marriage is difficult for a person who does not accept these activities. So is adjustment after marriage.

The Institutional-Authoritarian Group. The institutional-authoritarian churches tend to be the oldest. They have existed long enough to recognize the basic needs of personality and to take account of them in their philosophy of the family. They tend to emphasize authority, creed, and ritual. They regard the Bible and tradition as the sources of truth. They tend to be legalistic and dogmatic, and in their view conformity is the *sine qua non* of the good life. They generally stress the rewards of heaven

[10] From a case study in the author's files.

or of hell as the result of good or evil living. They have a broad outlook on the family and stress its relationship to both the church and society. They generally accept the value of sexual life in marriage but are very emphatic about the evil of any premarital sexual experimentation. Members of these groups tend to be liberal in their views on gambling and drinking as long as they are not indulged in to excess. They do not proscribe card-playing, dancing, or movies. These churches tend to do the thinking for their members and set forth conditions for divorce, use of birth control, religious education of children and all other important family concerns. The following excerpt from a case study indicates how sharply this group influences the conscience of its members:

> Mary Mooney, age 23, first year of graduate school, came to see the marriage counselor because, as her wedding date approached, she began to feel that she would not be able to say "I do" at the altar. She had no doubt about her love for the young man, no doubt about their "fitness" as to education, recreational, or religious harmony. But she felt she was slipping away from the boy. As she was to be married in three weeks, she was most alarmed at this feeling of deep estrangement and fear of marriage to him. The first interview produced no indications of any emotional reaction which might account for this feeling, other than the normal trepidation of entering a new relationship. However, her emotional reaction seemed too intense to allow this to stand as a sufficient explanation of her feelings.
>
> In the second interview Mary immediately introduced the idea that there was something in her background of experience which made her feel that she did not want to get married. She went on to explain that she had allowed her fiancé to caress her and had taken deep pleasure in it. Two days later, she had experienced profound remorse and had gone into something of a depression as a result. She later talked it over with him and they agreed on no more caresses until after the marriage. Nevertheless, when they were alone, they could not seem to escape making love and each time she experienced the same profound pleasure and the same guilt feelings. In trying to discover the cause for such reactions to petting she explained that she had grown up in a _____ home, and had attended a _____ church and that she knew very explicitly that petting was a severe sin. As she talked about it she began to realize that it was her extreme feelings of guilt which were tending to separate her from her fiancé whom she loved dearly.[11]

The institutional-authoritarian group influences family stability by its great insistence upon the religious value of the family by its marriage

[11] From a case study in the author's files.

ritual, and by its great power over the individual conscience. Some of the members of this church find it difficult to overcome the early linkage of sex with sin and conflict between the church's ideas on divorce, religious education of children, birth control, and those accepted by society. Also the tendency to depend upon the church for the answers, rather than upon the creative, problem-solving ability of each person, may cause maladjustments. This group of churches reinforces family cohesion by emphasizing family participation in the activities of the church.

The Liberal Churches. The liberal churches are differentiated from the others in that they accept no one authority for truth. They accept the Bible but they also depend on tradition, on science, and on human reason. They tend to accept divorce if they believe that it is in the interest of the developing personalities of the individuals in the family. They also accept birth control for the spacing of children, and grant the right of each member of the family to choose his own religion. They stress the realization of "eternal life" on earth rather than conformity to a moral code that will win entrance to heaven. They like to be considered "life-centered." Their members are secured by intellectual assent and they stress the intellectual side of religion, and the fellowship it provides, rather than emotional participation or dogmatic belief. Most of them put emphasis upon the full development of the various phases of human personality: physical and mental, social and religious. They fully accept most of the social customs such as card-playing, dancing, and going to the movies, but many of them have firm convictions against drinking and gambling. Many of them accept sex as a God-given aid to family cohesion and are developing ways of helping young people overcome ignorance in this field.

The Jewish Denominations. While all Christian denominations may be classified according to the types given, the Jewish groups have a unique heritage and must be considered separately. In general, the Jewish groups differ from all others in that they emphasize a rational rather than a supernatural, a democratic rather than an authoritarian approach; a "this-worldliness" as opposed to an "other-worldly" frame of ethical reference. There is very little asceticism in Judaism. Jews look on marriage as a way to find peace, to promote comradeship, to add to the enjoyment of life, and to perpetuate the race. "A man who has not a wife is not a complete man," says an ancient rabbi. Sex as such is accepted as a normal part of life and there are allusions to sexual intercourse in the Old Testament and in Rabbinical literature. Their rule has been continence before marriage and fidelity after marriage. Divorce is permitted under

445

circumstances but "The Altar of God sheds tears for one who sheds the companion of his early years." Birth control is accepted, but a family of children is one of the ideals of the group. All three branches of the Jewish church (orthodox, conservative, and reformed) condemn interfaith marriage and regard such marriages as "driving a nail in the coffin of Judaism."

The Agnostic or Nonchurch Groups. While the agnostics or nonchurch groups are religious groups only in a negative sense it is important to understand their concepts. Most of them have a humanitarian ethic which stresses good motives and sound living, but they do not believe it is necessary to refer such beliefs to any authority. Many of their members have carried this thought to its ultimate conclusion; one who has stated his point of view is Bertrand Russell:

> That man is the product of causes which had no prevision of the end they were achieving; that his origin, his growth, his hopes and fears, his loves and his beliefs, are but the outcome of accidental collocations of atoms; that no fire, no heroism, no intensity of thought and feeling, can preserve an individual life beyond the grave; that all the labors of the ages, all the devotion, all the inspiration, all the noonday brightness of human genius, are destined to extinction in the vast death of the solar system— all these things, if not quite beyond dispute, are yet so nearly certain that no philosophy which rejects them can hope to stand.[12]

The problem for young people who classify themselves as agnostics is one of values and motivations. Some navigators use the compass; others use the stars to guide them. But all have some means of establishing directions on the journey. The intellectual honesty of young people who state that they find themselves unable to accept some of the ideas of their forebears is admirable. But this is not enough. Such a declaration is only a negative statement for what one does not believe. How will these people weather the storms of life? By what values will they direct their family destinies? How will they compensate for the inspiration that comes to other individuals from worship? Adjustment to partners who have religious convictions may be a problem because of lack of communication and mutual interests.

The relationship of these religious groups to marital adjustment has been tested in a Los Angeles study of 420 husbands and wives.[13] The

[12] Bertrand Russell, *Mysticism and Logic* (London: Longmans, Green and Company, 1919), pp. 47 and 48. Reprinted by permission.

[13] James A. Peterson, "The Impact of Objective and Subjective Religious Factors on Adjustment and Maladjustment in Marriage," unpublished Ph.D. thesis, University of Southern California, February, 1951.

sample was obtained by utilizing a previous study made by Shevky and Williams of the characteristics of census tracts in Los Angeles County. The Shevky-Williams study rated the census tracts on the basis of two scales, one measuring socio-economic status and the other the degree of urbanization.

The census tracts were then arranged in a grid, and nine social areas were constructed on this grid. While the Shevky-Williams study also indicated those areas which were high in segregation, this part of the investigation was not utilized by the religious study. The sample consisted of all white persons.

The sample of 420 persons came from the group with a central urbanization index. One-third of the sample came from low-rating socio-economic census tracts, one-third from medium-rating census tracts and the other one-third from high-rating social areas. Houses were picked at random within representative blocks in each of these areas. Two interviewers visited each home, one to interview the wife and the other to interview the husband.

Each couple was asked detailed questions regarding their religious background, present church participation and religious activities. In addition they were asked the special questions which make up the Locke Adjustment Scale.[14] When the interviewing was completed the answers were transferred to Hollerith cards, and correlations were made between individual adjustment scores and religious factors. Comparisons were made regarding the impact of religious participation and membership in various types of churches in terms of marital adjustment. The Chi Square test was used as a measure of the significance of differences between these groups. This is a mathematical test which determines whether or not these differences might have been due to chance. A significance of .01 means that in ninety-nine out of one hundred times such a difference could not be due to chance.

Table 46 depicts the relation of high and low adjustment of men and women to religious types. The table indicates that men belonging to liberal religious groups have the highest level of adjustment while men belonging to institutional-authoritarian groups have the lowest level of adjustment. The high level of adjustment of the no-church group indicates some contradiction of the commonly held belief that those who are

[14] Harvey J. Locke, *Predicting Adjustment in Marriage: A Comparison of a Divorced and a Happily Married Group* (New York: Henry Holt and Company, 1951). Copyright Holt, Rinehart and Winston, Inc.

not members of churches fail in marital adjustment. The results for women are similar to those for men although women with no-church relationship have a somewhat lower adjustment score than men belonging to this group.

TABLE 46. Relation of High and Low Adjustment of Men and Women to Religious Types (by Per Cent) *

| | N = 196 (men) | | | | N = 186 (women) | |
	Sect Conservative- Orthodox	Institutional Authoritarian	Liberal	Jewish	No Church- Agnostic	Chi Square
	PER CENT	PER CENT	PER CENT	PER CENT	PER CENT	
MEN						
Low-adjust- ment score	28	45	22	23	23	22.21
High-adjust- ment score	72	55	78	77	77	Significant at .01 level
WOMEN						
Low-adjust- ment score	23	32	18	15	35	11.157
High-adjust- ment score	77	68	82	85	65	Significant at .03 level

* Adapted from Peterson, pp. 144–146.

DISAGREEMENT ON SEX AND RELIGIOUS BELIEF

It was important to see whether these differences in adjustment scores of men and women belonging to different religious types would be duplicated in other phases of family life. Questions were raised regarding disagreement on sexual matters and on guilt feelings regarding sexual relations. Tables 47 and 48 (p. 449) indicate that there are important differences recorded in this pilot study along the lines suggested by the descriptions of the types. Table 47 measures the degree of guilt experienced by men and women of different religious types, indicates again that the liberal, no-church, and Jewish groups experienced less guilt than

TABLE 47. Comparison of Church Members by Religious Types in Terms of Guilt Feelings Regarding Sexual Relations *

	Sect Conservative-Orthodox		Institutional Authoritarian		Liberal		Jewish		No church-Agnostic	
	NO.	PER CENT	NO.	PER CENT	NO.	PER CENT	NO.	PER CENT	NO.	PER CENT
TOTAL	56		66		106		20		141	
Those who had some guilt feelings	16	29	14	21	12	11	2	10	9	6

* Adapted from Peterson, p. 210.

the others. Table 48 compares church members by religious types on disagreement regarding sexual matters for both men and women. The liberal and no-church groups have the lowest degree of disagreement regarding sexual matters.

TABLE 48. Comparison of Church Members by Religious Types on Disagreement Regarding Sexual Matters, Both Men and Women N = 414 *

	Sect Conservative-Orthodox		Institutional Authoritarian		Liberal		Jewish		No church-Agnostic	
	NO.	PER CENT	NO.	PER CENT	NO.	PER CENT	NO.	PER CENT	NO.	PER CENT
TOTAL	56	100	66	100	106	100	20	100	141	100
No. who disagreed on sexual matters	14	25	21	31	20	18	5	25	13	9

* Adapted from Peterson, p. 210.

Guilt Over Birth Control and Religious Membership. A still further testing of the reactions of these religious types was made by comparing their guilt reactions to the use of birth control. Here the statistical material bears out very strongly previous findings. Table 49 presents a

TABLE 49. Comparison of Church Members by Religious Types in Terms of Guilt Feelings Regarding Birth Control   N = 420 *

	Sect Conservative-Orthodox		Institutional Authoritarian		Liberal		Jewish		No church-Agnostic	
	NO.	PER CENT	NO.	PER CENT	NO.	PER CENT	NO.	PER CENT	NO.	PER CENT
TOTAL	56		66		106		20		141	
No. who had some degree of guilt	7	12	13	20	4	4	4	20	3	2

* Adapted from Peterson, p. 214.

comparison of church members by religious type in terms of guilt feelings regarding birth control. Again the liberal group and the no-church group show the lowest percentage of guilt feelings.

These statistical conclusions indicate that there is a significant difference in adjustment to marriage according to membership in various types of religious groups. In terms of preparation for marriage and marriage adjustment, the student will want to review his religious background to see whether or not it may in some way present special problems for him. The student will wish to analyze such differences as may exist between himself and his intended mate, to discover whether or not those differences will be a special hazard to happiness in marriage. Case studies indicate some of the specific reasons why there is a difference in adjustment between religious groups. This material will now be presented.

TYPES OF RELIGIOUS INSTITUTIONS AND MARRIAGE ADJUSTMENT

The importance in marriage adjustment of membership and participation in these groups may be indicated by the following points:

1. Members of those groups (sect-conservative or institutional-authoritarian) which are very zealous about their denomination are apt to bring stress into their marriage, if the partner is not a member, by constantly putting pressure on him to join and to participate.

2. Members of those groups (sect-conservative-orthodox) which are

"other-worldly" and ascetic sometimes have great difficulty in sexual and social adjustment. The values to which they give allegiance and their life-time motivation are renunciatory of the "pleasures of the flesh." Consequently, problems of sexual and social adjustment arise unless both members of the marriage equally believe in this accent on their lives.

3. Members of those groups (institutional-authoritarian) which may be described as rigidly ethical have a tendency to be so forbidding in premarital education that individuals carry into marriage such restraints that their sexual adjustment is often unhappy. However, this group sometimes achieves a better social adjustment because they accept smoking, movies, dancing, and controlled drinking.

4. Members of those liberal groups who accept the sexual side of marriage and stress a "life-centered" approach sometimes fail to give their children and young people a sense of responsibility and value so that they enter marriage without determination to make it succeed.

5. Members of those groups which condemn birth control (institutional-authoritarian) may find themselves in conflict with their church or with their own consciences if they use this method of family planning. Many church members who develop these guilt feelings find that they interfere with their sexual adjustment.

6. Interreligious group marriages will be productive of conflict when the persons involved have differing attitudes toward such things as gambling, drinking, card-playing, movies, dancing.

7. Interreligious group marriages will be productive of conflict when they involve differing attitudes toward family planning and birth control.

8. Interreligious group marriages will be productive of conflict when they involve competition about the religious education of the children.

9. Interreligious group marriages will be productive of conflict when they involve a major difference in degree of religious interest or religious orientation.

10. Interreligious group marriages may not achieve the highest degree of integration because the family is not unified in celebrating the great festival occasions in life.

THE IMPACT OF RELIGION ON FAMILY INTEGRATION

What impact does religion have on the integration or diffusion of the family? Lenski's 1961 study of "The Religion Factor" gives some definitive answers to this question. Using a highly complex sampling procedure to obtain a representative group, his workers interviewed some 656 persons. To measure the relationship of membership in different religious groups to relatives, he undertook an analysis of visiting habits. The following table shows the results.

TABLE 50. Percentage Reporting Weekly Visits with Relatives and with Neighbors, by Socio-Religious Groups *

	A *Percentage Visiting Relatives Every Week*	B *Percentage Visiting Neighbors Every Week*	A/B
Jews	75	23	3.3
White Catholics	56	24	2.3
White Protestants	49	34	1.4
Negro Protestants	46	42	1.1

* Gerhard Lenski, *The Religious Factor* (Garden City, New York: Doubleday and Company, Inc., 1961). Copyright © 1961 by Gerhard Lenski. Reprinted by permission of Doubleday and Company, Inc.

Lenski added to this evidence his findings regarding the number of relatives outside the immediate family living in the same dwelling unit, the influence of friends, and the sources of political decisions.[15] In comparing the white Catholics, Jews, and white Protestants he concludes that

> White Protestants seem more involved in, and favorably disposed toward, groups and social ties where the bond of kinship is absent.[16]

In carrying his thought of the closer ties of the Catholic family into the realm of divorce, Lenski found that Jews and Protestants were much more likely to be divorced than Catholics, but because Protestants remarry in much higher proportions, the number currently divorced is not very much different.[17] Unfortunately, Lenski does not include figures for desertion, and this is a serious error because Catholics everywhere are underrepresented in divorce figures and overrepresented in desertion statistics.

Lenski developed a measure of child training practices which he put on a dimension moving from intellectual heteronomy (obedience to the dictates of others) to intellectual autonomy (thinking for oneself.)[18] In assessing the meaning of his findings and those of other studies, he concludes:

[15] Lenski, pp. 196–197.   [16] Lenski, p. 197.   [17] Lenski, p. 198.
[18] Lenski, p. 200.

452

If we may judge from the responses of Detroiters to our question concerning the importance of intellectual autonomy, Catholics and Negro Protestants are more likely than either Jews or White Protestants to be responsive to appeals to limit individual freedom and increase authority. The latter are more likely to respond to appeals to limit authority and increase individual freedom.[19]

Lenski raises far-reaching questions about the meaning of these findings for a "stable and effective democratic society," but he does not raise any question of the meaning of these conclusions for the future of the American family. Yet, these implications may be more important. If it is true that the American family is going through radical changes in function and role, one of the essential attributes of adjustment must be sensitivity to difference of relations between individual family and church, and the growth of creative adaptability in adjusting to these changes. Indeed, both the Locke and Burgess-Wallin study showed that adaptability was one of the major dimensions of good adjustment. If, then, significant sections of the religious population seem to be training the next generation in ways that preclude adaptability, we would not be surprised if there was maladjustment in marriage for that group. Some proof that this is already happening may be seen in the Peterson study which indicated a lower adjustment average score for sect and authoritarian church groups than for the liberal Protestants. Of course, a great deal more documentation is essential before one can be certain that one can generalize on the Lenski or Peterson research findings. Yet a religion provides a set of values and a norm for roles, and it is difficult to imagine that these have no relevance to family functioning. The future student of the American family must broaden the scope of inquiry and take cognizance of the possibility of a different influence on adjustment by various specific religious segments.

Here we quote Lenski by way of summary:

> Depending on the socio-religious group to which a person belongs, the probabilities are increased or decreased that he will enjoy his occupation, indulge in installment buying, save to achieve objectives far in the future, believe in the American Dream, vote Republican, favor the welfare state, take a liberal view on the issue of freedom of speech, oppose racial integration in the schools, migrate to another community, maintain close ties with his family, develop a commitment to the principle of intellectual autonomy, have a large family, complete a given unit of education, or

[19] Lenski, p. 204. Reprinted by permission of the publisher.

453

rise in the class system. These are only a few of the consequences which we have observed to be associated with differences in socio-religious group membership, and the position of individuals in these groups.[20]

THE POSITIVE CONTRIBUTIONS OF RELIGION TO THE FAMILY

Thus far we have discussed the ways in which religion may cause problems in marriage adjustment either by matching two very diverse religious types or by producing social and sexual inhibitions within the individual. In the concluding section we deal with specific ways in which religion contributes to family integration, family growth, and family happiness.

The Psychological Contributions of Religion. Since man is not perfect, life is often frustrating and irritating. Storms of temper and depressions born of fear and anxiety disturb men and women. They react emotionally and hurt one another. One hour they are lovers and the next hour there is hostility between them. One of the most difficult lessons to learn in life is to accept our own imperfections. When this is done, we are able to forgive others. Forgiveness promotes growth in cohesiveness in the family. Forgiveness is at the heart of all Hebraic-Christian beliefs. Hosea taught the Jewish nation to forgive as he forgave his erring wife, and Jesus forgave those who drove nails into His hands and feet. Those who have listened since childhood to Jesus' insistence that we cleanse the inside of the cup, and that no one is perfect are probably more humble than those who are nonreligious. Self-examination in prayer stimulates growth and induces humility. And the person who is humble, who recognizes the grossness of his own egocentricity and the wilfulness of his own personal aggressions, may truly forgive others. Thus, religion helps overcome those egocentric blocks to happiness in marriage that are well-nigh universal. As Bowman says:

> On the one hand, religion plays a part in reducing and eliminating destructive conflict within the individual, between one individual and others, and between an individual and the nonhuman elements in his environment. It produces a peace of mind, "the peace of God which passeth all understanding," important not only in and for itself but because of its contagious nature. By its focusing upon things bigger than self, religion plays a part in reducing the discomfiture, discouragement, anxiety, and confusion aris-

[20] Lenski, p. 289. Reprinted by permission of the publisher.

454

ing from personal problems. Again because of this focus, it makes possible working together for a common end without comparison of one person with another and even without measurement of the contribution of a given individual. It aids in eliminating competition, because success in moving toward a common end is felt to depend upon each one's doing his full share in the light of his capacities, rather than upon one's doing more than another. Such working together can produce a oneness second to none in human life. On the other hand, religion may intensify constructive conflict, for it sharpens the individual's determination to struggle against those elements in life that distort personalities, frustrate worthy purposes, and sacrifice one person to the selfish interest of another.[21]

The Character Contributions of Religion. The ideal of the church tradition is neighborliness and loving service. When the traveler fell among thieves it was a man with love in his heart who stopped and bound up the traveler's wounds and carried him to the inn. The ideal of loving service comes very close to the mutuality which contributes to happy marital relationships. Religion shifts the attention from the self to others. But it also takes motives into account. Attention to others which is part of a conscious effort to gain personal success or augment status is eventually productive of conflict. So Paul in his Hymn of Love says that even though one gives all he has, yes, even his body to be burned, if he does not have love, it is nothing. It is the love that is self-forgetting and spontaneous that makes the home a place of happy adjustment.

Religion helps marriage in that it tends to produce that type of character structure which is most productive of marital happiness.

The Contributions of Worship. Worship contributes to family unity by supplying a focus for family activity. Worship is a ritual, and like all rituals tends to have a binding force when it is performed consistently and persistently. Anything which the family experiences together with satisfaction makes the family more of a unity. The ritual of dressing for church, walking or riding together to church, sitting together and then discussing the service are experiences which strengthen the bonds of unity.

Worship also contributes to the growth of the spirit of the family by consistently holding up to its members aspirations that demand growth. The ideals stressed by churches are brotherhood, reconciliation, peace, kindness, and redemption. In worship one endeavors to relate oneself to the meaning of existence and to the core reality of life. Hours of worship

[21] Henry Bowman, *Marriage for Moderns*, 4th ed. (New York: McGraw-Hill Book Company, Inc., 1960), pp. 336–337. Reprinted by permission of the publisher.

are hours of the uplifted heart and the questing spirit. The frontiers of conscience and mind are pushed outward and the concern for others is sensitized. This experience may bring to a man and a woman a sense of trust, of faith, and of destiny that changes meaningless drifting into purposeful living, that transforms the confused, ambivalent individual into a person with perspective. In saying this we are not unmindful of the morbidity of some overly puritanical faiths which are barren of beauty and destructive of tenderness. Nevertheless, worship of God, the searching of conscience in prayer, the singing of hymns of brotherhood, and the relating of our experience to ideal goals and aims constitute for many a moving and constructive growth experience.

The Contribution of the Religious Counselor. Religious counseling includes not only the Catholic confessional but also Protestant and Jewish counseling. Catholics ease the burden on their souls by confessing their sins. They are assured of pardon when they have done penance and have promised not to repeat their mistakes. In Protestant churches this experience takes a different form. Men and women go to the study of their ministers and confess there. Today many of the modern Protestant seminaries are training their ministers in techniques of pastoral counseling. These ministers are learning ways to implement their religious concern for their members by counseling them about family problems. People in trouble often turn to their priests or ministers. The modern minister also is being trained to recognize those problems which are so severe that referral is wise. A priest or a minister contributes to the balance of the troubled individual who feels guilty by allowing the troubled person to unburden himself and by helping him to achieve a sense of his own worth.

A major contribution of ministers, priests, and rabbis is the growing practice of premarital counseling in which a couple is helped to prepare more adequately for marriage.

The Contribution of Fellowship. Urban life is generally a lonely life. Bars are often inviting to individuals not only because of the liquor they dispense but also because of the company they provide—people with whom to laugh and talk. Churches have specific fellowship groups and some of these are directly focused on family life. Young married peoples' groups concentrate on ways of achieving better harmony in marriage, on discovering new recreational patterns, and on raising the ideals of their members. Such groups often have a therapeutic value for couples who may not have solved all of their adjustment problems. Many churches have discussion groups on child psychology, adolescent problems, and

456

religious education. These groups bring to their members the best in modern thought about the rearing of children.

There are other groups in churches such as high school, college or young adult groups in which more and more stress is put on wholesome recreation, on developing values in dating and courtship, and on the discernment necessary for wise marriage choice.

Festival Occasions and Family Cohesion. Christmas, Easter, Thanksgiving, may only be seasons of drinking and hilarity. But for some families they are periods when their own pleasures are somewhat determined by institutional practices and broader contacts. The story of Mary and her Baby in the manger, of the shepherds and the wise men bringing gifts, in its simple, moving beauty touches all of the family, adds to family appreciation of itself, and gives added dimension to the gifts which are shared. In like manner all festival occasions are among the high points of life and those who have a religious orientation seem to find deep beauty and meaning in them which is reflected in their family attitudes.

CONCLUSION

Worship, prayer, religious festival occasions, and church fellowship tend to increase reverence for life. People are thus led to view their hours on earth with a special sense of mission and a sense of responsibility for those close and far from them; to see that personality has an eternal worth and that the family has a fundamental dignity that demands respect.

In this chapter certain of the important ways in which religion and religious participation are related to marital adjustment have been analyzed. It is impossible to generalize about the impact of a specific religious group on the married life or its members because of the great diversity of influences compounded under the general title of religion. Therefore a typing of religious groups was made to help the student objectify the way his or her religion may have influenced his or her preparation for marriage, or may influence adjustment with a person of another religion. The concluding section dealt with the positive benefits of religion to marriage.

PROJECTS

1. Invite a Catholic priest, a Jewish rabbi, and a Protestant minister to discuss their points of agreement and of difference in their beliefs about the family.

2. If any member of the class knows of such a situation, let that member report on the problems which are causing conflict in a marriage between people of different faiths.
3. If any member of the class knows of such a situation, let that member report on a family in which differences due to religion have been happily solved.

READINGS

BOVET, THEODOR. *A Handbook to Marriage*. New York, Doubleday and Company, Inc. (A Doubleday Dolphin Book C23), originally published as *Love, Skill and Mystery*. New York, Longmans, Green, and Company, Ltd., 1958.

BOWMAN, HENRY A. *Marriage for Moderns*. 4th ed. New York, McGraw-Hill Book Company, Inc., 1960.

GROVES, ERNEST R. *Christianity and the Family*. New York, The Macmillan Company, 1943.

LANDIS, JUDSON T. and MARY G. LANDIS. *Building a Successful Marriage*. 3rd ed., Englewood Cliffs, N.J., Prentice-Hall, Inc., 1958, Chapter XIII.

LENSKI, GERHARD. *The Religious Factor*. Garden City, New York, Doubleday and Company, Inc., 1961.

WIEMAN, REGINA WESCOTT. *The Family Lives Its Religion*. New York, Harper and Brothers, 1941. Copyright Harper and Row, Publishers.

RECORDING

The Hazards of Interfaith Marriage is a twenty-minute socio-drama illustrating the adjustment problems of those who belong to different religious faiths. It has an introduction to the socio-drama by James A. Peterson. Educational Recording Services, 5922 Abernathy Drive, Los Angeles 45, California.

CHAPTER 19

Recreational
Contributions
to Family
Life

If I had my life to live over again, I would have made it a rule to read some poetry and listen to some music at least once a week; for perhaps the parts of my brain now atrophied would then have been kept alive through use. The loss of these tastes is a loss of happiness, and may possibly be injurious to the intellect, and more probably to the moral character, by enfeebling part of our nature. CHARLES DARWIN

INTRODUCTION

SIGNS across the nation state: "the family that plays together stays together." There is no one of the various aspects of life, recreational, educational, religious, or economic, that in itself is the magic key to marital happiness. A blend of achievement in all of them insures the fullness of creative life that is the family goal. Of all these, recreation has been the one most often overlooked in the literature on preparing for marriage. Only one book in those canvassed for this study contained more than a brief reference to the basic importance of recreation in marital adjustment. A superficial glance at our environment is enough to convince us of the need for recreation. Properly developed, recreation is a major force for family cohesion.

LEISURE-TIME ACTIVITY AND MARRIAGE ADJUSTMENT

Many of us are destined to live and work in the great, gray canyons of cities where there is little sunshine and grass, where the sirens howl and crowds mill like cattle. There we worship the great gods of Speed, Efficiency, and Noise. Our campass becomes the clock, and our horizon is always a deadline. The tempo of the business world, of the social world, of the political world moves faster and faster, and man runs, anxious and driven, through the shadowy canyons. Small wonder that half of our hospital beds are filled with those who could not stand the smoke, the tension, the bustle, the nervous derelicts burned out by the friction of such an accelerated and frequently unlovely life.

But not everyone succumbs to the pace of modern life. Consider John Smith, for example. He seems very serene in the midst of the bustle of his office, calm when crises come, relaxed at the beginning and at the end of the day. Men in his office look at him and say, "I wonder what John's secret is, he is seldom troubled." There is not one, but several answers. But one of them is John's recreational life. In the middle of the week, he leaves his office early, he meets his wife for dinner, and they explore the various restaurants of different nationality groups. Sometimes they stay after dinner and dance to a Swiss accordion, sometimes they leave after a leisurely meal and see a play or hear a concert or visit friends. But the midweek ritual is never missed. On weekends, John is out in his garden, or is playing with a group of children who have come to know that they have fun at John's house on Saturdays, or is on a picnic or a ski trip with his family. John occasionally goes to church on Sunday, but on other occasions he may take his family to the beach or on a long drive. John is not overcome by the vastness of urban complexities; he uses these to enrich his life. He is not overcome by the nervous pressures of his occupation because he has a balanced existence. He has perspective. He knows that his economic life is important, that his contribution of energy and of his time is essential, but he does not give all of himself. He renders unto Caesar what is Caesar's but he keeps for his family and for his God that which is theirs. As a result, John Smith will not die of a premature heart attack, he will not have ulcers, he will not burn out. He will enjoy it all, laugh a great deal, and look back on his life as a worthwhile investment. Recreation not only gives him balance, it makes his other efforts worthwhile.

460

Despite the growth of spectator sports and commercialized leisure time activities there are contrary trends. The "do-it-yourself" market, the boating boom, the rise in family camping, home movies, the backyard swimming pool and barbecue all give evidence that there are also family-centered trends in recreation. It may be that these family activities are helping to slow down the "flight" from the home, and the tendency toward age-stratified and sex-stratified recreation. Nelson Foote summarizes this trend:

> Family living in the residential suburb has come to consist almost entirely of play . . . the seriousness with which homemaking is pursued should not conceal its playful nature, because work and play at their best are indistinguishable.[1]

Though authors of books on the family have not paid much attention to recreation, those who have studied family adjustment have asked questions about its importance. Locke studied two areas. One is exemplified by the following statement which individuals checked to indicate their use of leisure.

> In leisure time both husband and wife prefer to be "on the go," both prefer to stay at home, one prefers to be "on the go" and the other to stay home.[2]

The second dealt with agreement on recreation: the couples in his study were asked to check, on a six-point scale, the degree to which they felt they agreed on recreational pursuits. When Locke came to determine the importance of his findings about recreation in terms of their importance on how the answers to these questions were related to marital adjustment, he compared these answers to all the replies to his other adjustment questions. Then he determined the rank order of their importance among all the items that differentiated the happily married and the divorced. There were some thirty-four items in all. Leisure time rated in sixth place, while the question on agreement on recreational pursuits rated in twenty-sixth place. This seems to indicate that differences about doing things together are of more importance than what is done. Furthermore, it appears that differences in the way leisure time is used are highly important in determining the adjustment of a man and wife. On the other hand, Williamson found that the degree of agreement on recreation was signifi-

[1] Nelson Foote, "Family Living as Play," *Marriage and Family Living*, XVII, No. 4 (Nov., 1955), 297.
[2] Harvey J. Locke, *Predicting Adjustment in Marriage: A Comparison of a Divorced and a Happily Married Group* (New York: Henry Holt and Company, 1951), p. 48. Copyright © 1951 Holt, Rinehart and Winston, Inc.

cant in differentiating between the well-adjusted and the poorly adjusted groups in his sample. Williamson's study corroborates our conclusion that recreation is one of the major factors in marriage adjustment.

Kaplin interprets leisure as a composite of the following elements:

1. an antithesis to "work" as an economic function
2. a pleasant expectation and recollection
3. a minimum of involuntary social-role obligations *
4. a psychological perception of freedom
5. a close relation to the values of the culture
6. the inclusion of an entire range from inconsequence and insignificance to weightiness and importance
7. often, but not necessarily, an activity characterized by the element of play

"Leisure is none of these by itself but all together in one emphasis or another." [3]

In attempting to discover the degree to which the contemporary family uses money and leisure time, we shall follow several sociological studies. The first is a study of Crestwood Heights by Seeley, Seim and Loasley.[4] While this study was aimed primarily at child-rearing methods in the urban world, it produced several insightful conclusions which bear on the problems of shifting status and role functions. The first observation confirms our earlier conclusion that so much of the life of the individuals of the family is ordered by other institutions besides the family that any continuity of family interaction is difficult. They say:

> An urban population with its ramifying interdependence is also compelled to adopt synchronized schedules. Work and even play are regulated, not only because life is determined in numerous ways by the exactitudes of machines, but also because so many social activities . . . must occur at predetermined times in order that the day's events may run smoothly and the work of the city may be done.[5]

So both father and mother not only find their time schedules disrupted by delivering children to activities, but they, themselves, are endlessly involved in committees and meetings and planning activities outside the

---

* Kaplan means that during leisure pursuits individuals must be free from the constraints and duties associated with roles in more formal social settings; one can relax.

[3] Max Kaplan, *Leisure in America: A Social Inquiry* (New York: John Wiley and Sons, Inc., 1960), pp. 22 ff.

[4] John B. Seeley, R. Alexander Seim, and Elizabeth W. Loasley, *Crestwood Heights* (New York: Basic Books, 1956).

[5] Seeley, Seim, and Loasley, p. 64.

home. The functions of education, religion and recreation, once centered in the home, now take place in other places. But parents are expected also to leave the home for planning these events. Thus, they participate to some degree, but not in an intimate face-to-face relationship with their own children. Thus, the amount of time the family has to itself for its own leisure-time activities is strictly limited.

Furthermore, much of the leisure-time efforts of Crestwood Heights people is subtly directed towards status seeking. Participation in various social and recreational groups tends to be another "other-directed" activity for the sake of achieving status. So the authors say:

> A second set of activities generally follows but partly cross-cuts these (work tasks): the child's extra-curricular life; the father's quasi-social luncheon or business contact at the club; the mother's shopping and theater expeditions or her club work. These may not be "work," but they are much too seriously pursued, too near the heart of career goals, to be dismissed as "play." . . .[6]

In our second chapter we analyzed "the shift of importance from family role to occupational role." Seeley, *et al.* seem to confirm this shift in that they feel the emotional response that children, men, and women find in community associations is not only more important, but perhaps the inevitable result of the breakdown of intimacy of the family.

> Though mixed with other attractions, the element of intimacy in clubs and associations is none the less significant. Together with occupation, they have become important auxiliaries in creating a solidarity which cannot now be achieved solely with the primary group. It is perhaps inevitable that there should be many such external ties for each individual in a society which stresses independent activity dissociated almost entirely from the kinship system or other habitual primary ties. A man's business or professional affiliations in Crestwood Heights may hold out to him more emotional security than his family circle.[7]

One other study substantiates this conclusion. In their Detroit study, Blood and Wolfe discovered that the specialization and isolation involved in modern occupation leaves women so lonely that companionship in doing things together with the husband far outstrips love, understanding, standard of living, the chance to have children as the most valuable thing in marriage.[8] The most essential aspect of companionship is enjoyment of

[6] Seeley, Seim, and Loasley, pp. 74–75.   [7] Seeley, Seim, and Loasley, p. 293.
[8] Robert O. Blood, Jr. and Donald M. Wolfe, *Husbands and Wives* (New York: The Free Press of Glencoe, 1960), p. 150. Copyright The Macmillan Company.

leisure time with that person. It is not, then, surprising that Blood and Wolfe found that recreation ranks second out of eight in total disagreements between husband and wife. It is ironic that modern society in its organizational complexities not only increases man's need for intimate companionship at home, but at the same time precludes meeting those needs!

How does the employment of women affect the leisure-time activity of the family? Fortunately, there is research material available to illumine any such relationship. Nye has reported the results of his study of 1993 mothers in three Washington towns of from 10,000 to 30,000 population.[9] He found that employed mothers participate less in recreational activities that are time consuming, but they show no differences from nonworking mothers in spectator or commercial recreation.

But it is not only the degree to which husband and wife participate together that is important. Locke has shown that the nature of their shared activities differentiates two groups of happily married and divorced persons. The happily married group shared more frequently such activities as church, reading, radio, sports, and music. Conversely, a larger per cent of the divorced sample reported enjoying drinking and dancing. So Cunningham and Johannis conclude:

> Locke's study convincingly demonstrates that marital adjustment/maladjustment is, among other factors, dependent on the nature of the nonwork time behavior patterns of husband and wife.[10]

When we consider that projections of the work week to 1974 suggest a thirty-two to thirty-five hour employment span, we can visualize how significant patterns of leisure-time family behavior may be to the future of husband-wife interaction. Now, in summarizing the studies we have reported, we may conclude that:

1. Increasingly, leisure-time activities are being carried on separately by individual members of the family; they take place away from the home and sometimes serve emotional needs of individuals the nuclear family does not meet.

[9] Ivan Nye, "Employment Status and Recreational Behavior of Mothers," *Pacific Sociological Review*, II (Fall, 1955), 69–72.

[10] Kenneth R. Cunningham and Theodore B. Johannis, Jr., "Research on the Family and Leisure: A Review and Critique of Selected Studies," *The Family Life Coordinator*, IX, Nos. 1–2 (Sept.–Dec., 1960), 29. This review brings into focus by way of summary most of the significant research in this area.

2. Leisure-time activities are increasingly used as symbols of status or as means of enhancing status in the community.
3. Leisure-time activities for an undisclosed portion of our families, but certainly for families of employed wives, rarely involve social participation but lean towards spectator and commercial entertainment, thus repeating a pattern of dependence on the larger community already seen in other family functions.
4. Conflict over leisure-time activities is a highly important aspect of marital adjustment in terms of two considerations; Blood and Wolfe stress the factor of *time* shared in doing things together and Locke reports the importance of the *nature* of the activity itself.

More research is needed in this field. It is essential to study patterns of family nonwork time as related to stages in the family cycle, and as related to role definitions in terms of both family and nonfamily role expectations. Leisure is an important aspect of personal and family health, and young couples can enhance their prospect of adjustment by studying the way their leisure-time expectations complement or conflict with the expectations of their mates.

We now turn to a more subjective evaluation of the meaning of recreation to the family. How shall a family plan for constructive use of its leisure hours? Most of the studies of leisure have swiftly counted the number of hours individuals or families devote to recreation without paying basic attention to the meaning those activities have for the person or group.[11] Any given leisure-time pursuit can fulfill a variety of needs so it is impossible to classify all of them. It is more important to stress the dynamic function leisure performs. Gerson has attempted such an evaluation in his study of leisure and its contribution to the marital satisfactions of college married couples.[12] This study investigated the amount and uses of leisure time as these were related to the attitudes toward leisure of some fifty couples.

Over two-thirds of the individuals had less than twenty-one hours of leisure per week. The majority of couples were satisfied with their leisure-time activities, but those individuals who were "relatively dissatisfied" in marriage indicated that they:

[11] Marjorie N. Dodd and Robert J. Havighurst, "The Meanings of Leisure," *Social Forces,* XXXVII (May, 1959), 355–360.
[12] Walter M. Gerson, "Leisure and Marital Satisfaction of College Married Students," *Marriage and Family Living,* XXII, No. 4 (1960), 360–361.

(1) were dissatisfied with the kinds of their leisure pursuits;

(2) spent relatively little of their leisure time *together* with their spouses;

(3) were dissatisfied with the adjustments with their spouses in the area of leisure behavior;

(4) felt that their financial situations restricted their leisure activities to a great degree;

(5) disagreed quite often with their spouses about matters of leisure activity; and

(6) frequently had feelings that they had missed out on a lot of fun by marrying before one or the other had finished school.[13]

Couples who were more happily married reported just the reverse of the unhappy group. The author concludes that the amount of time given to leisure is not an important variable, but various attitudes about leisure are related to marital adjustment.[14]

This study indicates that the amount of time a couple spends together in leisure pursuits is not as important to good adjustment as is agreement on types of activities, and the way the couple interacts in any recreational situation. If a husband and wife come from homes characterized by different types of recreational activities, a concentrated effort to agree on those that please both is important. Furthermore, there must be adaptability in leisure-time activities because each phase of the family development cycle has special limitations and opportunities. The husband and wife cannot plan the same type of activity for a family that includes a boy of three and a girl of one as that type they enjoyed before the children arrived.

RECREATION AND FAMILY PATTERNS OF INTERACTION

What happens while the family is engrossed in a game of parchesi or ring-toss or tennis may influence what happens when it is planning the budget or discussing the family diet. There are personality clashes, competitions for status, difficulties in waiting for one's turn at speaking or moving or playing. The same personalities are involved. But the spirit of the occasion is different. The family organizing a game or the married couple setting out to play tennis are the same individuals who have been pondering the budget, but their orientation is different. Now they

[13] Gerson, p. 361.   [14] Gerson, p. 361.

are intent on having a good time. Memories of past good times come to their aid. Their expectation is that if there are clashes they will be resolved with humor, or at least with a minimum of difficulty. And when the conflicts do arise these expectations of fun, and the good-humored solutions of the past, help the couple or the family settle the conflict without too much difficulty. The whole spirit of the game influences their interaction. Consequently, they deal with these personality problems as something new and interesting. It is true that recreation may restore a family unity that has been sadly shredded by routine.

How does it do this? Thomas and Znaniecki, in their study, *The Polish Peasant,* concluded that every individual has a need or a wish for new experience. That which is repeated comes to be also drab. But play is never drab. In play a couple finds new stimulus, and if their play is full of adventure, it supplies the answer to this fundamental need of personality. A marriage marked by constant creative adventuring, in talk and in activities, in the home and outside it, will not be habit-worn and dry, but a union in which new interests and constant fun intensify companionship. So recreation contributes to the couple's real unity by adding appreciation and by multiplying common interests.

Psychological Contributions of Recreation to Marriage. Unless one partner is completely submissive or unless a couple is very dependent, they are bound to have conflicts. As has been pointed out, it is never easy for a person reared in one sort of family, with its particular set of expectations, to be joined to another person with an entirely different history. And if partners are full of life and energy, there will be many occasions when the gears grind. Again, few of us pass through childhood and adolescence or face the business of life without developing some hostilities. The outlet for hostility is aggression. We tend to express this aggression in irritation, annoyance or even anger at our partners, and, later, at our children. The very closeness of the partner produces tension. Many marriages break under the strain of aggressions which are expressed too violently and too persistently in the family circle.

Nevertheless these aggressions must somehow be expressed. If they are not verbalized or brought to the surface, serious strain is introduced into marriage. The family needs to develop a method of handling aggressions intelligently.

One answer to this problem is suggested by Dr. Karl Menninger, who, speaking before the American Association of Health, Physical Education and Recreation in Los Angeles, on April 10, 1952, had this to say:

467

Uncontrolled aggressions within us are major causes of mental illness. Adequate play is a means of channeling off excess aggressions. Play is one of the best antidotes for low morale and other conditions that might lead to mental illnesses.

In competitive family play, aggression is part and parcel of the activity. We take out our feelings in the game. We are, in a restricted way, carrying on a duel. Our needs to get even, to batter down, to let out latent hostility against our mates are all part of the motivation in a bridge game or a golf game. But the expression of those feelings is generally modified by the spirit of the game itself. We do get rid of the feeling but in a way that is not divisive of family unity.

> Slavson has pointed out that recreation can help release energies and give expression to hidden and unconscious motivations. He warns against undue repression of unconscious drives. In the formation of character, too strict repression sometimes begets disease, while sublimation and redirection lead to mental and emotional health. . . . Joyful activities help individuals forget their troubles, suppressed longings, and thwarted impulses. It must be remembered that leisure pursuits do not always accomplish desired results, and recreation does not always fit individual needs.[15]

Hard physical effort such as scaling a mountain or hiking a great distance or lugging a canoe around a portage or playing a hard-fought set of tennis—all these enable us to release some of the aggressions built up within us. We invest ourselves in these activities and when they are finished there has taken place a kind of catharsis that has value.

There is a type of psychological help for children called play therapy which is based on the definite recognition that creative play enables the child to release feelings hitherto inhibited. In the same way the play of husband and wife releases pent-up feelings and clears the way for more positive feelings.

Humor and Marital Adjustment. While humor is not limited to periods of leisure-time participation, we can discuss it in this chapter because psychologically recreation and humor have identical functions. The sociologist has long recognized that "many kinds of cultural patterns, among them jokes, games and sports, various kinds of ritual, and regu-

---

[15] Martin Neumeyer and Esther S. Neumeyer, *Leisure and Recreation*, 3rd ed. (New York: The Ronald Press Company, 1958), p. 180. Martin H. Neumeyer and Esther S. Neumeyer, *Leisure and Recreation*, A Study of Leisure and Recreation in Their Sociological Aspects, Third Edition. Copyright © 1958 The Ronald Press Company. Reprinted by permission of the publisher. The reference in the first line is to S. R. Slavson's *Recreation and Total Personality* (New York: Association Press, 1946).

lated forms of conflict, provide outlets for the tensions generated by social restraints and by cultural and structural inconsistencies." [16] One of the best known examples of diluting hostility by the use of humor is the mother-in-law joke. Duvall quotes many of these—this one does not disguise its hostility:

> "I thought you ought to know that your dog bit my mother-in-law yesterday."
> "He did? Then I suppose you want me to settle for damages."
> "No, not at all, I just came to see how much you want for your dog." [17]

There are a great many marriage jokes which likewise seem to have a core of hostility.[18] Many of their themes center around the conflicts between the old and the new roles for women. Duvall seems to feel that mother-in-law jokes likewise support "some older value system that may or may not have meaning for modern families." I do not think this is an accurate analysis of either marriage or mother-in-law humor. The structure of the family and the role functions of its members are changing. The change brings strain and hostile feelings. Jokes tend to dissipate that hostility and dissolve aggressions in laughter.

All humor is based partially on a sense of proportion. If the family has a sense of proportion it can laugh over "spilled milk" and not have an angry exchange over an inconsequential event. If the husband is mature enough to look at his wife's minor error with the checkbook in relation to the total value she has for him, he can laugh about it. So, too, the wife can laugh at his little exaggerations because compared to his general integrity they are nothing.

Shipman found in his study of speech thresholds of husbands and wives that "happiness is definitely related to the absence of irritation to voice tone. . . ." [19] It is very difficult to be irritated by laughter or humorous tones. Couples do well to cultivate a sense of proportion and thus a sense of humor.

Physical Contributions of Recreation. George Bernard Shaw, who lived to a great old age, contended that he got his exercise attending the funerals of his friends who exercised. But, Shaw to the contrary, good

---

[16] Ely Chinoy, *Society, An Introduction to Sociology* (New York: Random House, 1961), p. 343.

[17] Evelyn Duvall, *In Laws: Pro and Con* (New York: Association Press, 1954), p. 29.

[18] Mildred Perlis, "The Social Functions of Marriage Wit," *Marriage and Family Living* (Feb., 1954), 49–50.

[19] Gordon Shipman, "Speech Thresholds and Voice Tolerance in Marital Interaction," *Marriage and Family Living*, XXII, No. 3 (Aug., 1960), 203–209.

health is related to recreation. Good health is also related to happy marriages, while constant illness or poor vitality are associated with marital maladjustment.

The sluggish, anemic, devitalized individual can hardly be stimulating to a member of the other sex. Active recreation sends the individual's blood coursing through his arteries. When it returns to his lungs it is well purified because he is breathing deeply. His muscles harden, and every gland, bone, and sinew renews its youth. When he eats, it is with a natural hunger that makes eating a happy experience. His grace of movement and his attractiveness of form improve. His sexual capacity is augmented, and he becomes a more inviting sexual partner. Some gynecologists believe that much of the sexual frustration of modern women is due to their diet and lack of exercise. If they had a more normal physical routine, they would have sufficient energy to share vigorously in sexual pleasures. Not the least of the contributions of happy, zestful, outdoor participation in sports or games is the achievement of a more adequate body to carry on a more adequate life.

Recreation and Family Atmosphere. Recreational events are the "sunshine among shadows," the highlights of sometimes gray marital experience. But every experience in the family influences all other experiences. When a couple solves difficulties in a game, this provides them with a new pattern for solving difficulties in other areas. After several such recreational experiences the budget-planning session will be conducted in a little different atmosphere, with more gaiety and good humor.

The budget session will be conducted in a different atmosphere because those who participated in the game have come to think of each other in a different way. We say "think" but we should rather say "feel," for recreational experiences produce rather profound emotional changes.

What is this new interactive pattern? It has many ingredients. Instead of the picture of opposition and competition we have now a picture of the mate who cooperates in having a good time. There is a sense of "withness" rather than a sense of "againstness" which is so prevalent in many families. Again the buoyancy that goes with recreation changes the emotional approach to the rest of the marriage. If marriage is limited merely to facing problems, life is indeed a serious business. But if these problem-solving sessions are interspersed with fun sessions, the mood of the recreational hour carries over. Consequently the "tone" of the interaction is changed. Zest and enthusiasm have been introduced into this marriage and they cannot be compartmentalized and restricted to the

470

picnic, the game, or the trip; they "spill over" into the rest of the marriage.

The Contribution of Recreation to Parent-child Interaction. Wieman, in her chapter on "Fun," summarizes with great acuity the contribution of recreation to parent-child relationships:

> Creative interaction is a novel relationship where parents and children are equals under the immediate authority of the rules and courtesies of the game. This is more of a test for us parents than we always realize. For one thing, the children have the opportunity to observe how we interact with others when we are not the immediate authorities and cannot run things. The converse side of this is that we parents now having to obey orders taste the experience of our children who usually are the only ones who must do as they are told. We are reminded how it feels not to be boss but to be bossed. For another thing, quite often it is the children who excel in games or sports, and they then have the opportunity to observe us in the inferior position. Can we qualify as "good sports"? Third, it becomes apparent to the children what each of us parents values most in fun. We may be childish and think that winning is the big thing, or we may be mature and believe that playing *together* counts more than anything else.
>
> Of course, these possible values in creative fun are lost if we parents either pretend an interest in the fun or feign an indifference to losing or to acting under an unfavorable rule when the children sense that we actually do care.
>
> But the two best values that come out of the relation of equality required in fun are these: First, the parents, being relieved of management and responsibility, can release aspects of themselves usually subdued or inhibited. They can react more nearly with the full self and with joyful spontaneity. Second, the parents have a generous opportunity to balance their usual commands, requests and guiding standards with such graces as can be expressed through kindly jokes, through gracious subordination to the guidance of a child who plays well, and through tactful reinforcement of the child who is daringly experimenting or courageously holding to his own intention against the advice of others.[20]

We may add to this concise description of the values of family play the observation that the points made earlier regarding the contribution of recreation to the psychological adjustment between husband and wife apply equally to the relationship to parents and children.

The value of play in character building is more and more understood by leaders of recreation. Neumeyer says:

> In recent years recreation leaders have become definitely interested in character building, because of the close relationship between the child's play and his character. Possibly the greatest opportunity of a child's character lies in the proper attitude toward play and in the habits formed. . . .
>
> Recreation by means of games and sports is a valuable medium for lessons in gentlemanly and honorable sportsmanship. To win honestly, lose graciously, and to cooperate generously have made men out of selfish and cowardly individuals. Self-imposed discipline has moral values. Mastery over self fits a person to exert greater control over others and to meet critical situations more adequately.[21]

Finally, enthusiastic participation in games and play provides for children as well as for their parents an outlet which is highly necessary. There is no more basic need for child development than intensive and exertive play.

Recreation Results in Family Cohesion. Recreation in the sense of joyful, spontaneous participation not only gives a different tone to family interaction but changes the positions of those in the family. It reduces social distance. It results in greater solidarity. Of course anything that a couple does together that they view positively binds them closely together. Family rituals, admiring a new baby, handling a knotty problem of finance successfully, agreeing on a new purchase or on how to handle a mother-in-law or worshipping together or sharing a good meal brings them together more and more. But recreation contributes to cohesion in a special way.

When two people play together their mood is one of appreciation. They tend to say: "I had a wonderful time playing golf" or "It was a nice dance" or "Didn't we enjoy that bridge game?" When the activity has been spiced with laughter or very zestful participation, there is a hangover of happy memory. This extends to those who have shared the activity with them. The husband identifies his joy with his wife who made it possible, or, at least, who participated with him. One then does not tend to say as in a contemporary song, "I cannot understand why in a world full of peaches I had to choose a lemon," but one says, "Yes, that's my wife and my companion in life."

Balzac says that "there is a monster that devours everything in marriage

[21] Neumeyer and Neumeyer, pp. 158–160.

who must constantly be vanquished, his name is habit." So many marriages have been blighted by routines in which each partner comes to take the other one for granted or to think of the other as an uninteresting person that rule-of-thumb advice to families having difficulty is to go on a trip or take a second honeymoon.

Planning Family Recreation. There is no set form of recreation that gives the same stimulus to different types of individuals. A form of play that commands the entire allegiance of one family may be anathema to another. The first consideration in the choice of recreational activity is that it meet the needs of the individuals who are participating. A quiet game may provide as valuable results as a violent one. Dr. Menninger in the speech mentioned earlier said that "a chess game to one man may be as effective a relief as some violent sport like basketball to another."

The study made by Lehman and Witty and the National Recreation Association, published under the title of *The Psychology of Play Activities,* stressed the varieties of play. In endeavoring to discover the favorite leisure-time pursuit of thousands of children and youth under twenty-two they discovered that looking at the Sunday funny papers, reading books and newspapers, chewing gum, playing catch, drawing, running and romping, going to the movies, watching others participate in sports, participating themselves in games, riding in automobiles, playing cards, and many other individual interests were checked.[22] The final statistics indicated that less than 50 per cent of the group participated in any one special activity. This means that no one should attempt to find satisfaction in a sport or hobby simply because it is popular. He should rather follow his own inclination. One individual will prefer chess, another tennis, another will simply concentrate on conversation.

Recreational life should be an expression of an individual's interests and talents. While it is not necessary for every person to be a champion, one will probably not enjoy those sports or games in which he is hopelessly awkward or clumsy or in which his participation means an almost certain loss of status and a constant effort just to keep up with the others instead of a sense of freedom in participating. The development of some skill in trout-casting, serving a tennis ball, bidding a hand in bridge or in carrying on a conversation naturally adds to the enjoyment of the experience. Those who do very poorly in one area may do well in another. Whatever one chooses, one's recreational interests ought to have the

[22] H. C. Lehman and P. A. Witty, *The Psychology of Play Activities* (New York: A. S. Barnes and Company, 1927).

possibility of life-long enjoyment. Continuity makes for skill, for long-term friendships with partners, and for a host of happy memories.

It really makes little difference what hobby or what sport a family chooses. The important thing is that it represent an interest which will integrate the group and contribute to the growth of each member. It is the attitude of play associated with the activity that is important. If the activity ever comes to be thought of as a duty, or as work, it had best be quickly dropped. The degree of happiness and enthusiasm marking the participation of each member of the family is the final test of its value.

As more hours are released from occupational pursuits, there is more time available for leisure. Neumeyer lists ten over-all areas of leisure-time activity which have brought satisfaction to millions of Americans.[23] He lists reading, literary appreciation, creative writing, music, art, creative crafts, scientific experimentation, dramatics, pageantry, athletics, games, speech, traveling, and exploring. In addition he speaks of "sociability as an art" and stresses the satisfactions of parties, stimulating conversation and letter writing. With such a broad band of possible leisure-time activities every person should be able to find rewarding leisure-time pursuits. Furthermore, almost every community has a park or school facility where all noncontact sports can be played at moderate cost. It does not require an expensive outlay on equipment to fully enjoy group participation today.

Having considered these general principles of choice, we come to the question of exactly what leisure-time activities a woman and a man may take part in together. It was thought until quite recently that the physical endowments of a man and a woman are so different that they had best be separated for recreational pursuits. Today's stress on coeducational play has resulted in the awareness that both girls and boys may enjoy most activities. This is of value because skill and interest are developed in activities which both may enjoy throughout life. Certainly there is an absurd contradiction in the suggestion that a woman may stand beside a man in a factory and do the same work he is doing but not play beside him on a volleyball court.

Some students say that some leisure-time pursuits are very expensive financially and that they, therefore, will not have the resources to do these things after marriage. But this is generally an excuse and not a fact. The equipment for recreation is within oneself, and communitywise there are so many free opportunities that, irrespective of financial status, one may

[23] Neumeyer and Neumeyer, pp. 205 ff.

have a very full experience at any age. Marjorie Greenbie has described what is needed for recreation more poignantly than anyone else. She says:

> Because happiness is so personal, there is only one place for a man to begin his search for it, and that is in himself. The doctors of leisure now talk of equipment for the use of spare time, endowments for community recreation, swimming pools, workshops. All these things are good. But the primary equipment for leisure consists in the possession of two eyes, two ears, two hands and two feet, with the addition of numerous other items such as a heart, a memory, and a tongue—so long as they are all your own, and not mortgaged to any mass interest, mass habit, mass advertising, or mass hooey whatsoever. One can get along with a fraction of this equipment, if one really runs it one's self, for one's own satisfaction. But some personal possessions of this sort are fundamental, and if a man has all the Lord usually provides, he has so much equipment that it is any wonder he ever puts himself out to get any more.[24]

What is needed for a full recreational life is not a full purse but a bountiful imagination and a desire to make of one's married life a rewarding adventure in sharing many stimulating activities.

TELEVISION AND RECREATION IN THE HOME

One of the elements in family disintegration is "flight from the home." Does television tend to bring the family back? A series of interesting studies indicate that it may have the tendency. Dr. Edward McDonagh studied an anonymous community in Southern California to ascertain new family habits due to television. This study focused on a community large enough, and with sufficient range of social groupings, to be valid for wide generalization. Out of some eight hundred families, ranging from the professional class to the unemployed, the study staff selected a television-owning group and a nontelevision group, nearly identical in education, social, and economic composition. Personal interviews were conducted by trained interviewers, who employed a carefully compiled questionnaire.

That the "flight from the home" has been arrested is demonstrated by this table which shows a change in visiting habits of television and nontelevision families. Sixty-three per cent of the television families were visiting other families less often as compared to 16 per cent of the nontelevision families.

[24] Marjorie B. Greenbie, *The Arts of Leisure* (New York: McGraw-Hill Book Company, Inc., 1935), p. 5. Reprinted by permission.

TABLE 51. Difference of Television on Family Visiting *

	TELEVISION FAMILIES		NONTELEVISION FAMILIES	
	Number	Percentage	Number	Percentage
More	4	4.2	24	25.5
Less	63	66.3	16	17.0
Same	28	29.5	54	57.5

* Data from Edward C. McDonagh, "Television and the Family," *Sociology and Social Research*, XXXV (Nov.–Dec., 1950), No. 2, 121. Reprinted by permission.

New York University, collaborating with Cunningham and Walsh, a New York agency, in a continuing study of an anonymous community located forty miles from New York, sent sixteen researchers to interview some 3,007 television families and many nontelevision families. Their "census" showed that 16 per cent of the members of television families are away from home in the evening in contrast to 25 per cent of the nontelevision families.

If it is true that families spend more time at home after buying a television set, it logically follows that some of their activities outside the home have diminished. A clue to such a major shift of family life may be seen in reports of attendance at movies. McDonagh found an appreciable decline:

TABLE 52. Movie Attendance and Television *

	TELEVISION FAMILIES		NONTELEVISION FAMILIES	
	Number	Percentage	Number	Percentage
More	3	3.2	13	13.9
Less	76	80.0	24	25.5
Same	16	16.8	57	60.6

* Adapted from Edward C. McDonagh, p. 121. Reprinted by permission.

The Videotown Census shows that twice as many members of nontelevision families attend movies as do members of homes having television sets.

What has happened to radio listening in the family since the advent of television? This question also has received careful scrutiny by the researchers. McDonagh reported as in Table 53 on the increase or decrease

TABLE 53. Radio Listening and Television *

	TELEVISION FAMILIES		NONTELEVISION FAMILIES	
	Number	Percentage	Number	Percentage
More	0	0	17	18.1
Less	84	88.4	12	12.8
Same	11	11.6	65	69.1

* Adapted from Edward C. McDonagh, p. 120. Reprinted by permission.

in radio listening: 84 percent of the television families listened less to radio as compared to 12 per cent of the nontelevision families. These findings are corroborated by a study made in the Middle West for the John Meck Industries of Plymouth, Indiana, and reported in July, 1950 (Table 54).

TABLE 54. Radio Listening in Families Owning Television *

	High Income	Low Income
Listen about the same	22.2	14.3
Listen less	77.8	85.7

* Adapted from data from *Broadcasting* magazine, July 10, 1950, p. 3. Reprinted by permission.

Relatively few families are all at home together before 5:00 p.m.; hence television is making its bid precisely at the hour when the family gathers. What relative difference is there between the behavior of radio families and television families in respect to family participation when listening? The Princeton University study is the only one which has analyzed this difference statistically, and its findings are perhaps the most impressive of any research findings to date. This study shows that 91.6 of television families listen together as compared to 27.4 of radio families (Table 55). This means that there is a new cohesiveness in the family—a finding borne out by individual comments gathered by the University of Southern California and Princeton surveys. Typical comments from television homes were: "The family now stays home all the time and watches the

TABLE 55. Family Listening to the Same Program *

	Radio	Television
Family listens together	27.4	91.6
Family does not listen together	72.6	8.4

* Adapted from data from *Broadcasting* magazine, December 11, 1950, p. 40. Reprinted by permission.

same programs—turn it on at 3:30 p.m. and we watch until 10:00 p.m. We never go anywhere—my husband was awfully restless and never wanted to stay at home, but now he wants to watch the sports contests on TV." Sixty-six per cent of those who answered the questionnaires drawn up by Michael stated that "it was their frank opinion that TV served to bring all of the family closer together." However, television cuts down conversation, the intimate face-to-face communication that sociologists believe is so important in the formation of attitudes and friendships. McDonagh found a decrease in conversation. Sixty-two per cent of television families are talking less as compared with 15 per cent of non-television families.

Our Telecast Children. Parents who note the devotion of children to television viewing are sometimes disturbed by the extent of viewing time and the quality of programs the children watch. The following table,

TABLE 56. Children's Hours Spent Watching Television and at School *

AGE	SCHOOL TIME		TV TIME	
	Daily	Yearly	Daily	Yearly
3	0	0	.75	274
4	0	0	1.50	548
5	3	540	2.25	821
6–8	4.5	810	Wk. Days 2.50	936
			Holidays 3.00	
9–11	5.5	990	" "	936
12–17	6.	1,080	" "	936
Total for Age 3–17		12,420		12,875

* Adapted from Table IV-16, Comparison of Hours Spent on Television and in School, ages 3–17 (San Francisco), Wilbur Schramm, Jack Lyle and Edwin B. Parker, *Television in the Lives of Our Children* (Stanford University Press: Stanford California, 1961), p. 225. Reprinted by permission of the Board of Trustees of Leland Stanford Junior University.

adapted from the studies of Schramm, Lyle and Parker, show that children spend more time watching television than they do at school.

What the effects of such extensive viewing may be is another concern of parents. Schramm *et al.* indicate that the basic effect of both fantasy and reality type programs depends upon the mental ability, social norms, and social relationships of the child.[25] The child who is well adjusted and has incorporated social norms will not be adversely affected. Television does not harm children's eyes if proper viewing conditions are maintained.[26]

When they attempted to discover the impact of television viewing on learning experiences, the investigators found that the effect depended on the I.Q. of the watchers as the following summary table indicates.

TABLE 57. Effect of Television on Information Levels *

| Intelligence | AMOUNT OF VIEWING OF TELEVISION | |
	Above Average	Below Average
High	Probably less well informed than comparable children	Probably better informed if selects reality experiences
Middle	Probably not much difference	Probably not much difference
Low	Perhaps slightly better informed	Probably not much difference

* Adapted from material from Schramm, *et al.*, p. 152.

If television restricts the growth of our brightest children this is an unfortunate development.

On the other hand, television seems not to increase aggression, passivity, or delinquent tendencies of normal children.[27] But it may accentuate the difficulties of children who are already disturbed. An already aggressive child will learn mechanisms of aggression. A passive child will escape further by means of immersing himself in the fantasies of television. As far as juvenile delinquency is concerned, this study concludes that "the most television can do is to feed the malignant impulses that already exist." [28]

Nevertheless, television does bring to the child a great variety of exciting and deviant adult experiences. Parents have an obligation not

[25] Schramm, *et al.*, p. 144.　　[26] Schramm, *et al.*, p. 147.
[27] Schramm, *et al.*, pp. 157–166.　　[28] Schramm, *et al.*, p. 166.

only to help their children develop such stable personalities that they will not be influenced by such programs, but also to guide the child's television viewing. They must give their children a sense of inner security, of being loved and of belonging,[29] but they should also screen what comes on the screen. Many parents use television as a disciplinary tool or as a baby sitter and seem indifferent to the emotional diet furnished the child. With other parents, the type of program to be viewed and hours of viewing become focal points of tension and recrimination. As our evidence seems to indicate that television absorbs a child during more hours than does school, all of these questions must receive more and more attention from parents. As educational television develops, there will be more opportunity for parents to exercise selectivity in program choice.

Television and the Aged. More positive is the contribution of television to the older members of the family who have done their work in life and find their last decade or two filled with an exasperating number of empty hours. Such persons may have looked forward to retirement only to find it strangely empty of meaning. Many are unable to participate in the vigorous pastimes of their more virile years. Furthermore, a great many more individuals are living longer than before. For older persons television has much promise. Television is so virile, so enthusiastic, and so varied in its fare that a great many older people are finding it the answer to a long-felt need. For them, television provides a source of education and entertainment. Undoubtedly, it will become of increasing value to those who can no longer go to the ball game or the church service but may attend both at home.

CONCLUSION

One of the major trends of contemporary family life is the shift from home recreation to commercialized entertainment. This shift is accompanied by more and more watching and less and less participation. Furthermore, commercialized recreation tends to fragment the family by its organization on an age-level basis. Television has added to the limitation of activity, in that it requires only the minimum exertion of twisting a dial. On the other hand, television does bring the family together. It gives the family a core of common experiences which are binding in nature. It is particularly valuable to the shut-ins, the ill, and the aged who may find the television screen a window upon the world.

[29] Schramm, *et al.,* p. 182.

480

PROJECTS

1. Have each member of the class list his leisure-time interests which will later contribute to binding the family together.
2. Discuss commercialized recreation and analyze what percentage of recreational time each member of the class gives to it.
3. Analyze your own television habits, now and in preparatory school. Do you confirm the Schramm findings?

READINGS

CUNNINGHAM, K. R. "The Meaning of 'Leisure': An Analysis of Community Studies," *The Family Life Coordinator*, January, 1961.

DRAPER, E. *Entertaining Is Fun*. New York, Doubleday, Doran and Company, 1941.

GREENBIE, MARJORIE. *The Arts of Leisure*. New York, McGraw-Hill Book Company, Inc., 1935.

NEUMEYER, MARTIN H. and ESTHER S. *Leisure and Recreation*. 3rd ed. New York, The Ronald Press, 1958.

SCHRAMM, W., JACK LYLE and EDWIN B. PARKER. *Television in the Lives of Our Children*. Stanford, California, Stanford University Press, 1961.

SLAVSON, S. R. *Recreation and the Total Personality*. New York. Association Press, 1946.

CHAPTER 20

Contributions of Conflict to Family Cohesion

INTRODUCTION

AFTER the honeymoon, most couples face some conflict during their period of adjustment. These conflicts arise because of the necessity of bringing two distinct personalities into alignment. Marriage always imposes the obligation of compromising on some wishes, some habits, and some values which have been held sacred by one of the partners. The fact that two individuals come from different families and from different segments of a heterogeneous culture means that there must necessarily be problems in adjusting their life patterns. In this chapter we are concerned with the ways of achieving pair harmony and cohesion.

Conflict may be viewed in two ways: in the negative sense, conflict may be dreaded as a threat to marital stability. Those who have come from homes in which conflict has been continuous and disruptive may vow that they will sacrifice anything for harmony. Indeed in a recent discussion group on adjustment in marriage, a wife objected bitterly to the thought that there might be any positive outcome as the result of conflict. She said:

> The idea of marriage ought always to be an ideal of harmony. I resent any suggestion that conflict can bring anything but broken hearts and social distance into the relationship between a husband and a wife.

482

Later she said that in her home she had been victimized by twenty-five years of never ending conflict so that in her own marriage she wanted peace at all costs. But her parents' conflicts had never been adjusted. It was always a compromise with incompleteness. While the actual details of this marriage are not available, it is probable that the basic conflicts were never clarified or ventilated.

The second way to view conflict is to regard it as both a tribute to character depth and a means to the promotion of a final family cohesion. Individuals with values so superficial that they can easily adjust to anyone or to any situation generally have little of worth to share. It is the person with strong convictions and well-oriented values who comes into conflicts with others. So the very strength of some early family disturbances is an indication of the strength and resources which each of the partners will ultimately contribute to the partnership. Thus, "peace" may mean not only the absence of conflict but also the absence of personality substance. While it is not necessary to conclude that conflict is thus the prerequisite for every full marriage, it is often the harbinger of a union of deep meaning and finally of steady direction. Again, conflicts may be the stepping-stones to a marriage of maximum cohesiveness combined with a maximum development of personality for both partners. The ideal of marriage is not to eliminate areas of conflict but rather to face them courageously so that new values and new solidarity will appear. Some couples involved in an interfaith marriage solve their problem by dropping out of all religious participation. Likewise, some men try to solve the problem of conflict over the use of money by simply turning over their checks to their wives and allowing the wives to decide how the money shall be used. They eliminate the conflicts by never discussing them. The problems are solved by default. For the yielding individual, something of meaning has been sacrificed and the total family configuration of values has become weaker because of it. This type of resolution of conflict is a form of withdrawal which eventually weakens the structure of family unity and certainly weakens the interests and values of those in the family. On the other hand, in some matters about which one or both partners do not feel strongly, to overlook or forget the problem is not damaging. Many minor conflicts are solved in this way.

We are speaking here of the normal types of conflict which are contingent upon normal differences in temperament, cultural patterns, ritualistic systems, and expected roles in the family. Where conflict is rooted in severe neurotic needs, therapeutic help is essential as has been indicated in a preceding chapter. When the causes of conflict in the contemporary family have been established, it will be possible to develop ways of dealing with the conflicts that will promote family cohesion.

GENERAL CAUSES OF FAMILY CONFLICT

The more recent studies of marriage indicate the relative importance of areas of conflict. In Table 58, taken from Locke's study, it will be noted that much conflict centers about the traditional functions of the family—economic, recreational, social, religious, and sexual. There are important differences between the married and divorced samples. For instance only one item was checked by more than 20 per cent of the happy men but 13 items were checked by more than 20 per cent of the divorced men. The happily married and divorced differed significantly in the following five categories: (1) affectional and sex relationship, (2) socially disapproved behavior, (3) economic problems, (4) individualistic, and (5) miscellaneous difficulties.

DIFFERENCES IN PERSONALITY CONFIGURATIONS

Individuals expect different things from marriage because of their diverse experiences in the homes in which they grew up. They expect different patterns in marriage because they come from different regions, nationality groups, or social classes which have different definitions of marriage and family life. In our chapter on economic considerations in wise marriage choice, some attention was paid to the importance of clashes resulting from differences in work, status, and the use of money.

Other research findings seem to indicate substantial differences in various types of marital behavior in the various social classes. Kinsey's research, for example, shows radical differences in sexual behavior, and in sexual morality, among men of different social classes.[1] Because of the nature of his research, Kinsey's findings must be regarded as hypothetical, but they indicate that from lower social classes men have a greater intensity of sexual drive and less control of that drive than men from the middle and upper classes.

Another investigation studied practices in child training. A study of upper-middle- and upper-lower-class Chicago families showed that they

[1] Alfred C. Kinsey, W. B. Pomeroy, and C. E. Martin, *Sexual Behavior in the Human Male* (Philadelphia: W. B. Saunders Company, 1948).

484

T A B L E 58. Per Cent of Happily Married and Divorced Checking Items as Serious Marital Difficulties, with Critical Ratios of the Difference of Per Cents *

ITEM	MEN			WOMEN		
	Married N = 111	*Divorced* N = 123	CR	*Married* N = 125	*Divorced* N = 147	CR
A. Affectional and sex relationships.						
1. Mate paid attention to (became familiar with) another person	2.7	65.9	10.1	5.6	73.5	11.3
2. Lack of mutual affection (no longer in love)	4.5	60.2	9.0	1.6	61.2	10.3
3. Adultery	0.9	43.9	7.7	1.6	55.1	9.6
4. Unsatisfying sex relations	8.1	46.3	6.5	5.6	32.7	5.6
5. Venereal disease	0.0	1.6		0.8	12.2	3.7
6. Unsatisfied desire to have children	2.7	8.1	1.8	8.8	3.4	1.9
7. Sterility of husband or wife	0.9	3.3		4.8	0.7	2.1
B. Economic difficulties						
1. Mate's attempt to control my spending money	9.0	26.8	3.5	7.2	21.1	3.2
2. Other difficulties over money	14.4	34.1	3.5	19.2	38.1	3.4
3. Nonsupport	0.0	7.3	2.9	0.0	49.0	9.1
4. Desertion	0.0	20.3	5.0	0.0	27.2	6.3
C. Socially disapproved behavior						
1. Drunkenness	2.7	26.0	5.0	1.6	56.5	9.7
2. Gambling	2.7	6.5		3.2	26.5	5.2
3. Mate sent to jail	0.0	4.9	2.4	0.0	16.3	4.7
D. Individualistic behavior						
1. Do not have mutual friends	10.8	38.2	4.8	6.4	25.2	4.2
2. Selfishness and lack of cooperation	6.3	22.0	3.4	12.0	29.9	3.6
E. Miscellaneous items						
1. Interference of in-laws	17.1	52.8	5.7	20.0	29.9	1.9
2. Ill health	3.6	13.8	2.7	15.2	10.2	
3. Constant bickering	5.4	48.0	7.3	8.8	34.7	5.1
F. Undifferentiating items						
1. Different amusement interests	28.8	34.1		20.0	28.6	
2. Religious differences	6.3	8.1		4.8	7.5	
3. Cruelty to step-children	0.0	0.0		0.0	0.0	
4. Other reasons	6.3	12.2		15.2	19.0	
G. No difficulties at all	38.7	0.0	7.6	27.2	0.0	6.8

* Data from Table 12 in Harvey J. Locke, *Predicting Adjustment in Marriage: A Comparison of a Divorced and a Happily Married Group* (New York: Henry Holt and Company, 1951), pp. 75–76. Copyright © 1951, Holt, Rinehart and Winston, Inc. Reprinted by permission of the publisher.

differed markedly in their regulations regarding movie attendance, the enforcement of an afternoon nap, learning to wash dishes, cook, and sew, the age considered proper for weaning, training in bowel and bladder control.[2] These differences are reflected in the way individuals react when they are faced with these specific problems. The following excerpt from the case of Harry and Margaret illustrates what happens in terms of child training. Harry said:

> I came to you because I am losing respect for my wife. She gives in to the children at all times. When I get home I like a little order and at least some peace. In our home we always respected the wishes of Father when he got back from the office. But it isn't so with my kids. When I get home they climb all over me. They even sass me. They won't eat what is put before them and if I insist my wife says that modern child training methods are against forcing children to eat. The same thing happens when I reprimand them for being nasty or swearing. She says they need to get this out of their system. I think once in a while children need to learn to repress some things. I had to and it hasn't hurt me any. In fact I think I get along better because I learned to respect the wishes of others. No matter what it is my kids do my wife acts as though they were gods. I think she just doesn't want to run the risk of alienating them by making them behave.

But Margaret had an entirely different point of view:

> My husband doesn't understand children at all, Just because he was raised with the switch, he thinks that's the best way. But our little girl had polio when she was four and she needs all the love and all the encouragement she can get. We quarrel about their freedom because he wants them to learn to be quiet and mannerly. We quarrel about their eating because he wants them to learn to eat anything we happen to have on the table. We quarrel about their discipline because I think it's good for them to express themselves and get their feelings out in the open but he says it's disrespectful. If he were a little more tender and understanding, the children would love him more. They try to reach him by romping but he can't even respond to that. I think if he had been raised with more love and less severity he could love his children more and I want them to grow up to be loving persons.[3]

Both of these parents wanted the best for their children. Both thought they knew exactly what the best was. That best was the pattern of train-

[2] Allison Davis and Robert J. Havighurst, "Social Class and Color Differences in Child-Rearing," *American Sociological Review*, XI (1946), 698–710.
[3] From a case study in the author's files.

ing in which they had been reared. This illustration could be duplicated in dozens of case histories where basic differences in values or life patterns are related to social, class, or family backgrounds. The factor of interclass marriage is important because its accentuates conflict. As Burgess and Locke point out, "the United States has wide cultural differences in folkways by regions, by rural and urban areas, by various nationality stocks, and by social classes." [4] Over 50 per cent of the population in this country moved between 1940 and 1950. As individuals come into new neighborhoods and into new regions, it is inevitable that they will marry persons who have grown up with a different set of values and expectations regarding child rearing, sexual life, and other phases of matrimony. Since differences in personality configuration due to membership in different social classes or to residence in different regions are basic, they have very real potentialities for conflict.

VALUES AND MARITAL CONFLICT

Values are objects, or actions, or ideas which are viewed as having worth for an individual. They, too, vary with our cultural backgrounds. How important are differences in values, beliefs, customs, or family patterns in causing difficulty in the family? Of course there are some specific conflicts over certain traditional problems which seem important. Locke found that:

> Conflict over drinking, reading, sports, and parties was reported by a larger per cent of divorced men; conflict over drinking was reported by one fourth of the divorced and by one seventh of the married. For women, the activities where conflict was reported by a larger per cent of divorced than married were: going to church, drinking, and sports; drinking as a source of conflict was reported by one half of the divorced and by one fifth of the married.[5]

The importance of values, beliefs, ethical attitudes, and moral concepts has been strikingly indicated in an unpublished Ph.D. dissertation by Glover. Table 59 on page 488 illustrates the importance of values and beliefs to young people as well as the concern caused by differences between themselves and their prospective mates. Beliefs, values,

---

[4] Ernest W. Burgess, Harvey J. Locke and Mary Margaret Thomes, *The Family, From Institution to Companionship*, 3rd ed. (New York: The American Book Company, 1963), p. 375.

[5] Locke, pp. 260–261. Reprinted by permission of the publisher.

TABLE 59. Consensus of 218 Students Who Were Counseled on Difficulties by 36 Teachers of Marriage and the Family *

Rank	TITLE OF AREA OF CONCERN	Number of Students	Per Cent of 218 Students	Area Number
1.	Beliefs, values, attitudes, ethical and moral concepts	77	35.3	8
2.	Situations in dating, courtship, engagement	62	28.4	3
3.	Differences between self and prospective mate	53	24.3	5
4.	Money matters	40	18.4	9
5.	Attitudes toward parents and relatives	35	16.	1
6.	Feelings of insecurity and inadequacy	35	16.	6
7.	Sex adjustment, excluding homosexuality, of unmarried student	31	14.2	12
8.	Rearing of children or child	29	13.3	15
9.	Marital discord between self and mate	25	11.5	7
10.	Need for information relative to organs of reproduction or the reproductive process	20	9.2	4
11.	Marital discord between student's parents	20	9.2	13
12.	Spacing of children	18	8.3	16
13.	Physical or mental defects, known or suspected, in self, mate or prospective mate, or in a relative	11	5.6	2
14.	Legal implications of student's activities	6	2.6	10
15.	Venereal diseases	6	2.6	14
16.	Homosexuality	6	2.6	11

* Adapted from Leland Ellis Glover, "The Teacher of Marriage and the Family as Counselor," unpublished Ph.D. dissertation, University of Southern California, 1951, p. 87.

and attitudes constituted the most important problem area (35.3 per cent) while the values included in dating and courtship were an important second category (28.4 per cent). Psychological problems were also prominent (16.0 per cent), whereas differences between prospective mates troubled many students (24.3 per cent). In commenting on the meaning of this table, Glover said:

Students in the study who were counseled by their teachers indicated that the problems about which they were concerned most in common involved their beliefs, values, attitudes and ethical and moral concepts. They implied, thereby, their philosophical confusion and their need for clarification of their ideas and ideals. Therefore, it is recommended first, that teachers of marriage and the family should have a thorough knowledge and understanding of philosophers and religions, and second, that beliefs, values, attitudes, ethical and moral concepts as they apply to marriage and living in the family should be given considerable attention in the life-problems-centered course.[6]

These findings also suggest the confusion among young people confronted by the wide diversity of values in our society. If students have such concern for values, it is inevitable that these values will be important in marital adjustment. Twenty-four per cent of the students were concerned enough about differences between themselves and their prospective mates to seek counsel. They were aware of the potential of such differences for conflict in marriage. Every marriage counselor has dealt often with the task of helping couples adjust to differences concerning the training of children, the discipline of children, the use of money, the importance of luxuries, church attendance, drinking, gambling, and a great many other items. Because our society is so heterogeneous, most marriages must face a number of these differences.

The family counselor and the psychotherapist are seeing more and more difficulties in marriage that stem from character problems. Goode found in his analysis of divorced women that one of their chief complaints were men who generally drank and "helled around." The incidence of cheating in college and unethical business practices make us aware of characteristic problems in our society. The rate of major crime has increased 74 per cent faster than that of the population in the last ten years; a comparable figure shows juvenile delinquency increasing over 100 per cent faster than the population. Nothing can substitute for faithfulness, confidence and trust in the intimate relationship of husband and wife. Character problems inevitably result in loss of trust. Conflicts which are incidental to character difficulties are among the most difficult to solve, and the counsel of skilled therapists is essential when problems of this nature present themselves.

CONFLICTS OVER ROLE INCONGRUENCE

The student must by now be well aware of the shifting nature of the roles of modern men and women. We shall not duplicate that material here, but rather insist again on its basic importance. The following excerpt from a case illustrates one kind of role conflict that the counselor hears frequently:

Jim and Mary B. have been separated for five months. They have two children, both boys. Jim is twenty-six years of age and is out of law school

6 Glover, p. 248.

only three years. Mary is also twenty-six and supported Jim during his graduate work in the university. The presenting problem was mother-in-law trouble. Mary was very hostile as she spoke of her mother-in-law.

"She told me I was an unfit mother. Here I was supporting her son and she threw my working in my face. I had to ask her to watch the children or Jim could not have gone to school. Then Jim sided with her. I hate him for that. He never has really left home emotionally."

Jim had a different story. He said his wife loved a good time and dumped the children on either set of parents. He also had a long list of complaints about the way the children were being raised. Mary did not teach them—they were one and three years of age—to stay out of things. He said:

"She just lets them run and get into anything. They are going to be delinquent when they grow up if they don't learn some self-control. I don't believe in the new-fashioned permissiveness she reads in all those women's magazines. I'd like my children raised right."

There were also grave monetary and sexual difficulties. But no matter what the item, it was discussed loudly, angrily and punctuated with swearing and barbs. It was soon evident that it was not the mother-in-law, not the children, not sex, nor money that was at issue. These two were competing in every area for control. Not until they began to deal basically with this problem did they make any progress.[7]

Two issues finally emerged from this case. Jim's almost vitriolic denunciation rose out of his insecurity as a provider. He hated every minute of the years he had to endure during which Mary supported him. She added to his discomfort by often saying he was not a man or that he was weak. So he retaliated by condemning the way she played her role as a mother and a housewife. Mary was likewise a sensitive person and these allegations stung her because she was aware that when she worked she did have to neglect her house and children to some extent. Her husband's taunts only added to her own guilt over this neglect. So she struck out even more viciously at his role failure. In addition, both of them wanted to be ascendant in the relationship because they feared being submerged by the other. By the time the case got to the counselor these fundamental issues were obscured by the hard things both had said to hurt the other because they had been hurt themselves.

Our sense of personal worth is bound up with our sense of fulfilling the role expectations that cluster around our goals or status drives. When our mate frustrates these achievements or is in conflict with us about them,

[7] From a case study in the author's files.

our self-esteem is threatened and we react with anger. That anger may lead us to destructive quarreling but, on the other hand, it may also promote an honest inventory of role expectations on the part of both husband and wife. If it does this and is followed by efforts to assess ways of improving role perception and role congruence, progress in the relationship is almost assured.

Attitudes That Help in Role Adjustment. Indeed, the basic acceptance of the partner "at his worst" is the precondition for growth in closeness. If there is either a lack of acceptance of the mate *as he is* or a subtle attempt to handle him so that those aspects that are not acceptable will be eliminated, the inevitable result will be a defensiveness which will be a barrier to the growth of the individual. When we are condemned, we tend to become constricted and immobilized—we withdraw and defend ourselves. When we are accepted, we feel secure, and this security enables us to venture to change. So if anger, sorrow, grief, hatred and resentment can be freely expressed, they give catharses, they do not control us any more, and then the emotions of tenderness and love are more likely to find full and free expression. The individual who represses all negative emotions finds it equally and increasingly difficult to express positive feelings.

What we are saying is that a mature marriage is one where there is freedom of feeling. In such a marriage, both partners accept the fact that human beings are not solely thinking machines, but are individuals who become frustrated, who develop guilt feelings and feel defeat as well as exaltation. If the man and the woman are basically secure in their sense of the commitment of the other, they can afford to let the other be himself whether loving or hostile. The reward for that realistic acceptance is always a deeper union and a more profound appreciation of each other. Whenever a partner is forced to be wary, to "walk on eggshells" lest he upset the other, marriage becomes a difficult game of repression of natural impulses. Spontaneity is gone and so is joy.

But to accomplish this kind of mature acceptance an attitude of compassion is essential. Compassion presupposes a realistic assessment of human nature and life in the twentieth century. Compassion involves a gentle kindness without surrendering high standards for the other. It is the kind of love that "endureth all things" because of a capacity to understand another human being fully and tenderly. So when the husband comes home and speaks with irritation and rejection to his wife, she must feel with him enough to translate his mood into reality. She says to herself that this anger of my husband tells me something has gone wrong in his life. He is perplexed and unhappy. He is really asking for comfort and reassurance. So she mixes him a drink or brings him coffee or makes him comfortable, knowing that while he is acting like a little boy who has been hurt he is also crying out to her for help. Compassion involves this empathetic feeling which enables her to respond to his need with an appropriate feeling or act. In a lonely urban world marked by anxiety and competitiveness, the need for compassion is profound.

The expression of tender feelings are as vital as are expressions of hostility, and perhaps more so. In fact, all of us need to express all of our emotions. The marriage counselor listens often to the wife who insists that shortly after marriage her husband forgot how to demonstrate affection. This is a very common complaint. Why the wedding service changes men who were quite eloquent in protestation of love into mutes is not entirely understood. But the change is deeply resented. Many men say their wives "ought to know I love her, I'm working for her." But they misunderstand. Both men and women are hungry for affection, for companionship and evidences of devotion. And deprivation of these basic needs will lead to conflict.

DISCUSSION AS THE SOLUTION FOR CONFLICT

To stop on the note of a full and free emotional expression would be to leave the matter half-ended. Some conflicts may be resolved by the honest expression of emotions, but this is not true of conflict rooted in cultural values or social relationships. After the air has been cleared of tension, the couple needs to go on to a sane and intelligent discussion of the causes of that tension. There needs to be persistent and patient exploration of the basic roots of the differences that brought about the frustration. Often these roots have no relation to the matter at issue. The focal point of difficulty quite often obscures the more basic frustration. But couples who have learned how to talk together will sooner or later root out the cause of tension. The cue is communication of both ideas and feelings. Rewarding insight will come to the couple who are able to discuss their perplexities and irritations. It is for this reason that so many items dealing with discussion are included in the premarital test. There is no solvent for conflict more valuable than talking, and talking with a mate who is genuinely interested in knowing how the partner feels. If a couple cannot talk about problems or expectations, they need very soon to recognize this limitation and to practice on small matters until facing greater issues together comes more easily.

492

We have previously discussed communication as a basic tool in achieving cohesion. In this section we are sharpening its focus and relating it to conflict solution and the achievement of cooperation. Let us add one more research study which contributes to our judgment of its importance in marital adjustment.[8] The sample consisted of fifty-five couples randomly selected and another seventy-one couples made up of six groups of married couples affiliated with churches and other community institutions.

The study attempted to discover the relationship between primary communication and empathy and marital adjustment. Primary communication was measured by response of individuals to twenty-five questions about communication between husbands and wives. Marital adjustment was measured by the Locke marital adjustment test. The primary communication test included such questions as:

> Does your mate explain or express herself to you through a glance or gesture?
> Do you and your mate use words which have a special meaning not understood by outsiders? [9]

The correlations between primary communication and marital adjustment proved very meaningful; they were significant at the .01 level.[10] While this study does not prove that primary communication *causes* adjustment, it certainly reinforces our point of view that discussion is contributory to good adjustment.

If we are to isolate the mechanisms of good communication, we would like to present two factors; one, a subjective judgment that comes from observation of married couples in counseling, and the other an analysis by an expert of aspects of the process of conflict solution. One difficulty couples have is the inability to *really listen* to the other person. It is a difficult task for most of us to be completely *attentive* to another. Rather, we daydream or we think of what we will say in response to what we assume the other person is saying. Consequently, we often miss the overtone and the subtlety of another person's remarks and, as a result, our own words are often not responsive to the feelings and meaning of the other. Couples often need to practice listening, and such practice offers great rewards. This kind of attention is a compliment to the other person and it assures them of our real concern. When we have learned to listen in an

---

[8] Harvey J. Locke, Georges Sabagh and Mary Margaret Thomes, "Correlates of Primary Communication and Empathy," *Research Studies of the State College of Washington,* XXIV, No. 2 (June, 1956), 116–124.

[9] Locke, Sabagh, Thomes, p. 116.   [10] Locke, Sabagh, Thomes, p. 120.

understanding and nonjudgmental manner, our own response will be cued to move the discussion forward.

Communication is a process. It has its own forms and development, for it is keyed to attitudes that characterize the interactive process. John Spiegel has analyzed some of the characteristic ways that couples use communication for egocentric goals and to re-establish a better relationship. In this chart of methods we see how essential it is to analyze the attitudes that determine our stand in interaction. The chart also helps us understand the almost organic nature of conflict because Spiegel has also observed characteristic ways of countering or responding to these methods. There we see the interlocking pattern of attitudinal and communicative processes.

TABLE 60. Methods Employed by Partners in Attempting to Reestablish Role Equilibrium [11]

ROLE INDUCTIONS (based on unilateral decisions, manipulative—forcing the other person to "really give in" or adopt a counter-measure thus prolonging the disharmony)

METHOD	COMMENT
1. Coercing (the manipulation of present or future punishments)	Probably a universally used technique, readily used. The specific "neutralizer" is *defiance*.
2. Coaxing (manipulation of present or future rewards)	Less universally used and less readily available. The specific neutralizer is *withholding*.
3. Evaluation of the other (the rewards or punishments here are categorized and placed into a class of value judgments)	Examples: "you're nuts," "stop acting like a dictator!" Neutralization is specifically handled by *denial* (of the assigned category), and is often followed by efforts to employ methods 1 or 2 above.
4. Masking ("little white lies," shared silence around disturbing area, hypocrisy, major deceits)	Masking is universally used and is often very complex, often accomplished by self deception via "defense mechanisms," e.g., repression, displacement, projection. (Masking can be neutralized by *unmasking* confrontation) and such unmasking often leads to a major flare-up of hostility in the unmasked one.
5. Postponing (one person decides to wait until the other "has a change of mind")	Postponing is a bit more passive than 1, 2, 3, 4 above and may lead to a successful solution; often the other will not wait, and so postponing can be neutralized by *provoking*.

METHOD	*COMMENT*

There is a transitional phase, which is *essential*, to proceed from the above five *manipulative* measures toward role modifications which can lead to bilaterally agreeable solutions.

| 6. Role-reversal (here used in Mead's sense of "taking the role of the other" and understanding the other by empathic efforts) | This is signaled in by such remarks as: "I'm beginning to see how you feel," etc. Quite unlike the above 5 methods, it is essentially non-manipulative and, hence, does not require a specific neutralizer. This is an unstable phase, so that one person's efforts at role reversal may evoke any of the above 5 methods or any of the 5 listed below. Spiegel feels that the success of this phase depends on the amount and intensity of previous masking. |

ROLE MODIFICATIONS (unlike role inductions, both persons make some changes in their role enactment and role understanding, these changes being based on identifications and understandings of the other person. These lead to bilateral agreements through largely non-manipulative, noncoercive means.)

7. Joking	The first sign of role modification. Instead of the previous tension, a certain playfulness is introduced and the partners feel more free to try out absurd solutions, gradually abandoning unworkable ones and arriving at a novel and ingenious solution.
8. Referral to a 3rd party (mental health expert, marriage counselor, etc.)	At one level of awareness is the hope that the 3rd party will be less emotionally involved in the problem and can, through his training or particular viewpoint, be able to bring about favorable changes. At a more covert level, probably all such referrals find at least one partner assigning the role of "judge," "referee," or "ally," etc., to the expert. Thus, there are 2 difficulties: (1) the 3rd party may steer the relationship back to induction phases, or (2) a coalition may be formed between the expert and one of the partners.
9. Exploring	The assumption of new behavior, initiated via "joking," now takes on a more serious mien. The partners propose and reject possible solutions, but the relationship is largely "task oriented." Much of the activity of this phase is actually tried out in behavior, but verbal consideration

TABLE 60 (Cont.). Methods Employed by Partners in Attempting to Reestablish Role Equilibrium

METHOD	COMMENT
	of the solutions is probably also necessary.
10. Compromising (adjustment of and redistribution of goals)	After #9 (above) each partner recognizes some changes in his own role are necessary, adopts such, thereby making the new relationship something *qualitatively* different from the original.
11. Consolidating (adjustment and redistribution of rewards)	It is necessary to act out new behavior patterns for some time for the new compromise solution to endure. In this phase the learning of concrete details of the new roles leads to smoothness of execution and to easy rewarding of the other for his adoption of the new role. After the novelty and strain has worn off, a new "routine" is established which is mutually rewarding.

[11] Based on an article by John Spiegel entitled: "The Resolution of Role Conflict Within the Family," appearing in Greenblatt, Milton, *et al.*, *The Patient and the Mental Hospital* (Glencoe, Illinois: The Free Press, 1957), pp. 545–564.

When family decisions are made as the result of much communication and consideration of the wishes of all members of the family, a democratic type of organization is present. This type of participation results in solving problems by consensus. In this situation, members learn to give consideration to more than their own egocentric desires, and we say that cooperation has replaced conflict. We have yet to determine the contributions of this type of family to its members.

INTERPERSONAL RELATIONSHIPS AND MARITAL CONFLICTS

Conflicts which are the result of social relationships outside the immediate family are also important. A problem often arises over choice of friends. With reference to this kind of conflict Locke says:

The number of friends a husband and wife have in common is highly associated with marital adjustment, particularly for women. A wife who reported that she had "almost no" friends in common with her husband was much more likely to be in the divorced than in the happily married group, and, if she reported only "a few" friends in common with her husband, there was a fair probability that she would be in the divorced rather than in the married group.[12]

Locke gives the following excerpt from the life history of a divorced man to illustrate how chances of success in marriage seem to be reduced unless the husband and wife have mutual friends:

> We got along quite well, and I enjoyed married life. In fact I think I will marry the girl I am now going with. The main trouble with my marriage was that my wife resented the amount of time I spent with my friends. These were boyhood chums. I used to play basketball and go out evenings with them. She always wanted to do something else. She did not want me to hang around with them. They were perfectly fine fellows, and I resented this attempt on her part to keep me away from them. One quarrel gradually led to another, and we finally separated. My in-laws kept interfering, too, since she had been a little spoiled when she was a child. They took her side. Later on, when she had a child by another man, and we went through with divorce, her folks agreed that I was in the right.[13]

Perhaps it is a growing awareness that many man-woman friendships become serious and turn into affairs that cause suspicion and distrust. This may also reflect the need for companionship discovered in the research reported in discussing recreation. On the other hand, conflicts over friends may reflect more profound differences in socio-cultural backgrounds.

CONFLICT AND TENSION

There is a difference between conflict and tension. Conflict is an overt struggle of any sort and about anything. Tension may be defined as unsolved conflict. Tensions are the product of frustrations, or of conflict situations in which the vital interest of one person is never openly admitted, recognized, or discussed. If, in a series of problems, no solution is reached, the tension increases and causes social distance and withdrawal to take place. Waller uses a term, "the process of alienation," to describe the growth of increasing instability and social distance due to a series of tensions.[14] Mowrer indicates the manner in which conflict and tension result in the development of social distance in "The Diary of Miriam Donaven." [15] Burgess and Locke have diagrammed this development as shown in Figure 29. Burgess and Locke summarize this case as follows:

[12] Locke, p. 234.   [13] Locke, p. 235.
[14] Willard Waller and Reuben Hill, *The Family: A Dynamic Interpretation*, rev. ed. (New York: Dryden Press, 1951), pp. 539–557. Copyright Holt, Rinehart and Winston, Inc.
[15] Ernest R. Mowrer, *Family Disorganization* (Chicago: University of Chicago Press, 1927), pp. 231–250.

FIGURE 29. Development of Social Distance Between Alfred and Miriam Donaven *

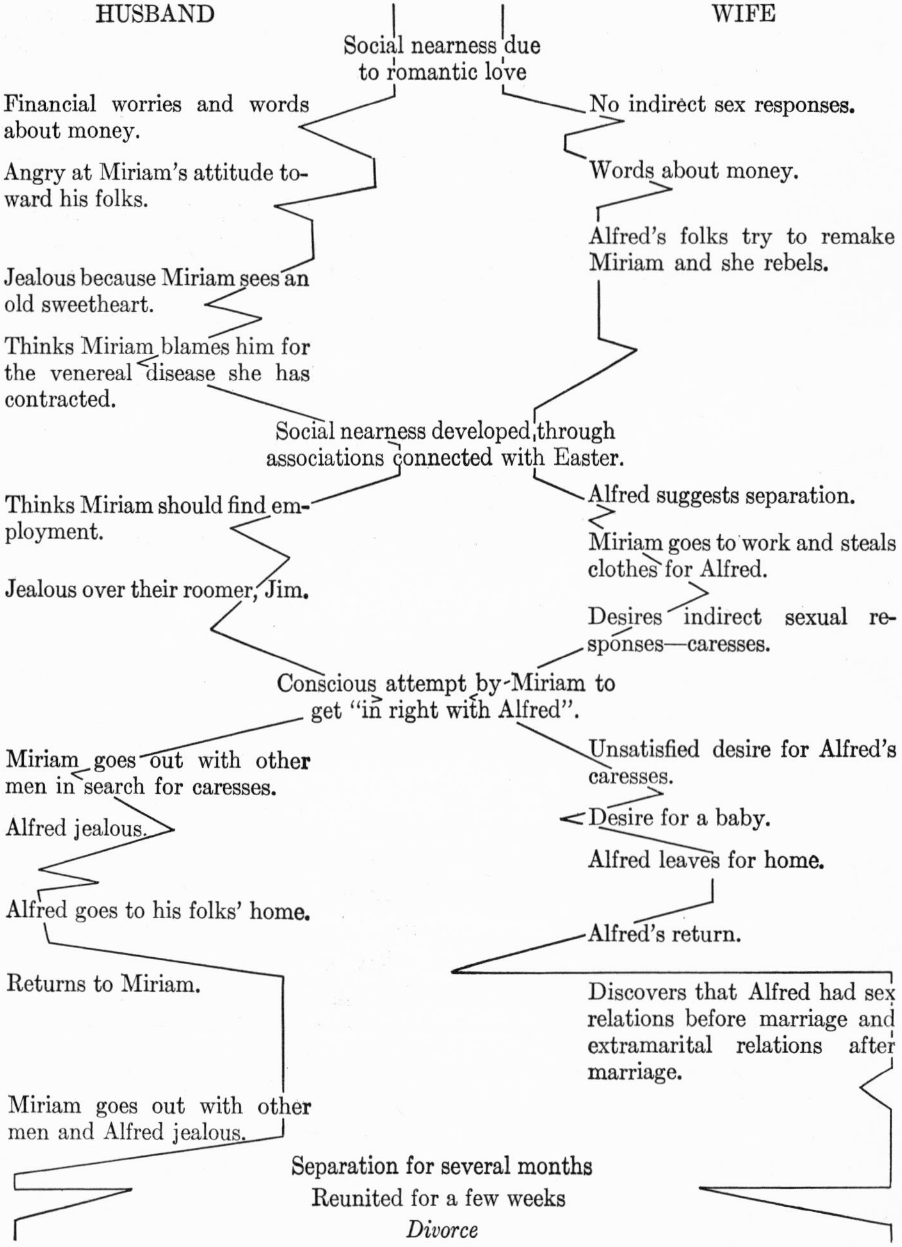

HUSBAND　　　　　　　　　　　　　　　　　　WIFE

Social nearness due
to romantic love

Financial worries and words about money.

No indirect sex responses.

Angry at Miriam's attitude toward his folks.

Words about money.

Alfred's folks try to remake Miriam and she rebels.

Jealous because Miriam sees an old sweetheart.

Thinks Miriam blames him for the venereal disease she has contracted.

Social nearness developed through associations connected with Easter.

Thinks Miriam should find employment.

Alfred suggests separation.

Miriam goes to work and steals clothes for Alfred.

Jealous over their roomer, Jim.

Desires indirect sexual responses—caresses.

Conscious attempt by Miriam to get "in right with Alfred".

Miriam goes out with other men in search for caresses.

Unsatisfied desire for Alfred's caresses.

Alfred jealous.

Desire for a baby.

Alfred leaves for home.

Alfred goes to his folks' home.

Alfred's return.

Returns to Miriam.

Discovers that Alfred had sex relations before marriage and extramarital relations after marriage.

Miriam goes out with other men and Alfred jealous.

Separation for several months
Reunited for a few weeks
Divorce

* From Burgess, Locke and Thomes, p. 391. Reprinted by permission.

An analysis of this case reveals tensions over money matters, the failure of the wife to adjust her conduct to the expectations of the husband's mother, the failure of the husband to give indirect sexual responses in the form of caresses, and sexual incompatibility. These tensions seem to have their roots in differences in the cultural background of the couple. While temporary periods of social nearness occurred, there was, nevertheless, an increasing distance between husband and wife.[16]

A careful scrutiny of Burgess and Locke's diagram will reveal almost all of the factors studied so far in the chapter as explanatory of conflict in marriage. No one item of conflict ever exists by itself. There is an interdependence of response and alienation that makes it very hazardous to attach importance to single factors. They are important, nevertheless, if we remember that they are parts of a whole.

PERSONALITY RESOURCES FOR MARITAL ADJUSTMENT

Whether or not a couple have indifferent or determined attitudes regarding the success of their marriage is important. Whether they invest their total loyalty or only a part of it in the new venture is important. Many marriages that might otherwise have succeeded have failed because of the tentative manner in which one partner has entered into the union. If the friction caused by a mother-in-law or a secretary is cushioned by the secure feelings that result from a complete transfer of loyalty and affection, that friction can be absorbed. If a wife knows that her husband will always be on her side in any quarrel with his mother, she can afford to be more generous. She will be more lenient, more understanding, and more tolerant of the mother-in-law. But even more basic is the fact that if friction does develop, facing the problem as a pair or a team brings the couple closer together. This is our first insight into the constructive handling of conflicts. It is the goal that is important. If the problem is faced by the couple as a unit and if they focus on achieving an outcome which will contribute most to their compatibility, no matter how strong the disagreement, the outcome will be constructive. It is when the couple is divided and the real problem is a struggle between their egos that social distance develops.

It is this willingness to abandon self-interest for the common good which gives both stability and motivation to the struggle for cohesion in

[16] Burgess, Locke, and Thomes, p. 390.

today's marriage. Christensen speaks strongly about the effect of selfishness in some marriages.

> Marriage is a cooperative adventure that fails when family members become self-centered rather than group centered, when they look towards "rights" and "privileges" rather than "obligations" and "contributions." Whether one looks at husband-wife relationships or those between parents and children, he will see that failure is almost invariably tied up with the selfishness of someone. There is too much emphasis on "I" and "me" rather than "we" and "us." Successful marriage is a process of give and take, but there are too many today who try to do all of the taking and none of the giving.
>
> In short, married mates prove most adjustable when they have a spirit of mutually accepted responsibility and cooperation, when they are realistic about the task before them, and when they are determined that they shall not fail. Success here does not spring from romanticizing alone, nor from temporizing, nor from exploiting; rather, it comes first and foremost from the attitude of regarding marriage as a challenging job and accepting it as a partnership.[17]

It is, then, the total investment of one's affectional, emotional, and intellectual self in the task of making the marriage succeed that gives a secure framework in which conflict and difficulties can be faced.

OVERT MARITAL CONFLICT AS A MECHANISM FOR ACHIEVING MARITAL ADJUSTMENT

By stressing the need for unselfish dedication of both partners to their marriage, we do not mean at all to overlook the fact that a marriage is never fully successful unless each partner achieves the full development of his own potentialities. While it is important to emphasize unselfishness and understanding as basic qualities in achieving marital compatibility, it is also important to stress selfhood. Often submission and ego-repression are the costs exacted in the name of unselfishness. These impoverish any human relationship and lead ultimately to hostility and social distance. One must be completely honest in one's dedication to one's mate at the altar; one must not reserve anything on any tentative basis. But one must also be prepared to be emotionally honest. If one is upset, or chagrined, or hurt, to interiorize these feelings is only to cause a long-lasting and basic

[17] Harold T. Christensen, *Marriage Analysis* (New York: The Ronald Press Company, 1950), pp. 313–314. Reprinted by permission of the publisher.

tension. When one feels anger, it is wise to express that anger honestly and openly. If it is kept under cover, it will be sure to appear in sexual withdrawal or irritability or under some other unfortunate guise.

Overt emotional conflict has many values. "Blowing up" may often release tensions which have stood in the way of a more enduring and more basic solution to the problem. The emotional release of feelings resulting from frustrations also brings the problem to the attention of the couple in such a dramatic way that it must be faced and cannot be forced underground again. Most of us in this day of change, loneliness, and tension have deep hostilities and daily frustrations. Wise is the husband or the wife who can recognize the need on the part of his or her mate for an aggressive expression of feeling. Duvall and Hill say:

> The modern couple will expect that in marriage they have a place of security and intimacy where they are free to behave like human beings with the normal variety of emotions. The workaday world, organized as it is, does not permit the frank expression of resentment, vanity, jealousy, and selfish ambition along with tenderness and love, all of which exist in the normal person. The individual must control his annoyances and his affections, he must often act like something more than human to get along in our complex industrial society. If he flies off the handle at his boss, he may lose his job. There needs to be some place, however, where the individual can give vent to his annoyances and be himself, and that place seems to be in marriage. If there is that kind of cantankerousness in a marriage, the couple should chalk it down as proof that their marriage is performing one of its main functions—providing a place to let off steam and re-establish emotional balance. If a marriage is so fragile that it must be maintained by the same kind of artificial manners that keeps an office force functioning, it is pretty precariously based. One insightful authority has stated in positive terms, "one of the functions of marriage is to weave a rope of relationships strong enough to hold each person at his worst." [18]

DEMOCRATIC FAMILY STRUCTURE
AND PROBLEM-SOLVING

If a couple are profoundly dedicated to their marriage, if they are honest with each other emotionally and intellectually, and if they have achieved the capacity for intelligent discussion, they will make progress

[18] Evelyn M. Duvall and Reuben Hill, *When You Marry*, rev. ed. (Boston: D. C. Heath and Co., 1945), pp. 187–188. Reprinted by permission of the publisher.

in solving conflicts constructively. However, in this process they will discover that they must work out some type of structure for their relationship so that ego-maximizing and the struggle for power will not engage energies which ought to go into constructive problem-solving. They must decide whether the husband or the wife is to be dominant or whether they will work together on a democratic basis of equality. In the past the patriarchal type of family organization, in which the father took the lead and made the decisions, was nearly universal. The changing role of women in today's world and the complexity of the conflicts to be faced raise the real question whether this type of organization will prove effective in the families of the future. What seems to be effective today for the adjustment of differences between partners and the solution of the problems continuously presented by our culture is the most fluid and flexible relationship a couple can achieve, a marital structure, in other words, which allows for the highest degree of give and take. This seems to be the equalitarian, democratic type of marriage in which both partners share in decision-making. Locke attempted to discover whether or not there was a difference between a married and a divorced sample in terms of democratic and individualistic behavior. Happily married and divorced persons were asked whether the lead was more often taken by the wife than by the husband, by the husband more often than by the wife, or by both equally in making family decisions, disciplining the children, handling family money, affectionate behavior, religious behavior, recreation and meeting people. His conclusion is as follows:

> The above analysis emphasizes the value attached by many persons, particularly women, to democratic behavior, in the family. The happily-married tended to feel that equality between husband and wife was present in their marriages, while the divorced felt that it was relatively absent.[19]

CONTRIBUTIONS OF THE DEMOCRATIC FAMILY

A study of the relationship of parental authority patterns to teen-age adjustments provides additional insights into the contribution of the democratic structure both to individuals and to family life as a whole. This study involved 4,310 high-school seniors, one-third of all high-school seniors in the State of Washington. The hypothesis of the study was that teen-agers reared in the democratic family suffer from "fewer serious per-

[19] Locke, p. 266.

sonal maladjustments and enjoy all-around happier homes than do young people reared in an atmosphere dominated by their parents' wishes or commands." [20] This hypothesis was upheld by the data. The authors concluded that a comparison of democratic and authoritarian families shows the superiority of the former in terms of parent-teenage adjustment because teen-agers in democratic families have fewer major problems and have a closer relationship with their parents than do boys and girls from authoritarian homes.[21]

Figure 30 records the reactions of boys and girls who were asked to

FIGURE 30. Responses of Teen-agers, by Sex and Family Administrative Pattern, to the Question, "When I am the age of my father or mother I would like to be": *

BOYS

	"Exactly like him or her"	"Somewhat different"	"Different"
Democratic	47.2	33.8	19.0
Intermediate	41.6	39.7	18.7
Authoritarian	23.3	35.0	41.7

GIRLS

Democratic	60.5	27.9	11.6
Intermediate	56.5	30.6	12.9
Authoritarian	23.5	41.0	35.5

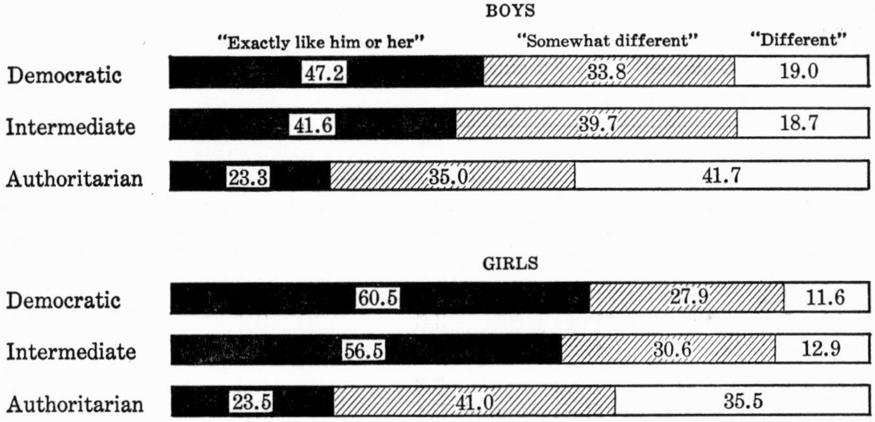

* Landis and Stone, p. 17. Reprinted by permission.

respond to the question, "When I am the age of my father or mother I would like to be exactly like him or her, somewhat different, or different?" This question is a very crucial one, for it measures the degree to which the boy or girl accepts the patterns of the home, their closeness to their parents, and their respect for them. Among both boys and girls, a substantially higher percentage of those who had been raised in a democratic family wanted to be exactly like their father or mother. For boys the difference in percentage was 47.2 per cent compared to 23.3 per cent

[20] Paul H. Landis and Carol L. Stone, "The Relationship of Parental Authority Patterns to Teen-age Adjustments," *Rural Sociological Series on the Family*, No. 3 (Washington Agricultural Experiment Stations, Institute of Agricultural Sciences, State College of Washington, September, 1952), p. 2.

[21] Landis and Stone, p. 28.

and for girls 60.5 per cent compared to 23.5 per cent. In interpreting these figures it is important to note that the degree of identification, the extent to which the boy or girl will adopt the way of life of the parents, depends on the degree of democracy in the home.

The principal thesis of Landis and Stone is that the growth of creative individuality of children and youth is one of the prime purposes of modern family living and that such individuality is essential to purposeful adjustment in modern society. Landis and Stone feel that "the superiority of the democratic family probably lies in the fact that, by and large, it substitutes cooperation for commands." [22] Cooperation undoubtedly gives a larger place for individual development and growth of ability to make decisions. That democratic living is more cooperative and less repressive is shown in Table 61, which emphasizes the differences in disagreements

TABLE 61. Percentage of Teen-agers Checking Items on Which They "Frequently Disagree" with Parents, Classified by Type of Family Administrative Patterns *

AREAS OF DISAGREEMENT		FAMILY ADMINISTRATION PATTERN		
	Sex	Democratic	Intermediate	Authoritarian
My spending money	Boys	20.2	28.8	39.4
	Girls	16.0	22.7	38.6
My friends	Boys	3.6	9.4	11.1
	Girls	3.9	10.4	23.1
My choice of clothes	Boys	6.6	9.2	11.9
	Girls	5.4	9.3	14.3
My attitude toward my parents	Boys	8.9	13.2	24.7
	Girls	11.5	15.8	34.1
My outside activities	Boys	13.8	22.7	27.8
	Girls	13.8	19.5	28.5
My school work	Boys	21.6	28.4	31.8
	Girls	8.0	12.7	15.6
My future plans	Boys	13.5	17.5	20.2
	Girls	12.1	19.5	25.5
My share of the work around the house	Boys	26.2	24.7	40.4
	Girls	27.4	27.6	40.3
My social life	Boys	8.2	15.8	22.7
	Girls	9.1	12.8	27.2

* Landis and Stone, p. 22. Reprinted by permission.

[22] Landis and Stone, p. 28.

504

between teen-agers and parents in democratic families as compared to authoritarian families. Two times as many teen-agers living in authoritarian homes frequently disagreed with parents as those living in democratic homes.

ADJUSTMENT OF DEMOCRATIC FAMILIES

The greater adjustment of teen-agers living in democratic families is emphasized again in Table 62 which shows that teen-agers from democratic homes have fewer family problems than those from authoritarian homes. However, this table also reveals that democratic families as a whole are happier than authoritarian families. There is only one-third the quarreling in the family (9.9 per cent compared to 27.8 per cent). Children from democratic homes get along better with their parents. Only 5.7 per cent of boys and 8.4 per cent of girls checked getting along with parents as a problem compared to 17.2 per cent of boys and 24.2 per cent of girls from authoritarian homes. Other revealing comparisons are to be found in the responses to such statements as "Wish I could live by myself," "I want to leave home," and "My parents are always quarreling." These items indicate that in general family adjustment the democratic family is superior to the authoritarian family. It would appear that in our society democratic home relationships make for more creative individuals and for better adjusted homes.

THE FAMILY COUNCIL

One of the ways in which many young couples are consciously structuring their relationship democratically is by providing a stated time when difficulties may be faced and new family opportunities may be explored. Many call this the family council. During these talks the monetary and time budgets of the family are prepared or revised, recurrent problems are discussed, and individual needs are considered. While problem-solving cannot be completely institutionalized, some form of continuous communication promotes family cohesion and certainly reduces family tension.

CONCLUSION

In this chapter we have reviewed some of the complex factors involved in conflict or tensional situations. These conflicts and tensions have been

505

T A B L E 62. Percentage of Teen-agers Living in Democratic, Intermediate, and Authoritarian Families Checking Family Problems Listed *

PROBLEM	Sex	FAMILY ADMINISTRATIVE PATTERN			CR Between Dem. and Auth.
		Democratic	Intermediate	Authoritarian	
Quarreling in the family	Boys	9.9	11.8	27.8	7.90
	Girls	12.7	16.2	37.0	9.21
Getting to use the car	Boys	22.3	25.0	34.8	4.58
	Girls	11.7	14.3	11.4	—
My folks understanding me	Boys	10.0	12.5	16.2	3.07
	Girls	13.4	16.7	28.3	5.92
I have to work to buy things	Boys	12.0	21.6	27.0	6.44
	Girls	8.2	11.3	18.8	5.08
Getting Mother to understand my problems	Boys	4.2	5.7	10.6	4.24
	Girls	6.5	12.1	26.3	8.62
Getting along with my parents	Boys	5.7	10.6	17.2	6.30
	Girls	8.4	10.8	24.2	13.59
Having no regular allowance	Boys	5.7	8.2	16.9	6.16
	Girls	8.6	12.6	21.2	5.79
Getting Dad to understand my problems	Boys	10.4	10.9	17.7	3.53
	Girls	12.5	16.0	20.6	3.57
Afraid I can't afford college	Boys	13.4	14.0	17.9	2.04
	Girls	10.2	12.5	16.3	2.94
I don't have any privacy at home	Boys	4.4	5.3	8.3	2.68
	Girls	2.6	7.1	17.8	8.22
Having a happy home life	Boys	7.8	10.5	12.1	2.55
	Girls	9.9	8.9	17.1	3.45
Understanding my folks	Boys	5.7	8.2	10.1	2.75
	Girls	7.4	12.0	15.8	4.29
Family always worried about money	Boys	6.9	7.5	10.4	2.08
	Girls	8.2	10.0	15.6	3.74
Wish I had my own room	Boys	6.2	6.9	11.4	3.10
	Girls	11.4	12.2	15.6	2.01
Don't have much spending money	Boys	6.8	7.9	11.4	2.68
	Girls	4.7	7.1	15.0	5.66
Mother has to work	Boys	7.0	6.9	6.8	—
	Girls	10.4	11.2	14.6	2.02
Treated like a child at home	Boys	4.8	6.1	11.6	4.27
	Girls	5.0	7.2	14.4	8.31

T A B L E 62 (*Cont.*). Percentage of Teen-agers Living in Democratic, Intermediate, and Authoritarian Families Checking Family Problems Listed

PROBLEM		FAMILY ADMINISTRATIVE PATTERN			CR Between Dem. and Auth.
	Sex	Democratic	Intermediate	Authoritarian	
Folks ridicule my	Boys	3.1	4.5	9.3	4.50
ideas	Girls	2.2	3.1	14.3	7.20
Wish I could live	Boys	2.7	2.2	9.1	4.79
by myself	Girls	3.2	3.7	14.1	6.36
My parents are al-	Boys	2.5	3.0	8.1	4.42
ways quarreling	Girls	3.4	5.2	13.5	5.95
Can't bring friends	Boys	2.3	3.5	8.3	4.73
to my home	Girls	3.1	4.9	13.3	6.01
Don't like the house	Boys	4.3	5.6	9.1	3.29
we live in	Girls	6.9	7.7	12.4	3.05
I want to leave	Boys	2.2	2.3	9.1	5.35
home	Girls	2.8	2.6	12.4	5.94

* The total check list contained sixty-three items. Only those checked by at least 10 per cent in one category, and which showed statistically significant differences, are reproduced here. Landis and Stone, p. 24. Reprinted by permission.

regarded not as threats but as opportunities to achieve greater closeness in marriage as well as avenues to self-realization for each marriage partner. Constructive approaches to conflict situations were found in a dedication to the success of the marriage, in emotional freedom and honesty of expression, in the development of ability to discuss creativity, and in the achievement of a democratic family structure which facilitates problem-solving. We have tried to show that conflict is inevitable and continuous, that it has its source in our culture, but that it may lead to new ways of achieving unity.

A FINAL WORD

This book has presented much new research material that is brought together to help the student understand the nature of the contemporary family. Much of it bears on the roles of husband and wife in their interaction with each other and with their children. The research of Mangus, Kotlar, and Luckey illustrated basic role adjustment problems, the work of Sears, Maccoby, and Levin the role of a wife as mother, the research of the Manpower Commission illustrated economic shifts in the role of women, and the material from Straus and Spiegel help us to understand methods of adjusting to these changes in role expectation and role behavior. This latter material was presented to help the student develop an awareness of his role expectations and then to become aware of possible ways of ameliorating role conflict.

This book has presented many ways in which marriage today may result in happiness. In the first part, the student was given an opportunity to investigate those background circumstances and experiences which might have conditioned him or her in such a way as to have an adverse effect on marital adjustment. It was suggested that by reviewing our past we could alter inhibitions and achieve more healthy attitudes. The emphasis was upon becoming a mature and marriageable person.

In the last part, psychological and sociological factors that influence marital choice and adjustment were analyzed so that the student might be better prepared when he or she faces the necessity of making similar choices or adjustments. In all of these sections, problem solving was regarded as a means to a way of enriching the dynamic bond between a man and his wife.

In conclusion, a word can profitably be said for using all the resources which are now being marshaled in the interest of better family living. Most families reach whatever degree of cohesion or happiness they achieve as a matter of chance. If husbands and wives gave only one-tenth as much time to discussing and planning the future of their relationship as they do to their business or even to their social life, their marriages would grow in meaning and cohesion. Many couples spend more time keeping their automobiles clean than in keeping their romance shining. We have said that contemporary social trends make it necessary for those who wish to be happy to plan consciously for that happiness. But we have also suggested that these same trends may mean that the contemporary couple may find new patterns of achievement in marriage which were not possible under the more rigid mores of several generations ago.

PROJECTS

1. Select any two members of opposite sex in the class. List on the board ten or fifteen important areas which will involve decisions in marriage such as child training, budget making, vacations, etc. Then ask each of the two to indicate their present ideas about each of these areas of interest.
2. Have a sharing session in which various members of the class indicate their

own habits or ways of solving conflicts. Which of these ways will be detrimental in marriage?

3. Select five areas of conflict in marriage. Let a male and a female student outline a very brief sociodrama to state the issues in one area. After they have done this, ask the class members to consider "Methods for Attempting to Re-establish Role Equilibrium." Classify the proposed methods, and evaluate their appropriateness.

VISUAL AIDS

Who's Boss? McGraw-Hill Marriage Series. McGraw-Hill Book Company.

READINGS

Blood, Robert O., Jr. *Anticipating Your Marriage.* New York, The Free Press of Glencoe, 1962. Copyright The Macmillan Company.

Burgess, Ernest W., Harvey J. Locke, and Mary Margaret Thomes. *The Family, From Institution to Companionship.* 3rd ed. New York, The American Book Company, 1963, Chapter 18.

Cavan, Ruth Shonle. *The American Family.* New York, Thomas Y. Crowell Company, 1953, Chapters 5, 6, 7.

Christensen, Harold T. *Marriage Analysis.* New York, The Ronald Press Company, 1950, Chapter 10.

Landis, Judson T. and Mary Landis. *Building a Successful Marriage.* 3rd ed. New York, Prentice-Hall, Inc., 1958.

Landis, Paul H. and Carol L. Stone. "The Relationship of Parental Authority Patterns to Teen-age Adjustments." *Rural Sociological Series on the Family,* No. 3, Washington Agricultural Experiment Stations, Institute of Agricultural Sciences, State College of Washington, September, 1952.

Lu, Yi-Chuang. "Marital Roles and Marriage Adjustment." *Sociology and Social Research.* XXXII, No. 6, Los Angeles, California, University of Southern California Press, July–August, 1952.

Peterson, James A. *Toward A Successful Marriage.* New York, Charles Scribner's Sons, 1960.

Ante-Nuptial Agreement
of the Catholic Church

To be signed in duplicate in the presence of the priest by the parties entering a mixed marriage, and by two witnesses.

To Be Signed by the Non-Catholic Party

I, the undersigned, not a member of the Catholic Church, wishing to contract marriage with the Catholic party whose signature is also hereinafter affixed to this mutual agreement, being of sound mind and perfectly free, and only after understanding fully the import of my action, do hereby enter into this mutual agreement, understanding that the execution of this agreement and the promises therein contained are made in contemplation of and in consideration for the consent, marriage and consequent change of status of the hereinafter mentioned Catholic party, and I, therefore, hereby agree:

1. That I will not interfere in the least with the free exercise of the Catholic party's religion;

2. That I will adhere to the doctrine of the sacred indissolubility of the marriage bond, so that I cannot contract a second marriage while my consort is still alive, even though a civil divorce may have been obtained;

3. That all the children, both boys and girls, that may be born of this union shall be baptized and educated solely in the faith of the Roman Catholic Church, even in the event of the death of my Catholic consort. In case of dispute, I, furthermore, hereby fully agree that the custody of all the children shall be given to such guardians as to assure the faithful execution of this covenant and promise;

4. That I will lead a married life in conformity with the Law of God and the teaching of the Catholic Church regarding birth control, realizing fully the attitude of the Catholic Church in this regard;

5. That no other marriage ceremony shall take place before or after this ceremony by the Catholic priest.

In testimony of which agreement, I do hereby solemnly swear that I will observe the above agreement and faithfully execute the promises therein contained, and do now affix my signature in approval thereof.

_____

Signature of the non-Catholic party

_____

Address

_____

City or Town

To Be Signed by the Catholic Party

I, the undersigned, a member of the Catholic Church, wishing to contract marriage with the non-Catholic party whose signature is affixed above to this mutual agreement, being of sound mind and perfectly free, and only after understanding fully the import of my action, do hereby enter into this mutual agreement, understanding that the execution of this agreement and the promises therein contained are made in contemplation of and in consideration for the consent, marriage and consequent change of my status, and I, therefore, hereby agree:

1. That I shall have all my children, both boys and girls, that may be born of this union, baptized and educated solely in the faith of the Roman Catholic Church. I understand that in case of my death, or in the event of a dispute, the custody of all the children shall be given to such guardians as to assure the faithful execution of this covenant and promise;

2. That I will practice my Catholic religion faithfully and will strive, especially by example, prayer and the frequentation of the Sacraments, to bring about the conversion of my consort;

3. That I will lead a married life in conformity with the Law of God and the teaching of the Catholic Church regarding birth control, realizing fully the attitude of the Catholic Church in this regard;

4. That no other marriage ceremony shall take place before or after this ceremony by the Catholic priest.

_____

Signature of the Catholic party

_____

Address

_____

City or Town

512

Signed in the presence of:

_____   _____
          Witness   Witness

I, the undersigned, do hereby attest that the parties whose signatures are affixed to the above agreement and promises appeared before me personally on the given date, and fully understanding the import and meaning of the aforementioned agreement and promises, freely entered here into this agreement and signed the above in my presence.

                              _____
                                   Pastor–Assistant

Date: _____

Two copies of this form should be filled in and sent to the Chancery. One copy, when duly signed, dated and sealed by the Chancellor, will be returned to the priest to be kept in the parish archives: the other copy will be retained in the Chancery. See "Synodus Diocesana Santi Ludovici Septima—1929" (Page 54, No. 95 under 2).

The Use and Meaning
of Statistical Terms

When social scientists make an investigation of the family or delinquency or any other social phenomena they wish to know whether or not the facts which they have discovered have meaning. They wish to know whether or not another scientist doing the same study would come to the same conclusions and have the same results. To discover that meaning, they have developed tools which enable them to measure rather precisely the relationship or association between two sets of data. They have other tools (statistical formulas) which enable them to know whether or not these associations are due to chance. If they are due to chance, no meaning can be ascribed to the supposed relationship they are studying. When, at the bottom of a chart describing the characteristics of two groups, the term $p = .01$ (or .02, .05 etc.) appears, the scientist is very simply telling us that there is less than one chance (or two chances, five chances, etc.) in a hundred that the differences reported in the table could be due to chance. Put in another way, this means that there is only one chance in a hundred that the differences reported in the study would disappear if a new sample were studied in the same way. If the term at the bottom of the table is $p < .01$, this tells us that there is *less than* one chance in a hundred that the findings reported are due to chance.

Many social scientists in the reports they make of their studies give the statistical formula they have used to discover p, or the *probability* that their findings are due to chance. In this book those formulas most frequently cited are *Chi Square* and the *Critical Ratio*. The term *Chi Square* is generally written out but the *Critical Ratio* is denoted by the letters, *CR*. A *CR* of 2.0 when translated into a probability ratio means that in only five cases out of a hundred the findings of the particular table are due to chance. As the *Chi Square* and the *CR* becomes larger, the greater the probability that the relationship to which it refers is not due to chance. On the other hand, the smaller the p the greater is the probability that the relationship to which it refers is not due to chance.

There are other statistical terms which need definition. In the Kotlar study, as well as in others, the term *correlation* is used. We use this tool when we want to study the association between two or more variables in order to estimate the magnitude of one variable as it relates to the magnitude of a second variable. It again

514

allows us to make some judgment about the significance of that relationship. If, as in the Luckey study of roles in the second chapter, the author refers to "differences in the means of the populations," she is simply referring to the differences in the two groups which are under study, i.e., the average happiness of one group that expresses its role behavior in one way is compared to the average happiness of a second group that expresses its role behavior in another way.

At the very top of some tables there is a term, $N = 1000$. This means that the number of subjects in the total study is 1000. But when N or $No.$ is at the head of a column it means the figures in the column are raw figures, in contrast to other columns headed by the term *Per cent*, where the raw figures have been turned into percentages.

These mathamatical terms are abstract and it may take the student a little time to use them meaningfully, but he should realize that statistical measurement is a tool that enables the scientist to become far more precise in his ability to think clearly and to draw valid conclusions about the family or any other social phenomenon. These devices enable the social scientist to avoid speculation and anchor his generalizations in meaningful research.

INDEX

517